A · COMPLETE · BIBLIOGRAPHY · OF ·

FENCING AND DUELLING

AS · PRACTISED · BY · ALL · EUROPEAN · NATIONS · FROM ·
THE · MIDDLE · AGES · TO · THE · PRESENT · DAY ·

BY
CARL · A ·
THIMM ·

With a Classified Index, in Chronological Order, according
to Languages (Alphabetically Arranged) ❧ Illustrated with
Numerous Portraits of Ancient and Modern Masters of the
Art, Title-pages & Frontispieces of some of the earliest works.

The Naval & Military Press Ltd

published in association with

ROYAL
ARMOURIES

Published by the
The Naval & Military Press
in association with the Royal Armouries

Unit 10 Ridgewood Industrial Park,
Uckfield, East Sussex, TN22 5QE
Tel: +44 (0) 1825 749494
Fax: +44 (0) 1825 765701

For a full listing of all N&MP titles, visit:
www.naval-military-press.com

MILITARY HISTORY AT YOUR FINGERTIPS

Online genealogy research:
www.military-genealogy.com

The Library & Archives Department at the
Royal Armouries Museum, Leeds, specialises
in the history and development of armour
and weapons from earliest times to the
present day. Material relating to the
development of artillery and modern
fortifications is held at the Royal
Armouries Museum, Fort Nelson.

ROYAL
ARMOURIES

For further information contact:
Royal Armouries Museum, Library, Armouries Drive,
Leeds, West Yorkshire LS10 1LT
Royal Armouries, Library, Fort Nelson, Down End Road, Fareham PO17 6AN

Or visit the Museum s website at
www.armouries.org.uk

*In reprinting in facsimile from the original, any imperfections are inevitably reproduced
and the quality may fall short of modern type and cartographic standards.*

Printed and bound by CPI Antony Rowe, Eastbourne

[The sword-hilt in the illustration, in the possession of Captain A. Hutton, is that of an early small-sword, of about 1650, the interesting period during which, in Western Europe, the old long Italian rapier evolved itself into the short-sword. The hilt in question is elaborately worked in silver, and, although fashioned mainly on the lines of the small-sword, it presents a trace of the rapier form in the strong outer ring immediately below the shell. That it is entirely of German make is evident from the manner in which the blade is set with a bias towards the old German "guard," a sort of "high seconde," which places the aforesaid ring in a position to protect the hand from a downward stroke. The blade is small, flat, and double-edged, bearing on both sides the lettering in gold, "ME . FECIT . SALINGEN . " and on it there are traces of that peculiar rust which is caused by blood alone. The shell is very interesting; it portrays four episodes of a siege, in which the landscape background is as carefully worked as the principal figures, and its interior edge is very much worn down by friction against the side of its original owner.]

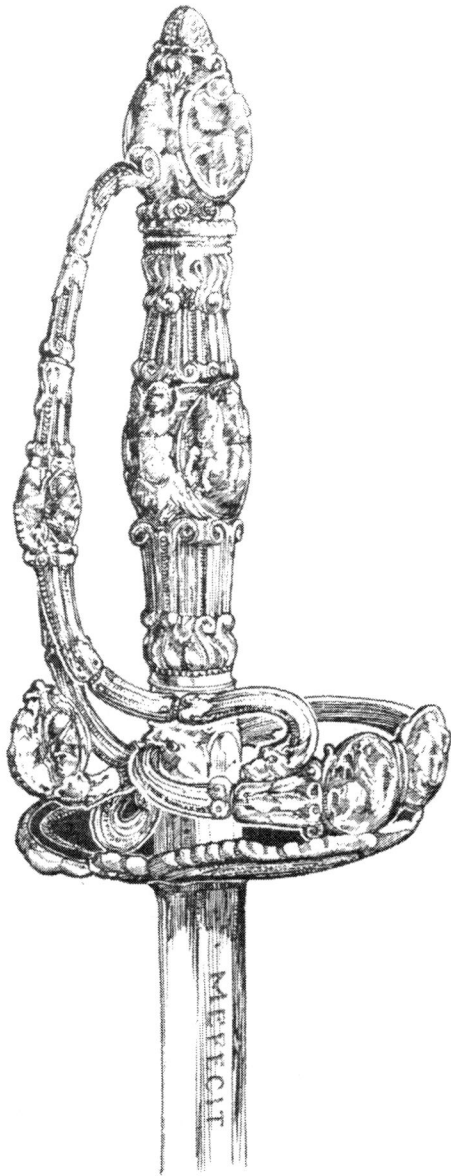

[*A full description of the sword-hilt in this illustration
is given on the opposite page.*]

PREFACE.

IN England, after a long period of abeyance, the pursuit of fencing in its various branches, an art which M. Ernest Legouvé, in his "Soixante Ans de Souvenirs," truly says, can "charm, console, calm, and even cure," has shown of late years unmistakable signs of revival.

This revival has created a demand for a work such as the present one. This is distinctly an age of accurate information, and, in a subject ranging so widely in, and appertaining (with differences) to, so many countries, the first and most useful help towards such information is plainly a good, accurate, and critical bibliography.

Its story is of especial interest to English readers, for, curiously enough, it is in England (the country which for so long has neglected the systematic practice of this fascinating sport) that the true character of ancient sword-play, and its evolution towards the highly perfect art which we now call fencing, was first elucidated.

Investigation of the doctrines of ancient masters of fence and bibliographic compilation of fencing works were things naturally bound to go hand in hand : both are virtually branches of what is now becoming the fashion to speak of as *Kernoozing*. And this investigation (at least in a really systematic manner) belongs to quite modern times.

It is true that such men as Pallavicini [1] in the seventeenth century, Kahn [2] in the eighteenth, Roux [3] and also Possellier [4] in the

[1] *Vide* PALLAVICINI (Giuseppe Morsicato). 1670. 1673.
[2] *Vide* KAHN (Anthon Friedrich). 1739. 1761.
[3] *Vide* ROUX (J. Ad. C.). 1798.
[4] *Vide* POSSELLIER (A. J. J.). 1845.

PREFACE

earlier part of the present, published bibliographical accounts of previous and contemporaneous works touching the art of the sword; but these accounts, useful as they may have been proved in some cases, contained at best but snippets of information concerning a very wide subject.

A first and, in its way, a very interesting attempt at reconstructing the story of the sword, duelling and military, was made in 1882 by M. Vigeant, the noted Parisian *maître d'armes* and *littérateur*, in the publication of "La Bibliographie de l'Escrime, Ancienne et Moderne." [1] This was a charmingly "got-up" little book, and contained much curious and valuable material available for a real History of the Art of Fence. It was trustworthy as regards French works, but it unfortunately fell woefully short of that high level in connection with books of other nationalities. Still, the volume was a most welcome adjunct to the literature of fence. It sent the price of works on the noble art at a premium almost at once, and thus promoted the search for unknown or rare books on that subject.

It may be said, moreover, to have had a much farther reaching effect on the study of ancient swordsmanship, for its appearance had no doubt some influence in suggesting to an Englishman the idea of a really systematic and critical work of research upon a subject hitherto fraught with much "legend and phantasy." This Englishman was Mr. Egerton Castle. In 1884 appeared a book which is still, and no doubt will remain long, a standard work, "Schools and Masters of Fence from the Middle Ages to the Eighteenth Century." [2] It was, at any rate, *princeps* on the matter, and has since been translated into French, as being a thoroughly comprehensive and methodical work. The Académie d'Armes de Paris (a body which, after an uninterrupted existence of two centuries, from Charles IX. to the Revolution, was revived with much importance in 1886) elected the author a member "in recognition of the service rendered to artistic swordsmanship."

[1] *Vide* VIGEANT (A.). 1882.
[2] *Vide* CASTLE (Egerton). 1884.

PREFACE

Since then, Mr. Egerton Castle had occasion to give, before a
select audience, an actual, living, panoramic display of the evolution
of the fencing art, in an "illustrated" lecture delivered, at Sir,
then Mr. Henry Irving's request, in the Lyceum Theatre, London,
under the title of the "Story of Swordsmanship." In this con-
ference the lecturer was assisted in his "illustrations" by (among
others) Captain Alfred Hutton (well known as a leading authority
on the subject, under the name of "Cold Steel"[1]), by Sir Frederick
Pollock[2] and Mr. Walter Pollock.[3]

The lecture, which explained picturesquely the concatenation of
all European fencing systems, from the two-hand sword to the
modern foil, was repeated at the same theatre by command of
H.R.H. the Prince of Wales, and had undoubtedly a far-reaching
effect in stimulating public interest in matters connected with
fencing, both historical and modern. Several displays of the same
kind have since been given in England, notably by Captain A.
Hutton and his friends of the London Rifle Brigade—one as recently as July 6, 1895, in the beautiful grounds of the Albany
Club,[4] Kingston-on-Thames, under the patronage of General H.H.
Prince Edward of Saxe-Weimar, K.P., G.C.B., in aid of the funds
of the Royal Cambridge Asylum for Soldiers' Widows—and have
been occasionally attempted on the Continent. Paradoxical as it
may seem, help, both in information and in *personnel*, had to be
sought in England. This was, perhaps, best shown in the case of
a recent and, it must be said, a truly magnificent display of historic fencing which took place in Brussels in the spring of 1894.
This show, under the apposite name of "Le Cycle de l'Epée,"[5]
was produced largely under the auspices of Monsr. A. Fierlants,
the President of the Cercle d'Escrime, translator of Mr. Castle's

---

[1] *Vide* HUTTON (Alfred). 1889.
[2] *Vide* POLLOCK (Frederick).
[3] *Vide* POLLOCK (W. H.). 1889.
[4] *Vide* ALBANY Club. 1895.
[5] *Vide* ESCRIME (L') à travers les Ages. 1894.

historical work,[1] and it derived its chief element of success from the presence and active help of Captain A. Hutton and several English officers of Volunteers, his companions in arms, who went over to lend the weight of their special and remarkable dexterity. Captain A. Hutton has left a permanent record of his skill and research by practically interpreting the complicated fence of ancient masters in a magnificent volume of actual "lessons," entitled "Old Sword-Play."[2]

This Bibliography is intended as a work of reference for all interested in fencing and duelling, bayonet exercise, &c., for a demand has been created for a standard work brought down to date, with a classified index, arranged in chronological order and division into languages, of books, &c., on these subjects, published or in manuscript, in all European languages and in all countries.

The works of many writers on fence and sword-play, both ancient and modern, have afforded useful *data*, but few such records can claim strict accuracy in their descriptions; I have therefore, when able, verified or corrected these references, and have little doubt they will now be of increased value.

I have accepted the definition that the subject of FENCE embraces *all works relating to the art of offence and defence with all weapons held in the hands,* for the science of arms should include the use of all non-ballistic weapons, from foil to bayonet, and from dagger to battleaxe.

I may be excused for having to "eke out the number of books of fence by the interpolation of so many drill-books;" but as these contain sword, bayonet, or lance exercises, to the student they are of much importance.

A Bibliography of DUELLING, an all-important subject in relation to fence, has not previously been attempted, and in the present volume I have endeavoured to enumerate all books and manuscripts

[1] *Vide* FIERLANTS (A.).   1888.
[2] *Vide* HUTTON (A.).   1891.

under this heading, together with such newspaper and magazine notices and articles as have come under my observation. All accounts of duels, &c., which have appeared in *The Times* from 1831–1895 will be found carefully noted in chronological order under the heading of that paper. In strict justice to this subject, a bibliographer is bound to chronicle all "poems, pamphlets, or sermons," and other such works, be they written for or against duelling.

My thanks are due to His Royal Highness the Duke of Connaught for graciously according me the honour of inscribing this volume to him; to Mr. Egerton Castle, M.A., F.S.A., for some advice and much information on a subject in which he is a recognised authority, not only in this country, but all over the Continent; and to Captain Alfred Hutton, F.S.A., late King's Dragoon Guards, for placing at my disposal his very valuable collection of books relating to the science of arms. He himself being, as I have mentioned, a distinguished master of the art of fence, and one of the most competent authorities on sword-play and bayonet-fencing; in all his works Captain Hutton writes with the completeness and clearness of a practised expert. To him also must be conceded the credit of having given an impetus to the recent revival; and he is doing valuable work in lecturing, and encouraging the practice of fencing in many of our public colleges and schools.

Mr. J. R. García Donnell's (of Buenos Ayres) magnificent collection of rare Spanish and other works deserves mention, for it contains many which have been omitted from my previous work.[1] I have, whenever possible, been careful to state where the old and rare volumes which I have consulted are to be found; and I trust that the Classified Index, now arranged chronologically, and grouped into languages (in alphabetical order), will be more useful, and that this work will continue to prove of value.

Great care has been taken to give fac-simile reproductions of portraits of certain leading masters of various centuries, whose

---

[1] *Vide* THIMM (C. A.). (1891.)

published works are known to us, as clearly and exactly as is possible by modern photography; in some instances they have had to be somewhat reduced in size.

In the selection of these reproductions of old portraits I have been guided by the advice and assistance of Captain A. Hutton. I should here mention that neither he nor Mr. Egerton Castle are *masters* in a professional sense, but merely private gentlemen devoted to the noble science.

To the modern authors my thanks are tendered for the loan of their original plates.

Knowing from past experience how impossible it is for a work such as this to be *complete*, I still claim the indulgence of all who consult its pages, and earnestly appeal to them to forward me information of omissions, errors, or corrections. In this latter respect I have to acknowledge Dr. Karl Wassmannsdorff's (of Heidelberg) article in *Monatschrift für das Turnwesen* (Mai 1892, Heft V.), and some carefully prepared notes of addenda and corrigenda from Sir Frederick Pollock, Bart.; for, as he truly observes, "Bibliography is nothing if not minute."

LONDON, *July* 1896.

TABLE OF CONTENTS.

LIST OF PORTRAITS,
TITLE-PAGES, FRONTISPIECES,
AND ILLUSTRATIONS.

XV

LIST OF PORTRAITS, &c.

XVI

[*Quarta guardia larga, diffensiva, imperfetta; formata dalla punta intiera sopramano, da cui nasce il rouescio ritondo.*—VIGGIANI (A.), 1575.]

BIBLIOGRAPHY OF FENCING, DUELLING, Etc.

[Note.—Authors' names, words, or letters printed in *ITALIC CAPITALS* refer to the name, word, or letter under which the full title of the reference will be found.]

A. (G.). — Pallas Armata. The Gentleman's Armorie; wherein the right and genuine use of the Rapier and of the Sword as well against the right-handed as against the left-handed man is displayed: and now set forth and first published for the common good by the author. 8°. 1639. *London:* J. D., for J. Williams, at the signe of the Crane in S. Paul's Churchyard.

    [6 *plates. The dedication is signed G. A. 96 pages. A different work from that with the same title by Sir T. Kellie.*]

        (*In the British Museum, G.* 2302.)

A. R. — *R. (A.).* — 1887.

ABÄNDERUNGEN zur Instruktion für den Betrieb der Gymnastik und des Bajonetfechtens bei der Infanterie vom 19. October 1860. Gr. 8°. 1865. *Berlin:* v. Decker.

    [14 *woodcuts in the text.*]

ABBAT (L'). — The Art of Fencing, or the Use of the Small Sword. Translated from the French of the late celebrated Monsieur L'Abbat (Labat), Master of that Art at the Academy of Toulouse, by Andrew Mahon, Professor of the Small Sword. 12°. 1734. *Dublin:* printed by James Hoey.

    [12 *copperplates, out of the text.*]

    (*In British Museum and Captain Hutton's Collection.*)

—— (—). — The Art of Fencing, &c. Translated from the French by Andrew Mahon. 2nd edition. 12°. 1735. *London:* Richard Wellington.

ABBONDATI (Niccolo). — Istituzione di arte ginnastica per le truppe di fanteria di S. M. Siciliana, compilata sulle teorie de' più accurati scrittori antichi e moderni. 2 vols. 8°. 1846. *Napoli.*

—— (—). — *VELLA* (G.). — 1857.

ABEL (C.). — Das Kreuz! Betrachtungen über das Duell Vering-Salomon. 3te Auflage. 8°. 1891. *Freiburg :* Fehsenfeld, Verlag.

ABRICHTUNGS-REGLEMENT f. d. k. k. Infanterie.   Mit 21 Tafeln (nach Geiger & Kollarz) darstellend d. Bajonettfechten. 8°. 1851. *Wien :* Sommer.

—— f. d. k. k. Pionniere. Mit 17 Tafeln über d. Bajonnett-fechten. 8°. 1853. *Wien :* Staatsdruckerei.

ACADÉMIE D'ARMES. Annuaire. 8°. 1889. *Paris.*
[*" Fencing,"* pp. 35.]

ACADEMY (The). — (Periodical.) 4°. *London.*
[Vol. XXV. p. 323. *Burton's " Book of the Sword."*]

ACCOUNT (An) of the damnable prizes in Old Nick's Lottery for men of honour only, where every man there ventures is sure to get the Lord knows what,—for ever! In a gradation of familiar thoughts arising from the not passing of the Duelling-bill brought in last session of Parliament. 8°. 1712. *London.*
(*In the Library of the London Institution.* [*Lansdowne Tracts,* Vol. CXCI. Art. III.])

ACCOUNT (An) of the abolishing of duels in France. 8°. 1713. *London.*

ACCOUNT of H. Paul's duel with Mr. Dalton in 1751.
[*MS. in British Museum.* (*Press mark,* 32,967, ff. 342, 344.)]

ACCOUNT (An) of the late Captain M[ountsey]'s Case.   4°. 1783. *Manchester.*
[*This pamphlet relates to the fatal duel between Cornet Hamilton and Captain Mountsey, fought with swords in Spencer's Tavern, Market Place, Manchester, on March 10, 1783. (Privately printed.)*]

A. C. O. [' Un afficionado ']. — Libro de armas y doctrina para el resguardo de los afficionados de dicha ciencia con contras y explicaciones de toda la arte que se encierra en la espada, hecho por un afficionado. [1750–60(?).] MS.
[*No date or place, bound 8° form, with engraved title-pages and 12 copper-plates by A. Sant Croos.*] (*In the possession of Captain A. Hutton.*)

CAMILLO AGRIPPA, Milanese. 1553.

ACTA ACAD. THEODORO-PALATINÆ. 4°. 1766-1794. *Mannheim :* Löffler.

> [Vol. III. (1773) *Schœpflin. Praebitio de duellis et ordaliis veteris Franciae Rhen.,* etc.]

ADAIR (DR.). — *SLOANIAN.* MS.

ADAM (JEHAN DE VILLERS, SEIGNEUR DE LISLE). — *MARCHE* (*O. Le*). MS.

ADAMS (C. F.). — *HARPER'S* Magazine.

ADKINS (M. T.). — *QUARTERLY* Review (The). — 1889.

ADMIRALTY and Horse Guards Gazette, and Naval and Military Forces. (Weekly Journal.) Folio. *London :* 98 Fleet Street.

> [*May* 23, 1891. *"The Art of Fence." (A review.)*
> *May* 28, 1891. (Page 343.) *Note pointing out that " Young officers take no interest in learning the use of the swords they bear."*]

ADMIRALTY and Horse Guards Gazette.—*NAVAL* and Military Argus.

ADVICE TO SECONDS. General Rules and Instructions for all Seconds. By a late Captain in the Army. 8°. 1793. *Whitehaven :* printed by John Ware.

AGER (H.). — *HARPER'S* Magazine.

AGOCCHIE (M. GIOVANNI DALL') [Bolognese]. — Del Arte di scrimia, libri tre. Ne' quali brevemente si tratta dello Schermire, della Giostra, dell' ordinar battaglie. Opera necessaria a Capitani, Soldati et a qual si voglia Gentil'huomo. 4°. 1572. *Venetia :* appresso G. Tamborino.

> [*Dedicated to Conte F. Pepoli.*] (*In the British Museum.*)

AGRIPPA (CAMILLO) [Milanese]. — Trattato di Scientia d'arme, con un dialogo di filosofia. 4°. 1553. *Roma :* per Antonio Blado, stampadore apostolico.

> [*Portrait of the author, 55 copperplates in the text.*
> " *The first author who introduced a desirable reduction in the number of guards was Camillo Agrippa, a Milanese. We say author advisedly, for Agrippa was no fence-master ; he was a gentleman, an artist, an architect, and, like Michael Cassio, a 'great arithmetician.' The needle erected in the middle of the Piazza San Pietro in Rome remains as one of the monuments of his engineering skill ; and among many treatises on various subjects, there is extant a book, illustrated, it is said, by Michael Angelo, in which we find the actions of sword-fence analyzed mathematically, and,*

what is of more practical importance, the number of recommended guards reduced to four, and an approximation to that cardinal action of fence, the 'botta lunga,' the long thrust or 'lunge.' Agrippa is also the first swordsman known to have advocated the almost sole use of the point."—Castle (E.), "The Story of Swordsmanship." ("The National Review," May 1891.)]
(In the British Museum, 64. d. 25.)

AGRIPPA (CAMILLO). — Modo da comporre il moto Spera conforme al Dialogo del trattato della scienza d'arme. 4°. 1557. *Romae :* Bladig.

[4 sheets and 1 large plate.]

—— (—). — Trattato di Scienza d'arme et un dialogo in detta materia. 4°. 1568. *Venetia :* appresso A. Pinargenti.

[Portrait of the author and 49 copperplates in the text.]
(In the British Museum.)

—— (—). — Trattato di Scienza d'Arme . . . &c. Third edition. 4°. 1604. *Venetia.*

(In the British Museum and Bodleian Library.)

AGUESSEAU (H. F. D'). — Lettres inédites. 2 vols. 8°. 1823. *Paris.*

[Vol. I. p. 211. "Duelling."]

AKERMAN (JOHN YONGE) [F.S.A.]. — Notes on the origin and history of the bayonet. 4°. 1861. *London :* printed by J. B. Nichols & Sons.

[1 plate. Reprinted from "The Archæologia," Vol. XXXVIII.]

ALBANESI (CARL). — Theorie der Fechtkunst, nebst e. Anleitung zum Hiebfechten und zum prakt. Unterrichte. Gr. 8°. 1862. *Wien :* Pichler's Wwe. und Sohn.

[3 folio plates photographed, containing 12 sketches.]

ALBANY CLUB, Kingston-on-Thames. Exhibition of Fence (Ancient and Modern). A Descriptive Account of the 16th Century Swordplay. By members of the School of Arms, London Rifle Brigade, under the direction of Captain Alfred Hutton, F.S.A., member of the Sports Committee, and Ernest Stenson Cooke, Esq., London Rifle Brigade, in aid of the Funds of the Royal Cambridge Asylum for Soldiers' Widows, Kingston-on-Thames, given in the Albany Club Grounds, on Saturday, July 6, 1895, at 4 P.M. punctually. With Notes on Ancient Fence by Captain A. Hutton, F.S.A., and on the Bibliography of the Art of Fence by Captain C. A.

TRATTATO DI

Scientia d' Arme, con vn Dia⸗
logo di Filofofia di
Camillo Aggrippa
Milanefe.

In Roma *per Antonio Blado ftampadore Apoftolico.*
M. D. LIII.

Con priuilegio della Santità di noftro
Signore Papa Giulio III.
per anni dicci.

[CAMILLO AGRIPPA. 4°. 1553.]

Thimm, F.R.G.S. 4°. 1895. *Kingston-on-Thames:* Drewett & Sons, Printers.

(In the British Museum, South Kensington Museum, and Captain Hutton's Collection.)

ALBERGATI (FABIO). — Trattato del modo di ridurre a pace l'inimicitie privato. 4°. 1583. *Roma.*

[*Woodcut title. (Another edition appeared in 1587. Bergamo.)*]

ALBIN (SAINT-). — *SAINT*-Albin.

ALBUM of copperplates representing various attitudes in fencing. Oblong 4°. Date about 1750.

ALBUM d'Escrime, (en couleur, de l'époque de Louis XIV.).

[*Les planches gravées et coloriées représentent des militaires de l'époque en costume, dans les attitudes d'escrime ; chaque planche contient en outre un pavillon français différent.*] (*In Monsr. Vigeant's Collection.*)

ALBUM d'Escrime. — XVIIIe Siècle. Escrimeurs du XVIIIe Siècle. 4°. [*vers* 1740.]

[*Recueil de douze planches humoristiques et magnifiquement gravées cuivre, en Allemagne.*]

ALCIATI (ANDREE). — De Duello (*pp. 204–212).

—— (—). — Consilium in materia duelli excerptum ex libro quinto responsorum (*pp. 212–213).

* [Vol. XII. "*Tractatus ex varis juris interpretibus Collecti.*" Folio. 1549. Lugduni.] (*In the British Museum, 5305. i.*)

ALCIATUS (A.). — De singulari certamine lib. Ejusd. consilium in materia duelli exceptum ex libro V. responsor. 8°. 1543. *Lugduni:* Jac. Giunta.

—— (—.). — Duello de lo eccellentissimo. Fatto de latino italiano. Tre consigli apresso de la materia medesima. 8°. 1545. *Venetia.*

—— (—.). — Duello, tre consigli appresso della materia medesima, uno del detto Alciato gli altri di Mariano Soncino, giureconsulto. 8°. 1552. *Vinegia.*

ALDEN (W. L.). — *IDLER (The).* — 1894.

ALEMBERT (D'). — *ANGELO (D.).* — 1787.

ALESSANDRI (TORQUATO E. D'). — Il cavaliere compito : dialogo nel quale si discorre d'ogni scienza e del modo d'imparare a schermir con spada bianca, e difendersi senz' armi. 8°. 1609. *Viterbo.*

—— (— —. —). — Precetti sulla Scherma. 8°. 1610. *Roma.*

ALESSANDRO (Giuseppe d'). — Pietra paragone de' Cavalieri di D. Giuseppe d'Alessandro Duca di Pescolanciano, divisa in cinque libri. 8° (?). 1711. *Napoli.*

—— (—— ——). — Opera di 1723. *Napoli.*
[*Con ritratto, figure e moltissimi ritratti di nomini illustri.*]

ALFIERI (Antonio). — Quesiti del cavaliero instrutto nell' arte dello schermo, con le riposte del suo maestro. 8°. 1644 (?). *Padova.*

ALFIERI (Antonio) [da Aquila]. — Pentateuco politico, ovvero cinque disinganni : spada, tamburo, piffero, scudo, tromba : al duca di Guisa per l'invasione del regno di Napoli l'anno 1654. 4°. 1655. *Aquila.*
[*Published under the anagrammatic pseudonym Arenif Atonoli.*]

ALFIERI (Francesco Ferdinando) [Maestro d'arme dell' illustrissima accademia Delia in Padova]. — La Bandiera. Obl. 4°. 1628. *Padova:* presso S. Sardi.
[*Numerous copperplates.*]

—— (—— ——). — La Scherma. Dove con nuove Ragioni e con Figure, si mostra la perfezione di quest' arte, e in che modo secondo l'arme e il sito, possa il Cavaliere restar al suo nemico superiore. Obl. 4°. 1640. *Padova:* per Seb. Sardi.
[*Portrait of author and 37 copperplates, after the manner of Callot.*]

—— (—— ——). — La picca e la bandiera. Nelle quale si mostra per via di figure una facile, e nuova pratica, ed il maneggio, e l'uso di essa, con la diffesa della spada. 2 parts. 4°. 1641. *Padova.*
[*Avec le portrait et blason de Lud. di Vidman, le portrait d'Alfieri, 12 gravures pour la picca, et 28 la bandiera, de l'école de J. Callot.*]

—— (—— ——). — L'arte di ben maneggiare la spada. 4°. 1643. *Padova:* Sebastiano Sardi.

—— (—— ——). — La Scherma . . . &c. 2nd edition. 4°. 1645. *Ancona.*

—— (—— ——). — L'arte di ben maneggiare la spada. 4°. 1653. *Padova.*
[*Copperplates.*] (*In British Museum and Captain Hutton's Collection.*)

—— (—— ——). — Lo Spadone. Dove si mostra per via di figura il maneggio e l'uso di esse. 4°. 1653. *Padova:* S. Sardi.
[*17 copperplates.*] (*In British Museum and Captain Hutton's Collection.*)

FRANCESCO FERDINANDO ALFIERI. 1653.

Maestro d'arme dell' Illma Accademia Delia in Padova.

ALFIERI (Francesco Ferdinando). — Arte di ben maneggiare la Spada . . . &c. 2nd edition. Obl. 4°. 1683. *Padova.*

—— (— —). — *HUTTON (A.).* — 1892.

ALLANSON-WINN (R. G.) and **WOLLEY** (C. Phillips). — Broadsword and Single-stick, with Chapters on Quarterstaff, Bayonet, Cudgel, Shillalah, Walking-stick, Umbrella, and other weapons of Self-defence. 16°. 1890. *London:* G. Bell & Sons.

[*Bohn's Handbooks of Athletic Sports. (All England Series.*)]

ALLAUCH (Richard d'). — Projet de Législation sur les duels. 8°. 1819. *Paris:* Bechet.

ALL ENGLAND SERIES. — *ALLANSON-WINN (R. G.).* — 1890.

—— —— —. — *DUNN (H. A. C.).* — 1889.

ALL THE YEAR ROUND (Periodical). 8°. *London.*

[Series 1. Vol. XX. pp. 469–500. *Duel Fighting.*
,,   1. ,,   VII. p. 214. *Duel between Lords Townshend and Bellamont.*
,,   1. ,,   VII. p. 212. *Duelling in Ireland.*
,,   1. ,,   XVIII. p. 329. *Duelling. Major Oneby's Case.*
,,   1. ,,   IX. p. 189. *Duels in France.*
,,   2. ,,   VII. p. 230. *Duel in Leicester Square.*
,,   2. ,,   X. p. 185. *Duel. The Duke of York and Colonel Lennox.*
,,   2. ,,   XXVII. p. 8. *Some Curious Duels.*
,,   2. ,,   XXXI. p. 139. *Duel. The Baron and Mr. Elliot.*
,,   2. ,,   XXXVIII. p. 298. *Duel with Broadswords.*
,,   2. ,,   XXXVIII. p. 133. *Duelling, Ancient and Modern.*
,,   2. ,,   XXXVIII. p. 546. *Duel. Sheridan and Matthews.*
,,   3. ,,   II. p. 322. *Duel. The Duke of York and Colonel Lennox.*
,,   3. ,,   II. p. 323. *Duel. Earl of Cardigan and Capt. Tuckett.*
,,   3. ,,   II. p. 377. *Some Curious Duelling.*
,,   3. ,,   II. p. 322. *Duels on Wimbledon Common.*
New Series, Vol. VII. p. 212. } *Duelling.*
,,   ,,   XX. pp. 469, 500.
,,   ,,   XXIII. p. 330. *Parisian Fencing.*
,,   ,,   XXVII. pp. 8–12. *The Comedy of the Duel.*
,,   ,,   XXXVII. p. 533. *Swords.*
,,   ,,   XLII. p. 271. *Swords of Celtic Chivalry.*
,,   ,,   LVIII. p. 133. *Ancient and Modern Duelling.*
,,   ,,   LXV. p. 376 (1889). *Curiosities of Duelling.*
,,   ,,   LXVII. p. 417 (1890). *Japanese Swords.*]

ALLEGATO istruzione per gli esercizi di ginnastica e di scherma col fucile. 8°. 1876. *Roma.*

[*With engravings.*]

ALMBERT (Alfred d'). — Physiologie du duel. 12°. 1853. *Paris:* Garnier Frères.

ALMBERT (Alfred d'). — Physiologie du duel. 8°. 1867. *Paris :* Amyot.

ALMIRANTE Bibliografia Militar de España. 1876. *Madrid.*
[*Contains a list of works on " Swordplay."*]

ALTONI (Francesco di Lorenzo).—Monomachia ovvero arte di scherma, cui segue un trattato del Giuoco della spada sola. 1550 (?). *Firenze.* MS.

ALVAREZ GARCÍA (D. Antonio). — *GARCÍA (Don Antonio Alvarez).*

ALVAREZ MARTINEZ. — *MARTINEZ (Don Cirilo Alvarez).* —1847.

AMERICAN LAW JOURNAL. *Philadelphia, U.S.A.*
[Vol. I. p. 1. *" Duelling." Trial for murder in France. Lola Montez.*]

AMERICAN LAW REGISTER. *Philadelphia, U.S.A.*
[New Series, Vol. XIV. p. 222. *Disqualification for office of carrying or accepting challenge. Annotated case.*]

AMERICAN MONTHLY MAGAZINE. *Boston, U.S.A.*
[Vol. II. p. 331. *" Duelling."*]

AMERICAN PRESBYTERIAN REVIEW. *New York, U.S.A.*
[Vol. V. p. 407. *" Duelling."*]

AMERICAN QUARTERLY REVIEW. *Philadelphia, U.S.A.*
[Vol. XXII. p. 1. *" Duelling."*]

ANAYA (Don Juan). — Dictamen sobre la espada encontrada en Peñafiel. 1759. MS.
(In the Bib. Nac. A. de la Historia.)

ANDEUTUNGEN für den Angriff und die Vertheidigung mit dem Bajonnet, in bestimmten taktischen Verhältnissen. Ein Supplement der bestehenden Vorschriften zur Einübung des Bajonnet-Fechtens. 8°. 1837. *Darmstadt.*

ANDRADE (Antonio Galvam d'). — Arte da cavallaria de Gineta, e Estardiota, bom primor de ferrar, & Alueitaria. Dividida en tres Tratados, que contem varios discursos & experiencias nouas desta arte. Folio. 1678. *Lisboa :* Joam da Costa.

ANDRÉ (Émile). — Coulisses et salles d'armes ; roman d'actualité. 12°. 1882. *Paris :* Bureau de l'Escrime Française.

—— (—). — Le Jeu de l'Épée. 8°. 1887. *Paris.*
[*278 pages.*]

ÉMILE ANDRÉ. 1896.

Fondateur de la Revue "l'Escrime Française."

ANDRÉ (ÉMILE). — L'Escrime Française. Revue bimensuelle. 4°. *Paris:* 270 Rue Saint-Honoré.

[*A commencé le 9 février* 1889.]

—— (—). — *JACOB* (*Jules*). — 1887.

ANDREW (A.). — Duelling in the 18th Century.

["*Colburn's New Monthly Magazine.*" (*London*) Vol. 103, p. 465.]

ANGE (J. D. L') [Fechtmeister]. — Deutliche und Gründliche Erklärung der Adelichen und Ritterlichen freyen Fechtkunst. Oblong 8°. 1664. *Heidelberg:* A. Weingarten.

[*Portrait of Daniel L'Ange, by Metzger, and 61 copperplates.*]
(*In Captain Hutton's Collection.*)

—— (—. —. —). — Erklärung der Fechtkunst, Lectionen auff den Stoss und deren Gebrauchs Wirkung. 4°. 1708. *Düsseldorf:* herausgegeben durch Ch. L'Ange.

[*With portrait and 61 copperplates.*]

ANGELINI (ACHILLE) [Tenente Generale]. — Osservazioni sul maneggio della sciabola secondo il metodo Radaelli. 1877. *Firenze.*

—— (—). — Codice Cavalleresco italiano. 8°. 1883. *Firenze:* G. Barbèra.

—— (—). — Ditto. Seconda edizione. Con schiarimenti ed aggiunte. 8°. 1886. *Firenze:* G. Barbèra.

—— (—). — Ditto. Terza edizione. Con nuove aggiunte e schiarimenti. 8°. 1888. *Roma:* E. Vercellini.

—— (—). — Ultima parola sulla risorta questione Angelini-Masiello, intorno alla scherma della sciabola del defunto Maestro Radaelli. 8°. 1888. *Roma:* C. Voghera.

—— (—). — *GELLI* (*J.*). — 1888.

ANGELO. — L'Ecole des Armes, avec l'explication générale des principales attitudes et positions concernant l'Escrime. Oblong folio. 1763. *Londres:* R. & S. Dodsley.

[*Dediée à Leurs Altesses Royales les Princes Guillaume-Henry et Henry-Frédéric.* 47 *copperplates by Gwyn, Ryland, and others, out of the text.*
"*Domenico Angelo Malevolti Tremamondo was the son of a very wealthy Italian merchant, and was born at Leghorn in 1716. His English friends persuaded him to abandon this too outlandish patronymic, and adopt the simple name of ' Angelo.' "—Castle's " Schools and Masters of Fence.*"]
(*In British Museum, South Kensington Museum, and Captain Hutton's Collection.*)

9

ANGELO. — L'Ecole des Armes, &c.   Oblong folio.   1765. *London :* S. Hooper.

[*A second edition of M. Angelo's work, containing same plates, but with two columns of text, in French and English.*]

——. — Conten. toute la théorie et la pratique de cet art, d'après l'excellent traité de M. Angelo. In-folio.   1765.   *Paris.*

[*Avec le texte descriptif et 14 intéressantes planches, représ. 47 figures de l'art d'escrime. (Extrait de Diderot, Encyclopédie.*)]

——. — L'Ecole des Armes, &c.   2nd edition.   Oblong folio. 1765.   *Londres.*

[*This edition contains the same plates as the first (vide 1763), but has two columns of text in French and English. It was printed by S. Hooper in London.*] (*Bodleian Library.*)

——. — L'Ecole des Armes, &c.   3rd edition.   Oblong folio. 1767.   *Londres.*

——. — *HUTTON (A.).* — 1892.

ANGELO (DOMENICO). — The School of Fencing, with a general explanation of the principal attitudes and positions peculiar to the Art.   Translated by Rowlandson.   Oblong 8°.   1787.   *London.*

[*47 plates. This work was translated into French, and reproduced, together with the plates, under the head "Escrime," by Diderot and D'Alembert in their "Encyclopédie."*] (*In British Museum and Hutton's Collection.*)

—— (—). — Escrime [1787 (?)] [Diderot et D'Alembert's Encyclopédie].   Folio.   1787.   *Paris.*

[*Avec le texte descriptif et 14 intéressantes planches, représ. 47 figures de l'art d'escrime.*
(*A reproduction and translation of Angelo's work published in London in 1787.*)]

—— (—). — The School of Fencing, &c.   Translated by Rowlandson.   2nd edition.   8°.   1799.   *London.*

ANGELO. — A treatise on the utility and advantages of fencing, giving the opinions of the most eminent Authors and Medical Practitioners on the important advantages derived from a knowledge of the Art as a means of self-defence and a promoter of health, illustrated by forty-seven engravings.   To which is added a dissertation on the use of the broad sword (with six descriptive plates). Memoirs of the late Mr. Angelo and a biographical sketch of Chevalier St. George, with his portrait.   Folio.   1817.   *London :*

published by Mr. Angelo, Bolton Row, and at his fencing academy, Old Bond Street.

> [*Containing the same plates as the "Ecole des Armes" of the author's father, a portrait of St. George, engraved by W. Ward from a picture of Brown, and six plates engraved and designed by Rowlandson, under the care of Angelo himself, in 1798–1799.*]

ANGELO. — Bayonet Exercise.   8°.   1829.   *London.*

> [*The first authorised edition by the Adjutant-General's Office, Horse Guards, appeared in July 1857.   London : J. W. Parker & Son.*]
> (*In Captain Hutton's Collection.*)

——. — *REGULATIONS* (Cavalry).   1819.

——. —   ——   (Infantry).   1819.

ANGELO (HENRY) [Superintendent of Sword Exercise to the Army]. — Instructions for the sword exercise selected from His Majesty's rules and regulations, and expressly adapted for the yeomanry.   8°.   1835.   *London :* Clowes & Sons.

—— (—). — Instructions for Cavalry Sword Exercise.   12°.   1840.   *London.*

—— (—). — *ROWLANDSON* (T.). — 1798–1799.

ANGELO (Reminiscences of Henry). — With memoirs of his late father and friends, with numerous original anecdotes, &c.   8°.   1828.

> (*In Captain Hutton's Collection.*)

ANGELO (ST.) [a pupil of — *sic*]. — The Art of Fencing, wherein the rules and instructions, with all the new thrusts and guards which have lately been introduced into the Fencing Schools, are in this work, that every one should be competent to meet his antagonist.   For of late years our neighbours on the continent have been our superiors in that of all others, the most useful, necessary, and gentlemanly Science.   Small 8°.   1830.   *London :* T. Hughes.

> [*1 folding plate.*]

ANGERSTEIN (E.). — *LENZ* (G. F.). — 1881.

ANLEITUNG zum Betrieb der Gymnastik und der Fechtkunst in der Armee.   8°.   1861.   *Berlin :* R. Decker.

> [*Zweite Abtheilung, pp. 85–120, "BAIONETFECHTEN." (66 figures in the text.)*]

ANLEITUNG zum Floretfechten für die K. Sächs. Infanterie. 8°. 1843. *Dresden* und *Leipzig:* Arnold.

ANLEITUNG zum Gebrauch des Bajonets, oder kurzer Unterricht des Wesentlichsten dieser Fechtart, für Unteroffiziere und Soldaten : Dem Schweizerischen Fussvolk gewidmet von einem Offizier des eidgenössischen Generalstabs. 8°. 1825. *Basel.*

ANLEITUNG zum Gewehrfechten. 8°. 1882. *Dresden:* Meinhold und Söhne.

ANLEITUNG zum Hieb- und Stossfechten mit dem Säbel. 8°. 1865. *Bern.*

[*Another edition.* 12°. 1876. Bern.]

ANNOT (A.). — Art Militaire des Chinois, ou recueil d'anciens traités sur la guerre, composés avant l'ère chrétienne par différents chinois, avec dix preceptes adressés aux troupes par l'Empéreur Yong-Tcheng, et des planches gravées et coloriées pour l'intelligence des exercises, habillement armes et instruments militaires des chinois, traduit en français par le P. Annot. 4°. 1772. *Paris:* Didot l'ainé.

[*Avec 33 belles planches représ. grand nombre de figures curieuses coloriées soigneusement à la main.*]

ANNUAIRE des Maîtres d'Escrime des armées de terre et de mer. 8°. [1894, &c.] *Nancy.*

[*In progress.*]

ANSALONE (ANTONIO). — Il cavaliere descritto in tre libri : nel primo si ragiona delle preminenze che hanno ottenuto i cavalieri ; nel secondo dei giuochi che tanto a cavallo, quanto a piedi esercitar si possono ; nel terzo come si debba comparire negli spettacoli e nelle maschere, ecc. 1629. *Messina:* presso Pietro Brea.

—— (—). — Il torneo a piede, discorso nel quale si ragiona con quanta magnificenza si sia combattuto nella sbarra da' signori cavalieri della Stella nell' anno 1636. 1637. *Messina:* presso Pietro Brea.

ANSWER (An) to the letter of Theophilus Swift, Esqr., on the subject of the Royal duel. 8°. 1794. *London:* Stalker.

ANTIDUELLO. — [*ESPAGNE (John d')*]. — 1632.

ANTI-PUGILISM, or the science of defence exemplified in short and easy lessons, for the practice of the Broad Sword and Single

Stick. Whereby gentlemen may become proficients in the use of these weapons, without the help of a Master, and be enabled to chastise the insolence and temerity, so frequently met with, from those fashionable gentlemen, the Johnsonians, Big Bennians, and Mendozians of the present Day; a work perhaps better calculated to extirpate this reigning and brutal folly than a whole volume of sermons. By a Highland officer. Illustrated with copperplates. 8°. 1790. *London:* printed for J. Aitkin.

[4 *copperplates, drawn by Cruikshank.*] (*British Museum.*)

ANTIQUARIAN REPERTORY.

[1807. Vol. I. p. 165. "*A breife note of three Italian teachers of offence.*" *By George Silver.*]

ANTIQUARY (Periodical). *London.*

[New Series, Vol. XV. p. 55 (1887?). "*Development of Fencing.*"]

ANWENDUNG (Die) des Bajonets gegen Infanterie und Kavallerie in d. königl. Dänischen Armee (aus d. Dänischen übertragen von dem Kapitän v. Jensen). 12°. 1829. *Braunschweig:* Vieweg.

ANWEISUNG (Gründliche und Vollständige) in der deutschen Fechtkunst. — [*ROUX (J. Ad. K.)*]. — 1798.

APPEAL or ASSIZE OF BATTLE.

[*By the old law of England, a man charged with murder might fight with the appellant, thereby to make proof of his guilt or innocence. In 1817, a young maid, Mary Ashford, was believed to have been violated and murdered by Abraham Thornton, who, on trial, was acquitted. In an appeal, he claimed his right by wager of battle, which the court allowed; but the appellant (the brother of the maid) refused the challenge, and the accused was discharged, April 16, 1818. This law was struck off the statute-book by 59 Geo. III., c. 46 (1819).*
In 1631 Lord Rea impeached Mr. David Ramsey of treason, and offered battle in proof; a commission was appointed, but the duel was prohibited by King James I.]

APPLETON'S JOURNAL. 8°. *New York, U.S.A.*

[Vol. XXV. p. 521. "*Comedy of Duel.*"]

ARAGÓN (MARTIN). — Proyecto de Ordenanza para los armeros de Córdoba presentado al Ayuntamiento. 1512. MS.

[*In the Arch. Municipal de Córdoba. (Inclúmos este "Proyecto" porque su carpeta dice equivocadamente: "Ordenanzas para los maestros de esgrima, yasi ha sido citado por algunos escritores.")*]

13

ARANDÍA Y MORENTIN (Don Juan Antonio Arrieta). — Resumen de la verdadera destreza y modo facil para saber los caminos verdaderos en la batalla, &c. 8°. 1688. *Pamplona:* Martin G. de Zabála.

ARAUJO (Don Jerónimo Salvador de). — Argvmento con qve se intenta probar qve la phylosophia, y destreza de las Armas es scientia, segvn Aristoteles. 4°. [N.D.]

[*Tiene, al principio un soneto de Don Juan Ignacio de las Muñecas, y concluye con otro, acróstico, "en aplavso de D. Jerónimo Carrança."*]

ARBEAU (Thoinot). — Orchésographie, métode et téorie en forme de discours et tablature pour apprendre à dancer, battre le tambour, jouer du fifre et arigot; tirer des armes et escrimer, avec autres honnestes exercices fort convenables à la jeunesse. . . . Jean Tabourot. Lengres par Jehan dez Preyz. 4°. 1596. *Lengres.*

[*Woodcuts.*]

ARCHÆOLOGIA. 4°. *London.*

  [Vol. VII. (1785) p. 374. *Letter on an ancient Sword. By Lieut.-General R. Melvill.*
  „ VII. (1785) p. 376. *Ditto. By Rev. J. Douglas.*
  „ XXIX. (1842) pp. 348–361. *Some Observations on Judicial Duels, as practised in Germany. In a letter from R. L. Pearsall (of Willsbridge), Esqr., to Sir Henry Ellis, K.H., F.R.S.* (*Contains 8 plates.*)
  „ XXXVIII. p. 422. *Akerman (J. Y.). Notes on the Origin and History of the Bayonet.*
  „ XLI. pp. 217–280. *Dillon (H. A.). Arms and Armour at Westminster, the Tower, and Greenwich.* 1547.]

ARCHÆOLOGICAL INSTITUTE (Journal of the).

  [Vol. XXXIII. p. 92. *Illustration of a Lansquenette or "Landsknecht's" sword. Showing the chief characteristics of the broadsword commonly worn by German foot-men in the sixteenth century. Its practice in fencing was essentially the same as that of the Düsack—length of blade, about 2 feet.*]

ARENIF ATONOLI. — *ALFIERI* (A.). — 1655.

ARGOSY (Monthly Magazine). — 8°. *London.*

  [Vol. XXVI. (*September* 1878) pp. 188–193. *"A Few Famous Duels." By W. M. Townsend.*
  Vol. XLVI. (1888) p. 353. *"The Duel." A Story by G. S. Godkin.*]

ARGUMENTOS que se ponen, y demonstraciones que se piden á los professores de la verdadera destreza de las Armas. 1694. *Madrid.*

[*Lorenz de Rada lo reprodujo integramente en su "Respuesta."*]

ARGY (CHARLES HENRI LOUIS D'). — Escrime du fusil, appliqué aux tirailleurs. 18°. 1842. *Lyon:* Dumoulin.

[71 *engravings and* 2 *plates.*]

ARIENTI (GIOVANNI SABBATINO DEGLI). — Il torneo fatto in Bologna il IV Ottobre MCCCLXX. 1888. *Parma:* L. Battei.

ARISTA (MARIA SALVATORE). — Dell progresso della scherma in Italia. Considerazioni sull' impianto della nuova scuola Magistrale per l'Esercito, fondata in Roma nel 1884. 8°. 1884. *Bologna:* Società Tipografica.

ARISTA (S.). — *DON GIOVANNI.* — 1888.

ARLOW (RITTER VON) [Hauptman] und **LITOMYSKY** (OBER-LIEUT.) [Militär-Fecht- und Turnlehrer]. — Systematisches Lehrbuch für den Unterricht im Säbelfechten aus der Hoch-Tierce-Auslage. Gr. 8°. 1894. *Wien:* W. Braumüller.

[141 *Seite mit* 16 *Lichtdr.-Bildern.*]

ARMAS (Las) y el duelo. Carta dirigida al Sr. D. Manuel Cardenal y Gómez, Maestro de esgrima, por uno de sus dicípulos. 8°. 1886. *Habana:* Romero Rubio.

[49 *pages.*]

A[RMAS] Y C[ÁRDENAS]. — Les Armas y el duelo. 4°. 1886. *Habana:* Romero Rubio.

ARMY AND NAVY GAZETTE (Periodical). Folio. *London.*

[1895. *August* 3. "*Swordsmanship in the Army.*"
1895. *September* 21. "*The New Infantry Sword Exercise.*"]

ARREGUI (TIRSO DE). — Tratado sobre el duelo, escrito en frances y traducido al castellano. 8°. 1871. *Barcelona.*

ARRIGHI (CLETTO). — Divorzio e duello. Drama sociale. 12°. *Milano:* Battezzati Successore.

[98 *pages.*]

ART OF DUELLING (The) by a Traveller. 12°. 1836. *London:* J. Thomas.

[*Dedicated to* "*the unfortunate General Torreijos and his brave companions in arms.*"] (*In Mr. J. R. Garcia Donnell's Collection.*)

ART OF FENCING. Corrected and revised by the author of the "Broadsword Exercise." 8°. 1831. *London:* T. Hughes.

ARTAGNAN (MONSIEUR D') [Capitaine-Lieutenant de la première Compagnie des Mousquetaires du Roi]. — Memoires. — Contenant

15

Quantité de choses particulieres et secrettes qui se sont passées sous le Regne de Louis le Grand. 3 vols. 12°. 1704. *Amsterdam:* Pierre Rouge.

[Tome I. p. 15.   *Duel. Athos, Porthos, Aramis, and D'Artagnan, v. Jussac, Cahusac, Biscarat, and Bernajoux.*

  „ I. p. 30.   *Rencontre with a "Garde de Mr. le Cardinal."*

  „ I. p. 84.   *Rencontre between Danueven and two other Mousquetaires and three of Richelieu's gardes.*

  „ I. p. 265. *Duel. D'Artagnan and Aramis v. Cox and another Englishman.*

(*Another edition.* 12°. 1700. *A* Cologne : *chez Pierre Marteau.*)]
(*In Captain Hutton's Collection.*)

ARTAGNAN (MONSIEUR D'). — *AURIAC* (*E. D'*). — 1847.

ASCHENBRENNER (MT.) — Betrachtt. über vorzügl. Gegenstände im Staatsleben. 8°. 1822. *Landshut:* Krüll.

[*Darin der Zweikampf als Probe des Muthes ansich betrachtet.*]

ASHMOLE (ELIAS). — The ancient method of usage of duels before the King. [N.D.] Out of an old MS. of Elias Ashmole, Esq. MS.

[*In* "*Brown's Miscellanea Aulica.*" 1702. Art. VI. pp. 161–172.]
(*In the Library of the London Institution.*)

ASHMOLEAN MANUSCRIPTS.

(*In the Bodleian Library, Oxford.*)

[A Discourse "Of the antiquity, use, and ceremony of lawfull combates in England." MS.

["*Ex MS. in Bibl. Hatton.*"] (*Ashmolean MS.* 856. 115.)

"Duello foild. The whole proceedings in the orderly dissolveing of a designe for single fight betweene two valient gentlemen ; by occasion whereof the unlawfulnesse of a duello is preparatorily disputed, according to the rules of honour and right reason. Written by the Lord Henry Howard, Earle of Northampton, Anno " . . .

["*Ex MS. in Bibl. Hatton.*" *Ascribed to Sir Edward Cook in Hearne's Collection of Curious Discourses* (ed. 1775, Vol. II. pp. 225–242); *and not known to be the Earl's production by either Walpole or Park.*] (*Ashmolean MS.* 856. 126.)

" A Discourse touching the unlawfulnesse of private combates, written by Sʳ: Edward Cooke, Lord Chiefe Justice of England, at the request of the Lord Henry Howard, Earle of Northampton." (3 Oct. 1609.)

["*Ex MS. in Bibl. Hatton.*"] (*Ashmolean MS.* 856. 146.)

ASHMOLEAN MANUSCRIPTS (*continued*)—

A Discourse "Of the antiquitie, use, and ceremony of lawfull combates in England, written by M^r: James Whitelock of the Middle Temple."

> ["*Ex MS. in Bibl. Hatton.*" *Printed in the* "*Curious Discourses,*" Vol. II. p. 190.] (*Ashmolean MS.* 856. 149.)

"The Antiquity, use, and ceremonyes of lawfull Combates in England, written by M^r: Francis Tate of the Midle Temple, London, 13 Februarij, Anno 1600."

> ["*Ex MS. in Bibl. Hatton.*" Not *printed among the* "*Curious Discourses.*"] (*Ashmolean MS.* 856. 154.)

"The Antiquity, use, and ceremony of lawfull combates in England."

> ["*Ex collect. Guil: Dugdale.*"] (*Ashmolean MS.* 856. 157.)

"His Ma^ts: declaration against duells, published at his Ma^ts: chappell at Bruxells upon sonday the 24th: of November 1658."

> (*Ashmolean MS.* 856. 172.)

"The manner of Donnald Ld Rey, and David Ramsey esq., their comeing and carriage at their tryall, upon monday, the 28 of November 1631, before the L^d of Lynsey, Lord High Constable of England, Tho: E. of Arundell, Earle Marshall, Phillip Earle of Penbroke and of Mountgomery Ld High Chamberlaine, and diverse others the Lords of his Matie most hon^ble Privie Counsell, and Sr Henry Martin joyned in commission for an assistant in the court."

> [*This is a very full and well-drawn-up Report of the Trial, and is more complete than No. 824 V. It ends with* "*Saturday the 18th of February* 1631." *A record of the trial is given in Dugdale's MS.* 30.] (*Ashmolean MS.* 856. 175–227.)

E rotulis publicis quædam annotationes; primo de Militibus Ordinis, et de Windesora; postea de constabulariis castri Windesoræ, de duello, et de insigniis armorum.

> [*Extracts by Ashmole, chiefly from the Patent Rolls and Close Rolls, Henry III. to Richard II.*] (*Ashmolean MS.* 1115. 225.)

A short extract by Sir W. Dugdale, "Out of a discourse in French concerning antient manner of Combates."

> ["*Ex vet. cod. MS.* (*temp. R. H.* 6^ti *ut videtur exarato*) *penes Semerum Shirley de Staunton-Harold in com. Leic: Baronettum ult: Martij* 1663." *This passage is not found in No.* 764.] (*Ashmolean MS.* 840. 211.)

ASHMOLEAN MANUSCRIPTS (*continued*)—

" De la droite ordonnance du 𝕮𝖆𝖎𝖌𝖊 𝖉𝖊 𝕭𝖆𝖙𝖆𝖎𝖑𝖑𝖊 par tout le royaume de France. Phelipe par la grace de Dieu Roy de France a touz ceulx qui ces presentes lettres verront salut."

> [*This letter of King Philip IV. (dated at Paris the Wednesday after Trinity, 1306), limiting the practice of wager of battle, is prefixed to Regulations for the whole course of combat. The last words are—* "*pour les aultres gaiges qui enssuire se pourroient.*"]
> (*Ashmolean MS.* 764. 44.)

A book " Of the manner and order of combating within listes, delivered by Thomas Duke of Gloucester unto King Richard the second."

> [*Transcribed* "*Ex MS. in Bibl. Hatton.*" *The first words are—*" *To his right high and mighty lord and leige Richard ;*" *and the last—* " *With the listes, scaffold, and tymber used at the said battaile.*" *This treatise is not mentioned in Tanner's* "*Bibliotheca.*" *Compare Art.* 23.] (*Ashmolean MS.* 856, 83.)

" The Earle Marshall's order in the quarrell betwixt Anthony Felton and Edmond Withepole, esquires, xxiij May 1598."

> ["*Ex. autogr. in Bibl. Hatton.*"] (*Ashmolean MS.* 856. 105.)

" The manner of the Challendge made by the Earl of Northumberland against Sr Francis Veare," both by letter dated 24 Apr. 1602, and by inter-messages, until forbidden by the Queen's commandment.

> ["*Ex MS. in Bibl. Hatton.*"] (*Ashmolean MS.* 856. 107.)

A statement of " The French King's edict constitutinge duellos to be punished in the nature of treason, within his dominions."

> ["*Ex MS. in Bibl. Hatton.*"] (*Ashmolean MS.* 856. 112.)

" Loo my leve lordes, here now next folowing is a Traytese, compyled by Johan Hill, armorier and sergeant in the office of Armorye w^t kynges Henry ye 4th and Henry ye 5te, of ye poyntes of Worship in Armes that longeth to a Gentilman in Armes, and how he shall be diversly armed and gouverned, under supportacion and favour of alle ye reders to correcte adde and amenuse where nede is, by the high commaundement of the princes that have powair soo for to ordeyne and establisshe—*The first honneur in armes is a gentilman to fight in his souverain lords quarell in a bataille of treason.*"

> [*This article (transcribed* "*Ex vet: MS: penes.* . . . *Keck de Medio Templo, ar:* ") *ends thus:* "*And thanne the Auctor Johan Hyll dyed*

ASHMOLEAN MANUSCRIPTS (*continued*)—

> *at London in Novembre the xiij^the yeer of Kyng Henry the sixt, so that he accomplisshed noo more of ye compylyng of this* [p. 383] *this trayties, on whos soulle God have mercy for his endles passion. Amen.*" (A.D. 1434.) *Bishop Tanner's knowledge of the author was obtained from this transcript only. See* " *Bibl. Brit.*," p. 403.]
> (*Ashmolean MS. 856. 376.*)

"And here next foloweth the maner and fourme of makyng of the thre Oothes that every appelant and defendant owe to make openly in the feelde before the **Kyng** and the Conestable and Mareschal, the same day that they shal do thair armes, both in Frensshe and in Englisshe; compyled and abstracte oute of a notable Traityes made of the rieule and gouvernance of the feelde in armes, by Thomas of Wodestoke, sumtyme Conestable of Englande and uncle to Kyng Richard [the Second], to whom he presented the said traities, submitting it to his noblesse to correct, adde, and amenuse as his highnes best liked."

> ["*Ex eodem MS.*" *It ends:* "*La fee du Mareshal est les listes, les barrers, et les estages dycelles, etc. Et sic finis de ista materia.*" *Compare Art. 4.*] (*Ashmolean MS. 856. 383.*)

ASSERCIONES hechas en favor de la destreça de las armas para la oposicion de maestro de su alteça, que está vaca, por muerte del Marqués de la Conquista. MS.

> [*Bibl. Nac. Madrid.* Cc. 46, p. 297.] (*En el indice figura con este titulo:* "*Noticia de la oposicion que se hacia para maestro de esgrima de los infantes de España.*")

ATHENÆUM (The). — (Periodical.) 4°. *London.*

> [1808. *Letter by N. N. on "Duelling."* (4 pages.)]

ATLANTIC MONTHLY (The). 1857–1876. *Boston:* H. O. Houghton & Co.

> [Vol. XXV. p. 626. "*Duel of the Spanish Bourbons*" (*Letter from Madrid*). By R. West.
> „ XVIII. p. 713. "*Sword of Bolivar.*" By J. T. Trowbridge.]

ATONOLI (ARENIF). — *ALFIERI* (A.). — 1655.

ATTENDOLO (DARUIS). — Il duello. 8°. 1560. *Venezia.*
> (*In Captain Hutton's Collection.*)

—— (—). — Il duello. 8°. 1562. *Venezia.*

—— (—). — Il duello con la giunta d'un Discorso del medesimo da ridurre ogni querela alla pace. 8°. 1565. *Venezia.*

19

ATTENDOLO (Daruis). — Discorso intorno all' honore, et la modo di indurre le querele per ogni sorte d'ingiuria alla pace.   8°.   1565.   *Venezia.*

AUDIGUIER (Vital d'). — Le vray et ancien usage des duels. Confirmé par l'exemple des plus illustres combats et deffys qui se soient faits en la chretienté.   8°.   1617.   *Paris:* Pierre Billaine.

> [*Pourquoy les seuls François se battent en duel.—Divers sujets pour lesquels les duels ont été permis.—Duel le Bayard et de Dom Alonse de Sainct-Major. —Combat de Créquy contre Philipe de Savoye.—Duel entre Carrouges et le Gris, &c.*]   (*In Captain Hutton's Collection.*)

AUERSWALD (Fabian von). — Ringer-Kunst.   Folio.   1539. *Wittenberg:* Hans Lufft.

—— (— —). — Ditto.   Erneuert von G. A. Schmidt, mit Einleitung von Dr. K. Wassmannsdorff.   8°.   1869.   *Leipzig:* M. G. Priber.

> [*Getreutes Facsimile des Originals.*]

AURIAC (Eugène d'). — D'Artagnan, Capitaine-Lieutenant des Mousquetaires, sa vie aventureuse, ses duels, ses rapports avec Athos, Aramis et Porthos ; ses amours, ses intrigues et ses missions politiques, ses combats, sa mort.   2 vols.   8°.   1847.   *Paris:* Baudry.

AYALA (Don Atanasio de). — El bisoño instruido en la disciplina militar.   8°.   1616.   *Madrid.*

> [*A military handbook for the instruction of recruits in the use of arms.*]

AYALA (Mariano d'). — Bibliografia Italiana Militare.

> [*Contains a list of works on "Swordplay."*]

AYRERI (G. H.). — Opuscula, ed. Jungius.   2 tomi.   8°.   1746. *Göttingen.*

> [*De per duellione seditiosorum de oguitibus legum, &c.*]

AZÉMAR (Baron d') [Colonel]. — Combats a la baïonnette. Théorie adoptée en 1859 par l'armée d'Italie commandée par l'Empereur Napoléon III.   16°.   1859.   *Torino.*

—— (— —). — Theorie der Kämpfe mit dem Bajonett, angenommen im J. 1859 von der italien.   Armee unter Napoleon III. aus (des verf.) System der neueren Kriegführg.   In's Deutsche übertragen von Lieut. Rich. Stein.   Gr. 8°.   1860.   *Breslau:* Kern.

B (Dr.). — Anleitung das Contraschlagen in kurzer Zeit gründlich zu erlernen, nebst einem Anhange über die steile Auslage und das Säbelschlagen. 8°. 1852. *Bonn:* Henry A. Cohen.
[*With figures.*]

B (Von). — Anleitung für Officiere und Unterofficiere beim Ertheilen d. Unterrichts im Turnen und Bajonettiren. 16°. 1881. *Hannover:* Helwing.

—— (—). — Anleitung für Officiere und Unterofficiere beim Ertheilen d. Unterrichts im Turnen und Bajonettiren. 2te nach den allerhöchsten und neuesten Vorschriften bearb. Auflage. 16°. 1885. *Hannover:* Helwing.

—— (—) [Univ. Fechtmeister]. — Die Fechtkunst mit dem krummen Säbel. Praktische Anleitung zum Militärfechten (Hieb und Stich) und zum deutschen kommentmässigen Studentenfechten. Gr. 8°. 1884. *Strassburg i. E.:* R. Schulz & Comp.
[22 *plates from photographs.*]

BACON (Francis) [Viscount of St. Albans.] — Charge touching duells, upon an information in the Star Chamber against Priest and Wright. With the decree of the Star Chamber in the same cause. 4° folio. 1614. [*London:*] printed for R. Wilson.

BADMINTON LIBRARY. — *POLLOCK* (*W. H.*). — 1889.

BADMINTON MAGAZINE (The) of Sports and Pastimes. Edited by Alfred E. T. Watson [Rapier]. 8°. 1895. *London:* Longmans, Green & Co.
[1895. September (No. 2). "*Fencing.*" *By Miss May G. Norris. Illustrated by E. Sparks and F. Craig from sketches by the author.*]

BADON (Edmond). — *LOCKROY.* — 1834.

BAÏONNETTE (La) française et le fusil à aiguille. 8°. 1867. *Paris:* Libr. du Petit Journal.

BAJONET-FECHTLEHRE für die Grossherzogliche Badensche Infanterie. 8°. 1823. *Mannheim.*
(*In Captain Hutton's Collection.*)

BAJONETTFECHTEN für die königl. Württenburg Infanterie. 1824. *Stuttgart.*
[1 *plate and* 44 *figures.*]

BAJONETTFECHTEN (Das). Leicht fassliche Darstellung, das-selbe in kurzer Zeit gründlich zu erlernen, nebst kurzer Auseinander-setzg., wie solches ohne hohe Kosten in der Schweiz einzuführen. 8°. 1852. *Chur :* Hitz.

[1 *folding plate containing 6 figures.*]

BAJONETT-FECHT-SCHULE in 21 Darstellungen mit Erläut. Texte. 4°. 1826. *Hermannstadt :* Thierry.

[*The text is lithographed.*]

BAJONETIR-REGLEMENT für die Grossherzogliche Hessische Infanterie. Lexicon-8°. 1836. *Darmstadt :* Leske.

[55 *plates containing* 70 *figures.*]

BAJONETTIR-VORSCHRIFT für die Infanterie. 16°. 1889. *Berlin :* Mittler u. Sohn.

BAKER (SIR SAMUEL WHITE). — Nile Tributaries of Abyssinia, and the Sword Hunters of the Hamram Arabs. 8°. 1867. *London.*

BALAN (C.) [Königl. Preuss. Konsistorialrath]. — Duell und Ehre. Ein Beitrag zur praktischen Lösung der Duellfrage unter besonderer Berücksichtigung der Verhältnisse im deutschen Offizier-korps. 8°. 1890. *Berlin :* Walther u. Apolant.

[*The German pamphlet just published, "Honour and Duels," has caused a sensation, particularly in army circles (Dalziel reports). The name of Herr Balan, lieutenant of the fourth Guard Landwehr regiment, is attached to the pamphlet as its author, but it is nevertheless believed to have been inspired by the Crown, some going so far as to attribute its authorship to the Emperor himself. It deals with the present mistaken idea concerning the demands of honour in relation to duelling, and rejects duelling as an absurd and unnecessary method of settling differences.—"Pall Mall Gazette," London, April 12, 1890.*]

BALASSA (C. K. K.) [Major]. — Fechtmethode. Eine rationelle, vereinfachte und schnell fassliche Fechtübung des Säbels gegen den Säbel, und dieses gegen das Bajonet und die Picke, zum Hauen, Stechen und Pariren. Eigens für die Cavallerie, nach den aus der Feld- und Friedens-Praxis geschöpften Grundsätzen in 25 Tabellen, nebst einem kleinen Anhang "Ueber das Kunstfechten." Mit 19 Abbildungen. Quer gr. 4°. 1844. *Pest.*

[26 *lithographed plates.*]

—— (—. —. —.) [Major]. — Die militärische Fechtkunst vor dem Feinde. Eine Darstellung der im Kriege vorkommenden Fechtarten des Bajonets gegen das Bajonet, des Säbels gegen den

Säbel, und der Lanze gegen die Lanze, mit Beseitigung aller beim Kunstfechten vorkommenden, vor dem Feinde aber nicht füglich anwendbaren Stiche, Hiebe und Paraden zum Gebrauche für Infanterie und Kavallerie, mit 26 (lith.) Abbildungen nebst einem Anhang über das Kunstfechten mit dem Säbel. Quer gr. 4°. 1860. *Pest :* Engel und Mandello.

[1 *lithograph containing 16 figures.*]

BALCK (V.). — Tabeller i sabelfäktning. Tvär 8°. 1876. *Stockholm :* Looström & Komp.

BANCROFT (G.). — *NORTH AMERICAN* Review.

BANE (Donald). — The expert sword-Man's companion : or the True Art of self-defence, with an account of the Author's life and his transactions during the wars with France. To which is annexed the art of gunnerie. 12°. 1728. *Glasgow :* printed by James Duncan.

[*Portrait of Bane, and 22 plates, out of the text.*]

BANVILLE (Teodoro de). — Duelo de Monstruos.

["*La España Moderna.*" *Revista Ibero-Americana.* 15 *Julio*, 1891. *Madrid.*]

BANWURA. Jacquot et Colas, duellistes. Comédie en un acte et en prose. 12°. 1783. *Paris :* Cailleau.

[*Représentée, pour la première fois, à Paris, sur le Théâtre des Variétés Amusantes en* 1781.]

BARESTE (Eug.). — Des plus anciens ouvrages publiés en France contre le duel. 8°.

[*Curiosités Bibliographiques.*] (*In Mr. J. R. Garcia Donnell's Collection.*)

BARIFFE (Wm.) [Captain]. — Military discipline, wherein is martially shown the order of drilling with the musket and pike, set forth in postures, with the words of command, and brief instructions for the right use of same. Exercise of the foot. Small 4°. 1642. *London :* T. Jenner.

[*Engraved portrait and plans.*]

BARR (Robert). — *IDLER* (*The*).—1894.

BARRINGTON (Sir Jonah) [Judge of the High Court of Admiralty in Ireland]. — Personal Sketches of his own Time. 2nd edition. 2 vols. 8°. 1830. *London :* H. Colburn & R. Bentley. [*Duelling.*]

BARROLL (G. W.). — Some Observations on Fencing. ["Illustrated Naval and Military Magazine," Nov. and Dec. 1888. 8º. *London.*]   [*With photolithographs.*]

—— (—. —.). — The Sabre. ["Illustrated Naval and Military Magazine," Feb., April, May, 1889. 8º. *London.*]
[*With photolithographs.*]

BARSEWISCH (Von) [Hauptmann]. — Praktische Bajonett-Fechtschule auf Grund der Bajonettir-Vorschrift für die Infanterie vom 15 August 1889. 2. Auflage. 12º. 1895. *Berlin:* E. S. Mittler & Son.
[*47 Seite mit 18 Abbildungen.*]

BARTHÉLEMY (Lhérie) et **CÉRAN** (Léon de). — L'Épée, le baton et le chausson. Vaudeville en quatre tableaux. 12º. 1830. *Paris:* J. N. Barba.

BAS (François). — Nouvelles et utiles observations pour bien tirer des armes. 8º. 1749. *Basle.*
[*Dedicated to the Colonels of the Basle troops and MM. J. Bourcard and Abel de Wettstein.*]

BAS (William). — Sword and Buckler, or Serving Mans Defence. 1602. 4º. *London:* imprinted for M. L. and are to be sold at his shop in S. Dunstons Church yard.
[16 *leaves.* "*Agimus hæc prœlia verbis.*"]

B[ASNAGE]. — Dissertation historique sur les duels et les ordres de Chevalerie. 12º. 1720. *Amsterdam.*

BASNAGE DE BEAUVAL (J.). — Histoire des ordres militaires ou des chevaliers, et un traité sur les duels. Nouvelle édition. 4 vols. Small 8º. 1721. *Amsterdam.*
[*Boston Public Library (U.S.A.),* 2234. 1.]

BASNAGE (Jacques). — Dissertation historique sur les duels et les ordres de Chevalerie, avec un discours preliminaire ou l'on entreprend de montrer, que le duel fondé sur les maximes du point d'honneur, est une vengeance barbare, injuste et fletrissante, par Pierre Roques. 8º. 1740. *Basle:* Jean Christ.
(*In Captain Hutton's Collection.*)

—— (—). — *ROQUES.* — 1747.

BASNIERRES (CHEVALIER DE). — De la beauté de l'escrime de l'épée, dedié au Maréchal de Villars.   8°.   1732.   *Paris:* chez Thiboust.

BAST (B. DE) [Ancien Professeur de Toute Arme et Gymnasiarque à la Société Royale et Chevalière de St. Michel à Gand]. — Manuel d'escrime.   8°.   1836.   *Bruxelles:* H. Dumont.

> [*Portrait of author and 7 folding plates in outline.*]
> (*In Captain Hutton's Collection.*)

—— (—. —). — Ditto.   8°.   1836.   *La Haye:* Kips.

BATAILLARD (C.). — Du Duel.   Suivi du combat et duel des seigneurs de la Chasteneraye et de Jarnac.   1829.   *Paris.*

BATIER [or BATTIER]. — La théorie pratique de l'escrime, pour la pointe seule, avec des remarques pour l'assaut.   12°.   1770.   *Paris.*

—— [—— ——]. — La théorie pratique de l'escrime pour la pointe seule, avec des remarques instructives pour l'assaut et les moyens d'y parvenir par gradation.   Dedié à S. A. S. le Duc de Bourbon.   8°.   1772.   *Paris:* Simon.

> [1 *engraving.*]

BATTLE (Trial by) (or Wager of).

> [*A trial by combat, formerly allowed by our laws, where the defendant in an appeal of murder might fight with the appellant, and make proof thereby of his guilt or innocence.   See APPEAL.*]

BAUDRY (AMBROISE). — L'Escrime pratique au XIXe Siècle.   8°.   1893.   En vente chez l'Auteur, 108, Rue de Richelieu.

> [*Préfaces de MM. Cloutier, Président de la Société d'escrime à l'épée de Paris, et Max Doumic, Vice-Président de l'École d'escrime pratique. Ouvrage orné de 16 gravures et de plusieurs vignettes.*]

BAUPRÉ (JEAN JAMIN DE) [Maître en fait d'armes de Son Altesse S. Electorale de Bavière, à la celebre Université d'Ingolstadt]. — Méthode très facile pour former la noblesse dans l'art de l'épée, faite pour l'utilité de tous les amateurs de ce bel art.   On trouvera en ce livre, rangés en ordre, tous les mouvements généralement bien expliqués qui sont necessaires à bien apprendre et à enseigner à faire des armes, en allemand et en français, avec 25 planches qui représentent toutes les principales actions, à la dernière perfection.   Ce jeu est choisi de l'Italien, de l'Allemand, de l'Espagnol et du Français, et composé de manière, par sa grande pratique, qu'on peut l'appeller le centre des armes.   Dedié à Son Altesse Electorale de Bavière.   4°.   1721.   *Ingolstadt :* Gedruckt bey T. Gran.

> [25 *copperplates, out of the text.*]   (*In Captain Hutton's Collection.*)

BAUPRÉ (Jean Jamin de). — Album d'escrime de quatorze planches gravées sur cuivre et coloriées (le traité en comporte vingt-cinq).   4° oblong.   1721.

> (*In Mons. Vigeant's Collection.*)

BAYARD et **GABRIEL** (J.). — Sa Salle d'Armes.   Comédie en un acte.   Mêlée de chant.   8°.   1843.   *Paris :* Beck.

> [*Représentée pour la première fois, à Paris, sur le Théâtre du Palais-Royal, le 4 Août 1843.*]

BAYONET EXERCISE.   12°.   1860.   *London :* Clowes.

> [*With plates.*]

BAYONET-FECHTLEHRE (Erste Abhandlung der).   8°.   1823. *Karlsruhe :* Müller.

> (*In Captain Hutton's Collection.*)

BAZANCOURT (Le Baron César de). — Les Secrets de l'Epée. 8°.   1862.   *Paris :* Amyot.

> [*Avec couverture ornée.*]   (*In Captain Hutton's Collection.*)

—— (⸺ ⸺ ⸺).   Ditto.   12°.   1876.   *Paris :* Amyot.

BEAUMONT (Edouard de). — L'Épée et les Femmes.   8°.   1882. *Paris :* Librairie des Bibliophiles.

> [*Avec dessins de Meissonier tirés hors texte.*]

BEAUVOIR (Edouard Roger de Bully) [dit Roger de]. — Duels et duellistes.   12°.   1864.   *Paris :* Lévy Frères.

—— (—— —— —— ——). — *BENTLEY'S* Miscellany.

—— (—— —— —— ——). — *GRISIER* (A.). — 1863.

BEECHER (L.). — Remedy for Duelling.   A Sermon [on Isa. lix. 14, 15], etc.   8°.   [1806 ?]   *Boston (U.S.).*

> (*In the British Museum,* 4485, *h.* 9.)

—— (—.). — Another Edition.   The Remedy for Duelling.   To which is annexed the resolutions and address of the Anti-duelling Association of New York.   8°.   1809.   *New York.*

> (*In the British Museum,* 4485, *i.* 27.)

BEHR (Fr. L.). — Flüchtige Bemerkungen über die verschiedene Art zu fechten einiger Universitäten, von einem fleissigen Beobachter. 8°. 1792. *Halle:* Dost.

BELGRAVIA MAGAZINE. 8°. *London:* Chatto & Windus.
> [Vol. XVII. p. 481. *"My First Duel."*
> „ XXXIV. p. 304. *"Duel in Herne Wood."* By W. Collins.
> „ LV. p. 155. *"French Duelling."* By H. R. Haweis.]

BELL (Ernest). — Boxing, Wrestling, Fencing, &c. 12°. 1890. *London:* Bell & Sons.
> [*Forming Vol. III. of Bohn's Handbooks of Athletic Sports.*]

BELLEVAL (Comte de). — Panoplie du XVe au XVIIe Siècle. 8°. 1873. [*Lille*]: A. Aubry.
> [*Dagger, Lance, Sword.*]

BELLEVAL (Le Marquis René de) [né à Abbeville en 1839]. — Nos pères, mœurs et coutumes du temps passé. 8°. 1879. *Paris:* Olmer.
> [*Un duel sous Mazarin.*]

BELLINI (Vincenzo). — Manuale del duello. 8°. 1881. *Napoli:* De Angelis e Figlio.

—— (—). — La sciabola. Trattato di scherma. 8°. 1882. *Napoli:* De Angelis.

—— (—). — Trattato di spada e sciabola (*in the press*).

BENARD. — Eleven plates on Fencing, containing 48 Positions. 4°. [n.d.]

BENNETT (John). — Discourse against the fatal effects of duelling. 4°. 1783. *Manchester.*
> [*This pamphlet relates to the fatal duel between Cornet Hamilton and Captain Mountsey, fought with swords in Spencer's Tavern, Market Place, Manchester, on March 10, 1783.*] (*Vide also ACCOUNT (An), 1783.*)

BENTLEY'S MISCELLANY. *London.*
> [Vol. II. p. 76. *Duelling.* By Captain Medwin.
> „ XXX. pp. 255, 353. *Anecdotes of Duelling.*
> „ XXXIII. p. 538. *Duel of D'Esterre and O'Connell.*
> „ LVII. p. 183. *Beauvoir on Duelling.*]

BERAUDIÈRE (Messire Marc de la) [Chevalier de l'ordre du Roy, Capitaine de cinquante hommes d'armes de ses Ordonnances, Seigneur de Mauvoisin]. — Le Combat de seul à seul en camp clos.

Avec plusieurs questions propres à ce sujet. Ensemble le moyen au gentilhomme d'éviter les querelles et d'en sortir avec son honneur, divisé en 4 parties. 1608. 4°. *Paris:* chez Abel l'Angelier.

[*Traité de duel renfermant des détails sur les pratiques du combat singulier.*]
(*In Captain Hutton's Collection.*)

BERGAUER (JOSEF) [Lieut. 1ter Klasse des k. k. 38. Linien-Infanterie-Regt.]. — Methodischer Leitfaden für das Säbelfechten. 12°. 1864.

[*Selbstverlag des Verfassers.* 1 *plate.*]

BERGER (A.). — Das sogenannte americanische Duell und die studentische Schlägermensur. Ein Beitrag zur Präcisierg. des Zweikampfdelictsbegriffes. 8°. 1892. *Leipzig:* Fock, Verlag.

BERICHT über den Fechtbetrieb von Ende 1877 bis Anfang 1881 im markischen Turngau im VIII. Kreise (Rheinland und West-falen) der deutschen Turnerschaft. Hierbei ein Anhang. Die Hiebfechtlehre. Klein 8°. 1881. *Iserlohn.*

BERLIN Kœnig. Bibliothek. (M. Germ. 9. 16, Gladiatoria). MS.
(*An anonymous work on fencing in the Royal Berlin Library.*)

BERLINGERO (GESSI). — La spada di honore. Libro primo delle osservazioni cavaleresche. 4°. 1671. *Bologna.*

[*Portrait and copperplates.*] (*In Captain Hutton's Collection.*)

BERNARDI (ANT.). — Episc. Casertani disputationes, in quibus monomachia (quam singulare certamen Latini, recentiores duellum vocant) astruitur et evertitur. Folio. 1562. *Basileae.*

BERNER. — 1828.
[*Ueber Bajonettfechten in der* "*Zeitschrift für Kunst u. s. w. des Krieges.*"]

BERRIMAN (W. M.). — Militiaman's Manual and sword-play. 12°. 1859. *New York:* D. van Nostrand.

—— (—. —.). — Militiaman's Manual and sword-play without a master. 2nd edition. 12°. 1861. *New York:* D. van Nostrand.

—— (—. —.). — Militiaman's Manual and sword-play. 3rd edition. 12°. 1863. *New York:* D. van Nostrand.

—— (—. —.). — Militiaman's Manual and sword-play. 4th edition. 12°. 1864. *New York:* Van Nostrand.

BERTELLI (PAOLO). — Trattato di Scherma ossia modo di maneggiare la spada e la sciabla. 8°. 1800. *Bologna :* U. Ramponi.
[*5 plates.*] (*In Captain Hutton's Collection.*)

BERTOLINI (BARTOLOMEO). — Trattato di sciabola, con 10 tavole. 8°. 1842. *Trieste.*
(*In Captain Hutton's Collection.*)

—— (—). — Teorie sulla sciabola per una scuola di contro-punta. 8°. 1856. *Ferrara :* Bresciani.

BERTRAND [Maître d'armes]. — L'escrime appliquée à l'art militaire. 8°. 1801. *Paris.*

—— (— —). — *LEGOUVÉ (E.).* — 1876.

BERTRAND (FILS). — Règlement de la Société d'armes de Paris, fait et présenté par M. Bertrand, président, et accepté par MM. les Membres. 18°. 1827. *Paris :* Demonville.

BESENZANICA (ERNESTO). — Come il sistema Radaelli fu esautorato. Considerazioni intorno la relazione della Commissione giudicante dei trattati di Scherma, presentati al Ministero della guerra, dietro concorso indetto il 21 Settembre 1882. 1886. *Milano :* Dumolard.

BESNARD (CHARLES) [Breton]. — Le maistre d'armes libéral, traittant de la théorie de l'art et exercice de l'espée seule, ou fleuret, et de tout ce qui s'y peut faire et pratiquer de plus subtil, avec les principales figures et postures en taille douce ; contenant en outre plusieurs moralitez sur ce sujet. Dedié à Nosseigneurs des Estats de la province et duché de Bretagne. 4°. 1653. *Rennes :* chez Julien Herbert.
[*4 copperplates, out of the text.*]

BETA (O.). — *ZWANZIGSTE* Jahrhundert. — 1891.

BETTENFELD (MICHEL). — L'art de l'escrime. 12°. 1885. *Paris :* Charpentier.

BIBESCO (G.). — Recueil. Politique — Religion — Duel. 8°. 1888. *Paris.*

BIBESCO (PRINCE). — *VAUX (Baron de).* — 1882.

BIBLE. Old Testament. Psalms. Latin. Duellum Poeticum. Contendentibus G. Eglisemmio . . . & G. Buchanano . . . pro Dignitate paraphraseos Psalmi cente simi quarti [containing two literal prose and the two rival poetical versions]. Adjectis prophylacticis adversus A. Melvini Cavillum in Aram Regiam [of which the text is given], aliisq; Epigrammatis (necnon Astrologicum de causis & effectibus novi Cometæ Judicum). 8°. 1618. *Londini :* E. Aldæus.

BIBLIOTHECA HISPANA NOVA. 1783. *Madrid :* Nicolas Antonio.

> [*Mentions the following MSS. :—*
> *Scripsit F. Franciscus Garçia, Mercenariorum Sodalis . . . &c. : Verdadera intelligencia de la destreza de las armas del Comendador Geronymo Sanchez Carranza de Barreda (Barameda ?).*
> *Extat MS. inter libros qui . . . nunc sunt excelentissimæ comitissæ.*
> *Scripsit Gundisalvus de Silva, qui se vocat Centurionem (seu Capitaneum vulgo) : Compendio de la verdadera destreza de las armas.* 4°. *MS.* (*In Villaumbrosana bibliotheca.*)
> *Anonymus, in bibliotheca Villaumbrosana extans, scripsit: De la destreza de las armas.* 4°. *MS.*
> *Anonymus alius scripsit : Libro del Exercicio de las armas. MS.* (*In bibliotheca Escurialensi regia.*)]

BINTZ (Dr. Jul.). — Die volksthümlichen Leibesübungen des Mittelalters. 4°. 1879. *Hamburg :* Nolte.

BIOGRAPHIE UNIVERSELLE. 52 vols. 8°. 1811–28. *Paris.*

> [Vol. V. pp. 402, 403 ; Vol. XXIII. p. 411 ; Vol. XLIV. pp. 127, 401 ; Vol. XLVIII. p. 522 ; Vol. XLIX. p. 130. "*Duelling.*"]

BIRAGO (F.). — Il secondo libro dei consigli cavallereschi. 8°. 1633. *Milano.*

> [*Portrait.*]

—— (—.). — Consigli cavallereschi né quale si ragiona circa il mondo del fare le paci con un' apologia Cavalleresca per il' Signor Torquato Tasso. 4°. 1686. *Bologna.*

BIRCH. — Historical Negotiations.

> [Page 467. "*Duelling.*"]

BISLAND (M.). — *OUTING.* — 1890.

BLACK AND WHITE (Weekly Periodical). Folio. *London,* Fleet Street.

> [1891. *May 30. Drawing by W. Frank Calderon of "Lance versus Sword," an incident at the Royal Military Tournament, Agricultural Hall, Islington.*
> 1891. *March 7. "Story of Swordmanship." By O. Crawfurd.*
> 1892. *June 11. "Cavaliere Pini's exhibition of Italian Fencing at St. Martin's Town Hall."*
> 1894. *February 24. "Fencing in all Ages."*
> 1895. *November 2. "The White Arm." Interview with Captain Cuthbert Keeson.*]

BLACKEVELL [? Blackwell]. — Album d'escrime. Oblong 8°. [*vers* 1680.]

[*Album de planches sur cuivre, destinées à un ouvrage d'escrime qui ne partul pas. Curieuses gravures. The spelling of the author's name is simply a mistake of M. Vigeant's. See note to Blackwell, 1730.*]
(*In Monsieur Vigeant's Collection.*)

BLACKSTONE (SIR WILLIAM). — Commentaries. 4 vols. 8°. *London :* Cadell.

[*Judge Blackstone lays down the law that if a man is killed in a duel, it should be regarded as murder, and the seconds should be treated as accomplices.*]

BLACKWELL (HENRY). — The English Fencing Master, or the Compleat Tutor of the Small-Sword. Wherein the truest Method, after a Mathematical Rule, is plainly laid down. Shewing also how necessary it is for all Gentlemen to learn this Noble Art. In a Dialogue between master and scholar. Adorn'd with several curious postures. 4°. 1702 and 1705. *London.*

[*5 woodcuts in the text. 24 copperplates, out of the text, folded. Dedicated to C. Tyron, Esq., of Bullick, Northants.*]
(*In British Museum, South Kensington Museum, and Captain Hutton's Collection.*)

B[LACKWELL] (H[ENRY]). — The Gentleman's Tutor for the Small Sword ; or the Compleat English Fencing Master. Containing the truest and plainest rules for learning that noble Art ; shewing how necessary it is for all gentlemen to understand the same, in thirteen various lessons between Master and Scholar. Adorn'd with several curious postures. Small 4°. 1730. *London.*

[*6 woodcuts. To this second edition is sometimes annexed, in addition to the 6 woodcuts in the text, a curious collection of folding plates, most of which are faithful reproductions of Capo Ferro's and Giganti's "attitudes," in which, however, the figures are "dressed" in the fashion of Queen Anne's reign, with large periwigs, lace ruffles, high-heeled square-toed shoes, &c.*]
(*In the Bodleian Library.*)

BLACKWOOD'S MAGAZINE. 8°. *London :* Blackwood.

[Vol. XXIV. p. 541. *The Duellists.* ·
 „ XLIII. p. 371. *How to avoid a Duel.*
 „ LXVIII. p. 712. } *Modern State Trials. By S. Warren.*
 „ LXX. p. 122. }
 „ CXXIX. p. 555. *The Sword.*]

BLENGINI (CESARE ALBERTO). — Trattato teorico-pratico di spada e sciabola, e varie parate di quest' ultimo contro la baionetta e la lancia. Operetta illustrata da 30 figure incise, con rittrato dell' autore. 8°. 1864. *Bologna :* Fava e Garagnani.

[*In 1879 a Russian translation was published in St. Petersburg.*]

BLENGINI (CRISTOFORO DI MONDOVI). — Teoria della scherma. 1850.

BLOT (JACQUES ANTOINE). — L'Ecole de l'escrime ; petit manuel pratique à l'usage de l'armée. 32°. 1862. *Paris :* Marpon.

[*Dédié au Prince Impérial.*]

—— (— —). — L'Ecole de l'escrime ; petit manuel pratique à l'usage de l'armée. Suivi du code du duel. Nouvelle édition. 12°. 1875. *Paris :* Tarride.

—— (— —). — L'Ecole de l'escrime. Petit manuel pratique à l'usage de l'armée. Suivi du code du duel. 32°. 1888. *Paris :* Marpon et Flammarion.

[*Another edition.* 8°. *1890. Paris.* (114 *pages.*)]

BLUETT (J. C.). — Duelling and the laws of honour examined upon principles of common sense and revealed truth. 8°. 1835. *London :* R. B. Seeley.

[*2nd edition, 1836.*] (*In Mr. J. R. Garcia Donnell's Collection.*)

BLUTH (PREM. LIEUT.). — Praktische Anleitung zum Unterricht im Hiebfechten. Nach der bei der königl. Central-Turnanstalt eingeführten Lehrmethode bearbeitet. 8°. 1878. *Berlin :* Schroeder. [18 *woodcuts in the text.*]

—— (HAUPTMANN). — Praktische Anleitung zum Unterricht im Hiebfechten. Nach der bei der königl. Militär-Turnanstalt eingeführten Lehrmethode bearb. 2te verb. Aufl. 8°. 1883. *Berlin :* Mittler u. Sohn. [18 *woodcuts in the text.*]

BOCCALINO. — Traj la bilansa politica. Folio. 1673. *Castel.*

[Tom. III. *Della natura di duella.*]

BOCER (HENR.). — De bello et duello tractatus denuo recogn. et auctus. Acc. oratio de privilegiis doctor. ab Joh. Halbrittero in actu doctoreo 30 julii 1604 dicta. 1607. *Tubingae.*

[*With portrait of author.*]

BOCERUS (HENRY). — Tractatus de Bello et Duello. 4°. 1591. *Tubingae.*

BODE (G. H.). — *NORTH AMERICAN* Review.

BODIN (Charles) [Sieur du Freteil.]. — Discours contre les duels. 8°. 1618. *Paris :* Toussainct du Bray.

BOEHEIM (Wendelin) [Custos der Waffensammlung des Österreichischen Kaiserhauses]. — Waffenkunde. Handbuch des Waffenwesens in seiner Historischen Entwickelung vom Beginn des Mittelalters bis zum Ende des 18. Jahrhunderts. 8°. 1890. *Leipzig :* E. A. Seemann.

> [*Mit* 662 *Abbildungen nach Zeichnungen von Anton Kaiser und vielen Waffenschwiedewanken.*]

BOEMERI. Jus eccles. Protestantium.

> [" *Duelling.*"]   (*Mentioned in Malcom's Theological Index.*)

* * * [**BOËSSIÈRE** (La)]. — Observations sur le traité de l'art des armes, pour servir de défense à la vérité des principes enseignés par les maîtres d'armes de Paris, par M. * * * maître d'armes des académies du Roi, au nom de sa compagnie. 8°. 1766. *Paris.*

> [*Cet opuscule tend à réfuter l'œuvre de Danet.*]

BOËSSIÈRE (M. La) [Maître d'Armes des Anciennes Académies du Roi, des Écoles Royales, Polytechniques et d'Équitation]. — Traité de l'art des armes à l'usage des professeurs et des amateurs. 8°. 1818. *Paris :* Didot.

> [20 *planches pliées, dessinées par Bodem et gravées par Adam.*]
> (*In Captain Hutton's Collection.*)

BOËSSIÈRE (La). — *CHAPMAN* (*G.*). — 1861.

—— (—). — *ROBAGLIA* (*A.*). — 1877.

—— (—). — *R.* (*A.*). — 1877.

BOGUSLAWSKI (A. von). — Die Fechtweise aller Zeiten. 8°. 1880. *Berlin.*

BOHN'S HANDBOOKS OF ATHLETIC SPORTS.

——. — *ALLANSON-WINN* (*R. G.*). — 1890.

——. — *BELL* (*E.*). — 1890.

——. — *DUNN* (*H. A. C.*). — 1889.

BOICCIO (G.) [edited by Antonio Quintino]. — Gioielo di sapienza, nel quale si contengono mirabili secreti e necessarii avertimenti per difendersi dagli huomini e da molti animali . . . &c. Nuovamente dato in luce da me Antonio Quintino, ad instanza d'ogni spirito gentile. 12°. 1613. Stampata in Milano et ristampata in Genova per Pandolfo Malatesta.

> [*Portrait of the author, and 15 woodcuts in the text.*]

BOIRIE. — *BONEL.* — 1805.

——. — *MELLESVILLE.* — 1818.

BOL (FERD. VAN). — 1559.

BOLGÁR (FRANZ VON) [Oberlieut.]. — Die Regeln des Duells. 8°. 1880. *Budapest.*

—— (— —). — Die Regeln des Duells. 2te verm. Auflage. 8°. 1884. *Wien:* Seidel u. Sohn.

[4. *Auflage,* 1891.]

BONAPARTE (PRINCE PIERRE-NAPOLÉON). — Le maniement de l'épée réduit à sa plus simple expression utile. 2e édition. 12°. 1869. *Paris:* Imprimerie Aubry.

BONDI' (DI MAZO) [da Venetia]. — La spada maestra. Libro dove si trattano i vantaggi della nobilissima professione della scherma, si del caminare, girare e ritirarsi, come del ferire sicuramente e difendersi. Oblong 4°. 1696. *Venetia:* Domenico Lovisa.

[80 *copperplates.*] (*In the British Museum and Captain Hutton's Collection.*)

BONEL et **BOIRIE**. — Storb et Verner, ou les suites d'un duel. Drame en trois actes. 12°. 1805. *Paris:* Barba.

BONIE (T.). — Étude sur le combat à pied de la cavalerie. 8°. [1870.] *Paris.*

BONNER (JOHN). — *HARPER'S* New Monthly Magazine.

[Vol. XII. p. 509.]

BONNET (B.). — Traité de l'art des armes, ou les principes de l'escrime mis à la portée de tout le monde. 12°. [N.D.] *Paris:* Delarue.

[*De nombreuses figures viennent, en regard du texte, aider aux explications, faisant comprendre à première vue les différentes positions de la main, de l'épée, du sabre ou de la canne.*]

[BONNOR (HONORÉ)]. — Arbre des Batailles. Folio. 1493. *Paris:* Antoine Verard.

[*Numerous fine woodcuts, the title in facsimile.* (*A treatise on arms and chivalry, duels, &c. Written about the year* 1370, *and dedicated to Charles V., whose name, by a printer's error, is altered to Charles VIII. in the opening lines of the book. From this mistake it is evident that the publication was in contemplation before the year* 1485.)]

BONONIEN (C. VON). — Neu Künstlich Fechtbuch. 4°. 1611. *Leipzig.*

BOOKE of Honor and Armes, wherein is discoursed the Causes of Quarrell, and the nature of injuries with their repulses. 4°. 1590. Printed by R. Jhones.

> [*Woodcut, title, and curious illustrations. A rare work, probably alluded to by Shakespeare in his "As You Like It," where Touchstone says, "O Sir, we quarrel in print, by the book." The copy which passed through my hands had the duplicate title-page (frequently wanting). The cuts, having been set out too large for the size of the pages, have the appearance of being cut into; it is the same in all copies.*]

BORDEAUX (A. B.). — Essai sur le duel. 1836.

> [*22 pages.*]

BORGERSEN (A.) — Vejledning i Kompagniets af Fægtning- slæren. 8°. 1887. *Nyborg :* Schønemann.

BORRÁS (José). — El Duelo; estudio histórico-crítico. 8°. 1888. *Madrid :* Imp. de M. Minnesa. Libr. de Fé.

> [*46 pages.*]

BOSQUETT (Abraham). — The young man of honour's vade- mecum : being a salutary treatise on Duelling : together with the annals of chivalry, the ordeal-trial, and judicial combat, from the earliest times. 12°. 1817. *London :* Chapple.

> (*In Captain Hutton's Collection.*)

—— (—). — A Treatise on Duelling : together with the annals of Chivalry, the ordeal-trial, and judicial Combat, from the earliest times. 1818.

> (*In the Library of the London Institution.* [*Reprint "Pamphleteer,"* Vol. XII., No. 23, Art. 4, pp. 79–83.])

BOTILLIER (Le). — Gages de Bataille.

> [*Quoted by Ollivier de la Marche in his "Livre des Duels," contained in the "Traitez et Advis," without sufficient data.*]

BOTKA (Theod. de). — De duellis hungarorum litisdecisoriis. 1829. *Pesth.*

BÖTTCHER (A. M.). — Die reine deutsche Stossfechtschule nach E. W. B. Eiselen ausführlich bearbeitet. Gr. 8°. 1849. *Görlitz :* Heinze & Co.

> [*25 figures.*]

—— (—. —.). — Die reine deutsche Stossfechtschule nach Eiselen. 2te Auflage. 8°. 1855. *Görlitz :* Heyn.

—— (—. —.). — *EISELEN (E. W. B.).* — 1882.

—— (—. —.). — *TURNKALENDER.* — 1888.

BOUFFÉMONT (H. DE JARRY DE). — Manuel de Gymnastique électique pour tous les âges.

> 1° Gymnastique pédagogique.
> 2° Gymnastique supérieure.
> 3° Gymnastique de chambre.
> 4° Lutte française, art du patin, canne, boxe française, jet de pierres, natation, javelot. 8°. 1871. *Paris.*
> [*With portrait, 14 plates, and 535 figures out of the text.*]

BOULLIER. — Maison Militaire des Rois de France.
> [Pages 87, 88. "*Duelling.*"]

BOURDEILLES (PIERRE DE) [Seigneur de Brantôme]. — Discours sur les Duels, . . . avec une préface par H. de Péne. 12°. 1887. *Paris.*
> [*256 pages.*]

BOWLES (G.). — *JOURNAL* of the Franklin Institute.

BOXERS AND FENCERS.
> [*Article in "New York Herald" (New York, U.S.A.), December 3, 1886.*]

BOYSSAT (P.). — Recherches sur les duels. Dediées au Sieur de Creqvi. 8°. 1610. *Lyon:* Irenée Barlet.

BRACKENRIDGE (HUGH HENRY). — *DUYCKINCK (E. A.).* — 1877.

BRADFORD CITIZEN (The). — (Periodical.) Folio. *Bradford.*
> [*February 6, 1892. "The Cowboy's Duel."*]

BRANDENBURG-BAYREUTHISCHES (Hochfürstlich) Duell-Edict. 1699.
> [*Contains also, "Eines Hochweisen Raths der Stadt Hamburg Edictum, wider die Duella," publicirt den 10 Februarii 1699.*]
> (*In Mr. J. R. Garcia Donnell's Collection.*)

BRANTING (G.). — *STRÖMBERG (N.).* — 1857.

BRANTÔME (PIERRE DE BOURDEILLE, SEIGNEUR DE). — Œuvres complètes, avec ceux d'André son frère aîné. 8 vols. 8°. 1822-23. *Paris.*
> [Vol. VI. "*Mém. sur les duels Rhodomontades.*"]

BRANTHÔME. — Œuvres complètes de Pierre de Bourdeilles, Abbé et Seigneur de Branthôme. Publiés pour la première fois selon

le plan de l'auteur, augmentées de nombreuses variantes et de frag-
ments inédits, suivies des Œuvres d'André de Bourdeilles et d'une
table générale, avec une introduction et des notes par M. Prosper
Mérimée et M. Louis Lacour. Tomes I. à VIII. 16°. 1858–1891.
Paris : E. Plon, Nourrit & Cie.

> [Tome VIII. " *Discours sur les duels.*" (*Bibliothéque Elzevirienne.*)]

BRANTÔME (Mémoires de).   [Contenans les Anecdotes de la
Cour de France sous les rois Henry II., François II., Henry III. et
IV. touchant les duels.]   Petit 18°. 1722. *Leyde :* I. Sambix.

> [" *There was that jovial personage mentioned by Brantôme, the redoubtable
> Tappa of Milan, who, it is said, could teach you to cut, whenever it pleased
> you, both eyes out of an adversary's face with a peculiar "rinverso tondo," a
> circular sweep of the point."—Castle (E.), " The Story of Swordsmanship."
> (" The National Review," May 1891.*)]   (*In Captain Hutton's Collection.*)

——. — Discours sur les duels.   Avec une préface par H. de Pène.
12°. 1888. *Paris :* Libraire des Bibliophiles.

BRAUNMÜHL (A.). — Ueber d. Zweikampf im Allgemeinen,
und über d. deszfallsige Straffgesetzgebung in Baiern, mit besond.
Bezieh. auf d. Studirenden und auf d. Militär-Ehren-Gerichte.
Abgehandelt nach prakt. Ansichten. 8°. 1826. *Landshut :*
Thomann.

BRAUNSCHWEIG (Herzogl.).   Edick und Verordnungen über
d. Duell. MS.

> [*Handschrift aus dem 17. Jahrhundert.* 132 pp. 4°.]

BRAUNSCHWEIG, Lüneburg, Landesordnungen. 1735. *Göttingen.*

> [*Duell-Edikt für d. Universit. Göttingen.*]

BREA (Don Manuel Antonio de) [Maestro Mayor y Examinador
de Todos los del Reyno]. — Principios universales y reglas generales
de la verdadera destreza del espadín, según la doctrina mixta de
francesa, italiana y española, dispueto para instrucción de los
Caballeros seminaristas del Real Seminario de nobles de esta Corte.
Small 4°. 1805. *Madrid :* Imprenta Real.

> [4 *hojas de prels.,* 68 *páginas y* 18 *láminas.*]
> (*In the B.B. Nacional, del Senado y de Fernandez San Roman.*)

BREEN (ADAM VAN). — Le maniement d'armes de Nassau avecq Rondelles, Piques, Espées et Targes ; répresentez par Figures. Folio. 1618. *La Haye:* Tavernier.

> [*Indispensables pour la connaissance de l'exercice et de la tactique de l'époque de Maurice de Nassau. C'est à lui et à son oncle Guillaume de Nassau, le Stathouder de Frise, qu'on doit le rétablissement de la tactique scientifique. "Nuict et jour sans cesse estudians" (v. Breen), surtout dans les auteurs latins (Vegetius), ils finirent par poser les règles, qu'on trouve dans ces deux ouvrages.*
> *Également sans titre, a 32 estampes sur la rondelle, l'épée et la pique, puis une suite de 15 sur la targe. Avec l'explication.*]

BRÉMOND (ALEXANDRE PICARD). — Trattato sulla scherma, aggiunta la notizia de' professori nonche de' dilettanti che si distinguono in quest' arte medesima nelle principali città d'Europa. Traduzione dalla francese nella lingua toscana. 8°. 1775. *Milano.*

> [*Portrait of Saint-George.*]

—— (— —). — Traité en raccourci sur l'art des armes. 8°. 1782. *Turin:* Impr. d'Ignace Soffietti.

> [*Avec attributs d'escrime dans le titre et une curieuse préface historique sur l'escrime de cette époque. Il y est parté du Chevalier de Saint-George.*]

—— (— —). — Trattato sulla scherma : traduzione dalla francese nella lingua toscana. 8°. 1782. *Milano:* Pirola.

BRENT (JOHN). — The Egyptian, Grecian, Roman, and Anglo-Saxon Antiquities in the Museum at Canterbury. 12°. 1875. *Canterbury:* W. Davey, printer, *Kent Herald* office.

> [*To the above is appended (pp. 52–62) a memoir and account of a duel between Sir John Heydon and Sir Robert Mansfield, fought in 1600, at Norwich, the severed hand of Sir John Heydon being preserved in the Lushington Room in the Museum.*]

—— (—). — *CANTERBURY* Museum.

BRESCIANI (MARIN) [Maestro d'armi Ferrarese]. — Li trastulli guerrieri. 8°. 1668. *Brescia.*

> [*With figures.*]

BRESLAUER [Rechtsanwalt]. — Duellstrafen, Materialien, gesammelt. Gr. 8°. 1890. *Berlin:* Rosenbaum & Hart.

BRICCIO (GIOVANNI). — Avisi necessarii per difendersi dall' inimico. 8°. 1613. *Vicenza.*

[**BRICHAMBAULT** (LE BARON ANTOINE CHARLES PERRIN DE) [Colonel du génie]]. — L'Escrime appliquée aux dames. Fragment d'un poëme inédit sur l'escrime. Par un amateur de Nancy. 8°. 1835. *Paris:* Impr. de Pihan-Delaforest.

[*4 pages.*]

BRIEF (A) of two proclamations and his Majesty's edict against duels. 1613.

[*MS. in British Museum. (Press mark,* 6297, *p.* 284.)]

BRIGHAM (W.). — *NORTH AMERICAN* Review.

BRILLAT DE SAVARIN (J. A.). — *SAVARIN (J. A. B. de).*

BRIMBLECON (E. E.). — *OVERLAND* Monthly. — 1891.

BRITISH (THE) CODE OF DUEL. 8°. 1824. *London:* Knight & Lacey.

(*In Mr. J. R. Garcia Donnell's Collection.*)

—— (—). — Ditto. 12°. 1824. *London:* Smith & Elder.

BRITISH (THE) CODE OF DUEL. A Reference to the Laws of Honour, and the Character of a Gentleman, also an Appendix in which is strictly Examined the Case *between the Tenth Hussars and Mr. Battier,* to which are now added Mr. Bric's and others. Post 8°. 1827.

BRITISH CRITIC (Periodical). *London.*

[Vol. III. p. 95. "*Advice to Seconds.*"
Vol. XIII. p. 471. "*Well-directed Reprehension of Duelling.*"]

BRITISH MUSEUM. The names of yor Pushes as they are to be learned gradually. [MS. Additional, No. 5540, folios 122, 123.]

[*Date, middle of the 17th century.*]

—— ——. A treatise on fencing, in Italian. 47 folios. [MS. Additional, No. 23,223.]

[*Date, end of 17th century.*]

—— ——. Three treatises, in German, on the art of fencing, as taught by Signor Sieg. Salvator and Signor Mornan, by H. A. V. [MS. Folio. Additional, No. 17,533, ff. 127.]

[*93 figures, drawn by the hand in Indian ink, copied from Fabris' plates. Date, middle of the 17th century.*]

BRITISH MUSEUM. The use of the two hand Sworde. MS. English.

(Harl. 3542.)

—— ——. *BRIEF (A.).* — 1613.

—— ——. *CARTAS* y Papeles Varios. MSS.

—— ——. *CHARLES II.* MS.

—— ——. *COMBATS.* MSS.

—— ——. *CORRESPONDENCE.* MS.

—— ——. *COTTONIAN* Library. MSS.

—— ——. *EDICT.* MS. 1613.

—— ——. *FENCING.* MSS.

—— ——. *HARLEIAN.* MSS.

—— ——. *LANSDOWNE.* MSS.

—— ——. *LEASES.* MSS.

—— ——. *MODUS* Faciendi, &c. MS.

—— ——. *ORDINANCES.*

—— ——. *SLOANIAN.* MS.

—— ——. *SWORDS.*

—— ——. *TRATADOS* Varios.

BRITISH SPORTSMEN (Periodical). *London.* — *CAMPBELL* (*Lady Colin*). — 1890.

BRITISH STANDARD HANDBOOKS. *London :* Spencer Blackett.

> [2nd Series, No. 21. "*Boxing, Wrestling, and Fencing, or the Art of Self-Defence.*"
> 3rd Series, No. 34. "*Fencing.*"]

BROCKHAUS' CONVERSATIONS-LEXICON. — 13. vollständig umgearb. Auflage. Lexicon 8°. 1882–1888. *Leipzig :* F. A. Brockhaus.

> [Vol. VII. p. 627. "*Fechtkunst.*"
> Vol. XVI. p. 973. "*Zweikampf.*"]

BROMMEL (C. A.). — Abhandlung von den Fechttänzen der ersten Christen. 8°. 1804. *Jena.*

BROSCHUREN (Frankfurter Zeitgemäsze). — *FÜRICH (W. von).* — 1886.

40

BROUILLET (J. A.) [Curé d'Avise, député à l'Assemblée Nationale]. — Opinion sur les duels. 1790. *Paris.*
[*Brochure de 16 pages.*]

BROWN'S Miscellanea Aulica, or a Collection of State Treaties, never before published, faithfully collected by T. Brown. 8°. 1702.
[*The ancient method and usage of Duels before the King. Out of an old MS. of Elias Ashmole, Esqr.*]

BRUCHIUS (JOHANNES-GEORGIUS) [Scherm- ofte Vecht-Meester der wyd-vermaerde Academie]. — Grondige Beschryvinge van de Edele ende Ridderlycke Scherm- ofte Wapen-Konste, &c. Oblong 4°. 1671. *Leyden.*
[*Portrait of the author by Van Somer, and 143 copperplates.*]
(*In Captain Hutton's Collection.*)

BRUNET (ROMUALD). — Traité d'escrime, pointe et contre-pointe. 12°. 1884. *Paris:* Rouveyre et G. Blond.
[*Ouvrage illustré de 5 dessins par Eugène Chaperon et de 27 planches inédites.*]

BRUXELLES. Musée Royal d'Antiquités et d'Armures. — *VINKEROY* (E. van). — 1885.

BRYE (J. DE) [Maistre en fait d'armes]. — L'art de tirer des armes, réduit en abrégé méthodique. Dédié à Monseigneur le Marechal Duc de Villeroy. 8°. 1721. *Paris:* D. L. Thibourt.
[*Frontispiece and medallion portrait of the Dauphin.*]

—— (—. —). — L'art de tirer des armes. . . . 2nd edition. 8°. 1731. *Paris.*

BUCHAN (GEORGE). — Remarks on the late Trial of David Landale, Esq., for killing Mr. Morgan in a duel. 8°. 1826. *Edinburgh.*

BUCKINGHAM (J. S.). — Legislation on duelling. 1835.

BUCKLE (H. T.). — History of Civilization in England. 8°. 1861. *London:* Parker & Son.
[Vol. II. p. 137. Note 71. *List of authorities on "Duelling."*]

BUGENHAGEN. Sammlung historischer Merkwürdigkeiten (Fechtergesellschaften). 1752. *Altenburg.*

BUJA (ANTONIO). — La scherma considerata sotto tutti i rapporti sociali, fisici e morali. 8°. 1875. *Lecce:* Salentina.

BULLA Clementis VII. P. M. prohibitiva duellorum et singular. Certaminum sub graviss. poenis. 4°. 1524. *Romae.*

BULLA super confirmat. ac innovat. prohibitionis Duellorum. Folio. 1561. *Roma.*

BURETTE (PETER JOHN). — Dissertation on single combat. [1740 ?]
> [*Mémoires de l'Acad. des Inscrip. et Belles Lettres.*]

BURGH (J.). — Political Disquisitions. 3 vols. 8°. 1774–75.
> [*Article on " Duelling."*]

BURGMAIER (HANS). — Der Weiss Kunig. [Suite de 237 planches gravées sur bois d'après les dessins et sous la conduite de Hans Burgmaier.] Folio. 1799. *Vienne.*
> [*Plates No. 37, 38, 39, and 56 interest the fencer.*]

BURTON (R. F.). — A complete system of Bayonet Exercise. 12°. 1853. *London :* Clowes.
> [*6 plates in text.*]

—— (—. —.). — A new system of Sword Exercise for Infantry. Crown 8°. 1875. *London :* Clowes.

—— (—. —.). — Book of the Sword. Being a history of that weapon from the earliest ages to the present day. 8°. 1884. *London :* Chatto.
> [*With numerous illustrations.*] (*This purports to be Vol. I. of a more extensive work. No continuation has been published, the author having died* [1890].)

—— (—. —.). — *ACADEMY* (*The*).

BYRON. — Account of the trial of Lord Byron for murder of Wm. Chaworth in a duel. Folio. 1765.

C. (VON SR.). — Der Geoffnete Fecht-Boden auf welchen durch kurtz gefast Regeln gute anleitung zum rechten fundament der Fecht-Kunst. 1706. *Hamburg.*

CACCIA (MASSIMILIANO) [Maggiore de Cavalleria]. — Trattato di scherma ad uso del R. esercito. 8°. 1853. *Torino :* Favale e Compagnia.
> [*With plates.*]

CAIMUS (F.) — De jure belli. 8°. 1678. *Patavii:* Frambatti.
[*Vi sono trattate varie questioni sul "duello."*]

CAIZO. —
[*There was Caizo, a teacher at the French Court under Henry II., who taught, in a few lessons, to the unjustly reviled Jarnac, that peculiar "falso manco," at the inside of the knee, by means of which that noted bully and duellist, La Chastaigneraie, was promptly disabled in the last of the judicial duels in France.—Castle (E.), " The Story of Swordsmanship." ("The National Review," May 1891.)*]

CAJOL (Francesco). — Guida pel Maestro di scherma e bastone. Teoria da uso civile e militare del maestro di scherma e ginnastica. 8°. 1865. *Torino:* V. Vercellino.

CALA (Cristóbal). — Luz de la destreza verdadera. 4°.

CALA (Cristóbal de). — Desengaño de la Espada y Norte de diestros. 4°. 1642. *Cádiz:* Fernando Rey.
(*In the Bibl. Nacional, Madrid.*)

CALARONE (Costantino) [detto l'Anghiel: maestro di scherma Messinese]. — Scienza prattica necessaria all' huomo overo modo per superare la forza coll' uso regolato della spada: parte prima. 4°. 1714. *Roma:* Luca Antonio Chracas.
[*Portraits, woodcuts in the text.*]

CALLOT. — Guerriers, Rodomonts, Spadassins, Matamores (Album d'escrime). [*vers* 1615.] Oblong 8°.
[*Suite complète de vingt-quatre gravures sur cuivre peu connues.*]
(*In Mons. Vigeant's Collection.*)

CALTON (R. B.). — Annals and Legends of Calais. 8°. 1852. *London:* J. R. Smith.
[*Duel between a sojourner in the town named Rook and the exiled desperado Montague.*]

CALVERT (Walter). — Duelling on the Stage—and off.
[(*With 3 illustrations*) "*The Theatre*" (*London*), *March* 1, 1891, *and April* 1, 1891.]

CAMELFORD (Lord) [Thomas Pitt]. — Life, adventures, and eccentricities of the late Lord Camelford, with particulars of the late fatal duel. 8°. 1804. *London.*

CAMERON (Charles Hay). — Two essays: on the sublime and beautiful, and on duelling. 8°. 1835.
[*Privately printed.*]

43

CAMPBELL (Archibald). — Duelling in German Universities.
![Letter in " The Times" (London), May 21, 1891.]

CAMPBELL (Lady Colin). — Fencing.
["British Sportsmen" (Periodical). No. 1. 1890. London.]

CAMPENON (Le Général). — Leçons d'armes. 4°. 1869. Lyon.

—— (— —). — Traité d'Escrime. 4°. 1869. Lyon.

CAMPIGNEULLES (Fougeroux de). — Histoire des duels anciens et modernes. 2 vols. 8°. 1835. Paris: Tessier et Cherbuliez.

CANADIAN MONTHLY. Toronto.
[" Sword Point." By M. Liebetren.]

CAÑIZARES (Don Joseph de). — La vanda de Castilla, y duelo contra si mismo. Comedia famosa.

CANNING [Right Hon., M.P. for Liverpool]. — Two letters to Earl Camden respecting the transactions of the late duel. 8°. 1809.

CANTERBURY MUSEUM (Antiquities in the). —
[MS. account of a duel which took place near Norwich, in January 1600. The manuscript is thus headed : " The hand of Sir John Heydon, Knight, who in the year 1600 fought a duell wth Sr Robert Mansfield, Knight, near Norwich city, which Sir John dyed of ye wounds he rec^d in the said duel, (as I'm infor'd). I had this hand from Mrs Lomax, whose mother was nearly related to the Heydon's."]

—— ——. — BRENT (John). — 1875.

CAPEFIGUE (Jean B. H. R.). — Histoire de la Réforme.
[Vol. VIII. p. 88. " Duelling."]

—— (— —. —. —.). — Richelieu. 8 vols. 8°. 1835–1836. Paris.
[Vol. I. p. 63. " Duelling."]

CAPODIVACCA (Paolo) [Nobile Padovano].—Massime et avverti-menti da praticarsi nella scherma. 4°. 1704. Padova: G. Corona.
(In Captain Hutton's Collection.)

CAPO FERRO (Ridolfo) [da Cagli. Maestro dell' eccelsa natione alemanna nell' inclita città di Siena]. — Gran simulacro dell' arte e

RIDOLFO CAPO FERRO, DA CAGLI. 1610.

Maestro dell' eccelsa natione alemanna nell' inclita città di Siena.

dell' uso della scherma. Dedicato al serenissimo Sig. don Federigo Feltrio della Rovere, principe dello stato d'Urbino. Oblong 4°. 1610. *Siena :* apresso Saluestro Marchetti e Camillo Turi.

[*Portraits of the Duke d'Urbino and of Capo Ferro, and 43 copperplates, out of the text, engraved by Rafael Schiamirossi. (A second edition appeared in 1652, with 44 plates.) Of all the Italian works on fencing, none ever had such a share in fixing the principles of the science.*]
(*In Captain Hutton's Collection; and South Kensington Museum [Art Library].*)

CAPO FERRO (RIDOLFO). — *HEUSSLER (Seb.).*—1616.

CAPPA E SPADA. Giornale di scherma, ginnastica, &c., diretto da Luigi Sestini. 4°. 1888. *Firenze,* Via Nazionale, 14.

[*Monthly review chiefly devoted to the interests of Italian swordsmanship.*]

CARAFA DE MONOMACHIA. —

[*" Duelling."*] (*Mentioned in Malcom's Theological Index.*)

CARANÇA. — *CARRANZA (J. S. de).*

CARBINE Exercises and Musketry Instruction for the Cavalry of the Army of India. 8°. 1875. *Calcutta.*

CARCANI (M.). — Il duello ed il codice penale. *Roma :* E. Voghera.

CARDENAL Y GÓMEZ (MANUEL). — Las Armas y el Duelo. Carta dirigida al Sr. D. M. Cardenal y Gómez, maestro de esgrima, por uno de sus discípulos. 8°. 1886. *Habano :* Romero Rubio.

[*49 pages.*] (*In the British Museum.* 8425, *bbb.* 42 (7).)

CÁRDENAS. — *A[RMAS] y C[árdenas].* — 1886.

CAREW. — State of France under Henry IV.

[*" Duelling."*]

CARIOLATO (CAV. DOMENICO, Principe de Belmonte). — *ROSARI.*

CARLYLE (T.). — Duelling 250 years ago.

[*" International Magazine "* (*New York*), Vol. III. p. 108.]

——— (—.). — Essays. 6 vols. 8°. 1870–71. *London :* Chapman & Hall.

[*" Duelling 250 Years Ago."*]

CARMONA (LUIS MENDEZ DE). — Compendio en defensa de la doctrina y destreza de Carranza. 4°. 1640. *Sevilla.*

[*Con un gran escudo de las armas de Manrique 41 hoj. fols. y una de tabla.*]

CARMONA (Tamaris Méndez de). — Libro de la destreza verdadera de las armas. 1640. MS.

[*Una lámina con escudo de armas y 240 hojas.*]

CARMOUCHE. — *THÉAULON.* — 1827.

CARNAZZA (Calcedonio). — Alcune idee su la scherma.

—— (—). — Figure dell' opera di scherma. 8°.

[*Autograph manuscript, contains 180 drawings.*]

—— (—). — Cenno storico su varii di scherma riconosciuti in Europa. 8°. 1828. *Catania:* F. Longo.

—— (—). — Critica sopra talune proposizioni che con altre moltissime grossolaneamente erronee campeggiano in alcuni opuscoli di scherma. 8°. 1840. *Catania:* M. Riggio.

—— (—). — Sobre la destreza de las armas. 4°. MS.

—— (—) [Professore nel Collegio di Cutelli]. — Fisiognomia schiamachiaca, ossia conoscenza d'intenzioni nella scherma, tratto idelogico. 8°. 1839. *Catania:* F. Pastore.

—— (—). — Cenno filosofico su i principii di scherma. 8°. 1840. *Catania:* Pietro Giuntini.

—— (—). — Ditto. 1841.

—— (—). — Poesie su la scherma. 16°.

[*Autograph MS. in Italian. 33 pages.*]

—— (—). — Preparazione allo studio pratico autodidattico della scherma. Assòlo di spada; seguono idee analitiche e sintetiche. 8°. 1845. *Catania:* Tip. del R. Ospizio di Beneficenza.

—— (—). — Nomenclatura di scherma. Voci tecniche e comuni che la riguardano.

[*Autograph MS. of 202 pages. Catania, 1852.*]

—— (—). — Nomenclature de l'Escrime Française par ordre alphabétique. 16°.

[*Autograph MS. of 88 pages. Catania ou Catanie, 1852.*]

—— (—). — Apotegmi su la scherma. 16°.

[*Autograph MS. of 317 pages. Catania, 1853.*]

—— (—). — Romanzo storico critico scientificartisticoletterario. 16°. 1856. *Catania.*

CARNAZZA (CALCEDONIO). — Scherma a Bisesso. Umana Comeddia. 1832.

[*Autograph MS.*]

—— (—). — Studio pratico autodidattico della scherma. 16°.

[*Autograph MS. of 172 pages. 4 plates.* Catania, 1858.]
(*All these MSS. belonged to M. Blasco Florio, and are now in the Bibliothèque de l'Université de Catane (Sicile).*)

CAROLINA LAW REPOSITORY. *Raleigh.*

[Vol. II. p. 385. *Speech of Mr. Nash on the suppression of duelling.*]

CARRANZA (JERÓNIMO SANCHEZ DE). — De la filosofia de las armas, de su destreza y de la agresion y defension Christiana. 4°. 1569. *Luciferi Fano* (vulgo San Lucar).

["*Carranza informs his reader that his book was finished in 1569, when a few copies were printed by command of the Duke of Medina Sidonia; but it was only issued for circulation in 1582, and appeared simultaneously at San Lucar de Barrameda and at Lisbon."—Castle (E.), "Schools and Masters of Fence."*]

—— (— — —). — Libro que trata de la filosofia de las armas y de su destreza y de la aggresion y defension Christiana. 4°. 1582. *Lisbon :* San Lucar de Barrameda.

[*Portrait of Carranza. 316 pages.*]

—— (— — —). — De la filosofia de las armas . . . &c. 2nd edition. 4°. 1600. *Madrid.*

[*Elizabethan comedies give us an echo of the great Carranza's fame, even from distant Castile: Carranza the "primer inventor de la Ciencia de las Armas," the royally and imperially favoured, the writer of treatises so abstruse on the "first and second cause" in matters of honour and sword-cuts that they never have been quite understood, we believe, to this day.— Castle (E.), "The Story of Swordsmanship." ("The National Review," May* 1891.)]

—— (— — —). — Los cinco libros sobre la ley de la lujuria, de palabra ó de obra, en que se incluyen las verdaderas resoluciones de la honra, y los medios con que se satisfacen las afrentas. 4°. *Sevilla.*

[*MS. of 300 pages.*]

—— (— — —). — Discurso de armas y letras, sobre las palabras del proemio de la instituta del Emperador Justiniano . . . &c. 4°. 1616. *Sevilla.*

[*MS. of 28 pages.*]

—— (— — —). — *ARAUJO* (*Don J. S. de*).

CARRANZA (Jerónimo Sanchez de). — *CARMONA* (*L. M. de*). — 1640.

—— (— — —). — *JONSON* (*Ben*).

—— (— — —). — *MUÑECAS MARMONTANO* (*Don J. I.*). — 1886.

—— (— — —). — *NARVAEZ* (*Don L. P. de*). — 1599–1600, 1602, 1618.

—— (— — —). — *PIZARRO* (*Don J. F.*). — 1623.

CARTAGHO.   El duelo ó desafío y sus reglas.   8°.   1873. *Madrid:* (Ariban).

CARTAS y Papeles Varios, 1520–1608.   MSS.   Folio.

[*British Museum. Add.* 8219. *A collection of historical and other tracts, mostly relating to the reign of Charles V., with an account of some of his journeys. By Pedro de Gante, Secretary to D. Manrique de Lara, Duke of Nagera.*
No. 7 [f. 19b] contains, " Carteles [de desafío] entre el Marques de Pescara [Ferrante Francesco Davalos d'Aquino] y Monsieur de Vendome."
No. 54 [f. 88]. " Desafío del Marques de Denia [D. Bernardo de Sandoval y Rojas] y Conde de Castro [D. Alvar Gomez Manrique de Mendoza]."
No. 105 [f. 192b]. " Cartel de desafío de Don Pedro Osorio á Balthasar Blasco ó de Velasco." Milan, 24th April 1547.
No. 106 [f. 193]. " Provision del Emperador sobre una differencia entre dos capitanes [Beltran de Godoy y Hieronymo de Guijosa]."]

CARVALHO (Theotonio Rodriguez de). — Breve resumo do jogo de florete, em dialogo para cualquier curioso se applicar ao serio estudio desta brilhante arte, etc., traduzido dos melhores Auctores Franceses.   8°.   1804.   *Lisboa:* impressão Regia.

[105 *pages and* 8 *plates.*]

—— (— — —). — Tratado completo do jogo de florete, em o qual se establecem os principios certos dos exercicios offensivos, e defensivos desta arte.   Traduzido dos melhores authores Francezes.   1804. *Lisboa:* impressão Regia.

[*Una hoja con una advertencia y* 8 *láms que se doblan, con* 17 *figuras.*]

CASALILLA Y GARCÍA (Don Carlos). — Methodo que deve observar el Maestro para enseñar á sus dicipulos la filosofia y destreza de las armas.   8°.

[*MS.* 62 *pages.*]

CASSAGNAC (P. de). — *JACOB* (*J.*). — 1887.

48

CASSANI (GIOVANNI ALBERTO) [di Frasinello di Monserrato]. —
Essercitio Militare, il quale dispone l'huomo à vera cognitione del
Scrimire di Spada et dell' ordinare l'Essercito à battaglia . . . &c.,
&c. 4°. 1603. *Napoli :* Longo.

[*This is rather a general handbook of the military art than a treatise on
fencing.*] (*In the British Museum, and Captain Hutton's Collection.*)

CASSELL'S MAGAZINE OF ART. — *FURNISS (H.).* — 1889.

CASSELL'S OLD AND NEW LONDON. By E. Walford and
W. Thornbury. 6 vols. Royal 8°. 1875. *London :* Cassell.

CASSELL'S SATURDAY JOURNAL 4°. *London :* Cassell.

[Vol. IV. No. 203 (*August* 20, 1887), pp. 741, 742. "*Duels of Famous
Men.*"]

CASTELLOTE (R.). — Handbook of Fencing. 18°. 1882.
London : Ward & Lock.

CASTILLO DE VILLASANTE (Diego Del) [*alias* de Villa-Sante]. — Remedio de desafíos sacado é vulgarizado del tractado del Duello, compuesto en lengua latina por el Dr. Diego del Castillo de Villa Sancte, en lengua castellana por un muy buen servidor de los Illustrísimos señores marqueses de Pescara é del Guasto, etc. Y á la vuetta : Al Ilmo. Sr. Don Alonso Dávalos de Aquino, Marqués del Guasto é capitan general de la infantería española en Italia, etc. 4°. 1525. *Taurini:* D. Antonium Ranatorum.

[*Habla del tratado que con éste se relaciona en asunto y título, de "Paris Dupuy," es decir, " Paris de Puteo ó Paride del Pozo."*]

—— (Jacobi) [*alias* villa sancte]. — De duello.

["*Tractatus ex varis juris interpretibus Collecti.*" (Vol. XII. pp. 197–204.) Folio. 1549. Lugduni.] (*In the British Museum.* 5305, *I.*)

—— (Jacobi de). — Tractatus de duello. 4°. 1525. *Taurini:* per D. Antonium ranatorum.

[*Anno domini M.CCCCC.XXV. Die xxv Octobris. En la 2ᵃ hoja dice: Jacobi Castillo alias de Villa Sancte. Juris utriusque Doctor, præfatio in tractatum "De Duello" ad illustrissimum Dominum Ferdinandum Franciscum Davalos Aquinaten, Marchionem Picariæ invictissimi; ac fellicissimi exercitus Cesarei magnum Ducem ac moderatorem. En el mismo vol. está la version castellana con portada aparte y este título.*] (*In Captain Hutton's Collection.*)

—— (Jacobi de) [*alias* de villa sanctæ]. — De duello.

[*Zilettus.* "*Tractatus Universi Juris.*" (Tomus XII. pp. 284–293.) Folio. 1584. Venetiis.] (*In the British Museum.* 449. *g.* 6.)

CASTLE (Egerton) [M.A., " Con Bretto di Nomina a Maestro di Scherma "]. — Schools and Masters of Fence from the middle ages to the 18th century. With a sketch of the development of the Art of Fencing with the Rapier and the Small Sword, and a bibliography of the fencing art during that period. Illustrated with reproductions of old engravings and carbon plates of ancient swords. 4°. 1884. *London:* George Bell & Son.

[141 *woodcuts in the text. Etched frontispiece, after a drawing of Louis Leloir, and 6 carbon plates.*]

—— (—) [Maître-ès-Arts. Membre du London Fencing Club]. — L'escrime et les escrimeurs, depuis le Moyen Age jusqu'au 18me siècle. Esquisse du developement et de la bibliographie de l'art de l'Escrime pendant cette periode. Illustré de reproductions de

Egerton Castle

ACADÉMIE D'ARMES DE PARIS, 1567 1886

From a Sketch by Seymour Lucas, A.R.A.

vieilles Estampes et de photogravures. Traduit de l'anglais par Albert Fierlants, Président du Cercle d'Escrime de Bruxelles. 4°. 1888. *Paris :* Ollendorff.

[*Etched frontispiece, 160 illustrations, 6 carbon plates.*]

CASTLE (Egerton) [M.A., F.S.A., "Con brevetto di nomina a Maestro di Scherma." Membre honoraire de l'Académie d'Armes de Paris]. — Schools and Masters of Fence, from the Middle Ages to the end of the Eighteenth Century, with a complete bibliography. Illustrated with reproductions of old engravings and representations of typical swords. A new and revised edition. 8°. 1892. *London :* George Bell & Sons.

[*Portrait of the author in photogravure (in fencing dress, armed with rapier and dagger of Elizabethan fashion, replacing the ideal frontispiece of the first edition). Frontispiece. Publisher's note. A few of the plates reduced.*]

—— (—). — Schools and Masters of Fence, &c. 3rd edition. 8°. 1893. *London :* G. Bell & Sons.

[*Bohn's Artist Library.*]

——(—). — Bibliotheca Artis Dimicatoriæ.

[*Being an excerpt from the volume "Fencing, Boxing, and Wrestling," in the Badminton Library* (vide *POLLOCK* (*W. H.*), 1889). *For private distribution; only 25 copies issued.* 8°. 1889. *Bound in vellum.*]

—— (—). — The Story of Swordsmanship, especially considered in its connection with the rise and decline of duelling.

[*A lecture delivered at the Lyceum Theatre, London, February 25, 1891, and repeated in March of the same year, by command of H.R.H. the Prince of Wales; reprinted, slightly enlarged, and published in the "National Review" (Monthly Periodical), London, May* 1891.]

—— (—). — Fencing.
[*Cassell's "Storehouse of Information."* 8°. 1892. London.]

—— (—). — Consequences; a novel. 3 vols. 8°. 1891. *London :* Bentley.

—— (—). — Ditto. 2 vols. 12°. 1891. *Leipzig :* Tauchnitz.

—— (—). — Ditto. 1 vol. 8°. 1891. *New York :* Appleton.
[*Contains a critical account of the German honour-code, the Heidelberger Fecht-Boden and a duel with the Krummer-Sabel.*]

—— (—). — La Bella and Others. 8°. 1892. *London :* Cassell.

CASTLE (EGERTON). — La Bella and Others. 8°. 1892. *New York:* Appleton.

—— (—). — Ditto. 12°. 1892. *Leipzig:* Tauchnitz.

[*Contains a collection, "Clank of Steel," descriptive of Italian Schools of Arms (La Bella), of duels between masters, and (the Renommist) of the Fecht-Comment in Prussian Universities at the beginning of this century.*]

—— (—). — Some Historic Duels.

[*" New Review" (Monthly Periodical), London, February and March* 1894. *Illustrations by Douglas Connah.*]

—— (—). — The Sword Duel, its history and its practice.

[*" The Daily Chronicle," March* 16, 1895.]

—— (—). — *CRAWFURD (O.).* — 1891.

—— (—). — *NATIONAL* Review. — 1891.

—— (—). — *NEW* Review. — 1894.

—— (—). — *POLLOCK (W. H.).* — 1889.
(*Badminton Library.*)

CASTLE (EGERTON) and **POLLOCK** (W. H.). — Saviolo. An original play in one act, written for Mr. (now Sir Henry) Irving. Privately printed. 8°. 1893.

[*The principal character is Vincentio Saviolo, the Italian master of fence, who taught the new art of the rapier in London during the last years of the sixteenth century.*]

CAUCHY (EUGÉNE) [Garde des archives de la Chambre de Paris]. — Du duel, considéré dans ses origines et dans l'état actuel des mœurs. 2 vols. 8°. 1846. *Paris:* Hingray.

[*New edition in* 1863. Paris: *Guillaumin & Cie.*
Savante étude historique sur le duel à toutes les époques de la monarchie, accompagnée de curieuses recherches juridiques. — Le duel chez les anciens. — Invasion des Barbares au règne de St. Louis. — Origine et progrès du combat judiciaire. — De St. Louis au règne de Charles IX. — Naissance du duel moderne. — Ordonnances de Philippe le Bel. — Du règne de Charles IX. à la Révolution de 1789. — Duels sous Henri III., Henri IV., Louis XIII., Richelieu, Louis XIV. — De 1789 à 1846, etc.]

CAUSA (CESARE). — Manuale di ginnastica, nuoto, scherma, equitazione e pattinaggio. 8°. 1880. *Firenze:* A. Salani.

CAVADA Y ESPADERO (DON BERNABÉ FERNANDEZ). — Sobre et Duelo. Discurso de su grado de doctor. 4°. 1860. *Madrid.*

CAVALCABO (H.) et **PATENOSTRIER**. — Traité, ou instruction pour tirer des armes, de l'excellent scrimeur Hyeronime Cavalcabo, Bolognois, avec un discours pour tirer de l'espée seule fait par le deffunt Patenostrier, de Rome. Traduit d'Italien en françois par le seigneur de Villamont, chevalier de l'ordre de Hierusalem et gentilhomme de la chambre du Roy. 12º. 1609. *Rouen:* chez Claude le Villain.

[*Dedicated to the Maréchal de Brissac.*]

CAVALCABO (HIERONIMO). — Neues kunstliches Fecht-Buch durch Mr. de Villamont in Frantzösische Sprach transferirt, verdeutscht durch C. Einsidell. Oblong 4º. 1611. *Leipzig.*

—— (—). — Neues Kunstliches Fechtbuch des Weitberümten und viel erfahrnen Italienischen Fechtmeister Hieronimo Cavalcabo, von Bononien Stievorn, aus dem geschrieben welchem Exemplar durch Monsieur de Villamont, Ritter des Ordens zu Jerusalem, &c., &c., in französische Sprache transferirt. Nun aber allen Löblichen Fechtkunst Liebhabern zu gefallen aus gemelter französischer Sprach verdeutscht durch Conrad von Einsidell. Oblong 4º. 1612. *Jena.*

[6 *copperplates, out of the text.*]

—— (—). — L'escrime à Lyon. 8º. 1889. *Lyon.*

[36 *pages.*] (*In the British Museum.* 7908. bbb. 45. (3).)

CAVALCABO, VINGTRINIER (AINÉ), **GAYET** (ERNEST). — L'escrime encore et toujours à Lyon. 8º. 1889. *Lyon:* Chanoine.

CAVALIERE (Il) compito. 1609. *Viterbo.*

CAVALRY SWORD EXERCISE. 8º. 1840. *London.*

CAVALRY SWORD EXERCISE. 8º. 1845. *London.*

CAVALRY SWORD, Carbine, Pistol, and Lance Exercises, together with Standing Gun Drill for the use of the Cavalry. Horse Guards, January 1858. 8º. 1858. *London:* J. W. Parker & Son.

CAVALRY SWORD EXERCISE. 8º. 1865. *London:* Horse Guards.

—— — —. — *RULES* and Regulations.—1796.

CENTURY (The). — (Illustrated Monthly Magazine.)   Large 8°. *London* and *New York.* — *ECKFORD (H.).* — 1887.

CENZANO Y ZAMORA (Don Luis). — Manual de esgrima de sable.   Recopilación de la principales tretas puestas por lecciones al alcance de todos los aficionados. 8°. 1882. *Burgos:* Imp. de la viuda de Villanueva.

[*20 figures.*]

CÉRAN (Léon de). — *BARTHÉLEMY.* — 1830.

CEREMONIES in connection with duels.   1096–1636.

[*French MS. in British Museum, 30,542.*]

CÉRÉMONIES des Gages de Bataille selon les constitutions du bon Roi Philippe de France, Representées en Onze Figures, etc., publiées d'après le Manuscrit de la Bibliothèque du Roi.   Par G. A. Crapelet.   Imperial 8°.   1830.   *Paris:* de l'impr. de Crapelet.

CERESA (Terenziano) [Parmegiano, detto l'Eremita]. — L'esercizio della spada regolato con la perfetta idea della scherma.   Opera utile e necessaria a chiunque desidera uscire vittorioso dalli colpi della spada nemica.   4°.   1641.   *Ancona:* M. Salvioni.

CERRI (Giuseppe). — Trattato Teorico-Pratico della scherma di bastone, col modo di difendersi contro varie altre armi, sia da punta che di taglio.   4°.   1854.   *Milano:* Civelli.

(*In Captain Hutton's Collection.*)

—— (—). — Trattato teorico-pratico della scherma per sciabola. 1861.   *Milano.*

—— (—). — Trattato teorico-pratico della scherma di bastone, col modo di difendersi contro varie altre armi sia di punta che di taglio.   1868.   *Milano:* Tip. F. Vallardi.

CESARANO (Federico) [di Napoli]. — Trattato teorico-pratico di scherma della sciabola, con appendice di tutti i regolamenti cavallereschi riguardanti la scherma.   1874.   *Milano.*

(*In Captain Hutton's Collection.*)

—— (—). — Il torneo internazionale di scherma a Milano nel 1881.   *Padova:* Tip. dei Fratelli Salmin.

CESARANO (FEDERICO). — La Palestra. Giornale di scherma e ginnastica. 1882. *Padova:* Veneta Carisi.

[CHABANNES (MARC-ANTOINE-JACQUES ROCHON DE)]. —Le Duel. Comédie en un acte et en prose, 1779. 8°. 1781. *Paris:* Veuve Duchesne.

CHALAUPKA (LIEUT. FRZ.). — Leitfaden zum Unterricht im Säbel-Fechten. Für Truppenschulen der k. k. Armee. 8°. 1875. *Teschen:* Prochaska.

[1 *lithographed plate.*]

CHALMERS (REV. P.). — Two Discourses on the sin, danger, and remedy of Duelling. With a view of the rise, progress, variations, prohibitions, and preventures of single combat. With notes. 12°. 1822. *Edinburgh:* Thomson Brothers.

(*In Mr. J. R. Garcia Donnell's Collection.*)

—— (—. —.). — Discourses on Duelling. 18°. [1850 ?] *London:* Whittaker.

CHAMBERS'S BOOK OF DAYS. Royal 8°. 1862. *London:* Chambers.

[Vol. II. p. 809. *A Balloon Duel in France in* 1808.]

—— **EDINBURGH JOURNAL.**

[Series 1. Vol. VI. p. 390. *Duelling Customs.*
  „   1.   „   X. p. 14. *Harrison on Duelling.*
  „   1.   „   IV. p. 24. *The Duellist.*]

—— **JOURNAL** (Periodical). Large 8°. *London.*

[Vol.   XI. p. 185. *Two Duels.*
  „   XXXI. p. 22. *History of the Sword.*
  „   XLIV. p. 305. *British Code of Duelling.*
  „   XLIV. p. 529. *Curiosities of French Duelling.*
  „   XLIV. p. 635. *Moorish and Toledo Swords.*
  „   XLIV. p. 807. *Duel in the Dark.*
  „   XLV. p. 107. *Arabian Sword Hunters.*
  „   XLV. p. 630. *Duels.*
  „   LVI. p. 763. *Droll Side of Duelling.*
1890. *April.* Vol. LXVII. p. 193. *S. Baring-Gould. Duelling in Germany.*
1895. *February* 1, Part 133 (5th Series), pp. 29–31. *Old London Duelling-Grounds.*]

C[HAMPDEVAUX] (M. DE). — L'honneur considéré en lui-même et relativement au duel, où l'on démontre que l'honneur n'a rien de commun avec le duel et ne prouve rien pour l'honneur. 12°. 1752. *Paris.*

CHANNING (E. T.). — *NORTH AMERICAN* Review.

CHAPITRE (F.). — Escrime à la baïonnette.   8°.   [1840 ?]
Bruxelles.
(In Captain Hutton's Collection.)

—— (—). — Escrime à la baïonnette.   2e Édition.   8°.   1872.
Bruxelles : E. Guyot.
[22 plates, out of the text.]

CHAPMAN (George). — Method of attack and defence in the
Art of Fencing.   Folio.   1860.   *London :* Clowes & Sons.

—— (—). — Foil practice; with a review of the art of fencing,
according to the theories of La Boëssière, Hamon, Gomard, and
Grisier.   8°.   1861.   *London :* Clowes & Sons.
[4 lith. plates.]   (In Captain Hutton's Collection.)

—— (—). — Notes and observations on the art of fencing.   A
sequel to "Foil Practice."   Part 1, No. 1.   8°.   1864.   *London :*
Clowes & Sons.
(In Captain Hutton's Collection.)

CHAPPON (Lajos). — A Párbaj Szabályai, mellyeket Gyakor-
latból meritve összeszedett.   8°.   1848.   *Budán :* Bagó Márton.
(In Mr. J. R. Garcia Donnell's Collection.)

—— (Louis). — Theoretisch-praktische Anleitung zur Fechtkunst.   Quer 4°.   1839.   *Pesth.*
[80 lithographed plates.]

—— (—). — Die Regeln des Zweikampfes.   Nach Erfahrung
abgefaszt mit deutschen und ungarischen Text.   8°.   1848.   *Ofen.*
[Mit 3 Abbild. und 1 Portrait.]   (In Mr. J. R. Garcia Donnell's Collection.)

CHAPTER (A) ON DUELLING.   Small 8°.   1840.
[Reprinted from "Fraser's Magazine."]

CHAPUIS (A.). — *MUZIO* (*G.*). — 1561.

CHAPUS (E.). — Le Sport à Paris.   Ouvrage contenant : Le
Turf, la Chasse, le Tir au pistolet et à la carabine, les Salles d'armes,
la Boxe, le Bâton et la Canne, &c.   16°.   1854.   *Paris :* Hachette
et Cie.

CHARLES II. (Declaration of) against duels.
[MS. in British Museum. 2542. f. 278.]

56

[**CHARLES II.**]. — Proclamation by King Charles II. against fighting of duells. Broadside. 1660. *London :* printed by John Bill & Christopher Barker.

[*A copy may be seen in the Guildhall Library, London.*]

CHARLES (J. B.) [Professeur d'Escrime]. — Ma Méthode. 12°. 1890. *Paris :* Maison Quantin.

[*Préface par Pierre de Coubertin.*]

CHARPENTIÉ [de l'Académie du Roi de Lyon]. — Les vrays principes de l'épée, dediez à Monseigneur le duc de Villeroy. 8°. 1742. *Amsterdam.*

CHARRIN. — Le revolver, ses défauts et les améliorations qu'il devrait subir au point de vue de l'attaque et de la défense individuelles. 8°. 1866. *Bruxelles :* Tanera.

[*Avec fig.*]

CHASTELLAIN (GEORGES). — Histoire du Chevalier Jacques de Lalain, Compagnon de l'ordre de la Toison D'or. Édition par J. Chifflet. 4°. 1634. *Bruxelles.*

[" *Duelling.*"]
(*In the Library of the Society of Antiquaries, Burlington House, London.*)

CHASTENERAYE. — *DUPLEIX* (*S.*).

CHÂTAUVILLARD (COMTE DE). — Essai sur le duel. 8°. 1836. *Paris :* E. Proux et Comp.

(*In Captain Hutton's Collection.*)

—— (GRAF DE). — Duell-Code. Aus dem Französischen übersetzt von C. von L****. 8°. 1888. *Karlsruhe :* Bielefeld.

[*Inhalt :* (1) *Von der Beleidigung.* — (2) *Beschaffenheit der Waffen.* — (3) *Duell und Ausforderung.* — (4) *Pflicht der Zeugen.* — (5) *Stossdegen-Duell.* — (6) *Pistolen-Duelle.* — (7) *Pistolen-Duelle mit festem Standpunkte,* — (8) *mit freiem Schusse,* — (9) *mit Vorrücken,* — (10) *mit unterbrochenem Vorrücken,* — (11) *auf Parallel-Linien,* — (12) *auf Kommando.* — (13) *Säbel-Duell.* — (14) *Säbel-Duell, Stich ausgenommen.* — (15) *Ausnahme-Duelle.* — (16) *Pistolen-Duell mit geringen Entfernungen.* — (17) *Pistolen-Duell über's Schnupftuch.* — (18) *Ausnahme-Duell auf Parallel-Linien.* — (19) *Unterschriften.* — (20) *Erläuterungen.*]

CHATELAIN (LE CHEVALIER) [Officier supérieur de Cavalerie]. — Traité d'escrime, à pied et à cheval, contenant la démonstration des positions, bottes, parades, feintes, ruses, et généralement tous les coups d'armes connus dans les Académies.   8°.   1815.   *Paris :* Magimel, Anselin et Pochard.

[*A second edition appeared in* 1818, "*Augmentée de quelques leçons sur le sabre.*" 9 *lithographed plates.*] (*In Captain Hutton's Collection.*)

CHATELAIN. — Theorie der Fechtkunst.   Eine analyt. Abhandlung, frei nach dem Französischen bearbeitet.   Nebst einer Anleitung über das Hiebfechten von A. Lüpscher und F. Gömmel.   8°. 1819.   *Wien.*

[*Mit* 20 *Tafeln und* 2 *Tabellen.*]

CHATIN (Le Capitaine). — Escrime à la Bayonette.   12°.   1854. *Paris.*

(*In the Royal United Service Institution Library, Whitehall, London.*)

—— (— —). — Escrime à la baïonnette.   12°.   1856.   *Paris :* Blot.

[24 *figures, out of the text.*]   (*In Captain Hutton's Collection.*)

—— (— —). — *THEORIE* der Fechtkunst. — 1819.

CHAWORTH (Wm.). — *BYRON.*

CHÉTARDYE (La). — Instructions pour un jeune Seigneur, ou l'Idée d'un galant homme.   En deux parties.   18°.   1683.   *Paris :* Girard.

CHEVALIER (Le Sieur de). — Les ombres des défunts sieurs de Villemor et de Fontaines.   Discours notable des duels, etc.   12°. 1609.   *Paris.*

[CHEVALLIER (Le Sieur Guillaum de)]. — Discours des querelles et de l'honneur.   8°.   1598.   *Paris :* Leger Delas.

—— (— — — —). — Discours de la Vaillance.   8°.   1598. *Paris :* Robert le Fizelier.

—— (— — — —). — The Ghosts of the Deceased Sievrs de Villemor and de Fontaines.   A most necessarie discourse of duells, wherein is shewed the meanes to roote them out quite.   With the discourse of valour.   Translated from the French by T. Heigham. 3rd edition.   8°.   1624.   *Cambridge :* C. Legge.

CHEVIGNY (De). — Science des personnes de cour et d'épée. 2e edition.   12°.   1752.   *Amsterdam.*

[Tome VII. Chapter X., *dedicated to the art of fencing.* 8 *folded copperplates.*] (*In British Museum.*)

CHEVIGNY (DE). — *MASSUET* (P.). — 1752–1757.

CHÉZY (W.). — Die sechs nobeln Passionen. (Das Waidwerk. —Die ritterlichen Uebungen. — Das Mäcenat. — Die Galanterie. — Das Spiel. — Das Zechen.) 16°. 1842. *Stuttgart:* Krabbe.

CHIFFLET (J.). — *CHASTELLAIN* (George). — 1634.

CHILD (T.). — *HARPER'S* Magazine. — 1887.

CHISHULL (EDMUND) [D.D.]. — Against duelling : a sermon on Rom. XII. 19. 8°. 1712. *London.*
> [*Preached before the Queen at Windsor Castle.*]

CHRISTENSEN (F. C. A.). — Infanteristens Forhold i Fægt-ningen. 8°. 1882. *Kjøbenhavn:* Viborg.

CHRISTFALS (P. E.). — Jüdische Fechtschule. 8°. 1760. *Onoldsb.* und *Schwabach:* Enderes.

CHRISTIAN OBSERVER. *London.*
> [Vol. XLIII. p. 564. *"Dunlop's Anti-Duel."*]

CHRISTIAN QUARTERLY SPECTATOR. *New Haven.*
> [Vol. X. p. 353. *"Duelling."*]

CHRISTMANN (F. C.) und **PFEFFINGER** (DR. G.). — Theo-retisch-praktische Anleitung des Hau-Stossfechtens und des Schwad-ronhauens, nach einer ganz neuen Methode, nebst einem Anhange "Verhalten des Degen- oder Säbelführenden gegen den Bajonetisten und Lancier," &c., &c. 8°. 1838. *Offenbach a. M.*
> [12 *plates containing* 119 *figures, out of the text.*]
> (*In Captain Hutton's Collection.*)

CHURCHILL (CHARLES). — The duellist, a poem in 3 books. 4°. 1764. *London:* Peter Wilson.

CIEN conclusiones de la destreza de las Armas.
> [*MS. Español con dibojos exist. en la B. de Middelhill de Lóndres* (?), *cit. por Haenel en su Cat. Libr. MSS. Leguina's "Libros de Esgrima,"* 1891.]

CIULLINI. — *WRIGHT* (F. V.). — 1889.

CIVILITÉ Françoise (Traité de la).

————— ————— (Suite de la) ou traité du Point-d'honneur, et des Régles pour converser et se conduire sagement avec les Incivils et les fâcheux. 24°. 1680. *Paris:* Helie Josset.

CIVY (ULRIC GUELFE DE) [Viscount]. — Discours sur l'escrime. 16°. 1893. *Paris.*

[*8 pages.*]

CLADEL (LÉON). — Ompdrailles le tombeau des lutteurs, avec 16 eauxfortes hors text, et sept dans le texte. Par Rodolphe Julian. 4°. 1879. *Paris:* Cinqualbre.

CLAIR (G. DE SAINT). — *SAINT*-Clair (G. D.). — 1887.

CLARETIE (JULES). — *GRAVE (Th. de).* — 1868.

CLARK (H.). — History of Knighthood. 2 vols. 8°. 1784.
[*Ancient ceremonies used at Duels, Combats, Jousts, and Tournaments. 82 copperplates.*]

CLERC (LE). — Bibliothèque Universelle.
[*Vol. XX. p. 242. "Duelling."*]

CLERMONT (LE COMTE DE). — *MÉMOIRE.* — 1763.

CLESIO (MAESTRO).
[*Although this author has been mentioned by some writers, I have not been able to trace his works.*]

COCKBURN (JOHN) [Rector of Northaw, Midx., D.D.]. — The History and Examination of Duels, shewing their Heinous Nature, and the Necessity of Suppressing them. In two parts. 8°. 1677.
[*Another edition appeared in 1720.*]

—— (—). — History of Duels. 2 vols. in 1. 8°. 1888.
[*Only 275 copies privately printed.*]

CODE OF DUEL (The). — A reference to the laws of honour & the character of gentlemen, with the case between the 10th Hussars and Mr. Battier, Captain Callan, Mr. Finch, etc. Small 8°. 1824.

CODICUM MANUSCRIPTS.

(*In the Bodleian Library, Oxford.*)

[Codex chartaceus, in folio, ff. 266, sec. xvii. :—

1. Sir Robert Cotton's discourse of the lawfulness of combats in England (fol. 1).
   [*Printed in Hearne's "Curious Discourses of Antiquaries," 1775, London, Vol. II. p. 172.*]

2. Mr. [afterwards Sir] John Davies on the same subject (fol. 7, 13b).
   [*Ibid., pp. 180, 187.*]

CODICUM MANUSCRIPTS (*continued*)—

3. James Whitelock on the same subject (fol. 16).
   [*Ibid.*, p. 190.]

4. Duello foil'd; the whole proceedings in the orderly dis-
   solving of a single fight, written by Henry Howard, earl
   of Northampton (fol. 20).
   [*Printed and ascribed to Edward Cook [Coke].* *Ibid.*, p. 225.]

5. An edict by Henry IV., King of France, constituting
   duellos to be punished in the nature of treason (1609)
   (fol. 37*b*).
   [*Printed in Gutch's "Collectanea,"* 1781, *Oxford,* Vol. I. p. 20.]

6. Discourse touching the unlawfulness of private combats,
   written by sir Edw. Coke, lord chief justice (fol. 39*b*).
   [*Ibid.*, p. 9.]

7. Of a lie; how it may be satisfied, &c. (fol. 42).
   [*Ibid.*, p. 12.]

8. The antiquity, use, and ceremonies of lawful combats in
   England, by Francis Tate (fol. 48).
   [*Ibid.*, p. 6.]

9. The manner and order of combating within lists, set down
   by Thomas [Plantagenet], duke of Gloucester, uncle to
   Richard II. (fol. 51).
   [*See also Codicum MSS.* 278.   Nos. 10, 11, 12, 13, 14, 15.]

Regulations for the trial of single combat, with the duties
of the several officers employed, &c.
   [*It is entitled, " The way of Duells before the King."*
   (*Codex chartaceus, in folio, ff.* 6, *sec. xvii.* *C.C.C. cccxlii.*)]

The way of duelling before the king.
   [*Chartaceus, in folio, ff.* 294, *sec. xvii.* *Reg. cxxi.* 276.]

On the Duellum or laws of single combat.
   [*Exon. cxxxvii.* 153.   *Chartaceus, in folio, ff.* 285, *sec. xvii.* (*Gl.* 57).]

COENALIS (ROB.). — Axioma de utriusque gladii facultate usuque
legitimo.   8°.   1546.   *Paris.*

COKE (SIR E.), **COTTON** (SIR ROBERT), and Others. — On Duels.
Seventeenth century.
   [*MSS. in British Museum.* 25,247 *passim.*]

COKE (Sir Edward) [Lord Chief Justice of England]. — *ASH-MOLEAN* MSS.

—— (— —). — *CODICUM* MSS.

—— (— —). — *COOK (Sir E.).*

—— (— —). — *COOKE (Sir E.).*

COLBOURN'S MAGAZINE. — *DUELLING* in Olden Times.

——   ——   . — *DUELLING* in Modern Times.

COLBOURN'S NEW MONTHLY MAGAZINE. 8°. *London.*
[Vol. XL. p. 470. *"German Duelling." By T. C. Grattan.*]

—— — — —. — *ANDREW (A.).*

COLBOURN'S UNITED SERVICE MAGAZINE. 8°. *London.*
[*September* 1866. *Bayonet Exercise in the French Army.*
January 1867. *The Bayonet, a short historic sketch.*
March 1867. *Notes on the Bayonet.*
January 1869. *Cavalry Sword Competition.*]

COLE (Benjamin). — The Soldier's Pocket-Companion, or the Manual Exercise of our British Foot. To which is added a short view of the use of the small sword. 8°. 1749. *London:* B. Cole.
[*96 plates.*]

COLECCION de 30 figuras que demuestran las señales del mando militar con la espada Dedicada al Exercito Nacional. Se halla en las Librerias de Escribano y Gomez, calle de Carretas, á 12rs (Sin 1, ni a).
[*Port. grabada y 30 láms.*]

COLIGNY-SALIGNY (Comte de). — Mémoires publiés pour la Société de l'Histoire de France. Par A. Monmerqué. 8°. 1841. *Paris:* Renouard.
[*Le Marquis de Cessac tué en duel.*]

COLLIER (Jeremy). — Essays: upon Pride, Cloaths, *Duelling,* General Kindness, the office of a Chaplain, the Weakness of Human Reason. 2nd edition. 12°. 1697.

COLLINS (W.). — *BELGRAVIA* Magazine.

COLOMBEY (ÉMILE) [Pseudonyme de M. Émile Laurent né à Colombey en 1819]. — Histoire anecdotique du duel dans tous les temps et dans tous les pays. 12º. [N.D.] (1860?) [Bruxelles.] *Paris:* Michel Lévy Frères.

COLOMBIÈRE (VULSON DE LA). — Le vray théâtre d'honneur et de chevalerie ou le Miroir héroïque de la noblesse, contenant les combats, les triomphes, les tournois, pas d'armes, combats à la barrière et en champs clos, carrousels, courses de bagues, duels, dégradations de noblesse, obsèques, pompes funèbres et tombeaux des anciens nobles et chevaliers. 2 vols. Folio. 1648. *Paris.*

> [*Frontispices gravès, planches signées par Michel Lasné, Chaveau et autres. Portrait de Vulson. Le grande planche représentant un carrousel sur la Place Royal à Paris s'y trouve.*]

COLTON (W.). — Remarks on duelling. 1828.
> (*In the New York State Library, U.S.A.*)

COMBAT (Le) au vray d'entre le seigdom Ph. de Savoie et le sieur de Crequy: avec la coppie de deffit, etc. 8º. 1599. *Paris:* G. Lombard.

COMBAT (Le) des seigneurs d'Aguerre et de Fendilles, accompli à Sedan (en l'année 1549, sous Henry II.). 8º. 1621. *Sedan.*

COMBAT (Le). 8º. 1887. *Paris:* Berger-Levrault.
> [*Extrait de la " Revue de Cavalerie."*]

COMBAT (Single).
> [*Trial by this commenced by the Lombards, 659. Baronius. It was intro-duced into England for accusations of treason, if neither the accuser nor the accused could produce good evidence; see " Appeal of Battle."*
> *A battle by single combat was fought before the king, William II., and the peers, between Geoffrey Baynard and William, Earl of Eu, who was accused by Baynard of high treason; and Baynard having conquered, Eu was deemed convicted, and blinded and mutilated, 1096.*
> *A combat proposed between Henry of Bolingbroke, Duke of Hereford (after-wards Henry IV.), and Thomas, Duke of Norfolk, was forbidden by Richard II., Sept. 1398.*
> *A trial was appointed between the Prior of Kilmainham and the Earl of Ormond, the former having impeached the latter of high treason; quarrel taken up by the king, decided without fighting, 1446.*
> *A combat was proposed between Lord Reay and Mr. David Ramsey in 1631, but the king prevented it.*
> *In a combat in Dublin Castle, before the Lords Justices and Council, between Connor MacCormack O'Connor and Teig Mac-Gilpatrick O'Connor, the former had his head cut off and presented to the Lords, 1553.*]

COMBATS. — On the certain kinds of combats, with the order of marshalling in the field on such occasions (Gall).   MS.
(In the British Museum. Add. 4101.)

COMBATS. — Collections relative to judicial combats, and the Earl Marshal's court.   MS.
(In the British Museum. 9023.)

COMBATS. — Proceedings belonging to Judicial Combat.   MS.
(In the British Museum. 6297. p. 60.)

COMBATS. — A Catalogue of such combats as have been anciently granted by the Kings of England.   MS.
(In the British Museum. Harl. 7021.)

COMBATS. — A Collection of papers on duels, *i.e.,* lawful combats.   MS.
(In the British Museum. MSS. in the Cottonian Library. Titus, C. 1. [B. 26-44.])

COMBATS. — De la droite ordonnance du gaige de bataille, partout le Royaume de France.   MS.
(In the British Museum. Titus, C. 1.)

COMBATS. — An heraldical tract, beginning with a proclamation from "Arthour Soñ to the Duke of Bertaignie, erle of Richemont," &c.   From the title of the first chapter the tract seems to be called "the Gaige of Battail."   MS.
(In the British Museum. Harl. 6149.)

COMBATS. — Ex Libro quodam vetere, M. Joannis Feronij, des Gaiges de Bataille, Ordonnance du Charles Roy de France, donné a Paris, le Mercredi apres la Trinitie, l'an 1306.   MS.
(In the British Museum. Harl. 902.)

COMBATS. — Ten original instruments, being chiefly royal mandates of Henry VI., several of them signed by him; concerning lists and combats.   MS.
(In the British Museum. Titus, C. 1.)

COMBATS. — The case of trial by combat.   MS.
(In the British Museum. Slo. 4297.)

COMBER. — Discourse on duels.   1710.
64

C[OMBER] (T[HOMAS]) [Dean of Durham, D.D.]. — A Discourse of Duels, showing their sinful nature and the mischievous effects of them ; and answering the usual excuses made for them by challengers, acceptors, and seconds. Small 4°. 1687. *London : L. Roycroft.*
(Library of the London Institution. Vol. CIX. Art. XI.)

COMMANDO für d. Fechtunterricht. 8°.
[*About* 1865.]

CONGREGATIONAL MAGAZINE. *London.*
[Vol. V. p. 460. "*Duelling.*"]

CONNOISSEUR (The). By Mr. Town-Critic and Censor General. 4 vols. 8°. 1757.
[*Contains a paper on "Duelling."*]

CONTEMPORARY REVIEW (The). — (Periodical.) 8°. *London.*
[1880. Vol. XXXVIII. p. 595. "*Mythical and Mediæval Swords.*" By *Lady F. P. Verney.*]

CONVENTIONELLEN (Die) Gebräuche beim Zweikampf. 8°. 1883. *Berlin.*

COOK (EDWARD). — Duello-Foiled : or the whole proceedings in the orderly disposing of a design for single fight, in which the un-lawfulness and wickedness of a duello is preparatively disputed according to the rules of honour and right reason.
[Vide "*Hearne's Collection,*" Vol. II. p. 223.]

COOK (SIR EDWARD) [COKE]. — *ASHMOLEAN* MSS.

—— (— —) [COKE]. — *CODICUM* MSS.

COOKE (E. STENSON) [Lieutenant, London Rifle Brigade].
[*Lectures delivered at Haileybury College, March* 31, 1894; *at Toynbee Hall, London, October* 20, 1894, *and January* 22, 1895, "*On Swordsman-ship.*"]

COOKE (SIR EDWARD) [COKE] [Lord Chief Justice of England]. — *ASHMOLEAN* MSS.

COOMANS [Aîné]. — De la Repression du duel. 8°. 1836. *Gand.*

CORAZZI (DAVID). — *ESGRIMA.* — 1883.

CORBESIER (A. F.). — Theory of fencing ; with the small sword exercise. 1873. 8°. *Washington.*

CORDELOIS [Professeur d'escrime]. — Leçons d'armes. Du duel et de l'assaut. Théorie complète sur l'art de l'escrime. Gr. 8°. 1862. *Paris :* Tanera.

[*Édition illustrée de 28 planches gravées sur acier par M. Brown, professeur à l'Académie des Beaux-Art des Bruxelles.* (28 plates comprising 42 figures.)] (*In Captain Hutton's Collection.*)

——. — Leçons d'armes. Du duel et de l'assaut. Théorie complète sur l'art de l'escrime. 2e édition. 8°. 1873. *Paris :* J. Dumaine.

[*Portrait and 28 plates.*]

CORNHILL MAGAZINE (Monthly). 8°. *London.*

[Vol. XXII. p. 715. "*Trial by Battle.*"
1890. *December.* Vol. LXII. p. 618. "*The Duello in France.*"]

CORNWALL (Sir J.). — *CORRESPONDENCE.* MS.

CORR (M.). — Reminiscences of duelling in Ireland.

["*Macmillan's Magazine*" (*London*), Vol. XXIX. p. 304.]

CORRADINO. — *VELLA* (G.). — 1857.

CORRESPONDENCE of the seneschal of Hainault with Henry IV. and others, on a proposed combat. Sir J. Cornwall. 1404–1449.

[*French MS. in British Museum,* 21,370.]

CORTÉS (Don Balbino). — El palo y el sable, ó teoría para el perfeccionamiento del manejo del sable por la esgrima del palo corto. En 25 lecciones, ilustrada con 37 láminas y 74 figuras. Obl. 12°. 1851. *Madrid :* Zaragozano.

[37 *lithographs.*] (*In Captain Hutton's Collection.*)

CORTÉS Y DOMÍNGUEZ (Don José). — Enseñanza general de la esgrima del sable. 8°. 1882. *Albacete :* Luciano Ruiz.

[*With plates.*]

CORTHEY (A.). — Le fleuret et l'épée. Etude sur l'escrime contemporaine. 8°. 1885. *Paris :* Giraud.

—— (—.). — Petit traité d'Escrime à la Baïonnette. 12°. 1889. *Paris.*

[24 *pages.*] (*In Captain Hutton's Collection.*)

—— (—.). — Français et Prussiens armes blanches et armes à feu. Deuxième édition. 12°. 1889. *Paris :* J. Delorme.

(*In Captain Hutton's Collection.*)

CORTHEY (A.). — Histoire de l'Épée.

[*Pour paraître prochainement.*]

COSMOPOLITAN (The). — (Periodical.) *New York, U.S.A.*

[1892. *January.* Vol. XII. p. 361. "*Fencing and Fencers in Paris.*" By *C. De Kay.*]

COSTI (A.). — De ratione puniendi duella. 8°. 1860. *Berol.*

COTEREAU (CLAUDE). — Du devoir d'un capitaine et chef de guerre, assi du combat en camp cloz ou duel. Mis en langue françoyse par Gabr. du Preau. 8°. 1549. *Poictiers.*

COTTON (SIR ROBERT). — Cottoni Posthuma, Divers Choice Pieces of that Renowned Antiquary, Preserved from the injury of Time and exposed to Public Light for the Benefit of Posterity by James Howell. Small 8°. 1672.

[*Among the contents of this curious volume are* "*Valour anatomized in a Fancy,*" *by Sir Philip Sidney* (*containing a poem,* "*Wooing-stuff*"); *a Discourse of the Legality of Combats,* "*Duels,*" *or Camp-fight.*]

—— (— —). — *CODICUM* MSS.

—— (— —). — *COKE (Sir E.).*

COTTONIAN MANUSCRIPTS.

(*In the British Museum.*)

[Tib. E. viii. 14. " Modus faciendi duellum coram rege (Gallice)." (50 *b.*)

——. ——. ——. 42. " Declaration of a combat within lists ; set forth by Tho. D. of Gloucester." (190.)

Nero, D. vi. 12. " Modus faciendi duellum coram rege (Gallice)." (82.)

Vitel. C. iv. 10. " De certamine singulari coram constabulario et marescallo Angliæ (Gallice)."   (129.)

Tit. C. i. B. A collection of papers on duels, *i.e.*, lawful combats.

——. ——. ——. 26. " A brief historical dissertation on duels ; by R. Cotton. 1609." (201.)

——. ——. ——. 27. " Seven tracts on the antiquity, use, and ceremony of lawful combats in England ; by Davies, Whitlock, Holland, Agard, and others." (205.)

COTTONIAN MANUSCRIPTS (*continued*)—

Tit. C. i. 28. "A challenge for a duel between Henry Inglose, Esq., and sir John Tiptoft, Knt., to be fought before the Duke of Bedford, high constable. (Fr.) 1415." (229.)

——. —. —. 29. "Five writs relating to combats before the constable and marshal." (230.)

——. —. —. 30. "A list of patents relating to the office of marshal; from 27 Edw. III. to 8 Hen. VI." (232.)

——. —. —. 31. "Ten original instruments, being chiefly royal mandates of Henry VI., several of them signed by him; concerning lists and combats." (234.)

——. —. —. 32. "Notes of certain turns to be put in form, and then to be concluded by the whole council, touching the regulation of duels: in the hand-writing of K. James I." (238 *b.*)

——. —. —. 33. "A treatise on duels, in two books." (239.)

——. —. —. 34. "A collection of notes, papers, &c., on duels. (Chiefly French.)" (346.)

——. —. —. 35. "What manner of duels they use in Italy; and why they hold it not fit to answer a challenge. (Ital.)" (370 *b.*)

——. —. —. 36. "Forme di pace fatte da diversi; being compromises of quarrels." (374.)

——. —. —. 37. "Duello foil'd, being a treatise in which the lawfulness of duels is disputed according to the rules of honour and right reason." (393.)

——. —. —. 38. "Two papers on measures taken against duels." (402.)

——. —. —. 39. "Of a lye; how it ought to be dealt in by an E. marshal." (404.)

——. —. —. 40. "Notes of the laws in Spain for preventing single combats." (407.)

COTTONIAN MANUSCRIPTS (*continued*)—

Tit. C. i. 41. "Notes out of the D. of Bullion's discourse, touching the lye and the blow." (408.)

——. —. —. 42. "Three questions proposed to the count d'Angosciola (banished from Parma and living in Savoy) in matter of duel. (Italian.)" (409.)

——. —. —. 43. "Placcart des Archiducs contre les defis et duels. (Printed.) Bruxelles. 1610." (413.)

——. —. —. 44. "A paper concerning laws against duels." (416.)

——. —. iv. 1. "Certain humble petitions, to be obtained by the King's assent, before any regular and just order can be set down for the suppression of duellos and challenges." (1.)

——. —. —. 2. "Collectanea under the running titles 'Mendacium, provocatio, leges civiles, jus naturæ, &c.,' all relating to duels." (3.)

——. —. —. 3. "A tract in 4to. under the heads of 'lye, injury, blows, provocation, and satisfaction.'" (111.)

——. —. —. 4. "A letter of thanks from Count de Cartignano, to the Earl of Northampton; on his leaving England. (Orig. Ital.) Gravesend, Jan. 13, 1612." (131.)

——. —. —. 5. "Continuation of the above Collectanea, under the heads 'provocatio, recontre, precedentes, pena delle prove, ferite, satisfactio, honos non in nostra potestate, regis potestas;' and many others, all on the subject of duels." (131 b.)

——. —. —. 6. "A treatise against duels, written by, or in the name of, K. James I." (422.)

——. —. —. 7. "A discourse concerning duels: anonymous." (460.)

COTTONIAN MANUSCRIPTS (*continued*)—

Tit. C. iv. 8. "Francis Cottington to Ld. Northampton (?) on the laws of duels in Spain. (Orig.) Lond. Sept. 12, 1613." (503.)

——. ——. ——. 9. "Sir John Finet to the E. of Northampton (Ld. privy seal) on the practice of duelling in France. (Orig.) Paris, Feb. 19, 1609–10." (504.)

——. ——. ——. 10. "The Earl of Northumberland's challenge sent unto sir Francis Veere; with an account of the proceedings thereupon." (510.)

Vesp. C.xiv. 234. "The manner how the defendants do answer the Prince's highness challenge; being a list of names." (568.)

——. ——. ——. 235. "Of combats, in Mr. Garter's house. May 22, 1601. (A draught.)" (569.)

——. ——. ——. 236. "The ordinances that belong in gayging of battayle, made by qwarrell, after the constitutions made by King Philip of France." (570.)

Faust. E. v. 2. "Of single combat." (4.)]

COUBERTIN (Pierre de). — *CHARLES* (*J. B.*).—1890.

COUDRAY (Jean Baptiste le Perche du). — *PERCHE* (*B. le*) [du Coudray].—1676. 1750.

COURCELLES. Mémoires de la Marquise de Courcelles, née Marie Sidonia de Lénoncourt, et sa correspondance, précédés d'une histoire de sa vie et de son procès, revue et augmentée d'après des documents inédits, par C. H. de S. D. 8°. 1869. *Paris:* Librairie de l'Académie des Bibliophiles.

    [*Duel des Marquis de Cavais et De Courcelles.*]

COURT CIRCULAR (The). — (Periodical.) Folio. *London,* 2 Southampton Street, W.C.

    [*May* 30, 1891, p. 527. *"Bibliography of the Art of Fence."*
    Sept. 26, 1891. *"The Pope on Duelling."*]

COURTIN (ANT. DE). — Suite de la civilité française, ou traité du point d'honneur et des règles pour se conduire sagement avec les incivils et les fâcheux. 12º. 1717.

[*Another edition.* 12º. 1676. *Paris: Josset.*]

CRAIG (ROBERT H.). — Rules and regulations for the sword exercise of the cavalry. 8º. 1812. *Baltimore.*

[26 *plates.*]

CRAPELET (G. A.). — *CÉRÉMONIES* des gages de bataille.— 1830.

CRAWFURD (OSWALD). — *BLACK AND WHITE* (Periodical). —March 7, 1891.

[*Article on Egerton Castle's lecture, "The Story of Swordsmanship." Illustrated by J. Finnemore.*]

CREMER (PROF. D. H.). — Duell und Ehre. 8º. 1894. *Gütersloh:* C. Bertelsmann.

[*Aus "Gütersloher Jahrbuch," 1892. (23 pages.)*]

CREMONY (J. C.). — *OVERLAND* Monthly.

CRIVELLARI (GIULIO). — Il duello nella dottrina e nella giurisprudenza. 4º. 1884. *Torino:* Unione Tipografico.

CROABBON (A.) [Avocat]. — La Science du point d'honneur, commentaire raisonné sur l'offense et le duel. 8º. 1894. *Paris:* Librairies-Imprimeries réunies (ancienne Maison Quantin).

[*Lorsqu'un homme essuie une offense pour laquelle les lois ordinaires n'accordent aucune réparation, ou n'accordent que des réparations insuffisantes, il est tenté de recourir au seul juge qui reste : " soi-même," et d'en appeler à la seule législation qui le reconnaisse comme tel : "la législation du point d'honneur." Mais, comme ce recours peut entraîner des conséquences très graves, il ne doit point l'exercer sans s'être renseigné préalablement sur l'issue d'une telle entreprise, et avoir consulté pour cela l'ouvrage que M. Croabbon vient de publier sous le titre un peu ambitieux peut-être, mais très justifié, de "Science du point d'honneur."*

L'auteur y envisage en effet le duel au point de vue de l'offense et des règles du combat, de la responsabilité pénale, pécuniaire, religieuse, en France et à l'étranger.

Un appendice contenant les pièces justificatives, un résumé aide-mémoire, des modèles annotés de procès-verbaux, un index bibliographique, complètent cet ouvrage, qui constitue la première partie, spéciale à la France, mais intéressante pour l'étranger, d'une vaste encyclopédie où M. Croabbon étudiera le duel "chez tous les peuples civilisés."

Cette synthèse, basée sur une masse considérable de documents, est faite par un homme qui possède admirablement son sujet, le fouille dans tous ses

replis, l'expose avec méthode et sait demeurer personnel tout en restant
scrupuleusement fidèle à la doctrine véritable.
Les éditeurs ont donné leurs meilleurs soins typographiques à cet ouvrage,
unique dans son genre, et que voudront posséder tous ceux qui à un titre
quelconque peuvent devenir tributaires de l'inexorable " Point d'honneur."]

CROSNETTE. — Une théorie du double jeu de la crosse et de la baïonnette. (1811 ?)

> [*According to Pinette, this work, with drawings, was sent to the Emperor Napoleon about 1811 (?), but was lost sight of in the offices of the Ministry of War. Hutton's " Fixed Bayonets."*]

CRUSE (P. H.). — *NORTH AMERICAN* Review.

CRUZADO Y PERALTA (MANUEL). — Las tretas de la vulgar y comun esgrima de espada sola y con armas dobles, que aprobó don Luis Pacheco de Narvaez, y las oposiciones que dispusó en verdadera destreza contra ellas. 4º. 1702. *Zaragoza.*

(In Libraries of Fernandez San Roman y de Mariátegui.)

CUCALA Y BRUÑÓ (DON JOSÉ) [Caballero Teniente Mayor del Reino y examinador en la cienca filosófica y matemática de la destreza de las armas en todos los dominios de España]. — Tratado de esgrima. Comprende la esgrima del florete, tres guardias de sable de infantería . . . &c. &c. 4º. 1854. *Madrid :* J. Peña.

> [24 *plates.*]

—— (— —). — Tratado de la esgrima del fusil ó carabina armada de la bayoneta. 1861. *Habana.*

[**CUISIN** (J. P. R.)]. — Les Duels, suicides et amours du bois de Boulogne. Recueil historique, contenant un grand nombre d'événements tragiques, rendez-vous galants, intrigues piquantes, comiques et romanesques ; mystères et secrets étonnants, soit en fait de galanterie, soit en complots criminels dont ce bois fameux n'est que trop souvent le théâtre. Par un rôdeur caché dans un arbre creux de ce bois. 2 vols. 12º. 1830. *Paris :* Imp. de Belin.

CUPÉRUS (N. J.). — *LENZ (G. F.).* — 1881.

CURSORY reflections on single combat, or modern duel. Addressed to gentlemen in every class of life. 4º. 1789. *London :* Baldwin.

CURTIS (GEORGE WILLIAM). — *MOTLEY (J. L.).* — 1889.

CUVELIER. — [Trouvère du xiv⁰ siècle.] Chronique de Bertrand Du Guesclin. 2 vols. 4°. 1839. *Paris :* Firmin Didot Frères.

[Vol. II. p. 365. *Duel between two Jews. (A very curious description.*)]
(*In the British Museum* [*see FRANCE—Collection de documents inédits sur l'histoire de France,* 1⁰ Serié, Vol. XL.].)

CYPRIEN (LE PÈRE). — La destruction du duel, par le jugement des Mareschaux des France, sur la protestation de plusieurs gentil-hommes de marque. 4°. 1651. *Paris.*

D. (LE CAPITAINE). — Manuel du Tireur, armes de guerre, armes de précision, armes de chasse, armes a répétition. Tir au pistolét et au revolver à l'usage des amateurs et des Sociétés de tir. 8°. [N.D.] *Paris :* Delarue.

[*Un fort volume illustré de très nombreuses figures.*]

DAILY CHRONICLE (The). — (Periodical.) Folio. *London.*

[1894. *April* 20. *" Duelling in the Austrian Army."*
1895. *March* 16. *" The Sword Duel—its history and its practice."* By *Egerton Castle.*]

DAILY GRAPHIC (The). — (Periodical.) Folio. *London.*

[*May* 15, 1892. Vol. X. No. 740, p. 4. *" Duelling in France. A word for the defence."* By a *Fire-Eating Englishman.*]

DAILY NEWS (The). — (Periodical.) Folio. *London.*

[*May* 5, 1891. *A Duel at Agram in Hungary.*
May 18, 1891. *Fencing and Duels (leading article).*
Sept. 14, 1891. *A Duel of an original character in Antwerp.*]

DAILY TELEGRAPH (The). — (Periodical.) Folio. *London.*

[1890. *April* 8. *Duelling in the German Army.*
1891. *April* 4. *Combats on the Stage. Letter by W. Terriss.*
1891. *June* 30. *Duel with swords between Comte de Lahens and M. de Lamothe, the latter twice wounded.*
1891. *July* 3. *Do Women Fence?*
1892. *April* 25. *Duel between Americans near Ostend (Mr. Edward Fox and Mr. Hallet Borrowes).*
1892. *August* 27. *Duel between Marquis Morès and Captain Mayer.*
1894. *August* 21. *Duelling in Russia.*
1895. *January* 28. *" Professor Wagner, a Christian Socialist, has, says a Berlin telegram, declined to fight a duel with Baron Stumm, who challenged him on account of certain insulting comments made by him on a speech of the Baron's in the Reichstag. Herr Wagner, at the same time, refuses to retract the offensive remarks."*
1895. *February* 1. *" Several well-intentioned and enthusiastic gentlemen are making laudable efforts to revive the art of fencing in England. It may interest them to know the opinion of a nobleman who lived at the end of last century and the beginning of the present respecting the effect of that accomplishment on national character. In the new volume of the Report*

of the Historical Manuscripts Commission, dealing with the papers pre-
served in Belvoir Castle, is a letter dated January 23, 1786, from the
Marquis of Lothian to the Duke of Rutland, in which the following
passage occurs: 'I most thoroughly approve of the education you mean to
give your sons. There is only one part, I think, Granby should not be
much flattered upon. I mean fencing, as I am convinced that great part
of the flippancy of the Irish is owing to an early knowledge of that science.'"
1895. *February* 14. *Duel between Lieutenant Canrobert, son of the late*
Marshal, and M. Hubbard, a Member of Parliament. The Deputy
received a deep puncture in the breast.
1895. *March* 2. *Fatal Sword Duel. (Between M. Hippolyte Percher*
("Harry Alis") and M. le Chatelier. The former killed.)
1895. *March* 27. *Duel at Constantine, in Algeria, between M. Souleyre, a*
Government engineer, and M. Masson, the manager of "Silhouette."
Former transfixed by his adversary's rapier a moment after the encounter
commenced.
1895. *April* 15. *A Desperate Duel. (Between Herr von Kotze, Master of*
Ceremonies to the Court, and Baron von Reischach, one of the Kaiser's
Chamberlains, and Court Marshal to Her Majesty the Empress Frederic.
The former wounded.)
1895. *April* 16. *Leading Article against Duels in Berlin.*
1895. *July* 1. *A duel between a Minister and a private soldier. (Senator*
Gadaud, Minister of Agriculture, and M. Mirman, representing Rheims
in the Chamber.)
1895. *October* 8. *The History of the Sword.*
1895. *November* 25. *Duel with swords between M. Albert Carré, manager*
of the Vaudeville and Gymnase theatres, and M. Possien, a journalist.
Latter wounded.]

DAMBREVILLE (E.). — Abrége Chronique de l'histoire des
ordres de chevalerie. *Paris.* 1807.

[28 plates.]

DANET [Syndic-garde de la Compagnie des maîtres d'armes de
Paris]. — L'art des armes, ou la manière la plus certaine de se
servir utilement de l'épée, soit pour attaquer, soit pour se defendre,
simplifiée et démontrée dans toute son étendue et sa perfection,
suivant les meilleurs principes de théorie et de pratique adoptés
actuellement en France. Ouvrage nécessaire à la jeune noblesse,
aux militaires et à ceux qui se destinent au service du Roy, aux personnes même qui, par la distinction de leur état ou par leurs charges,
sont obligées de porter l'épée ; et à ceux qui veulent faire profession
des armes. Dedié à Son Altesse Monseigneur le Prince de Conty.
Tome premier. 8°. 1766. Tome second contenant la réfutation
des critiques et la suite du même traité. 1767. 8°. 1766–1767.
Paris: Hérissant.

[1 *portrait*, 1 *frontispice gravé*, 1 *fleuron aux armes du Prince de Conti et* 45

GME. DANET. 1767.

Ecuyer, Syndic-Garde des Ordres de la Compagnie des Maîtres en fait d'armes des Académies du Roi en la Ville et Fauxbourgs de Paris, aujourd'hui directeur de l'Ecole Royale d'Armes.

planches pliées gravées par Taraval. Raccommodage au premier feuillet de l'épître dédicatoire.
Frontispiece, and 43 copperplates, out of the text, engraved by Taraval from designs by Vaxeillère.]
(*In British Museum, South Kensington Museum, and Captain Hutton's Collection.*)

DANET [Ecuyer, Syndic-Garde des ordres de la Compagnie des Maîtres en fait d'armes des Académies du Roi en la ville et Faux-bourgs de Paris, aujourd'hui directeur de l'Ecole Royale d'Armes]. — L'art des armes, où l'on donne l'application de la théorie à la pratique de cet art avec les principes méthodiques adoptés dans nos écoles royales d'armes. Ouvrage aussi que nécessaires . . . etc. 2e edition. 2 vols. 8º. 1787. *Paris.*

[*Avec approbation et privilège du Roi. 45 copperplates, out of the text.*]

———. — L'art des armes. . . . 3e edition. Bélin. Rue St. Jacques. 2 vols. 8º. 1798. [An VI.] *Paris.*

[*Enrichi de 47 figures gravées en taille-douce.*]

DANIEL (GABR.). — Histoire de la milice françoise. 2 vols. 4º. 1721. *Paris.*

[Tome I. pl. 22, p. 415. *Representation of a plug bayonet, and in pl. 33, p. 466, of a socket bayonet.*
Tome II. p. 582. "*Duelling.*"
Tome II. p. 592. *Reference to the introduction of the bayonet into the French army.*]

DARBEY D'AUREVILLY (JULES). — Les Diaboliques. 12º. 1874. *Paris:* Dentu.

["*Le Bonheur dans le Crime.*"]

DARCIE (ABRAHAM). — Annals of Elizabeth.

[*Recounts how "Rowland Yorke, a desperado who betrayed Devanter to the Spaniards in 1587, was the first who brought into England that wicked and pernicious fashion to fight with a rapier, called a Tucke, only fit for the thrust.*"]

DARESSY (HENRI) [membre honoraire de l'Académie d'armes]. — Statuts et règlements faits par les maître en faits d'armes de la ville et faubourgs de Paris, 1644. 8º. 1867. *Paris.*

——— (—). — Archives des maîtres d'armes de Paris. 8º. 1888. *Paris:* Quantin.

[*Avec portrait et facsimiles.*]

D'ARTAGNAN. — *ARTAGNAN (D').* — 1704.

D'AUDIGUIER. — *AUDIGUIER (D').* — 1617.

D'AURIAC (Eugène). — *AURIAC (E. D').* — 1847.

DAVIES (John). — *CODICUM* MSS.

D'AZÉMAR. — *AZÉMAR (D').* — 1859.

DE BRYE (J.). — *BRYE (J. de).*

DE CHEVIGNY. — *CHEVIGNY (De).* — 1752.

D'EON. — *EON (F. d').*

DÉCLARATION du Roy pour la deffence du port d'armes.   8°. 1610. *Paris.*

DÉCLARATION du Roy portant deffences d'user d'appels, ny de rencontres suyvant l'édict des duels, 1609.   8°.   1611.   *Paris.*

DÉCLARATION du Roy sur les édicts de pacification des duels. 8°. 1614. *Paris.*

DE KAY (C.). — *KAY (C. de).* — 1892.

DELANY (Patrick). — Discourses.
>["*Duelling.*" *Mentioned in Malcom's Theological Index.*]

DE LA TOUCHE [Philibert]. — *TOUCHE (De La).* — 1670.

DELBRÜCK (Fd.). — Der akademische Zweikampf.   Eine Rede. 8°. 1836. *Bonn :* Weber.

DELEBECQUE (Alphonse). — Commentaire législatif de la Loi sur le duel. 8°. 1841. *Bruxelles :* Durand.

DEL FRATE. — *FRATE (S. Del).*

DEMEUSE (N.). — Nuevo Tratado de Arte de las Armas.   4°.
>[*MS. 322 pages. Mentioned in Leguina's "Libros de Esgrima."* 1891.]

—— (Nicolas) [Garde-du-Corps de S. A. S. le Prince Evêque à Liège et Maître en fait d'armes]. — Nouveau traité de l'art des armes, dans lequel on établit les principes certains de cet art, et où l'on enseigne les moyens les plus simples de les mettre en pratique.   Ouvrage nécessaire aux personnes qui se destinent aux armes et utile à celles qui veulent se rappeler les principes qu'on leur a enseignés.   12°.   1778. *Liège :* Desoer.
>[*4 copperplates, out of text.*] (*In Captain Hutton's Collection.*)

DEMEUSE (NICOLAS). — Suite complète de 14 planches in-4, pour Le Traité de l'art des armes par Demeuse. In-4 obl., *en ff.* 1778. *Liège.*

—— (—). — Nouveau traité de l'art des armes. . . . 2e edition. 12°. 1786. *Liège :* Desoer.

[*Contains* 14 *plates.*]

—— (—). — Nouveau traité de l'art des armes. . . . 3e edition. Imprimerie de Blocquel. (To the original text is added a Dictionnaire de l'art des armes.) 12°. 1800. *Lille & Paris.*

[14 *copperplates, different from the previous editions.*]
(*In Captain Hutton's Collection.*)

DEMOCRATIC REVIEW. *New York (U.S.A.).*

[Vol. XL pp. 311, 413.
„ XXIX. p. 547. ⎱-"*Duelling.*"]
„ XXXVI. p. 116.

DENNIE'S PORTFOLIO. *Philadelphia (U.S.A.).*

[Vol. XXVIII. p. 60. "*Duelling.*"
„ XXXIII. pp. 239, 431. "*British Code of Duelling.*"]

DE QUINCEY (THOMAS). — Works. 15 vols. 2nd edition. 8°. *Edinburgh :* A. & C. Black.

[Vol. VII. p. 279. "*Duelling : reason why not in vogue among the Greeks and Romans, the unlimited licence of foul language among them.*"]

DÉRUÉ (LE CAPITAINE). — Nouvelle méthode d'escrime à cheval. 12°. 1885. *Paris :* Lahure.

[*Illustrated.*]

—— (LE COMMANDANT). — L'Escrime dans l'armée. 16°. 1888. *Paris :* Quantin.

[*Avec couverture en chromotypographie.*]

DESBORDES. — Discours de la théorie, de la pratique et l'excellence des armes. 4°. 1610. *Nancy :* chez Andre.

DESCARES (JACQUES). — 1568.

[*M. Buja (ouvrage "La scherma," etc., 1875, cité pag. 113) affirme que Jacques Descares, Français, écrivit et fit imprimer un ouvrage sur l'escrime en 1568.*]

DESCRIPTION des accessoires de la lance modèle 1890 (22 Août 1893). 8°. *Paris.*

DESJARDINS (ALBERT). — *THUREAU (P.).* — 1862.

DESMEDT (Eugène). — La science de l'escrime. Avec une préface de Max Waller, un Dictionnaire de l'épée et un Guide des escrimeurs. 8°. 1888. *Bruxelles.*

[Illustré de quinze planches en photogravure d'après nature.]
(In Captain Hutton's Collection.)

DESTREZA Á CABALLO. Recuerdos de otros tiempos.

[MS. moderno.]

DESTREZA (DE LA) DE LAS ARMAS. 4°. MS.

[Bibl. Villaumbrosana.]

DEUTSCHE FECHTSCHUL-ZEITUNG. 8°. *Lahr* (Baden).

DEUTSCHE HIEBFECHTSCHULE für Korb- und Glockenrapier. Eine kurze Anweisung zur Erlerng. d. an unseren deutschen Hochschulen gebräuchl. Hiebfechtens. Hrsg. vom Verein deutscher Universitätsfechtmeister. 8°. 1887. *Leipzig:* Weber.

DEUTSCHE REICHSFECHTSCHULE. Redacteur, W. Forke. 4°. 1886. *Magdeburg:* Faber.

[52 numbers per annum.]

DEUTSCHE STOSZFECHTSCHULE nach Kreusslerschen Grundsätzen. Zusammengestellt und herausgegeben vom Verein deutscher Fechtmeister. 12°. 1892. *Leipzig:* J. J. Weber.

[Mit 42 Abbildungen. xiv. and 104 pages.]

DEUTSCHE ZEIT-FRANGEN. — *THÜMMEL (C.).* — 1887.

DEUTSCHLAND (Von den in) gewohnlichen Gebräuchen bei Duellen und über die Mittel die Duelle abzustellen. 12°. 1804. *Leipzig:* im Comptoir für Literatur.

DE VOS (W.). — *VOS (W. de).* — 1805.

DICTIONNAIRE DES ARTS ACADÉMIQUES. Equitation, Escrime, Danse et art de Nager. 4°. 1786. *Paris.*

DICTIONNAIRE DES ARTS ACADÉMIQUES. Equitation, Escrime, Danse, Natation: faisant partie de l'Encyclopédie. 8°. [1840?] *Paris.*

[16 plates.]

DIDEROT et **D'ALEMBERT**. — Encyclopédie des sciences. Tome V. 1775. *Paris.*

[*Il reproduit le traité d'escrime d'Angelo Malevolti de Livourne.*]
(*In Captain Hutton's Collection.*)

——. — *ANGELO (D.).* — 1787.

DIERICKX (JACQUES) [Président de la grande société académique d'escrime de Bruxelles]. — Traité et théorie d'escrime. 12°. 1849. *Bruxelles :* Polack-Duvivier.

[10 *planches contenant* 40 *figures coloriées.*]

DIERKES (A.). — Leitfaden für den Unterricht im Säbelfechten. 8°. 1857. *Prag :* Hess.

DIETZ (HEINR. WILH. SCHÄFFER VON). — Fechtkunst. 4°. 1620. Marpurgh.

[Vide *Schäffer (H. W.),* 1620, *for the full title.*]

DIEULAFOY et **GERSIN**. — Le duel par la Croisée, ou le Français à Milan. Comédie-Vaudeville en un acte. 12°. 1818. *Paris :* Fages.

[*Représentée pour la première fois sur le Théâtre du Vaudeville, le* 17 *Janvier* 1818.]

DIGBY. — Sr. Kenelme Digbyes Honour maintained. By a most couragious Combat which he fought with Lord Mount le Ros, who by base and slanderous words reviled the King. Also the true relation how he went to the King of France, who kindly intreated him, and sent two hundred men to guard him so far as Flanders. And now he is returned from Banishment, and to his eternall honour lives in England. [1641.]

[*Pamphlet. Title-page with woodcut of duel and two leaves.*]
(*In the possession of Sir Frederick Pollock, Bart.*)

DILICH (W.). — Beschreibung und Abriss dero Ritterspiel so Moritz, Landgraff zu Hessen, etc., auff die Fürstliche Kindtauffen Frewlein Elizabethen ; zu Cassel angeordnet, und halten hassen, etc. 2 Parts. Folio. 1598–1601. *Cassel :* W. Wessel.

[*Numerous plates of the Ceremony, Tournament, Processions, &c.*
An excessively rare pageant. Contains "H. Fabronii carmen de equestri Certamine in Honorem Elizabethæ Reginæ Angliæ a Mauritio Landgravio Hessiæ dum ejusdem Elizabetham sacro Baptismati per Legatos offerebas ; "
a full account of the Entrance of the English Ambassadors.]
(*In the British Museum.* 813. *h.* 29.)

DILICHII (Wilhelmi). — Hochvernünsstig gegründet und aussgerichtete in gewisse Classen eingetheilte bisher verschlossen gelegen, numehr aber eröffnete Krieges-Schule. Folio. 1689. *Frankfurt am Mayn:* J. D. Zunners.

> [*Portrait of the author, and numerous plates.*
> Page 104.   *Vom Nutzbarkeit des Fechtens in dem Kriegs-Wesen.*
> ,,   107.   *Wie die Musquetirer zu exerciren und erstlich in Ladung der Musqueten sich stellen müssen.*
> ,,   116.   *Von dero Piquenirer-Exercitio und erstlich wie die Pique zur hand zu nehmen.*
> ,,   117.   *Wie ferner die Piquenirer auff Schildwachten und im Marchiren sich verhalten sollen.*
> ,,   118.   *Von Exercitien dero Treffen beyden Piquenirern.*
> ,,   119.   *Von Unterricht und Ubung der halben Piquen, Helleparten, Rondartschen und Spadonen.*
> ,,   127.   *Von Lanzirer Exercitien.*]

DILLON (Honble. Harold Arthur) [F.S.A.]. — Arms and Armour at Westminster, The Tower, and Greenwich. 1547.

> [*Read February* 16, 1888, *at the Society of Antiquaries, London* (Vol. LI. "*Archæologia,*" pp. 217–280).]

DISCOURS SUR LES DUELS. 1761.

DISCOURS DE L'ESPÉE SEULE. MS. (fin XVIIIe Siècle). 8°.

> [*Plaquette manuscrite: petites notes sans suite sur l'escrime, de l'époque Louis XIV. La dernière note concerne la danse.*]
> (*In Mons. Vigeant's Collection.*)

DISCOURSE AGAINST DUELLING (Rom. xii. 19). 12°. 1831. *Hereford.*

DISCOURSE (A) OF DUELS, shewing the sinful nature and mischievous effects of them, and answering the usual excuses made for them by challengers, accepters, and seconds, by T. C., D.D. 4°. 1687. *London:* S. Roycroft.

DISNEY (John). — Laws against duelling. Folio. 1729. *Cambridge.*

DITCHFIELD (P. H.) [M.A.]. — Old English Sports and Pastimes. Post 8°. 1891. *London:* Methuen.

> [*Quarterstaff.* (*Illustrated.*)]

DOCCIOLINI (Marco) [Florentino]. — Trattato in materia di scherma. Nel quale si contiene il modo e regola d' adoperar la spada cosí sola, come accompagnata. 4°. 1601. *Firenze:* Nella stamperia di Michelagniolo Sermatelli.

> [*Dedication to Don Giovanni Medici.*]

DODGE (THEODORE C.) [Colonel U.S.A.]. — Fencing. ("Harper's Young People," New York, U.S.A., April 14 and April 21, 1888.)
> [*Numerous cuts in the text, reproduced from Egerton Castle's "Schools and Masters of Fence."*]

DOLCH (O.). — Geschichte des deutschen Studententhums. 8°. 1858. *Leipzig :* Brockhaus.
> [Page 72. "*Die Kunst der Feder- oder Freifechter.*"]

DON GIOVANNI. — Rivista mondana in illustrata. 1888. *Bologna.*
> [*Among the writers for this Revue are Sig. Salvatore Arista, Maestro della Società Bolognese di Scherma, Sig. Carlo Pilla, dilletante di scherma, and Sig. Georges Robert, maestro di scherma a Pirigi.*]

DONON [Ex-Adjutant-Major des ci-devant lanciers polonais]. — L'escrime moderne, ou nouveau traité simplifié de l'art des armes. 8°. 1830. *Vers. :* Lithog. de Helbig.
> [*13 plates in outline.*]

——. — Manuel des Armes, ou guide de professeurs. Nouveau traité simplifié. 12°. 1843. *Paris :* imprimerie de A. Appert.

DORAN (JOHN). — Habits and Men. Post 8°. 1855. *London :* Bentley.
> [Page 164. "*The Swearing of the Sword.*"]

—— (—). — Knights and their Days. Post 8°. 1856. *London :* Bentley.
> [Page 65. "*Duelling in the Times of Chivalry.*"]

DOUGLAS [General]. — Note respecting the introduction of the Bayonet into the English Army, 18th Century.
> [*MS. British Museum,* No. 27,892. *f.* 211*b.*]

DOUGLAS (REV. J.). — *ARCHÆOLOGIA.*

DOUGLAS (W.). — Duelling days in the Army. 8°. 1887. *London :* Ward & D.
> [*280 pages.*]

DOUHAIRE (M. P.). — Le Décaméron Russe. Histoires et Nouvelles, traduits des meilleurs auteurs. 12°. *Paris :* C. Douniol.
> [Pages 62–77. "*Le duel.*"]

DOUX (CLEMENTE). — Il maneggio della sciabola secondo il metodo di scherma Radaelli. 1875–6. *Roma.*

DOWNIE (SIR JOHN). — Colleccion de laminas del ataque y defensa del arma de la lanza. 4°. 1814. *Madrid.*

DOYLE (ALEXANDER). — Neue Alamodische Ritterliche Fecht- und Schirm-Kunst. Das ist Wahre und nach neuester Französischer Manier eingerichtete Unterweisung wie man sich in Fechten und Schirmen perfectioniren und verhalten solle. Denen respectiven Herren Liebhaberen zu besserer Erleuterung mit 60 hierzu deut- lichen Figuren herausgegeben von Alexander Doyle, aus Irrland geburtig. (i) Ihrer Churfurstl. Gnaden zu Maintz verordneten Hof-Fechtmeistern. Obl. 4°. 1715. *Nürnberg :* Paul Lochmern.

(In the British Museum.)

—— (—). — Neue Alamodische Ritterliche Fecht- und Schirm- Kunst. 2te Auflage. Oblong 4°. 1729. *Nürnberg.*

DRESKY (VON) [Oberst a. D.]. — Anleitung zum Fechten mit dem Stoszdegen. Bearbeitet für Offizier-Fechtvereine und militär. Bildungsanstalten an der Hand der Vorschriften vom Jahre 1884. 16°. 1891. *Berlin :* E. S. Mittler & Sohn.

[Mit 11 Abbildungen.]

DREYER. — *SCHLICHTEGROLL (Dr. N.).* — 1817.

DRUY (LE COMTE DE). — Traité de la beauté de la valeur et la lâcheté du duel.

DUARTE I. (REY DE PORTUGAL). — Regimento para aprender a jogar as armas. MS.

DU CHAILLU (PAUL B.). — Viking Age, History, &c. 2 vols. 8°. 1889. *London :* Murray.

[Vol. I. p. 563. "Duelling."]

DUDAS que se ofrecen á un aficionado de la verdadera destreza de las armas, á que pide solucion con razones satisfactorias. 8°. 1696. *Madrid.*

[A printed pamphlet of 3 pages, dated September 20, 1696.]

DUDEFFAND (MARIE DE VICHY — CHAMBROND, MARQUISE). — Correspondance à Horace Walpole.

[Vol. III. p. 249, Vol. IV. pp. 27, 28, 152. "Duelling."]

DUEL between the Duke of Hamilton and Lord Mohun. A letter from Mr. Maccartney at Ostend (Lord Mohun's second) to a friend in London, giving a relation of the above duel. Small 4°. 1713. *Dublin.*

DUEL (Het). — Een Ethisch-Sociale Studie. Uit 't Hoogduitsch. 12°. [N.D.] *Zutfen :* W. C. Wansleven.

DUEL (Le). 18°. 1868. *Paris :* Lebigre-Duquesne.

DUEL (Le) et l'escrime.
[*Paris Illustré.* No. 31 (1 *Juin* 1885).]

DUEL (Le) et les duellistes. 18°. *Paris.*
[*Ce volume fait partie de la Bibliothèque des Curiosités.*]

DUEL (The); a Play, as it is performed at the Theatre-Royal in Drury Lane. 8°. *London :* Davies.

DUEL'S ANATOMIE (The). — With the manner and form of Combats anciently observed before the Kings of England ; and a catalogue of certain Combats. Small 4°. 1613. *London.*
(*In the Library of the London Institution.* [Vol. V., Art. 9. *Imperfect.*])

DUELL (Das). 8°. 1856. *Münster :* Theissing.
[*Aus dem Münsterschen Sonntags-Blatte abgedruckt.*]

DUELL von Manteuffel-Twesten. 8°. 1861. *Berlin :* Rahn.

DUELL (Das) in seinem Ursprunge und Wesen. 8°. 1864. *Padborn :* Schönigh.

DUELL (Das) in seiner moralischen und gesellschaftlichen Berechtigung. Eine ethischsoziale Studie. 8°. 1871. *Leipzig :* Luckhardt.

DUELLE (Über das) d. Studirenden. 8°. 1829. *Altona :* Aue.

DUELLE und Paukereien oder der "geadelte Mord," v.e. "alten Herrn." 8°. 1885. *Leipzig :* Bredow.

DUELL (Das) als Emancipation der Ehre oder Beleuchtung des Duells vom geschichtlichen, moralischen und politischen Standpunkte. 8°. 1846. *Freiburg :* Herder.
(*In the British Museum, and Mr. J. R. Garcia Donnell's Collection.*)

DUELL (Das), oder die Freundschaft als Schutzgeist der Liebe. Erzählung aus den Leben gegriffen.　2 Thle.　8°.　1834–35. *Weimar :* Tantz u. Comp.

DUELL (Ein). — Trauerspiel in 5 Akten von F. A. * * *.　8°. 1848.　*Frankfurt a. M. :* Literar. Anstalt.

DUELL Holzapfel-Oehlke vor d. Schwurgericht.　8°.　1885. *Berlin :* Eckstein Nachf.

[*6 pages.*]

DUELLING.
[" *Southern Literary Messenger* " (*Richmond, U.S.A.*), Vol. XXXII. p. 226.]

DUELLING DAYS IN THE ARMY.
[" *United Service Magazine* " (*London*), Vol. I. pp. 90–209, Vol. II. p. 45.]

DUELLING DAYS IN THE NAVY.
[" *United Service Magazine* " (*London*), 1882, Vol. II. p. 81.]

DUELLING IN GERMANY.
[" *Chambers's Journal* " (*London*), *April* 1890.]

DUELLING IN ITALY.
[" *Spectator* " (*London*), Vol. LVII., No. 1072.]

DUELLING IN MODERN TIMES.
[" *Colbourn's Magazine* " (*London*), Part 123, p. 116.]

DUELLING IN OLDEN TIMES.
[" *Colbourn's Magazine* " (*London*), Part 122, p. 476.]

DUELLING and Suicide repugnant to revelation, reason and common sense.　8°.　1774.　*London.*

DUELLING and Suicide repugnant to revelation, reason and common sense.　8°.　1775.　*London :* Meigham.

DUELLING (Thoughts on) and the Christian Character.　8°. 1839.　*London :* Longman.

DUELLIST. — The Female Duellist, an afterpiece, with songs. 8°.　1793.　*London.*
(*In the British Museum. King's Pamphlets*, 163. *l.* 7.)

DUELLIST ; or a cursory review of the Rise, Progress, and Practice of Duelling, with illustrative anecdotes from history.　8°.　1822. *London :* Longman.

DUELLISTS, or Men of Honour. 12°. [Between 1800–1818.] *London :* Cundel.

DUELLO (Un) al buio : scherzo comico in un atto : parole di V.M. Musica di Ricardo Martini. 16°. 1889. *Firenze :* U. Boninsegni e C.

[*23 pages.*]

DUELLO, civè il libro de re militare. 8°. 1544. *Vinegia.*

DUELLO de Fausto da Longiano regolato a le leggi de l'honore. 8°. 1559. *Vinegia.*

(*In Captain Hutton's Collection.*)

DUELLO DI MERCY. 4°. *Milano :* E. Sonzogno.

[*Con 5 incisioni.*]

DUELLO DUJARIER-BEAUVALLON. 4°. *Milano :* E. Sonzogno.

[*Con 5 incisioni.*]

DUELLO. — Libro de Re Imperatori. Principi Signori Gentilhomini et di tutte Armigeri Continente Disfide Concordie Pan, Casi Accadenti e Indicii con pagione Exempla, &c. 12°. 1525. *Venetia.*

[*Another edition, 1554.*] (*In Captain Hutton's Collection.*)

DUELLO. — Tractatus inter Militem Sacrum et Militem Secularum Editus Latium zanchum. 4°. 1588. *Verona.*

DUELS (Les), Suicides et Amours du Bois de Boulogne. Recueil historique par un Rôdeur. 2 vols. 8°. 1821. *Paris.*

——. — [*CUISIN (J. P. R.*)]. — 1830.

DUEÑAS (D. GREGORIO MARÍA) [Caballero de la órden del Mérito militar y Profesor de esgrima en la academia de infantería]. — Ensayo de un tratado de esgrima de florete. 4°. 1881. *Toledo :* Fando é hijo.

[*7 láminas plegadas con 20 figuras. 135 pages.*]

DUFOUR (LOUIS). — Répression du duel. Recherche du meilleur mode de pénalité. 8°. 1840. *Paris :* Durand.

[*Extrait de la " Revue de législation et de jurisprudence."*]

DUGDALE (SIR W.). — *ASHMOLEAN* MSS.

DUGUÉ (E.). — Les Trente-deux duels de Jean Gigon; drame en cinq actes. Tiré du roman de M. A. Gandon. 12°. 1861. *Paris :* Barbré.

DULAURE (J. A.). — Histoire physique, civile et morale de Paris. 3e édition. 7 vols. 8°. 1825. *Paris.*

> [Vol. IV. p. 567, and Vol. V. pp. 300, 301. *"Duelling."*]

DUMAS (ALEXANDRE). — Le Maître d'Armes (Mémoires de A. Grisier). 3 vols. 8°. 1840. *Paris :* Dumont.

—— (—). — Ditto. 12°. 1848. *Paris :* Lévy frères.

—— (—). — Ditto. 12°. 1861. *Paris :* Lévy frères.

—— (—). — Le Maître d'Armes (Episodes). Edited with English notes by H. Lallemand and Eugene Joel. 8°. 1891. *London :* Nutt.

—— (—). — *GRISIER (A.).* — 1863, 1864.

—— (—). — *VAUX (Baron de).* — 1888.

DUMANIANT et **TOMEONI**. — Le Duel de Bambin. Comédie en un acte et en prose, mélée d'ariettes. 12°. 1880. *Paris :* Tiger.

DUNCAN (P. B.). — Motives of Wars, an Essay, together with a paper on duelling. Small 8°. 1844. *Bath.*

DUNCOMBE (THOMAS SLINGSBY) [M.P.]. — Life and Correspondence. 2 vols. 8°. 1868. *London.*

> [*Contains notices of French duels.*]

DUNLOP (J.). — Anti-Duel, or a plan for the abrogation of Duelling, which has been tried and found successful. 8°. 1843. *London :* Houlston.

—— (—.). — *CHRISTIAN* Observer.

—— (—.). — *MONTHLY* Review.

DUNN (H. A. COLMORE). — Fencing. 16°. 1889. *London :* George Bell & Sons. (The All England Series.) (Bohn's Handbooks of Athletic Sports.)

> [*With illustrations by H. C. Willink.*]

DUPLEIX (Scipion) [Conseiller du roi Louis XIII.]. — Le combat et duel des Seigneurs de la Chasteneraye demandeur et assaillant et de Jarnac défendeur et soustenant. 8°.

[*Avec gravure combat ajoutée.*]

—— (—). — Les loix militaires touchant le duel, en IV livres. 4°. 1602. *Paris.*

[*Another edition appeared.* 12°. 1611. Paris.]

DÜRER (Albrecht). — Oplodidaskalia, sive armorum tractandorum meditatio. [1512.]

[*MS. in the Magdalenenbibliothek, Breslau. Quoted by Lenz in his "Zusammenstellung von Schriften über Leibesübungen."*]

—— (—). — *WASSMANNSDORFF (K.).* — 1871.

DURFORT (Genl. de). — Supplément à la défense du Genl. de Durfort dans le procès de la prétendue contrefaçon de l'escrime de cheval. 8°. 1827. *Paris.*

DÜVAL (Jeanet). — Theoretische Anweisung zur Fecht- und Voltigirkunst. Quer 4°. 1822. *München :* Fleischmann.

[*1 plate and 60 figures, lithographed.*]

DU VERGER de Saint-Thomas (Comte). — *SAINT-*Thomas. — 1879.

DUYCKINCK (Evert A.) and **DUYCKINCK** (George L.). — Cyclopædia of American Literature. 2 vols. 4°. 1877. *Philadelphia :* William Rutter & Co.

[Vol. I. p. 310. "*Captain Farrago's Instructions to Teagul on the Duello.*"
  By Hugh Henry Brackenridge.
  „   II. p. 949. "*The Duel*" (a poem). By Lucy Hamilton Hooper.
  „   II. p. 450. "*Notes on Duels and Duelling.*" By Lorenzo Sabine.]

DWARF (The). — (Periodical.) 8°. *London :* 12 Crane Court, E.C.

[Vol. III., No. 57 (*January* 12, 1892). "*Pistols and Coffee for Two.*" By J. A. C., "*The Special Commissioner.*" Illustrated by Paul Frenzény.]

DWIGHT (Henry Edwin) [A.M.]. — Travels in the North of Germany in the years 1825 and 1826. 8°. 1829. *New York :* G. & C. & H. Carvill.

[Pages 49-56. "*Duelling Customs in Germany.*"
  Engraved frontispiece, showing Combatants, Seconds, Umpire, and Witnesses. The Surgeon and Spectators are not represented.]
  (*In the British Museum,* 1428. *f.*)

DWIGHT (TIMOTHY) [D.D., President of Yale College]. — The folly, guilt and mischiefs of Duelling. A sermon [on Prov. xxviii. 17] preached in the College Chapel at New Haven, . . . September 1804. 8°. 1805. *Hartford.*

(In the British Museum, 4436. f. 46.)

—— (——). — [Another edition]. A Sermon on Duelling, &c. 8°. 1805. *New York.*

(In the British Museum, 4486. cc. 14 (6).)

EASY AND FAMILIAR RULES for attaining the art of attack and defence on foot with the broadsword, to which are added instructions for using of the single-stick. 8°. 1831. *London:* T. Hughes.

[*One folding plate with 12 figures, being the same as those given in the pamphlet by " a pupil of St. Angelo."*]

ECHO (L') DES SPORTS DE PARIS. (Journal Hebdomadaire, paraissant le Samedi.) Folio. *Paris:* 108 Rue de Richelieu. (Le Numéro 25 centimes.)

[*Escrime, Sports Athletique, etc.* No. 1 *en* 1890.]

ECHO (The). — (Periodical.) Folio. *London.*

[1892. *February* 15. *Duel between M. Rateau, former editor of a Boulangist paper, and M. Gabriel Baume, a member of the Staff of the " Autorité."*
1892. *February* 17. " *Duelling in Hungary."* M. Edmund Gajary, editor *of the " Memzet," and M. Ludwig Csavolsky, editor of the " Egyetertes." Duel with swords between M. Aurel Muennich and Kornell Abranyi. Both slightly wounded.*]

ECKFORD (HENRY). — Fencing and the New York Fencers.

[*The " Century Illustrated Monthly Magazine,"* Vol. XXXIII., No. 3 (*January* 1887), pp. 414–421.]

ECKLER (G.). — *LENZ* (G. F.). — 1881.

ECKSTEIN (E.). — *VOM* Fels zum Meer. — 1891.

ECLECTIC MAGAZINE. 8°. *New York, U.S.A.*

[Vol. XXIV. pp. 53, 233, 407. *Anecdotes of Duelling.*
　,,　XXIX. p. 392. *Duel of D'Esterre and O'Connell.*
　,,　XXXVI. p. 170. *Duelling.*
　,,　LIV. p. 376. *Duelling in Modern Times.*
　,,　LXX. p. 566. *Arabian Sword Hunters.*
　,,　LXXVI. p. 168. *Trial by Battle.*
　,,　XCVII. p. 145. *The Sword.*
　,,　CIV. p. 222. *French Duelling. By H. R. Haweis.*]

EDICT (An), or Statute lately set forth by the French King, concerning the Prohibition and Punishment of Single and Private Combats, translated out of French. 4°. 1609.

EDICT. — A brief of two proclamations and his Majesty's Edict against duels. 1613. MS.

(*In the British Museum, 6297. p. 284.*)

EDICT (A publication of his Maties) and severe Censure against Private Combats and Combatants. Whether within his Highnesses' Dominions or without: with their seconds, accomplices and adherents. Small 4°. 1613. *London :* Robert Barker.

(*In the Library of the London Institution.* [Vol. V. Art. 8.])

EDICT du roy contre les duels et rencontres Vérifié en parlement le roy (Ludwig XIV.) y seant le 7 Sept. 1651. 4°. 1651. *Paris.*

EDICT du Roy sur la prohibition et punition des querelles et duels. 8°. 1609. *Paris.*

EDINBURGH REVIEW. 8°. 1802–1874. *Edinburgh.*

[Vol. V. p. 470. *Sword, the Queen of Arms.*
  „ XXII. p. 74. *Duelling, by the law, is a capital offence, yet a mere dead letter owing to the discrepancy between it and the manners of the country.*
  „ XXXIV. p. 196. *Duels, remarks on the practice of, among the ancient Scandinavian nations and their descendants.*
  „ XLI. p. 84. *Duels, the code of, among the associated German students.*
  „ LXXV. pp. 422–452. *Duelling. By Millingen.*
  „ LXXIX. p. 374. *Duels in Russia—both a civil and military offence.*
  „ LXXX. p. 229. *Duels, progress and limitations of private.*]

EDIT du Roy contre les duels. 4°. 1723. *Paris :* Louis-Denis Delatour.

(*In Mr. J. R. Garcia Donnell's Collection.*)

EDIT du Roy portant réglement général sur les Duels, donné à Saint-Germain-en-Laye au mois d'août 1679, avec le nouveau réglement de messieurs les Maréchaux de France sur le même sujet. 8°. 1679. *Paris :* Théodore Girard.

EEKHOUD (GEORGES). — *ESCRIME* (*L'*) à travers les Ages. [1894.]

EFFENBERGER (ANT.). — Leitfaden zur praktischen Erlernung d. Rappier- und Säbelfechtens. 8°. 1878. *Pola :* Schmidt.

EGENTER (F. J.). — Ueber Duell und Ehre. Mit besond. Rücksicht auf Studentenduelle. 3. Auflage. 16°. 1878. *Leipzig:* Wölfert.

EGERTON (HONBLE. WILBRAHAM) [M.A., M.P.]. — An illustrated Handbook of Indian Arms; being a classified and descriptive catalogue of the arms exhibited at the Indian Museum. Large 8°. 1880. *London:* W. H. Allen & Co.

     [*Published by order of the Secretary of State for India in Council.*]

EICHHOLZ (F.). — Der Paukarzt. 8°. 1886. *Jena:* Doebereiner.

         [*24 pages.*]

EINSIDELL (C.). — *CAVALCALO (H.)* — 1611.

EISELEN (E.). — *JAHN (F. L.).* — 1816.

EISELEN (E. W. B.). — Das deutsche Hiebfechten der Berliner Turnschule. 8°. 1818. *Berlin:* Dümmler.

     (*In Mr. J. R. Garcia Donnell's Collection.*)

—— (—. —. —.). — Abriss des deutschen Stossfechtens, nach Kreusslers Grundsätzen dargestellt. 8°. 1826. *Berlin:* Dümmler.

—— (—. —. —.). — Das Säbelfechten. Manuscript, aufgezeichnet von dessen Schüler G. im J. 1825. 8°. 1881. *Berlin:* Lenz.

—— (—. —. —.). — Das deutsche Hiebfechten der Berliner Turnschulen. Neu bearbeitet und mit Abbildungen versehen von Turnlehr. A. M. Böttcher und Dr. K. Wassmannsdorff. 8°. 1882. *Lahr:* Schauenburg.

—— (—. —. —.). — Abrisz des deutschen Säbel und Stoszfechtens. Nach Kreuslers Grundsätzen dargestellt. Herausgegeben von dessen Schüler F. Gierow. 12°. 1889. *Berlin:* Lenz.

     [*Mit 35 Abbildungen von P. Gierow.*]

—— (—. —. —.). — *BÖTTCHER (A. M.).* — 1849. 1855.

EISENBERGS FECHTSCHULE. — 1748.

EJERCICIOS DE LAS ARMAS.

     [*16th century. MS. in Bibliot. del Escorial* (52 *foj. iv. a.* 23).]

ELDON (LORD). — *MEDLAND (W. M.).* — 1808.

ELIOT (T.). — *LOQUE (B. de).* — 1591.

ELLERO (P.). — Dei mezzi più opportuni a bandire dalla società il duello. 8°. 1864. *Modena.*

ELLIOT. — A collection of 4 plates of broadsword and Spanish and Italian Fencing, with figures in military costumes of various nations. 4°.

ELLIOTT (MAJOR W. J.) [late of H.M. War Department].—The Art of Attack and Defence in use at the present time. Fencing: Sword *v.* Sword, Sword *v.* Bayonet, Single-stick, Bayonet against Sword or Bayonet; Boxing. 8°. 1884. *London :* Dean & Sons.
> [*With 61 figures.*] (*In Captain Hutton's Collection.*)

ELLIOTT [MAJOR]. — Art of Attack and Defence; Fencing, Sword and Bayonet Exercise, Singlestick, Boxing. Foolscap 8°. [N.D.] *London :* Dean & Son.
> [*Champion Series of Illustrated Sixpenny Useful Handbooks.*]

EMBRY (J. A.). — Dictionnaire raisonné d'escrime, ou Principes de l'art des armes d'après la méthode enseignée par les premiers professeurs de France, précédé de l'histoire de l'escrime et de l'analyse de l'histoire de France dans ses rapports avec le duel. 1re et 2e parties. In-8, avec 8 pl. 1856. *Toulouse.*
> [*L'ouvrage, composé d'environ 700 pages, sera divisé en 4 parties, et paraîtra en 2 séries : 1re serie, comprenant l'histoire de l'escrime ; l'analyse de l'histoire de France, dans ses rapports avec l'escrime et le duel. Une nouvelle édition de cette 1re série a été annoncée en 1859, en vente à Paris chez M. Bohin de Corday, 18, quai de la Mégisserie. La 2e série, qui sera publiée en deux parties, renfermera un Traité théorique sur l'art des armes et le Dictionnaire raisonné d'escrime.*]
> (*In Captain Hutton's Collection.*)

EMPLOI (L') DU SABRE. Etude raisonnée du combat à l'arme blanche d'après les principes posés par le règlement sur les exercices de la cavalerie du 31 mai 1882. 32°. 1882. *Paris.*
> [48 *pages. Ouvrage accompagné de 11 figures en photogravure, hors texte.*]

ENCYCLOPÆDIA BRITANNICA. 9th edition. 1888. *Edinburgh :* A. & C. Black.
> [*Articles on " Fencing " and " Duelling."*
> Vol. XXII. p. 800. " *Sword.*" *By Frederick Pollock.*]

ENCYCLOPÉDIE. La science de cour, d'épée et de robe. — De l'art de faire des armes. — Extrait. 8°. 1770.

[*Résumant les théories de l'ouvrage de Girard et reproduisant sur cuivre ses gravures réduites.*]

ENCYCLOPÉDIE MÉTHODIQUE. Traité d'escrime. 1782. *Paris.*

—— ——. Equitation, Escrime, Danse, et art de Nager. 4°. 1786. *Paris.*

—— —— (Planches de L'). — Nouvelle édition enrichie de remarques. Dediée à la serenissime Republique de Venise. Art Militaire, Equitation, Escrime, &c. Folio. 1795. *Padova.*

ENCYCLOPÉDIE Moderne, XII. au mot : Escrime. 1828. *Paris.*

ENRICHETTI (CESARE) [Maestro-capo e direttore di scherma alla scuola centrale di Parma]. — Trattato elementare teorico-practico di scherma. 8°. 1871. *Parma.*

[6 *lithographs.*]

—— (—). — *MARCHIONNI (A.).* — 1868.

ENTWURF einer Vorschrift über das Fechten mit dem Kavallerie-Degen. Modell. 1886. 8°. 1887. *Berlin :* Mittler & Sohn.

[*With illustrations.*]

EON (FREDERICK D'). — System of fencing as arranged and systematically taught by Frederick d'Eon, fencing-master. In thirty-one sections, for the first quarter's tuition. 12°. 1823. *Boston.*

EPITOME (AN) OF THE WHOLE ART OF WAR. 8°. 1692. *London :* Philip Lee.

[*Contains the whole exercise of the Pike and Musquet, with plain directions for the various postures.*]

ERCILLA (FORTUN GARCIA DE). — Tratado del Desafio de Francisco I. y del Emperador [Carlos V.], de Alemania. MS. paper, in folio.

[*British Museum, Eg.* 537. *Being an account of the challenge offered by that monarch and accepted by Charles, with historical and juridical observations, &c. A note at the beginning states this treatise to have been composed by Ercilla, a native of Bermeo, in Viscay, and a lawyer by profession. His birth is fixed in* 1486, *and it is added that his life was written by D. D. B. G.*]

ERLASS DES RATHS DER STADT STRASSBURG gegen die Herausforderungen und Zweikämpfe. Folio. 1609. *Strassburg.*

ERLASS GEGEN DAS DUELIREN, Rauffen, Balgen und Schlagen, 23 Feb. 1748. Folio. 1748. *München.*

ERSCH und **GRUBER.** — Encyklopädie. Gr. 8°. 1840–1846. *Leipzig:* Brockhaus.

> [1te Sec., 42, S. 204 u. ff. *Scheidler (H.),* "*Fechtkunst.*" 1884 (?).]

ERSTE ABHANDLUNG DER BAYONET-FECHTLEHRE. 8°. 1823. *Karlsruhe:* Müller.

> (*In Captain Hutton's Collection.*)

ERSTE ANLEITUNG DES SOLDATEN in der eigentlichen zerstreuten Fechtart. Auszug aus d. Werke des Obersten Grafen v. Waldersee, "Die Methode zur kriegsgemässen Ausbildung der Infanterie f. das zerstreute Gefecht." 8°. 1850. *Mainz:* V. von Zabern.

ESCHER (J. B.). — Anweisung zur Fechtkunst auf Hiebe in verhängter und steiler Auslage. 4°. 1833. *Freiburg:* Groos.

> [18 *engravings.*]

—— (—. —.). — Méthode d'escrime. 8°. 1843. *Fribourg.*

ESCOTT (A.). — Fencing and Fencers.

> ["*The Theatre*" (*London*), S. III. Vol. II. No. 12, pp. 347–350.]

ESCRIME.

> [*L'Encyclopédie de* 1755 *est la première à nommer et à enseigner la* "*botte d'octave.*" *Une nouvelle édition en* 1763 *reproduisit le traité de Angelo Malevolti.*]

ESCRIME (L'). — Gazette des salles d'armes, paraissant le Dimanche. 4°. *Paris.*

> [*Adolphe Tavernier fonda ce journal en* 1882 *et le dirigea pendant deux années. La collection complète du journal forme deux gros volumes d'environ* 1200 *pages chacun; mais il est presque impossible de les trouver.*]

ESCRIME (L') DU FANTASSIN À LA BAÏONNETTE. Oblong folio. [About 1830.] MS.

> [*In possession of Captain A. Hutton, and described by him in* "*Fixed Bayonets*" *as follows:* "*Contains* 37 *pages of fine clearly written text;* 61 *illustrations, of which* 10 *have been removed, consisting of carefully drawn pen-and-ink outline figures. The writer draws attention to three German works published at Vienna* 1819, *Dresden* 1821, *and Stuttgart* 1824, *but the titles are not given.*"]

ESCRIME À LA BAÏONNETTE. 1841. *Strasbourg.*
[*Extrait de " L'Instruction des bataillons des Chasseurs.*"]

ESCRIME À LA BAÏONNETTE. (Extrait de l'instruction provis. sur l'exercise et les manœuvres des bataillons des Chasseurs à pied.) 32°. 1842. *Strasbourg :* Levrant.

ESCRIME DE CHAMBRE, méthode pour s'exercer seul à faire des armes, par le commandant E. T. 32°. *Paris.*
[24 *pages.*]

ESCRIME (L') À TRAVERS LES AGES. Le Cycle de l'Épée. Prologue en vers, de M. Félix Hecq. 8°. [1894.] *Bruxelles :* J. Lebègue et Cie.
[*Histoire vivante de l'épée en dix Tableaux Épis odiques Livret de M. Georges Eekhoud. With 8 illustrations and a frontispiece drawn from " L'Escrime et les Escrimeurs," by Egerton Castle.*] (*In Captain Hutton's Collection.*)

ESCRIME (L') ENCORE ET TOUJOURS À LYON 1889. *Lyon :* Léon Delaroche et Cie.

ESCRIME (L') RECUEIL de 38 gravures reprod. des exercices, évolutions d'infanterie et de cavalerie, fortification, artillerie, avec texte.
[*Ce recueil est indiqué dans un des catalogues d'Albert Foulard, Paris, No. 3847.*]

ESCRIME (L') FRANÇAISE. Rédacteur en chef, Emile André. 4°. 1889. *Paris :* 270 Rue Saint-Honoré.
[*The first number appeared on the 9th February 1889. Revue bi-mensuelle paraissant le 5 et le 20 de chaque mois, avec numéros supplémentaires ou supplément de Décembre à Juin. 60 centimes.*]

ESGRIMA DE LA BAYONETA ARMADA, traducida del Italiano por un Oficial de Milicias Provinciales. 8°. 1830. *Madrid :* León Amarita.
[56 *págs.*]

ESGRIMA (LA). — Colección de apuntes, datos y noticias, tomadas de autores antiguos y modernos. MSS.
[*Es una reunión de extractos y copias de varias Enciclopedias, como la de Bouillet, Suárez de Figueroa, Mellado, Serrano, &c.*]

ESGRIMA ORNADA, con 10 gravuras, David Corazzi, editor. 8°. 1883. *Lisboa.*
[63 *págs.*]

94

ESPAGNE (JOHN D')]. — Antiduello; or a treatise in which is discussed the lawfulnesse and unlawfulnesse of single combats. Together with the forme of several Duels performed in this kingdome on sundry occasions. 4°. 1632. *London :* T. Harper for B. Fisher.

—— (— —). — Anti-Duello. The anatomie of Duells, with the symptomes thereof. 4°. 1632. *London :* printed by Thomas Harper for B. Fisher.

ESPAÑA MODERNA (LA). — Revista Ibero-Americana. 8°. *Madrid.*
  [15 *Julio* 1891, p. 86. "*Duelo de Monstruos*" *por Theodoro de Banville.*]

ESSAI SUR LE DUEL. Par A. B. 8°. Août 1836. *Bordeaux.*

ESSAY (AN) ON DUELLING; written with a view to discountenance this barbarous and disgraceful practice. 8°. 1792. *London :* Debrett.

ESTEVA (GONZALO A.). — Consejos para el Duelo á espada y á pistola. 4°. 1878. *México :* G. A. Esteva.

ETTENHARD (DON FRANCISCO ANTONIO DE) [Cavallero de la Orden de Calatrava]. — Compendio de los fundamentos de la verdadera destreza y filosofía de las armas. Dedicado á la Cathólica, Sacra y Real Magestad del Rey, nuestro Señor Don Cárlos Segundo, Monarca de España y de las Indias. 4°. 1675. *Madrid :* Antonio de Zafra.
  [18 *hoj. de prels*, 391 *págs.* y 17 *láminas.*
  To the above is generally found joined a smaller work entitled, "*Siguese el papel de Juan Caro, en que impugna la obra con Quince Oiepciones, y la respuesta de el Autor a ellos* (1 *copperplate*).]
  (*In the British Museum.*)

ETTENHARD Y ABARCA (DON FRANCISCO ANTONIO DE). — Diestro Italiano y Español. Explican sus doctrinas con evidencias mathemáticas conforme á los preceptos de la verdadera destreza y filosofía de las armas. 4°. 1697. *Madrid :* Manuel Ruiz de Murga.
  [4 *copperplates.*] (*In the British Museum ; and in the BB. de Ingenieros, del Senado, de Fernandez San Roman.*)

EUDEL (PAUL). — Collectionneurs, — Vigeant, une collection d'escrime (Extrait). 8°. 1885. *Paris :* Charpentier.

EULER (Prof. Dr. Carl). — Handbuch der Leibesübungen. Eine encyklopädische Darstellung des gesamten Turnwesens und der verwandten Gebiete in alphabetischer Ordnung. *Wien:* A. Pickler's Witwe & Sohn.

> [(*In the Press.*) *Das Fechten sowohl in allgemeinen als in den Haupt-fechtarten.*]

EVELYN (John) [F.R.S.]. — Diary and Correspondence. 4 vols. 8°. 1850. *London:* H. Colburn.

> [Vol. II. p. 328. "*Duel, fatal one.*" (*Wilson and Laws, a Scotchman.* 1694.)]

EVENING NEWS AND POST (Periodical). Folio. *London.*

> [1891. *August* 11. "*Why not revive Duelling!*"]

EVERY SATURDAY (Periodical). Boston.

> [Vol. IV. p. 336. *Curiosities of French Duelling.*
>   ,, VI. pp. 618, 661. ⎱ *Duelling.*
>   ,, IX. p. 235.   ⎰
>   ,, IX. p. 199. *Parisian Fencing.*
>   ,, XVI. p. 288. *Reminiscences of Duelling in Ireland.*
>   ,, XVII. p. 383. *Laws of Duelling.*]

EXERCISES (THE) OF ARMES FOR CALIUERES, Muskettes and Pikes; set forth in figures. Folio. 1608.

EŸCH (J. H.). — Deutliche Explication der adelichen und ritter-lichen Fechtkunst. 8°. MS.

> [*Eÿch was State Fencing-Master in Cologne, and dedicates his work to Burgermasters Krufft and Kerich. Autograph 8° MS. in the possession of Captain A. Hutton, date about 1740. M. Vigeant has also a copy in his collection, and which he describes as follows:* "*Explication du noble et chevaleresque art de l'escrime.* Cologne.
> *Petit manuscrit allemand in 4° oblong, avec nombreuses planches dessinées à la plume par le maître lui-même. Ce manuscrit n'a jamais été imprimé. Reluire ancienne en veau, tranche jaspée et filets sur les plats.*"]

F. (G.). — Duell-Ease. A worde with Valiant Spiritts, shewing the abuse of Duells, that Valour refuseth Challenges and Private Combates. Sett forth by G. F., a defendour of Christian Valoure. 4°. 1635. *London:* Ann Griffin.

> [*Title-page engraved.*]

FABRI (Antonio). — Per la inaugurazione della sala di scherma e del Maneggio nel quartière del reggimento cacciatori a cavallo in Palermo.

SALVATOR FABRIS. 1606.

Capo del' Ordine dei sette cori.

FABRIS (SALVATOR) [Capo dell' ordine dei sette cori]. — Sienza [*sic*] e pratica d'Arme. Divisa in dui Libri : Nel Primo, si dismotra [*sic*] le suttilita sopra le quali é fondata la professione. Nel Secondo, Alcvne Raggioni, non piu da altri intese. Con la tauola, di quanto nell' opera si Contiene. Folio. 1606. *Copenhaven :* Henrico Waltkirch.

> [*Engraved title-page. With a second title-page also engraved, which reads,* "*De lo Schermo, overo scienza d'arme.*" *Frontispiece. Portraits of Christian IV. of Denmark, to whom the work is dedicated, and of the author. 190 copperplates by J. Halbeeck in the text.*
> *The seizure in Dagger Play, or the method for an unarmed man attacked by one armed with a knife, is touched upon by this author.*
> "*Fabris divides his work into two books and six parts. The first book treats thoroughly the question of broad principles and of the more 'academic' actions with the rapier, alone or accompanied with dagger or cloak; it discusses in a very exhaustive manner the relative value of the past and present methods. The second book is one 'wherein is demonstrated certain rules with which it will be possible to strike the enemy from the moment the sword is drawn, without halting or waiting any time, principles which have never been treated by any master or writer.'*"—*Castle's* "*Schools and Masters of Fence.*"]
> (*In the British Museum,* 534. *m.* 13. (*imperfect*); *and Captain Hutton's Collection.*)

—— (—). — Neu künstlich Fechtbuch. 1617. *Neurenberg.*

—— (—). — Della vera practica e scienza d'armi . . . &c. Opera di Salvator Fabris. Folio. 1624. *Padova :* per Pietro Paoli Tozzi.

—— (—). — Des kunstreichen und weitberümeten Fechtmeisters S. Fabris Italienische Fechtkunst. Folio. 1619. *Leyden.*

> [*Printed by Isaack Elzevier, and dedicated by the same to Gustavus Adolphus. The copperplates of the first edition are replaced by woodcuts* (192).]

—— (—). — Scienza e pratica d'arme di Salvatore Fabris, Capo dell' ordine dei sette cuori. Das ist : Herrn Salvatore Fabris, Obersten des Ritter-Ordens der Sieben Hertzen, Italienische Fechtkunst. Von Johann Joachim Hynitzchen, Exercitien Meister. 4°. 1677. *Leipzig :* gedruckt bey Michael Boge.

> [*German translation parallel with the Italian text. The plates are the same as in the original edition, with the addition of one representing the monument erected to Fabris's memory in Padua, his native town; and of a portrait of a certain Heinrich, who seems to have patronised this reproduction of the great master's work.*]

FABRIS (SALVATOR). — [A second edition of the Italian and German reproduction.] 4°. 1713. *Leipzig.*

—— (—). — *HEUSSLER (Seb.).* — 1616.

FAIRFAX (LORD THOMAS). — Two declarations from him and the General Council of his Army; the first to the Lord Mayor, &c., of London; the second to the whole Kingdom in general, concerning the resolution of his Excellency, and the officers and soldiers under his command, touching the power of the Sword, &c. 4°. 1647. *London.*

FALCIANI (ALBERTO). — La scherma della sciabola o del bastone a due mani, brevemente insegnata nella lingua del popolo. 12°. 1870. *Pisa.*

FALLOPIA (ALFONSO) [Lucchese. Alfiere nella fortezza di Bergamo]. — Nuovo et breve modo di schermire. 4°. 1584. *Bergamo :* appresso Comin Ventura.

FALSE HONOR, a Poem. 1720.
[*" Duelling."*] (*In the New York State Library, U.S.A.*)

FAMBRI (PAULO). — Relazione al Ministro della Guerra sul trattato di scherma di Masaniello Parise. 8°. 1884. *Roma :* Tip. Nazionale.

—— (—). — Novelle Cavalleresche. 8°. 1888. *Torino :* E. Loescher.

FAMBRI (P.). — La giurisprudenza del duello. 16°. *Firenze.*

FARINA (SILVESTRO LA). — Risposta ad un articolo anonimo pubblicato in occasione di un accademia di scherma data dal sig. P. Fonsio. 8°. 1836. *Messina :* Tip. del *"Faro."*
[*Estratto dal "Faro" fascicolo 2°, febbraio 1836, pag. 7.*]

FAUSTO (S.) [de Longiano]. — Duello . . . con due risposte ad una scrittura consultata dal M., etc. 8°. 1560.

—— (—.). — La seconda difesa, . . . risposta alla Faustina del Mutio. 8°. 1560.

FAVINE (ANDREW). — The Theatre of Honour and Knighthood, &c. Folio. 1623.
[*" Of duelles of Single Combat, with their Original Laws and Observations."*]

FAVYN (ANDRÉ). — Le Théatre d'honneur et de chevalerie ou l'hist. des ordres militaires des Roys et Princes de la chrestienté et leur généalogie, etc.   2 vols.   4°.   1620.

[Figures.]

FAYET (AUGTE. NOUGARÈDE DE). — Du duel sous le rapport de la législation et des mœurs suivi de l'ordonnance de Louis XIV. en 1651, du réquisitoire de M. Dupin, procureur général, et de l'arrêt de la Cour de Cassation du 22 Juin 1837.   8°.   1838.   *Paris:* Capelle.

FAZY (GEORGES). — Le Duel.   Dissertation présentée à la Faculté de droit de l'Académie de Genève.   8°.   1871.   *Genève:* H. Georg.

FECHT-BODEN (Der Geöffnete) auf welchen durch kurtz gefasste Regeln gute Anleitung zum rechten Fundament der Fecht-Kunst gegeben und gewiesen wird.   Worinnen die Haupt-Lectiones bestehen, und wie sie nach heutiger Manier ausgeübt, auch vortheilhafftig mit guter Adress können angebracht werden.   Mit dazu dientlichen Figuren verfertiget von Sr. C.   12°.   1706.   *Hamburg:* B. Schillern.

[10 copperplates.]
(In the British Museum, and Captain Hutton's Collection.)

FECHT-BODEN (Der Geöffnete) auf welchen durch kurtz gefasste Regeln gute Anleitung zum rechten Fundament der Fecht-Kunst gegeben wird.   Mit 8 Kupfertaf.   8°.   1715.   *Hamburg.*

FECHTBUCH (Die Ritterliche) mannliche Kunst und handarbeyt Fechtens und Kempffens, &c.   1558.

[At the end: Zu Franckfurt am Meyn, bei Chri. Egen. Erben. MDLVIII.]

—— (Die Ritterliche) mannliche Kunst und handarbeyt Fechtens und Kempffens.   Aus warem ursprunglichen grund der Alten, mit sampt heymlichen Geschwindigkeyten, in leibs nöten sich des Feinds tröstlich gemalt [about 1530–58 ?].   *Franckfort am Meyn:* bei Chr. Egenolff.

[46 pages.]

FECHTER (DER ALTENN) AN FENGLICHE KUNST. — Mit sampt verborgenen heymlicheytten, Kämpffens, Ringens, Werffens, &c.   Figürlich fürgemalet, bisher nie an tag kommen.   1531 (?).   *Frankfurt am Meyn:* Chr. Egenolff.

[46 pages.   Woodcut on title-page.   At the end: Zu Franckfurt am Meyn, bei Christian Egenolff.]

FECHTER (DER ALTENN) GRÜNDLICHE KUNST. — Mit sampt verborgenen heymlichten, Kämpffens, Ringens, Werffens, &c. Figürlich fürgemalet. Bisher nie añ tag komen.

[48 pages. Woodcut on title-page about 1530–58 ?]

FECHTKUNST (DIE) AUF UNIVERSITÄTEN. 8°. 1802. *Köthen :* Aue.

[Copperplates.]

FECHTSCHULN-REIMEN vom Jahre 1579. MS.

(Im germanischen National-Museum zu Nürnberg.)

FECHTWEISE (DIE NEUE) DER FRANZÖSISCHEN INFAN-TERIE. — Nach dem französ. Infanterie-Exerzier-Reglement vom 29. Juli 1884, und der Instruction pour le combat vom J. 1887. Bearb. v. e. deutschen Infanterie-Offizier. Mit zahlreichen Skizzen auf 6 Taf. 8°. 1887. *Darmstadt :* Zernin.

FEHN (A.) [Fechtlehrer an der Königl. Hannov. Cadetten-Anstalt]. — Die Fechtkunst mit Stoss- und Hiebwaffen. Gr. 8°. 1851. *Hannover :* Rümpler.

[Mit 34 Abbildungen. Stossfechten, Hiebfechten, Säbelschlagen, Pallasch-
fechten, Bajonetfechten.] (In Mr. J. R. Garcia Donnell's Collection.)

—— (—.). — Die Fechtkunst mit Stoss- und Hiebwaffen. 2te Auflage. 8°. 1856. *Hannover :* C. Meyer.

[34 figures.]

—— (—.). — Fechtschule, mit Originalzeichnungen von Ferdinand Liebsch. 2te Auflage. 8°. 1856. *Hannover :* C. Meyer.

—— (—.). — Fechtschule. 8°. 1876. *Heidelberg.*

FEHN (Aug.) [Univ. Fechtlehrer]. — Die Schule d. Manschett-fechtens. 8°. 1878. *Heidelberg :* Koester.

[With drawings.]

FEHN (W.). — Anleitung für Officiere und Unterofficiere beim Ertheilen d. Unterrichts im Turnen und Bajonettiren. 2te nach den allerhöchsten und neuesten Vorschriften bearb. Auflage. 16°. 1885. *Hannover :* Helwing.

—— (—.) [Univ. Fechtmeister]. — Das kommentmässige Fechten mit dem deutschen Haurappier Rechts und Links. Gr. 8°. 1885. *Strassburg i. E. :* Schultz & Comp.

[24 plates from photographs.]

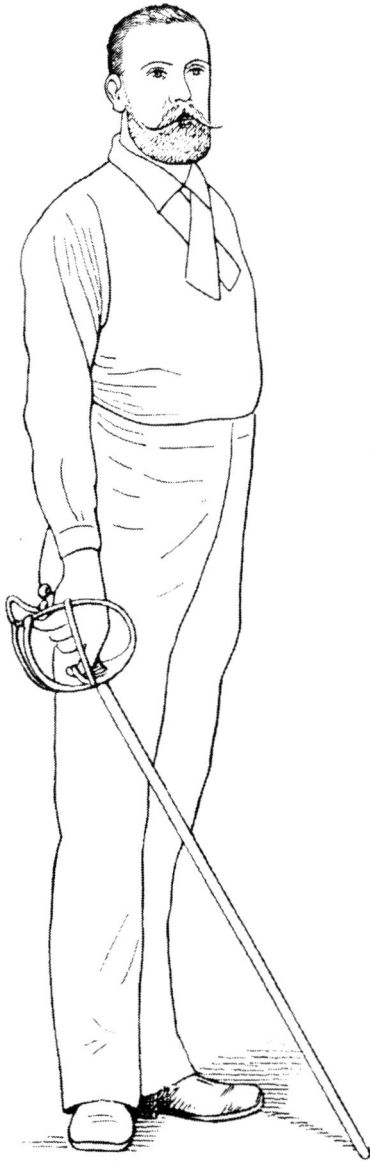

WILHELM FEHN. 1885.

Fechtmeister an der Universität zu Strassburg.

FEHN (W.). — Entwurf einer Instruction für deutsche Hieb-fechtschulen. 8°. 1885. *Strassburg i. E. :* Schultz & Comp.
[*With photographic plates.*]

—— (—.) — Die Fechtkunst mit dem krummen Säbel. Praktische Anleitung zum Militärfechten (Hieb und Strich) und zum deutschen kommentmässigen Studentenfechten. 8°. 1885. *Strassburg :* R. Schultz & Comp.
[*26 pages.*]

FEHRENBACH (C.). — *NEUMANN (L.).* — 1890.

FELDMANN (Jos.) [Major]. — Leitfaden zum Unterrichte im Rappier-, Säbel-, Bajonet- und Stockfechten. Gr. 8°. 1882. *Wiener-Neustadt :* Lentner.
(*In Captain Hutton's Collection.*)

—— (—.). — Leitfaden zum Unterrichte im Stock-, Rapier-, Säbel- und Bajonettfechten. 2te Auflage. Lexicon-8°. 1886. *Wien :* Seidel und Sohn.
[*56 plates containing 77 figures, out of the text. 116 pages.*]

FÉLIX. — Encyclopédie. 1773. *Paris.*
[*Au mot "Escrime."*]

FÉLIZET (Docteur). — *LAMARCHE (Claude).*

FELTON (C. C.). — *NORTH AMERICAN* Review.

FEMALE DUEL (The); or, the Ladies' Looking Glass. 8°. 1661. *London.*
[*With a frontispiece.* ("*Duelling.*") (?)]

FENCING. — Billes for pryses at fencing as M[aste]rs Pryses and schollers pryse[s]. Licensed conditionally to T. Purfoot in 1587.
[*Mentioned in Hazlitt* (*W. Carew*)—*Handbook* (p. 194). 8°. 1867. London : J. R. Smith.]

"FENCING (On) with two-handed Sword."
[*A poem from MS. Harleian* 3542, *of the 15th century, British Museum.*]

FENCING (Rules for).
[*MS. in the British Museum,* 5540. *f.* 120.]

FENCING (Treatise on the Art of). With marginal notes. 17th century. Small 4°.
[*Italian MS.* (*imperfect*), *written in two different hands, in British Museum,* No. 23,223.]

FENCING. — Three Treatises on the Art of Fencing, as taught by Signor Salvator and Signor Mornan, by H. A. V.; with illustrations in Indian ink. Folio.

[*MSS. Paper*, 18*th century.* (*MS. in the British Museum, Add.* 17,533.)]

FERBER (WOLFGANG). — Fechtschule 27. September 1614 bei Gelegenheit des Armbrustschieszens zu Dresden. 1615.

[*Mentioned by Schmied-Kowarzik* (*J.*) *und Kufahl* (*H.*), "*Fechtbüchlein,*" 1894.]

FERGUSSON (HARY). — A dictionary explaining the terms, guards, and positions used in the art of the small sword. 8°. 1767. [No place, no printer's name.]

["*Hary*" *is thus on the title and at page ii.*]

FERRERO (GIO. BATTISTA). — Breve Trattato di scherma sul maneggio della sciabola. 1868. *Torino.*

FERRETTI (J.). — Consilia de duello. 8°. 1538. [*Ravennae ?*]

FERRETTI (JUL.). — Consilia et Tractatus. 4°. 1562. *Venetiis.*

[*In quasi* 100 *luoghi di quest' opera si tratta del duello e dei duellanti.*]

—— (JULII). — [Rauennatis] De duello.

[*Zilettus.* "*Tractatus Universi Juris.*" Tomus xii. (pp. 307–313). *Folio.* 1584. *Venetiis.* (*In the British Museum,* 499. *g.* 6.)]

FERRÉUS. — Annuaire du duel, 1880–1889. 12°. 1890. *Paris :* Perrin.

["*L'Annuaire du duel*" *est le répertoire des affaires d'honneur. L'intérêt de cette publication nous a paru être de constituer, pour ainsi dire, le dossier d'honneur de contemporains. A l'aide de ce répertoire (et avec la table alphabétique de noms propres qui y renvoie), ou trouvera la liste et le compte rendu des affaires d'honneur auxquelles, à titre d'adversaire, ou de témoin, ou d'arbitre, chacun a pu participer. Pour ce premier volume, nos comptes rendus ont été faits d'après les notes publiées par les journaux de Paris.*]

FERRO (R. CAPO). — *CAPO FERRO (R.).* — 1610.

FEUQUIÈRE (MARQUIS DE). — Memoires historical and military. Translated from the French. 1735. *London.*

[*In the glossary appended is given a description of the* "*Bagonet*" (*bayonet*) *then in use.*]

FÉVAL (PAUL). — Le fils du diable. 12 vols. 8°. 1846. *Paris :* Comon.

[*Has an account of Grisier's* "*Salle,*" *and a lesson given by him.*]

FEVERSHAM (EARL OF). — Exercize of Dragoons. Composed for his Ma^ies Roy^l Regiment by ye R^ht Honble Louis, Earl of Feversham, Colonell.

[*MS. volume in the possession of John Yong Akerman, Esq., F.S.A., Secretary, Society of Antiquaries, London, written in the latter half of the 17th century. Bayonet Exercise.*]

FEWTRELL. — The science of manual defence. 1790. *London.*

FIELD (The). — (Periodical.) Folio. *London :* Bream's Buildings.

[Vol. LXXIX. No. 2039 (*January* 23, 1892), " *The Art of Fence* " and *Prévost and Jollivet's* " *L'Escrime et le Duel.*"]

FIERLANTS (ALBERT). — *CASTLE (E.).* — 1888.

FINET (SIR JOHN).—A Letter from Paris upon the subject of Duelling. 1720.

[*The original letter is in the Cottonian Library (deposited in the British Museum). Titus, C. iv. 9. " Sir John Finet, to the E. of Northampton (Ld. Privy Seal) on the practice of duelling in France. (Orig.) Paris, Feb. 19, 1609–10." (510.)*]

FIRME (MANUEL MARTINS). — Espada firme, ou firme tractado para o jogo da espada preta e branca. 8°. 1744. *Evora.*

[xxxvi—68 *pág.*] (*En la B. de J. C. de Figaniere.*)

FISCHER (JONATH.). — Der Mann mit der Lanze. 8°. 1848. *Freiberg :* Craz und Gerlach.

FLORIO (BLASCO) [Siciliano]. — Il progresso della scienza della scherma delle Due Sicilie.

—— (—). — Di risposta ad alcune dimande di scherma, lettere di Blasco Florio . . . &c. 8°. 1820. *Catania.*

—— (—). — La stessa opera, al quanto modificata, fu pubblicata in Catania dal Pappalardo. 8°. 1823. *Catania.*

—— (—). — Discorso sull' utilità della scherma. 4°. 1825. *Messina :* G. Fiumara.

—— (—). — Discorso sull' utilità della scherma. 2nd edition. 4°. 1828. *Catania.*

(*In Mr. J. R. Garcia Donnell's Collection.*)

FLORIO (BLASCO). — La scienza della scherma. 8°. 1844. *Catania :* Tip. del R. Ospizio di Beneficenza.
> [*Con 3 fig.*] (*In Captain Hutton's Collection.*)

—— (—). — Giustificazione di Blasco Florio ai signori del Fôro Catanese. 8°. 1850. *Catania :* Fratelli Giuntini.

—— (—). — Osservazioni critico-apologetiche all' opera intitolata : "Istituzione di arte ginnastica," dirette ai professori di scherma in Napoli. 8°. 1856. *Catania.*

—— (—). — Ai signori Claudio Inguaggiato, Giovan Battista Vella e Francesco Pinto, professori di scherma in Palermo. Terzo Indirizzo.
> [*In risposta alle lettere del 12 giugno e 26 agosto 1857 del maestro Fonzio di Palermo.*]

—— (—). — Blasco Florio ai professori di scherma. 1858. *Catania.*

—— (—). — Lettera al signor Marchesino Carlo Mortillaro. 1858. *Catania.*
> [*Con una tavola dimostrativa : pag.* 15.]

—— (—). — Sul coraggio e sul combattere del soldato siciliano colla tattica garibaldina, lettera al cittadino Carlo Ardizzone. 1860. *Catania.*
> [*La lettera è in data 10 agosto 1860. Come è da supporsi, il Florio basa tutte le sue argomentazioni sulla " Scherma delle Due Sicilie."*]

—— (—). — La scienza della scherma delle Due Sicilie. Seconda edizione riveduta ed accresciuta dall' autore. Volume 1°. 8°. 1860. *Catania :* C. Galatola.

—— (—). — Alla Patria. Al cittadino Signor Antonio Alonzo, qual funzionante da Presidente del Consiglio civico della città di Catania. 1861. *Catania.*

—— (—). — Sulla autonomia schermistica della Spada sopra le armi da presso. Lettera seconda al cittadino Carlo Ardizzone. 1861. *Catania.*
> [*La lettera porta la data del 21 maggio 1861. In questa l'autore sostiene con argumentazioni, qualche volta cavillose, che " La spada vince la spadancia " — " La spada vince la sciabola lunga de cavaliere e quella corta de fante " —" La spada vince le armi doppi, cioè la spada e pugnale "—La spada vince la bajonetta innastata al fucile."*]

FLORIO (Blasco). — Il palladio della scuola di Scherma Romana antica napolitanizzato, socio onorario della Grande Accademia di Scherma per le Guardie Nazionali di Napoli. 8°. 1865. *Catania:* V. Metitiero.

—— (—). — Lettera al cav. Agostino Longo da servire di preludio alla ristampa delle cose edite ed inedite relativamente alla scienza della scherma. 8°. 1865. *Catania:* Tip. V. Metitiero.

—— (—). — Nuove osservazioni filosofiche-schermistiche. 8°. 1866. *Catania:* V. Metitiero.

—— (—). — *INGUAGGIATO (C.).* — 1857.

—— (—). — *MESSINEO (P.).* — 1858.

—— (—). — *VELLA (G.).* — 1857.

FLORONUS (Lucas de Solarolo). — Tract. de Prohibitione Duelli. 4°. 1610. *Venetia.*

FOELCKERSAHM (Hamilcar Baron). — Duell und Ehrengericht. 8°. 1893. *Leipzig:* E. G. Naumann.

FONSIO (P.). — *FARINA (S. La).* — 1836.

FONT SANMARTÍ (A.). — El Duelo. 8°. 1888. *Barcelona.*
　　　[31 *pages.*] (*In the British Museum,* 8425. bbb. 28 (4).)

FORGE (A. de la). — *JACOB (J.).* — 1887.

FORKE (W.). — *DEUTSCHE REICHSFECHTSCHULE.*

FÖRSLAY till gymnastik-og bajonettfaktnings-reglemente för infanteriet. 12°. 1869. *Stockholm:* Norstedt & Söner.

FORSYTH (J. S.). — *ROLANDO (Le Sieur G.).* — 1822, 1826.

FORTE (Capitano Luigi). — Sul metodo di scherma Radaelli, lettera critica. 1878. *Catania.*

FOSTER. — Sermons.
　　　[" *Duelling.*"] (*Mentioned in Malcom's Theological Index.*)

—— (F. A.). — *HARPER'S* Magazine.

FOUGÈRE. — L'art de ne jamais être tué ni blessé en Duel, sans avoir pris aucune leçon d'armes, et lors même qu'on aurait affaire au premier Tireur de l'univers. 12°. 1828. *Paris:* Galerie de Bois.

[1 *copperplate.*]

FOUGÈRE (J.) [Fechtmeister]. — Die Kunst, aus jedem Zwei-kampfe lebend und unverwundet zurückzukehren, selbst wenn man niemals Unterricht im Fechten gehabt, und es auch mit dem grössten Schläger oder Schützen der Welt zu thun hätte. In 10 Vorlesungen. Aus dem Französischen. 8°. 1829. *Leipzig.*

FOUGÈRE (M.). — In dieci lezioni. L'arte di non essere mai ferito, nè ucciso in duello, quand' anche non si conosca la scherma e si abbia a che fare col primo spadaccino della terra. 1828. *Lugano.*

FOX (G. M.) [Lieut.-Col., late First Battalion "The Black Watch"]. — Physical Drill, with and without arms, and the new Bayonet Exercise. 12°. 1889. *London:* Clowes & Son.

[*With illustrations.*]

FOX (the Sword-maker).

["*M. N.* (7th S., XI. 307), *who asks for information respecting Fox the sword-maker, has confounded a brand with a name. Fox blades were celebrated all through the sixteenth and seventeenth centuries for their excellent temper, and mention of them is frequent in English drama. This is their history: There was a certain Julian del Rei, believed to be a Morisco, who set up a forge at Toledo in the early part of the sixteenth century, and became famous for the excellence of his sword-blades, which were regarded as the best of Toledo. That city had, for many ages previous, been renowned for sword-making, it being supposed that the Moors introduced the art, as they did so many good things, from the East. Julian del Rei's mark was a little dog (perrillo), which came to be taken for a fox, and so the 'fox-blade,' or simply 'fox,' for any good sword. See 'Henry V.,' iv. 4, ' Thou diest on point of fox.' The brand came to be imitated in other places, and there are Solingen blades, of comparatively modern manufacture, which still bear the little dog of Julian del Rei. For a note on the 'espada del Perrillo,' see my edition of ' Don Quixote,' Vol. IV. p. 194.—H. E. Watts, 24 Bedford Gardens, Campden Hill, W.*" ("*Notes and Queries,*" 7th S., XI. No. 279, p. 356.)]

FRADIN (G. Letainturier-). — *LETAINTURIER-FRADIN* (G.). — 1892.

FRAGEN (Gelöste und ungelöste), aus dem akademischen Leben der Gegenwart. Aufsätze über das Verbindungswesen,

Mensur und Duell, sowie über verschiedene hervorrag. Greignisse in der akadem. Bewegg. der Gegenwart. Hrsg. von der Redaktion der Akadem. Monatshefte. 1. Reihe. 8°. 1886. *Stuttgart :* Bonz' Erben.

FRANCKENBERG-LUDWIGSDORFF (M. von). — Das Fleurettiren oder Stossfechten, als Vorübung f. d. Hiebfechten und Bajonettiren. 8°. 1845. *Münster :* Wundermann.

[*3 plates of figures.*]

—— (—. —). — Das Bajonetfechten. Nach den Grundsätzen der neueren Zeit umgeändert. 8°. 1845. *Münster :* Wundermann.

[*6 copperplates.*]

—— (—. —). — Betrachtungen über das Bajonettfechten und den bisherigen Betrieb desselben in der Armee. Ein Vortrag gehalten zur Anregg. der Besprechung im Officier-Corps. 8°. 1861. *Berlin :* Mittler & Sohn.

(*In Captain Hutton's Collection.*)

FRANKFURTER zeitgemäsze Broschüren. — *FURICH* (*W. von*). — 1886.

FRASER'S MAGAZINE. 8°. *London :* 39 Paternoster Row.

[Vol. **XXI.** p. 594. "*Duelling.*"
„ **LXXI.** p. 316. "*Laws of Honour.*"]

FRATE (Settimo del) [Capitano-aiutante maggiore nei Cavalleggieri di Montferrato]. — Istruzione pel maneggio e scherma della sciabola. 8°. 1869. *Milano :* G. Baroffio.

[*19 plates with 50 figures.*]

—— (— —). — Istruzione per la scherma di sciabola e di spada del professore Giuseppe Radaelli scritta d'ordine del Ministero della Guerra. 4°. 1872. *Milano :* G. Baroffio.

[10 *lithographs. 2nd edit.* 1876.] (*In Captain Hutton's Collection.*)

—— (— —). — Istruzione per la scherma di punta di Giuseppe Radaelli, professore di scherma e ginnastica, scritta d'ordine del ministero della guerra. 8°. 1885. *Milano.*

[10 *lithographed plates.*]

—— (— —). — Istruzione per la scherma di sciabola e di spada del professore Giuseppe Radaelli scritta d'ordine del Ministero della Guerra. 8°. 1885. *Milano :* Fratelli Dumolard.

[7 *lithographed plates and 30 figures.*]

FRATE (Settimo del). — *RADAELLI (G.)*. — 1868, 1876.

FRÉVILLE (Chevalier de). — Maximes et instructions sur l'art de tirer des armes. 8º. 1775. *Saint-Pétersbourg.*

—— (— —). — Maximes et instructions sur l'art de tirer des armes. . . . 2nd edition. 8º. 1776. *Leipzig.*

—— (— —). — Maximes et instructions sur l'art de tirer des armes. 3rd edition. 8º. 1799. *Leipzig.*

FREYTAG (F. A.). — De Duello. 4º. 1840. *Heidelberg.*
> [*36 pages.*]

FRIAS (Don Simon de) [Maestro de todas armas examinado, aprobado y titulando por el superior Gobierno de Nueva España]. — Tratado Elemental de la destreza del Sable. Small 4º. 1809. *Mexico :* en la imprenta de Arizpe.
> [*13 plates. 2 folding, with 27 figures ; at end.*]
> (*In Mr. C. A. C. Keeson's Collection.*)

FROISSART (Sir John). — Chronicles of England, France, Spain, Portugal, Scotland, Brittany, Flanders, and the adjoining Countries ; translated from the original French, at the command of Henry VIII., by John Bourchier, Lord Berners. Reprinted from Pynson's edition of 1523 and 1525. 2 vols. 4º. 1812. *London :* F. C. & J. Rivington.
> [Vol. II. p. 203. *Duel " at Parys, before the king and his court, in mortal combat, ordained by the parliament, between Sir John of Carongne and Jaques le Grys* (1386)."
> The " gage de bataille" incidental to the coronation of the English kings is also described, and many "deeds of arms."]

FROUDE (J. A.). — Two Chiefs of Dunboy : Irish Romance of last Century. Post 8º. 1889. *London :* Longmans.
> [" *Has a duel in which, according to our humble theory, almost all possible errors are committed. The novelist's common error is to give the challenged party the choice of weapons."—The " Daily News," May* 1891. *Article on " Fencing and Duels."*]

FUN (Periodical). 4º. *London :* 153 Fleet Street.
> [1891. *September* 30 (p. 145). " *The Slicers' Club.*"]

FUNCKE. — Der geadelte Mord oder das Duell. 8º. 1885. *Bremen :* Müller.
> [*15 pages.*]

FÜRICH (W. von). — Das Duell. Kritisch beleuchtet. 8°. 1886. *Frankfurt-am-Main :* Foesser Nachfolger.

[No. 6. *Frankfurter Zeitgemäsze Broschüren. Neue Folge, herausgegeben von Dr. Paul Hoffner. Band 7, Heft 2–7.*]

FURLAN (Fiore) [De Civida].

[*Vellum MS., with pen-and-ink and gold sketches. See "Notes and Queries,"* Series V., Vol. IV. p. 414.]

FURNISS (Harry). — The Kernoozer's Club. Glimpses of Artist-Life. Text by M. H. Spielmann. 4°. 1889. *London :* Cassells.

[*Reprinted from "The Magazine of Art." 4°. 1889. London : Cassells. One full-page illustration represents the studio of Mr. Seymour Lucas, A.R.A., during a meeting of the Club, on the occasion of a disquisition on "Elizabethan Sword-Play," by Mr. Egerton Castle, F.S.A.—Another delineates the demonstration of the "Stramazzone" and "Punta Riversa" by the lecturer.*]

G. (P. A.). — *NOTES* sur l'instruction. — 1894.

GABRIELLE (Mme. Adrienne). — French Swordswomen.

[*The "New York Herald," London (May 17, 1891, p. 7).*]

GAIANI (A. G. B.). — Discorso del tornear a piedi. 4°. 1619. *Genova.*

GAIANI (Gio. Battista) [Alfiero]. — Arte di maneggiar la Spada a piedi et a cavallo. Opera per le nuove osservationi già desiderata. 4°. 1619. *Loano :* appresso Francesco Castillo.

[*Dedicata ai Serenessimi Principi Vittorio Amadeo e Francesco Tomaso di Savoia.*] (*In the British Museum.*)

GALAXY (Periodical). *New York, U.S.A.*

[Vol. XIX. p. 405. "*Duels in German Universities.*" By J. Hawthorne.]

GÁLVEZ DE ZEA (Don Francisco). — Ensayo sobre la Esgrima de la bayoneta para el manejo del fusil como arma blanca. 8°. 1855. *Valencia :* I. M. Garin.

[*16 figures.*]

GAMBOGI (Conte Michele). — Trattato sulla scherma. Adorna di figure incise da Giuseppe Rados. Oblong 4°. 1837. *Milano :* R. Fanfani.

[*Portrait of author and 56 lithographed plates.*]
(*In Captain Hutton and Mr. J. R. Garcia Donnell's Collections.*)

GANDOLFI (Giovanni) [Maestro d'armi]. — Metodo teorico-pratico per la scherma di sciabola e norme generali per il duello. 8°. 1876. *Torino :* Borgarelli.

GANDON (ANT.). — Les trente-deux duels de Jean Gigon ; histoire d'un enfant-trouvé. 12°. 1860. *Paris :* Librairie nouvelle.

[*Avec vignette. Souvent réimprimé. 14e édition en 1863.*]

—— (—.). — *DUGUÉ (E.).* — 1861.

GANFALDONI (FERDINANDO). — Tratto di sciabola.

[*Mentioned by Bertolini in " Tratto di Sciabola" (1841), but without data.*]

GARAY (DON SALVADOR JACINTO DE). — Tratado de la Philosophia y Destreza de las Armas. 4°. 1672. *Málaga :* Pedro Castera.

[*Another edition. 4°. 1664. Cádiz.*]

GARCÍA (D. ANTONIO ALVAREZ). — Nociones de esgrima del sable español. 8°. 1883. *Remedios :* imprenta de " La Constitución," Gloria, 16.

[*The first edition appeared in 1882.*]

—— (—. — —). — Tratado de esgrima de sable y florete. 4°. 1886. *Jerez :* imprenta de " El Cronista," Consistorio, 2 (Puerta Real).

—— (—. — —). — Manual de esgrima de Espada y Palo-bastón. 1887. *Granada :* imprenta y libr. de Paulino V. Sabatel.

GARCÍA (F. FRANCISCO). — Verdadera intelligencia de la destreza de las armas del comendador Geronymo Sanchez Carranza de Barreda. MS.

[*17th century.*]

GARCÍA Y DELGADO DEL PINO (JUAN ROGEL). — Tratado de las armas. 8°. 1693. *Valladolia :* M. de Lago.

GARTER (MR.).—Of Combats in Mr. Garter's house. 1601.

[*Cottonian MSS. Vesp. C. xiv. 235 (569).*]

GARZONIUS. — Allgemeiner Schauplatz. 1619. *Franckfurt.*

GASSION (J.). — Advis sur les duels. 1609.

—— (—.). — Anti-duel, ou discours pour l'abolition des duels. 1612.

—— (—.). — Invective ou discours satyrique contre les duels. 1629. *Paris.*

GAUTHIER (PAUL). — L'Escrime à Lyon. Préface par François de Veyssière. 8°. 1888. *Lyon :* imprimerie Waltener et Cie.
[*Avec vignette. Tiré à 250 exemplaires.*]

GAUVAIN (H. VON). — Das Duell und seine Rechtfertigung. 8°. 1866. *Berlin.*

GAYA (LOVYS DE). — Traité des armes, des machines de guerre, des feux d'artifice, des enseignes et des instrumens militaires anciens et modernes ; avec la manière dont on s'en sert présentment dans les armées, tant Françoises qu'Etrangères. 1678. *Paris :* S. Cramoisy.

GAYET (ERNEST). — *CAVALCABO.* — 1889.

GEBRÄUCHE (DIE CONVENTIONELLEN) BEIM ZWEI-KAMPF, unter besond. Berücksicht. d. Offizierstandes. Von e. älteren aktiven Offizier. Nebst Anhang : Verordnung über die Ehrengerichte der Offiziere im preusz. Heere vom 2. Mai 1874, und strafrechtl. Bestimmgn. über den Zweikampf. 3. umgearb. und verm. Auflage. 8°. 1888. *Berlin :* Eisenschmidt.

GEIGER. — *ABRICHTUNGS-REGLEMENT.* — 1851.

GELLI (JACOPO) [Cavaliere]. — Il duello nella storia della Giurisprudenza e nella pratica italiana (Codice cavalleresco). 8°. 1886. *Firenze :* Loescher et Seeber.

—— (—). — Resurrectio. Critica alle osservazioni sul maneggio della sciabola secondo il metodo Radaelli del Generale Achille Angelini. 8°. 1888. *Firenze :* Tipografia Niccolai.

—— (—). — Reponsabilità penale dei duellanti (aggiunte al Codice cavalleresco). 8°. 1888. *Firenze :* Loescher et Seeber.

—— (—). — Corte d'onore permanente in Firenze. Note e Regolamento. 8°. 1888. *Firenze :* C. D. Angelis.

—— (—). — Nuovo Codice cavalleresco. Parte Prima. — Tecnica del duello. — Nuova edizione. 8°. 1888. *Firenze :* F. Stianti e Comp.
[5a ediz. 16°. 1892. Milano.]

—— (—). — Poche Parole in sostegno del Giuoco collettivo di sciabola. — Ai signori componenti la commissione per la Ginnastica, nominata con Regio Decreto del 27 dicembre 1888. 8°. 1889. *Firenze :* L. Niccolai.

GELLI (JACOPO). — Brevi note sulla scherma di sciabola per la cavalleria. 8°. 1889. *Firenze :* L. Niccolai.

—— (—). — La scherma collettiva quale mezzo di educazione fisica. Con 32 tavole dimostrative. 8°. 1889. *Firenze :* Tipografia Niccolai.

[*Con 37 tavole. Figures in the text.*]

—— (—). — Bibliografia generale della scherma con note critiche, biografiche et storiche. Testo italiano e francese. Large 8°. 1890. *Firenze :* L. Niccolai.

[*" An outrageously careless compilation." — Saturday Review, June* 28, 1890.]

—— (—). — Manuale di Scherma italiana sui principii ideati da Ferdinando Masiello. 8°. 1890. *Milano :* Hoepli.

[*Con 63 tavole.*]

—— (—). — Statistica del duello. 8°. 1892. *Milano.*

—— (—). — Bibliografia generale della scherma. Nuova ediz. economica con aggiunte. Testo italiano e francese. Large 8°. 1894.

[*Di pagine 816. A new but " uncorrected" edition.*]

—— (—). — Levi (Baron Georges Henri). La bibliographie du duel, avec notes.

[*In the press.*]

—— (—). — Le dictionnaire technique italien-français de l'escrime, avec notes critiques et historiques. Ouvrage destiné aux philologues, aux bibliophiles et aux escrimeurs.

[*In the press.*]

—— (—). — Les escrimeurs d'autrefois et ceux d'aujourd'hui. Dictionnaire biographique et historique, ancien et moderne.

[*In the press.*]

—— (—). — *SCHERMA* Italiana. — 1891.

GENERAL RULES AND INSTRUCTIONS for Seconds in Duels. By a late Captain in the Army. 8°. 1793. *Whitehaven.*

GENERAL RULES AND INSTRUCTIONS for all Seconds in Duels. By a late Captain in the Army. 8°. 1809. *London :* Cadell.

GENEVOIX (GUSTAV). — Duel feminin (Roman). 12°. 1892. *Paris :* C. Lévy.

GENLIS (Mémoires de).

>   [Vol. II. p. 191, Vol. VII. p. 215, Vol. IX. p. 351. "*Duelling.*"]

GENNARDO (NICOLA DI) [dottore avvoccato]. — Componimento I. : della scherma e de' Gladiatori. Componimento II. : di aggiunta al primo, sulla lode della scherma e de' Gladiatori, &c. 8º (?). 1783. *Venezia.*

GENTILSHOMMES FAISANS PROFESSION DES ARMES. Déclaration du Roy sur ses Lettres-patentes et closes du mois passé touchant le devoir des Gentilshommes et autres personnes faisans profession des armes, et tenans fiefs et sur l'association générale permise ès provinces de ce Royame. 8º (de 8 pag.). 1577. *Paris :* Fred Morel.

>   [*Ordonnance leue et publiée à son de trompe et cry public par les Carrefours de ceste ville de Paris, par Simonet, Sergent à verge au Chastellet, Pasquet Rossignol, Crieur-Juré et Phillipe Noiret, Trompette du Juré. Cette ordonnance donnée par Henry II. est datée de Chenonceaux du 23 Mai 1577.*]

GENTLEMAN'S MAGAZINE (The). — (Selections from, by John Walker.) 4 vols. 1814.

>   [Vol. I. p. 376. *Copy of a writ issued in the 8th year of Henry VI. to the Sheriffs of London to provide lists and bars for a duel between John Upton and John Down.*]

GENTLEMAN'S MAGAZINE. 8º. *London.*

>   [1853. *September.* "*A Duel which took place in 1609.*"]

GEORGENS (J. D.). — Illustriertes Sportbuch. 4 parts. 8º. 1890. *Leipzig:* Spamer.

GERDIL (HYACINTH SIGISMOND). — Traité des combats singuliers. 8º. 1761. *Turin:* impr. roïale.

>   (*In Captain Hutton's Collection.*)

GERHARD (E.). — De judicio duellico vulgo vom Kampf und Kolben gericht. 4º. 1732. *Francof.*

GERMAN DUELLING.

>   ["*Saturday Review*" (London) Vol. LX. No. 748.]

GERONA Y ENSEÑAT (D. FEDERICO) [Oficial de caballeria]. — Esgrima del sable. 8º. 1877. *Madrid.*

>   [19 *plates.*
>   (*Segunda edition aumentada.* 8º. 1882. *Madrid: Fortanet.*)]

G[ERONIMO?] (J.). — *GRASSI* (*G. di*). 1594.

[" *Another popular teacher was Geronimo, the same who, in 1594, ' Englished' Grassi's fence-book; but he met with a melancholy and premature end one fine morning, ' being in a coch with a wench that he loved well,' says George Silver, the champion, in print at least, of the Corporation of Masters of Defence, at the hands of one Cheefe, ' a tall man in his fight naturall English.' "—Castle (E.), " The Story of Swordsmanship." (" The National Review," May* 1891.)]

GERSTER (J.). — De per duellione. 1752. *Marburg.*

GESCHLOSSENE (Die) und zerstreute Fechtart [das Exerciren und Plänkeln] der Infanterie. 1.–3. Abth. 8°. 1868-9. *Stuttgart :* Lindemann.

GESELLIGE (Der). Eine moral. Wochenschrift. 1764. *Halle :* Gebauer.

[*Band 1 darin von den Zweikampfen.*]

GESSI (Senator Berlingiero). — La Spada di Honore. 12°. 1622. *Venetia :* presso Paolo Balioni.

—— (— —). — La spada di honore, libro I. (unico) delle osservazioni cavaleresche. 4°. 1671. *Bologna.*

—— (— —). — La spada di honore, libro I. (unico) delle osservazioni cavaleresche. 8°. 1672. *Milano.*

GHERSI. — Traité sur l'Art de faire des Armes. 8°. 1830. *Paris.*

GHEYN (J. DE). — Wapenhandelinghe von Roers Musquetten ende Spiessen. 117 plates. Folio. 1607. *Amsterdam.*

(*In the Royal United Service Institution Library, Whitehall, London.*)

—— (—. —). — [English translation of his work from the Dutch.] Folio. 1608. *Amsterdam.*

—— (—. —). — Maniement d'armes d'arquebuses, mousquetz et piquez. En conformité de l'ordre de Monseigneur le Prince Maurice d'Orange, représenté par figures par Jaques de Gheyn. Ensemble les enseignements par escrit, a l'utilité de tous capitaines et commandeurs, pour par cecy pouvoir plus facilement enseigner à leurs soldatz inexperimentez, l'entier et parfait maniement d'icelles armes. Folio. 1608. Imprimé à *La Haye*, en Hollande.

> [*Titre, 6 ff. d'explications, 1 f. de privilège et 117 planches gravées en taille-douce par J. de Gheyn. On a relié à la suite : " De Wapen-handelinge van Schilt, Spies, Rappier, en Targis . . . door A. van Breen." In s'Gravenhaghe, 1640, titre grave, 4 ff. d'explications et 51 pl. gravées. Quelques feuillets remontés.*
> *Another edition. Folio. 1608. Amsterdam : R. de Baudous. (Titre monté et 117 figures.)*]

GHISLIERO (FEDERICO) [da Alessandria]. — Regole di molti cavagliereschi esercitii. 4°. 1587. *Parma.*

GIEROW (F.). — *EISELEN* (G. W. B.). — 1881. 1889.

GIFFORD (W.). — *JONSON* (Ben). — 1816.

GIGANTI (NICOLETTO) [Vinitiano]. — Scola overo teatro nel qual sono rappresentate diverse maniere e modi di parare et di ferire di spada sola, e di spada e pugnale; dove ogni studioso potrà essercitarsi e farsi prattico nella proffessione dell' Armi. Oblong 4°. 1606. *Venetia :* appresso Gio. Ant. et G. de Franceschi.

> [*Frontispiece with the Medici arms, portrait of the master, and 42 copperplates, out of the text.*
> " *Wonderfully perfect and complete in comparison with the mass of those which were written before it. One of the plates represents an action which closely resembles the modern 'flanconnade' — the 'fianconata' of the Italians."—Castle's " Schools and Masters of Fence."*]
> (*In the British Museum.*)

—— (—). — Teatro . . . &c. 2nd edition. Oblong 4°. 1608. *Venegia.*

> [" *In which he advocates a guard with the left foot foremost, and announces his intention of bringing forth another treatise, 'wherein he will show that all actions can be performed with the left foot forward.' This incomprehensible retrogression to faulty principles is not accounted for, neither did the book in question ever make its appearance."—Castle's " Schools and Masters of Fence."*]

—— (—). — Escrime nouvelle ou théâtre auquel sont représentées diverses manières de parer et de frapper, d'espée seul et d'espée et poignard ensemble, démontrées par figures entaillées en cuivre, publié en faveur de ceux qui se délectent en ce tres noble exercice des armes, et traduit en langue françoise par Jacques de Zeter. Apud Ja. de Zeter. Oblong 4°. 1619. *Francofurti.*

> [*Portrait of the author, and 42 copperplates, out of the text.*]
> (*In the British Museum.*)

GIGANTI (NICOLETTO). — Theatre (*vide* Giganti, 1606; Giganti, 1619). Oblong 4°. 1622.

—— (—). — Fecht-Kunst darinnen gezeyget, wie beydes mit dem Rappier allein, vnd mit Rappier vnd Dolchen zusammen ohne Still-haltung, mit Vortheil auff d. Gegentheyl hinan zu gehen. Quer 4°. (Pergament.) 1622. *Franckfort a. M.:* Hartm. Palthenius.

[*Der beschreibende Text ist französisch und deutsch abgefasst.* (*A French and German translation.*)]

—— (—). — Teatro . . . &c. 2nd edition. Oblong 4to. 1628. *Padua :* per Paolo Frambotto.

(*In Captain Hutton's Collection.*)

GIGON (JEAN). — *DUGUÉ (E.).* — 1861.

—— (—). — *GANDON (Ant.).* — 1860.

GILCHRIST (J. P.). — A Brief Display of the origin and History of Ordeals, Trials by Battle, Courts of Chivalry or Honour; and the decision of private quarrels by single combat, Duels, &c. 1821. *London :* W. Sams.

[*Chronological Register of the principal duels fought since the commencement of the reigns of His late Majesty, George III., and His present Majesty, George IV., up to the present time* (1821).]
(*In Mr. J. R. Garcia Donnell's Collection.*)

GILLET (AUGUSTE). — L'escrime rendue facile et classique. Traité théorique et pratique à l'usage de l'enseignement et des amateurs d'après les leçons de M. Lacrette. 18°. 1875. *Paris :* Dumaine.

[*With figures.*]

GIORGI (LODOVICO) [di Fano]. — Istruttione per soldati novelli di Fanteria, nella quale con stile facile e breve, se li danno Avverti-menti e Regole, etc., etc. . . . e maneggiare l'Armi, cioè picca, moschetto et archibugio. Con alcuni brevi documenti di scherma. 8°. 1629. *Urbino :* L. Ghisani.

GIRARD (P. J. F.) [Ancien officier de Marine]. — Nouveau traité de la perfection sur le fait des armes, dedié au Roi. Enseignant la manière de combattre, de l'épée de pointe seule, toutes les gardes etrangères, l'espadon, les piques, hallebardes, bayonnettes au du fusil,

fleaux brisés et baton à deux bouts. Ensemble à faire de bonne
grâce les saluts de l'esponton, l'exercice du fusil et celui de la gréna-
diere, tels qu'ils se pratiquent aujourd'hui dans l'art militaire en
France. Orné de figures en taille douce. Oblong 4°. 1736-7.
Paris : chez Moétte.

> [*Frontispiece, and 116 copperplates, out of the text, engraved by Jacques de
> Favanne, representing the various attitudes of the French School, and the way
> of successfully opposing them to the Italian, German, and Spanish guards.
> (Elle contient le premier tirage du titre, du beau portrait de l'auteur et
> des 116 planches gr. sur cuivre, hors texte par Thevenard.)*
> (" *The most splendid work on fencing, with the exception of Angelo's, that ever
> appeared since Thibaust's ponderous folio. Besides its historical value to
> the military antiquarian, Girard's work is important among fencing works
> as registering some innovations introduced into the theory of the small sword
> during the last forty years."—Castle's " Schools and Masters of Fence."*)]
> (*In the British Museum, and Captain Hutton's Collection.*)

GIRARD (P. J. F.). — Nouveau Traité de la Perfection sur fait
des Armes, &c. 4°. 1740. *La Haye :* P. de Hondt.

> [*With portrait by J. de Favanne, and 116 copperplates, out of the text, engraved
> by Thevenard. A 4th edition appeared in 1755.*]

—— (—. —. —.). — *ENCYCLOPÉDIE.* — 1770.

GIRÓN. — *MANCHA Y GIRÓN (M. C.).* — 1708.

GIULIANI-BOLOGNINI (GIUSEPPE). — Sul maneggio della sciabola. 1850. *Ferrara.*

—— (—). — Teorie sulla sciabola per una scuola di contrapunta
di genere misto. 1856. *Ferrara.*

GLOBE (The). — (Periodical.) Folio. *London.*

> [1890. *August 28. Duelling in the French Army.*
> 1890. *December 23. The Brousse-Dumay Duel.*
> 1891. *February 24. A Boys' Duel.*
> 1892. *February 19. Duel near Paris (M. Drumont and M. Isaacs).*]

GLOUCESTER (THOMAS, DUKE OF). — *ASHMOLEAN* MSS.

—— (—, — —). — *CODICUM* MSS.

—— (—, — —). — *COTTONIAN* MSS.
> [*Tib. E. viii.* 42. (190.)]

GNEIST (R.). — Der Zweikampf und die germanische Ehre. 8°.
1848. *Berlin.*

GODESCARD (C.) [Chanoine de Saint-Honoré à Paris]. — Réflexiones sur le Duel, et sur les moyens les plus efficaces de le prévenir. Opuscule traduit de l'Anglais. 12°. 1801. *Paris :* Fuchs.

GODFREY (JOHN) [Captain]. — A Treatise upon the useful Science of Defence connecting the Small and Back Sword, and shewing the Affinity between them. Likewise endeavouring to weed the Art of those superfluous, unmeaning Practices which overrun it, and choke the true Principles, by reducing it to a narrow Compass, and supporting it with Mathematical Proofs. Also an Examination into the Performances of the most noted masters of the Back-Sword, who have fought upon the Stage, pointing out their Faults, and allowing their Abilities. 4°. 1747. *London :* printed for the Author by T. Gardner.

> [*This work is said to have been first published in 1735, but the edition commonly met with is dated 1747.*] (*In Captain Hutton's Collection.*)

GODINS (Des) de Souhesmes. Du Duel. 8°. 1878. *Alger.*

GODKIN (E. L.). — Southern and other duelling.
> [*"Nation" (New York),* Vol. XXXVI. p. 397.]

—— (G. S.). — *ARGOSY (The).* — 1888.

GODWIN (WILLIAM). — An enquiry concerning Political Justice and its influence on general virtue and happiness. 2 vols. 4°. 1793. *London.*

> [Vol. I. pp. 94–96. *"Of Duelling."* Appendix, No. 11. *Motives of Duelling :* 1. *Revenge ;* 2. *Reputation for Courage. Fallacy of this motive. Objection answered. Illustration.*]
> (*In the British Museum,* 521. *l.* 20.)

GÖLER-HABER. — Die reine Wahrheit über d. Streitsache zwischen M. von Haber und Freiherr Göler von Ravensburg (Duell-Sache). 8°. 1843. *Strassburg.*

——. — *SARACHAGA* (*G. von*). — 1843.

GOMARD. — *CHAPMAN* (*G.*). — 1861.

——. — *PINETTE* (*Joseph*). — 1847.

——. — *POSSELLIER* (*A. J. J.*). — 1845.   1847.

——. — *R.* (*A.*). — 1877.

——. — *ROBAGLIA* (*A.*). — 1877.

GÖMMEL (Fr.). — *CHATELAIN.* — 1819.

—— (—.). — *LUPSCHER (Ant.).* — 1819.

GONZÁLES DE VILLAUMBROSA (Don Santiago). — Destierro vulgar y compendio sucinto en que se incluyen los términos mas essenciales y propios del Arte, y Ciencia de la Espada y sus apropiados : Con verdad, claridad, y distincíon para toda mediana inteligencia y razón natural. 4°. 1724. *Madrid :* L. F. Mojados.

GONZÁLEZ (Hilario) [Capitán de infantería]. — La fábrica de armas blancas de Toledo. Resumen histórico ó breves noticias sobre el origen, progressos, vida, decadencia y renacimiento de la fabricación de armas blancas en Toledo, desde los tiempos más remotos hasta nuestros días. Se añaden ligeras noticias acerca de la construcción de la fábrica y las grandes mejoras introducidas últimamente en ella. 8°. 1889. *Toledo :* imprenta de Menor, hermanos.

[104 *páginas y 2 láminas plegadas.*]

GORDINE (Gérard) [Capitaine et maître en fait d'armes]. — Principes et quintessence des armes. Dedié à S. A. Jean-Theodore, duc des Deux-Bavières, cardinal de la sainte église romaine, évêque et prince de Liège, &c. 4°. 1754. *Liège :* S. Bourguignon.

[20 *copperplates, out of the text, by Jacob.*]

GORDON (Anthony). — A treatise on the science of defence for the sword, bayonet, and pike in close action. Dedicated to Field-Marshal H.R.H. The Duke of York. 4°. 1805. *London.*

[(19 *plates.*) " *This is the earliest known work giving any idea of attack and defence with the bayonet.*"—*Hutton's* " *Fixed Bayonets.*"]
(*In Captain Hutton's Collection.*)

—— (J.). — *OVERLAND* Monthly.

GORGUEREAU (F.). — Le Duel considéré dans tous les rapports historiques, moraux et constitutionnels et moyens de l'anéantir radicalement. 8°. 1791. *Paris.*

GORIO (Gio. Pietro) [Milanese]. — Arte di adoprar la spada per sicuramente ferire e perfettamente diffendersi. Dedicata e consegrata al nome e merito dell' illustriss^mo Sig. Conte Pirro Visconti Borromeo Aresi. 8°. 1682. *Milano :* Federico Francesco Maietta.

[*Portrait of the author.*]

GÖRNE (Von), **SCHEFF** (Von), und **MERTENS**. — Die Gymnastik und die Fechtkunst in der Armee. 8°. 1858. *Berlin :* Mittler.

[xiv *and* 231 *pages.*]

GOTHA BIBLIOTHEK.

[*Codex memb.* 115–1091.   *An anonymous MS. on Fencing in the Gotha Library.*]

GÖTTINGEN (Neues) histor. Magazin.   Herausgegeben von E. Meiners und L. T. Spittler.   3 vols.   8°.   1791–1794.   *Hannover :* Helwing.

[*Band 3. " Zweikampf."*]

GÖTTLING (Prof.). — Ueber die thüring. Fechterfamilien Kreussler.   1829.

[Vide " *Thüringer Volksfreund,*" 1829, Nr. 43, Seite 345.]

GOUFFÉ (Armand) et **LEDOUX** (P.). — Le Duel et de Déjeuner. Comédie-Anecdote et un acte et en prose, mêlée de complets.   8°. 1835. *Paris :* Barba.

GOULD (S. Baring). — Duelling in Germany.

[" *Chambers's Journal*" (*London*), *April* 1890.]

GRANDEFFE (Arthur de). — Discours prononcé le 3 janvier 1884, à Chatou, sur la tombe du maître d'armes Pons.   8°.   1884. *Paris :* Chaix.

GRANDGAGNAGE (J.). — Lettre sur le duel.   8°.   1836. *Liège.*

GRANGE [Maître d'armes au 25° d'artillerie]. — Réglement d'une salle d'escrime.   8°.   1879.   *Châlons :* Martin.

GRANGIER (Louis). — L'oncle Ernest.   12°.   [1892.]   *Paris :* Marpon & Flammarion.

[*Pages* 125–152. " *Un Duel.*" *Dessins de Guy Thomery.*]

GRAPHIC (The). — (Periodical.)   Folio.   *London.*

[1890. *November* 1.   No. 1092, Vol. XLII. *Plate showing the new English, French, and German Magazine Rifles.*
1891. *March* 28.   No. 1113, Vol. XLIII. *Engraving showing Old English Sword-and-Buckler play by Capt. A. Hutton and Dr. Mouatt Briggs, at Captain Egerton Castle's lecture before the Prince of Wales at the Lyceum Theatre, London, on " The Story of Swordsmanship.*"

RAGIONE
DI ADDOPRAR
SICVRAMENTE L'ARME
SI DA OFFESA COME DA DIFESA,

Con un Trattato dell'inganno, & con un modo
di eſſercitarſi da ſe ſteſſo, per acquiſtare
forza, giudicio, & preſtezza.

Di Giacomo di Graſſi da Modena.

CON PRIVILEGIO.

IN VENETIA,
Appreſſo Giorgio de' Caualli. MDLXX.

[GIACOMO DI GRASSI. 4°. 1570.]

GRAPHIC (The) (*continued*)—

1891. *November* 21. No. 1147, Vol. XLIV. *A Fencing class at the People's Palace. A bout with foils. Drawn by Paul Renouard.*

1892. *March* 5. *The assault-at-arms given by the Oxford University Fencing Club at the Clarendon Rooms.*

1892. *July* 2. No. 1179. *French Duellists and Italian Fencers.*

1894. *March* 10. *An "at home" at the Ladies' Fencing Club, Brompton Road.*

1894. *April* 14. No. 1272. *Types of Old Swordsmanship. Exercises with the Double-handed Sword. Drawn by Percy Macquoid.*

1894. *October* 6. *Pages* 397, 406. *Types of Old Swordsmanship. II. The Sword and Dagger Duel. Drawn by Percy Macquoid.*

Page 408. 16*th Century Rapiers and Daggers.*]

GRASSI (GIACOMO DI) [da Modena. (Some copies bear "da Corregio")]. — Ragione di adoprar sicuramente l'arme si da offesa come da difesa; con un trattato dell' inganno et con un modo di esercitarsi da se stesso per acquistare forza, giudicio et prestezza. 4°. 1570. *Venetia:* appresso Giorgio de' Cavalli.

[*Some copies bear the indication "appresso Giordano Ziletti." Portrait of Grassi, and copperplates, in the text.*]

(*In Captain Hutton's Collection, the British Museum, and Bodleian Library.*)

—— (— —). — Giacomo di Grassi, his true Arte of Defence, plainlie teaching by infallable demonstrations, apt Figures, and perfect Rules the manner and forme how a man, without other Teacher or master may safelie handle all sortes of weapons as well offensive as defensive. With a treatise of Disceit or Falsinge: and with a waie or meane by private industrie to obtaine Strength, Judgment, and Activitie. First written in Italian by the foresaid Author, and Englished by J. G[eronimo?], gentleman. 4°. 1594. *London:* sold within Temple Barre at the sign of the Hand and Starre.

["*Plusieurs auteurs ne semblent pas accorder à Grassi la place qui lui revient dans l'escrime de son époque sans vouloir le comparer à Marozzo et à Agrippa, il faut lui reconnaître certaines tendances artistiques qui ont dû être pour quelque chose dans le choix qu'a fait Saint-Didier, notre premier auteur français. Ce dernier, en effet, dans la composition de son ouvrage, a pris Grassi pour guide principal, et à ce titre le traité du maître italien, a pour nous un caractère éminemment intéressant.*"—*Vigeant.*]

(*In Captain Hutton's Collection, and Bodleian Library.*)

GRATTAN (T. C.) — *COLBOURN'S* New Monthly Magazine.

GRAVE (THÉODORE DE). — Les duellistes. Préface par Jules Claretie. 12°. 1868. *Paris:* Barba.

—— (— —). — Les drames de l'Epée. 12°. 1879. *Paris:* Dentu.

GREENWOOD (GEORGE) [Colonel]. — Cavalry Sword Exercise. 12°. 1840. *London:* Clowes.

GRIBBLE (SAMUEL). — Treatise on Deportment, Horsemanship, &c., comprising likewise instructions for the Lance and Carbine Exercises. 8°. 1829. *London:* Whittaker. *Derby:* W. Bemrose & Co.

> [*Small folding plate. Dedicated to Colonel Wildman of Newstead Abbey.*]
> (*In Mr. J. R. Garcia Donnell's Collection.*)

GRIFFITHS (T.). — Modern Fencer, with the most recent means of attack and defence. 12°. 1862. *London:* Warne.

—— (—.). — The Modern Fencer, with the most recent means of attack and defence. 12°. 1868. *London:* Warne.

GRIMALDI (GIUS. MARIA). — Nuova asta d'Achille a soppressione del Duello e della Vendetta, per ridurre a pace ed aggiustamento ogni querela in via cavalleresca. 3 libri. 8°. 1693. *Bologna.*

GRISETTI (PIETRO). — *SCORZA* (*Rosaroll*). — 1803. 1811. 1871.

GRISIER (AUGUSTIN). — Les armes et le duel. 8°. 1847. *Paris:* Garnier.

> [*Engraved portrait of the Chevalier de Saint-Georges, and 10 lithographed plates.*] (*In Captain Hutton's Collection.*)

—— (—). — Les armes et le duel. Préface anecdotique par Alexandre Dumas. Notice sur l'auteur par Roger de Beauvoir. Épître en vers de Méry. Lettres du comte d'H * * * et du comte d'I * * *. 2e édition, revue, corrigée et augmentée. Gr. in-8°. 1863. *Paris:* Dentu.

> [*Dessins par E. de Beaumont, Portrait de Grisier par E. Lassalle.*]

—— (—). — Les armes et le duel. 3e édition, revue, corrigée et augmentée. 8°. 1864. *Paris:* Dentu.

> [*Ouvrage agnée par S. M. l'Empereur de Russie. Préface anecdotique par Alexandre Dumas. Avec portrait, vignette et planches.*]

—— (—). — *CHAPMAN* (*G.*). — 1861.

—— (—). — *DUMAS* (*A.*). — 1840. 1848. 1861. 1891.

—— (—). — *FÉVAL* (*Paul*). — 1846.

—— (—). — *ROBAGLIA* (*A.*). — 1877.

GRISIER (Eugène). — Des duels à différentes Époques. Un mot sur l'influence des Lois qui le Regissent.

[" *Journal du Dimanche,*" p. 7 (Paris).]

—— (Georges). — *MARY (Jules).* — 1892.

GROVE (F. C.). — *POLLOCK (W. H.).* — 1890.

(*The Badminton Library.*)

GRÜNDLICHE BAJONNET-FECHTSCHULE zur Ausbildung der Lehrer und Vorfechter in der Armee. Gr. 8°. 1863. *Cassel:* Freyschmidt.

[15 *figures and diagrams in text.*] (*In Captain Hutton's Collection.*)

GRÜNDLICHE und vollständige Anweisung in der deutschen Fecht-Kunst auf Stoss und Hieb. — [*ROUX (J. Ad. K.)*] — 1798.

GRÜNEBUSCH. Liv. I. 26. [De per duellionio.] 1814.

GUALDO (Galeazzo). — Il maneggio delle armi. 8° (?). 1643. *Bologna:* per Tebaldini.

GUARDIAN (The). — (Essayist.)

[Paper 129. " *Duel between Monsieur Sackville and Monsieur le Baron de Kinloss.*"]

GUERRA DE LA VEGA (D. Alvaro). — Comprehensión de la destreza. 4°. [1681.] MS.

(*Bibl. Nac. Madrid.*)

[**GUIL** (De La Gaye)]. — Le Duelliste malheureux. Tragi-Comédie. Pièce nouvelle pleine d'intrigues à la mode, suivant le temps, non jamais veue ou imprimée. 8°. 1636. *Rouen:* Guill. de la Haye.

GUILLET (Le Sieur de). — Les arts de l'homme d'épée ou le dictionnaire du gentilhomme. 12°. 1680. *La Haye.*

—— (—— ——). — L'arte dell' Huomo di Spada. Translated by Narbonte Prodoni. 12°. 1683. *Venice.*

(*In the Royal United Service Institution Library, Whitehall, London.*)

—— (—— ——). — Les arts de l'homme d'épée ou le dictionnaire du gentilhomme. 12°. 1878. *Paris:* Clouzier.

[*A reprint. 1 planche.*]

GUN AND BAYONET DRILL. "The exercise of the Firelock and Bayonett, with ye Doublings and Hollow Square," with copies of orders and regulations by the Duke of Marlborough. 1711.

[*MS. in British Museum, No. 29,477. ff. 107–117.*]

GUNNERY DRILL BOOK for Royal Naval Reserve. 12°. 1890. *London :* Her Majesty's Stationery Office.
[" *Cutlass Exercise,*" pp. 80–88.
" *Sword-Bayonet Exercise,*" p. 141.]

GUNTERRODT (HENRICUS λ.). — De veris principiis artis dimi-catoriæ. 4°. 1579. *Vvittemberg.*

GÜNTHER (W. A.). — Ueber Ehe, Adel, Duell, Leben, Eid. 8°. 1869. *Berlin :* Kortkampf & Co.
[v *and* 198 *pages.*]

GÜTERSLOHER JAHRBUCH. — *CREMER* (*Prof. D. H.*). — 1894.

GUTSMUTHS (I. C. F.). — Gymnastik für die Jugend. 2te Auflage. 8°. 1804. *Schnepfenthal.*
[*Contains an article by J. A. C. Roux.* "*Das Fechten auf Stoss und Hieb.*"]

GYMNASIUM (The). — (Periodical.) *London.* — *NOAKES* (*S. G.*).

GYMNAST AND ATHLETIC REVIEW. — (Periodical.) 4°. *London.*

[1895.   *September 1st*
1895.   *October 1st*   ⎱ *Infantry Sword Exercise.*]
1895.   *November 1st* ⎰

GYMNASTE (LE) SUISSE. — (La Gymnastique et le Gymnaste réunis). Organe de la Société fédérale suisse de gymnastique. 8°. 1859. *Genève.*

GYMNASTIC EXERCICES, system of fencing, and exercices for the regulation clubs. Demy 12°. 1863. *London :* Horse Guards.
(*In Captain Hutton's Collection.*)

GYMNASTIK (DIE) UND DIE FECHTKUNST in der Armee. 16°. 1858. *Berlin :* Mittler.
[*Von v. Görne, v. Scherff und Mertens.* (xiv *and* 231 *pages.*)]

GYMNASTIK - MILITÄRISK tidskrift för ungd. 8°. 1873. *Stockholm :* Bergegrens bokh.

GYMNASTIK-REGLEMENTE für Kongl. flottan, utarb. af L. M. Törngren. 12°. 1879. *Stockholm :* Norstedt.
[*Atlas,* 34 *plates in folio.*]

GYMNASTISCHER UNTERRICHT f. d. bad. Truppen. 8°. 1847. *Carlsruhe.*
[*With atlas containing 298 plates.*]

H. (W.). — *UEBUNGS-TABELLE.* — 1890.

HABER [Göler-Haber]. — *SARACHAGA* (*G. von*). — 1843.

HABER-GÖLER von Ravensburg. — Die reine Wahrheit über die Streitsache zwischen M. v. Haber und Frhr. Göler von Ravensburg (Duell-Sache). 8°. *Strassburg.*

HAINAULT (The Seneschal of). — *CORRESPONDENCE.* MS.

HALES. — The Private School of Defence. 1640 (?).
[*This work is mentioned in Walton's "The Compleat Angler," edition* 1653, p. 3.]

HALEVY (Léon). — Le Duel. Comédie et un acte et en prose. 12°. 1826. *Paris:* Carpentier-Méricourt.
[*Représentée pour la première fois sur le premier Théâtre Français, le 29 août* 1826.]

HALLIWELL (J. O.). — *SHAKSPERE* (*William*).

—— (—. —.). — *WRIGHT* (*T.*). — 1845.

HALM (Fr.). — Fechter von Ravenna. 8°. *Wien:* Gerold.
[*A novel.*]

[HAMILTON (Joseph)]. — Some short and useful reflections upon Duelling, which should be in the hands of every person who is liable to receive a challenge or an offence. By a Christian Patriot. 12°. 1823. *Dublin:* C. Bentham.

HAMILTON (Joseph). — The only approved guide through all the stages of a quarrel, containing the Royal Code of Honor, Reflections upon duelling, and the outlines of a court for the adjustment of disputes, with anecdotes, documents and cases, interesting to Christian moralists who decline the combat; to experienced Duellists, and to benevolent legislators. 12°. 1829. *London:* Hatchard & Sons.
(*In Captain Hutton and Mr. J. R. Garcia Donnell's Collections.*)

HAMMER (Guido). — *SPORT* (*Der*). — 1880.

HAMON (P. G.). — Manuel de gymnastique suivi d'un Traité sur l'art des armes. 8°. 1827. *Londres.*

[*Lithographed plates.*] (*In Captain Hutton's Collection.*)

—— (—. —.). — Spinal Deformities. To which is subjoined a treatise on Fencing and Bodily Exercises. 8°. 1832. *London :* Carpenter & Co.

[*Illustrated with 8 coloured engravings.*] (*In Captain Hutton's Collection.*)

—— (—. —.). — *CHAPMAN* (*G.*). — 1861.

HANDBOOK FOR MARTINI - HENRY RIFLE : Containing Manual, New Bayonet and Firing Exercises, Aiming Drill, and Care of Arms and Ammunition. With Practical Questions on the Same, Corrected to June 1891. Fully Illustrated. 32mo. 1891. *Chatham :* Gall & Polden.

HANDBUCH DER LEIBESÜBUNGEN. Eine encyklopädische Darstellung des gesamten Turnwesens und der verwandten Gebiete in alphabetischer Ordnung. *Wien :* A. Pickler's Witwe & Sohn.

[(*In the press.*) *Das Fechten sowohl im allgemeinen als in den Hauptfecht-arten.*]

HANDBUCH für die Offiziere des Beurlaubtenstandes der Infanterie. 4 Theile. 12°. 1890. *Berlin :* Mittler u. Sohn.

[Theil III. 6. Abschnitt : "*Turnen und Bajonettiren.*" 9. Abschnitt "*Gefechtslehre.*"]

HAPPEL (J.). — Das Freifechten. 8°. 1865. *Leipzig :* Weber.

—— (—.). — Das Geräthfechten. Das Stock-, Stab-, Säbel- und Schwertfechten. 8°. 1877. *Antwerpen.*

[15 *figures, in the text.*]

HARLAND (HENRY). — *IDLER* (*The*). — 1894.

HARLEIAN. — Henry the Marquis of Newcastle, his Book of honour of the Sword, or the Art of Fencing : written with his own hand. MS. XVIIth Century.

[*A large-paper book, with the signature of the Duke in several places.*] (*In the British Museum, Harl.* 4206.)

HARLEIAN. — The mathematical demonstration of the Sorde. MS. XVIIth Century.

[*Only 6 pages, with 2 plates.* "*Henry Duke of Newcastle his booke,* 1676."] (*In the British Museum, Harl.* 5219.)

HARLEIAN MS. 3542. — *FENCING* (*On*).

HARLEIAN MANUSCRIPT.

[*Copy of an old Broadside announcing* "*At the Bear-Garden in Marrow-bone-Fields, the Backside of Soho Square, at the Boarded-House, a tryall of Skill to be perform'd this present Monday, the 17th of May, 1714, by two Masters of the Noble Science of Defence.*"]
(*In the British Museum, Harl.* 5961.)

HARLEIAN MANUSCRIPTS.

(*In the British Museum.*)

[Accounts of Tournaments, viz.:—

	Vol.	Page.	Cod.	Art.
On Marriage of Richard, Duke of York, Son of Edward IV. . .	I.	17	69	1–3
Mary (?), Princess (Daughter of Henry VIII.), Birth of . .	I.	17	69	4, 5
Henry VIII., Creation of . .	I.	17	69	6, 7
At Greenwich (temp. Hen. VIII.) .	I.	18	69	13
Westminster (temp. Hen. VIII.) .	I.	18	69	16
Arthur (Prince), on Marriage of .	I.	18	69	24
Challenges to Tournaments of Philip de Barton and others . .	I.	18	69	11
Uladislaus of Bodna and others .	I.	18	69	*12
Frederick de Toledo and others .	I.	18	69	20
Challenge (General) by Earls of Lenox, &c.	III.	215	4888	20
Duels—				
The Way of Duells before the King; with the Office of the Constable and Earl Marshal, &c., upon such occasions	I.	249	424	13
Of legal Duels, or Combats . .	I.	492	980	134
Of the antiquity, use, and ceremony of Combats in England, by James Whitlock, &c. . . .	III.	122	4176	2
Concerning Duells in Spaine .	III.	122	4176	4
"Extracts out of the D. of Bullyon's Discourse, touching the Lye and the Blow; by Mr. Luekenor" .	III.	122	4176	5
De Duellis	III.	332	6149	19
[*Contains* 173 *leaves.*]				
Instances of Trial by Duel . .	I.	490	980	36

HARLEIAN MANUSCRIPTS (*continued*)—

Regulations concerning Tournaments—		Vol.	Page.	Cod.	Art.
By Parliament of England	. .	I.	18	69	14
By Richard I.	. . . .	I.	165	293	123, 124
By John Tiptoft (Earl of Worcester)		I.	18	69	17
,,	,,	II.	12	1354	11 *et seq.*
,,	,,	II.	226	1776	43
,,	,,	III.	316	6064	80
Single Combats—					
Tracts on	. . . . .	III.	319	6069	66, 67
,,	. . . . .	III.	505	7021	22
Instances of Trial by	. . .	I.	490	980	46
Between the Dukes of Hereford and Norfolk	. . . . .	III.	322	6079	36
Between Mr. Dan. Archdeacon and Francis Mowbray	. . .	III.	370	6495	1
Whitlock (James), Discourse on Combats in England	. . . .	III.	122	4176	2]

HARO (RAMIREZ DE). — *Tratado de la brida y gineta.* MS.

HARPER'S NEW MONTHLY MAGAZINE. 8°. 1850–1887. *New York:* Harper Brothers.

[Vol. III. p. 360. *Incidents of Duelling.*
  ,,   V. p. 399. *Duel in 1830.*
  ,,   VIII. p. 239. *Sword of Mauley. By W. D. O'Connor.*
  ,,   VIII. p. 846 ; XI. 411 ; XXXV. 666 ; LXVII. 631. *Duelling.*
  ,,   XI. p. 609. *The Duel. By F. J. O'Brien.*
  ,,   XII. p. 509. *Pistol-shot at Duellists. By John Bonner.*
  ,,   XV. p. 79. *Duel in Russia.*
  ,,   XV. p. 516. *Code of Honor. By H. Ager.*
  ,,   XVI. p. 471. *Duelling-ground at Bladensburg. By F. A. Foster.*
  ,,   XVI. p. 473. *Marson and M'Carty Duel.*
  ,,   XVII. p. 416. *Pène Duel in France.*
  ,,   XVII. p. 559. *Fournier-Blumm Duel.*
  ,,   XVII. p. 861. *Duelling: Affair of Honor (Comic).*
  ,,   XXII. p. 393. *Duellists. By E. Bulwer-Lytton.*
  ,,   XXIII. p. 183. *Duelling-ground, Weehawken, N.J.*
  ,,   XXIII. p. 415. *Manteuffel-Twesten Duel.*
  ,,   XXV. p. 70. *Burr and Hamilton Duel.*
  ,,   XXVIII. p. 453. *Bayonet-making.*
  ,,   XXXIII. p. 221. *Sword of Damocles (Poem).*
  ,,   XXXVII. p. 401. *Duels and Duellists. By T. B. Thorpe.*
  ,,   XLV. p. 752. *Duer-Meade Affair.*
  ,,   XLVI. p. 270. *Washington Duels.*

HARPER'S NEW MONTHLY MAGAZINE (*continued*)—
   Vol. XLVII. p. 924. *Mrs. Grundy and Duelling.*
    „ XLVIII. p. 741. *Duelling. By Thomas F. Marshall.*
    „ L. p. 135. *William of Prussia on Duels.*
    „ LVIII. p. 460. *Decline of Duelling.*
    „ LXXIV. p. 519. *Duelling in Paris. By T. Child.*]

HARPER'S YOUNG PEOPLE. — *DODGE (T. C.).* — 1888.

HARRISON [PROFESSOR].—Indian Clubs, Dumb-Bells, and Sword
Exercises. Foolscap 8º. [N.D.] *London:* Dean & Son.
    [*With diagrams. Expert feats with the sword.*]
   (*Champion Series of Illustrated Sixpenny Useful Handbooks.*)

HARTELIUS (T. J.). — *TIDSKRIFT* i Gymnastik, 1876–1885.

HASPELMACHER (JH. GEO. HNR.). — Systematische Abhandlung von den schädlichen Folgen einer nicht auf sicheren Regeln
gegründeten Fechtkunst, nebst einer Anweisung wie man solche
vermeiden kann. Gr. 8º. 1783. *Helmstadt:* Fleckeisen.

HAUSNER (O.). — Rede über den Zweikampf. Geschichte,
Gesetzebung und Lösung. 8º. 1880. *Wien:* Perles.

HAWEIS (H. R.). — *BELGRAVIA.* London.
    [Vol. LV. p. 155.]

—— (—. —.). — *ECLECTIC* Magazine.

HAWK (The). — (Periodical.) Folio. *London.*
    [1892. *February 2. " Duelling at Jena University."*]

HAWTHORNE (J.). — *GALAXY.*

HAYDN'S Dictionary of Dates. 20th edition, by Benjamin
Vincent. 8º. 1892. *London:* Ward Lock & Co.
    [*Duelling took its rise from the judicial combats of the Celtic nations. The
    first formal duel in England, between William, Count of Eu, and Godfrey
    Baynard, took place 1096. Duelling in civil matters was forbidden in
    France, 1305. Francis I. challenged the Emperor Charles V., 1528,
    without effect. The fight with small swords was introduced into England,
    1587. Proclamation that no person should be pardoned who killed
    another in a duel, 1679.* Duelling was checked in the army, 1792, and
    has been abolished in England, by the influence of public opinion, aided by
    the Prince Consort. A society "for the discouraging of duelling" was*

---

    * "*As many as 227 official and memorable duels were fought during my
    grand climacteric.*"—*Sir J. Barrington. A single writer enume-
    rates 172 duels, in which 63 individuals were killed, and 96
    wounded; in three of these cases both the combatants were killed,
    and 18 of the survivors suffered the sentence of the law.*—*Hamilton
    (J.), 1829.*

HAYDN'S Dictionary of Dates (*continued*)—

established in 1845. " The British Code of Duel," published in 1824, was approved by the Duke of Wellington and others. See BATTLE (Wager of), COMBAT, and JARNAC.

MEMORABLE DUELS.

1712. *Between the Duke of Hamilton and Lord Mohun, fought 15th November.*
    (*This duel was fought with small swords, in Hyde Park. Lord Mohun was killed upon the spot, and the Duke expired of his wounds as he was being carried to his coach.*)
1728. *Captain Peppard and Mr. Hayes; latter killed.*
1748. *Messrs. Hamilton and Morgan; former killed.*
1763. *S. Martin wounded Mr. Wilkes, M.P., 16th November.*
1765. *Lord Byron killed Mr. Chaworth, 26th January.*
1773. *Lord Townsend wounded Lord Bellamont, 1st February.*
1778. *Comte d'Artois wounded by Duc de Bourbon, at Paris, 21st March.*
1779. *Mr. Donovan and Captain Hanson; the latter killed, 13th November.*
1779. *Charles James Fox wounded by Mr. Adam, 30th November.*
1780. *Colonel Fullerton wounded Lord Shelburne, 22nd March.*
1782. *Reverend Mr. Allen killed Lloyd Dulany, 18th June.*
1783. *Colonel Thomas killed by Colonel Gordon, 4th September.*
1786. *Lord Macartney wounded by Major-General Stuart, 8th June.*
1788. *Mr. M'Keon killed George N. Reynolds, 1787; executed 16th February.*
1788. *Mr. Purefoy killed Colonel Roper, December.*
1789. *Duke of York and Colonel Lennox, afterwards Duke of Richmond (for an insignificant cause), 26th May.*
1790. *Sir George Ramsay and Captain Macrea; Sir George killed.*
1790. *Mr. Curran and Major Hobart, 1st April.*
1790. *Mr. Macduff and Mr. Prince; latter killed, 4th June.*
1790. *Mr. Harvey Aston and Lieutenant Fitzgerald: the former severely wounded, 25th June.*
1790. *Mr. Anderson killed Mr. Stevens, 20th September.*
1791. *Mr. Julius killed Mr. Graham, 19th July.*
1792. *Mr. John Kemble and Mr. Aitken; no fatality, 1st March.*
1792. *Earl of Lonsdale and Captain Cuthbert; no fatality, 9th June.*
1792. *M. de Chauvigny wounded Mr. Lameth, 8th November.*
1796. *William Pitt and George Tierney, 27th May.*
1796. *Lord Valentia wounded by Mr. Gawler, 28th June.*
1796. *Mr. Carpenter killed by Mr. Pride, 20th August.*
1800. *Henry Grattan wounded Isaac Corry, 15th January.*
1801. *Lieutenant Willis killed Major Impey, 26th August.*
1802. *George Ogle and Bernard Coyle; no fatality.*
1802. *Sir Richard Musgrave and Mr. Todd Jones; Sir Richard wounded, 8th June.*
1803. *Captain MacNamara killed Colonel Montgomery, 6th April.*
1804. *General Hamilton and Colonel Aaron Burr (in America); the General killed.*
1804. *Captain Best killed Lord Camelford, 6th (died 10th) March.*
1806. *Surgeon Fisher killed Lieutenant Torrens, 22nd March.*
1806. *Baron Hompesch wounded Mr. Richardson, 21st September.*
1807. *Sir Francis Burdett and Mr. Paull; both wounded, 5th May.*

HAYDN'S Dictionary of Dates (*continued*)—

1807. *Mr. Alcock killed Mr. Colclough, and lost his reason, 8th June.*

1808. *M. de Granpré and M. Le Pique, in balloons, near Paris, and the latter killed, 3rd May.*

1808. *Major Campbell and Captain Boyd; latter killed (former hanged, 2nd October 1808), 23rd June.*

1809. *Lord Paget and Captain Cadogan; neither wounded, 30th May.*

1809. *Lord Castlereagh wounded George Canning, 21st September.*

1810. *Mr. Clarke killed George Payne, 6th September.*

1811. *Ensign de Balton killed Captain Boardman, 4th March.*

1812. *Lieutenant Stewart killed Lieutenant Bagnal, 7th October.*

1813. *Mr. Edward Maguire killed Lieutenant Blundell, 9th July.*

1814. *Captain Stackpole (of "Statira" frigate) and Lieutenant Cecil; the Captain killed (arose on account of words spoken four years previously), April.*

1815. *Mr. D. O'Connell killed Mr. D'Esterre, 31st January.*

1815. *Colonel Quentin and Colonel Palmer, 7th February.*

1815. *Mr. O'Connell and Mr. Peel; an affair, no meeting, 31st August.*

1816. *Major Greene and Mr. Price (in America); the latter killed, greatly lamented.*

1817. *Lieutenant Conroy killed Lieutenant Hindes, 8th March.*

1817. *Major Lockyer killed Mr. John Sutton, 10th December.*

1818. *Mr. O'Callaghan killed Lieutenant Bayley, 12th January.*

1820. *Mr. Grattan and the Earl of Clare, 7th June.*

1820. *Mr. Henshaw and Mr. Hartinger; both desperately wounded, 18th September.*

1821. *Mr. Christie killed Mr. Scott, 16th February.*

1821. *M. Manuel and Mr. Beaumont, 9th April.*

1822. *Mr. James Stuart killed Sir Alexander Boswell, 26th March.*

1822. *The Duke of Buckingham and the Duke of Bedford; no fatality, 2nd May.*

1823. *General Pepe wounded General Carascosa, 28th February.*

1824. *Mr. Westall killed Captain Gourlay.*

1826. *Mr. Beaumont and Mr. Lambton; no result, 1st July.*

1826. *Mr. Hayes killed Mr. Bric, 26th December.*

1827. *Rev. Mr. Hodson wounded Mr. Grady, August.*

1829. *Duke of Wellington and the Earl of Winchelsea; no injury, 21st March.*

1829. *Captain Helsham killed Lieutenant Crowther, 1st April.*

1830. *Mr. W. Lambrecht killed Mr. O. Clayton, 8th January.*

1830. *Captain Smith killed Mr. O'Grady, 18th March.*

1833. *Mr. Storey wounded Mr. Matthias, 22nd January.*

1833. *Sir John W. Jeffcott and Dr. Hennis; the latter wounded (and died on the 18th), 10th May.*

1835. *Lord Alvanley and Mr. Morgan O'Connell; two shots each, 4th May.*

1835. *Sir Colquhoun Grant and Lord Seymour; no fatality, 29th May.*

1835. *Mr. Roebuck, M.P., and Mr. Black, editor of the "Morning Chronicle;" two shots each, 19th November.*

1836. *Captain Dickson wounded General Evans, 8th April.*

1836. *Mr. Ruthven and Mr. Scott, and Mr. Ruthven and Mr. Close (Mr. Scott's second); the latter wounded, 23rd May.*

1836. *Emile de Girardin killed Armand Carrel (both journalists), 24th July.*

131

HAYDN'S Dictionary of Dates (*continued*)—

1840. *The Earl of Cardigan and Captain Tuckett; two shots each; the latter wounded (the Earl was tried in the House of Lords and acquitted, 16th February 1841), 12th September.*

1842. *Captain Boldero and Hon. Craven Berkeley; no fatality, 15th July.*

1843. *Lieutenant Munroe killed Colonel Fawcett, 1st (died 3rd) July.*

1845. *Lieutenant Hawkey killed Lieutenant Seton, 20th May.*

1862. *Duc de Grammont Caderousse kills Mr. Dillon at Paris, for a newspaper attack, October.*

1868. *Paul de Cassagnac and M. Lissagaray, journalists; latter run through, 4th September.*

1870. *Don Enrique de Bourbon killed by the Duc de Montpensier, near Madrid, after much provocation, 12th March.*

1873. *Paul de Cassagnac (wounded) and M. Ranc, Paris, 7th July.*

1873. *Prince Soutza kills N. Ghika at Fontainebleau, 27th November.*

1875–84. *Duels (often nominal) still frequent in France.*

1878. *MM. Gambetta and De Fortou; neither hit, 21st November.*

1884. *Captain Fournier and H. Rochefort, for attack in "Intransigeant;" both slightly wounded, 11th October.*

1888. *Habert killed M. Felix Dupuis (artist), who resented satirical verses, Paris, 29th April.*

1888. *General Boulanger seriously, and M. Floquet slightly, wounded, 13th July.*

1892. *Captain Mayer killed Marquis de Mores, Paris, 23rd June.*]

HAYES (SAMUEL). — Duelling, a Poem. 4°. 1775. *London.*

(*In the British Museum. King's Pamphlets*, 163. *l.* 7.)

HEARNE (TH.). — Collection of curious discourses written by eminent antiquaries, with appendix and notes. Edited by J. Ayloffe. 2 vols. 8°. 1773.

[*Contains discourses on "Duelling."*]

HEBERT (ROLAND). — Remonstrance du roy contre les duels, prononcée à Fontainebleau le 19 juin 1625. 8°. 1625. *Paris.*

HÉBRARD DE VILLENEUVE. — Propos d'Épée. 1882–1894. 8°. 1894. *Paris.*

[*viii and 207 pages.*]

—— — ——. — *ROBERT* (G.). — 1887.

HECQ (FÉLIX). — *ESCRIME* (L') à travers les Ages. — [1894.]

HEERUSKIRSCH. 1552.

[*Engravings on copper of two-handed sword fights, rapier, &c.*]

HEIDELBERGER Studentenleben, Einst und Jetzt. Sechsund-
dreissig Lichtdruck-Bilder nach Naturaufnahmen, Handzeichnungen
und Kupferstichen mit erläuterndem Texte. Quer 4°. 1886. *Heidelberg :* Otto Petters.

> [*Aeltestes Mensurbild auf der Hirschgasse* (1826).]

HEINZE (A. C.). — Katechismus der Bajonetfechtkunst. 8°.
1851. *Leipzig :* Weber.

HENKE (Jos.). — Kurzgefasste Anleitung für den Unterricht
im Säbelfechten. Gr. 8°. 1893. *Wr.-Neustadt. (Wien :* L. W.
Seidel & Sohn.)

HENRY. — Sur l'art de l'escrime en Espagne au moyen âge
[*Revue Archéologique,* tome 6, p. 583. 8°. 1849–50. *Paris.*]

HENRY IV. — *CORRESPONDENCE.* MS.

HENRY VI.—*COTTONIAN* MSS.

> [*Tit. C. i. B.* 30. (232.)]

HENRY VIII. (Creation of).—Account of Tournament.

> [*Harleian MSS. vol. i. pag.* 17. *cod.* 69. *art.* 6, 7.]

HERALD (The). — (Sunday Periodical.) Folio. *London.*

> [1891. *September* 13. " *The Italian Sword-Cane Fencing introduced in
> London.*"]

HERAUD Y CLAVIJO (D. A., de Soria). — Manual de esgrima,
en el que se trata de la esgrima de la espada, espada y daga, del
sable y del florete. 12°. 1864. *Paris.*

> [*A few figures, in the text.
> A reprint was published in* 1877. 8°. Paris: *Ch. Bouret.*]

HERBELOT (D') [Colonel]. — Traité des armes, par le Chevalier
Xylander. Traduit de l'allemand. 8°. 1860. *Paris.*

HEREDIA (Narcisco Antonio José Guillermo Juan Nepo-
muceno de) [Marqués de Heredia]. — Verdades en pocas palabras
(sobre la esgrima y los esgrimidores). Small 8°. 1892. *Madrid :*
Est. Tip., "Sucesores de Rivadeneyra."

> [*112 pages.*]

HEREFORD (Duke of).—*HARLEIAN* MSS.

> [*Single combat between the Dukes of Hereford and Norfolk.
> (Vol. iii. pag.* 322. *cod.* 6079. *art.* 36.)]

HERGSELL (GUSTAV). — Die Fechtkunst. 8°. 1881. *Wien :* Hartleben.
[*22 plates. 2. verm. Auflage 1892.*]

—— (—). — Unterricht im Säbelfechten. Gr. 8°. 1885. *Wien :* Hartleben.
[*128 pages.*]

—— (—) [Hauptmann und Landesfechtmeister]. — Talhofer's Fechtbuch aus d. Jahre 1467. Large 4°. 1887. *Prag :* Calve.
[*268 photographic plates.*]

—— (—). — Duell-Codex. Gr. 8°. 1891. *Wien :* Hartleben.
[*Mit 7 Tafeln.*]

—— (—). — *TALHOFFER.* — 1889 (2).

—— (—). — *WASSMANNSDORFF (K.).* — 1887.

HERMANN (A.). — Grundzüge einer Anleitung zum Säbelfechten. 16°. 1859. *Pest :* Geibel.

—— (—.). — Schlüssel zur Kunst des Rapier- und Säbelfechtens à la contrepointe. 16°. 1861. *Linz :* Danner.

HESSE (G.) [Schermmeester in de G. Vg. Lycurgus-Achilles en Olympia, &c.,&c.]. — Handboek ten gebruike bij het schermonderwijs op den degen en de sabel, ten dienste van liefhebbers, meesters en onderwijzers. Opgedragen aan den weledelen zeergeleerden Heer Dr. Johan Georg Mezger. 8°. 1887. *Apeldoorn :* Laurens Hansma.
[*42 figures, in the text.*]

HEUSSLER (SEB.). — New Künstlich Figuren Büchlein, darinnen etlich schöne Stellungen vom Rappier vnd Mantel fechten.
[*20 Kupferstiche ohne Text.*]

—— (—.). — Neu Künstlich Fechtbuch. 4°. 1615. *Nürnberg.*

—— (—.) [Kriegsmann vnd Freyfechter von Nürnberg]. — Neu künstlich Fechtbuch zum andern Mal auffgelegt, vnd mit vielen schönen Stücken verbessert, als dess Sig. Salvator Fabri de Padua, vnd Sig. Rudol. Capo di Ferro, wie auch anderer italienischen vnd frantzösischen Fechter beste Kunststücklein im Dolchen und Rappier zusammengetragen und mit schönen Kupfferstücklein geziert. Oblong 4°. 1616. *Nürnberg.*
[Theil I. *Rappierfechten.* Theil II. *Das Fechten im Rappier und Dolch.* 177 *copperplates.*]

HEUSSLER (Seb.). — New Künstlich Fechtbuch zum dritten mal auffgelegt und mit vielen schoenen Stücken verbessert. Als des Sig. Salvator Fabri de Padua und Sig. Rud. Capo di Ferro, wie auch anderer Italienischen und Französischen Fechter, &c. Oblong 4°. 1630. *Nürnberg :* Simon Halbmayern.

   (*In British Museum, and Captain Hutton's Collection.*)

—— (—.). — Künstliches Abprobirtes und Nützliches Fecht-Buch von Einfachen und doppelten Degen Fechten, damit ein ieder seinen Leib defendirn kan. Oblong 4°. 1665. *Nürnberg :* Paulus Fürsten.

   [124 *copperplates.*]

—— (—.). — Neues Künstliches Fechtbuch, darinnen 54 Stuck in einfachen Rappier, &c. 2 Theile. 1716–17. *Nürnberg.*

HEWES (Robert) [of Boston, U.S.]. — Rules and regulations for the sword exercise of the Cavalry. To which is added the review exercise. The 2nd American from the London Edition. Revised and corrected by Robert Hewes, teacher of the sword exercise for cavalry. 8°. 1802. *Philadelphia :* M. Carey.

   [28 *plates.*]

HEWITT (John). — Ancient Armour and Weapons in Europe ; from the Iron Period of the Northern Nations to the End of the 13th Century. 2 vols. 8°. 1845. *London & Oxford :* J. H. & J. Parker.

  [Vol. I. p. 375. *Pictorial representation of the Legal Duel or wager of battle. This drawing has been carefully traced from one of the " Miscellaneous Rolls " in the Tower, of the time of Henry III. The combatants are Walter Blowberme and Hamun le Stare, the latter being the vanquished champion, and figuring a second time in the group as undergoing the punishment incidental to his defeat. The names of the duellers are written over the figures, the central one being that of the victor. Both are armed with the quadrangular bowed shield and a "baston" headed with a double beak. Britton (" De Jure Angliæ," fol. 41) describes their arming.* Vol. II. pp. 342–343. *Judicial Duel.*]

HEY (Richard) [LL.D.]. — A dissertation on duelling. 8°. 1784. *Cambridge.*

  [*Published by appointment as having gained a prize in the University of Cambridge.*] (*Another edition appeared in* 1812.)

HILDER (G. O.) [Major a. D.]. — Das Duell und die Offiziere. Zeitgemäsze Betrachtungen. [No. 5. Flugschriften-Sammlung. No. 4–9.] 8°. 1887. *Berlin :* Eckstein Nachf.

HILL (JOHAN). — *ASHMOLEAN* MSS.

HINT (A) ON DUELLING. In a Letter to a Friend. 8°. 1751. *London.*

> (*In the Library of the London Institution.* [*Reed Tracts,* Vol. XLIX.
> (Vol. 442) Art. 8.])

HINT (A) ON DUELLING: in a letter to a friend. 8°. 1765. *Stamper.*

HIS MAJESTY'S severe censure against private Combats. 4°. 1613.

HISTORICAL MANUSCRIPTS COMMISSION (Report of the).
— *DAILY* Telegraph (The). — 1895. February 1 (4th column, p. 5).

HISTORY OF DUELLING, in two parts, containing the Origin, Progress, Revolutions, and present state of duelling in France and England, including many curious Historical Anecdotes. 12°. 1770. *London :* E. & C. Dilly.

> [1*st Part contains the History of Duelling in France, translated from the French by M. Coustard de Massi; and the 2nd Part, on Duelling in England.*] (*In Mr. J. R. Garcia Donnell's Collection.*)

HISTORY (THE) OF DUELLING; containing the origin, pro gress, revolutions & present state of duelling in France & Eng land, including many curious historical anecdotes. 12°. 1774. *London :* Dilly.

HISTORY (The) of the most remarkable Tryals in Great Britain and Ireland in Capital Cases. Faithfully extracted from Records and other Authentick Authorities as well Manuscript as printed. 8°. 1715. *London :* A. Bell.

> [Pages 55–61. *The history of a trial by Combat between Sir John Annesly, Kt., and Thomas Katrington, Esq., in the 3rd and 4th of King Richard II. Anno* 1380.
> „   62–72. *The history of the Combat between Henry Plantagenet, or Bolingbroke, then Duke of Hereford, afterwards of Lancaster, and King of England, by the name of Henry IV., and Thomas Mowbray, Duke of Norfolk, Earl Marshal of England, in the year* 1397, *and 21st of Richard II.*
> „ 244–247. *The history of an interchangeable and doubtful accusation, try'd by Combat between Mr. Newton and Mr. Hamilton, in the reign of Edward VI. Anno* 1548.
> „ 399–404. *A Law-suit determined by Combat between the Champions of a Plaintiff and Defendant.*]

HODGHE (ROMEYA DI). — *PETTER.* — 1674.

HOFMANN (FRHR. VON) [Prem. Lieut.]. — Systematischer Lehr-gang zur Ausbildung der Infanterie im Bajonettiren. 1. und 2. unveränd. Auflage. 16°. 1893. *Metz:* G. Scriba.

[*23 pages.*]

HOLBROOK (ANTHONY) [Rector of Waltham Parva, Essex, M.A.] — Against duelling; [on 1 Sam. xviii. 48, 49]. Preached at St. Paul's. 8°. 1727. *London.*

(*In the British Museum*, 1413. *e.* 12. (20.))

HOLLAND. — *COTTONIAN* MSS.

[*Tib. C. i. B.* 27. (205.)]

HOLZAPFEL-OEHLKE (Das) Duell vor dem Schwurgericht. Stenographischer Bericht über die Berhandlungen. 8°. 1885. *Berlin:* Eckstein Nachf.

[*6 pages.*]

HONE. — *STRUTT* (*Jos.*). — 1850.

HONE'S POPULAR WORKS. 8°. 1873. *London:* Tegg.

[*Year Book*, p. 17. *Jeffery Hudsons.*
  ,,   p. 247. *D'Urfey and Bello.*
  ,,   p. 1355. *Lord Mohun and Coote.*
Every Day Book. Vol. I. p. 451. *Duelling characterised.*
  ,,   ,,   ,,   ,, I. p. 911. *Duel, K. B. Sheridan and Mathews.*
  ,,   ,,   ,,   ,, II. p. 942. *Memorandum of Vice-President of United States.* 1804.
Table Book, p. 20. *Duel with a bag.*
  ,,   p. 720. *Duels, A.D.* 1763, 1764, 1765, 1772, 1789, 1790, 1797, 1803.
  ,,   p. 724. *Poetical answer to a challenge.*
  ,,   p. 225. *Sir E. Sackville and Lord E. Bruce, &c.*]

HONOUR'S PRESERVATION without Blood, or a Sober Advice to Duellists. Small 4°. 1680.

HOOGE (ROMEYN DE). — Klare Onderrichtinge der Voortreffe-lijcke Worstel - Konst. 4°. [1674.] *Amsterdam:* W. van Lansvelt.

—— (— —). — *PETTER* (*N.*). — 1674.

HOOGUE (ROMAIN DE). — L'Académie de l'admirable Art de la Lutte, montrant d'une maniere très exacte non seulement la force extraordinaire de l'Homme, mes assi les mouvemens merveilleux, l'usage singulier, & les souplesses des principales parties ou membres du corps humain. Avec une instruction claire et familiaire, comment on peut, en toutes les occasions, repousser sûrement et adroitement toutes sortes d'insultes et d'attaques. 4°. [1712 ?] *Leide:* Isac Severinus.

> [*Première édition avec un texte français. Superbes tirages des belles eaux-fortes au nombre de 71. (A translation from the Dutch.) (The seizure in Dagger Play, or the method for an unarmed man attacked by one armed with a knife, is touched upon by this author.)*]
> (*In Captain Hutton's Collection.*)

HOOPER (LUCY HAMILTON). — *DUYCKINCK (E. A.).* — 1877.

H[OPE] (W[ILLIAM]). — Scots Fencing Master, or Compleat small-swordman, in which is fully Described the whole Guards, Parades, and Lessons belonging to the Small-Sword, &c. By W. H. Gent. 8°. 1687. *Edinburgh:* John Reid.

> [*12 copperplates, out of the text.*]

—— (—). — The Sword-Man's Vade-Mecum, or a preservative against the surprize of a sudden attaque with Sharps. Being a Reduction of the most essential, necessary, and practical part of Fencing, into a few special Rules. With their Reasons: which all Sword-Men should have in their Memories when they are to Engadge; but more especially if it be with Sharps. With some other Remarques and Observations, not unfit to be known. By W. H. Gentleman. 12°. 1691. *Edinburgh:* John Reid.

> (*In Captain Hutton's Collection.*)

—— (—). — The Fencing-master's advice to his scholar: or, a few directions for the more regular assaulting in schools. Published by way of dialogue for the benefit of all who shall be so far advanced in the art as to be fit for assaulting. Small 8°. 1692. *Edinburgh:* John Reid.

—— (—). — The compleat Fencing-Master: in which is fully Described the whole Guards, Parades, and Lessons, belonging to the Small-Sword, as also the best Rules for Playing against either Artists or others, with Blunts or Sharps. Together with Directions how to behave in a single Combat on Horse-back: illustrated with figures Engraven on Copper-plates, representing the most necessary

Postures. 2nd edition. 8°. 1692. *London:* printed for Dorman Newman, at the King's Arms in the Poultrey.

> [*12 copperplates, out of the text. This work, with a different title, is in every other respect a reproduction of the "Scots Fencing Master."*]
> (*In Captain Hutton's Collection.*)

H[OPE] (W[ILLIAM]). — Sword-man's Vade-Mecum. 2nd edition. 12°. 1694. *London:* printed by J. Tailor.

> [*The title of the 2nd edition only shows a little difference in the spelling.*]
> (*In the British Museum.*)

—— (—). — The Sword-man's Vade-Mecum. 12°. 1705. *Edinburgh:* J. Reid.

> (*In Captain Hutton's Collection.*)

HOPE (SIR WILLIAM, of Balcomie, Bart.) [Late Deputy-Governour of the Castle of Edinburgh]. — A New, Short, and Easy Method of Fencing : or the Art of the Broad and Small Sword, Rectified and Compendiz'd, wherein the Practice of these two weapons is reduced to so few and general Rules, that any Person of indifferent Capacity and ordinary Agility of Body, may, in a very short time, attain to, not only a sufficient knowledge of the Theory of this art, but also to a considerable Adroitness in Practice, either for the Defence of his life, upon a just occasion, or preservation of his Reputation and Honour in any Accidental Scuffle, or Trifling Quarrel. 4°. 1707. *Edinburgh:* James Watson.

> [*One large folded sheet, containing 16 figures engraved on copper.*]
> (*In Captain Hutton's Collection.*)

—— (— —). — New Method of Fencing, or the True and Solid Art of Fighting with the Back-Sword, Sheering-Sword, Small-Sword, and Sword and Pistol; freed from the Errors of the Schools. 2nd edition. 4°. 1714. *Edinburgh:* printed by James Watson.

—— (— —). — A Vindication of the True Art of Self-Defence, with a proposal, to the Honourable Members of Parliament, for erecting a Court of Honour in Great Britain. Recommended to all Gentlemen, but particularly to the Soldiery. To which is added a Short but **very** useful memorial for Sword Men. 8°. 1724. *Edinburgh:* William Brown and Company.

> [*The same plate as that which appears in the work published by Sir W. Hope in 1707, and a frontispiece, representing the badge "Gladiatorum Scoticorum."*] (*In British Museum, and Captain Hutton's Collection.*)

HOPE (SIR WILLIAM, of Balcomie, Bart.). — Observations on the Gladiators' Stage-Fighting. 8°. 1725. *London.*

—— (— —). — A Vindication of the True Art of Self-Defence, &c. 2nd edition. 8°. 1729. *London :* printed by W. Meadowes.

[*Same plate and frontispiece. Dedicated to the Right Honourable Robert Walpole.*

"*In these islands the great advocate and exponent of French fencing at the end of the seventeenth and in the early eighteenth century was Sir W. Hope, of Balcomie, at one time Deputy-Governor of Edinburgh Castle. He wrote a great number of quaint treatises of great interest to the 'operative' as well as to the 'speculative' fencer, and yet was instrumental in endeavouring to push through Parliament a Bill for the establishment of a 'Court of Honour,' the office of which was to have been the deciding of honourable quarrels, if possible, without appeal to fencing skill. The House, however, being at the time very excited and busy on the question of the union of England and Scotland, the Bill never became Act. And gentlemen, in consequence, continued to discuss their knotty point 'sur le pré.'"—Castle (E.), "The Story of Swordsmanship." ("The National Review," May 1891.)*]

HORMAYER. — Geschichte, Fechten.

[HORNE (R. H.)]. — History of duelling in all countries. Translated from the French. 12°. [N.D.]

HORNSTEIN (L.). — Die Fechtkunst auf den Hieb. Eine Skizze. 8°. 1869. *München :* J. A. Finsterlin.

[*38 figures.*]

HOUDETOT (CÉSAR FRANÇOIS ADOLPHE, COMTE D'). — Le Tir au pistolet ; causeries théoriques, contenant l'art de tirer le pistolet à pied et à cheval, le choix des armes, la manière de les guidonner, etc. 8°. 1847. *Paris.*

[*Avec gravures dans le texte.*]

—— (— — —, — —). — Ditto. 12°. 1847. *Paris :* Tresse.

H[OUDETOT] (M. A. D'). — Le Tir au Pistolet. Causeries Théoriques. 12°. 1843. *Paris :* Tresse.

[*Deuxième édition, Revue, augmentée et ornée de vignettes.*]

HOUSEHOLD WORDS (Periodical). Large 8°. *London.*

[Vol. XV. pp. 596–614. "*Duelling in England.*"
„ XVIII. p. 97. "*Extraordinary Duelling.*"]

HOUSSAYE (ARSÈNE). — Le duel de la tour. 12°. 1856. *Paris :* Lévy frères.

[*Comédie en un acte et en prose.*]

—— (—). — *VAUX (Baron de).* — 1884.

HOWARD (LORD HENRY) [Earl of Northampton]. — *ASH-MOLEAN* MSS.

HOWELL (JAMES). — *COTTON* (*Sir Robert*). — 1672.

HOYER (G. v.). — Geschichte der Kriegskunst (Fechten). 2 Bände. 1798–1801. *Göttingen :* Röwer.

HUDSON (FREDERIC). — Journalism in the United States from 1690 to 1872. 8°. 1873. *New York :* Harper Brothers.
[Chap. LV. "*The Duels of Editors.*"] (*In the British Museum*, 2308. *e.* 7.)

HUGHES (T.). — Tom Brown's School Days. New edition. 18°. 1872. *London :* Macmillan.
["*Our old 'single-stick' play, as described in that delightful book ' Tom Brown's School Days,' was strangely similar, yet had not departed quite so far from the fundamental laws of swordsmanship.*"—*Castle* (E.), "*The Story of Swordsmanship.*" ("*The National Review,*" May 1891.)]

HUGOT (EUGÈNE). — Un duel en Chambre. 18°. *Paris :* Lèvy.
[*Scène de la vie parisienne en 1 acte.*]

HÜLFS- UND HANDBUCH für Offiziere und Unteroffiziere d. preuss. Infanterie zum Gebrauch bei Ausbildung der Mannschaft in d. Gymnastik und im Bajonettfechten. 5te Auflage. 16°. 1874. *Potsdam :* Döring.

HÜLFS- UND HANDBUCH für Offiziere und Unteroffiziere d. preuss. Infanterie zum Gebrauch bei Ausbildung der Mannschaft im Turnen und Bajonettfechten. Nach den allerhöchsten Vorschriften vom 6. April 1876, in tabellar. Form bearbeitet von e. preuss. Offizier. 8te Auflage. 16°. 1877–8. *Potsdam :* Döring.

HÜLFSBUCH ZUM BETRIEBE d. Turnens und d. Bajonettfechtens der Infanterie. Zusammengestellt nach den neuesten Vorschriften zum prakt. Gebrauch und zum Anhalt von B. 16°. 1878. *Torgau :* Jacob.

HÜLFSBUCH FÜR DEN INFANTERIE-UNTEROFFIZIER zum Gebrauch bei Ausbildung der Mannschaft im Turnen und Bajonettfechten. Zusammengestellt nach den bis 9. Nov. 1882 ergangenen Bestimmungen. 1te u. 2te Auflage. 24°. 1884. *Potsdam :* Döring.

HÜLFSBUCH FÜR DEN INFANTERIE - UNTEROFFIZIER zum Gebrauch bei Ausbildung der Mannschaft im Turnen und Bajonettfechten. Zusammengestellt nach den Vorschriften über das Turnen vom 27. Mai 1886 und das Bajonettfechten vom 9. Novbr. 1882. 4te Auflage. 16°. 1887. *Potsdam :* Döring.

> [*6te Auflage.* 16°. 1892. *" Und der Bajonettir-Vorschrift vom* 15. *Aug.* 1889." (*56 pages.*)]

HÜLFSBUCH ZUM BETRIEBE d. Turnen und d. Bajonett-Fechtens, etc., von v. S. 15. Auflage. 32°. 1889. *Nordhausen :* Koppe.

——. — Ditto. 16. Auflage. 32°. 1890. *Nordhausen :* Koppe.
> [18. *Auflage,* 1891.]

HUME (D.). — Essay on suicide and the immortality of the soul. 8°. 1799. *Strasburgh.*

HUMÉ (EUGÈNE) et RENKIN (J.). — Escrime. Traité et théorie de canne royale. 18°. 1862. *Bruxelles :* Poot et Cie.

HUME (MARTIN A. SHARP). — Chronicle of Henry VIII. of England, written in Spanish by an unknown hand. Translated with notes and introduction. 8°. 1889. *London :* G. Bell & Sons.
> [Page 129, Chapter LIX. *" How Captain Julian went to France and fought with Captain Mora."*]

HUNDFELDER. — *LIECHTENHAUER.* — MS.

HUNDT (MICH.). — Ein new Künstlich Fechtbuch im Rappier zum Fechten und Balgen, u. s. w. 4°. 1611. *Leipzig.*

HUNZFELD (MARTEIN). — Für das Fechten im Harnisch und zu Rosz mit langem Schwerte.
> [*Mentioned in Schmied-Kowarzik und Kufahl's " Fechtbüchlein."* 1894.]

HUTCHINSON (H. D.) [Major]. — Physical Drill with Arms. Strictly in accordance with the New Drill, and fully illustrated, as taught at Aldershot. Urdu edition and Nagri edition. 32°. 1890. *Chatham :* Gale & Polden.

HUTER. — Fechtbuch. 1532. *München.* MS.

HUTH (J. H.). — Works on Horses and Equitation. A bibliographical record of Hippology. 4°. 1887. *London :* Quaritch.
> [*Contains many works on Sword and Lance Exercise.*]

Yours very Truly
Alfred Hutton

HUTTON (ALFRED) [Lieut. Her Majesty's Cameron Highlanders]. — Swordsmanship. Written for the members of the Cameron Fencing Club. 8°. 1862. *Simla:* printed at the "Simla Advertiser" Press.

—— (—). — Swordsmanship, for the use of Soldiers. 8°. 1866. *London:* W. Clowes & Sons.

—— (—) [Lieut. King's Dragoon Guards]. — Swordsmanship and Bayonet-fencing. 8°. 1867. *London:* W. Clowes & Sons.

—— (—). — The Cavalry Swordsman. 8°. 1867. *London:* W. Clowes & Sons.

—— (—) [late Captain, King's Dragoon Guards]. — Bayonet-fencing and Sword Practice. 8°. 1882. *London:* W. Clowes & Sons.

—— (—). — Cold Steel: a practical Treatise on the sabre, based on the old English backsword play of the eighteenth century, combined with the method of the modern Italian school. Also on various other weapons of the present day, including the short sword-bayonet and the constable's truncheon. Illustrated with numerous figures, and also with reproductions of engravings from masters of bygone years. 8°. 1889. *London:* W. Clowes & Sons.
[Portrait of the author, and 55 plates, out of the text.]

—— (—). — Fixed Bayonets. A complete system of Fence for the British Magazine Rifle, explaining the uses of point, edges, and butt, both in offence and defence; comprising also a glossary of English, French, and Italian terms common to the art of fencing, with a bibliographical list of works affecting the bayonet. 8°. 1890. *London:* W. Clowes & Sons.
[Frontispiece, and 23 illustrations, out of the text.]

—— (—). — The Swordsman. A manual of Fence for the three arms, foil, sabre, and bayonet. With an appendix consisting of a code of Rules for assaults, competitions, &c. 8°. 1891. *London:* H. Grevel & Co.
[With 42 illustrations.]

—— (—). — Old Sword-Play. A glance at the systems of Fence in vogue during the XVIth, XVIIth, and XVIIIth Centuries, with lessons arranged from the works of various Ancient Masters for the practical study of the use of the picturesque arms borne of our forefathers. 4°. 1892. *London:* H. Grevel & Co.

[*Illustrated by 56 typical examples from Marozzo, Di Grassi, Thibault, Alfieri, De la Touche, De Liancour, Angelo, Weischner, &c., with photogravure portrait of the author by Boussod, Valadon, & Co. The edition limited to 300 numbered copies.*]

HUTTON (ALFRED). — Our Daggers.

[" *The Illustrated Naval and Military Magazine* " (*London*), *July* 1890.]

—— (—). — Our Swordsmanship.

[*Lecture delivered at the Royal United Service Institution, Whitehall, February* 10, 1893.]

—— (—). — Lecture and Exhibition of Swordsmanship (Mediæval and Modern) at the Gentlemen's Concert Hall, Manchester, December 2, 1893. 4°.

—— (—). — Notes on Ancient Fence. — *ALBANY CLUB.* — 1895.

—— (—). — *ILLUSTRATED* Naval and Military Magazine.

—— (—). — *JOURNAL* of the Royal United Service Institution.

—— (—). — *NAVAL* and Military Argus.

—— (—). — *PALL MALL* Budget.

—— (—). — *PALL MALL* Gazette.

—— (—). — *SATURDAY* Review.

HYNITZCHEN (JOHANN JOACHIM). — *FABRIS.* — 1677.

IDLER (The). — (Monthly Magazine.) 8°. *London:* Chatto & Windus.

[1894. *March.* Pages 184–192. *A Duel. By Henry Harland. Illustrations by R. Jack.*
1894. *March.* Pages 212–224. *The Idlers' Club—Duels and Duelling. By Robert Barr, Henri Rochefort, Morley Roberts, R. H. Sherrard, Henry Harland, Bronson Howard, and W. L. Alden.*]

ILLUSTRATED LONDON NEWS (The). — (Periodical.) Folio. *London.*

[1851. *May* 31. Page 498. *Toledo Swords. By Don Manuel de Ysasi.* — *Pistole d'Honneur. By Devisme.*
1851. *June* 14. Page 570. *Sword Handle. Delacour.*
1851. *July* 26. Page 136. *Group of Arms, Swords, &c. By Gueyton.*
1851. *September* 6. Page 292. *Swords. By Reeves, Greaves, & Co., Birmingham.*]

ILLUSTRATED LONDON NEWS (The) (*continued*)—

[1891. *March 7. The Story of Swordsmanship. By E. Castle.*
1891. *May 16. Regulation Swords (Naval).*
1891. *June 13. Page 675. The French Fencing Masters.*
1892. *June 4. Page 681. Italian Fencers at the Royal Military Tournament.*
1892. *July 9. Old Sword-Play. Review of Captain A. Hutton's Work. By W. H. Pollock.*]

ILLUSTRATED NAVAL AND MILITARY MAGAZINE. 8°.
London : W. H. Allen & Co.

[1888. *November and December. Some Observations on Fencing. By G. W. Barroll.*
1889. *Vol. I. Nos. 3 and 4. The Sabre. By G. W. Barroll.*
1890. *July. Our Daggers. By Alfred Hutton.*
1890. *September 1. The Coup de Jarnac. By Captain A. Hutton.*]

ILLUSTRATED SPORTING AND DRAMATIC NEWS
(Periodical). Folio. *London.*

[1886. *April 24. No. 646. Pages 1666–1668. Shakespearian Swordsmanship.*
1895. *April 13. Page 187. Public Schools Gymnastic, Fencing, and Boxing Competitions at Aldershot.*]

ILLUSTRIRTE ZEITUNG (Periodical). Folio. *Leipzig.*

[1892. *2nd April. Band 92. Nr. 2544. Pages 359–360. "Auf der Mensur." Aus den Erinnerungen eines crassen Fuchses von A. Oskar Klauszmann. Original zeichnung von Werner Zehme.*]

ILUSTRACION (LA) GALLEGA Y ASTURIANA. — *LABRA*
(*R. M.*).

IMMISCH. — Ueber das "Pauken." 8°. 1885. *Heidelberg :*
Bangel & Schmitt.

[*15 pages.*]

IN DIECI LEZIONI, l'arte di non essere mai ferito, ecc.

[*Vide : Bibl. italienne et française. Fougère.*]

INDEX OF DATES (An). 1858. *London :* Bohn.

[" *Duels," Private—dates of memorable duels from* 1772 *to* 1843. " *Combats," Judicial, from* 501 *to* 1819.]

INDIAN DAGGERS. — Collection of the Prince of Wales.
(*In the Art Library, South Kensington Museum. Portfolio* 215.)

INDIAN DAGGERS. — Madras Exhibition, 1857.
(*In the Art Library, South Kensington Museum. Portfolio* 34.)

INDIAN DAGGERS. — Royal Armoury, Windsor Castle.
(*In the Art Library, South Kensington Museum. Portfolio 2.*)

INDICTMENT FOR MURDER of Mr. Edward Grayson, of Liverpool, Ship-builder, against William Sparling, Esqr., late Lieutenant 10th Dragoons, S. M. Colquitt, Esqr., Captain, Royal Navy, at the Lancaster Assizes on April 4, 1804. Full account of trial and proceedings. 8°. 1804. *Liverpool.*

INFANTRY (THE) SWORD EXERCISE. 8°. 1817. *London.*
(*In Captain Hutton's Collection.*)

——. — Ditto. 1819.
(*In the Royal United Service Institution Library, Whitehall, London.*)

——. — Ditto. Revised edition. 8°. 1842. *London:* W. Clowes & Sons. (23rd April.)

——. — Ditto. Revised edition. 8°. 1845. *London :* Parker, Furnivall & Parker. (January 1845.)

——. — Ditto. Revised edition. Adjutant-General's Office, Horse Guards. 12°. 1862. *London.*

——. — Ditto. Revised edition. 12°. 1875. *London.*

INFANTRY SWORD and Carbine Sword-Bayonet Exercise. 12°. 1880. *London.*

——. — Ditto. 32°. 1885. *Chatham :* Gale & Polden.
[*Another edition.* 16°. 1891. London : *Stationery Office.* (31 *pages.*)]

INFANTRY. — Revised Infantry Sword Exercise. 12°. 1887. *London :* W. Clowes & Sons.

INFANTRY SWORD EXERCISE, 1895. 8°. 1895. *London :* Stationery Office.

[78 *pages.* 17 *illustrations.*
The system of swordsmanship is that of Il Cavaliere Ferdinando Masiello, of Florence, and the work contains the essence of his teaching. The illustrations are designed to show, not only the position of the body, but the action of the muscles and joints in the various exercises.
"*The new sword exercise has not met with favour from those competent to judge. It has been condemned by all experts of the art of fence in England, and it has not been received with open arms by the Army. The fact is, the Italian system is, by universal consent, acknowledged to be*

inferior to that of the French school, and I am puzzled to understand why Sir Redvers Buller and the authorities should have revived a faulty and exploded method. That it is tiring, trying, and a great strain on the muscles, I can, from personal experience, vouch; and I am not surprised to find that the new exercise is condemned by the medical profession as productive of unnecessary strain on the muscles, nerve exhaustion, fatigue, and unsteadiness. *Few officers in our Army know anything of fencing or of the sword, the Adjutant-General is too independent and too proud to consult Captain Hutton and other independent authorities, and the result is, we have a sword exercise which no sensible nation would adopt.*"—" *The Globe,*" *August* 10, 1895.

" *The Lancet,*" *July 27, 1895.—*" *Infantry Sword Exercise and the Recent Handbook from the War Office.* (*To the Editors of* ' *The Lancet.*')—*Sirs,* —This handbook of instructions in the use of the sword has just been issued by the War Office. As the document is official, and imposes on the British soldier certain methods of attack and defence, it is not out of place to inquire into the soundness of the principles involved in the teaching, both from physiological and practical points of view. *The system here ordered for adoption is that of the Italian school, as modified by Cavaliere Masiello, of Florence.* The Italian system has been weighed in the balances of experience and found wanting; it is now almost universally superseded by the French school. We fail, therefore, to understand why our authorities should have revived a faulty and more or less exploded method. The position of the body and limbs now recommended (we should say ordered) are essentially faulty, entailing, as they do, unnecessary outlay of muscular power, and leading by their unnatural conditions to rapid nerve exhaustion. *The* '*guard*' *itself, with the feet widely separated,* ' *with both shoulders and sword parallel to the directing line,*' and the attacking arm prone and fully extended, involves an attitude quickly inducing fatigue and unsteadiness, and this without any adequate compensation. The brachial and deltoid muscles get easily tired, *the more so as the elbow-joint is fixed as completely as if it were anchylosed, and the suggestion in the handbook that it should* '*serve as a pivot*' *is an anatomical impossibility.* From such a position it is evident that rapid recovery after the lunge is most difficult, *and thus the fencer is exposed to great risk if engaged with an active opponent skilled in the French method.* We write as representing the feelings and judgment of many members of the medical profession who are interested in fencing as an amusement and exercise, as well as a discipline for the officers and soldiers of the British Army. That a method so faulty and unsound should be now presented to the British soldier for his instruction and guidance appears to us a measure distinctly retrograde and dangerous.— We are, Sirs, yours faithfully,   *I. D. Chepmell, M.D.* " *July* 23rd, 1895.   *G. H. Savage, M.D., F.R.C.P.*"]

INGLOSE (HENRY). — *COTTONIAN* MSS.
        [*Tib. C. i. B.* 28. (229.)]

INGRAM (ROWLAND). — Reflections on duelling.   8°.   1804. *London.*

INGUAGGIATO (CLAUDIO). — A Blasco Florio, risposta all' indirizzo fatto ai maestri di scherma di Sicilia.   1857.   *Palermo.*

IÑIQUEZ (Eusebio). — Ofensas y desafíos ; recopilación de las leyes que rigen en le duelo, y causas originales de este, tomadas de los mejores tratadistas, con notas de autor. 4°. 1890. *Madrid :* Evaristo Sánchez.
[*190 páginas.*]

INSTITUTIONS MILITAIRES.   24°.   1759.   *Paris :* David Jeune.
[*De l'escrime*, pp. 20, 21.]   (*In Captain Hutton's Collection.*)

INSTRUCCIÓN PARA LA ESGRIMA de la Bayoneta. Para el uso del Regimiento Infanteria de Toledo No. 35.   8°.   1859.   *San Sebastian.*
[*With figures.*]

INSTRUCTION POUR L'ENSEIGNEMENT de la gymnastique dans les corps de troupes et les établissements militaires.   18°. 1847.   *Paris :* Dumaine.
[*Avec 3 tableaux et un atlas de 24 planches in folio pliées in 4°.*]

INSTRUCTION POUR LE MANIEMENT et l'emploi de la lance, approuvée par le Ministre de la guerre le 6 avril 1889.   32°.   1889. *Paris.*
[*4e édition, 1894.*]

INSTRUCTION PROVISOIRE sur l'exercice et les manœuvres des bataillons de Chasseur à pied.   32°.   1841.   *Strasbourg :* Levrant.
[*Page 100.   Cinquième leçon :* "*Escrime à la Baïonnette.*"]

——. — Ditto.   32°.   1842.   *Strasbourg :* Levrant.

INSTRUCTION PROVISOIRE sur l'exercice et les manœuvres des bataillons de Chasseurs d'Orléans.   1845.   [July 22.]
[*Page 62, Part I.* "*Escrime à la Baïonnette.*"]

INSTRUCTIONS FOR THE SWORD, Carbine, Pistol and Lance Exercise, &c., &c.   8°.   1858.   *London :* J. Parker & Sons.

INSTRUCTIONS FOR THE SWORD, Carbine, Pistol and Lance Exercise, &c., &c.   For the use of Cavalry.   16°.   *London :* War Office.

INSTRUCTIONS POUR UN JEUNE SEIGNEUR, ou l'idée d'un galant homme.   12°.   1686.   *Paris :* Théodore Girard.

INSTRUCTIONS POUR L'ENSEIGNEMENT préparatoire de l'escrime à l'épée. 18°. 1866. *Paris :* Dumaine.

———. — Ditto. 1868. *Paris :* Dumaine.

INSTRUCTIONS POUR L'ENSEIGNEMENT préparatoire de l'escrime à l'épée, suivie du règlement provisoire pour l'organisation de l'enseignement gratuit et obligatoire de l'escrime dans l'armée, 28 avril 1872, modifié par la circulaire du 7 décembre 1872. 18°. 1875. *Paris :* J. Dumaine.

[*With plates.*]

INSTRUCTIONS SUR L'ESCRIME du sabre et de la lance à Cheval. 1867. *Paris.*

INSTRUCTIONS SUR LE TRAVAIL individuel dans la cavalerie, le tir du fusil et du pistolet. Traité sur la ferrure. 4°. 1862. *Paris :* Dumaine.

[*With 23 plates.*]

———. — Ditto.   Edition in 8°.

———. — Ditto.   Edition in 18°.

INSTRUKTION I FÄKTNING och gymnastik för svenska kavaleriet. [Utdrag ur Handbok för Kavaleriet.]   8°.   1882. *Stockholm :* Norstedt & Söner.

[*Another edition.* 8°. 1889. Stockholm : *Norstedt & Söner.*]

INSTRUKTION I GYMNASTIK och bajonettfäktning för infanteriet [af d. 26 mars 1872].   8°.   1872.   *Stockholm :* Norstedt & Söner.

[*2nd edition.* 12°. 1876. Stockholm : *Norstedt & Söner.*]

INSTRUKTION ÜBER DAS BAJONETFECHTEN für das K. Preuss. 31. Inf.-Regt.   8°.   1842.   *Erfurt.*

ISLE-ADAM (L'). — *TRAITÉS* du duel judiciaire. — 1872.

ISNARDI (MICH.). — *THALHOFER (K.).* — 1838.

ISTRUZIONE PER LA SCHERMA di sciabola-bajonetta e bastone. 12°. 1853. *Cuneo :* Fenoglio.

ISTRUZIONE PER LA SCHERMA del bastone ad uso dei bersaglieri. 12°. 1864. *Livorno.*

[*Another edition.* 12°. 1868. Firenze & Torino : *Tipografia Fodratti.*]

ISTRUZIONE PER LA SCHERMA del bastone. 12°. 1867. *Livorno :* F. Vigo.

(In Captain Hutton's Collection.)

ISTRUZIONE PER GLI ESERCIZI di ginnastica e di scherma col fucile. 12°. 1876.

(In Captain Hutton's Collection.)

ISTRUZIONE SULLA SCHERMA di baionetta pei bersaglieri. 12°. 1868. *Firenze :* Fodratti.

[1 *folding plate, containing* 7 *figures.*]

IVANOWSKI. — Nouveau système d'escrime pour la cavalerie, fondé sur l'emploi d'un nouveau sabre. 8°. 1834. *Paris.*

JACAMBO (M.). — Il duello e la moderna civiltà. 8°. 1860. *Napoli.*

[2*nd edizione di molto ampliata.* 16°. 1879. Napoli : *Cav. Antonio Marano.*]

JACOB (JULES). — Le jeu de l'épée. Leçons de Jules Jacob, rédigées par Emile André, suivies du duel au sabre et du duel au pistolet et de conseils aux témoins. Préfaces de MM. P. de Cassagnac, A. Ranc et A. de la Forge. 12°. 1887. *Paris :* Paul Ollendorff.

[" *Is the most clear, concise and practical work I have yet met with.*"—*Hutton's* " *Cold Steel.*" 1889.]

JACOBILLI (FRANCESCO) [da Foligno]. — Compendio del giuoco moderno di ben maneggiare la spada. 8°. 1654. *Padova.*

JACQUES [le Grand]. — Premier duel de Pierrot, parodie en un acte et en vers. 8°. *Paris :* Librairie de l'eau-forte.

[3 *eaux-fortes de H. Somm et de Courtois.* (*Tiré à* 100 *exemplaires.*)]

JAHN (F. L.) und **EISELEN** (E.). — Die deutsche Turnkunst. Gr. 8°. 1816. *Berlin :* Reimer.

[*Contains a list of* " *ältere Fechtbücher.*" 2 *copperplates.*]

JAHN (F. L.). — Deutsche Turnkunst. Gr. 8°. 1847. *Berlin :* G. Reimer.

[*Seite* 281 — " *Ordnung der Fechtschulen.*"]

JAHRBUCH der Vereine Deutschlands [Vereins-Adressbuch]. — In 7 Abtheilungen. Unter Mitwirkg. der Vereine selbst zusammengestellt von Paul Wiesenthal. Gr. 8°. 1890. *Berlin :* Wiesenthal.

[*Inhalt : Schützen- u. Schiess-, Alpen-, Touristen-, Sammler-, Schach-, Kartenspiel-, Rauch-, Kegler-, Fussball-, Billard- u. Fecht-Vereine.*]

JAILLE (Hardouin de la). — *TRAITÉS* du duel judiciaire. — 1872.

—— (— — —). — *TRAITÉS* et Advis. — 1586.

JAIME. — *LÉON.* — 1833.

JAITNER. — Exercir-Regl., Turn-, Bajonett- und Fecht-Unterricht. 8°. 1862. *Wien.*

[JAMES I.]. — A publication of His Majestie's (James I.) Edict and severe censure against private combats and Combatants, whether within his Highnesse Dominions, or without, with their seconds, accomplices and adhærents. Small 4°. 1613. *London :* Barker.

JAMES I. (KING). — *COTTONIAN* MSS.
[*Tit. C. i. B.* 32. (238 *b.*)
Tit. C. iv. 6. (422.)]

JANIN (JULES). — Contes Fantastiques et Contes Litteraires. 4 vols. 12°. 1832. *Paris :* A. Levavasseur.
[Tome III. pp. 1-28. "*Les Deux Duels.*"]

JAPAN (Duelling in).
["*The Times*" (*Newspaper*). *Folio.* London. *September* 27, 1890.]

JARNAC (W. FRANCE).
[*A Jarnac Stroke—an unjust term of opprobrium—is derived from the Seigneur de Jarnac, who, in a duel with La Chataigneraye, for a great insult, disabled his antagonist by an unexpected wound in the ham,* 1547.]

——. — *DUPLEIX* (S.).

——. — *ILLUSTRATED* Naval and Military Magazine.

JAY (W.). — On Duelling. (Prize Essay.)
[1842. Vol. XXXII. "*New World.*"]

JEAN-LOUIS. — *NOTICE* biographique sur. — 1866.

——. — *ROBAGLIA* (A.). — 1877.

JEFFREY (FRANCIS). — Contributions to the Edinburgh Review. Small 4°. 1853. *London :* Longman.
[Page 622. *Bentham's substitute for Duelling.*]

JENNINGS. — System of attack and defence. 8°. [Between 1800-18.] *London :* Cadell.

JENSEN (Kapitän v.). — *ANWENDUNG (Die).* — 1829.

JHONES (Richard). — The Booke of Honor and Armes. Small 4°. [*circa* 1500.] *London.*
(In Captain Hutton's Collection.)

JOANNE DE LIGNANO et Alias de Villa Sante tractatus duplex de duello. Folio.
[A clear MS., date about the beginning of the 17th century.]

JOB. — Les épées de France. Album contenant 48 planches color. 4°. 1895. *Paris:* H. Geffroy.

JOLLIVET (G.). — *PRÉVOST (C.).* — 1891.

JOLLY (Jules). — Du duel et de sa législation. 8°. 1838. *Paris.*

JONES (Thomas). — A sermon on duelling. 4°. 1792. *London.*

JONSON (Ben). — Works, with notes critical and explanatory, and biographical memoir by W. Gifford. 9 vols. 8°. 1816. *London.*
[Vol. VI. p. 69. "Duelling."]

—— (—). — Every Man in his Humour.
[Where Captain Bobadil, the Paul's man, is so full of the Great Carranza.]

JOURNAL OF THE FRANKLIN INSTITUTE. *Philadelphia.*
[Vol. VIII. p. 307. "Toledo Sword Blades." By G. Bowles.]

JOURNAL OF THE ROYAL UNITED SERVICE INSTITU-TION. 8°. *London.*
[1894. "School Swordplay." By Captain A. Hutton.]

JOVE Y HEVIA (Don Plácido). — Estudios sobre el duelo. 1848. *Madrid.*

JUDICIAL COMBATS (Collections relative to) and the Earl Marshal's Court.
[MS. In the British Museum. 9023.]

JUSTINOPOLITANO (Il Gentilhuomo, del Mutio). 8°. 1575. *Venetia.*

—— (—). — Le Risposte Cavalleresche. 12°. 1576. *Venetia:* Domenico Farri.

Exprimit os Kahni sculptor; sed gloria famæ
Armorum potius cuspide sculpta manet.

In honorem nobilissimæ Autoris adf...
C.R. ab Alvensleben.

ANTHON FRIEDRICH KAHN. 1739.

K. (C. DE) [Le Colonel]. — Annotations méthodiques et succinctes de l'escrime. 8°. 1872. *Paris :* Léautey.

KAHN (ANTHON FRIEDRICH) [Fechtmeister auf der Georgius Augustus-Universität zu Göttingen]. — Anfangsgründe der Fechtkunst nebst einer Vorrede von dem Nutzen der Fechtkunst und den Vorzügen dieser Anweisung. 4°. 1739. *Goettingen :* J. C. L. Schlultzen.

> [*Portrait of Kahn and 25 copperplates, out of the text, engraved by F. Fritsch.*
> *The principal authority on the subject of University fence schools, and an account of what he calls the " Kreussler'sche Schule" is given at some length.*]
> (*In the British Museum, 7905. bbb.* 6 (*in this copy the portrait is missing*) ; *and Captain Hutton's Collection.*)

—— (— —). — Anfangsgründe der Fechtkunst, &c., &c. Neue Auflage. Mit e. Anhang über d. Kunst, auf d. Hieb zu fechten. 4°. 1761. *Helmstädt :* C. F. Weygand.

> [25 *copperplates.* (*Contains a bibliography,* pp. 16, 17.)]

KAL (PAUL). — *KARL (Paul).*

KARL (PAUL) [PAULUS KALL, also PAUL CARL]. — (A collection of drawings on vellum, displaying the fencing stratagems employed in combats with the different weapons of the 15th century.)

> [*MS. München Bibliothek* (*Codex Germ.* 1507).
> *Dated* 1400. *See the monograph on judicial duels, published by R. L. Pearsall in "Archæologia,"* Vol. XXIX., *which is based on Paul Kall's MS.*]

KARUS (HUGO). — Schläger, Säbel und Pistole. Ein wort an die deutsche Studentenschaft und die Freunde derselben. 8°. 1888. *Halle :* Mühlmann's Sortiment.

KAY (C. DE). — *COSMOPOLITAN (The).* — 1892.

KELLIE (SIR THOMAS). — Pallas Armata, or Militarie Instructions for the learned, and all generous spirits who affect the profession of Armes. The first part containing the Exercise of Infanterie, as well ancient as moderne, etc. 4°. 1627. *Edinburgh :* printed by the Heires of A. Hart.

> (*In the British Museum.* 534. *f.* 26. (2.))

KELTON [Lieut. 6th Regiment, United States Infantry]. — A New Manual of the Bayonet for the Army and Militia of the

United States. Small 8°. 1861. *New York :* D. Van Nostrand, 192 Broadway.

[" *It is simply the theory of the attack and defence of the sword applied to the bayonet on the authority of men skilled in the use of arms."—Author's Preface.*

108 *pages ;* 30 *folding plates at end.*]

KENRICK (WILLIAM). — The Duellist. Comedy. 8°. 1773.

[*Acted at Covent Garden (Theatre, London). Taken from Fielding's "Amelia."*]

KEYMEULEN (L. VAN). — Études de Genre. 4°. 1882. *Anvers :* Jos. Theunis.

[Pages 71–77. " *Le Duel de Carl Weisfeld."*]

KEYSERLING (H.). — Erörterungen über das Duell. 3. Auflage. 8°. 1883. *Dorpat :* Schnakenburg.

[32 *pages.*]

KIEFER.—Duell e fideles. 1894.

KING-HARMANN (COLONEL). — Officers and their Weapons.

[*Lecture delivered at the Royal United Service Institution, Simla, June 16, 1892.*

(" *The Journal of the United Service Institution of India."* Vol. XXI. No. 94. 1892.)]

KINLOSSE (EDWARD BRUCE, BARON OF). — *LANSDOWNE MSS.*

—— (— —, — —). — *SACKVILE (Sir E.).*

KIRCHE, DUELL, Freimaurerei nebst einem anhange : Ueber Wohlthätigkeit, &c. 1858. *Berlin.*

KLAUSZMANN (A. OSKAR). — *ILLUSTRIRTE* Zeitung.

KLEMM (G.). — Die Werkzeuge und Waffen, ihre Entstehung und Ausbildung. 8°. 1858. *Sondershausen.*

[*Illustrations of swords and daggers.*]

KLOSS (M.). — Hantel-Büchlein für Zimmerturner. 16°. 1858. *Leipzig :* Weber.

[2*te Auflage.* 1860.]

KLUGE (H. O.). — Commando - Tafeln für das Degen- und Bajonettfechten. Nach dem Schwedischen Systeme entworfen für die Schüler der Königlichen Central-Turn-Anstalt zu Berlin. 8°. 1852. *Berlin :* Dümmler.

KLUGKIST (H.). — De veris duellorum limitibus vom Kampf-Recht. 4°. 1736. *Halæ.*

KNICKERBOCKER MAGAZINE. *New York, U.S.A.*
    [Vol. XXXVII. p. 40. *"Duelling."*
    „ LXII. p. 525. *"Anecdotes of Duelling."*]

KNYGHTON [The Historian]. — *LANSDOWNE* MSS.

KOCK (H. F. DE). — Het duel. Acad proefschrift. 8°. 1876. *Leiden.*

KOHUT (DR. ADOLPH). — Das Buch berühmter Duelle. 2te Auflage (Neue Titel-Ausgabe). 8°. 1891. *Berlin:* A. H. Fried & Co.
        [1*st edition.* 1888. Berlin. (263 *pages.*)]

KOLLARZ. — *ABRICHTUNGS-REGLEMENT.* — 1851.

KOLLOCK (S. K.). — The guilt of duelling. A Sermon. 1842.
    [*In the New York State Library* (*U.S.A.*) (*P.* 908.)]

KÖPPEN (JOACH.). — Newer diskurs von der rittermässigen und weitberühmten Kunst des Fechtens, u. s. w. Small folio. 1619. *Magdeburg.*

—— (—.). — Cours von der Fechtkunst. Small folio. 1619. *Magdeburg.*

KORWIN-DZBANSKI (MAJ.-AUDIT. DR. STANISL. RITTER VON). — Der Zweikampf mit besond. Verücksickt. des neusten Entwurfes e. österreichischen allgemeinen Strafgesetzes. Gr. 8°. 1893. *Wien:* Verlagsanstalt "Reichswehr."
            [55 *pages.*]

KÖTHE (FRIED.). — Das Ganze der Fechtkunst, oder ausführliches Lehrbuch die Fechtkunst in ihren verschiedenen Zweigen gründlich zu erlernen. 8°. 1841. *Nordhausen:* Fürst.
        [*Band I. Das Stossfechten, mit Figuren.*]

—— (—.). — Das Ganze der Fechtkunst. 8°. 1849. *Leipzig.*

—— (—.). — Das Stossfechten. 8°. 1851. *Leipzig.*
            [16 *figures.*]

    [*Another edition.* 12°. 1849. Leipzig: *Schmidt. (Mit 16 Figuren auf* 1 *lith. Tafel.*)]

KRASINSKI (LE COMTE CORVIN). — Essai sur le maniement de la lance. 4°. 1811. *Paris.*

KREUSSLER. — Fechtschule MS. in the Kgl. Bibliothek, Dresden.

——. — *DEUTSCHE* Stoszfechtschule. — 1892.

——. — *EISELEN (E. W. B.).* — 1826.

——. — *GÖTTLING (Prof.).* — 1829.

——. — *KAHN (A. F.).* — 1739.

——. — *RIEMANN (H.).* — 1834.

——. — *ROUX (F. A. W. L.).* — 1849.

——. — *ROUX (H.).* — 1786.

KRIEGSDIENST-VORSCHRIFTEN für die Grossherzoglich Badischen Truppen. 8°. 1841. *Karlsruhe :* Gutsch und Rupp.

> [*XV. Abtheilung. Fünftes Hauptstück. Erster Abschnitt. "Bajonett-Fechtunterricht."* (6 *folding plates.*)]

KRÜNITZ. — Encyclopädie. 8°. 1785. *Berlin.*

> ["*Fechterspiele.*"]

KUNSTREICHES FECHTBUCH. MS. 1579.

> (*In the Wolfenbüttel Library.*)

L * * * * (C. von). — *CHÂTAUVILLARD (Graf de).*

LABAÑA (Pedro de).

> ["*Aunque le cita como escritor de esgrima Pérez de Mendoza en sus 'Principios,' creo que debe ser Juan Bautista, el cosmógrafo del Rey de Portugal.*"]

LABAT. — L'art de l'espée. 12°. 1690. *Toulouse.*

> [*With copperplates.*]

LABAT [Maître en fait d'armes de la ville et Académie de Toulouse]. — L'art en fait d'armes, ou de l'épée seule, avec les attitudes ; dédié à Monseigneur le Comte d'Armaignac, Grand Ecuyer de France, &c. 8°. 1696. *Toulouse :* J. Boude.

> [12 *copperplates by Simonin, out of the text.*
> "*Labat's two works, although of unpretending dimensions, rank among the soundest treatises on practical fencing. Indeed, from the days of Liancour and Labat till quite the latter part of the eighteenth century, all the books written by the followers of the French school are more or less close imitations of their works.*"—*Castle's " Schools and Masters of Fence.*"]

LABAT [Maître en fait d'armes de la ville et académie de Toulouse].
— Questions sur l'art en fait d'armes, ou de l'épée, dédié à Monseigneur le Duc de Bourgogne. 4°. 1701. *Toulouse:* G. Robert.
(*In Captain Hutton's Collection.*)

——. — *ABBAT (L').* — 1734. 1735.

L'ABBAT. — *ABBAT (L').*

LA BOËSSIÈRE (M.). — *BOËSSIÈRE (M. La).* —1766. 1818.

LABORDE Y NAVARRO (Don Angel). — Ejercicio del sable.
4°. 1832. *Habana.*

LABRA (Rafael María de). — Las armas en Madrid. 4°.
1879. *Madrid :* Aurelio J. Alaria.
[*Cartas sobre la Esgrima.*]

—— (— — —). — Las armas en Madrid . . . observaciones sobre
la esgrima.
[*See "La Ilustracion Gallega y Asturiana,"* Tome II. p. 81.]

LACOMBE (Paul). — Les armes et les armures. 12°. 1867.
Paris : Hachette et Cie.
[*Avec 60 vignettes.* (*Fait partie de la "Bibliothèque des merveilles."*)]

LACRETTE. — *GILLET (A.).* — 1875.

LAFAUGÈRE (Louis-Justin). — Traité de l'art de faire des
armes. 8°. 1820. *Lyon.*
[2 *folding plates.*]

—— (—). — Traité de l'art de faire des armes. 8°. 1825.
Paris : Bouchard.
[*Portrait et 2 grandes planches pliées.*] (*In Captain Hutton's Collection.*)

—— (—). — L'Esprit de l'escrime : poëme didactique. 8°. 1841.
Paris : Garnier.
[*Portrait of author, by E. Sam.*] (*In Captain Hutton's Collection.*)

—— (—). — Nouveau manuel complet d'escrime, ou Traité de
l'art de faire des armes. Nouvelle édition, entièrement refondue et
ornée de vignettes intercalées dans le texte. 18°. 1865. *Paris :*
Roret.
[*Woodcuts in the text.*
The 1st edition appeared in 1838. 16°. Paris: *Roret.* (*Ornée de
planches.*)] (*In Captain Hutton's Collection.*)

157

LAFAUGÈRE (Louis-Justin). — Nouveau manuel complet d'escrime. Nouvelle édition, entièrement refondue. 18°. 1884. *Paris:* Roret.

[*With figures in the text.* (*Manuels-Roret.*)]

—— (—). — *LAFFARGÈRE (F.).* — 1841.

—— (—). — *MARÍN (D. Antonio).* — 1841.

—— (—). — *ROBAGLIA (A.).* — 1877.

LAFAYETTE. — Mémoires.

[Vol. I. p. 86, *contains a curious letter regarding chivalry and duelling in* 1778.]

LAFFARGÈRE (F.) [Lafaugère (J.) (?)]. — Tratado completo de esgrima compuesto por el célebre profesor maestro Mr. F. L. adoptado últimamente en Francia, y traducido al Español por el profesor D. Antonio Marín. 8°. 1841. *Madrid:* Alegría y Charlain.

LAGRANGE (Fernand). — La Médication par l'Éxercice. 8°. 1894. *Paris:* Félix Alcan.

[Page 400. "*Rôle orthopédique de l'escrime.*"]

—— (—). — L'escrime et ses effets sur la colonne vertébrale.

[*J. Soc. de méd. et pharm. de la Haute-Vienne.* Limoges. 8°. 1885. IX. pp. 133–139.]

LALAING (Jacques de). — *CHASTELLAIN (George).* — 1634.

LAMARCHE (Claude) [Pseudonyme du Docteur Félizet]. — Traité de l'épée. 16°. 1884. *Paris:* Marpon et Flammarion.

[*Illustrations dans le texte et 15 planches à part par Marius Roy. Un beau volume sur papier teinté avec couverture tirée en couleur. Exemplaires numérotés, papier du Japon.*] (*In Captain Hutton's Collection.*)

LAMBERTINI (Vittorio) [Maestro d' armi]. — Trattato di scherma teorico-pratico illustrato della moderna scuola italiana di spada e sciabolo. 8°. 1870. *Bologna.*

[*Frontispiece and 29 lithographed plates.*]

LÁMINAS DEL ATAQUE y defensa del arma de la lanza. Publicado con superior permiso. Folio. 1814. *Madrid.*

[25 *láminas.*]

LANCKE (Jul.) [Prem. Lieut.]. — Praktische Anleitung zur Ausbildung und Vorstellung der II. Bajonetfechtklasse. Nach den Vorschriften über das Bajonetfechten der Infanterie aus dem Jahre 1876 und eigenen Erfahrungen zusammengestellt. 8°. 1878. *Mainz :* V. von Zabern.

L'ANGE (J. D.). — *ANGE (J. D. L').* — 1664. 1709.

LANGE (L.). — De duelle vocabuli origine et fatis. 4°. 1878. *Lipsiæ.*

LANGLOIS (V.). — Notice sur le Sabre de Constantin XIV., dernier Empereur de Constantinople.
[" *Revue Archéologique,*" Vol. XIV. p. 292. 8°. 1857-58. Paris.]

LANSDOWNE MSS.
[*Duel on appeal of murder, notes on (dcccxxv. 55).*
Duelling, speech against (dccxlvi. 37).
Duels, King James I.'s speech concerning (clx. 91).
     „   " *The way of, before the kinge, written as is supposed by Mr. Selden.*"
           (This is a translation from the French.) (ccxi. 2).
     „   " *The way of duells before the king.*" *(cclv. 21).*
     „   *discourse of. Partly in the handwriting of Henry Howard, Earl of*
           Northampton. (cclv. 26).
The Combat between Edward Bruce, Baron of Kinlosse, and Sir Edward
     Sackvile, brother of the Earl of Dorset (ccxiii. 8).
An Extract from Knyghton the historian concerning the intended Duel at
     Paris between Otho, Duke of Brunswick, and Henry, Earl of Lancaster
     (cclv. 22).]
         (In the British Museum.)

LAPANOUSE (M. J.) [ancien capitaine de dragons]. — Le duel jugé au tribunal de la raison et de l'honneur. 8°. 1802. *Paris :* impr. de Munier.

—— (—. —.). — El duelo, juzgado en el tribunal de la razon y del honor. 8°. 1807. *Madrid.*

LARA (D. Gaspar Agustin de). — Cornucopia numerosa. Alfabeto breve de principios assentados, y rudimentos conocidos de la verdadera filosofía y destreza de las armas. Colegidos de las obras de Don Luis Pacheco de Narvaez. 4°. 1675. *Madrid :* A. Gonçalez de Reyes.
[32 *hoj. prels.,*136 *págs. de texto, una hoja de indice y otra con versos.*]
(*In the BB. Nacional, de Fernandez San Roman, de Mariátegui, and in Don E. de Leguina's Collection.*)

LÄROBÖCKER, Finska värnepligtiges. 8°. 1881. *Helsingfors :* G. W. Edlund.

[*I. Handledning i militärgymnastik.*]

LAROUSSE (PIERRE). — Dictionnaire (Grand) universel du XIXᵉ Siècle. 4°. 1864–1868. *Paris :* Larousse et Boyer.

[*Contains an article on " Duel."*]

LARRIBEAU [Professeur d'escrime et de canne]. — Nouvelle théorie du jeu de la canne, ornée de 60 figures, indiquant les poses et les coups. 12°. 1856. *Paris* [chez l'auteur, passage Verdeau].

[*Portrait of the author and 4 plates.*]

—— (——). — Théorie du jeu de la canne. 16°. 1884. *Paris.*

LARWOOD (JACOB) [L. R. Sadler]. — Story of the London Parks. 2 vols. 8°. 1871. *London :* Hotten.

[Pages 52,	69.	*Duel, Hamilton and Mohun.*
Page	81.	*Duelling, Hyde Park.*
,,	94.	*Duel, fatal, Hyde Park.*
,,	110.	*Duels, numerous.*
Pages 125,	127.	*Duel, Wilkes and Martin.*
Page	126.	*Duelling, Reign George III.*
,,	136.	*Duels about Wilkes.*
Pages 140,	176.	*Duelling Mania.*
Page	142.	*Duel, Sheridan and Mathews.*
,,	143.	,, *Whately and Temple.*
,,	154.	,, *Garrick and Baddeley.*
,,	155.	,, *Fox and Adam.*
,,	156.	,, *Dudley and Stoney.*
,,	157.	,, *Shelburne (Earl) and Fullerton.*
,,	158.	,, *Allan and Dulaney.*
,,	172.	,, *Biggs (Lieut. R.N.) and Wilson (Lieut. 67th foot).*
,,	172.	,, *Gordon (Honble. Colonel) and Thomas (Lieut.- Colonel).*
,,	173.	,, *Randall (Wm., Earl of Antrim) and Mr. M-n-n.*
,,	173.	,, *Lowther (Sir James) and Bolton (Sergeant).*
,,	184.	,, *Macpherson and Major Brown.*
,,	184.	,, *Townshend (Honble.) and Faulkner (Wm.).*
,,	198.	,, *Parkhurst (Captain) and Kelly (Lieut. R.N.).*
,,	198.	,, *Price and Carpenter.*
,,	199.	,, *King (Colonel) and Fitzgerald (Colonel).*
,,	199.	,, *Lonsdale (Earl of) and Vane (Sir F. F.).*
,,	217.	,, *R-d-n and Steward (Captain).*
,,	217.	,, *Buckingham (Duke of) and Bedford (Duke of).*
,,	217.	,, *Montgomery (Colonel) and Macnamara (Captain).*
,,	217.	,, *H. C. (Honble.) and T. John.*

LARWOOD (Jacob)—*continued.*

Page 218. *Duel Interrupted.*
    „ 277. „ *Howard (Thomas, Captain) and Jermyn.*
    „ 291. „ *Colt (Sir Havey) and Beau Fielding.*
    „ 291. „ *Pulteney (Wm., Earl of Bath), and Harvey (John, Lord).*
    „ 300. „ *Powell (Charles) and Captain Henry Newton.*
    „ 304. „ *Ligonier (Edward, Viscount) and Alfieri (Count).*]

LATHAM (John) [F.S.A.]. — Arms and the Men.
[" *Time* " (*Periodical*). London. (*About* 1879.)]

—— (—). — The Shape of Sword Blades. 1862.
[*Reprinted from* " *The Journal of the United Service Institution,*" Vol. VII., No. 29, 1862. *Contents: Introduction—The Sword as a Weapon for Cutting, Thrusting, and Guarding—Principles of Cutting Weapons— Centre of Percussion—Curved Blades, their Principles and Effect—Different Methods of Cutting—Expression of Force in Moving Bodies— Weight and Velocity—Centre of Gravity—Balance of Sword — Sections of Cutting Weapons—Angles of Edge and Point—Principles of Thrusting Weapons— Methods of Thrusting—Straight Thrust—Schools of Fencing in Europe— Curved Thrust—Guarding—Principles and Shape required—Form of Hilts —Comparison of English Regulation Swords—Remarkable Feats of Swordsmanship—Conclusion.*]

LA TOUCHE ([Philbert] De). — *TOUCHE* (*De La*). — 1670.

LAURENT (Émile). — *COLOMBEY* (*E.*).

LAVALLÉE (Henri). — De la répression du duel en Belgique.
8°. 1836. *Bruxelles.*

LAW MAGAZINE or **QUARTERLY REVIEW.** *London.*
[Vol. X. p. 367. " *Laws of Duelling.*"
  „ XXVI. p. 318. " *French Laws on Duelling.*"]

LAW TIMES (Periodical). 4°. *London.*
[Vol. II. pp. 484, 509. " *Duelling.*"]

LAWS OF HONOUR, or an Account of the Suppression of Duels in France, published for the use of English Gentlemen who have had the honour to carry Arms. 12°. 1685.

LAYARD (Charles Peter) [Prebendary of Worcester, D.D., F.R.S.]. — A poetical essay on duelling. 4°. 1775. *Cambridge.*
[*Another edition.* 4°. 1776. London.]

LEA (H. C.). — Superstition and Force. 8°. 1866. *Philadelphia.*
[" *Duelling.*"]

LEACH (RICHARD) [Sergeant in the Norfolk Rangers]. — The words of command and a brief explanation, embellished with engravings, representing the various cuts and attitudes of the new sword exercise. 8°. 1797. *Newcastle.*

LEASES from the Company for making hollow Sword-blades. 1704–1709.

> [*MSS. in British Museum. Add. Ch.* 24,473. 24,474.]

LEBER (J. M. C.) [Salgues (J. B.) and Cohen (J.)]. — Collection des dissertations relatives à l'histoire de France. 8°. 1838. *Paris.*

> [Vol. V. p. 6. " *Dissertation sur les duels.*"]
> (*In the Boston Public Library, Upper Hall.* 2618. 1.)

LEBKOMMERS (HANS). — *LECKÜCHNER (Hans).* — 1531 (?).

LEBOUCHER (Professeur d'escrime, de Rouen). — Théorie pour apprendre à tirer la canne en Vingt-cinq leçons. 8°. 1843. *Paris :* Rigaud.

> [*The portrait and* 37 *plates.*]

LEBRUN. . . . 1750 (?). *Paris.*

LECKÜCHNER (HANS). — Der alten Fechter gründliche Kunst. Mit sampt verborgenen heymlichten, Kämpffens, Ringens, Werffens, &c. Figürlich fürgemalet. Bisher nie añ Tag komen. [1531 (?)].

> [48 *pages, woodcut on title-page, described by some as being the work of Hans Lebkommers, this being a printer's error for Hans Lecküchner, which appears on the original MS.*]

LECOMTE (L. HENRY). — Vers et Chansons. Première série. 12°. 1882. *Paris :* A. Patay.

> [Pages 34–36. "*Le Duels.*"]

LEDELI (MORITZ). — *SPORT (Der).* — 1880.

LEGAL OBSERVER (Periodical). *London.*

> [Vol. XVI. p. 489. *Laws of Duelling.*
>   ,,   XVII. p. 72. *Ancient Duelling Cases.*
>   ,,   XXVI. p. 242. *Laws of Honour.*
>   ,,   XLIX. p. 498. *Trial before Mr. Justice Bayley,* 1830.]

LEGENDRE (P.). — The Exercise of the Broad Sword, and its use fully explained; with the various cuts and guards, and every mode of Defence amply detailed; according to the system used in the French Army. By order of the late Emperor. Also, some short lessons for the practice of Single stick. 8°. [N.D.] [1810 (?).] *London :* J. Bailey.

> [*Illustrated frontispiece, containing* 16 *positions of cuts and guards.*]
> (*In Captain Hutton's Collection.*)

LEGOUVÉ (ERNEST). — Un tournoi au XIXe siècle. 4°. 1872. *Paris :* Lemerre.

—— (——). — Deux épées brisées (Bertrand et Robert). 8°. 1876. *Paris :* Ollendorff.

> [2 *portraits. Partly repeated in Preface to C. Prévost's "Théorie pratique de l'escrime."* 1886.—*Since included in Legouvé's "Soixante ans de souvenirs"* (Vol. I. Chap. XIII.). 2 *vols.* 8°. 1886-7. Paris : *Hetzel.*]

—— (——). — *PARIS* Guide. — 1867.

—— (——). — *PRÉVOST (C.).* — 1886.

—— (——). — *ROBERT (G.).* — 1887.

LEGUINA (DON ENRIQUE DE). — La Espada. Apuntes para su historia en España y Portugal. Datos. Duelo. Bibliografía. 8°. 1885. *Sevilla :* C. Rasco.

> [271 *págs. Tirada de* 100 *ejemplares numerados.*]

—— (— — —) [Barón de la Vega de Hoz]. — Libros de Esgrima, Españoles y Portugueses. Indice formado. 8°. 1891. *Madrid :* De los Huérfanos.

> [*Tirada de* 100 *Ejemplares.*]

LEIPSIG, Verein Universitäts Fechtmeister. Deutsche Hieb-fechtschule für Korb- und Glockenrapier. 8°. 1887. *Leipzig.*

> [95 *pages.*]

LEISURE HOUR (Periodical). 8°. *London.*

> [Vol. XVIII. p. 460. "*Duelling.*"
> „ XXIV. p. 214. "*Duelling in England.*"]

LEITFADEN FÜR DEN UNTERRICHT im Stockfechten zum Gebrauche der K. K. Militär-Bildungs-Anstalten. 8°. 1854. *Wien.*

LEITFADEN FÜR DAS TURNEN und Bajonettiren im Königl-preuszischen Cadetten-Corps. 12°. 1890. *Berlin :* Mittler & Sohn.

LEMOINE (AL.). — Traité d'éducation physique, comprenant la natation, l'escrime à la baïonnette, la boxe française, l'escrime à l'épée, la gymnastique. Gr. 8⁰. 1857. *Gand.*

[*With an atlas of 56 plates.*] (*In Captain Hutton's Collection.*)

LENOX (EARLS OF).—General Challenge by.

[*Harleian MS.* Vol. III. p. 215. cod. 4888. art. 20.]

LENTZ (G. F.). — Hiebfechtlehre für d. deut. Turner z. Ausbildg. im Vorfechten. 16⁰. 1862. *Zwickau.*

—— (—. —.). — Zusammenstellung von Schriften über Leibesübungen. 3. Auflage. 8⁰. 1865. *Berlin :* Lenz.

—— (—. —.). — Zusammenstellung von Schriften über Leibesübungen. [Turnen, Heilgymnastik, Ringen, Spiele, Turnlieder, Schwimmen, Eislauf, Fechten und Turniere.] Herausgegeben von G. F. Lenz, unter Mitwirkg. von E. Angerstein, N. J. Cupérus, G. Eckler, &c. 4te stark verm. Auflage. Gr. 8⁰. 1881. *Berlin :* Lenz.

LÉON et **JAIME**. — M. Mouflet, ou le duel au 3ᵐᵉ étage. Comédie-Vaudeville en un Acte. 12⁰. 1833. *Paris :* Barba.

LE PERCHE (JEAN-BAPTISTE). — *PERCHE (Jean-Baptiste Le).*

LEROY (CHARLES). — Guide du duelliste indélicat. 8⁰. 1884. *Paris :* Tresse.

[*Illustrations de d' Ulzès.*]

LESSING. — De duellis. 4⁰. 1738. *Vitemburg.*

LETAINTURIER (GABRIEL). — Le Duel. 8⁰. 1890. *Nice.*

[85 *pages.*]

LETAINTURIER-FRADIN (GABRIEL). — Le Duel à travers les Âges : Histoire et Législation. Duels Célèbres. Code du Duel. Avec une Préface de A. Tavernier. Gr. 8⁰. 1892. *Paris :* Marpon et Flammarion.

[*Avec figures et planches.*] (*In Captain Hutton's Collection.*)

LEVI (BARON GEORGES HENRI). — *GELLI (J.).*

LEVI (*Refer.* DR. ERNST). — Zur Lehre vom Zweikampfverbrechen. 8⁰. 1889. *Leipzig :* Duncker & Humblot.

ANDRÉ WERNESSON, SIEUR DE LIANCOUR. 1686.

LEWAL (LE GÉNÉRAL). — L'Escrime et ses obligations nouvelles. 12°. 1891. *Paris :* Dentu.

[*177 pages.*]

LEYSER (AUGUST V.). — Meditationes ad pandectas. 4°. 1735. *Halle.*

> [J. 8.　"*De satisfactione de per duellione.*"
> J. 9.　"*De duellis.*" (1741. Leipzig.)]

LHÉRIE. — *BARTHÉLEMY.* — 1830.

L[HOMANDIE] (P. F. M.) [Amateur, élève de feu Texier de la Boëssière]. — La Xiphonomie ou l'art de l'escrime, poëme didactique en quatre chants. 8°. 1821. *Angoulème :* imprimerie Broquisse.

[*Another edition appeared in* 1840.]

—— (—. —. —.). — *ROBAGLIA (A.).* — 1877.

LIANCOUR (WERNESSON DE). — Le maistre d'armes, ou l'exercice de l'espée seule dans sa perfection.　Dédié à Monseigneur le Duc de Bourgogne.　Les attitudes de ce livre ont esté posées par le Sieur de Liancour et gravées par A. Perelle.　Oblong 4°.　1686.　*Paris :* chez l'auteur, Fauxbourg Saint-Germain, rue des Boucheries.

> [*Portrait of the author by Langlois, and* 14 *copperplates, out of the text.*
> "*This book was obviously used as a model by many French and English masters until the latter part of the* 18*th century.*"—*Castle* (E.), "*Schools and Masters of Fence.*"]

—— (— —). — Le maistre d'armes. . . . 2nd edition.　Oblong 4°.　1692.　*Amsterdam.*

—— (— —). — *HUTTON (A.).* — 1892.

LIBRARY (The). — (Magazine.)　8°.　*London :* Elliot Stock.
[Vol. III.　No. 31.　*July* 1891.　"*Bibliography of the Art of Fence.*"]

LIBRO DE RE DUELLO, imperatori, principi, signori, gentil' homini, et de tutti Armi geri, continenti disfide, concordie, pace, casi accadenti, et judicii con ragione, exempli et authoritate de poeti, hystoriographi, philosophi, legisti, canonisti ecclesiastici.　8°.　1521.　*Venetia.*

LIBRO DE ARMAS y arte de la espada.　8°.　1748.
[*MS.* 67 *págs. Mentioned in the* "*Catalogue des livres de la Bibliothèque de M. C. de la Serna Santander.*" Bruxelles. 1803.]

LIBRO DE FIGURAS que demuestran todas las posiciones del manejo de arma del exercicio establecido por S. M. en su Infanteria y Dragones. Con privilegio de S. R. M. 8°. 1762.

[28 *láminas.*]

LIEBETREN (M.). — *CANADIAN* Monthly.

LIECHTENAUERS (JOHANNES ODER HANS). — Fechtregeln.

[*Im germanischen National Museum, Nürnberg. MS. nach Liechtenauer,* 1389. *Mentioned in Schmied-Kowarzik & Kufahl's "Fechtbüchlein"* 1894].

LIECHTENHAUER (JOHANN). — Ritterlich Kunst des langen Schwerts. [1389 (?).]

[*MS. in the Dresden Bibliothek (C. 487). Other copies in the Gotha Bibliothek (Chart 553 fol.), Wien Bibliothek (Ambr. Sammlung 57), and the Vatican Library (Rome), (called Fechtbücher).*]   ★

LIECHTENHAUER (MEISTER). — Kunstbuch. Darinnen auch Meister Lion's, Meister Hundfelder's v. w. Huter.

[*MS. München Bibliothek (Codex Germ. 3712).*]

LIFE (Periodical). 4°. *London.*

[*March 29, 1890. Note on "Bibliography of the Art of Fence."*]

LIGNANO (JOANNIS DE). — Tractatus amenus de duello, excellentisimi viri domi. Cum Additioni bus do Pauli de Lignano.

[" *Tractatus ex varis juris interpretibus collecti.*" Vol. XII. pp. 193–196. *Folio.* 1549. *Lugduni.*] (*In the British Museum.* 5305. *i.*)

—— (— —). — De Duello.

[*Zilettus.* "*Tractatus Universi Juris.*" Tomus XII. pp. 281–284. *Folio.* 1584. *Venetiis.*] (*In the British Museum.* 499. *g.* 6.)

LIKA JOKO (Periodical). Folio. *London :* 12 St. Bride's Street, E.C.

[1895. *January* 26. No. 15, p. 297. "*How Honour was, is, and will be satisfied.*"]

LIMIERS. — *MAUSSUET* (P.). — 1752.

LING (P. H.). — *ROTHSTEIN* (H.). — 1853. 1860. 1872.

—— (—. —.). — *STRÖMBORG* (N.) — 1857.

—— (—. —.). — *TOLLIN* (F.). — 1851.

LINSINGEN (A. VON). — Handbuch zur Anweisung des Soldaten in der Gymnastik und im Bajonetfechten. 8°. 1854. *Hannover:* Hahn.

> [*Mit 30 Abbildungen auf 5 Tafeln.*] (*In Captain Hutton's Collection.*)

LION (J. C.). — Das Stossfechten, zur Lehre und Uebung in Wort und Bild dargestellt. Gr. 8°. 1882. *Hof:* Grau & Co.

> [26 *woodcuts, in the text.*]

—— (—. —.). — Übungsgang der Stossfechtkunst in Beispielen. 8°. 1890. *Hof:* R. Lion.

> [*Aus:* "*Das Stossfechten.*"]

LION (MEISTER). — *LIECHTENHAUER.*   MS.

LIPPINCOTT'S MAGAZINE.   8°.   *Philadelphia, U.S.A.*

> [Vol. IV. p. 540. "*Duelling.*" *By J. J. Reed.*
>   ,, LI. p. 107. "*Fencing.*" *By E. van Schaick.*]

LIPSIUS (JUSTUS). — Ivsti Lipsi Saturnalivm sermonum libri duo; qui de Gladiatoribus. Editio ultima et castigatissima. Cum æneis Figuris. 4°. 1604. *Antverpiæ,* ex officina Plantiniana, apud Joannem Moretum.

> [*Avec grandes gravures sur cuivre et gravure sur le titre. Un des beaux ouvrages de l'imprimerie Plantin, d'Anvers.*]
> (*In Captain Hutton's Collection.*)

LITERARY REPOSITORY. — *RICHARDSON* (S.). — 1765.

LITOMYSKÝ (OBER-LIEUT.). — *ARLOW* (R. von). — 1894.

LITTELL'S LIVING AGE.   *Boston, U.S.A.*

> [Vol. IV. p. 178. *The Duellist's Vow. A Tale.*
>   ,, XV. p. 467. *Duelling in America.*
>   ,, XXVIII. p. 545. *Duelling in England.*
>   ,, XXXVII. p. 39. *Duelling.*
>   ,, LXXXV. p. 17. *Laws of Honor.*
>   ,, CXLIX. p. 707. *The Sword.*]

LITTELL'S MUSEUM OF FOREIGN LITERATURE.   8°. *Philadelphia.*

> [Vol. VII. p. 317. *British Code of Duelling.*
>   ,, XIV. p. 59. *The Duellist.*
>   ,, XXXV. p. 18. *Duelling.*]

LIVINGSTON (Opinion de) sur le Duel et sur la manière le reprimer. 8°. 1829. *Paris.*

LLAVE (D. Pedro de la). — Grabados y temas de armas blancas seguido de algunas consideraciones sobre el mismo asunto por Martinez (D. Guillermo). 4º. 1882. *Madrid:* Gregorio Hernan.

LOCKROY et **BADON** (Edmond). — Un duel sous le Cardinal de Richelieu. Drame en trois actes, mêlé de couplets. 8º. 1834. *Paris:* J. N. Barba.

LOCKWOOD (Henry H.) and **SEAGAR** (E.). — Exercises in small arms and field artillery; arranged for the naval service under an order of the Bureau of Ordnance and Hydrography of the Navy department. Large 8º. 1852. *Philadelphia:* printed by P. K. & P. G. Collins.

[104 *plates*. (Part IV. pp. 151–168. "*Small and Broad Sword Exercises.*")]

LOMBARDELLI (Orazio). — Gioiéllo di sapienza, nel quale si contengono gli avisi d' arme. Con l' inclinazione dei dodici segni celesti et il memorial dell' arte del puntar gli scritti. 8º. 1618. *Firenze:* alle scale di Badia.

[8 *woodcuts*.]

LONDON FIGARO (The). — (Periodical.)   4º.   *London:* 2 Tavistock Street, Covent Garden, W.C.

[1891. *November* 18. *Article on Duelling with reference to the Count of Paris and Captain Armstrong (husband of Madame Melba).*]

LONDON MAGAZINE.   *London:* [1732–1758.]

[Vol.	IV. p. 451.	*Duels. One fought.*
,,	XI. p. 198.	*British Code of Duelling.*
,,	XV. p. 424.	*Duel.*
,,	XIX. p. 139.	*Duel between two sea officers.*
,,	XIX. p. 216.	*Wickedness and impiety of Duelling.*
,,	XX. p. 243.	*Remonstrance against that pernicious practice of Duelling.*
,,	XXII. pp. 471, 473.	*An essay on Duels, and a method of preventing them.*
,,	XXVII. p. 186.	*How far the spirit of Duelling is connected with the manly spirit of defence.*]

LONGIANO (Fausto da). — Duello regolato a le leggi de l' honore con tutti li cartelli missivi e risponsivi in querela volontaria del tempo de cavallieri erranti, de' bravi e de l' età nostra. 1552. *Venetia.*

LONGOLII (CHRIST.). — Civis romanis per duellionis rei defensiones dual. Small 8°. [N.D.] *Venetiis:* Aldus.

[*Circa* 1510.]

LONGOLIUS (CH.). — Per duellionis rei defensiones duæ. [N.D.] *Venetiis:* Aldus.

[*Circa* 1518.]

—— (—.). — Ditto. 8°. 1559. *Vinegia.*

[*Ristampato con un discorso quali sieno armi da cavallieri.*]
(*In Captain Hutton's Collection.*)

LONNERGAN (A.). — The Fencer's Guide, being a Series of every branch required to compose a Complete System of Defence, Whereby the Admirers of Fencing are gradually led from the First Rudiments of that Art, through the most complicated Subtilties yet formed by imagination, or applied to practice, until the Lessons, herein many ways varied, also lead them insensibly on to the deu Methods of Loose Play, which are here laid down, with every Precaution necessary for that Practice. In four parts. Part I. and II. contains such a general explanation of the Small Sword as admits of much greater Variety and Novelty than are to be found in any other work of this kind. Part III. shews, in the Use of the Broad Sword, such an universal knowledge of that Weapon, as may be very applicable to the use of any other that a man can lawfully carry in his hand. Part IV. is a compound of the Three former, explaining and teaching the Cut and Thrust, or Spadroon Play, and that in a more subtile and accurate manner than ever appeared in Print. And to these are added Particular Lessons for the Gentlemen of the Horse, Dragoons, and Light Horse, or Hussars, with some necessary Precautions and an Index, explaining every term of that Art throughout the book. The whole being carefully collected from long Experience and Speculation, is calculated as a Vade-Mecum for Gentlemen of the Army, Navy, Universities, &c. 8°. 1771–2. *London:* sold by W. Griffin, in Catharine Street.

[" *One of the most reliable and complete writers of the ' back-sword' period.*"
—*Hutton's " Cold Steel."*] (*In Captain Hutton's Collection.*)

LOQUE. — Traitez de la guerre et du duel. 12°. 1589. *Lyon.*

[**LOQUE** (BERTRAND DE)]. — Discourses of Warre and single Combat, translated out of [the] French [of B. de L.] by T. Eliot. 2 parts. 8°. 1591. *London:* J. Wolfe.

[*Black Letter. Each part has a separate title-page.*]

LORD BYRON. — *CHAWORTH* (*William*). — Account of his duel with Lord Byron. 1765.

> [*MS. 5832. f. 224. b., in the British Museum.*]

—— —. — *BYRON.*

LORENZ DE RADA (DON FRANCISCO). — *RADA* (*Don F. Lorenz de*).

LORENZINI (F.). — Il duello in generale. 8°. 1852. *Torino :* Tipografia economica.

LOSA (DON MANUEL) [?]. — Nueva ciencia de la destreza de las armas.

—— (— —). — *SOSSA* (*D. Manuel*).

LOTHIAN (MARQUIS OF), on Fencing.

> [*In a letter dated Jan. 23, 1786, to the Duke of Rutland.—Historical Manuscripts Commission (Report of the).*]

LOUIS XIV. — Edict against duels. 1679.

> [*A clause of the edict ran to the effect that "those who doubting their own courage, shall have called in the aid of seconds, thirds, or a greater number, &c.," were to have their coats of arms dishonoured.*]

LOVINO (GIOVANNI ANTONIO) [Milanese]. — Opera intorno alla Practica e Theorica del ben adoperare tutte le sorti di arme ; overo, la Scienza dell' Arme. 4°. Vellum. MS.

> [*MS. in the Bibliothèque Nationale, Paris.*
> *Mentioned in G. F. Bure's "Bibliographie Instructive."* 1764. Paris. (*Vol. "Jurisprudence et Arts."*)]

—— (— —). — Sull' arte di ben maneggiare la spada. Dedicata a Enrico III.

> [*"Codice della bibliot. reale di Parigi, in cui leggesi la dedica a Enrico III."* —Ayala (M. D').—" *Bibliografia.*" 1854.]

LOW (ERNEST W.). — *WINDSOR* Magazine. — 1895.

LOWENHJELM (GREFVE G.). — *MENTZER* (*T. A. v.*). — 1843.

LOZANO (JUAN ANTONIO) [de Ibdes]. — Destierro y azote del libro del Duelo en forma vulgar y predicable. 1640. *Zaragoza.*

LOZÈS (BERTRAND) [Ex-professeur d'escrime aux Écoles Polytechniques]. — Théorie de l'escrime simultanée. 18°. 1862. *Paris :* Dumaine.

(*In Mr. J. R. Garcia Donnell's Collection.*)

LÜBECK (W.). — Lehr- und Handbuch der deutschen Fechtkunst. 8°. 1865. *Frankfurt a. d. O. :* Harnecker.

[*3 lithographs and 7 tables.*]

—— (—.). — Lehr- und Handbuch der deutschen Fechtkunst.
2. Ausgabe. 8°. 1869. *Frankfurt a. d. O. :* Harnecker & Co.

[*Mit 3 Steindruck und 7 Uebungstafeln.*]
(*In Mr. J. R. Garcia Donnell's Collection.*)

LUCA (GUIDO ANTONIO DI). — (?) . . . 1532.

LUCAS (WILLIAM). — The Duellists ; or Men of Honour. 12°.
1805. *London.*

LUCHESI (C.). — Essame dell' Honore cavalleresco de tempi
presenti. 16°. 1625. *Venetia.*

LUDEWIG (D. J. DE). — De veris duellorum. 4°. 1736.
Halæ.

LUEKENOR [MR.]. — Extracts out of the D. of Bullyon's Discourse touching the Lye and the Blow.

[*Harleian MS.* Vol. III. p. 122. cod. 4176. art. 5.]

LUIZ (THOMÁZ). — Tratado das liçõens da Espada preta, e destreza com que hão de usar os jogadores della. Folio. 1685.
Lisboa : Domingos Carneiro.

[29 *páginas y* 1 *lámina.*
Another edition. 8°. 1688. 29 *páginas,* 2 *hojas y* 1 *lámina.*]

LUNAR (D.). — Impugnación fisico-moral á los desafios, dedicada
á la memoria de Cervantes y publicada. 8°. 1806. *Madrid.*

LÜPSCHER (ANT.) und **GÖMMEL** (FR.). — Theorie der Fechtkunst. Eine analytische Abhandlung sämmtl. Stellungen, Stösse,
Paraden, Finten u. s. w., überhaupt aller Bewegungen im Angriffe
u. d. Vertheidigung. Nach der Traité d'escrime par le Chevalier
Chatelain frei bearbeitet. Nebst einer Anleitung über das Hiebfechten. 8°. 1819. *Wien :* Strauss.

[*With 2 tables and 20 plates.*]

—— (—.) —— —— (—.). — *CHATELAIN.* — 1819.

LÜRMANN (J. F.). — Das Ringerbuch des berühmten Faust-
fechters und Ringers Jos. Petter. Aus d. Holländ. übersetzt. 8°.
1814. *Berlin :* Maurer'sche Buchhandlung.

LYANCOUR (WERNESSON DE). — *LIANCOUR* (*W. de*). — 1686.

LYON. — L'escrime à Lyon. Une passe d'armes à la salle Voland. 1874. *Lyon.*

LYTTON (E. BULWER-). — *HARPER'S* New Monthly Magazine. [Vol. XXII. p. 393.]

MAÇA (DON PEDRO). — Duelo y Campo de Batalla que en el año de 1487 tuvieron Don Pedro Maça [de Licana y Cornele] y [Don Frances de Proscita] el Conde de Almenara en la Corte y a presencia de Rey de Navarra. MS. Paper; VIIth cent. Folio.

[*Containing copies of letters and official documents recording the circumstances of the duel.*] (*In the British Museum.* 25,443.)

M'ARTHUR (J.) [of the Royal Navy]. — The Army and Navy Gentleman's Companion: or a new and complete treatise on the theory and practice of Fencing, displaying the intricacies of small sword play, and reducing the Art to the most easy and familiar principles by regular progressive Lessons. Illustrated by mathematical figures, and adorned with elegant engravings after paintings from life, executed in the most masterly manner, representing every material attitude of the Art. Large 4°. 1780–1. *London:* James Lavers.

[*Frontispiece engraved by J. Newton from a drawing by Jas. Sowerby, and 8 plates drawn by the author and engraved by J. Newton.*] (*In Captain Hutton's Collection.*)

—— (—.). — The Army and Navy Gentleman's Companion, &c. 2nd edition. Plates. 4°. 1784. *London:* J. Murray.

[*Dedicated to John, Duke of Argyll.* 19 *large folding plates* (1 *coloured*). 3rd edition. 4°. 1810. London : *Macready.*] (*In the South Kensington Museum.*)

M'BANE (DONALD). — The expert Sword-man's companion: or the True Art of self-defence, with an account of the Author's life and his transactions during the wars with France. To which is annexed the art of gunnerie. 12°. 1728. *Glasgow:* printed by James Duncan.

[*Portrait of M'Bane, and 22 plates, out of the text.*]

M'CARTHY (T. A.). — Quarter-Staff. A practical manual. 12°. 1883. *London:* Sonnenschein & Co.

[*With 25 figures.*]

MACCARTNEY. — Letter concerning the duel between Duke of Hamilton and Lord Mohun. 4°. 1713. *London.*

MACERONE (FRANCIS) [late Aide-de-Camp to Joachim, King of Naples (Murat)]. — Defensive instructions for the people, containing the new and improved combination of arms called Foot-Lancers; miscellaneous instructions on the subject of small arms and ammunition, street and house fighting, and field fortification. 8°. [1832.] *London : J. Smith.*

[*6 folding plates, of which 5 are coloured.*]

MACHRIE (WILLIAM). — Essay upon duelling. 8°. 1711. *Edinburgh.*

MACKAY (CHARLES). — Extraordinary Popular Delusions. 3 vols. 8°. 1841. *London : Routledge.*

[*Vol. I. p. 160. "Duels and Ordeals."*]

M'LAREN (A.). — The Elopement; or a Caution to Ladies. Dramatic Piece. To which is added, The Duellists. 12°. 1811.

MACLAREN (ARCHIBALD). — A Military System of Gymnastic Exercises, and a System of Fencing, for the use of Instructors. To which is appended a Series of Excercises for the Regulation Clubs. By Lieut. Anderson, 64th Regt. 8°. 1868. *London :* Printed under the Superintendence of Her Majesty's Stationery Office.

[*Adjutant General's Office, Horse Guards, April* 1868.
This [1868] *edition contains on pages* 279, 280, *" An Exercise for a Bayonet engaged with a Bayonet," taken entirely from the " Swordsmanship for the Use of Soldiers," by Lieut. Alfred Hutton,* 1866, *without any acknowledgment of the real authorship.*]

MACLAREN (ARCHIBALD). — A Military System of Gymnastic Exercises, and a System of Fencing, for the Use of Instructors. To which is appended a Series of Exercises for Regulation Clubs. 12°. 1877. *London : W. Clowes & Sons.*

[*Another edition. Crown* 8°. 1864. London : *Whittaker.*]

M'CLELLAN (G. B.). — Manual of Bayonet Exercise prepared for the use of the Army of the United States. 8°. 1861. *Philadelphia :* Lippincott & Co.

> [*24 plates, containing 58 figures, out of the text.*
> "*It is confessedly not original. but a mere translation of a foreign author.*"—
> Hutton's "*Fixed Bayonets.*"]
> (*In Captain Hutton's Collection.*)

MACMILLAN'S MAGAZINE. 8°. *London :* Macmillan.

> [Vol. XXIX. p. 304. "*Reminiscences of Duelling in Ireland.*" *By M.* Corr.
> „   XLVIII. p. 195. "*Forms and History of the Sword.*" *By F.* Pollock.]

M'CRINGER (Joel). — A compendious treatise of Modern Education, in which the following subjects are liberally discussed : The nursery, private schools, gallantry, duelling, &c., &c. Folio. 1804. *London.*

> [*Coloured designs both characteristic and illustrative.*]
> (*In Captain Hutton's Collection.*)

MACY (De La). — The Duel in High Life ; or, De la Macy and Emily Clifforde. A Romantic Tale. 2 vols. 8°. 1839. *London :* Holmes.

> (*In the British Museum.* 12,614. i. 12.)

MADAN (Spencer) [Chaplain in Ordinary to His Majesty, Chancellor & Prebendary of Peterborough, D.D.]. — The fatal use of the sword : a Fast Sermon. 8°. 1805.

MADER (J. J.). — De duello. 4°.

> [120 *pages.*]

MADERI (J. J.). — De duello ut ordalei quondam specie dissertatio. 4°. 1679. *Helmstadii.*

MAFFEI (F. S.). — La scienza cavalleresca. 4°. 1710. *Roma.*

MAFFEI (Scipione) [Veronese, Accademico della Crusca]. — Della Scienza chiamata Cavalleresca. Libri Tre. Inquesta quarta edizione visono inserte le Aggiunte del Signor Conte Giovanni Bellincini Modonese, Gentiluomo della Camera secreta del Serenissimo Signor Duca di Modona. All' Illustrissimo Signor Francesco Crivelli di Craizperg. Small 4°. 1717. *Trento :* Giovanni Parone, Stampator Vescovale.

> (*In Captain Hutton's Collection.*)

MAFFIOLI (J. P.). — Dissertation sur le duel, destinée aux écoles de droit. 8°. 1822. *Paris:* A. Bertrand.

MAGAZINE OF AMERICAN HISTORY (Periodical).
[1891. *January.* Vol. XXV. p. 18. "*The Blandensburg Duelling Ground.*"
1891. *December.* Vol. XXVI. p. 443. "*The Duelling Code in North Carolina.*" *By S. B. Weeks.*]

MAGAZINE OF ART (The). — *FURNISS (H.).* — 1889.

MAHON (ANDREW). — *ABBAT (L').* — 1734. 1735.

MAHON (THE O'GORMAN) [M.P.].
["*The O'Gorman Mahon, M.P. for county Carlow, died at noon yesterday, at his residence in Chelsea, in his 88th year. He was called to the Irish Bar in 1834, but never practised. Sixty-one years ago he entered Parliament as member for Clare, and represented Ennis from 1847 to 1852, and Clare from 1879 to 1885. On the death of Mr. J. A. Blake he was elected for county Carlow. The O'Gorman Mahon was one of the most notable characters in the Irish history of the past three-quarters of a century. He was one of the band of Irishmen who fought in the early political campaign of Daniel O'Connell. Half a century ago political duelling was not uncommon, and The O'Gorman Mahon was "out" more than a dozen times. After O'Connell's fatal duel with D'Esterre, O'Connell vowed never to send or accept a challenge. At a public meeting, after O'Connell had spoken, The O'Gorman Mahon rose and said, 'I have made no such resolution—God forbid.'*"—"*The Standard*" (*London*), June 17, 1891.

"*He had fought—popular tradition now converted into history alleges—at least a dozen of 'jules,' whether doing or receiving any harm in any of them does not appear. He was the second of O'Connell in the duel with D'Esterre, which was fatal to the latter. O'Connell, as is well known, refused ever afterwards either to send or to accept a challenge. His success was accidental, and the accident might have been on the other side. He could not count on having the same luck always. The O'Gorman Mahon had no such qualms, and may possibly have had some suspicion as to his friend's motives. 'God forbid,' he piously said, 'that he should ever make such a resolution,' and report has it that he carried this temper far beyond his eightieth year, and was, less than a year ago, with difficulty persuaded from challenging Mr. Parnell for insulting Mr. Gladstone. When, however, The O'Gorman Mahon was dexterously reminded that the last English challenge, of which there is any knowledge, was sent by Mr. Labouchere to the proprietor of the 'Daily Telegraph,' and declined by the latter gentleman, who did not wish to incur the remorse of Emile de Girardin, he felt that duelling in England had become ridiculous. This, at least, is our inference.*"—"*The Saturday Review,*" June 20, 1891.

"*In an article which Mr. Gladstone contributed to the 'Nineteenth Century' some two or three years ago, there occurs a pretty compliment to The O'Gorman Mahon. It was 'à propos' of O'Connell's duel with D'Esterre, and it ran:—'In this connection the House of Commons is now familiar with the stately appearance of an Irish gentleman advanced in life, who*" *carries with him the halo of an extraordinary reputation as a duellist, but who is conspicuous among all his contemporaries for his singularly beautiful and gentle manners.' The O'Gorman's faith in the duello as a means of settling difficulties among gentlemen survived long after the Repeal days, and during the Parliament of 1874–80 he was very anxious to fight a Ministerialist who had given him offence. The last person whom he wished to call out was (as we mentioned yesterday) Mr. Parnell."—" Pall Mall Gazette," June 18, 1891.]*

MAIER (HECTOR) [Burger zu Augsburg]. — Kunstfechtbuch. Folio. 1542.

    [MS. in Dresden Bibliothek. (Coloured drawings.)]

—— (—). — *MAIR (Paul Hector).*

MAINDRON (M.). — Les Armes. 8°. 1891. *Paris:* Librairies-Imprimeries réunies.

    [Illustré. Fait partie de la Bibliothèque de l'Enseignement des Beaux-Arts.]

MAIR (PAUL HECTOR). — Ein Fechtbuch.

    [MS. in the Kgl. Bibliothek, Dresden.
    Dr. K. Wassmannsdorff fully describes this MS. in his reprint of Auerswald's " Ringerkunst," 1869.]

MAITLAND (PROFESSOR F. W.). — Select Pleas of the Crown. Edited for the Selden Society.

    [Contains a fac-simile of a fight from a thirteenth-century legal MS. preserved in the Record Office, Chancery Lane, London.]

MALCOM (HOWARD). — Theological Index. References to the Principal Works in every department of Religious Literature. 8°. 1868. *Boston (U.S.):* Gould & Lincoln.

    [Pages 156, 157. *Duelling.*] *(In the British Museum. BB. A. b. 15.)*

MALENZA (G. B.). — Cenni critici sull' opera "La Giurisprudenza del duello di Fambri." 4°. 1871. *Venezia.*

MALEVOLTI (D'ANGELO). — *DIDEROT* et d'Alembert. — 1775.

[**MALIGRE** (P. F.)]. — Le Duel de Niort, ou histoire d'un plaisant mariage, petit poëme dédié aux amateurs de la gaieté françoise, par un ancien condisciple de l'auteur du " Baron de Brac." 12°. An IX. (1803).

MALLET (A. MANUSSON). — Les Travaux de Mars, ou l'Art de la Guerre. 1685. *Amsterdam.*

    [Tome III. p. 30. *Description and engraving of the bayonet then in use.*]

MALVUS (Franz). — Die Gebräuche beim Zweikampf. 8°. 1887. *Berlin:* Mayer & Müller.

[*42 pages.*]

MANCHA Y GIRON (Don Martin Cerón). — Fiel Dispertador y Mayor amigo la malicia: confundiendo su exaltacion en la duda que padece en la destreza y Filosofia de las Armas. 4°. 1708. *Granada:* T. Copado.

MANCIOLINO (Antonio) [Bolognese]. — Opera nova, dove sono tutti li documenti e vantaggi che si ponno havere nel mestier de l'armi d'ogni sorte, novemente correcta et stampata. 16°. 1531. *Vinegia:* Per N. d'Aristotile, detto Zoppino.

[*A few woodcuts, unconnected with the text.*] (*In the British Museum.*)

MANDAT d. König von Pohlen und Churfürst von Sachsen wider Selbstrache und Duelle, de dato Crahan, 15 April 1706. Folio. *Dresden.*

MANDAT wider Selbstrache und Duelle de dato anno 1712. *Weissenfels.*

M[ANDERVILLE] (B[ermardede] de). — Christianity. An enquiry into the origin of honour and the usefulness of Christianity in War. 8°. 1732.

[*An English advocate for duelling, quoted by Sir Lucius O'Trigger.*]

MANEGGIO DELLA SCIABOLA per uso della brigata lancieri, redatta da una guardia di ufficiali della stessa arma. 1840. *Napoli.*

MANGANO (Guido Antonio del) [Pavese]. — Riflessioni filosofiche sopra l'arte della scherma. 8°. 1781. *Pavia.*

MANGIN (Edw.) [of Bath]. — An Essay on Duelling, translated from the French. 8°. 1832. *Bath.*

MANUAL DEL BARATERO ó arte de manejar la navaja, el cuchillo y la tijera de los gitanos. 8°. 1849. *Madrid:* A. Goya.

[*Engravings in the text.*] (*In Captain Hutton's Collection.*)

MANUAL EXERCISES FOR THE RIFLE and Carbine and Bayonet Exercise. 32°. 1885. *London:* Horse Guards.

MANUAL OF INSTRUCTION FOR SINGLE-STICK DRILL.
8°. 1887. *London :* Harrison & Sons.

MANUAL OF NEW BAYONET and Firing Exercises for
Martini-Henry Rifle. 32°. 1889. *London :* Simpkin.

MANUEL D'ESCRIME MILITAIRE, approuvé par le Ministre
de la Guerre, le 18 mai 1877. 18°. 1877. *Paris.*
(In Captain Hutton's Collection.)

MANUEL D'ESCRIME, approuvé par le Ministre de la Guerre.
32°. 1878. *Paris :* J. Dumaine.
[40 *figures.*]

MANUEL D'ESCRIME, approuvé par M. le Ministre de la
Guerre, le 18 mai 1877. 32°. 1881. *Paris :* J. Dumaine.
[*Avec figures dans le texte.*]

MANUEL D'ESCRIME, approuvé par M. le Ministre de la Guerre,
le 18 mai 1877. 32°. 1883. *Paris :* L. Baudoni et Cie.
[2nd *edition,* 1888.
3rd *edition.* 18°. 1890. Paris : *L. Baudoni et Cie.*
4th *edition,* 1893.]

MANUEL DE GYMNASTIQUE (gymnastique d'assouplissement
et gymnastique appliquée, natation, boxe française, bâton et canne);
approuvé par M. le Ministre de la Guerre, le 26 juillet 1877. 18°.
1879. *Paris :* J. Dumaine.
[*With numerous figures.*] (*In Captain Hutton's Collection.*)

MANUEL D'HYGIÈNE ATHLÉTIQUE. A l'Usage des Lycéens
et des Jeunes gens des Associations Athlétiques. 12°. 1895. *Paris :*
Felix Alcon.
[Pages 53–56, *L'Escrime.*]

**MANUEL POUR L'ENSEIGNEMENT DE LA GYMNASTIQUE
ET DE L'ESCRIME,** publié par ordre de M. le Ministre de la
Marine et des Colonies. 18°. 1875. *Paris :* J. Dumaine.
[*With numerous figures.*]

MANZINI (G. B.).—Del torneo ultimamente fatto in Bologna.
4°. 1639. *Bologna.*
(In the Art Library, South Kensington Museum.)

MARCELLI (Francesco Antonio) [Maestro di scherma in Roma].—
Regole della scherma insegnate de Lelio e Titta Marcelli, scritte da

FRANCESCO ANTONIO MARCELLI. 1686.

Figlio e nipote, e Maestro di Scherma in Roma.

Francesco Antonio Marcelli, figlio e nipote, e maestro di scherma in
Roma. Opera non meno utile che necessaria a chiunque desidera
far profitto in questa professione. Dedicata alla sacra rael Maestà
di Christina Alessandra regina di Suetia. Parte prima : Regole
della spada sola. Parte seconda : Regole della scherma. Nella
quale si spiegano le regole della spada e del pugnale insegnate da
Titta Marcelli ; con le regole di maneggiar la Spada col brochiere,
targa, rotella, cappa, lanterna ; col modo di giocar la spada contro la
sciabola. In 2 parts. 4°. 1686. *Roma.*

[*Frontispiece, containing the portraits of the Marcelli who were fencing-
masters, seven in number. Copperplates, in the text, from designs by the
author himself.*]
(*In the British Museum ; Bodleian Library ; Art Library, South Kensington
Museum ; and Captain Hutton's Collection.*)

MARCHE (CLAUDE LA).—*LAMARCHE* (*Claude*).

MARCHE (OLIVIER DE LA). — Les mémoires. Small 4°. 1567.
Bruxelles.

[*3e édition, reuë & augmenté d'un Estat particulier de la maison du Charles
Le Hardy, composé du mesme Auteur, & non imprimécy-devant. Sm. 4°.
1616. Bruxelles : Hubert Antoine.*]

—— (— — —).—*TRAITÉS* du Duel Judiciaire. — 1872.

—— (— — —).—*TRAITÉS* et advis. — 1586.

MARCHE (OLIVIER LE) [Count of]. —Sur le Gage de Bataille.

[*A treatise. Dedicated to Philip, Arch-Duke of Austria. Inserted by the
same author, " Le livre du Seigneur de Lisle Adam, pour gaige de bataille.
(This author calls himself Jehan de Villers, Seigneur de Lisle Adam.) It is
addressed to the grandfather of the other Philip. A French MS. of 35
leaves of very thick vellum.*]
(*In the British Museum. Harl. 5217.*)

MARCHEGAY (PAUL). — Duel Judiciaire entre deux commu-
nantés religieuses. 1098.

[*Article paru dans la " Bibliothèque de l'École des Chartes,*" 1839–1840, 1e
Série, Tome I. pp. 552–564.]

MARCHINI (ANTONIO).

[*M. Buja à page 114 de son ouvrage, dit qu' Antonio Marchini de Rome
écrivit.*]

MARCHINI (J.). — Il duello esaminato. 16°. 1879. *Savona.*
[*31 pages.*] (*In the British Museum. 8425. aa. 9.*)

MARCHIONNI (ALBERTO). — Trattato di scherma sopra un nuovo sistema di guoco misto di scuola italiana e francese. 8°. 1847. *Firenze.*

     [*5 lithographed folding plates, and woodcuts in the text.*]

MARCHIONNI (ALBERTO) e **ENRICHETTI** (C.). — Trattato di scherma. 8°. 1868. *Firenze:* Tip. Fioretti.

MARCO (ALESSANDRO DI) [Professore di scherma Napoletano maestro de due collegj Capece e Macedonio e d'altri cavalieri]. — Ragionamenti accademici intorno all' arte della scherma. 8°. 1758. *Napoli.*

—— (— —). — Discorsi instruttivi ne' quali si tratta in particolare intorno all' arte della scherma. 8°. 1759. *Napoli.*

—— (— —). — Riflessioni fisiche e geometriche circa la misura del tempo ed equilibrio di quello e della natural disposizione ed agilità dei competitori in materia di scherma e regolamenti essenziali per saggiamente munirsi da ogni inconsiderato periglio sul cimento della spada nuda. 12°. 1761. *Napoli.*

MARCY [COLONEL]. — Memoir on Swords. 8°. 1860. *London:* Weale.

MAREY-MONGE (GUILLAUME STANISLAS) [Général français, né à Nuits en 1796]. — Mémoire sur les armes blanches. 8°. 1841. *Strasbourg:* Imprimerie Silbermann.

—— (— —). — Memoir on Swords, translated by Lieut.-Colonel H. H. Maxwell. 12°. 1860. *London:* Virtue (Weale's Series).
     [*Another edition.* 8°. 1856. London.]
     (*In the Royal United Service Institution Library, Whitehall, London.*)

MARÍN (DON ANTONIO). — Esgrima á la bayoneta, ó manejo de dicha arma aplicado á los ejercicios y maniobras de la infantería aprobado por S. M. y mandado observar por Real órden de 13 de setiembre de 1859. Traducido del francés de Th. Pinette. 1859. *Cádiz.*
     [*168 pp., 3 láminas. Tiene un "Apéndice sobre el Manejo de Sable."*]

—— (— —). — Tratado completo de esgrima, compuesto por el célebre profesor y maestro M. F. Lafaugère, adoptado últimamente

OPERA
NOVA DE
ACHILLE MA
ROZZO BOLOGNE
SE, MASTRO GE
NERALE DE
LARTE
DE LAR
MI.

[ACHILLE MAROZZO, DI BOLOGNA. 4°. 1536. MUTINÆ.]

en Francia, y traducido al español. 8°. 1841. *Madrid :* Alegría
y Charlaim.

[*3 hojas de tables y 6 láminas que se doblan.*]

MARÍN (Don Antonio). — Esgrima á la bayoneta por J.
Pinette. Traducido al Castellano. 4°. 1850. *San Fernando :*
Libreria Española.

——— (— —). — *LAFFARGÈRE (F.).* —1841.

MARMIETTA (Pierre). — L'Académiste françois qui propose
des moyens pour bannir les duels e pour déraciner les vices qui sont
aujourd'huy si. frequens purmy la noblesse de cet estat. 1615.
Paris.

MAROZZO (Archille) [di Bologna]. — Opera nova. 4°. 1517.
Venetia : M. Sessa.

[" *Marozzo is generally looked upon as the first writer of note on the art of
fencing. It would be perhaps wiser to consider him as the greatest teacher
of the old school, the rough and undisciplined swordsmanship of which
depended as much on dash and violence and sudden inspiration as on carefully cultivated skill.*"—*Castle's* " *Schools and Masters of Fence.*"]

——— (—) [Maestro generale de l'arte de l'armi]. — Opera nova.
Chiamata duello, o vero fiore dell' armi de singulari abattimēti offen-
sivi et diffensivi . . . che tratta de casi occorēti ne l'arte militare
. . . e tratta de gli abattimēti de tutte l'armi . . . cō le figure che
dimostrano cō l'armi ī mano tutti gli effetti et guardie possano far,
&c. 4°. 1536. *Mutinæ*, in ædibus venerabilis D. Antonii Bergolæ
sacerdotis ac civis Mutin. XXIII. Idus Maii.

[82 *woodcuts.*]

(*In the British Museum* (7907. c. 5), *South Kensington Museum, and Captain
Hutton's Collection.*)

[*Another edition.* 4°. (1540. *Modena* (?).)]
(*In the British Museum.* 7906. cc. 8.)

——— (—). — Opera nova . . . &c. 2nd edition. 4°. 1550.
Venetia : Stampata per Giovane Padouano, ad instantia de Mar-
chior Sessa.

(*In the British Museum.* 7906. e. 13.)

——— (—). — Opera nova . . . &c. 3rd edition. 4°. 1568.
Venetia : Ant. Pinargenti.

[76 *figures, out of text.*]

MAROZZO (ARCHILLE). — Arte dell' Armi. Ricorretto, et ornato di nuove figure in rame. 4°. 1568. *Venetia:* Appresso Antonio Pinargenti.

> [24 *copperplates in the text. The colophon bears the date* 1569. *Contains more matter than the previous editions, and brought under the care of the painter Giulio Fontana.*]
>
> (*In the British Museum, and Captain Hutton's Collection.*)

—— (—). — Arte dell' Armi . . . &c. 5th edition. 4°. 1615. *Verona.*

—— (—). — *HUTTON* (*A.*). — 1892.

> [*Marozzo gives the most copious instructions as to the mode of procedure in an encounter, with the seizure in dagger-play, or the method for an unarmed man attacked by one armed with a knife.*
>
> *Marozzo est le premier qui ait traité cette matière d'une façon presque complète et bien définie. Ses précurseurs ne firent qu'ébaucher quelques principes; les auteurs qui écrivirent après lui l'ont souvent consulté.—Les nombreuses estampes gr. sur bois qui décorent ce rare et beau volume, sont assez curieuses et intéressantes pour les costumes de l'époque.*
>
> "*There was in Bologna, in the second quarter of the sixteenth century, a celebrated school of arms, which, no doubt, owed much of its wide reputation to the perpetual influx and exodus of students into and out of the University. It is there that, about* 1530, *flourished one Achille Marozzo, who proclaimed himself on the title-pages of his books ' Master-General of the Art of Arms.' He was the first to set forth in print something which approached to a regular system of fence.*"—*Castle* (E.), "*The Story of Swordsmanship.*" "*The National Review,*" *May* 1891.]

MARS HIS FEILD, or The Exercise of Armes, wherein in lively figures is shewn the Right use and perfect manner of Handling the Buckler, Sword, and Pike. With the wordes of Command and Brefe instructions correspondent to every Posture. 12°. [1611 ?] *London.*

> [16 *copperplates, with explanatory legends. No text.*]
>
> (*In the Bodleian Library.*)

MARS [*pseudonyme* de Maurice Bonvoisin, dessinateur et caricaturiste, né à Verviers (Belgique) en 1849]. — L'Escrime à l'Elysée. Album in folio. 1882. *Paris.*

> [*Silhouettes destireurs, préface par A. Tavernier, portrait de Mars par Carolus Duran, Paris, ateliers de reproductions artistiques. Tirage à cent épreuves numérotées.*]

MARTAINVILLE (ALPHONSE). — Le Duel impossible. Comédie en un acte et en prose. 12°. 1803. *Paris:* Barba.

> [*Représentée, pour la première fois, sur le théâtre Louvois, le 7 ventose, an xi.*]
>
> (*In the British Museum.* 11,738. i. 7. (3.))

MARTELLI (C.) — An improved system of fencing, wherein the use of the small sword is rendered perfectly plain and familiar : being a clear description and explanation of the various thrusts used, with the safest and best methods of parrying, as practised in the present age. To which is added a treatise on the art of attack and defence. 8º. 1819. *London :* J. Bailey.

[1 *folding plate, with 12 figures.*]
(*In Captain Hutton and Mr. J. R. Garcia Donnell's Collections.*)

MARTIN (EDMOND). — Étude Juridique. Le Duel. 8º. 1877. *Paris :* Durand.

MARTIN (LE SIEUR) [Maistre en fait d'armes de l'académie de Strasbourg]. — Le Maistre d'armes, ou l'abrégé de l'exercice de l'épée. Orné de figures en taille-douce. 12º. 1737. *Strasbourg :* Chez l'auteur, au Poële des Maréchaux.

[16 *copperplates, out of text. Contains a curious proof of the influence of the Paris Academy on matters of fence in the shape of an approbation of the professed and privileged " maistres en fait d'armes" of that corporation.*]

MARTINEZ (DON CIRILO ALVAREZ). — Ensayo histórico-filosófico-legal sobre el duel. 4º. 1847. *Madrid.*

MARTINEZ (D. GUILLERMO). — *LLAVE* (D. Pedro de la). — 1882.

MARTINEZ (DON JUAN JOSÉ). — Ejercicio del sable, mandado observar por el Gefe de Escuadra D. Angel Laborde y Navarra, á bordo de los Bageles de S. M. del Apostadero de la Habana. Traducido del inglés. 4º. 1832. *Habana :* José Boloña.

[1 *plate.*]

MARTINS FIRME (MANUEL). — Espada firme o firme tractado para o jogo da espada preta e branca. Folio. 8º. 1744. *Evora :* na offico da Univ.

[xxxvi *and* 86 *pages.*]   (*In the Library of J. C. de Figaniere.*)

MARY (JULES) & **GRISIER** (GEORGES). — Le Maître d'Armes, drame en cinq actes [and in prose]. 12º. 1893. *Paris.*

[155 *pages.*
A play produced in Paris on October 13, 1892, at the Théâtre de la Porte Saint Martin, where it was favourably received. Translated from the French, and adapted "to the usages" of the British stage, by Messrs. Brandon Thomas and Clement Scott, under the title of " The Swordsman's

Daughter," and given for the first time in London at the Adelphi Theatre, August 31, 1895.

" *Here is another striking instance of the old adage that truth is stranger than fiction.* Attention was very naturally drawn both in Paris and in London to the apparent improbability and glaring inconsistency of the climax to the French play ' Maître d'Armes,' which has been faithfully retained in the new Adelphi version of the drama known as ' The Swordsman's Daughter.' The so-called improbability, or absurdity, as it has been called, is where Vibrac, the fencing-master, appears in open court apparently as a witness favourable to Rochefiere, his friend and pupil, who has ruined his child ; whereas in reality he desires to avenge his daughter's dishonour. The evidence that Vibrac has to give is turned, by the request of the jury, into a practical illustration of a duel in which Rochefiere, by a foul stroke, had killed his adversary. By a repetition of the same stroke Vibrac kills Rochefiere, and it is recorded by the judge as an accident.

" *Now the French authors are anxious that it should be known that this very climax—which is, so to speak, the pivot of the play—was based on an actual case which did occur in Paris, not earlier than the year 1850. It is described in the ' Causes Célèbres,' a book which is the French equivalent to our ' Newgate Calendar.' In this case the duel was repeated, and, as in the play, the professor who undertook to demonstrate the stroke, wounded the accused principal, though, happily, not fatally. But this is not all. In 1869, at Tlemcen, in the French provinces of Algeria, an almost identical case occurred, and, although the one combatant had only wounded his adversary in the duel, yet, when it was re-enacted before the presiding judge, a Professor Gautier, who came from Cairo to give evidence, ' inadvertently' guided the other man's sword to his own breast,' his lungs were pierced, and he died shortly afterwards. Boulanger, it will be well remembered, made the same slip in his duel with Floquet, but ' guided' the sword to his neck, not his breast.*

" *With regard to the re-enactment of a dramatic incident in open court, which appears so strange to an English audience, it is unnecessary for me to state that this ' reconstruction' of a case, as it is called in France, is quite commonly resorted to in the French courts of law, and it is not at all an unusual occurrence to have the entire ' mise en scène' of a murder, for example, built up in the court, and people are engaged to go through the event, as it is judged to have occurred, in order to assist a jury to arrive at a verdict with greater decision. This must be a survival of the old ' Ordeal by Touch,' which, by the way, was the subject of a very admirable drama, written by Richard Lee, and produced some years back at the Princess's Theatre.*

" *The French authors of ' Maître d'Armes,' MM. Jules Mary and Georges Grisier, have courteously asked that these facts should be placed before the public that has received their work with such interest in England, so I hasten to comply with their request.*

" *It may be noted that M. Cotis, who gives an exhibition of fencing in the second act of the new play, has a small Salle d'Armes on the Boulevard St. Martin, opposite the Porte St. Martin Theatre, where he gives occasional lessons, and sometimes ' coaches' French actors in the art of fencing. His opponent, M. Beau, is a distinguished amateur, not a professional fencer, and he has served the usual term in the French Army. It is proposed, in a few weeks' time, to bring over from Paris two experienced professors in the French exercise known as ' la savate,' a veritable kicking match, and a*

wonderful sight when well done."—("*Drama of the Day,*" *by Clement Scott.*)—"*The Daily Telegraph,*" *September* 14, 1895.
(*A review of the play appears in the Appendix at the end of this volume.*)]

MARZIOLI (FRANCESCO). — Precetti Militari, consacrati all' immortal nome dell' altezza Serenissima, di Ferdinando Maria, Dvca dell' vna e dell' altra Baviera, e del Svperiore Palatinato Elettorale del Sacro Romano Impero, etc. 1670. *Bologna.*

> [*La première partie de cet ouvrage traite du* "*Maneggio Militare della picca*" *et l'escrime de la pique y est démontrée en* 17 *feuillets et par* 60 *figures gravées sur cuivre.*]

—— (—) [Bresciano]. — Precetti Militari. Folio. 1673. *Bologna.*
> [*Numerous plates.*]

MASCOT (The). — (Periodical.) Folio. *London.*
> [1895, *December* 7. "*An Affair of Honour.*"]

MASIELLO (FERDINANDO). — La Scherma Italiana di spada e di sciabola. 8°. 1887. *Firenze :* G. Civelli.
> [70 *lithographed plates and figures in the text.*]
> (*In Captain Hutton's Collection.*)

—— (—). — La Scherma di sciabola a Cavallo. 8°. 1891. *Firenze.*
> [104 *pages.*]

—— (—). — *ANGELINI* (*A.*). — 1888.

—— (—). — *GELLI* (*J.*). — 1890.

—— (—). — *NINI* (*Conte Giuseppe*).

—— (—). — *WRIGHT* (*F. V.*). — 1889.

MASON (R. O.). — Reasons that exist for reviving the use of the Long Bow, with the Pike. 8°. 1798. *London :* Egerton.
(*In the Royal United Service Institution Library, Whitehall, London.*)

MASSA (ANT.). — Contra usum duelli. 4°. 1554. *Roma.*
> [99 *pages.*]

—— (—.). — Contra l'uso del duello. . . . Con una lettera . . . del medesimo soggetto [by A. Stellino]. 8°. 1555. *Venetia.*
(*In the British Museum.* 526. *f.* 5. (1.))

—— (—.). — Contra usum duelli. 1620. 8°. *Tübingœ.*
(*In the British Museum.* 500. *a.* 15. (4.))

MASSAE (ANTONII). — Gallesii civis Romani contra vsum duelli. [*Zilettus, "Tractatus Universi Juris."* Tomus XII. pp. 313–321. *Folio.* 1584. Venetiis.] (*In the British Museum.* 499. g. 6.)

MASSI (COUSTARD DE). — Histoire de duels en France. 8°. 1768. *Londres:* P. Elmsly.

[" *Very few copies of this little but curious compilation were printed; and those distributed only among select friends, because, as the performance would be considered in France as an effort to revive a ferocious practice, against which so many rigorous edicts have been enacted, it might probably subject the author to a prosecution, especially on account of his warm panegyric on duelling at the conclusion."—Sir L. O'Trigger.*]

—— (—— ——). — Duelling in all Countries. Translated from the French of M. C. de M. . . . With introduction and concluding chapters by Sir Lucius O'Trigger [pseud.]. 8°. [1880.] *London:* Newman & Co.

[xxxix *and* 116 *pages.*] (*In Mr. J. R. Garcia Donnell's Collection.*)

—— (—— ——). — *MASSY* (*Coustard*). — 1770.

MASSON. — Répression du duel. 8°. 1838. *Auch:* P. Roger.

MASSUET (P.). — La science des personnes de cour, d'épée et de robe. Commensée par de Chevigny, continué par de Limiers, revue, corrigée et augméntée par P. Massuet. 12°. 1752. *Amsterdam.*

—— (—.). — Suite de la science personnes de cour, etc. Contenant les elemens de la philosophie moderne. 12°. 1757. *Amsterdam.*

MASSY (COUSTARD). — The history of duelling. In two parts. Containing the origin, progress, revolutions and present state of duelling in France and England ; including many curious historical anecdotes. (The history of duelling in France, translated from the French of M. C. de M.) 12°. 1770. *London :* E. & C. Dilly.

[176 *pages.*] (*In the British Museum.* T. 1830. (2.))

MATHEWSON (T.) [Lieutenant and Riding Master in the late Roxbrough Fencible Cavalry]. — Fencing familiarised, or a new treatise on the art of the Scotch broad sword, shewing the superiority of that weapon when opposed to an enemy armed with a spear, pike, or gun and bayonet. 8°. 1805. *Salford:* Printed by W. Cowdray, junr.

[13 *plates, out of the text.*] (*In Captain Hutton's Collection.*)

MATTEI (Francesco Antonio). — Della scherma napoletana, discorso primo, dove, sotto il titolo dell' impossibile possibile, si prova che la scherma sia scienza e non arte si danno le vere norme di spada e pugnale; discor o secondo, dove si danno le vere norme di spada sola. 4°. 1669. *Foggia :* Novello de Bonis.

MAUPASSANT (Guy de). — *VAUX (Baron de).* — 1882.

MAUROY (Victor). — Mémento de l'escrimeur. 12°. 1887. *Paris :* Libraire des Bibliophiles.

MAXWELL (H. H.) [Colonel]. — *MARCY (Colonel).* — 1856.

MAŸR (Paulus). — MS. (A small 4° volume with 36 copper-plates of armed men. No letterpress. A short Latin sentence under each figure. (Hainrich Ullrich in Normbergæ Schulp. excudit.)

MAZO (Bondi di). — *BONDI (Di Mazo).* — 1696.

MEDEM (Landger.-R. Prof. Dr. Rud.). — Die Duellfrage. 2. verm. Auflage. Gr. 8°. 1890. *Greifswald :* J. Abel.
[45 *pages.*]

MEDLAND (W. M.) and **WEOBLY** (Charles). — A Collection of Remarkable and Interesting Criminals' Trials for Murder, Assault, Duelling, &c., with biographical sketches of Lord Eldon and Mr. Mingay. 2 vols. 8°. 1808.
[*Portraits of Lord Eldon and Mr. Mingay.*]

MEDWIN (Captain). — *BENTLEY'S* Miscellany.

MEICKLE (R.). — The Fencer's Manual, a practical treatise on the small sword, &c. 8°. 1859. *Melbourne.*
[*With illustrations.*]

MEINERS (C.) und **SPITTER** (L. T.). — Neues Göttingisches historisches Magazin. 8°. 1793. *Hannover :* Helwing.
[Band II. pp. 471–523. "*Ueber die gymnastischen, und kriegerischen Uebungen verschiedener Völker.*"]

MEISTER. Prakt. Bemerkungen aus dem Criminalrecht. 2 Bände. 1751–55. *Göttingen.*
[*In direckten Vorsatz in Anwendung auf Duell.*]

MÉLESVILLE et RAOUL. — Une Affaire d'Honneur. Comédie-vaudeville en un acte. 12°. 1832. *Paris :* Barba.

MÉLESVILLE. — *THÉAULON.* — 1827.

MELINA (ALMERICO). — La nuova scherma mista e la vera italiana. 8°. 1888. *Napoli :* de Angelis.

MELLESVILLE, MERLE, et BOIRIE. — Le Duel et le Baptême. Drame en trois actes, en prose. 12°. 1818. *Paris :* Fages.

MELLO PACHECO DE RESENDE (JOSÉ DE). — Instrucção do jogo d'espada a pé e a cavallo para ser posto em pratica na eschola militar, e nos corpos de cavallaria e artilheria montada do exercito do Brasil. 1839. *Rio de Janeiro :* Brasileira.

— — — — (— —). — Instrucções de cavalleria para uso do corpos d'esta arma, de primeira linha e da Guardia Nacional contendo alem da eschola a pé, e jogo de espada e as evoluções convenientes. 8°. 1859. *Rio de Janeiro.*

[198 *pages.*]

MELVILLE (ROBERT)[Lieutenant-General].—*ARCHÆOLOGIA.*

MELZO (FR. LVDOVICO). — Reglas Militares sobre et govierno y servicio particolar de la Cavalleria. Folio. 1619. *Milan :* Baptista Bidelo.

[17 *figvra.*]

MENDÈS (CATULLE). — *VAUX.* — 1885.

MENDEZ (TH. A.). — Essai sur le Duel. 8°. 1854. *Paris :* Appert et Vavasseur.

MÉNDEZ DE CARMONA (TAMARIS). — *CARMONA (T. M. de).*

MENDIETTA-MAGLIOCCO (SALVATORE) [Furiere : maestro di scherma alla scuola normale di fanteria]. — Manuale della scherma di sciabola. 12°. 1868. *Parma.*

[*With plates.*]

—— (—). — Manuale della scherma di sciabola. 8°. 1878. *Parma.*

MENDOZA (DON MIGUEL PEREZ DE). — Defensa de la doctrina y destreza de las armes. 4°. 1665. *Madrid.*

188

MENDOZA Y QUIJADA (Don Miguel Pérez de). — Espejo de la Filosofia y Mathemática de las Armas. Breve resumen de la verdadera destreza. MSS.

——— — — (— — — —) [Maestro de la destreza]. — Principios de los cinco svjetos principales de que se compone la Philosofia y matemática de las armas, practica y especulativa. 8°. 1672. *Pamplona:* M. G. de Zabala.

(*In the Bibl. de Ingenieros, del Senado, de Fernandez San Roman.*)

—— — **QUIXADA** (— — — —). — Resúmen de la verdadera destreza de las armas, en treinta y ocho asserciones refuidas y advertidas con demonstraciones prácticas deducido de las dos obras principales que tiene escritas su autor. 4°. 1675. *Madrid:* Francisco Sanz.

[*Dedicada á Cárlos II. 1 lámina plegada, 21 hojas prels. y 73 foliadas.*]
(*In the Bibl. de Ingenieros, del Senado, de Fernandez San Roman.*)

MENESSIEZ. — Mémoire pour le sieur Menessiez, Maître en fait d'armes, et maître des pages de M. le Comte de Clermont. Contre la Communauté des Maîtres en fait d'armes. 4°. 1763. *Paris:* de l'Imprimerie Simon.

[**MENESTRIER** (Clavde François)]. — Traite de Tovrnois, Jovstes Carrovsels, et avtres spectacles pvblics. 4°. 1669. *Lyon:* Jacqves Mvgvet.

MENSUR, DUELL UND VERRUF in Beziehung zu den studentischen Korporationen. Von e. Couleurstudenten. 8°. 1890. *Leipzig:* Bouman.

MENTZER (T. A. v.). — Svenska Kavalleriets fäktning, enligt Generalen m. m. Grefve G. Löwenhjelm's method. 8°. 1843. *Stockholm.*

MENZA (G. di). — Il duello leale e il duello sleale. 4°. 1875. *Palermo.*

MERCURIALIS (Hieronymus). — Artis Gymnasticæ apud antiquos celeberrimæ, nostris temporibus ignoratæ, libri sex, Palestræ descriptio ex Vitruvio. 4°. 1569. *Venetiis:* Apud Juntas.

(*In the British Museum. 785. h. 2.*)

MERCURIALIS (HIERONYMUS). — De arte Gymnastica libri sex. 4°. 1569. *Venetiis :* Apud Juntas.

(In the British Museum. 785. h. 2.)

—— (—). — Ditto. 4°. 1573. *Venetiis :* Apud Juntas.

(In the British Museum. 557. e. 26.)

—— (—). — De arte Gymnastica libri sex. In quibus ex exercitationum omnium vetustarum genera, loca, modi, facultates et quidquid denique ad corporis humani exercitationes pertinet, diligenter explicatur. 4°. 1577. *Parisiis :* apud Jacobum du Puys.

—— (—). — Ditto. 4°. 1587. *Venetiis :* Apud Juntas.

[Très-belles figures en bois.]

—— (—). — De arte Gymnastica libri sex. In quibus exercitationum omnium vetustarum genera, loca, modi, facultates et quidquid denique ad corporis humani exercitationes pertinet, diligenter explicatur, opus non modo medicis, verum etiam omnibus antiquarum rerum cognoscendarum, et valetudines conservandæ studiosis admodum utile. 4°. 1601. *Venetiis :* Juntas.

[Avec nombreuses superbes et grandes figures en bois.]

—— (—). — De arte gymnastica. Small 4°. 1672. *Amstelodami.*

(In Captain Hutton's Collection.)

—— (—). — De arte Gymnastica libri sex. In quibus exercitationum omnium vetustarum genera, loca, modi, facultates et quidquid denique ad corporis humani exercitationes pertinet, diligenter explicatur. Edit. noviss. aucta et figuris authenticis Christophori Coriolani exornata. 4°. 1672. *Amsterdam.*

[Avec joli frontispice par Rom. de Hooghe, gravures et beaucoup de jolies figures sur bois. (Brunet : "Bonne édition de cet ouvrage estimé.")]

MERELO Y CASADEMUNT (DON JAIME) [Professor de esgrima en el colegio de infantería]. — Tratado de la verdadera esgrima del fusil ó carabina armados de bayoneta. 4°. 1858. *Toledo :* Severiano López Fando.

[3 hojas de indice y erratas y 22 figuras.

2nd edition.	4°.	1861.	Toledo : *S. L. Fando.*	(3 *láminas con* 17 *figuras.*)	
3rd „	8°.	1864.	„ „	„	„
4th „	8°.	1865.	Madrid : *Fando é hijo.*	„	„
5th „	8°.	1865.	Toledo : *Fando é hijo.*	„	„
6th „	8°.	1867.	„ „	(dos *láms. con* 12 *fig.*)	
7th „	8°.	1871.	„ „		
8th „	8°.	1875.	Valencia : *C. Verdejo.*	(2 *láms. con* 12 *fig.*)	
9th „	8°.	1878.	„ *V. de Ayoldi.*	(3 *láms. con* 17 *fig.*)]	

MERELO Y CASADEMUNT (Don Jaime). — Tratado completo de la esgrima del sable español. 8°. 1862. *Toledo:* Severiano Lopez Fando.

> [204 *páginas y* 4 *láminas plegadas.*
> 2nd *edition.* 4°. 1862. Valencia.]

—— — — (— —). — Elementos de esgrima para instruir al soldado de infantería en la verdadera destreza del fusil ó carabina armados de bayoneta. 8°. 1865. *Toledo:* Fando.

> [1 *plate.*]   (*In Captain Hutton's Collection.*)

—— — — (— —). — Manual de esgrima, recapitulación de las tretas más principales que constituyen la verdadera esgrima del sable español y del florete. Oblong 8°. 1878. *Madrid:* R. Labajos.

MERELO Y FORNÉS (Don Alfredo). — Manual de esgrima de sable y lanza para toda el arma de caballeria y sable de infantería. Corregido y aumentado por su señor padre, Professor que ha sido de varias Academias militares y que los es en la actualidad de la del Cuerpo administrativo de Ejército, D. José Merelo y Casademunt, Condecorado por sus publicaciones de Egrima con la Cruz blanca de primera clase del mérito militar. 8°. 1880. *Madrid:* Establ. tip. de M. Minuesa, Juanelo, 19 y Ronda de Embajadores.

> [*Una gran lámina con* 17 *figuras.*]

MERELO Y SAYRÓ (Don Luis). — Apuntes sobre la esgrima en general. MS.

MÉRIGNAC (Emile). — Histoire de l'escrime dans tous les temps et dans tous les pays. Tome I., Antiquité. Gr. 8°. 1883. *Paris:* Rouquette.

> [*Avec portrait, nombreuses figures, planches et eaux-fortes de M. de Malval, dessins de M. Dupuy.*]   (*In Captain Hutton's Collection.*)

—— (—). — Histoire de l'escrime dans tous les temps et dans tous les pays. Tome II., Temps modernes. Gr. 8°. 1886. *Paris:* Rouquette.

> [*Illustrated.*]   (*In Captain Hutton's Collection.*)

MERJAY (J. B. N.). — *SELMNITZ.* — [1840 ?].

MERLE. — *MELLESVILLE.* — 1818.

MERLIN (M.). — Table Générale alphabétique et raisonée des matières contenues dans le Répertoire de Jurisprudence et dans le recueil alphabétique des Questions de Droit.　Par L. Rondonneau.　*Paris :* J. P. Roret.

[Pages 267–268. *Duel.*]

MERTENS. — *GORNE* (*Von*). — 1858.

MESSINEO (PIETRO). — A Blasco Florio in risposta all' ultimo indirizzo fatto ai professori di scherma.　1858.　*Palermo :* A. Russitano.

METZ (ALEX. EDLER VON) [Gen. Major]. — Fechtbuch für die Prim-Auslage.　8°.　1864.　*Wien :* Braumüller.

—— (—. — —). — Fechtbuch für die Prim-Auslage.　Hrsg. im J. 1863, nach genauer Durchsicht neu aufgelegt im J. 1883.　8°. 1883.　*Wien :* Seidel & Sohn.

[*112 pages.*]

MEYER (JOACHIM) [Freyfechter zu Strasburg]. — Gründliche Beschreibung der Freyen, Ritterlichen und Adelichen Kunst des Fechtens in allerley gebreuchlichen Wehren, mit vil schönen und nützlichen Figuren gezieret und furgestellet.　Oblong 4°.　1570. *Strasburg.*

[*Getruckt zu Strasburg bey Thiebolt Berger am Weynmarkt zum Treubel.*
Numerous woodcuts.]
(*In the Bodleian Library and Captain Hutton's Collection.*)

—— (—). — Gründliche Beschreibung der Freyen, &c., &c.　2nd edition.　Oblong 4°.　1600.　*Augspurg.*

[*Getruckt zu Augspurg bey Michael Mauger, in verlegung Eliae Willers.* 73 *woodcuts.*
" *Contains in a more systematic shape an equally complete account of the use of the popular weapons ' Düsack,' 'Schwerdt,' ' Helleparten,' and 'Pflegel' (halbert and flail), together with a thorough system of the rapier, imitated from that of Grassi and Viggiani.*"—*Castle's* "*Schools and Masters of Fence.*"] (*In the British Museum.*)

—— (—). — Gründliche Beschreibung der Freyen, &c., &c.　3rd edition.　Oblong 4°.　1660.　*Augsburg.*

[*Numerous woodcuts.*]

MEYER (OSCAR). — Das Fechten des Cavalleristen mit den blanken Waffen (dem Säbel und Pallasch), zu Fuss und zu Pferde. Mit Zeichnungen.　8°.　1859.　*Trier.*

[*6 plates.*]

CAPTAIN JAMES MILLER. 1738.

MEYER.—Konversations-Lexikon. 4. Aufl. 8°. 1885. *Leipzig:* Bibliogr. Institut.

[*Article on "Fechtkunst."*]

MEZGER (Dr. Johan Georg). — *HESSE (G.).* — 1887.

MICHELI (Michele). — Tratatto in lode della nobile e cavalleresca arte della scherma. Diretto ai nobili e cittadini Toscani. 8°. 1798. *Firenze:* Nella stamperia granducale.

MICHELS (R.). — Der Chassépot-Karabiner z. Unterr. f. Unteroffiziere. 8°. 1874. *Paderborn.*

MICHIELS (Alfred).— Drames politiques. 12°. 1865. *Paris:* Dentu.

[Pages 1–92. "*Le duel sans fin.*"]

MILITARY DISCIPLINE, or the Art of War. Shewing directions for the Postures in exercising of the Pike and Musket. 2nd edition, with many additions and corrections. Improved and designed by Capt. J. S. 8°. 1689. *London:* Robert Morden.

[22 *copperplates.*] (*In Captain Hutton's Collection.*)

MILITARY MENTOR, a series of letters written by a General Officer to his son, comprising a course of Instruction calculated to unite the Accomplishments of the Gentleman and the Soldier. 2 vols. 12°. 1804.

[*Contains letters on "Duelling."*]

MILLA (Francisco). — Dictamen sobre la espada en contra da en Peñafiel y el origen y hechos de la espada en todas las naciones. MS.

MILLAUD (Albert). — *PERRIÈRES (C. des).* — 1874.

MILLER (J.) [Captain]. — A Treatise on Backsword, Sword, Buckler, Sword and Dagger, Sword and Great Gauntlet, Falchon, Quarterstaff, in the shape of an album of fifteen copperplates, engraved by Scotin, with one column of text. Folio. 1738. *London.*

[*This "Mr." Miller in the reign of Queen Anne was a sergeant in a foot regiment. Later on he seems to have gradually established his position as that of a gentleman, and received a captaincy from George II.*]
(*In Captain Hutton's Collection.*)

MILLINGEN (J. G.). — History of Duelling : including narratives of the most remarkable personal encounters that have taken place from the earliest period to the present time. 2 vols. 8°. 1841. *London :* R. Bently.

(*In Mr. J. R. Garcia Donnell's Collection.*)

MILLINGEN. — *EDINBURGH* Review.

———. — *MONTHLY* Review.

MILLOTTE (Lieutenant au 39ᵉ Régiment de Ligne). — Traité d'escrime, pointe. 18°. 1864. *Paris :* Dumaine.

MILTON (ROBERT). — *SAINT-ALBIN* (*A. de*).

MINCKWITZ (H. E.). — De duello. 4°. 1842. *Leipzig.*

MINGAY. — *MEDLAND* (*W. M.*). — 1808.

MODERN SOCIETY (Periodical). 8°. *London.*

[1872. *August* 13. Page 1223. "*Duel at Dos Agnas between two young ladies.*"]

MODI di metter mano alla spada. Oblong 24°. 1560. *Venice.*

[*42 plates of fencing, the text also engraved.*]

MODUS faciendi duellum coram rege.

[*MS. in British Museum.* 32,097. *f.* 34 (*temp. Richard II.*).]

MOLINE. — Le duel comique. Opera bouffon. 12°. 1776. *Paris :* Duchesse.

[*Représenté pour la première fois, par les Comédiens Italiens, ordinaires du Roi, le Lundi,* 16 *septembre* 1776.]

MOLINIER (JOSEPH VICTOR). — Du duel. Examen du dernier projet de loi sur le duel, approuvé en 1851 par une commission de l'assemblée législative, et du rapport préparé par M. Auguste Valette, président de cette commission. 8°. 1861. *Toulouse :* Bonnal et Gibrac.

MOMAN. — *BRITISH* Museum. MS.

MONASTERIO (RICARDO). — La casa del duelo ; sainéte cómico en un acto y en prosa. 1892. 8°. *Madrid :* R. Velasco.

[33 *páginas. Estrenado en el Teatro de Lara el* 15 *de Diciembre de* 1892. (*Galeria dramática de Hidalgo.*)]

MONATSCHRIFT für das Turnwesen (Periodical). 8°. *Berlin :* R. Gaertner.

> [*XI. Jahrgang. Mai* 1892. *Heft* 5. *Das älteste in französischer Sprache gedruckte Fechtbuch von J.* 1538 *ist eine Uebersetzung des ältesten deutschen Fechtbuch v. J.* 1516. *Von Dr. Karl Wassmannsdorff.*]

MONCIO (PIETRO). — Opere di scherma. 1509.

> [*Mentioned by Pallavicini and Marcelli, but the work does not seem to be extant.*]

MONICA (FRANCESCO DELLA). — La scherma napolitana, discorsi due. 4°. 1680. *Parma.*

MONITEUR OFFICIEL DE L'ESCRIME et de la Gymnastique (Journal). *Paris.*

> [*20 novembre et 5 décembre* 1886.]

MONNOYE (DE LA). — Le duel aboli.

> [*" Poema premiado por la Academia Francesa."—Leguina's " Espada."*]

MONTAG (J. B.). — Neue praktische Fechtschule auf Hieb und Stoss, sowie auf Stoss gegen Hieb und Hieb gegen Stoss. Für Militärschulen und Turnanstalten wie auch zum Selbst-Unterricht für die Liebhaber der Fechtkunst eingerichtet und durch 30 Figuren-Tafeln verauschaulicht. 8°. 1868. *Erfurt :* Bartholomäus.

> [*30 figures.*]

—— (—. —.). — Neue praktische Fechtschule auf Hieb und Stoss, &c., &c. 2. verb. sehr verm. Auflage. 8°. 1882. *Leipzig :* Gracklauer.

> [*Plates. 125 pages.*]

MONTEIL (AMANS ALEXIS). — Histoire des Français des divers états. 5 vols. 12°. 1827. *Paris.*

> [Vol. VI. p. 48. *" Duelling."*]

MONTELIUS (O.). — Sur les poignées des épées et des poignards en bronze.

> [*" Congrès d'Anthropologie," &c., Stockholm,* 1874, Vol. II. p. 882. 8°. 1876. Stockholm.]

MONTENEGRO (DON JOSEPH DE). — Tratado de esgrima. 4°. Imprenta de Villalpando (Siglio XVIII.).

> [16 *págs.*]

MONTEPIN (XAVIER DE). — Les tragédies de l'épée. Roman. 2 vols. 8°. *Paris :* Dentu.

MONTESQUIEU (Baron de) [Charles de Secondat]. — De l'esprit des loix. 2 vols. 4°. [1748.] *Geneve :* Barillot & Fils.

[*Duelling.—Table of Contents noted in the English translation beneath.*]
(*In the British Museum.* 1233. *f.* 1.)

—— (— —). — The Spirit of Laws. With D'Alembert's Analysis of the Work. Translated from the French by Thomas Nugent, LL.D. 2 vols. 8°. 1878. *London :* George Bell & Sons.

MONTFAUCON (Abbé de). — The Count de Gabalis. 12°. 1680.

MONTHLY LAW MAGAZINE. *London.*

MONTHLY REVIEW (The). 1749–1844.

MONTHLY REVIEW (The) (*continued*)—

Vol. LXIV. p. 92.   *Fencing, Various Rules to be observed in.*
,,   XXI. p. 326.   *Bayonet, Inconveniences and Defects of, compared with the Pike.*
,,   LXXII. p. 199.   *Duelling, Invective against.*
,,   LXXVI. p. 115.   *Duelling, Strictures on.*
,,   LXXVII. p. 504.   *Duelling, Lord Rawdon's Sentiments on.*
,,   LXXIV. p. 272.   *Sword, Observations on an Ancient.*
,,   LXVII. p. 509.   *Bayonets, when first used by the French.*
,,   XVIII. p. 248.   *Duel, Account of a Remarkable One, with all the ceremonies of chivalry.*
,,   XLIV. p. 30.   *Duelling, A Lady's Remarks on.*
,,   XLIV. p. 183.   *Duelling, Regulations against, by the Order of Malta.*
,,   LXXIV. p. 251.   *Duelling, its Prevalence in America.*
,,   L. pp. 520, 521.   *Swords, Ancient, Memoirs on.*
,,   CLV. p. 72.   *On Duelling.   By Milligan.*
,,   CLXI. p. 169.   *Anti-Duel.   By Dunlop.*]

MONTLOSIER. — Monarc. Franç.

[Vol. II. p. 436.   "*Duelling.*"]

MONTMORENCY (R. H. DE) [Lieut.-Col.]. — Exercise and Manœuvres of the Lance.   With account of the most celebrated Banners and Orders of Chivalry.   4°.   1820.   *London.*

(*In the Royal United Service Institution Library, Whitehall, London.*)

MONTRET [Sous officier du 12e Léger]. —["Est l'auteur du premier traité que ait été fait sur le sujet dont nous vous occupons. Ce traité contenait plûtot des exercices pour le maniement du bâton que pour l'escrime à la baïonnette."—PINETTE.]

[*This work does not seem to have been published; apparently it did not get beyond the MS. stage (1811 ?).*]

MOORE (CHARLES) [M.A., Rector of Cuxton, Kent]. — A Full Inquiry into the subject of Suicide: to which are added (as being closely connected with the same subject) two treatises on duelling and gaming.   2 vols.   4°.   1790.   *London.*

(*In Captain Hutton's Collection.*)

MORA (DOMENICO) [gentilhuomo grisone]. — Il soldato, nel quale si tratta di tutto quello che ad un vero soldato si conviene sapere. 4°.   1569.   *Venezia:* Griffio.

MOREAU. — Essai sur l'art de l'escrime.   8°.   1815.   *Nantes.*

MOREAU (J.). — Moreau, maître en fait d'armes à la jeunesse nantaise. Réimpression de la brochure originale de Joseph Moreau et d'un portrait d'après un dessin du temps. 8°. 1886. *Nantes:* Vier.
[24 *pages.*]

MORENO VINIEGRA (PEDRO). — Esgrima.

MORENTIN (A. A.) — *ARANDÍA* y Morentin.

MORI (DR.). — Duelling in Japan.
[*An article in " Von West nach Ost," a German magazine, published in Tokio.*]

MORISON (SIR WILLIAM) [Major-General]. — The advantages of the Pike-Musket and Pike-Rifle, as compared with the arms at present in use. 8°. 1850. *London.*
(*In the Royal United Service Institution Library, Whitehall, London.*)

MORNAN (SIGNOR). — *FENCING* (*Three Treatises on, &c.*).

MORNING LEADER (The).—(Daily Newspaper.) Folio. *London.*
[1895. *May* 31. *" Duel with Swords.—Paris, May* 30.—*A duel with swords was fought to-day between Prince Arsene Karageorgevitch, who is a lieutenant of cavalry in the Russian guard, and M. Paul Dollfus, the writer of a violently-worded article recently published in the ' Evènement.' M. Dollfus was wounded in the hand in the seventh encounter.—Reuter.*"
"1895. *September* 17. *As a result of a dispute between the staffs of two Madrid journals, the ' Pais' and the ' Nacion,' no fewer than four duels have taken place, and in each case the representative of the ' Pais' wounded his opponent. Swords were the weapons used. The report of these duels has led to further disputes, and 24 more meetings have been arranged.*"]

MOROSONI (GIUSEPPE). — Trattato elementare di scherma. Parte prima. 1808. *Verona:* Moroni.

—— (—). — Parte seconda. 1810. *Verona:* Mainardi.

—— (—). — Parte terza. 1811. *Verona:* Giuliari.

—— (—). — Parte quarta. 1811. *Verona:* Mainardi.

—— (—). — Trattato elementare di cavallerizza. Parte prima. 1811. *Verona:* Giuliari.

MOSER (CURT.). — *SÄCHSISCHE* Fechtzeitung.

MOTLEY (JOHN LOTHROP) [D.C.L.]. — The Correspondence of J. L. Motley. Edited by George William Curtis. 2 vols. 8°. 1889. *New York:* Harper & Brothers.
[Pages 20–23. *" Duelling Customs in Germany."*]

MOURIER — *VALORY.* — 1830.

MOWBRAY (FRANCIS). — *HARLEIAN* MSS.
[*Single combat between Mr. Dan. Archdeacon and Francis Mowbray.* (Vol. III. p. 370. cod. 6495. art. 1.)]

MÜHLEN (LANDR. A. V. ZUR). — Eine Landtagsrede auf dem Landtage im Jan. 1893 zur Vertheidigung e. Antrags auf Einführung von Ehrengerichten in der est ländischen Ritterschaft und Anerkennung der Gewissensfreiheit. 8°. 1893. *Neval:* F. Kluge.
[*Eine Landtagsrede über das Duell* (24 *pages*).]

MULLER (A.). — Théorie sur l'escrime à cheval, pour se défendre avec avantage contre toute espèce d'armes blanches. 4°. 1816. *Paris:* Cordier.
[51 *plates.*]
(*In Captain Hutton's Collection; and Art Library, South Kensington Museum.*)

—— (—.). — Ditto. 2e édition. 8°. 1828. *Paris:* Cordier.
[*L'atlas seul, contenant 54 figures représentées en 44 planches.*]

—— (—.). — Maniement de la baïonnette appliqué à l'attaque et à la défense de l'infanterie. 12° oblong. 1828. *Paris:* Moreau et Anselin.
[*Illustré de 21 planches.*]

—— (—.). — Extrait de la théorie du maniement de la bayonette. 4°. 1832.
[*Lithogr.*]

—— (ALESSANDRO). — Il maneggio della baionetta all' attacco ed alla difesa, delle fanterie, individual mente ed in massa con 53 figure. Traduzione italiana dalla 2ª francese del 1835. 8°. 1851. *Torino:* Tipografia Canfari.

—— (—). — Maniement de la baïonnette appliqué à l'attaque et à la défense de l'infanterie. 4°. 1835. *Paris.*
[20 *plates.*]

MÜLLER (CAPITAINE). — Maniement de la baïonnette. 12°. 1845. *Paris:* Léautey.
(*In Captain Hutton's Collection.*)

MÜLLER (FRZ.). — Fecht-Unterricht mit dem Feuer-Gewehre, eigentlich Bajonetfechten. Small 8°. 2te Auflage. 1841. *Prag :* Haase Söhne.

[*6 lithographs.*]

MUÑECAS MARMONTANO (DON JUAN IGNACIO). — Panegirico á D. Francisco de Añasco. Dirigido a Don Cipriano de Alberro, Cavallero del Orden de Santiago. 4°.

[(" *Fué uno de los mejores maestros sevillanos, en careciendo su destreza Luis Diaz de Viedma, en su 'Metodo,' y Méndez de Carmona en la ' Defensa de Carranza.' Discipulo de este maestro, siguió puntualmente los principios del Commendador.*) (30 *págs. prelms. y* 49 *de texto.*)
Segunda edición. 4°. 1886. Sevilla.
Tercera edición. 4°. 1887. Sevilla.]

MUONI (DAMIANO) [Membro di più Istituti scientifici nazionali e stranieri]. — Il duello, appunti storici e morali. 8°. 1865. *Milano :* F. Gareffi.

[*Memoria letta all' " Accademia Fisio-Medico-Statistica " di Milano del giorno* 16 *marzo* 1865.]

[MURATORI (L. A.)]. — De duello ejusque origine ac usu. Dissert. Folio.

[*14 pages.*]

MURATORI (LODOVICO ANTONIO). — Introduzione alle paci private. S'aggiungono un ragionamento di sperone speroni intorno all duello, e un trattato della pace di G. B. Pigna, non publicati finora. 8°. 1708. *Modena.*

(*In the British Museum.* 232. e. 9.)

MURZ (F.) [Hauptmann im Infanterie-Regiment Nr. 39]. — Degen, Säbel und Duell-Fechten. 8°. 1890. *Debreczen :* Gedruckt in der Buchdruckerei des " Debreczeni Ellenör."

[*Mit* 21 *vom Verfasser nach photographien Gezeichneten Figurentafeln.* iv *and* 234 *pages.*]

MUSÉE D'ARTILLERIE, Paris. L'Art ancien.

[*Daggers. Chinese Swords. French Swords of Henry II. Gallic Swords. French Swords,* 18*th century, belonging to M. Meissonier. Gallo-Greek Swords. Greek Swords. Indian Daggers. Japanese Swords.*]
(*In the Art Library, South Kensington Museum. Portfolio* 366.)

MUSEUM OF FOREIGN LITERATURE.
[*"Duelling."* Vol. VII. p. 317.
„ „ XIV. p. 59.
„ „ XXVI. p. 498.
„ „ XXXV. p. 18.]
(*Mentioned in Malcom's Theological Index.*)

MUTIO (GIROLAMO). — La Faustina del Mutio Justinopolitano, delle arme cavalleresche. Con privilegio. 16º. 1560. *Venetia:* V. Valgrisi.

—— (—). — *MUZIO (G.).*

MUTIO (HIERONIMO). — Il duello del Mutio Justinopolitano. Con le risposte cavalleresche. Di nuouo corretto e ristampato; 2 parti in 1 vol. 8º. 1551. *Vinegia:* Gabriel Giolito de' Ferrari e fratelli.
[*Con privilegio del Sommo Pontefice Giulio III. & dello Illustriss. Senato Veneto, & d'altri Prencipi.*
Other editions appeared in 1554, 1558, 1564, 1575, 1576, 1585.]
(*In Captain Hutton's Collection.*)

—— (—). — *MUZIO (G.).*

MUYART DE VOUGLANS [Conseiller au Grand-Conseil].— Les loix criminelles de France, dans leur ordre naturel. Dédiées au Roi. Folio. 1780. *Paris:* Merigot le jeune.
[*Duel, Crime; son origine,* p. 194.
„ *Divers réglement à ce sujet,* p. 165 & suiv.
„ *Moyens de le prévenir,* p. 197.
„ *De combien de manières on peut se rendre coupable ou complice de crime, & quelles sont peines dans tous ces différens cas,* p. 197 & suiv.
„ *Juges qui en doivent connoître,* p. 203.
„ *Ce que ce crime a de particulier par rapport à l'instruction,* pp. 204 & suiv.]
(*In the British Museum.* 24. i. 8.)

MUZIO (GIROLAMO). — Traité du duel. 8º. 1553. *Venetia.*

—— (—). — Le combat de Mutio Justinopolitain, avec les responses Chevaleresses, traduit nouvellement d'Italien en Françoys par A. Chapuis. 4º. 1561. *Lyon.*
(*In the British Museum.* 31. c. 20.)
[*Another edition.* 8º. 1582. Lyon: *A. Tardif.* (436 *pages.*)
(*In the British Museum.* 1193. i. 35.)

—— (—). — Il Gentilhuomo. 4º. 1571. *Venetia.*
(*In the British Museum.*)

—— (—). — *MUTIO.*

201

NACHERTANICH PRAVIL FECHTOVALJNAVO iskoostva
risoonkami **v** pyakti tchnactyahkh. Sochinenich Pomoshtchnika
glavnavo. Fekhtovaljnavo Ootchitelyah Otdyailjnavo Gvardeickavo
Korpoosa. 4°. 1843. *Sanktpeterboorg:* Sokolova.

NACHWORT (EIN RUHIGES) zum Duell Salomon-Vering. 8°.
1890. *Hannover:* Verlag. d. hannov. Rundschau.
[*Aus " Hannoversche Rundschau."*]

NAHLOWSKY (Jos. W.). — Das Duell. Sein Widersinn und
seine moralische Verwerflichkeit. 8°. 1864. *Leipzig:* Pernitzsch.
[viii *and* 267 *pages.*]

NAPOLÉON. — *BONAPARTE (Prince Pierre-Napoléon).* — 1869.

NARVÁEZ (DON LUIS PACHECO DE) [Maestro del Rey]. — Libro
de las grandezas de la espada, en que se declaran muchos secretos
del que compuso el comendador Geronimo de Carrança. En el qual
cada uno se podrà liçionar y deprender à solas, sin tener necessidad
de maestro que le enseñe. 4°. 1599–1600. *Madrid:* J. Iñiquez
de Lequerica.
[80 *pliegos.*
Portrait of Don Luis, 2 figures, and 155 diagram woodcuts, in the text.
Si increible parece que puedan Uenarse tantas páginas con esgrima, aún la
parece más el número de Autores que Pacheco cita:—Jaime Pons de
Perpiñan—Pedro Moncio—Achile Marozzo—Camilo Agrippa—Giacomo
de Grassi—Joachim Meyer—Joannis de la Agocchie—Ridalfo Capo Ferro
—Nicolao Giganti—Angelo Vizani—Federico Ghisliero—Maestre Vico—
Maestre Claso—Rabote—Marco Docciolini—Alférez Fallopia—Francisco
Roman—Pedro de la Torre—Salvador de Fabris—D. Atanasio de Ayala
—Gerónimo de Carranza—Giraldo Thibault.
Sobre " destreza" á caballo han escrito:—Camilo Agrippa—Federico Ghisliero
—Gerónimo de Carranza—D. Diego Ramirez de Haro—D. Juan de
Peralta—Conde de Puñonrostro—D. Bernardo de Vargas Machuca—
D. Simon de Villalobos—D. Diego Silvestre y Ludovico.]
(In the British Museum, and Captain Hutton's Collection.)

—— (— — — —). — Compendio de la filosofía y destreza de las
armas de Geronimo de Carrança. 4°. 1612. *Madrid:* Luis
Sanchez.
[*Woodcuts, in the text.*]

—— (— — — —). — Cien conclusiones, o formas de saber, de la
verdadera destreza, fundada en ciencia, y diez y ocho contradicciones
a las de la comun. Folio. 1608. *Madrid:* Luis Sanchez.

NARVÁEZ (DON LUIS PACHECO DE). — Carta al Duque de Cea diciendo su parecer acerca del libro de Geronimo de Carrança. De Madrid en quatro de Mayo. 8°. 1618. *Madrid.*

—— (—— —— —— ——). — Modo fácil y nuevo para examinarse los maestros en la destreza de las armas ; y entender sus cien conclusiones, ó formas de saber. 8°. 1625. *Madrid :* Luis Sanchez.
[92 *hojas.*] (*In the British Museum.* 785. *a.* 78.)
[*Another edition.* 8°. 1659. Madrid : *Juan de Paredes.*]

—— (—— —— —— ——). — Engaño y desengaño de los errores que se han querido introducir en la destreza de las armas. 4°. 1635. *Madrid.*

—— (—— —— —— ——). — Advertencias para la enseñanza de la filosofía y destreza de las armas, asi a pie como a cavallo. 4°. 1639. *Madrid.*

—— (—— —— —— ——). — Modo fácil para examinarse . . . &c. [2nd edition, to which is often added : Adicion á la filosofía de las armas. Las diez y ocho contradicciones de la comun destreza, por el mismo autor. Año M. DC. LX.] 8°. 1658. *Zaragoça :* Pedro Lanaja.
(*In the British Museum.*)

—— (—— —— —— ——). — Adicion á la filosofía de las armas. Las diez y ocho contradicciones á la comun destreza, y las cien conclusiones, ó formas de saber la destreza de las armas, fundada en sciencia. 1659.

—— (—— —— —— ——). — Nueva cienca y filosofía de la destreza de las armas, su teórica y práctica. 8°. 1672. *Madrid :* Melchor Sanchez.
[*Sin fig.*]

—— (—— —— —— ——). — Apología contra Carranza.
[*"La cita Nic. Ant°, pero no hemos conseguido ner ningún ejemplar ni tenemos noticia de su existencia, por lo que suponemos sea la que salió con el nombre de Pizarro."*
"Mine host in the 'New Inn,' commenting on the glories of past fencemasters, remarks, as an incontrovertible statement : 'They had their time, and we can say they were. Don Lewis, of Madrid, is now the sole remaining master of the world.' This was Don Luis Pacheco Narváez, Carranza's pupil, successor and vindicator, both in print and by 'cutting and pointed' argument, during the first quarter of the seventeenth century."— Castle (E.), "The Story of Swordsmanship." ("The National Review," May 1891.)]

NARVÁEZ (Don Luis Pacheco de). — *CRUZADA Y PERALTA* (*M.*). — 1702.

—— (— — — —). — *LARA* (*D. G. A. de*). — 1675.

NATION (Periodical), *New York.* — *GODKIN* (*E. L.*).

NATION (The). July 1865–September 1880. *Boston.*
[Vol. XIV. p. 306. *"Bayonets."*
 „ VI. p. 207. *"Duelling."*
 „ XXII. p. 63. *"Fencing."*]

NATIONAL ART LIBRARY (South Kensington Museum). A list of books and photographs in the National Art Library, illustrating Armour and Weapons. 8°. 1883. *London :* Printed by Eyre & Spottiswoode.
[Pages 31–32. *"Fencing and Sword Exercise."*]

NATIONAL POLICE GAZETTE (The). Folio. *New York.*
[1891. *November 7.* *"Earl Dorsey and William Statler fight a duel in a Moundsville, W. Va., Theatre for the favour of a handsome chorus girl."*]

NATIONAL REVIEW (The). — (Monthly Periodical.) 4°. *London :* W. H. Allen & Co.
[*May* 1891. Pages 312–330. *"The Story of Swordsmanship."* By Captain Egerton Castle.]

NAVAL AND MILITARY ARGUS (Periodical). Folio. *London*
[No. 45. *May* 15, 1890. *Article on "Want of Encouragement by the War Office given to Fencing."*
 „ 46. „ 22, 1890. *Letter to Captain A. Hutton, advocating establishment of a National School of Fence.*
 „ 47. „ 29, 1890. *Ditto.*
 „ 48. *June* 5, 1890. *"Swordsmanship for Boys."*
 „ 49. „ 12, 1890. *Article on ditto.*
 „ 50. „ 19, 1890. *Letter to Lord Wolseley. "Military Swordsmanship."*]

—— — — —. — *ADMIRALTY* and Horse Guards Gazette.

NAVARRE (C.) [Maître d'armes de la première compagnie de la maison du Roi]. — L'art de vaincre par l'épée, dédié à messieurs les Gardes-du-Corps du Roi de la compagnie de Noailles. Avec approbation de la compagnie. 18°. 1775. *Paris.*

NEILSON (George). — Trial by Combat. 8°. 1890. *Glasgow :* W. Hodge & Co.
[xvi *and* 348 *pages.*]

NERLING (F.). — Der Blutbann des Duells vor dem Richter-stuhle d. Gewissens und der Vernunft. 8°. 1883. *Dorpat :* Schnakenburg.

[*55 payes.*]

NEUMANN (L.) und **FEHRENBACH** (C.). — Das Duell Vering-Salomon. Stenographischer Bericht über d. Verhandl. d. Schwur-gerichts Freiburg am 16. April 1890. 8°. 1890. *Freiburg i/B. :* J. Elchlepp.

NEW BUDGET (The). — (Periodical.) Folio. *London :* 69 Fleet Street.

> [1895.   *April* 18 (p. 9).   "*At a Fencing Class.*"   *By A. J. B. Salmon.*
> 1895.   *May* 23 (p. 9).   "*The Trained Bands of London.*"   *Pikeman.*
> 1895.   *August* 8 (p. 5).   "*The New Infantry Sword Exercise.*"   *Illustrations showing Fencing by the Royal Horse Guards: Engage—Parried.*]

NEWCASTLE (HENRY, THE MARQUIS OF). — *HARLEIAN* MSS.

NEW REVIEW (Monthly Periodical).   8°.   *London.*

> [1894.   *February* (pp. 177–185), *March* (pp. 353–364).   "*Some Historic Duels.*"   *By Egerton Castle.   Illustrated by Douglas Connah.*]

NEW YORK DAILY TRIBUNE (Periodical).   Folio.   *New York, U.S.A.*

> [1892.   *August* 14 (p. 18).   "*Duelling in the Navy.*"]

NEW YORK HERALD (Periodical).   *New York, U.S.A.*

> [1891.   *December* 6.   "*Methods and Styles of Fencing.*"]

—— — — (Periodical).   *London.*

> [1890.   *November* 23.   "*Another Duel and Another Scratch.*"
> 1890.   *August* 17.   "*Bibliography of the Art of Fence.*"
> 1891.   *May* 17.   "*French Swordswomen.*"   *By Mme. Adrienne Gabrielle.*]

—— — —. — *BOXERS* and Fencers.

NEW YORK TIMES (The). — (Periodical.)   Folio.   *New York, U.S.A.*

> [1890.   *September* 16.   "*A Deadly Duel in the Street.*"
> 1891.   *June* 2.   "*Emperor William is challenged to a Duel.*"]

NINI (CONTE GIUSEPPE).

> [*The Conte Giuseppe Nini has written some remarkable articles in* "*Cappa e Spada,*" "*Dritto,*" *and* "*Sport Illustrato,*" *on Masiello's treatise on Fencing.*]

NOAKES (S. G.). — Swords and how to Use them.

[" *The Gymnasium* " (*Periodical*), *London, December* 1890, *January* 1891.]

NOBILI (FLAM.). — Trattato dell' amore con discorsi sopra questione d'honore.   4º.   1580.   *Bologna.*

NOBLE SCIENCE (La) des joueurs d'espée.   4º.   [1533 ?]   *Paris.*

[*This is the first known French work of Fence, and is curiously enough shown to be a translation from the German of Paurnfeindt.*]

—— — (—) des joueurs d'espée.   [Ici commence un très beau livret, contenant la chevaleureuse science des joueurs d'espée, pour apprendre à jouer de l'espée à deux mains et aultres semblables espées, avec aussi les braquemars et aultres courts cousteaux lesquels lon use à une main . . .] — (At the end : Imprimé en la ville Danuers par moy, Guillaume Vosterman, demourant à la Lycorne dor.)   4º.   1538.   *Antwerp.*

[*Black letter.   14 whole-page and 12 half-page woodcuts.*]
(*In the British Museum.*)

—— — (—). — [*PAURNFEINDT* (A.)]

NODIER (C.). — *PALAYE* (*La Curne de Ste*). — 1826.

NORD WILLARDS. — *WILLARDS* (*Comte de Nord*).

NORFOLK (DUKE OF). — *HARLEIAN* MSS.

[*Single Combat between the Dukes of Hereford and Norfolk.* (Vol. III. p. 322. cod. 6079. art. 36.)]

NORRIS (MAY G.). — *BADMINTON* Magazine (The).—1895.

NORTH AMERICAN REVIEW.   8º.   1815–77.   *New York, U.S.A.*

[Vol. XXVI. p. 498.	*Duelling, by P. H. Cruse.*		
„ XXVII. p. 87.	,,	„ G. H. Bode.	
„ XXIX. p. 400.	,,	„ J. de Wallenstein.	
„ XXXI. p. 7.	,,	„ G. Bancroft.	
„ XLVI. p. 352.	,,	„ E. T. Channing.	
„ L. p. 348.	,,	„ W. Brigham.	
„ LI. p. 436. } „ LXIII. p. 149. }	„	„ C. C. Felton.	
„ LXIII. p. 195.	,,	„ C. F. Adams.]	

NORTHAMPTON (EARL OF) [Lord Henry Howard]. — *ASHMOLEAN* MSS.   (856. 126.)

NORTHAMPTON (EARL OF). — *COTTONIAN* MSS.

[*Tit. c. iv.* 4. (131.)
Tit. c. iv. 10. (510.)]

NORTHUMBERLAND (EARL OF). — *ASHMOLEAN* MSS.

NOTES AND QUERIES (Periodical). 4°. *London.*

NOTES AND QUERIES (*continued*)—

NOTES SUR L'INSTRUCTION des recrues dans la cavalerie. Par P. A. G.   4e édition.   32°.   1894.   *Paris.*

  [(148 *pages.*)
  Première partie : Instruction à Pied—Escrime.
  Deuxième partie : Emploi du Sabre—Emploi du Revolver.]

NOTICE BIOGRAPHIQUE sur Jean-Louis et son ecole.   8°. 1866.   *Montpellier :* Richard.

  [*Attributed to General D——, a pupil of Jean-Louis. Lithographed portrait.*]

——. —*SURDUN.*—1866.

NOUVELLE REVUE (La). — (Periodical.)   8°.   *Paris :* 18 Boulevard Montmartre.

  Tome LXX. 3e livraison. 1 *Juin* 1891. Pages 587–595. "*Du Duel,*" par *G. Sénéchal.*]

NOVALI (K. VON). — Germanisches Turnbuch, oder die Reit-, Jagd- und Fechtkunst, nach den neuesten Grundsätzen dargestellt. Ein Hand- und Hausbuch für Ritterguts-Besitzer, Offiziere, Forstbeamte, Akademiker, &c. Gr. 8°. 1837. *Augsburg :* Jenisch und Stage.

―― (―. ―). ― Germanisches Turnbuch, oder die Reit-, Jagd- und Fechtkunst, &c. 2te Auflage. 8°. 1839. *Augsburg :* Jenisch und Stage.

NOVELI (D. NICOLÁS RODRIGO). — Crisol especulativo demostrativo o practico, mathematico de la destreza de las armas. 8°. 1731. *Madrid :* Alonso Balvás.

[12 *lámas grabadas, por P. Minguet.*]

―― (―. ― ―). ― Cartilla de torear á caballo. 8°. 1726. *Madrid.*

NUGENT (THOMAS). — *MONTESQUIEU (Baron de).*

NYBLÆUS (GUSTAF). — Allmän gymnastik, fäktlära. 8°. 1876. *Stockholm :* Norstedt & Söner.

[3 *figuren.*]

―― (―). ― Militärgymnastik el. den allm. gymnastikens användning för militärisk utbildning. 8°. 1876. *Stockholm :* Norstedt & Söner.

―― (―). ― Öfningstabeller till ledning för undervisningen i gymnastik och bajonettfaktning vid indelta arméns Korprals-och volontärskolor. På anmodan af statsrådet och chefen för Kongl. landtförsvarodepartementet utarbetade. 8°. 1887. *Stockholm :* Norstedt & Söner.

O. (A. C.). — *A. C. O.*

OBERKIRCH (BARONESS D'), Memoirs of. 2 vols. 8°. 1852. *London.*

[Vol. I. p. 71. *"Duelling."*]

O'BRIEN (F. J.). — *HARPER'S* New Monthly Magazine.

[Vol. XI. p. 609.]

O'BRIEN (WILLIAM). — The Duel. A comedy. 8°. 1772. *London.*

(*In the British Museum. King's Pamphlets,* 161. e. 14.)

[O'BRIEN (WILLIAM).] — The Duel. A play ; as performed at the
Theatre-Royal in Drury Lane. 2nd edition. 8°. *London.* 1773.

[*Acted at Drury Lane,* 1772. *This piece deserved more success than it met
with. It was taken from "Le Philosophe sans le Sçavoir" of Sedaine, and
was acted only one night.*]

OBSERVATIONUM SELECTARUM ad rem Litterariam Spec-
tantium. 24°. 1704. *Halæ Magdebvrgicæ.*

[Tomus IX. pp. 101–126. *" Variis duellorum generibus."*
      ,,   ,,   126–161. *" Duellorum varii generis moralitate."*]

O'CONNOR (D.). — *HARPER'S* New Monthly Magazine.
[Vol. VIII. p. 239.]

OEHKE. — *HOLZAPFEL.* — 1885.

OETTINGEN (ALEX. VON). — Zur Duellfrage. 8°. 1889. *Dorpat :*
Karow.

OFENHEIM (ADOLF [RITTER] VON). — Das Wesen des Duells,
und ein Reform-Vorschlag. 8°. 1887. *Wien :* Manz.
[vi *and* 184 *pages.*]

O'KEEFE (ADEL). — Broken Sword ; or, A Soldier's Honour. A
Tale. 12°. 1854. *London :* Groombridge.

OLEVANO (GIOV. BATT.). — Trattato nel quale col mezzo di
cirquanta casi vien posto in atto il modo di ridurre a pace ogni sorte
di privata inimicitia nota per cagion d'honore. 1620. *Milano :*
Bidelli.

OLIVER (DON ANTONIO). — Historia de la esgrima y de los
desafíos. 4°. 1837.

[*Es opúsculo muy erudito dividido en dos partes :*—1. *De la esgrima.* 2. *De
los desafíos. Empieza la primera por el origen de la espada, que la en-
cuentra en la época en que los escitas la veneraban como imágen de Marte.
Se ocupa en la segunda del tiempo en que fueron permitidos los desafíos, y
de las causas que más adelante hicieron necesaria su prohibicion.*]
(*MS. in the Library of D. Joaquín María Bover.*)

OLIVIER (J.) [Professor of Fencing in St. Dunstan's Court, Fleet
Street, London. Of the Royal Academy of Paris]. — L'Art des
armes simplifié. Nouveau traité sur la manière de se servir de
l'épée. Enrichi de figures en taille douce représentant les différentes
attitudes d'où dépendent les principes et la grâce de cet art, peintes

d'après nature, exécutées supérieurement et de la manière la plus élégante. 8°. 1771–72. *Londres:* Jean Bell.

> [*Frontispiece, and 8 plates, out of text.*
> *This work is very sound, and thoroughly justifies its French title, as it contains a simplified system, shorn of all unnecessary and obsolete details.*]
> (*In Mr. J. R. Garcia Donnell's Collection.*)

OLIVIER (J.) — Fencing Familiarized, or a New Treatise on the Art of Sword Play. Illustrated by Elegant Engravings, representing all the different Attitudes in which the Principles and Grace of the Art depend ; painted from life, and executed in a most elegant and masterly manner. 8°. 1771–72. *London:* John Bell.

> [*Facing the above title is its exact translation into French. The text is in both languages. Frontispiece and eight folded plates, engraved by Ovenden.*]
> (*In Captain Hutton's Collection, and South Kensington Museum.*)

—— (—.). — Fencing Familiarized, &c. 2nd edition. Revised, corrected, and augmented by an original set of prints. 8°. 1780. *London :* J. Bell.

> [*Dedicated to the Earl of Harrington. Same frontispiece as in first edition ; but the plates* (14) *are different, being drawn by J. Roberts, and engraved by D. Jinkins, Goldar, W. Blake, and C. Grignon.*]
> (*In Captain Hutton and Mr. J. R. Garcia Donnell's Collections.*)

ONEBY (JOHN). — True and Faithful Narrative of the Life and Actions of John Oneby, Esqr., commonly called Major Oneby : of his career with the army in Flanders, under Marlboro, his duels, gaming, and murder of Mr. Gower, and subsequent suicide in prison. Small 8°. [1727.] *London.*

> (*In the British Museum. 518. f. 73.*)

ORDENANZA DE SU MAGESTAD, en que se prescribe la formacion, manejo de arma, y evoluciones, que manda se establenzca, y observe en la Infanteria de su Exercito. 1761. 4°. *Madrid:* A. Marin.

> [*162 págs. y 5 lámas. que se doblan.*]

ORDENANZES DE SU MAGESTAD, para el regimen, disciplina, subordinacion, y servicio, de la infanteria, cavalleria y dragones, de sus exércitos en guarnicion, y en campaña. Folio. 1728. *Madrid:* J. de Ariztia.

> [*303 págs. Contiene algunas nociones de esgrima de la bayoneta.*]

ORDINANCES FOR SINGLE COMBATS within Lists, before the King, submitted to Richard II. by Thomas, Duke of Gloucester, Lord High Constable. (*Temp.* Richard II.)

[*MSS. In the British Museum. Fr.* 28,549. *f.* 28. *b.*]

ORDONNANCE DU ROI du 4 mars 1831 sur l'exercice et les manœuvres des bataillons de l'infanterie. 3 vols. Small 8°. 1831. *Paris.*

[*64 plates.*]

ORDONNANCE. — Escrime à la bayonnette, extraite de l'ordonnance du 22 juillet 1845 sur l'exercice et les manœuvres des bataillons des chasseurs à pied. 8°. 1852. *Paris.*

ORDONNANCE DU ROI du 22 juillet 1845 sur l'exercice et les manœuvres des bataillons de chasseurs à pied. 2 vols. 16°. 1862. *Paris.*

ORUS (DON MIGUEL DE). — Esgrima de la bayoneta. 4°. 1861. *Madrid.*

[*2 plates.*]

OSORIO Y GÓMEZ (DON PEDRO). — Tractado de esgrima a pée a cavallo, em que se ensina por principios o maneo do florete ou o jogo da espada, que se usa hoje. Large 8°. 1842. *Lisboa :* Typ. Commercial.

[*24 plates.*]

OSSBAHR (CARL ANTON). — Studier i Nordiska museets rustkammare. [Samfundet för Nordiska museets Främjande 1888.] 8°. 1890. *Stockholm :* Norstedt & Söner.

O'SULLIVAN (DANIEL) [Maître en fait d'armes des académies du Roi]. — L'escrime pratique, ou principes de la science des armes. 8°. 1765. *Paris :* Sebastien Jorry.

O'TRIGGER (SIR LUCIUS). — *MASSI (M. C. de).* — 1880.

OTT (JOSEF) [Unterlieut.]. — Das System der Fechtkunst à la contrepointe für den Stoss und Hieb. Zum Unterricht in Fecht schulen, sowie zur Selbstbildung, nebst den Verhaltungen im Zweikampfe, General-Assaut, Duell oder Wettkampf, mit Rechts-Links-Kunst- und Naturfechten, und einem Anhange : "Geschichte des Duells." 3 Bücher. Gr. 8°. 1851. *Olmüz :* Hölzel..

[1 *Buch des Stossfechten,* 192 *S., mit* 47 *lith. Taf. in qu.* 4°.]

OTT (Josef). — Das System der Fechtkunst à la contrepointe für den Stoss und Hieb. Nebst Anhang : Geschichte der Fechtkunst. 2. Auflage. 8°. 1853. *Olmüz :* Hölzel.

[*Mit 43 lithogr. Tafeln Abbildungen.*]

—— (—.). — Das System der Fechtkunst à la contrepointe f. den Stoss und Hieb. 3. Auflage. 8°. 1855. *Olmüz :* Hölzel.

[*Mit 90 lithogr. Tafeln in qu. 4°.*]

—— (—.). — Geschichte des Zweikampfes aller Völker und Zeiten, nebst der Schilderung der nationalen Kampfspiele und bezüglichen gymnastischen Übungen. 8°. 1855. *Olmüz :* F. Slawik.

[*258 pages.*]

OUTING (Periodical). *New York.*

[1887 (?). Vol. II. p. 1. *Fencing. By E. van Schaick.*
1890 (February). Vol. XV. p. 341. *Fencing for Women. By M. Bisland.*]

OVERLAND MONTHLY (Periodical). *San Francisco.*

[Vol. I. p. 496. *Duelling in West Indies. By J. C. Cremony.*
  „   IX. p. 251. *Instances of Duels. By J. Gordon.*
  „   XIII. p. 330. *Duel on Boston Common. By A. Young.*
1888 (New Series). Vol. XII. p. 128. *Duels to the Death. By D. S. Richardson.*
1891 (New Series). Vol. XVIII. p. 287. *Sword of Luis Gonzales. By E. E. Brimblecon.*]

OXFORD UNIVERSITY FENCING CLUB. — *SPORTSMAN (The),* February 25, 1892.

OZAETA (Joseph J.). — Instruccion de bayoneta, traducida del italiano. 4°. MS.

[88 *págs. y 22 láms. que se doblan.*]

P. (J. V. M. DE). — Manejo del sable. Coleccion de cuarenta diseños que representan las diversas posiciones de este exercicio á caballo. Once cuad. Folio. 1819.

[40 *figures by Horace Vernet.*
Notable, por ser los dibujos del célebre "Horacio Vernet," y la litografia de "Engelmann," reciente su invencion en aquella fecha. Los uniformes tienen suma exactitud.]

P. (M. D. L. P.). — Pieces intéressantes et peu connues pour servir a l'histoire et la litteratures. Nouvelle édition. 12°. 1790. *Bruxelles :* Prault.

[Tome Huitième, pp. 437-450. "*Relation du fameux duel entre le Lord Bruce et le Chr. Edouart Sackville, par ce dernier.*"]

PAALZOW (Christian Ludwig). — Magazin d. Rechtsgelehrsamkeit in den preussischen Staaten. 7 vols. 8°. 1802–4. *Berlin:* Schöne.

[*Contains " Untersuchung und Erkenntniss über ein Duell."*]

PAGANO (Marc' Antonio) [gentil'huomo napolitano]. — Le tre giornate d'intorno alla disciplina dell' arme, espezialmente della spada : al duca di Sessa. 8°. 1553. *Napoli.*

PAGE (T.). — The Use of the Broad Sword. In which is shown the true method of fighting with that weapon, as it is now in use among the Highlanders ; deduc'd from the use of the scymitar, with every throw, cut, guard, and disarm. 8°. 1746. *Norwich:* M. Chase.

[*48 pages.*]

PAGLIUCA (Giovanni). — Cenni di critica sul sistema di scherma Radaelli. 1880. *Torino.*

PALAYE (La Curne de Ste.). — Mémoires sur l'ancienne chevalerie, avec une introduction et notes historiques par Ch. Nodier. 2 vols. 8°. 1826. *Paris.*

[*Avec figures.*]

PALESTRA (La). — *CESARANO (F.).* — 1882.

PALEY (William) [M.A., Archdeacon of Carlisle]. — The Principles of Moral and Political Philosophy. 2nd corrected edition. 4°. 1786. *London:* Printed by J. Davis, for R. Faulder.

[*Page 225. " Duelling."*]
(*In the British Museum. 29. e. 17.*)

PALLADINI (Camillo) [Bolognese]. — Discorso sopra l'arte della scherma ; come l'arte della scherma é necesseria a chi si diletta d'arme. Oblong 4°. [*Circa* 1560.]

[*MS. renfermant quarante-deux dessins d'escrime du xvie siècle, à la sanguine. Plusieurs sont en costume. Le choix du papier, la beauté de l'écriture, la valeur de bon nombre de ses dessins, font de ce manuscrit, qui n'a jamais été imprimé, une précieuse curiosité bibliographique de l'escrime. Riche reliure doublée de Marius Michel attributs d'escrime. Reliure dans un doublé étui.*
42 *drawings in red chalk, imitated from the plates of Agrippa's work.*]
(*In M. Vigeant's Collection, Paris.*)

PALLAVICINI (Giuseppe Morsicato) [Maestro di scherma Palermitano]. — La scherma illustrata, per la di cui teorica e prattica si può arrivare con faciltà alla difesa ed offesa necessaria, nel occasioni d'assalti nemici. Opera utilissima alle persone che si dilettano di questa professione, con le figure della scienza prattica dichiarate coi loro discorsi. Folio. 1670. *Palermo:* Domenico d'Anselmo.

[Frontispiece and 31 *copperplates.]*
(In British Museum (558. **c.* 6.) *and Captain Hutton's Collection.)*

PALLAVICINI (GIUSEPPE MORSICATO). — La seconda parte della scherma illustrata, ove si dimostra il vero maneggio della spada e pugnale et anco il modo come si adopera la cappa, il brochiero e la rotella di notte, le quali regole non sono state intese da nessuno autore. Folio. 1673. *Palermo:* Domenico d'Anselmo.

[Frontispiece and 36 *copperplates.]*
(In the British Museum.)

PALL MALL BUDGET (Periodical). Folio. *London.*

[1889. *August* 15. *Cold Steel. (A review of Captain Hutton's work.)*
1891. *February* 26. *Fencing at the Lyceum Theatre (London). With 3 portraits.*]

PALL MALL GAZETTE (Periodical). Folio. *London.*

[1885.	*January*	12.	*Schools and Masters of Fence. (A review of Mr. Egerton Castle's work, with two illustrations.)*
1889.	*August*	9.	*Cold Steel. (A review of Captain Hutton's work.)*
,,	*October*	17.	*Fencing for Everybody. A visit to M. B. Bertrand.*
1890.	*March*	1.	*On the Advantages of Teaching Girls to Fence.*
,,	,,	12.	*German Emperor on Fencing.*
,,	,,	29.	*German Emperor on Duelling.*
,,	*April*	10.	*American Journalists and Duelling.*
,,	,,	12.	*Honour and Duels in Germany.*
,,	*August*	2.	*Duel between Lieutenant Castenschiold and Baron von Rathen.*
,,	,,	27.	*Duel between Ross Hamilton and Robert Ferguson.*
,,	,,	30.	*Fatal Military Duel in Germany.*
,,	*September*	3.	*Duel between an Editor and an Officer.*
,,	,,	13.	*Should Women Fight Duels?*
,,	,,	15.	*Duel in Mexico.*
,,	,,	16.	*Duel between Boys in Berlin.*
,,	,,	17.	*Duels between French Politicians.*
,,	*October*	6.	*Duelling Statistics (Italian).*
,,	,,	28.	*Fatal Duel in France.*
,,	*November*	8.	*Duel over Madame Bernhardt.*
,,	*December*	17.	*Serious Duel between Frenchmen.*
1891.	*January*	1.	*A Duel in the Cavalry Barracks at Vienna.*
,,	,,	3.	*The Recent Duels in France.*
,,	*February*	7.	*Duel between M. Larroumet and M. Saul Lordon.*
,,	,,	24.	*Desperate Duel in America.*
,,	*March*	3.	*Duel between Fencing-masters. (M. Mérignac and M. Vigeant.)*

PALL MALL GAZETTE (*continued*)—

1891.	April	4.	*Fatal Duel in America.*
,,	,,	10.	*M. Jules Lamaitre's Duel.*
,,	,,	24.	*Duelling in France.*
,,	,,	25.	*A Circus Incident followed by a Duel.*
,,	,,	30.	*Fatal Duel between Gamblers.*
,,	May	11.	*The Isaac-Rochefort Duel.*
,,	,,	13.	*M. Rochefort's Duel stopped by Police.*
,,	,,	16.	*The German Emperor and Duelling.*
,,	,,	25.	*An Austrian Baron's Duel in Chicago.* (*Baron Rudolf Kalnoky de Korös-Patak.*)
,,	July	13.	*Duel between Hungarian Deputies.* (*Deputy Gayary and Herren Vecsey and Polonyi.*)
,,	,,	24.	*Duel between French Journalists.* (*M. Charles Simon and M. Chironte.*)
,,	,,	30.	*Paris Duellists Injured.*
,,	September	4.	*Duel between French Journalists.* (*M. Charles Laurent and M. René de Hubert.*)
,,	,,	9.	*Mr. Coventry Patmore, Second at a Duel.*
,,	,,	11.	*Mr. Coventry Patmore, Second at a Duel.* (*Contradicted.*)
,,	,,	23.	*The Essence of the Duel.* (*Leading Article.*)
,,	,,	26.	*A Duel in Corsica.*
,,	October	30.	*Desperate Duel with Daggers.* (*Count Bertazzoli and Signor Calderoni.*)
,,	November	7.	*A Spanish Admiral's Duel.* (*Vice-Admiral Beranger.*)
,,	,,	11.	*Fatal Duel in Italy.* (*Signor Contarini and the Marquis Dosi.*)
,,	,,	23.	*Municipal Duel in France.* (*Mayor of Dax and the Sub-Prefect.*)
,,	,,	23.	*A British Vice-Consul as Duellist's Second.* (*Mr. J. F. D. Bowden second in a duel between a Mr. Lucas and a Mr. Chandor.*)
,,	December	8.	*A Non-Duelling Colonel Expelled the (French) Army.*
,,	,,	15.	*Paris Duellists Injured.* (*M. Charles Soller and Colonel Andruzzi.*)
1892.	March	29.	*Spanish Duel.* (*Don Jose Maria Beranger and the Editor of the "Resumen."*)
,,	May	19.	*Four Mighty Men of Fence.* (*M. Bourgeois, M. Vital Labailly, M. Danguy, and Cavaliere Eugene Pini.*)
,,	,,	20.	*The Quadruple Duel.* (*M. Roulez*). [*See also "Standard," May 19, 1892.*]
,,	June	10.	*Duel in Paris.* (*M. Ernest Jubet and M. Bonnefoi.*)
,,	,,	25.	*The Fatal Duel. Arrest of the Marquis de Morès.* (*The Marquis and Captain Meyer.*)
,,	,,	30.	*M. Maxime Le Comte, Senator for the Nord, to introduce a Bill providing a Penalty against Duelling.*
,,	July	11.	*Sequel to the "Series of Duels." ("M. Roulez, whose imaginary duels went the round of French papers a few weeks ago, has been sent to a private asylum." —Reuter.*)

MASANIELLO PARISE. 1895.

PALL MALL GAZETTE (*continued*)—

1892.   *July*   19.   *Fatal Accident to a Fencer.* (*The button of the foil used by Professor Castaldi became detached in fencing with Mr. C. Terry, physician at Fall River, Mass., U.S.A., and the weapon pierced the doctor's mask, and entering his right eye, penetrated to the brain.*)

   „   *August*   23.   *Duel between Princess Pauline Metternich and Countess Kilmannsegg, with Rapiers.* (*At the third round the Princess was slightly wounded on the nose, and the Countess on the arm.*)

   „   *September*   8.   *The Tzar and Duelling in the Russian Army.*

1893.   *May*   2.   *Ancient and Modern Swordplay. Exhibition at Windsor by the Officers of the King's Dragoon Guards.*]

PALL MALL MAGAZINE (Periodical).   8°.   *London:* 18 Charing Cross Road.

[1896. *February.* "*Phyllis is my only Joy.*" *By C. J. Wills. Illustrated by Arthur B. Buckland.* "*Duel,*" pp. 199–200.]

PAMPHLETEER (The). (Periodical.)   *London.*

[Vol. XII. p. 79. "*Duelling.*"]

PAPELES VARIOS, manuscritos è impresos trasladados de mano de D. Juan Francisco Marañon y Pumarejo.   Folio.

[*MSS. In the British Museum. Eg.* 349. Vol. XIX. *Containing papers and tracts relating to part of the reign of Philip IV.* (1639–66); No. 12 (f. 104), "*Copia del cartel de desafio que el duque de Medina Sidonia* [*D. Gaspar*] *envió al de Berganza* [*D. Juan*];" 29th Sept. 1641 (*printed in folio at the time*).]

PAREJA (P. FRANCISCO). — Disertacion sobre si sería justa ta la ley que diese por infame al que no venció ó quitó la espada á su adversario ó le permitió quedar libre.

[*MS. In the Bibl. Nacional, Madrid. CC.* 84.]

PARISE (MASANIELLO). — Trattato teorico-pratico della scherma di spada e sciabola.   Preceduto da un cenno storico sulla scherma e sul duello.   8°.   1884.   *Roma:* Tip. Nazionale.

[*4th edition,* 1889. (xxxi *and* 328 *pages.*) *Numerous figures in the text. Approvato dal Ministero della Guerra e della Marina.*] (*In Captain Hutton's Collection.*)

—— (—). — *FAMBRI* (*Paolo*). — 1884.

PARIS GUIDE; par les principaux écrivains et artistes de la France.   12°.   2 vols.   1867.   Librairie Internationale.

[Tome II. pp. 981–986. *Legouvé* (*E.*), "*Les salles d'armes.*"]

PARIS ILLUSTRÉ (Periodical).   Folio.   *Paris.*
[1885. 1 *juin.* No. 31. " *Le duel et l'escrime.*"]

PARISIAN DUELS.
[" *Saturday Review* " (*London*), Vol. LIII., No. 804.]

PARISIAN FENCING.
[" *All the Year Round.*" Vol. XXIII. p. 330.]

PARKYNS (SIR THOS.) [of Bunny, Baronet]. — The Inn-Play, or Cornith-Hugg Wrestler. Digested in a method which teacheth to break all holds and throw most falls mathematically. Easy to be understood by all gentlemen, &c., and of great use to such who understand the Small Sword in Fencing. Small 4°. 1727. *London :* Tho. Weekes.

—— (—— —.). — Ditto. 8°. [N.D.] [1809 ?] *London :* J. Bailey.
[*Curious folding frontispiece, partly coloured.*]

PASCHA[LL] (JOHANN GEORG). — Kurze Unterrichtung belangend die Pique, die Fahne, den Jägerstock, das Voltesiren, das Ringen, das Fechten auf den Stoss und Hieb, und endlich das Trincieren verferrtigts. 8°. 1657. *Wittenberg.*

—— (— —). — Kurze doch Gründliche Unterrichtung den Pique, den Trillens in der Pique, die Fahne, den Jägerstock, Trincieren, Fechten auf den Stoss und auf den Hieb, &c. 8°. 1659. *Osnabruck.*

—— (— —). — Kurtze doch Gründliche Unterrichtung der Pique, den Trillens in der Pique, der Fahne, des Jägerstocks, Trincierens, Fechtens auf den Stoss und auf den Hieb, &c. Mit Kpf. 8°. 1659. *Osnabruck.*

—— (— —). — Kurze, jedoch deutliche Beschriebung handelnd. vom Fechten auf den Stoss und Hieb. Folio. 1661. *Halle in Sachsen.*

—— (— —). — Ditto. Mit sonderbaren Fleiss auffgesetzt, und mit . . . Kupffern aussgebildet von J. G. Paschen. 2te Auflage. 3 parts. Folio. 1664. *Halle in Sachsen.*
[*With an engraved general title-page, as follows :* " *Vollständiges Fecht-, Ring- und Voltigier-Buch,*" *and bearing the imprint :* Leipzig, 1667.]
(*In the British Museum.* 7905. *h.* 17.)

PASCHA[LL] (JOHANN GEORG). — Vollständige Fecht-, Ring- und Voltigier-Kunst. Small folio. 1667. *Leipzig.*

—— (— —). — Deutliche Bescreibung von dem Exerciren in der Mussquet . . . nach heutiger Kriegs-Art . . . beschrieben, und mit vielen nöthigen Kupffern ausgebildet. Folio. 1667. *Halle in Sachsen.*

—— (— —). — Vollständige Fecht-, Ring- und Voltigier-Kunst. Small folio. 1673. *Leipzig.*

—— (— —). — Der adelichen gemüthen wohlerfahrne Exercitien-Meister ; das ist :—Vollständige Fecht-, Ring- und Voltigier Kunst. Small folio. 1683. *Franckfurt und Leipzig :* C. Weidermannen.

PASQUIER (EST.). — Gages de batailles. 2 vols. Folio. 1723. *Trevoux.*

PASTOR DE CASAL (JULIÁN). — Arte de las armas, ó sea instruccion de florete, sable y pistola. 4°. MS.

PATEK (FRANZ). — *SPORT* (*Der*). — 1880.

PATENOSTRIER. — *CAVALCABO* (*H.*). — 1609.

PATIN (GUY). — Lettres. 3 vols. 8°. 1846. *Paris.*
[Vol. III. p. 536. *"Duelling."*]

PATRONI (GUIS). — Duello. 8°. 1881. *Siena.*

PATTEN (GEORGE W.). — Cavalry Drill and Sabre Exercise. 16°. 1863. *New York.*

PAUL. — Account of H. Paul's Duel with Mr. Dalton in 1751.
[*MS. in the British Museum.* 32,967. *ff.* 342, 344.]

PAULI. — Schimpf und Ernst. 8°. 1546. *Augsburg :* Steyner.
[*Zweikampf mitgetheilt.*]

PAULSEN (HECTOR MAIR) [Bürger zu Augsburg]. — MS. in the Royal Library, Dresden.
[*Contains numerous well-drawn coloured illustrations of Fencing.*]

PAURNFEINDT (ANDRE) [Freyfechter* czu Vienñ in Osterreich]. — Ergrundung ritterlicher Kunst der Fechterey nach klerlicher

begreiffung vnd kurczlicher verstendnusz. Oblong 4°. 1516.
Viennæ : Hieronm ū Vetoıē.

[*Ornamental title-page, with the arms of the Bishop of Gurck. 22 woodcuts
showing the use of the long sword (Schwerdt) ; 8, that of the cutlass (Messer,
Tesak, Düsack) ; 4, that of the quarterstaff (Stange).*
" *This is the oldest printed book in German, and is exceedingly rare. It is
an admirable exponent of the ways of using long and short sword, knife,
or dagger to the utmost of their lethal capacity, quite irrespective of any
sense of decorum. It must have met what would now in journalistic style
be called a long-felt want, for it was reproduced under various attractive
titles, very confusing to the bibliographer, in Frankfort, Augsburg, Strasburg, and finally done into French, under the name of ' La Noble Science
des Joueurs d'Espée,' published in Paris and Antwerp in 1538.*
" *Thus is the first French book of fence known, curiously enough shown to be
a translation from the German."—Castle (E.), " The Story of Swordsmanship." (" The National Review," May 1891.)*
 * *The Freyfechter was a teacher certificated by the central committee of the
Marxbrüder. The ordeal which the candidate for this freedom had to
undergo was very severe.*]
(*In Dr. Karl Wassmannsdorff's Collection in Heidelberg.*)

[PAURNFEINDT (ANDRE).] — La noble science des joueurs
d'éspée. [Ici commence un tres beau livret, contenant la chevaleureuse science des joueurs d'éspée, pour apprendre à jouer de l'éspée à
deux mains et aultres semblables éspées, avec aussi les braquemars et
aultres courts cousteaux lesquels lon use à une main. . . .] — (At
the end : Imprimé en la ville Danuers par moy, Guillaume Vosterman, demourant à la Lycorne dor.) 4°. 1538. *Antwerp.*

[Black letter. 14 *whole-page and 12 half-page woodcuts.*
" *Das älteste in französischer Sprache gedruckte Fechtbuch v. J. 1538 ist eine
Uebersetzung des ältesten deutschen Fechtbuch vom Jahre 1516."—Dr.
Karl Wassmannsdorff.* (" *Monatsschrift für das Turnwesen." 1892.
Mai. Heft 5.)* (*In the British Museum.*)

PAZ (D. FRANCISCO SANCHEZ, SANTOS DE LA). — Ilustracion de
la destreza indiana ; epístola oficiosa que escribó al maestro de campo
Don F. Lorenz de Rada, órden de Santiago, Marqués de la Torres,
. . . &c. &c., sobre varios discursos publicados por el referido marqués,
en la que intituló defensa de la verdadera destreza de las armas.
Sácala á luz el Capitan Diego Rodriguez de Guzman, guarda mayor
de la Real Casa de Moneda desta ciudad de Lima, corte de Perú.
4°. 1712. *Lima :* Gerónimo de Contreras y Alvarado.

PEARSALL (R. L.). — Some Observations on Judicial Duels, as
practised in Germany. In a letter to Sir Henry Ellis, K.H., F.R.S.
[*Read at the Society of Antiquaries, London, February* 20, 1840. (" *Archæologia," Vol. XXIX. pp.* 348–361. 8 *plates.*)]

PEARS' PICTORIAL. An Illustrated Quarterly. Edited by Joseph Grego. Folio. *London:* New Oxford Street.

> [1895. *March* 1. Vol. I., No. 7. "*Rowlandson and his Works.*" Page 16.
> *The Assault, or Fencing-match, which took place at Carlton House on the 9th April 1787, between Mademoiselle La Chevalière d'Eon de Beaufort and Monsieur Saint-George, in the presence of the Prince of Wales and many eminent fencing-masters of London and Paris.* "*A Fencing-match* (1788)."]

PELLEGRINI (C.). — Considerazione sulla razionalità e punibilità del duello. 8°. 1868. *Venezia.*

PEN AND PENCIL (Periodical). *London.*

> [1887. *February* 5. Vol. I., No. 4, p. 27. "*The Last Duel in Scotland.*" (*Sir Alexander Boswell, Bart., and Mr. James Stuart.*)]

PÉNE (HENRY DE). — *BOURDEILLES* (*Pierre de*). — 1887.

—— (— —). — *BRANTÔME.* — 1888.

PENNSYLVANIA LAW JOURNAL. *Pennsylvania (U.S.A.).*

> [Vol. VII. p. 45. "*Duelling.*"]

PENNY ILLUSTRATED PAPER (The). — (Periodical.) Folio. *London.*

> [1894. *June* 2. "*Ladies' Duel at the Goldsmiths' Institute, New Cross.*"]

PENNY MAGAZINE. (Periodical.) *London.*

> [Vol. V. p. 31. "*Remarkable Duel in* 1664."]

PEPPER (W.) [of the Notts Yeomanry Cavalry]. — Treatise on the New Broad Sword Exercise, with 14 Divisions of Movements as performed at Newmarket. 12°. 3rd edition. 1798.

> [12 *plates.*
> 6th *edition* 1803.]

PEPYS (SAMUEL) [F.R.S.].—Memoirs and Diary, with his Private Correspondence. Edited by Lord Braybrooke. 5 vols. 8°. 1828. *London:* Colburn.

> [*Many brilliant portraits and plates.*
> "*For graphic accounts of gory stage-fights the reader is referred to various contemporary accounts of foreigners on a visit to England (among others to that of one Monsieur Jorevin de Rocheford, who seems to have been much horrified by the blood-letting he saw in the* 'Bergiardins,' *or bear-gardens, of the Surrey side), to the pages of the* 'Spectator' *[No. 436], and to the Diary of the immortal Mr. Pepys.*"—*Castle* (E.), "*The Story of Swordsmanship.*" ("*The National Review,*" *May* 1891.)]

PEPYS (SAMUEL). — Diary and Correspondence. 3rd edition. 5 vols. 8°. 1849. *London:* H. Colburn.

> [Vol. II. p. 165. *"Art of Fencing."*
> *"And I with Sir J. Minnes to the Strand May-pole; and there light out of his coach, and walked to the New Theatre, which, since the King's players are gone to the Royal one, is this day begun to be employed by the fencers to play prizes at. And here I came and saw the first prize I ever saw in my life: and it was between one Mathews, who did best at all weapons, and one Westwicke, who was soundly cut several times both in the head and legs, that he was all over blood: and other deadly blows they did give and take in very good earnest, till Westwicke was in a sad pickle. They fought at eight weapons, three boutes at each weapon. This being upon a private quarrel, they did it in good earnest; and I felt one of their swords, and found it to be very little, if at all, blunter on the edge than the common swords are. Strange to see what a deal of money is flung to them both upon the stage between every boute. So, well pleased for once with this sight, I walked home."*]

PERALTA (SUÁREZ DE). — Tractado de la Cavalleria de la Gineta y Brida. 1580. *Sevilla.*

PERCHE (JEAN BAPTISTE LE) [du Coudray]. — L'exercice des armes ou le maniement du fleuret. Pour ayder la mémoire de ceux qui sont amateurs de cet état. Oblong 4°. 1676. *Paris:* chez N. Bonnard.

> [35 *copperplates. Avec titre en frontispice; les planches et le texte encadrés sont gravés sur cuivre.*]

—— (—— —— ——). — L'exercice des armes, etc. 2e édition. Oblong 4°. 1750. *Paris:* N. Bonnard.

> [*With the addition of 5 plates.*]

PEREGRINUS (AL.). — Tractatus de duello. 4°. 1614. *Venetia.*

PÉREZ (DON CAYETANO POBLACIÓN). — Esgrima, ó sea la destreza del florete. 4°. 1832. *Valladolid:* Roldán.

> [7 *plates.*]

PÉREZ (G.). — Il sistema di spada Radaelli, giudicato dall' arte della scherma. 4°. 1878. *Verona:* Tip. di Gaetano Franchini.

> [7 *folded lithographed plates.*]

PÉRIGNON (BARON) [Député de la Marne]. — Rapport et discours sur une pétition qui avait pour de provoquer la présentation d'une loi spéciale sur le duel. 1847. 8°. *Paris:* Panckoucke.

> [16 *pages.*] (*In Mr. J. R. Garcia Donnell's Collection.*)

PERINAT (D. Juan Nicolás) [Maestro de esgrima en la real academia de Cavalleros Guardias - Marinas]. — Arte de esgrimir florete é sable por los principios mas seguros, faciles y intelligibles. Oblong 4º. 1758. *Cádiz :* Cavalleros Guardias-Marinas.

> [36 *copperplates.*]

PERRIÈRES (Carle Des). — Les figures de cire. Avec une préface par Albert Millaud. 12º. 1874. *Paris :* Sartorius.

> [Pages 141–156. *"Premier duel."*
> Pages 157–169. *"Du duel, notes et conseils."*]

—— (— —). — Paris au club. 12º. 1890. *Paris :* Calmann Lévy.

> [Pages 13–30. *"Duels d'autrefois et duels d'aujourd'hui."*]

PERSON (David). — Varieties, or a Surveigh of Rare and Excellent Matters Digested into Five Books. Small 4º. 1635.

> ["*Duels and Combats.*"]

PERSUASIVE (A) from the Practice of Duelling. By a Minister of the Church of England. 4º. 1784. *London :* Cadell.

PERVANCHÈRE (De la). — Essais sur l'escrime. 1869. *Nantes :* Ev. Mangin.

PESTEL (Thomas) [Chaplain to Charles I.]. — Sermons preached at several Courts to King Charles the First of ever blessed memory, and to our most gracious Sovereign King Charles II., together with some Devotions [in verse], and a Treatise of Duels. Small 8º. 1660.

PETIT GLANEUR (Le). 32º. 1815. *Paris.*

> [*Almanach de 1815, renfermant la chanson : L'Amour maître en fait d'armes.
> Avec gravures en couleur, chez L. Fuel.*]

PETTER (Nicolaes). — Klare onderrichtinge der voortreffelijcke Worstel-Konst, verhandelende hoemen in alle voorvallen van Twist en Handtgemeenschap, sich kan hoeden : en alle aengrepen, borst-stooten, Vuyst-slagen, &c., versetten. 4º. 1674. *Amsterdam :* Willem van Lamsvelt.

> [*Met 71 naeuwkeurige Verbeeldingen in 't Kooper gebracht door R. de Hooge.
> The seizure in dagger-play, or the method for an unarmed man attacked by
> one armed with a knife, is touched upon by this author.*]
> (*In the British Museum.* 556. e. 9.)

PETTER (NICOLAES). — Der künstliche Ringer, oder . . . An-
leitung zu der Fürtrefflichen Ringe-Kunst . . . in mehr als 70 . . .
Figuren vorgestellet, und ins Kupffer gebracht durch . . . R. de
Hooge. 4°. 1674. *Amsterdam :* J. Jansson von Waesberge.

(*In the British Museum.* 7905. *e.* 13.)

—— (—). — [Another copy, with a different title-page.]   4°.
[1674 ?] *Amsterdam :* W. van Lamsvelt.

(*In the British Museum.* 556. *e.* 8.)

—— (—). — [Another edition.]   Folio.   1675.   *Mümpelgart.*

(*In the British Museum.* 7905. *h.* 2.)

—— (—). — *HOOGE* (*R. de*). — 1674.

—— (—). — *HOOGUE* (*R. de*). — [1712 ?]

—— (—). — Ring-Kunst vom Jahre 1674.   Mit deutschem und
holländischem Text und 71 Lichtdrucken der Kupferstiche Romein
de Hooghe's neu herausgegeben von Dr. K. Wassmannsdorff.   4°.
1887.   *Heidelberg :* K. Groos.

[**xvi** *and* 39 *pages. A reprint of Petter's work, with a German translation.*]

PFEFFINGER (DR. G.). — *CHRISTMANN* (*F. C.*). — 1838.

PHILIP OF FRANCE (KING). — *COTTONIAN* MSS.

[*Vesp. C. xiv.* 236. (570.)]

PHYSICAL DRILL with Arms and Bayonet Exercise.   32°.
1889.   *London :* Harrison & Sons.

[21 *plates, out of the text.*]

PHYSICAL DRILL, NEW BAYONET EXERCISES, and Attack
and Defence made Easy.   6th edition.   32°.   1895.   *Chatham :*
Gale & Polden.

PICK-ME-UP (Periodical).   4°.   *London.*

[1893.   *November* 23.   *" Naval Manœuvres."* (*Humorous sketch of Cutlass
Exercise.*)]

PICOT (V. M.). — [Fencing Print.   Curious old Engraving by
Picot, after Robineau, of the " Assault or Fencing-match which
took place between Mademoiselle La Chevalière d'Eon de Beaumont
and Mons. Saint-George, 9th April 1787."   Size, exclusive of margins,

18 in. × 16 in.   Dedicated by permission to H.R.H. the Prince of Wales.   1789.   *London :* V. M. Picot, 6 Greek Street, Soho.]

[*The match was fought at Carlton House in the presence of the Prince of Wales (whose portrait appears), several of the nobility, and many eminent fencing-masters of London.*
From a picture of Robineau's in the possession of H.R.H. the Prince of Wales.]

PICTORIAL WORLD (Periodical).   Folio.   *London.*

[1884.   *November* 13.   "*Sword-making.*"]

PIETSCH (ALBERT). — Der Papst gegen den Zweikampf.

[1891–92.   "*Die Residenz.*"   Heft 1.   Seite 23–26.   (4°.   Wien : *Backerstrasse* 24.)]

PIGNA (GIOUAN BATTISTA). — Il duello, al S. Donno Alphonso da este Prencipe di Ferrara, diviso in tre libri.   Ne quali dell' honore, et dell' ordine della cavalleria con nuouo modo si tratta.   4°.   1554.   *Vinegia :* Vincenzo Valgrisi.

(*In Captain Hutton's Collection, and British Museum* [713. c. 1. (1.)].)

—— (— —). — Il duello, al S. Donno Alphonso da este Prencipe di Ferrara, in tre libri.   Ne quali dell' honore e dell' ordine della cavalleria.   Con nuovo modo si tratta.   12°.   1560.   *Vinegia.*

—— (— —). — *MURATORI (L. A.).* — 1708.

PILLA (CARLO). — Arte e scuole di scherma.   Conferenza tenuta alla Società Bolognese di scherma nel febbraio 1886.   8°.   1886.   *Bologna :* Società Tipografica già Compositori.

PINAUD (L.). — L'Académie d'armes de la rue Saint-Honoré en 1876.   Portraits, esquisses.   8°.   *Paris :* Dupont.

[*Non mis dans le commerce.*]

PINETTE (JOSEPH). —École du tirailleur, ou maniement de la baïonnette appliqué aux exercices et manœuvres de l'infanterie.   18°.   1832.   *Paris :* Dumaine.

[32 *figures.*]

—— (—). — École du tirailleur, ou maniement de la baïonnette.   5e édition.   12°.   1843.   *Paris :* J. Dumaine.

(*In Captain Hutton's Collection.*)

PINETTE (JOSEPH). — École du tirailleur, &c. 8e édition. 18°.
1846. *Paris:* Dumaine.

> [32 *figures.* Vide 1*st edition,* 1832.]

—— (—). — Théorie de l'escrime à la baïonnette. 18°. 1847.
Paris: Dumaine.

> [16 *figures.*]

—— (—). — Réfutation de l'escrime à la baïonnette, de M.
Gomard. 8°. 1847. *Paris:* Dumaine.

> (*In Captain Hutton's Collection.*)

—— (—). — Katechismus der Bayonnetfechtkunst. 8°. 1851.
Leipzig: Weber.

> [*Mit* 16 *Abbildungen.*]

—— (—). — Dissertation sur l'emploi de la baïonnette, les
travaux et les sacrifices que l'auteur du maniement de cette arme a
faits pour répandre sa méthode dans l'armée. 8°. 1860. *Montrouge.*

> (*In Captain Hutton's Collection.*)

—— (—). — *MARÍN* (*Don Antonio*). — 1850. 1859.

PISAN (CHRISTINE DE).—The fayttes of armes and chyualrye,
whiche translaycyon was fynysshed the viij day of juyll the said
yere (1489), was emprynted the xiiij day of juyll the next folowing.
B. L. Folio. [1489. Westminster.] Per Caxton.

> [*This work was translated and printed by William Caxton from the French
> of Christine de Pisan. MS. notes. Without title-page or pagination.
> Signatures A–Siij and A–R have 8 leaves each. 144 leaves, the last blank;
> 30 and 31 lines to a full page.*]
> (*In the British Museum. C. 21. d. 33.*)

PISE (CHRISTINE DE). — Livre des faits d'armes et de chevalerie.
Folio. 1488. *Paris:* Anth. Verard.

PISTOFILO (BONAVENTURA) [Ferrarese]. — Oplomachia, nella
quale, . . . &c., si tratta per via di teoria et di practica del maneggio
e dell' uso delle armi, di picca, &c. 4°. 1621. *Sienna:* Ecole
Gori.

> (*In the British Museum. 785. a 16.*)

—— (—). — Il torneo. 4°. 1627. *Bologna:* per il Ferrone.

> [*Frontispiece and 114 copperplates; no text.*]
> (*In the South Kensington Museum.*)

Ipse ensem, et calamum.   *galeamq̃, gerog̃, galerum.*
Sic docco, et scribo.   *sic nocco, el tucor.*

BONAVENTURA PISTOFILO. 1621.

Nobile Ferrarese Dottore e Caualiere.

[BONAVENTURA PISTOFILO. 4°. 1621.]

PIZARRO (D. Juan Fernando). — Apología de la destreza de las armas. (Defensa del libro de Carranza sobre ello.) 8°. 1623. *Trujillo.*

PLAISTER (Gabriel Sticking). — Duelling. 8°. 1840. *Bath.*

PLAN (A) TO ABOLISH DUELLING. 8°. 1844. *London.*

PLUMER (W. S.). — *PRINCETOWN* Review.

POCKET VOLUNTEER CAVALRY INSTRUCTOR in the Sword Exercise ; in five parts. 24°. *London.*

POLANCO (Juan Claudio Aznar de). — Carta, de la destreza de las armas, respuesta a un papel de titulo : destreza vulgar, . . . &c. 4°. 1724. *Madrid.*

PÖLLNITZ (G. L. von). — Das Hiebfechten zu Fuss und Pferde. Gr. 8°. 1820. *Halberstadt :* Brüggemann.

—— (—. —. —). — Ditto. Neue Auflage. Large 8°. 1825. *Halberstadt :* Brüggemann.

POLLOCK (Frederick). — [" Sword." *Encyclopædia Brittanica.* 9th edition. Vol. XXII. p. 800.]

—— (—). — Oxford Lectures and other Discourses. 8°. 1890. *London :* Macmillan.
[" *The Forms and History of the Sword.*"]

—— (—). — Lecture on "The Sword" at the School of Arms, Inns of Court Rifle Volunteers.
[" *The Times,*" *Weekly edition, Nov. 20, 1891.*]

—— (—). — *MACMILLAN'S* Magazine.

—— (—). — *SATURDAY* Review (The). — 1891. Vol. LXXII. p. 587.

POLLOCK (W. H.), **GROVE** (F. C.), and **PRÉVOST** (Camille). — Fencing. With a complete Bibliography of the Art by Egerton Castle. (The Badminton Library.) 8°. 1890. *London :* Longmans.
[*Illustrated with* 18 *intaglio plates.*
" *Mr. Walter Herries Pollock, editor of the ' Saturday Review,' is, like Sir Charles Dilke, one of the most expert swordsmen in the country.*"—" *The Star* " *(London), August 31, 1891.*]

POLLOCK (W. H.). — *ILLUSTRATED* London News.—July 9, 1892.

—— (—. —.). — *CASTLE (E.).* — 1893.

POLYCARPE (DE ST.). — Sonnets contre les escrimeurs et duellistes. Petit in-4°. 1588. *Paris :* Jamet Mattayer.

PÖNITZ (KARL EDUARD). — Die Fechtkunst auf den Stoss ; nach den Grundsätzen des Herrn von Selmnitz. 8°. 1822. *Dresden :* Arnold.

—— (— —). — Ditto. Neue wohl. Ausgable. 8°. 1828. *Dresden :* Arnold.

PONS (DE MAJORCA) [or **PONA**] (JAYME) [JAUME or JACOBUS]. — (A Treatise on the Art of the Sword.) 1474. *Perpiñan.*

> [*Dr. Thomas Windsor (Manchester) writes, under date of May 21, 1891 :* "*A very good reason for the extreme rarity of this work is that no such book was printed at or near that time. I am speaking from memory, but I think I made myself, many years ago, quite certain of what I say.*"]

PONS (MAÎTRE D'ARMES). — *GRANDEFFE (A. de).* — 1884.

POPULAR SCIENCE MONTHLY (Periodical). *New York.*
[Vol. XXI. p. 79. "*Genesis of the Sword.*"]

PORATH (DIEDERICH). — Palaestra Suecana, eller den adelige Fachtare-Konsten, &c., &c. Folio. 1693. *Stockholm.*
[24 *copperplates, in the text.*]

PORCACCHI (THOMAS). — Haym a inséré une collection d'ouvrages italiens sur le point d'honneur, dans la liste qu'il a donnée de la collection dite Collana, imaginée ; et imprimée par Gab. Giolito de Ferrari.
[*Crevena l'a reproduite dans son catalogue de 1776. 4°. Voy. le t. vi. p.* 204 *et* 205.]

PORONI (MARCHESE DI). — Breve, e distinto dialogo nel quale si ragiona del duello, et si decidono cento, e piu dubi e questione. 12°. 1692. *Colonia :* V. Vr-sager.
(*In Captain Hutton's Collection.*)

PORRES (D. GOMEZ ARIAS DE). — Resúmen de la verdadera

destreza en el manejo de la espada. 4°. 1667. *Salamanca :*
Melchor Estevez.

[*Dedicale al Illustrissimo Señor Don Fernando de Villalolos y Porres su tio,
&c.* 12 *hoj. de prels.*, 147 *págs. con algunos grab. y* 3 *hoj. de tabla.*]
(*In the Bibl. Nacional y de Fernandez San Roman.*)

PORTFOLIO (The). 8°. 1820.
[*Contains celebrated Duels.*]

POSSELLIER (A. J. J.) [dit Gomard]. — La théorie de l'escrime,
enseignée par une méthode simple, basée sur l'observation de la
nature ; précédée d'une introduction dans laquelle sont résumés tous
les principaux ouvrages sur l'escrime qui ont paru jusqu'à ce jour.
8°. 1845. *Paris :* Dumaine.

[20 *planches, par Ch. Guérin.*] (*In Captain Hutton's Collection.*)

—— (—. —. —.). — L'Escrime à la baïonnette, ou école du
fantassin pour le maniement du fusil comme arme blanche. 8°.
1847. *Paris.*

[36 *plates.*]

POSSÉVINI. — *POSSEVINO (A.).*

——.— *POSSEVINO (G. B.).*

POSSEVINO (A.) [the Elder]. — Libro nel quale s'insegna a
conoscer le cose pertinenti all' honore, et a ridurre ogni querela
alla pace. 4°. 1559. *Vinegia :* Giolito.

(*In the British Museum.* 30. *b.* 23.)

—— (—.). — Ditto. 8°. 1564. *Vinegia :* Giolito.
(*In the British Museum.* 232. *c.* 8.)

POSSEVINO (G. B.) [the Elder]. — Dialogo dell' honore, nel
quale si tratta à pieno del Duello. 8°. 1553. *Vinegia.*
[*Edited by A. Possevino.*]

—— (—. —.). — Dialogo dell' honore, nel quale si tratta à pieno
del duello con la tavola di quanto vi si contiene fatta con diverso
ordine dall' altre. 4°. 1556. *Vinegia.*
(*In Captain Hutton's Collection.*)

—— (—. —.) [Mantovano]. — Dialogo dell' honore, nel quale si
tratta a pieno del duello. Di nuovo aggiuntovi un trattato di M.

Antonio Possevini, nel quale s'insegna a conoscere le cose apparenenti all' honore, & a ridurre ogni querela alla pace, & con le Apostille nel margine. 4°. 1558. *Vinegia:* Gabriel Giolito de' Ferrari.

(In the British Museum. 713. *c.* 3.)

POSSEVINO (G. B.). — Ditto. Di nuovo aggiunto un trattato di M. A. Possevini, nel quale s'insegna a conoscere le cose appartenenti all' honore, etc. 2 parts. 4°. 1559. *Vinegia.*

(In the British Museum. 30. *b.* 23.)

—— (—. —.). — Ditto. 8°. 1564. *Vinegia.*

—— (—. —.). — Ditto. 8°. 1568. *Venetia.*

—— (—. —.). — Ditto. 8°. 1583. *Venetia.*

PRADET (Jean Eleonord du) [Maître en faites d'armes en la ville et université du Pont-à-Mousson]. — Abrégé de l'art des armes, ou l'exercice de l'épée seule avec les attitudes. Oblong 8°.

[*MS. de 245 pages, avec 13 planches semblables à celles du Danet, gravées sur cuivre, de la Bibl. Nationale à Florence ("Magliabechiana," XIX. 196). Date, end of the eighteenth century.*]

PRAGMÁTICA que su magestad ha mandado promulgar reiterando la del año 1716 por la que prohibe los duelos, retos y desafíos baxo de graves penas. 8 pages in folio. 1757. *Madrid:* A. Sanz.

PRAKTISCHE ANLEITUNG ZUM UNTERRICHT IM STOSS-FECHTEN. 8°. 1872. *Berlin:* Schroeder.

[*With woodcuts.*]

——. — Ditto. 2te Auflage. Klein 8°. 1874. *Berlin:* Schroeder.

[*Figures in the text.*]

——. — Ditto. Nach der bei der königl. Central-Turnanstalt eingeführten Lehrmethode. 3te verb. Auflage. 8°. 1879. *Berlin:* Schroeder.

[*Figures in the text.*]

PRAKTISCHE BAJONETT - FECHTSCHULE auf Grund der Bajonettir - Vorschrift für die Infanterie vom 15. August. 8°. 1889. *Berlin:* Mittler u. Sohn.

[*17 plates, in text.*]

CAMILLE PRÉVOST. 1895.

PRAKTISCHER UNTERRICHT IN DER BAJONETFECHT-KUNST, der schweizerischen Infanterie gewidmet. 8°. 1835. *Bern.*

[52 *figures.*]

PREAU (GABR. DU). — *COTEREAU (Claude).* — 1549.

PREUSSISCHEN GROSSEN GENERALSTABES (Königlich), Katalog der Bibliothek des. 8°. 1878. *Berlin:* E. S. Mittler und Sohn.

[Page 50. " *Fechten.*"]

PRÉVOST (CAMILLE). — Théorie pratique de l'escrime. Avec préface et notice, par Ernest Legouvé de l'Académie française ; et la biographie de Prévost père, par A. Tavernier. Gr. in-8°. 1886. *Paris:* De Brunhoff.

[*With plates.*
Dessins de Bourgoin d'après l'épreuves photographiques instantanées de Nadar.]

—— (—). — *POLLOCK (W. H.).* — 1890.

(*The Badminton Library.*)

PRÉVOST (C.) et **JOLLIVET** (G.). — L'Escrime et le duel. 8°. 1891. *Paris:* Hachette & Cie.

[*Avec 21 héliogravures en taille-douce, et 25 gravures insérées dans le texte.* (*Fait partie de la " Bibliothèque du sport."*)]

PRÉVOST (M. C.).

[" *Wrote a short pamphlet on 'Fencing,' at Prince Albert's request, but owing to the latter's sudden death it was never published. His son has, however, utilised it in his 'Théorie Pratique de l'Escrime,' in which he aims at explaining as clearly and precisely as possible Bertrand's and his father's method of fence."—" Fencing," by May G. Norris. (" The Badminton Magazine," September 1895.)*]

PRÉVOST (PIERRE). — Théorie pratique de l'escrime simplifiée pour l'enseignement mutuel. 8°. 1860. *Londres:* Nissen et Parker.

—— (—). — Theory and Practice of Fencing, for Mutual Instruction. 8°. 1860. *London:* Nissen & Parker.

(*In Captain Hutton's Collection.*)

PRINCETOWN REVIEW (Periodical). *Princetown (U.S.A.).*

[Vol. XX. p. 542. " *Duelling." By W. S. Plumer.*]

PRINCIPES pour apprendre à tirer des armes par M. . . ., Dragon au Régiment du Mestre de Camp Général des Dragons.

> [*MS. Vers.* 1750. *Manuscrit d'une belle écriture avec trois planches dessinées à la plume, la première coloriée ornée en frontispice. In-8°. N'a jamais été imprimé. Reliure ancienne en veau avec deux fermoirs de cuivre, dos orné, tranche rouge.*] (*Vigeant's Collection.*)

PROBST (Em.) [Hauptmann]. — Anleitung zum Säbelfechten (Stichsäbel) mit Reglement zum Preisfechten. 8°. 1889. *Zürich :* Orell Füssli & Co.

> (*In Mr. J. R. Garcia Donnell's Collection.*)

—— (—.). — Instruction sur l'escrime au sabre [contre-pointe] avec réglement pour les concours. 8°. 1889. *Zürich :* Orell Füssli & Co.

PRODONI (Narbonte). — *GUILLET.* — 1683.

PROST (Bernard). — Traicté de la forme et devis comme on faict les tournois, par Olivier de La Marche, Hardouin de La Jaille, Anthoine de La Sale, etc. Mis en ordre par B. Prost. Enrichi de 16 planches, dont 9 doubles, coloriées au pinceau et rehaussées d'or. Gr. in-8°. 1878. *Paris :* A. Barraud.

> [*C'est le même volume qui a été publié en 1872 par l'éditeur Willem (tirage à 400 exemplaires numérotés) sous le titre, " Traités du duel judiciaire." Le libraire Barraud a acheté en 1878 le restant de l'ouvrage (260 exemplaires), en a modifié le titre comme ci-dessus, y a joint les planches (qui, du reste, ne se rapportent pas au texte) et l'a remis en vente avec le millésime de 1878, et la mention : " Il n'a été tiré que 260 exemplaires de cet ouvrage, avec les 16 planches coloriées, tous numerotés de 1 à 260."*]

—— (—). — *TRAITÉS* du duel judiciaire. — 1872.

PROZESS-VERHANDLUNGEN des Assisen-Hofes der untern Seine (Rouen) in Sachen des Duells zwischen des Journalisten Dujarier und von Beauvallon zu Paris. Aus dem Französ. des Journals "die Presse" übersetzt. 8°. 1846. *Berlin :* Tacco.

PRYME (George). — Autobiographic Recollections. 8°. 1870. *London :* Bell & Dalby.

> [Pages 233–236 *relate to Duels and Duelling.*]

PUJOS (MAURICE). — Essai sur la repression du duel. 12°. 1862. *Paris :* Dupray de la Mahérie.

PUÑONROSTRO. — Discurso para estar á la Gineta con gracia y hermosura. 1590. *Madrid.*

PUTEO (PARIS DE). — Solemnis et vtilis tractatus de re militari ubi est tota materia duelli pel singularis certamis.   Gr. in-folio. 1515. *Mediolani :* Aug. Scinzenzeler.

> [*La belle marque de l'imprimeur gravée e. b. au titre.*]

PUTEO (PARIS DE). — Duello : libro de re, imperatori, principi, sígnori, gentil' homini ; et de tutti armigeri, continente disfide, concordie, pace, casi accadenti ; et judicii con ragione, exempli., etc.   8°. 1521. *Venetia.*

> [*Numerous engraved initial letters ; title within woodcut border of swords, axes, bows, armour, guns, and cannons.*]
> (*In the British Museum. C. 62. a. 9. In Mr. J. R. Garcia Donnell's Collection.*)
> [*Other editions appeared in 1523, 1525, 1536, 1540, and 1544.*]

PUTNAM'S MONTHLY MAGAZINE (Periodical).   *New York.*
> [Vol. X. p. 254. "*Philosophy of the Pistol.*"]

PUYSEGUR (SEIGNEUR DE). — Les mémoires de Messire Jacques de Chastenet, Chevalier, Seigneur de Puysegur.   1747.   *Paris.*
> [Tome XI. p. 306, *refers to the use of the bayonet.*]

—— (LE MARÉCHAL DE). — Art de la guerre par principes et par règles. 1748. *Paris :* Jombert.
> [Tome I. chap. vi. p. 57, *refers to the introduction of the bayonet into the French army.*]

PYRGOS (N.). — Hoplomachetiké Xiphaskía kaì Spathaskìa hypo N. Pýrgu, didaskálu en têi stratiotikêi scholêi. 8°. 1872. En *Athénaès :* Typographeion S. K. Blastu, hodos Hermû. arith. 178.

—— (—.). — Encheiridion praktikes Spathaskias. Meros proton. Askesis kata xiphon hypo N. Pyrgu, didaskálu tês hoplomachetikês en têi scholêi tôn euelpídon kaì tû ekpaideutikû lóchu. 8°. 1876. *Athenesi :* (timâtai drachmês).   Typois Andreu Koromeda.

QUARTERLY REVIEW (Periodical). 8º. *London :* John Murray.

QUEHL (Fr. W.). — Anweisung auf Fechten auf Stoss und Hieb, mit einer Anleitung zum Unterricht grösserer Abtheilungen im Fechten ins besondere in Turnvereinen. 16º. 1866. *Erlangen :* Besold.

[26 *plates.*]

—— (—. —.). — Anweisung zum Bajonetfechten. 8º. 1866. *Berlin.*

QUESITI del cavaliere instrutto nell' arte della scherma. 8º. 1664. *Padova.*

QUINCEY (Tho. de). — *DE QUINCEY (Tho.).*

[*Paper on " Duelling." See under " Quincey " in Bohn's " Lowndes."*]

—— (—. —). — *TAIT'S* Edinburgh Magazine.

QUINTINO (Antonio). — *BOICCIO (G.).* —1613.

QUIXADA. — Destreza de las armas. 1675. *Madrid.*

R. (A.). — De l'escrime d'après les règles et les principes de nos meilleurs professeurs, Laboëssière, Gomard, Lhomandie, Jean-Louis, Lafaugère et Grisier ; précédé d'une notice historique sur le fleuret et les salles d'escrime. 8º. 1877. *Paris :* Vernay.

[*Avec 16 planches.*]

R. (Hauptmann von). — Anleitung zum Kontra-bajonettfechten im Anschluss an den Entwurf der provisorischen Vorschriften für das Bajonettfechten der Infanterie. 12°. 1882. *Berlin :* Liebel.

R. (P. DE). — Dialogue de salle sur l'art de l'escrime. Essai soi-disant didactique par un amateur, secondé d'un artiste. 8°. 1882. *Genève.*

RACHEL (SAM.). — Disputatio de duellis. 4°. 1666. *Kiloni.*

RADA (DON FRANCISCO LORENZ DE). — Arte y manejo de la espada. Sobre la formación del atajo. 4°. *Cádiz.*
　　　　[*Beristain y Souza. Biblioteca Hispano-Americana.*]

—— (— — — —). — Crisol de la destreza, donde se purifica el oro de la verdad. 4°.
　　　　[*Beristain y Souza. Biblioteca Hispano-Americana.*]

—— (— — — —). — Respuesta filosófica y matemática en la qual se satisface á los Argumentos y Proposiciones que á los professores de la verdadera destreza y filosofía de las armas se han propuesto por un papel expedido sin nombre de autor. 4°. 1695. *Madrid :* Diego Martinez de Abad.
　　　　(*In the Biblioteca Nacional y de Fernandez San Roman.*)

—— (— — — —). — Experiencia del istrumento armigero espada. 4°. 1705. *Madrid :* D. Martinez.

—— (— — — —). — Nobleza de la espada, cuyo esplendor se expressa en tres libros, segun ciencia, arte y experiencia. Folio. 1705. *Madrid :* Joseph Rodriguez Escobar.
　　　　[16 *copperplates.*] (*In the Biblioteca Nacional y de Fernandez San Roman.*)

—— (— — — —). — Defensa de la verdadera de las armas, y respuesta á la carta apologetica de Diego Rodriguez de Guzman, graduado de maestro de esgrima en la Universidad del Engaño. 4°. 1712. *Mexico :* Vinda de Miguel de Ribera Calderon, en el Empedradillo.

RADAELLI (GIUSEPPE). — Istruzione pel maneggio della sciabola, pubblicata dal Capitano S. del Frate. 1868. *Firenze.*

RADAELLI (GIUSEPPE). — Istruzione per la scherma di scia-
bola e di spada del Prof. Giuseppe Radaelli, scritta d' ordine del
Minisetro della Guerra dal Capitano S. del Frate. 4°. 1876.
Milano.

[*10 folded lithographs.*]

—— (—). — *ANGELINI (A.).* — 1877. 1888.

—— (—). — *BESENZANICA (E.).* — 1886.

—— (—). — *DOUX (C.).* — 1875. 1876.

—— (—). — *FORTE (L.).* — 1878.

—— (—). — *FRATE (S. del).* — 1872. 1885.

—— (—). — *GELLI (J.).* — 1888.

—— (—). — *PAGLIUCA (G.).* — 1880.

—— (—). — *PEREZ (G.).* — 1878.

RAILTON. — The Army's Regulator ; with a Vindication of the
Sword. 8°. 1738. *London.*

RAMBACH (F. E.). — *ROQUES und BASNAGE.* — 1747.

RANC (A.). — *JACOB (J.).* — 1887.

RANIS (HEINRICH CHRISTOPH) [Königl. Commissarrii und Fecht-
meisters]. — Anweisung zur Fechtkunst für Lehrer und Lernende.
8°. 1771. *Berlin :* A. Mylius.

[*4 copperplates folded.*]
(*In Captain Hutton's Collection, and in the British Museum* [785. b. 34].)

RANZATTO (A.). — Istruzioni per la scherma di sciabola. Illustrata da 18 figure con aggiunte alcune norme per il duello. 8°.
1885. *Venezia :* Fratelli Visentini.

RAOUL. — *MÉLESVILLE.* — 1832.

RAPIERS. Spanish. 16th century.
(*In the Art Library, South Kensington Museum. Portfolio* 556.)

RAVANNE (CHEVALIER DE). — Page du Régent et Mousquetaire.
3 vols.   12°.   1751.   *Londres.*

> [Tome I. p. 141.   *Duelling.*
> ,,   II. p. 135.   ,,
> ,,   III. p. 40.   *Pistol Duel between the Marquise de Nesle and Madame*
>   *de Polignac.*
> ,,   III. p. 68.   *Duel with Comte de Bre . . ., Mousquetaire dans la*
>   *Première Compagnie.*
> (*Mémoires curieux remplis d'anecdotes sur la vie privée des personnages de la*
> *Cour du Régent dans les quels Alexandre Dumas père a puisé pour la com-*
> *position de ses romans " Régence."*)]

RAVIZZA (C.). — Il suicidio, il sacrifizio della vita e il duello.
8°.   1843.   *Milano.*

RÉCIT (Le) **DU DUEL** déplorable entre Messieurs le Duc de Beaufort et de Nemours, avec ce qui s'est passé dans le Luxembourg
entre Monsieur le Prince et le Comte de Rieux.   4°.   1652.
Paris: Simon le Porteur.

RECUEIL DE DIVERS ÉDICTS du roi et autres pièces touchant
les duels et rencontres.   4°.   1653.   *Paris.*

RECUEIL DE DIVERSES PIÈCES touchant les duels et rencontres.   4°.   1663.   *Paris:* Sebastien Cramoisy.
                    (*In Captain Hutton's Collection.*)

RECUEIL DES ÉDITS, déclarations et arrests de la Cour de
Parlement, contre les duels, publiez depuis l'année 1599 jusque à
present.   4°.   1660.   *Paris.*

RECUEIL DES ÉDITS, déclarations, arrests et autres pièces concernant les duels et rencontres.   12°.   1669.   [1679?]   *Paris:*
Cramoisy.

RECUEIL DES ÉDITS, déclarations, arrêts, etc., concernant les
duels.   12°.   1689.   *Paris:* Léonard.

RECUEIL DE THÉORIES ÉTRANGÈRES sur le maniement du
sabre ou l'escrime à cheval.   Traduit de l'allemand par un officier
général.   8°.   1826.   *Paris:* Anselin et Pochard.
                    (*In Captain Hutton's Collection.*)

REDIVIVUS (LATIMER) [*pseud., i.e.,* the REV. JOHN DAVIES,
D.D.]. — Splendid Sins.   A Letter addressed to . . . the Duke of
Wellington.   2nd edition.   8°.   *London.*   1830.
                    [Page 35.   "*Duelling.*"]
                    (*In the British Museum.   T.* 1290 (10.))

REED (J. J.). — *LIPPINCOTT'S* Magazine.

REFEREE (The). — (Periodical.) Folio. *London.*
[1890. *November* 23. "*Duelling.*" *By* "*Dagonet*" (*George R. Sims*).]

REFLECTIONS ON DUELLING, and of the most Effectual Means of Preventing it. 8°. 1790. *Edinburgh.*

RÉFLEXIONS (Quelques) d'un homme du monde sur les spectacles, la musique, le jeu et le duel. 8°. 1812. *Paris.*

REFORM. — Zur Reform des ackademischen Lebens. Wider Duellzwang. 8°. 1885. *Leipzig.*
[32 *pages.*] (*In the British Museum.* 8304. *aa.* 10. (4.))

REGLAMENTO de duelo ó juicio de batayla.
[*Copia en la Acad. de la Historia de un MS. lemosin que existió en el monasterio de Ripoll.*]

REGLAMENTO para instruccion especial de los regimientos de artilleria. 8°. 1874. *Madrid.*
[Titulo IV. pp. 90–116. "*Manejo del sable.*"
   „   V. pp. 119–125. "*Manejo del machete.*"]

REGLAMENTO para la instruccion táctica de las tropas de artilleria. 8°. 1888. *Madrid.*
[Cap° IV. "*Manejo y empleo del sable y machete.*"]

REGLAS PARA LA DESTREZA de las Armas, fundada en Ciencia, Philosophia, Mathemática, Arithmetica, Geometria, Música y Astronomia. 16°. 1727. *Madrid.*
[*MS.* 78 *págs.*]

REGLAS PARA LA LUCHA, uso de las armas, modo de atraer, acometer y defenderse del contrario.
[*MS.* (16*th century*). *Bibl. del Escorial.*]

REGLEMENT FOR BAYONETFÄGTNING. 8°. 1837. *Christiania.*

REGOOR (M.). — De Schermkunst voor het volkzonderwijs geschikt gemaakt. 8°. 1866. *s'Gravenhage.*

REGULATIONS AND INSTRUCTIONS for the Cavalry Sword Exercise. Adjutant-General's Office, Horse Guards, 10th June 1819. 8°. [1819.] *London:* W. Clowes.
[*With plate of Angelo's Sword Exercise.*]

REGULATIONS AND INSTRUCTIONS for the Infantry Sword Exercise. Adjutant-General's Office, Horse Guards, 10th September 1819. 8°. 1819. *London:* W. Clowes.

> [*Contains plate of Angelo's Sword Exercise.*]

REGULATIONS AND INSTRUCTIONS for the Cavalry Sword Exercise. 4°. [1824.] *London:* Horse Guards.

> [*With a large target and another plate.*]

REGULATIONS FOR THE CARBINE, Pistol, and Lance Exercises. 4°. [1824.] *London:* Horse Guards.

REICHSFECHTSCHULE. — *DEUTSCHE* Reichsfechtschule.

REIFFENBERG (BARON DE). — Frère Jacques-le-Mineur, ou le duel et le rendez-vous, anecdote belge. 8°. 1837. *Paris:* Rue de la Rochefoucaud, 12.

> [*31 pages.*]   (*In Mr. J. R. Garcia Donnell's Collection.*)

REIHENFOLGE DER KOMMANDOWÖRTER für das Bayonnet-Fechten der königlich bayerischen Infanterie. Gr. 16°. 1860. *München:* Kaiser.

RELAZIONE DEL TORNEO A CAVALLO, e a piedi fatto questo carnerate in Ferrara. 8°. 1612.

RELAZIONE DE TORNEO A PIEDI fatto in Ferrara questo carnevale dell anno 1624. 8°. 1624.

RELIQUIÆ WOTTONIANÆ. 1665. [Extract of a letter to Sir E. Bacon, dated 18th April 1633, relative to a Duel between Lord Fielding and Mr. Goring in Hide Park.]

REMARKABLE DUELS.

> [*"Saturday Review"* (*London*), Vol. LIV. No. 567.]

RENKIN (J.). — *HUMÉ* (*E.*). — 1862.

RESIDENZ (DIE). — Illustrirtes Familienblatt. 4°. *Wien:* Bäckerstrasse 24.

> [1891–92. Heft 1, pp. 23–26. "*Der Papst gegen den Zweikampf.*"—*Von Albert Pietsch.*]

REVUE ARCHÉOLOGIQUE. — *HENRY.*

REVUE DE CAVALERIE. — " Le Combat." 8°. 1887. *Paris :*
Berger-Levrault.

REVUE DE LÉGISLATION ET DE JURISPRUDENCE. —
DUFOUR (L.). — 1840.

REVUE DE PARIS. 8°. 1790. *Paris :* de l'Imprimerie
patriotique.

> [*Détail du combat qui a eu lieu hier au soir au bois de Boulogne, entre M.
> Charles de Lameth et M. de Castries, dans lequel M. de Lameth a été
> malheureusement blessé. Avec gravure sur cuivre.*]

REYNOLDS (JOHN). — The Triumphes of God's Revenge against
the Crying and execrable Sinn of Murther, exprest in thirty severall
Tragicall Histories ; to which is added, God's Revenge against the
Abominable Sinn of Adultery, containing severall Histories never yet
printed. Small folio. 1679. *London :* A. Matthewes. Printed for
Thomas Lee.

> [*Illustrated with curious old title-page (mounted), divided into seven com-
> partments, each containing an illustration depicting the various punish-
> ments, such as hanging, burning, "duelling," breaking-on-the-wheel, &c.,
> &c. ; also a large number of other extraordinary engravings, all divided into
> compartments, and printed on the text at the head of each history, which
> they depict very vividly from first to last—very brilliant impressions. The
> histories are of various nations, French, German, Italian, Greek, Portu-
> guese, &c.*]

RHEIN (A. VON). — Das Bajonetfechten. 8°. 1840. *Wesel :*
Bagel.

> [8 *lithographed plates.*]

—— (—. —). — Das Bajonetfechten. 2te Auflage. 1844.
Wesel : Bagel.

> [10 *plates, giving* 35 *figures.*] (*In Captain Hutton's Collection.*)

RICE (J. M.) [Lieutenant-Colonel, United States Army]. — Ex-
periments with Rice's Trowel Bayonet. 8°. 1874. *Springfield,
Mass., U.S.A.*

> (*In the Royal United Service Institution Library, Whitehall, London.* 8°
> Pamphlets, 3rd Series, Vol. XXXI.)

RICHARD I. — Regulations concerning Tournaments.

> [*Harleian MSS.*, Vol. I. p. 165, cod. 293. art. 123, 124.]

RICHARDSON (D. S.). — *OVERLAND* Monthly. — 1888.

RICHARDSON (SAMUEL).
[*Six original letters of Richardson upon "Duelling" were printed in the "Literary Repository," 1765. Page 227.*]

RICHELIEU (MARÉCHAL DE). — Vie privée, contenant ses amours et intrigues. 3 vols. 8°. 1791. *Paris :* J. P. Roux & Co.
[Vol. I. Chapitre **xvi.** "*Duel du Duc de Richelieu avec le Prince de Lixen, parent de sa femme.*"
    ,,   ,,   **xvii.** "*Il se bat avec M. de Peuterieder et le tue.*"]
(*In Captain Hutton's Collection.*)

RIELECH (F.). — Lose Worte über die Bestimmungsmensuren der deutschen Couleurstudenten. 8°. 1885. *Breslau :* V. Zimmer.
[*24 pages.*]

RIEMANN (HEINR.). — Vollständige Anweisung zum Stossfechten, nach Kreussler's Grundsätzen. 8°. 1834. *Leipzig :* Engelmann.
(*In the British Museum.* 785. d. 21.)

RIFLE AND FIELD EXERCISES and Rifle Practice for H.M. Fleet. 12°. 1888. *London.*
[Page 38. "*Sword-bayonet Exercise.*"]

ROBAGLIA (A.). — Escrime-pointe. Nouvelle théorie, dédiée à l'armée, sur le maniement de l'épée. 16°. 1855. *Metz :* Verronnais.
[*8 plates.*]

—— (—.). — Cours complet d'escrime. Théories sur le maniement de l'épée ou l'art de faire des armes, simplifié et démontré suivant tous les principes théoriques et pratiques ; précédé de quelques notices et de recueils historiques. 12°. 1864. *Paris :* Fontenay.

—— (—.). — De l'escrime d'après les règles et les principes de nos meilleurs professeurs : La Boëssière, Gomard, Lhomandie, Jean-Louis, Lafaugère et Grisier, précédée d'une notice historique sur le fleuret et les salles d'escrime. 8°. 1877. *Paris :* F. Vernay.
[*16 plates.*]

ROBAGLIA (LE CAPITAINE). — L'Escrime et le duel. 12°. 1884. *Paris :* Dejey.
[*269 pages.*]

—— (—— ——). — Le duel et l'escrime mis à la portée de tous. 18°. [1890.] *Paris :* Kolb.
[*17 plates. 294 pages.*]

ROBAGLIA (LE CAPITAINE). — L'Escrime ou le jeu de l'épée enseigné par l'image à l'usage des enfants et des adolescents sans crainte d'accidents et sans dépenses. 12°. 1893. *Paris :* Dubois.

ROBERT (GEORGES) [Professeur d'escrime au Lycée Henri IV. et au collège Sainte-Barbe]. — La science des armes, l'assaut et les assauts publics, le duel et la leçon de duel. Avec une notice sur Robert aîné par Ernest Legouvé de l'Académie française, et une lettre de M. Hébrard de Villeneuve, président de la Société d'encouragement de l'escrime. Large 8°. 1887. *Paris :* Garnier.

[*Portrait of Robert the Elder, vignettes, 57 figures, and 8 folding analytical tables.*]

—— (—). — *DON GIOVANNI.* — 1888.

—— (—). — *LEGOUVÉ (E.).* — 1876.

ROBERTS (MORLEY). — *IDLER (The).* — 1894.

ROBINEAU. — *PICOT (V. M.).* — 1789.

" ROCCO " (SIGNIOR).

[*" Vincentio Saviolo was not the only foreign master of note established in London during the latter part of Elizabeth's reign. A ' Signior Rocco ' had a very gorgeously appointed ' academie' in Warwick Lane, near St. Paul's, where he seems to have been coining money rapidly at the expense of gulls and gallants alike. This man came to grief ultimately in an encounter with the long sword of an English master of fence."—Castle (E.), " The Story of Swordsmanship." (" The National Review," May 1891.) See also the account of " Rocco " in this author's " Schools and Masters of Fence."*]

ROCHEFORD (LOREVIN DE). — An Account of a Journey to the British Isles. 1672. *Paris.*

[*Contains graphic description of gory stage-fights, and the manner in which they were heralded and conducted.*]

ROCHEFORT (HENRI). — *IDLER (The).* — 1894.

ROCHEMONT (PICTET DE). — Dialogue de salle, sur l'art de l'escrime. Essai soi-disant didactique, par un amateur secondé d'un artiste. 8°. 1882. *Genève.*

[*Vignettes de Castan. En vers fantaisistes, non mis dans le commerce.*]

ROCHI (ROCCO). — Exercitio militare della scherma. 8°. 1643. *Mantova.*

RODRÍGUEZ DEL CANTO (D. DIEGO). — El discipulo instruido y diestro aprovechado en la ciencia philosophica y mathematica de la destreza de las armas.
[*17th century MS. 4 tomos con numerosos dibujos.*]

RODRÍGUEZ DE GUZMÁN (DIEGO). — Doce conclusiones de la destreza de la espada. Dedicadas al Marqués de Castelldosrius, Virey de estos Reinos. 4°.

ROEDENBECK (S.) — Zweikampf im Verhältniss zur Tötung. 8°. 1883. *Halle:* Niemeyer.
[*56 pages.*] ·

ROGER (M.). — Principes d'escrime. 12°. *Paris.*

—— (—.). — *BEAUVOIR* (*É. R. de B.*). — 1864.

ROHNE (K.). — Gründlicher Unterricht im Heibfechten. Zum Selbstunterricht und zur Fortübung. Gr. 8°. 1840. *Quedlinburg und Leipzig:* Basse.
[*Mit 10 Tafeln Abbildungen.*]
(*In Mr. J. R. Garcia Donnell's Collection.*)

ROLAND (GEORGE). — A Treatise on the Theory and Practice of the Art of Fencing. Illustrated with twelve highly finished plates, and continued by easy and progressive lessons, from the simplest position to the most complicated movements. 8°. 1823. *Edinburgh.*
[*12 plates.*]
(*In the British Museum.* 556. e. 10.)

—— (—). — A Treatise on the Theory and Practice of the Art of Fencing. Royal 8°. 1824. *London:* William Sams.
[*12 plates. A duplicate of the preceding, with a new title-page.*]
(*In Mr. J. R. Garcia Donnell's Collection.*)

—— (—) [Fencing-master of the Royal Academy, the Scottish Naval and Military Academy, &c., &c.]. — An Introductory Course of Fencing by George Roland. 8°. 1827. *Edinburgh.*
[*5 lithographed plates*]

—— (—). — An Introductory Course of Fencing. 8°. 1837. *London:* Simpkin, Marshall.
[*5 plates.*] (*In Captain Hutton's Collection.*)

—— (—). — Introductory Course of Fencing. 8°. 1846. *London:* Simpkin.

ROLAND (GEORGE). — Introduction to Fencing and Gymnastics. Royal 8°. 1854. *London:* Simpkin.

ROLAND (JOSEPH) [Fencing-master of the Royal Military Academy at Woolwich]. — The Amateur of Fencing, or a Treatise on the Art of Sword Defence. 8°. 1809. *London:* T. Egerton.
(In Captain Hutton's Collection, and in the British Museum [7907. bbb. 12.])

ROLANDO (LE SIEUR GUZMAN). — The Modern Art of Fencing, carefully revised, and augmented with a Technical Glossary, by J. S. Forsyth. 24°. 1822. *London:* S. Leigh.
[22 *coloured plates.*]
(In Captain Hutton's Collection; and Art Library, South Kensington Museum.)

—— (— — —) [de la academia de armas]. — Nuevo arte de esgrima conforme á la práctica de los mejores maestros de Europa. Aumentado y corregido por J. S. Forsyth, y traducido del inglés por un Militar Español. 12°. 1826. *Lóndres:* Ackermann.

—— (— — —). — *RADA (F. L. de).* — 1712.

ROMÁN (FRANCISCO). — Tratado de esgrima, con figuras. Folio. 1532. *Sevilla:* Bartolomé Peréz.
[Given on the authority of Almirante's Bibliografía Militar.]

ROMEI (ANNIBALE) [Gentil' hvomo Ferrarese]. — Discorsi, etc. 4°. 1586. *Ferrara:* Vittorio Baldini.
[Pages 58–94. *Giornata terza. Nella quale si tratta dell' honore.*
Pages 95–136. *Giornata quarta. Nella quale si tratta dell' iniquità dell' duello, del combatter alla Macchia, e del modo di accommodar le querele, e ridur' à pace le inimicitie priuate.*]
(In the British Museum. 525. e. 11. (3.))

RONDELLE (LOUIS) [Maître d'Armes at Boston Athletic Association and the Harvard University Fencing-club]. — Foil and Sabre. A Grammar of Fencing in Detailed Lessons for Professor and Pupil. 8°. [1892.] *Boston:* Estes & Lauriat.
[With 52 illustrations.]

RONDONNEAU (L.). — *MERLIN (M.).* — 1829.

ROOFER (ROOF). — The Fencing-Girl, a London New Soul. 8°. 1895. *London:* Gay & Bird.
[A novel.]

244

ROQUELAURE (Aventures du Duc de).   3 vols.   12°.   [N.D.]
Paris : Fayard.
[*Ses duels.*]

ROQUES und **BASNAGE.** — Histor. und Moral. Betrachtungen
über d. Duelliren. Aus dem Franz. von F. E. Rambach.   8°.   1747.
Jena.

ROQUES (PIERRE). — *BASNAGE* (*M.*). — 1740.

ROSARI [con Cariolato e Belmonte]. — Relazione del torneo
internazionale di scherma tenuto in Milano.   8°.   1881.   *Napoli :*
Ferrante.

ROSAROLL (SCORZA GUISEPPE) [da Napoli]. — *SCORZA* (*Rosaroll*).

ROSE (A.). — Gymnastique militaire escrime à la baïonnette,
reflexions sur la théorie du sabre.   8°.   1885.   *Bruxelles :* Etterbeek
(*In Captain Hutton's Collection.*)

RÖSENER (CHRISTOFF) [Bürger in Dressden, Meister des
Schwerts]. — Ehren Tittel und Lobspruch der Ritterlichen Freyen
Kunst der Fechter, auch ihrer Ankunfft, Freyheiten und Keyfer-
lichen Priuilegien, etc.   1589.   *Dressden :* Gimel Bergen.
[Vide *Wassmannsdorff* (*K.*), "*Sechs Fechtschulen,*" 1870.]

ROSENKRANZ (KARL). — Der Zweikampf auf unsern Universitäten.   Eine Rede.   8°.   1837.   *Königsberg :* Unzer.
(*In the British Museum,* 8356. bb. 56. (2.))

—— (—). — Die Abschaffung des Duellzwanges.   8°.   1845.
Königsberg.
(*In the British Museum.*   6875. c.)

ROSENTRETER. — Betrachtungen, über Betriebsmethode der
Militärgymnastik.   8°.   1873.   *Kiel :* Universitäts Buchhandlung.
[32 *pages.*]

ROSIS (LUIGI DE). — Codice italiano sul duello, scritto dal professore di scherma.   8°.   1865.   *Napoli :* de Angelis.
[*A second edition appeared in* 1869.]

ROSNY (LUCIEN DE). — L'epervier d'or, ou description des joutes
et des tournois qui sous le titre de nobles Roi l'Epinette, se célé-
brèrent à Lille au Moyen-Age.   Small 4°.   1830.   *Paris.*
[31 *plates of arms, and* 16 *of jousts and tournaments.*]

ROSSI (GIORDANO). Scherma di spada e sciabolo. Manuale teorico-pratico, con cenni storici sulle armi e sulla scherma, e principali regole del duello. 8°. 1885. *Milano :* Fratelli Dumolard.

[54 *figures, in the text.*] (*In Captain Hutton's Collection.*)

ROTHSTEIN (H.). — Anleitung zum Bajonetfechten. 8°. 1847. *Berlin :* Schroeder.

—— (—.). — [Another edition.] 1. und 2. unveränd. Abdruck. 8°. 1853. *Berlin :* Schroeder.

[1 *lithograph, containing* 11 *figures.*]

—— (—.). — [Another edition.] 8°. 1853. *Berlin :* Schroeder.

[*Mit* 11 *erläuternden Figuren.* (3. *unveränd. Abdruck.* 1857.)]
(*In Captain Hutton's Collection.*)

—— (—.). — Das Bajonetfechten nach dem System P. H. Ling's reglementarisch dargestellt. 8°. 1853. *Berlin :* Schroeder.

[2 *lithographs, comprising* 32 *figures.*]

—— (—.). — [Another edition.] 2. Auflage. 8°. 1860. *Berlin :* Schroeder.

(*In Captain Hutton's Collection.*)

—— (—.). — Das Stoss- und Hiebfechten mit Degen und Säbel. 8°. 1863. *Berlin :* Schroeder.

[40 *figures.*]

—— (—.). — Das Bajonetfechten nach dem System P. H. Ling's reglementarisch dargestellt. 3. Auflage. 8°. 1872. *Berlin :* Schroeder.

ROUX (F. A. W. L.). — Deutsches Paukbuch. 4°. 1857. *Jena :* Mauke.

[6 *photo-lithographed figures.*]

—— (—. —. —. —.). — Deutsches Paukbuch. 2. Auflage. Folio. 1867. *Jena :* Mauke.

[*Mit sechs Tafeln photographischer Abbildungen.*]

—— (—. —. —. —.) [Lehrer der Fechtkunst an der Universität Jena]. — Anweisung zum Hiebfechten mit graden und krummen Klingen. Nebst einer Einleitung vom Prof. Dr. K. H. Scheidler. Qu. 8°. 1840. *Jena :* Mauke.

[36 *figures. Einleitende Bemerk. über die Geschichte der Fechtkunst, namentlich auf unsern deutschen Universitäten, Seite* 22.
2. *Auflage. Qu.* 4°. 1849. Jena : *Mauke.* (*Mit* 36 *Abbildungen.*)]

ROUX (F. A. W. L.). — Die Kreussler'sche Stossfechtschule, zum
Gebrauch für Academien und Militärschulen, nach matematischen
Grundsätzen. Imp. 4°. 1849. *Jena :* Mauke.

[*Portrait of the author, and 120 figures drawn from nature, lithographed.*
2. *Auflage.* 1857.]

—— (—. —. —. —.). — *ROUX* (*J. A. C.*). — 1841.

ROUX (HEINRICH FRIEDRICH). — Versuch über das Contrafechten
auf der rechten und linken Hand nach Kreuzler'schen Grundsätzen.
4°. 1786. *Jena :* Cröker.

—— (— —) [Französischen Sprachmeister in Jena]. — Lehrbuch
der deutschen Fechtkunst. 1786. *Jena.*

—— (— —). — Grundriss der Fechtkunst als gymnastische
Uebung betrachtet. Gr. 8°. 1798. *Leipzig.*

[2. *Auflage.* 1799. Leipzig : *Barth.*]

[**ROUX** (JOHANN ADOLF CARL)]. — Gründliche und vollständige
Anweisung in der deutschen Fechtkunst auf Stoss und Hieb aus
ihren innersten Geheimnissen wissenschaftlich erläutert, für kenner
zur Ausbildung und als kunstschatz, für Lernende systematisch und
deutlich entworfen. 4°. 1798. *Jena :* Wolfg. Stahl.

[*Mit 5 Kupfern.*]

ROUX (JOHANN ADOLF CARL) [Fechtmeister und öffentlicher
Lehrer der Turnkunst auf der Köngl. Bayrischen Universität zur
Erlangen]. — Das Fechten auf Stoss und Hieb.

[*Article in Gutmuth* (*E. C. F.*), "*Gymnastik für die Jugend.*" 2. *Auflage.*
8°. 1804. Schnepfenthal.]

—— (— — —). — Die deutsche Fechtkunst, enthaltend eine
theoretisch-praktische Anweisung zum Stossfechten. Gr. 8°. 1803.
Leipzig : J. A Barth.

[2. *verbesserte und vermehrte Auflage.* 1817. Leipzig : *J. A. Barth.*]

—— (— — —). — Die deutsche Hiebfechtkunst. 1803. *Erlangen.*

[2. *Auflage.* 1817. Fürth.]

—— (— — —). — Theoretisch - practische Anweisung zum
Hiebfechten, e. Leitfaden für d. mündl. Unterricht. Gr. 8°. 1803.
Fürth.

ROUX (Johann Adolf Carl). — Grundriss der Fechtkunst als gymnastiche Uebung betrachtet. Gr. 8°. 1817. *Jena* und *Leipzig:* Barth.

—— (— — —). — Ueber das Verhältniss der deutschen Fechtkunst zum Ehrenduell sowohl im Allgemeinen, als auch für Universitäten insbesondere mit Berücksichtigung der Mittel, die Duelle zu verhüten, oder sie wenigstens unschädlich zu machen und zu mindern von demselben, auf besonderes Verlangen des Verfassers nach seinem Tode zum Druck befördert und vollendet von F. A. W. L. Roux. 8°. 1841. *Erfurt:* Hennings & Hopf.

ROUX (J. W.). — Anleitung zur Fechtkunst nach mathematisch-physikalischen Grundsätzen. 4°. 1808. *Jena:* im Verlag der akademischen Buchhandlung.

[*10 copperplates.*]

ROUX (Ludwig Caesar) [Fechtmeister an der Königl. Sächs. Universität zu Leipzig]. — Die Hiebfechtkunst. Eine Anleitung zum Lehren und Erlernen des Hiebfechtens aus der verhangenen und steilen Auslage, mit Berücksichtigung des akad. Comments. Gr. 8°. 1885. *Jena:* Pohle.

[*100 tinted lithographic figures. xvi and 120 pages.*]
(*In Mr. J. R. Garcia Donnell's Collection.*)

—— (— —). — [Another edition.] 2. Auflage. 8°. 1889. *Jena:* Pohle.

ROUX (W.). — *ROUX* (J. A. C.). — 1841.

ROWLANDSON (T.). — Hungarian and Highland Broad-sword. Twenty-four plates, designed and etched by T. Rowlandson, under the direction of Messrs. H. Angelo and Son, Fencing-masters to the Light Horse Volunteers of London and Westminster. Dedicated to Colonel Herries. Oblong folio. 1798–99. *London:* Printed by C. Roworth.

(*In Captain Hutton's Collection.*)

—— (—.). — *ANGELO* (D.). — 1787. 1799.
—— (—.). — *PEARS'* Pictorial. — 1895.

[*Rowlandson as a delineator of fencing enjoyed extensive practice.*
The Assault, or Fencing-match, which took place at Carlton House, 9th April 1787, between Mdlle. la Chevalière d'Éon de Beaumont and M. de Saint-George, in the presence of the Prince of Wales and many eminent masters, was treated pictorially by artists, the best version being engraved by Rowlandson.
Henry Angelo, the well-known "maître d'armes" who had the princes as his

pupils, while his father had similarly taught the king's brothers when young, has recorded, concerning the famous "assaut d'armes" in 1787, under the auspices of the Prince of Wales and his guests: "There was a meeting appointed at Carlton House of the nobility then resident in this country, among whom was the Duc de Fitzjames, together with all the celebrated fencing-masters of the time, which were at that period considerable; the occurrence of the French Revolution shortly after occasioned their return to France. The Prince of Wales was much gratified with the performance, and smiled at the violent noises of Saint-George during his attacks, which resembled more the roaring of a bull than sounds emanating from a human being!"

The antagonists in Rowlandson's picture are Mdlle. la Chevalière d'Éon de Beaumont and M. de Saint-George, the accomplished Creole, a sort of Admirable Crichton of his day, musician, composer, athlete, horseman, and swimmer. In the practice of fencing "he surpassed all his contemporaries and predecessors. No professor or amateur ever showed so much accuracy and such strength," writes Angelo, who had practical evidence of the Chevalier's prowess, "such length of lunge and such quickness; his attacks were a perpetual series of hits; his parade was so close that it was in vain to attempt to touch him—in short, he was all nerve."

In Rowlandson's picture D'Éon is attacking vigorously. The spectators are ranged behind a barrier; George, Prince of Wales, and Mrs. Fitzherbert are the most conspicuous. The heir-apparent's French intimates, and his political friends of the time, members of the Opposition—North, Fox, Sheridan, and Burke, &c.—and the various fencing celebrities of London and Paris, are shown as spectators. The picture contains very numerous portraits. The original engraving was published in both London and Paris, and being much sought after by professors and amateurs of fencing, commands a high figure.]

ROWORTH (C.). [of the Royal Westminster Volunteers]. — The Art of Defence on Foot with the Broad-sword and Sabre, uniting Scotch and Austrian Methods into one Regular System. To which are added Remarks on the Spadroon. 2nd edition. 8°. 1798. *London:* Egerton.

[*Plates.*] (*In Captain Hutton's Collection, and in the British Museum.*)

[ROWORTH (C.)]. — The Art of Defence on Foot with the Broadsword and Sabre. Adapted also for the Spadroon, or Cut-and-thrust Sword. Improved and augmented with the Ten Lessons of Mr. John Taylor, late Broad-sword Master to the Light Horse Volunteers of London and Westminster. Illustrated with Plates by R. K. Porter, Esq. 8°. 1804. *London.*

[*With a diagram.*

This is a reproduction of Roworth's book (1798), with a number of alterations and additions, and fresh drawings.

"*Mr. Angelo confessedly borrowed his system of broadsword instruction, on which the infantry sword-exercise of 1842 was based, from this work.*"— Hutton (A.), "Cold Steel."]

(*In Captain Hutton's Collection; the South Kensington Museum; and British Museum, 7906. ee. 19.*)

ROY (MARIUS). — *MARCHE* (*Claude La*). — 1884.

RÜCKER (PREM. LIEUT.). — Vergleichung der Bajonnettfechtens der preussischen und französischen Armee. 16°. 1865. *Luxemburg:* Heintze.

[9 *lithographed plates.*]

RULES AND REGULATIONS for the Sword Exercise of Cavalry. Royal 8°. 1796. *London.*

[29 *folding plates.*]
(*In Captain Hutton's Collection, and in the South Kensington Museum.*)

RUMPF (H. F.). — Allgemeine Literatur der Kriegswissenschaften. 8°. 1824. *Berlin:* G. Reimer.

[Pages 212-220. "*Fechten*" (*Bibliographie*).]

RUSH (JACOB) [the Honorable President of the Third District of the Court of Common Pleas and Quarter Sessions for the State of Pennsylvania]. — Charges, and Extracts of Charges, on Moral and Religious Subjects; delivered at sundry times. 8°. May, 1804. *Philadelphia:* Printed [reprinted by Geo. Forman : *New York*].

[*On Duelling* (pp. 148-167). *Delivered at Reading, before the Grand Jury of Berks County, Nov. 1802.*] (*In the British Museum.* 722. f. 15.)

RUTZ (CASPAR). — Omne pene gentium imagines. 1557.

[*Plebii adolescentis in Anglia habitus.* (*Showing the sword and hand buckler then in fashion.*)]

S. (E. VON). — Die Grundsätze der zerstreuten Fechtart in ihrer praktischen Anwendung näher beleuchtet. 16°. 1864. *Wien:* Seidel & Sohn.

[3 *lithographed plates.*]

S. (V.). — Hülfsbuch zum Betriebe der Gymnastik und Bajonetfechtens für Offiziere und Unteroffiziere der preussisch-norddeutschen Infanterie. 2te u. 3te Auflage. 32°. 1870. *Nordhausen:* Eick.

—— (—.). — Hülfsbuch zum Betriebe des Turnens und Bajonetfechtens für Offiziere und Unteroffiziere der deutschen Infanterie. 32°. 1890. *Nordhausen:* J. Koppe.

[*This work has gone through 18 editions.*]

SABBADINO DEGLI ARIENTI (G.). — *ARIENTI* (*G. S. Degli*). — 1888.

SABINE (LORENZO). — Notes on Duels and Duelling alphabetically arranged, with a preliminary Historical Essay. 8°. 1855. *Boston:* Crosby, Nichols, & Co.

[*Another edition.* 1859.]

SABINE (Lorenzo). — *DUYCKINCK (E. A.).* — 1877.

SÄCHSISCHE FECHTZEITUNG. — Eigenthum d. Wohlthätig Keits-Vereines "Sächsische Fechtschule." Unterhaltungsblatt und Organ sämmtl. 62 Verbände d. Königr. Sachen.   Redacteur C. Moser.   Gr. 4°.   *Dresden :* Schönfeld.
  [*1st number appeared in* 1884.]

SACKVILL (Sir Edward) [Earle of Dorsett]. — "All the passages concerninge Combate between the late [Edward and] Lord Bruce [of Kinloss] deceased, and the then Sir Edward Sackvill, nowe Right honorable Earle of Dorsett," etc.; consisting of letters between the parties, and an account of the duel in a letter of Sir E. Sackvill.   1613.
  [*MS. ˙ Paper. 17th century folio.*]   (*In the British Museum.   Add.* 18,644.)

—— (— —). — A Chalenge by Mr. Edward Sackvill, Esq., from the Lord Brus, a Scottish Baron, who fought together in Zealand, 1614, where the said Lord Brus was slaine ; and the letters that passed between them.
  [*MS.   In the British Museum.   Add.* 4149.]

[SADLER (L. R.)]. — *LARWOOD (Jacob).* — 1871.

SAILLET (Alexandre de). — Histoire des duels célèbres.   Tome 1er.   8°.   1857.   *Paris :* Chabot-Fonteney.

SAINT-ALBIN (Albert de) [Robert Milton]. — Les salles d'armes de Paris.   Roy. 8°.   1875.   *Paris :* Glady frères.
  [*Frontispiece et portraits à l'eau-fort par Courtry.*]

—— (— —). — A travers les salles d'armes, avec une préface de Vigeant.   8°.   1887.   *Paris :* Librairie illustrée.
  [12 *engravings in photogravure by Frédéric Régamey, and* 1 *vignette in the text.*]

—— (— —). — Les sports à Paris.   12°.   1889.   *Paris :* Librairie moderne.

SAINT-CLAIR (G. de). — Sports athlétiques et exercices en plein air.   16°.   1887.   *Paris :* Arnould.
  [*2nd edition.* 1889.   12°.   *With* 24 *figures.*]

SAINCT-DIDIER (Henry de)[Gentilhomme Provençal]. — Traicté contenant les secrets du premier livre sur l'éspée seule, mère de toutes armes, qui sont éspée, dague, cappe, targue, bouclier, rondelle, l'éspée à deux mains et les deux éspées, avec ses pourtraictures, ayant les armes au poing pour se deffendre et offencer à un mesme temps des coups qu'on peut tirer, tant en assaillant qu'en deffendant, fort utile et profitable pour adextrer la noblesse et suposts de Mars : redigé par art, ordre et pratique.   Dedié à la Maiesté du Roy tres chrestien Charles neufiesme.   4°.   1573.   *Paris :* Imprimé par Jean Mettayer et Matthurin Challenge.   Avec privilège du Roy.

> [*Portrait of the author, of Charles IX., and 64 woodcuts in the text.*
> *This is the second known French work of Fence.*
> *Issued under royal favour in Paris, on the first anniversary of St. Bartholomew's Day.   Has been shown to be a précis and adaptation of two Italian treatises—to wit, the " Trattato di scienza d'arme," of Camillo Agrippa, and Grassi's " Ragione di adoprar sicuramente l'arme," published in Venice in 1568 and 1570 respectively.*
> "*The first who adopted the convenient method of referring to two typical persons in order to explain their respective actions.   Beyond this improvement, and the introduction of numerous figures arranged in series so as to show the progressive stages of the antagonistic actions, it will be seen to be a mere rearrangement of that part of Grassi's method which treats of the sword alone."—Castle's " Schools and Masters of Fence."*]
> (*In the British Museum.*)

SAINT-GEORGE (Chevalier). — *ANGELO.*—1817.

ST. JAMES'S GAZETTE (Periodical).   Folio.   *London.*

> [1890.   *December* 4.   "*Broadsword and Singlestick.*"
> 1891.   *April* 2.   "*A Fatal Stage Duel.*"
> 1891.   *May* 9.   "*The Emperor William on Students' Duels.*"]

SAINT-MARTIN (J. DE) [Maître d'armes imperial de l'Académie Theresienne]. — L'art de faire des armes réduit à ses vrais principes. Contenant tous les principes nécessaires à cet art, qui y sont expliqués d'une manière claire et intelligible.   Cet ouvrage est composé pour la jeune noblesse et pour les personnes qui se destinent au métier de la guerre, ainsi que pour tous ceux qui portent l'épée.   On y a joint un traité de l'espadon, où l'on trouve les vrais principes de cet art, qui y sont expliqués d'une façon aisée, et qui est rempli de découvertes vraiment nouvelles.   Dédié à S. A. R. Monseigneur l'Archiduc Charles.   4°.   1804.   *Vienna :* Janne Schramble.

> [*72 figures.*]

ST. PAUL'S.   An Illustrated Journal of the Day (Weekly). Folio.   *London :* Arundel Street, W.C.

> [1894.   *July* 7.   "*Swordsmanship.*"
> 1895.   *May* 18 (No. 54, Vol. IV. pp. 319–320).   "*The Duel.*"
> 1895.   *December* 7.   "*A Study in Fencing.*"]

SAINT-PIERRE (L'Abbé de). — Mémoire pour perfectionner la police contre le duel. 4 juillet 1715. À *Ruel.*

SAINT-THOMAS (Comte Charles, Du Verger de). — Nouveau code du duel. Histoire, législation, droit contemporain. 12°. 1879. *Paris :* Dentu.

[*Nouvelle édition revue et corrigée,* 1887.]

SALA (George Augustus). — *SUNDAY* Times.

SALAFIA-MAGGIO (E.). — Codice cavalleresco nazionale. Sua procedura. 8°. 1895. *Palermo :* R. Sandron.

[168 *pages, con* 12 *tavole fototipiche.*]

SALATS (Jules). — Essai sur la législation pénale applicable au duel. 8°. 1840. *Paris :* Didot.

SALAVILLE (J. B.). — Essai sur le duel, sur la nécessité et sur le moyen d'en abolir l'usage. 8°. 1819. *Paris.*

SALGEN (Joh.). — Kriegsübung u. s. w. den frischanfahenden Fechtern und Soldaten für erst nutzlich und nöthig zu wissen. 1637.

SALLE (Antoine de). — *TRAITÉ* du duel judiciaire. — 1872.

SALM. — Uebungs-Tafeln für den systematischen Betrieb der gesammten Militär-Gymnastik. A. Infanterie-Ausgabe. 2. Auflage. 16°. 1890. *Berlin :* Mittler & Sohn.

———. — Dasselbe. B. Gessamt-Ausgabe. (Für Kavallerie und militär. Bildungs-Anstalten.) 2. Auflage. 16°. 1890. *Berlin :* Mittler & Sohn.

SALUT (LE) DES ARMES. — (Issued under the authority of the Académie d'Armes. Attributed to Vigeant.) 8°. 1888. *Paris :* Paul Schmidt.

SALVATOR (Sieg.). — *BRITISH* Museum. MS.

SALVATORE. — Legittimità e limiti dell' aggravante nella recidiva : memoria. 8°. *Palermo :* Nicolò Carosio edit. (tip. dello *Statuto*).

[vi *and* 91 *pages.*]

253

[**SALVO** (J.) y **VELA**]. — Duelo. Comedia famosa. Tambien ay duelo en los Santos. De un Ingenio esta Corte. 4°. 1744. *Madrid.*

(In the British Museum. T. 1734. (22.))

SAMMLUNG SCHLESISCHER PROVINZIALGESETZE. 1771.

[Bd. I. "*Kaiserl. Duell Edikt v. 23. Sept. 1682.*"]

SAMPSON (W.) — Trial of Lieutenant Renshaw. 1809.

[*Duelling.*] (*In New York State Library, U.S.A.*)

SÁNCHEZ (DON JOSÉ CASADO) [Capitan Graduado]. — Esgrima de la bayoneta. 12°. 1853. *Madrid :* Pedro Montero.

[3 *folding plates.*]

SANCHEZ DE LA CRUZ (MATEO). — Apartamiento del cuerpo y del alma, con un juego de esgrima á lo diuino. 4°. 1628. *Servilla.*

SANTIAGO PALOMARES (FRANCISCO DE). — Noticia de la fábrica de espadas de Toledo, que por tantos siglos existió hasta fines del XVII. en que acabó; y del método que tenian aquellos artifices armeros para forjarlas y templarlas, aceros de que usaban y ostras particularidades que las hicieron tan famosas en todo el mundo, como apetecidas al presente. 1760.

[*MS. Acad. de la Historia, Madrid.*]

SANZ (ADELARDO). — Esgrima del sable y consideraciones sobre el duelo. 4°. 1886. *Madrid :* Fortanet.

[223 *pages.*] (*In the British Museum.* 7907. i. 13.)

SANZ (DON GREGORIO). — Arte académico de la esgrima, traducido del francés al castellano. Folio. 1791. *Madrid :* Sancha.

[11 *grandes láminas que se doblan y contienen* 53 *figuras hechas con singular esmero.*]

SARACHAGA (G. VON). — Vermächtniss oder Neue Folgen in der Göler-Haberschen Duell-Sache. Mein letztes Wort in der Sache gegen Herrn Moritz von Haber. 8°. 1843. *Stuttgart :* Rieger'sche Buchhandlung.

[*Portraits of Jul. von Göler, Sarachaga, and Werefkin.*]

—— (——. ——). — Vollständige Darstellung der Streitsache zwischen Freiherrn Julius Göler von Ravensburg und Herrn Moritz von Haber, so wie des daraus entstandenen Duells des erstern mit Herrn von Werefkin, wie vor Gericht niedergelegt wurde. 4. Auflage. 8°. 1843. *Karlsruhe :* Macklot.

SARACHAGA (G. VON). — Précis du différend entre Monsr. le Baron Jules Goeler de Ravensburg et Monsr. Maurice de Haber, et du duel né de ce différend entre Monsr. de Goeler et Monsr. de Verefkine, etc. 8°. 1483. *Karlsruhe:* Macklot.

SATURDAY REVIEW (Periodical). Folio. 1882–1895. *London.*

[1882. *June* 24. *Parisian Swordsmen.* Vol. 53, p. 804.
„ *Oct.* 28. *Duelling Dramas.* Vol. 54, p. 567.
1883. *July* 14. *The Sword.* Vol. 56, p. 43.
1884. *Jan.* 5. *Fencing and Fencing Masters (Review of Emile Merignac and M. Vigeant's books).* Vol. 57, pp. 29–30.
„ „ 19. *Backsword and Schläger.* Vol. 57, p. 74.
„ *April* 12. *Rapier and Dagger.* Vol. 57, pp. 469–470.
„ *May* 15. *An Assault-at-Arms (given at Willis's Rooms by M. A. Thieriet).* Vol. 61, p. 678.
„ *Nov.* 22. *La Scherma.* Vol. 58, p. 657.
„ „ 29. *Schools of Fence, Old and New.* (*A review of Mr. Egerton Castle's book.*) Vol. 58, p. 687.
1885. *Mar.* 21. *The Theology of Duelling.* Vol. 59, p. 376.
„ *May* 23. *A Sword of Honour.* Vol. 59, p. 689.
„ *June* 6. *The Lawless Duello.* Vol. 59, p. 757.
„ *Sept.* 5. *Books on Fencing.* Vol. 60, p. 321.
„ „ 12. *The Chevalier d'Éon.* Vol. 60, p. 362.
„ *Dec.* 5. *Schlägerei (German Duelling).* Vol. 60, p. 748.
1886. *April* 10 and 17. *The Good English Backsword.* Vol. 61, pp. 497, 553.
„ *June* 19. *Military Tournaments.* Vol. 61, p. 843.
„ „ 26. *Latest Book of Fence.* (*Review of Camille Prévost's book.*) Vol. 61, pp. 900–901.
„ *July* 10. *Drumont-Meyer Duel.* Vol. 62, p. 56.
„ *Oct.* 9. *Fencing Scene in Hamlet.* Vol. 62, pp. 479–481.
„ *Nov.* 6. *M. Vigeant on Hamlet's Duel.* Vol. 62, pp. 613–614.
1887. *Feb.* 5. *Swordsmen's Clubs.* Vol. 63, pp. 191–192.
„ *May* 28. *Thieriet's Assault of Arms.* Vol. 63, pp. 765–766.
„ *July* 23. *Le Jeu de l'Épée.* Vol. 64, pp. 115–116.
„ *Dec.* 3. *Parisian Fencing-rooms.* Vol. 64, pp. 767–768.
1888. *Oct.* 27. *L'Escrime et les Escrimeurs.* Vol. 66, p. 502.
„ *Nov.* 10. *Judicium Dei.* (*Evolution of the Duel.*) Vol. 66, p. 551.
„ *Dec.* 29. *Fencing Literature (twelve months).* Vol. 66, pp. 783–784.
1889. *July* 6. *Cold Steel.* (*A review of Captain Hutton's work.*) Vol. 68, pp. 24–25.
„ *Nov.* 23. *Queer Duels.* Vol. 68, p. 574.
„ „ 30. *Fencing.* Vol. 68, pp. 621–622.
1890. *Jan.* 4. *Musashi of the Two Swords.* Vol. 69, p. 10.
„ *Mar.* 8. *Trial by Combat.* (*Review of Mr. George Neilson's book.*) Vol. 69, pp. 299–300.
„ *May* 31. *A Parisian Assault of Arms.* Vol. 69, pp. 674–675.
„ *June* 14. *Fixed Bayonets.* (*A review of Captain Hutton's work.*) Vol. 69, pp. 744–745.
„ „ 21. *Swordsmen at Play.* (*From the Diary of Sir W. Hope, of Balcomie, Bart., during his stay in London.*) Vol.

SATURDAY REVIEW (*continued*)—

		69, p. 765. [*Causerie d'Armes. Given by Mr. A. Forbes Sieveking at Bertrand's "Salle d'Armes," 10 Warwick Street, London, W., June 14, 1890. The quotation—"Qu'est-ce que faire des armes? C'est causer! car causer, n'est-ce pas parer, riposter, attaquer. . . . Toucher sur-tout?"—explanatory of the title of the programme, is from Legouvé's article in the "Paris Guide," 1867* (Tome II. pp. 981–986). *Mr. Sieveking was, I believe, the first to use the phrase "causerie d'armes."*]
1890.	June 28.	*Bibliografia della Scherma.* (*A review of Gelli's work.*) Vol. 69, p. 809.
„	July 5.	*The Knife-Bayonet and the Mounted Soldier.* Vol. 70, p. 13.
„	„ 12.	*The Fatal Duel.* Vol. 70, pp. 33–34.
„	Aug. 9.	*Truth of the Sorde, by the Marquis of Newcastle.* Vol. 70, pp. 164–165.
„	Oct. 4.	*Sword Inscriptions.* Vol. 70, p. 393.
1891.	Jan. 17.	*Lances.* Vol. 71, p. 71.
„	Feb. 21.	*Broadsword.* Vol. 71, p. 219.
„	„ 28.	*The Story of Swordsmanship.* (*Mr. E. Castle's lecture.*) Vol. 71, p. 255.
„	May 9.	*Lance v. Sword.* Vol. 71, p. 556.
„	„ 16.	*Stage Duels.* Vol. 71, pp. 582–583.
„	„ 16.	*The Swordsman.* (*Review of Captain Hutton's book.*) Vol. 71, pp. 596–597.
„	„ 23.	*The German Duel.* Vol. 71, pp. 614–615.
„	„ 30.	*The Converys Sword.* Vol. 71, p. 648.
„	June 6.	*Royal Military Tournament.* Vol. 71, p. 679.
„	„ 20.	*L'Escrime et le Duel.* (*Review of C. Prévost and G. Jollivet's book.*) Vol. 71, p. 750.
„	„ 27.	*Bibliography* [*of Fencing and Duelling*]. (*A review of Carl A. Thimm's work.*) Vol. 71, p. 781.
„	Nov. 21.	*"The Sword," at Lincoln's Inn.* Vol. 72, p. 587.
„	Dec. 26.	*Fencing as an English Art.* Vol. 72, p. 720.
1892.	Feb. 27.	*The O. U. F. C.* (*Oxford University Fencing Club*). Vol. 73, p. 243.
„	May 28.	*Hutton's Old Swordplay.* Vol. 73, p. 637.
„	June 11.	*Italian Fencing.* Vol. 73, p. 683.
„	July 9.	*Duelling in France.* Vol. 74, p. 38.
1893.	Mar. 11.	*Swordsmanship in the Army.* Vol. 75, p. 264.
„	Oct. 21.	*Bobadill, Carranza, and Saviolo.* Vol. 76, pp. 464–465.
„	Nov. 4.	*Sword Tests.* Vol. 76, p. 514.
„	„ 25.	*A Memorial of Fencers.* Vol. 76, p. 596.
„	Dec. 9.	*Swords at Manchester.* Vol. 76, p. 648.
1894.	Feb. 24.	*Mr. Brett's Arms and Armour.* Vol. 77, p. 204.
„	April 28.	*The Judging of Swordplay.* Vol. 77, p. 442.
„	July 21.	*The Point of Honour.* (*Review of Monsr. A. Croabbon's book.*) Vol. 78, pp. 81–82.
„	Sept. 1.	*Fencing and Fighting circa* 1600. Vol. 78, p. 234.

(*Among the contributors to this Review were Mr. Egerton Castle, Captain A. Hutton, and Sir Frederick Pollock, Bart.*)]

VINCENTIO
SAVIOLO

his Practife.

Jn two Bookes.

*The firft intreating of the vfe of the Rapier
and Dagger.*

*The fecond, of Honor and honorable
Quarrels.*

LONDON
Printed by I oHN WOLFE.
1 5 9 5.

[VINCENTIO SAVIOLO. 4°. 1595.]

SAVARIN (J. A. BRILLAT DE). — Essai historique et critique sur le duel d'après notre législation et nos mœurs. 8°. 1819. *Paris :* Caille et Ravier.

[*Table des Chapitres :*—1. *Origine du duel.* 2. *Législation des duels jusques à Louis XIV.* 3. *Louis XIV.-suite.* 4. *Louis XV.* 5. *Louis XVI.* 6. *Mœurs.* 7. *Législation depuis 1791.* 8. *Question de Législation criminelle sur la qualification du duel.* 9. *Faut-il faire une loi ?* *Notes supplementaires et anecdotes.*]
(*In Captain Hutton's Collection.*)

SAVARON (JEAN) [Maistre, Sieur de Villars, Conseiller du Roy, President & Lieutenant General en la Seneschaussée d'Auvergne, & siege Presidial à Clairmont]. — Traicté de l'Espée Françoise. 8°. 1610. *Paris :* Adrian Perier.

[*Au Roy Tres-Chrestien.*]   (*In the British Museum.* 501. *a.* 18. (2.))

—— (—). — Traicté contre les duels. Avec l'Edict de Philippes le Bel de l'an M.CCC.VI., non encores imprimé. 8°. 1610. *Paris :* A. Perier.

[*Au Roy Tres-Chrestien, Lovys XIII.*]
(*In the British Museum.* 501. *a.* 18. (1.))

—— (—). — Ditto. Avec les ordonnances et arrests du Roy S. Lovys. 8°. 1614. *Paris :* Pierre Chevalier.

SAVIOLO (VINCENTIO). — His Practise, in two bookes ; the first intreating of the Use of the Rapier and Dagger, the second of Honour and Honourable Quarrels. 4°. 1595. *London :* Printed by John Wolfe.

[*Without pagination. 6 woodcuts, in the text. Dedicated to the Earl of Essex.* "*This work is generally believed, and with good reason, to be alluded to by Shakespeare in 'As you Like it.' It is very illustrative of allusions both in Shakespeare and Ben Jonson. Some copies contain eleven leaves less than the above, marked with a kind of flower. The first leaf of sheet 'I' was cancelled, and twelve additional leaves inserted in its place, forming the complete book, as in this copy. The second leaf of sheet 'I' is erroneously marked 'H 2.' In some copies both the cancelled leaf and the additional sheet occur ; but the former is certainly out of place, being repeated. There are therefore three different kinds of copies, all virtually perfect. Between 'Gg' and 'Hh' are also two leaves, the first marked ¶, forming a chapter 'Of the Duello or Combats.'*"—"*Quaritch's Catalogue of Books.*" *Supplement 1875–77, p. 138.* "*The first writer on the rapier in this country was Vincentio Saviolo, the great expounder of that Italienated fence so much reviled by the old-established master, withal much admired of Elizabethan courtiers, Shakespeare's fencing-master.*"—"*The Story of Swordsmanship.*" ("*The National Review,*" *May* 1891.)]
(*In Captain Hutton's Collection ; British Museum ; and Bodleian Library.*)

SAYAS Y ALFARO (CRISTOBAL). — Libro de la verdadera destreza. MS. [Siglio XVI.]

SCALES (LORD). — *WIDVILE* (*Antony*).

SCALZI (PAOLO DE'). — La scherma esposta in lezioni. 8°. 1852. *Genova.*

―― (―― ――). — La ginnastica educativa e la scherma. 8°. 1852. *Genova.*

―― (―― ――). — La scuola della spada. 8°. 1853. *Genova.*

―― (―― ――). — Ditto. Seconda edizione con aggiunte. 8°. 1868. *Firenze.*

[*With figures.*]

SCARRON (LE JODELET). — Duelliste. Comedie. 16°. 1668. *Paris* (suivant la copie imprimée à).

SCHÄFFER (HEINRICH WILHELM, VON DIETZ). — *SCHÖFFER* (*H. W.*). — 1620.

SCHAICK (E. VAN). — *LIPPINCOTT'S* Magazine. — 1893.

―― (―. —). — *OUTING.* [1887 ?]

SCHEIDLER (PROF. DR. K. H.). — Ueber die Abschaffung der Duelle unter den Studirenden; mit besonderer Rücksicht auf die hierauf bezüglichen Schriften des Herrn Geh. Kirchenrath Dr. Paulus und des Herrn Kirchenrath Dr. Stephani. 8°. 1829. *Jena :* Bran.

[*Aus der Minèrva abgedruckt.*] (*In Mr. J. R. Garcia Donnell's Collection.*)

―― (―. —. —. —.). — Ueber die Geschichte der Fechtkunst, so wie über den wahren Werth und die Vorzüge des Hiebfechtens.

―― (―. —. —. —.). — Nochmalige Erörterung der Frage : Hieb oder Stoss ?　Eine hodegetische Vorlesung. 8°. 1843. *Jena :* Frommann.

―― (―. —. —. —.). — Fechtkunst. 1844 (?).

[Vide *Ersch u. Gruber's Encyklopädie.* 4°. *Leipzig.* 1te Sec., Bd. **42**, pp. 190-206.]

―― (―. —. —. —.). — *ROUX* (*F. A. W. L.*). — 1840.

SCHEME submitted to the Officers of the Army and Navy. 12°. 1767. *London.*

[*Against Duelling.*]

SCHEMPP (A.) [Hauptmann]. — Die Fechtweise der russischen Infanterie in der Kompagnie und im Bataillon. [Anhang zum Reglement über den Infanterie-Frontdienst vom J. 1881/85. Aus dem Russ. übersetzt. 8°. 1888. *Hannover:* Helwing.

SCHERFF. — *GORNE (Von).* — 1858.

SCHERMA DEL BASTONE e della baionetta. 1867.
(*In Captain Hutton's Collection.*)

SCHERMA ITALIANA. — Rivista bimensile redatta dal cav. J. Gelli. Folio. (15 gennaio.) 1891. *Milano:* tip. degli Operai.
[*Direttore Magis Massimiliano. Cent. 75 il numero. (In progress.)*]

SCHERMA (La). — Giornale di sport. 4°. 1887. *Palermo.*
[*In* 1888 *the title was altered to* " *La Scherma—L'Arte universale—Sport Italiano illustrato.*"]

SCHERZ (F. G.). — Friederici I. imperat indicum de Henrico Leone altera de duellis principum. 1749. *Leipzig.*

SCHILDE (Constantin von). — Das Hau-Stosz-Fechten. 1888.

[**SCHLEGEL** (G.)]. — Über das Duelle auf den Universitäten. 8°. 1782. *Lübeck.*

SCHLEIDT (Gust.). — Die Fechtkunst. Kurze Anleitung für die Stosz- und Hiebkunst [Degen, Gewehr, Lanze, Säbel und Stock], Waffentänze und Waffenreigen. 8°. 1890. *Leipzig:* Strauch.

SCHLICHTEGROLL (Dr. N.). — Talhofer, ein Beitrag zur Literatur der gerichtlichen zweykaempfe im Mittelalter mit Dreyer's Anmerkung von den Duellgesetzen. Oblong 4°. 1817. *München.*
[6 *large plates of Legal Duelling.*
Talhofer was a professional champion, and wrote in 1443 *a book on the* " *Law of Trial by Battle*," *which is now preserved in manuscript at the Royal Library, Vienna.*]

SCHMIDT. — Fechtkunst auf Stoss und Hieb. 8°. 1780. *Leipzig.*

——. — Lehrschule der Fechtkunst. 1te Theil, oder Lehrbuch für die Cavalerie zum vortheilhaften Gebrauche des Säbels. 4°. 1797. *Berlin:* Maurer.
[8 *copperplates.*]

SCHMIDT. — Instruction pour la cavalerie, sur le maniement le plus avantageux du sabre publiée en 1796. Traduit par un Officier Général, et précédée d'une dissertation [de 333 pp.] sur l'antiquité de l'art de s'escrimer à cheval. 8°. 1828. *Paris :* Anselin.

> [*Avec 8 planches.*
> *Translated from the German by a General Officer.*]
> (*In Captain Hutton's Collection.*)

SCHMIDT (G. A.). — *AUERSWALD* (*F. von*). — 1869.

SCHMIDT (JOHANN ANDREAS) [des H. Röm. Reichs Freyen Stadt Nürnberg, bestellter Fecht- und Exercitien-Meister]. — Leib-beschirmende und Feinden Trotz bietende Fecht-Kunst ; oder leicht und getreue Anweisung auf Stoss und Hieb zierlich und sicher zu fechten ; Nebst einem curieusen Unterricht vom Voltigiren und Ringen. Deutlich und gründlich beschrieben und mit saubern darzu gehörigen nach den Actionen gezeichneten Kupffern an das Licht gestellet. Oblong 8°. 1713. *Nürnberg :* J. C. Weigel.

> [376 *pages. Portrait of the author in his own fencing-school ;* 84 *copperplates, in and out of the text.*]
> (*In Captain Hutton's Collection, and in the British Museum.*)

—— (— —) [Fecht- und Exercitien - Meister]. — Gründlich lehrende Fecht-Schule. 8°. 1749. *Nürnberg.*

—— (— —). — Fecht-Kunst. 8°. 1750. *Nürnberg.*

—— (— —). — Lehrende Fechtschule. 8°. 1760. *Nürnberg :* Stein.

> [*Copperplates.*]

—— (— —). — Fechtkunst, oder Anweisung in Stoss und Hieb, wie auch zum Ringen und Voltigiren. 12°. 1780. *Nürnberg :* Schneider u. W.

> [*Mit* 82 *Figuren.*]

SCHMIDT (JH. FR.). — Gründliche Anweisung zur deutschen Fechtkunst auf Stoss und Hieb. 4°. 1817. *Dresden :* Arnold.

SCHMIED-KOWARZIK (JOSEF) und **KUFAHL** (HANS). — Fechtbüchlein. 18°. [1894.] *Leipzig :* Philipp Reclam, jun.

> [*Universal-Bibliothek,* 3301–3303. *Mit* 20 *Abbildungen. Frontispiece, portraits of authors.*]

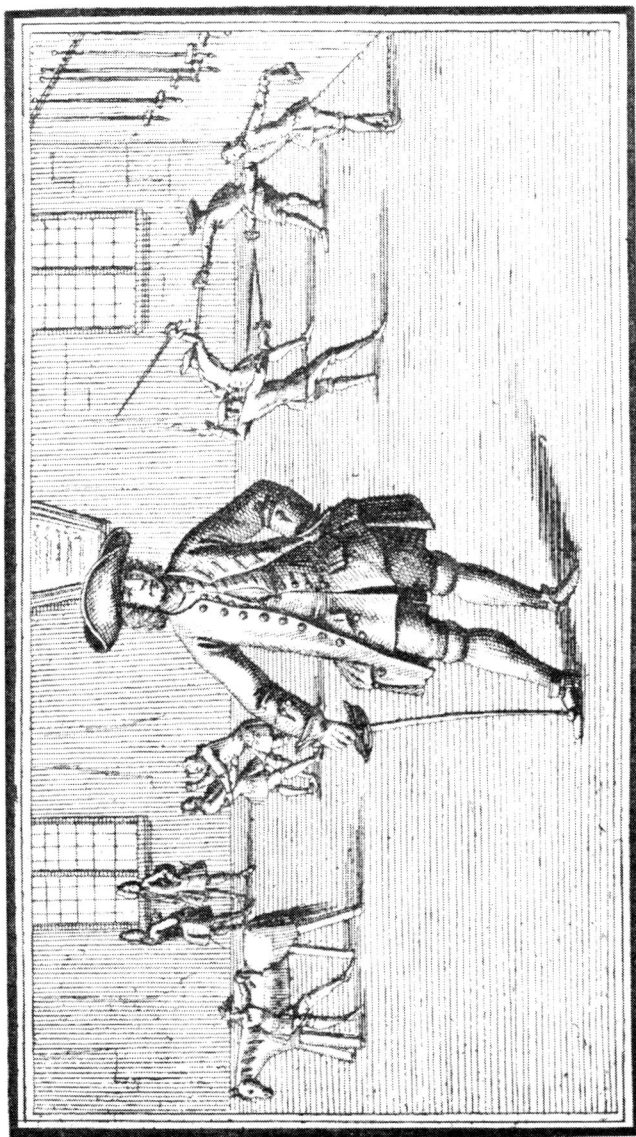

JOHANN ANDREAS SCHMIDT. 1713.

Der H. Röm. Reichs Freyen Statt Nürnberg, bestellter Fecht- und Exercitien-Meister.

SCHNEEGANS (L.). — Die unterbrochene Fechtschule in dem
Jahrbuch für elsässische Geschichte 1853 aus der Strassburger
Chronik.

[Mentioned in Schmied-Kowarzik und Kufahl's " Fechtbüchlein" (1894).]

SCHNEIDER (Fr.) [Hauptmann]. — Anleitung zum Unterricht
im Säbelfechten. 12°. 1887. *Bern :* Nydegger & Baumgart.

[Mit 6 lith. Tafeln. 32 pages.]

SCHÖFFER (Hans Wilhelm) [von Dietz, Fechtmeister in Mar-
purg]. — Grundliche und eigentliche Beschreibung der freyen
Adelichen und Ritterlichen Fechtkunst im einfachen Rappir und
im Rappir und Dolch, nach Italischer Manir und Art, in zwey
underschiedene Bücher ferfast, und mit 670 schoenen und nothwendigen Kupfferstucken gezieret und for Augen gestellt. Oblong
4°. 1620. *Marpurg :* John Saurn.

*[In Rumpf's (H. F.) "Allgemeine Literatur der Kriegswissenschaften"
(8°, 1824, Berlin), the author's name is given as " Heinrich" Wilhelm
"Schäffer" von Dietz. Both Monsr. Vigeant and Mr. Egerton Castle
quote the author as above described.]*

SCHOLL (A.). — *TAVERNIER* (A.). — 1885. 1888.

—— (—.). — *VAUX* (*Le Baron L. de*). — 1881. 1882.

SCHOTTEL. — De singul. quibusdam et antiq. in Germania juribus
et observatis. 1671. *Erfurt* u. *Leipzig.*

[Seite 538. " Erzählt ein Paar Weispiele deutschen Duelle."]

SCHRAMM (H.). — Ein Pereat den Duellen ! 8°. 1869. *Leipzig :* Denicke.

(In the British Museum, and Mr. J. R. Garcia Donnell's Collection.)

SCHULZE (Friedrich) [Fechtlehrer]. — Die Fechtkunst mit dem
Haurapier unter besonderer Berücksichtigung des Linksfechtens,
mit Uebungsbeispielen. Gr. 8°. 1885. *Heidelberg :* Bangel u.
Schmitt.

[5 Tafeln in Lichtdruck.]

—— (—). — Die Säbelfechtkunst. Eine gründliche Anleitung
zum Rechts- und Linksfechten, zugleich ein Lehr- und Lernbuch für
den Gebrauch an Universitäten und Militärbildungsanstalten sowie
für Turn- und Fechtvereine. 8°. 1889. *Heidelberg :* Petters.

[7 plates.]

SCHWARZ (Dr. Adolf). — Grabrede auf den im Duell gefallenen cand. med. Eduard Salomon. 8°. 1890. *Karlsruhe :* A. Bielefeld.

SCIENCE (Periodical). *New York.*
　　　　[Vol. VII. p. 93. *" Worthless Bayonets."*]

SCORZA (Rosaroll) [capitano de' zappatori]; **GRISETTI** (Pietro) [capitano di artiglieria]. — La scienza della scherma espota dai due amici. 4°. 1803. *Milano.*
　　　　　　[10 *folding plates.*]

—— (—); —— (—). — Ditto. 2nd edition. 4°. 1811. *Napoli.*
　　　　(*In Captain Hutton's Collection.*)

—— (—); —— (—). — Ditto. Nocera infer. Gr. 8°. 1871.
　　　　　　[*Con travole.*]

SCORZA (Rosaroll). — La scienza della tattica. 4°. 1814. *Napoli.*

—— (—). — Scherma della baionetta astata. 8°. 1818. *Napoli.*

—— (Giuseppe Rosaroll). — La scienza della scherma. 12°. 1806. *Milano.*
　　　　[*Another edition.* 12°. 1814. Napoli.]

—— (— —) [da Napoli]. — Trattato della spadancia o sia della spada larga. 8°. 1818. *Napoli.*

SCOTS MAGAZINE (Periodical). 1790. *London.*
　　[1790. *April 7. " Duel betwixt Sir George Ramsay and Mr. Macrae."*]

SCOTT (Clement). — *MARY (Jules).*

SCOTT (Rev. William). — The Duellist, a bravo to God, and a coward to man, and therefore impossible to be " a Man of Honour," being a discourse. 8°. 1774. *London.*

SCOURGE (A) FOR ADULTERERS, DUELLISTS, gamesters, and self-murderers.

SCRIBNER'S MONTHLY (Magazine). — *New York.*
　　　　[Vol. XI. p. 546. *French Duels.*]

SEAGER (E.). — *LOCKWOOD* (H. H.). — 1852.

SEBETIĆ (RAIMUND). — Theoretisch-praktische Anleitung zum Unterrichte im Säbelfechten. Zum Gebrauche für Truppenschulen sowie zur Selbstbildung leichtfasslich und vollständig nach der k. k. österreichischen Armee eingeführten Fecht - Methode bearbeitet. Gr. 8º. 1873. *Wien:* Gerold's Sohn.

> [2 *lithographed plates, comprising* 14 *figures.*]
> (*In Mr. J. R. Garcia Donnell's Collection.*)

—— (—) [Oberlieut.]. — Duell-Regeln. 3te unveränderte Auflage. 16º. 1881. *Debreczin:* Czáthy.

> [57 *pages.*
> *4te Auflage.* 12º. 1887. Graz: *Cieslar.*]

SEEHORST (A. VON). — Deutschland's Militair - Literatur im letzten Jahrzehent 1850 bis 1860. 8º. 1862. *Berlin:* A. Bath.

> [Pages 42–43. "*Fechten.*"]

SEGA (J.). — What is True Civilization? 12º. 1830. *Boston.*

> [*Suppression of Duelling.*]
> (*In the New York State Library, U.S.A.*)

SEGAR (W.). — Honor, military and ciuill, contained in four books. Folio. 1602. *London:* R. Barker.

> (*In Captain Hutton's Collection.*)

SEGERS (J.). — Anleitung zum Hiebfechten mit Korbrappier, Säbel und Pallasch, zum Selbstunterricht auf deutschen Universitäten und mit besonderer Rücksicht auf das Militär herausgegeben. 8º. 1834. *Bonn:* Habicht.

> [38 *figures.*]

—— (—.). — Anleitung zum Stossfechten, nach eigenen Grundsätzen und Erfahrungen herausg. Gr. 8º. 1836. *Bonn:* Habicht.

> [16 *figures.*]

—— (—.). — Anleitung zum Hiebfechten mit Korbrappier, Säbel und Pallasch, zum Selbstunterricht auf deutschen Universitäten und mit besond. Rücksicht auf das Militär herausgegeben. 2te verm. Auflage. 8º. 1837. *Bonn:* Habicht.

> [*Mit* 38 *neues Figuren.*]

SEIDLER (E. F.) [Stallmeister]. — Anleitung zum Fechten mit dem Säbel und dem Kürassierdegen, zuvörderst dem Unterrichte in

Kavallerie-Abtheilungen angeeignet, nebst Bemerkungen für den ernstlichen Kampf zu Fuss und zu Pferde. 8°. 1840. *Berlin.*
[1 *copperplate.*
2te verm. Auflage. Gr. 8°. 1843. Berlin : *Mittler.*]

SEITZ (FRANZ). — Über die Pflege der Leibesübungen auf d. deutschen Universitäten. 4°. 1861. *München.*

SEITZ (PROFESSOR OTTO). — *SPORT (Der).*—1880.

SELDEN (JOHN). — The Duello, or Single Combat from antiquitie derived into this Kingdome of England, with seuerall kindes and ceremonious formes thereof, from good authoritie described. Small 4°. 1610. *London :* Printed by G. E. for J. Helme.
[*The first work of authority on Duelling in the English language.*
A reprint. 4°. [1711?] London. (*In the British Museum.* 501. c. 29.)]

SELF-INSTRUCTOR (A) of the new system of Cavalry and Infantry Sword Exercise : comprehending directions for preparatory motions, assaults, guards, attack and defence, and divisions, as performed on foot, also as performed when mounted, with instructions for the old sword exercise and its attack and defence : together with directions and some useful remarks on the Lance Exercise. 8°. 1822. *Manchester :* Bancks & Co.
[1 *large folding plate, coloured, showing target and numerous figures.*]

SELMNITZ (ED. VON) [Ritter]. — Die Bajonettfechtkunst, oder Lehre des Verhaltens mit d. Infanterie-Gewehre als Angriffs- und Vertheidigungswaffe. 1er Theil. Gr. 8°. 1825. *Dresden.*
[10 *folio copperplates and 1 vignette.*]

—— (—. —). — Die Bajonettfechtkunst. (Vorrede zur 2ten Auflage.) 8°. 1831. *Leipzig.*

—— (—. —). — Die Bajonettfechtkunst. 2. Auflage. 1832. *Berlin :* Mittler.
[10 *copperplates.*] (*In Captain Hutton's Collection.*)

—— (—. —) [Capitaine de l'armée saxonne]. — De l'escrime à la baïonette, ou instruction pour l'emploi du fusil d'infanterie comme arme d'attaque et de défense. Traduit de l'allemand par J. B. N. Merjay. 12°. [N.D.] [1840?] *Paris et Bruxelles.*
[4 *plates, comprising 12 figures.*] (*In Captain Hutton's Collection.*)

SELMNITZ (ED. VON). — *PÖNITZ (K. E.).* — 1822.　1828.

SEÑALES DEL MANDO con la espada ó bastón para los toques de guerra, inclusas las del suplemento, para uso de todos los Señores Oficiales de Infanteria del Exercito, y en particular para los jóvenes, por tenerlo demostrado al golpe de vista : puede servir igualmente de suplemento à las Ordenanzas Militares.　Los puntos que tienen algunas figuras junto à la punta de la espada, denotan el giro que debe uevar el brazo, haciendo un molinete.　4°.　*Madrid :* Libreria de Escribano.

　　[18 *láms. dibujadas por Bernardo Medina, y grabadas por Francisco Jordan.*]

SÉNÉCHAL (G.). — Du duel.
　　[1891.　*Juin* 1.　"*La Nouvelle Revue.*"　Tome LXX. 3e Livraison, pp. 587–595.]

SÉNÉMAND (P.). — Étude sur le duel.　8°.　1873.　*Poitiers :* Imprimerie Dupré.

SENESCHAL OF HAINAULT. — Copies of Cartels or Challenges to Feats of Arms sent by the Seneschal of Hainault to King Henry IV. of England, &c.　Folio.
　　[*MS. French. On vellum.*]　(*In the British Museum.*　21,370.)

SENESE (ALESSANDRO) [gentil' huomo Bolognese]. — Modi di metter mano alla spada.　Oblong 24°.　1660.　*Venetia.*
　　[42 *plates.*]　(*In Captain Hutton's Collection.*)

—— (—). — Il vero manneggio della spada.　Folio.　1660. *Bologna :* L'Herede di Benacci.
　　　　[14 *copperplates, out of text.*]

—— (—). — Quesiti del cavaliere istrutto nell' arte della scherma. 1664.　*Padova.*

SERENO (B.). — Trattato dell' uso della lancia à cavallo, del combattere a piede, alla sbarra et dell' imprese et inventioni cavaleresche.　4°.　1610.　*Napoli.*

SERMON (A) intended as a Dissuasive from the Practice of Duelling.　4°.　1783.

SESSA (DUCA DI). — *PAGANO (M. A.).* — 1553.

SESTINI (LUIGI). — *CAPPA* e spada.

SHAKESPEARE (WILLIAM). — Hamlet.
> [*The last act contains stage direction concerning the fencers.*]

—— (—). — Romeo and Juliet.
> [*The chief characteristic of Elizabethan sword-play is the concerted action of the left hand parrying while the right attacks. It is brilliantly described in Benvolio's account of Tybalt's fight :—*
>
> > ". . . . he tilts
> > *With piercing steel at bold Mercutio's breast,*
> > *Who, all as hot, turns deadly point to point,*
> > *And, with a martial scorn, with one hand beats*
> > *Cold death aside, and with the other*
> > *Sends it back to Tybalt, whose dexterity*
> > *Retorts it. . . ."—"Romeo and Juliet,"* Act 2, Scene 4.
>
> (*See* APPENDIX, *Captain Alfred Hutton's memorandum on the fighting of the Shakespearian era, "The Single Combats."*)]

—— (—). — The Complete Works. Revised from the original edition by J. O. Halliwell. 2 vols. 8°. *London :* The London Printing and Publishing Co.
> [2nd Part of "King Henry VI.," p. 255. "*The trial by combat between the armourer Horner and his 'prentice, Peter Thump. Duels of this character are of great antiquity, and in them the vanquished was considered to be the guilty party. Men of low condition were not permitted to fight with the sword or lance—these were honourable weapons reserved for knights and nobles ; therefore the common people in these trials fought with an ebon staff, at the end of which was fixed a bag crammed hard with sand, which made a more formidable weapon than might at first be conceived, and one with which a powerful man might easily strike his opponent dead. With this instrument the timorous Peter kills his master, the latter having drank so freely with his neighbours as to be incapable of defending himself.*"]

SHAKESPEARIAN SWORDSMANSHIP.
> [*An article in the "Illustrated Sporting and Dramatic News" (Periodical). Folio.* London. No. 646 (*April* 24, 1886), pp. 1666–68.]

SHARMAN (JULIAN). — The Library of Mary, Queen of Scots. 8°. 1890. *London :* Elliot Stock.
> [*Contains a curious notice of works on Duelling.*]

SHARP (GRANVILLE) [Philanthropist]. — A Tract on Duelling, wherein the opinions of some of the most celebrated writers on Crown Law are examined and corrected, either by the authority of the *same writers,* declared in contradictory sentiments on the same subject collated from other parts of their works, or by the solemn decisions of *more ancient writers of* (at least) *equal* authority, in order to ascertain the due distinction between Manslaughter and Murder. 2nd edition. Small 8°. 1790. *London :* B. White & Son.

> [*In " The Duel" the author has attempted to ridicule that wicked and too prevalent custom, and he hopes that no immoral tendency will be found in that. He endeavours to prove that the plea of sudden anger cannot remove the imputation and guilt of murder when a mortal wound is wilfully given with a weapon.*
> *First edition was printed in 1773.*]
> (*In Mr. J. R. Garcia Donnell's Collection, and in the British Museum* [S425. *b.*].)

SHARP (GRANVILLE). — *WESTERN* Law Journal.

SHAW (L. O.). — The Duel. A satirical poem, in four cantos; with other poems. 12°. 1815. *Blackburn :* T. Rogerson.

SHERRARD (R. H.). — *IDLER (The).* — 1894.

SHORT (SOME) AND USEFUL RECOLLECTIONS upon Duelling. 12°. 1823. *Dublin :* C. Bentham.

> [Vide *Hamilton (J.)*] (*In Mr. J. R. Garcia Donnell's Collection.*)

SHURLOCK (MANWARING). — Tiles from Chertsey Abbey, Surrey, representing early romance subjects. Folio. 1885. *London :* W. Griggs.

> [Plate 19. "*The Legal Duel or Wager of Battle.*"]

SIBBALD (A. T.). — *UNITED* Service Magazine. — 1888.

SIEBENHAAR (C.). — Handleiding voor het onderwijs in de Schermkunst. Zevende verbeterde druk. 8°. 1888. *S' Graven-hage :* J. & H. van Langenhuysen.

> [*Met platen. 126 pages.*
> *6e verb. druk. Met 4 platen. 122 pages.* 8°. 1885.]
> (*In the British Museum.* 7907. *bb.* 39.)

SIERRA Y VALENZUELA. — Duelos, rieptos y desafíos. Ensayo filosófico-jurídico sobre el duelo. 1878. *Madrid.*

SIEVEKING (A. FORBES). — *SATURDAY* Review (The). — 1890 (June 21).

SIEVERBRÜCK (J.). — Manuel pour l'étude des règles de l'escrime au fleuret et à l'espadon. 4°. 1860. *Paris :* Tanera.

> [*Portrait et figures.*] (*In Captain Hutton's Collection.*)

[**SIGNOL** (ALPHONSE)]. — Le duel. Drame en deux actes. Musique de M. Sergent; représenté pour la première fois à Paris sur le théâtre du Cirque-Olympique, le 26 mars 1828. 8°. 1828. *Paris:* J. N. Barba.

—— (—). — Apologie du duel. 8°. 1829. *Paris:* Chaumerot.

SILFVERSVÄRD (REINH.). — Handbok för undervisning i sabelfäktning till fot. 8°. 1868. *Stockholm:* Eklunds.

SILVA (DON DIEGO REJÓN DE). — Compendio de las definiciones, y principios de la ciencia de las armas. 8°. 1697. *Orihuela:* J. Mesnier.

SILVA (GONZALVO DE) [Capitan]. — Compendio de la verdadera destreza de las armas. 4°.
> [*MS. In Villaumbrosana Bibliotheca.*]

SILUER (GEORGE) [**SILVER**]. — Paradoxes of Defence, wherein is proued the true groundes of fight to be in short auncient weapons, and that the short sword hath aduantage of the longe rapyer or long sword, and the weakenes and imperfection of the Rapyer fightes displeyed; together with an admonition to the noble, anncient, wictorius, valiant, and most brave nation of Englishmen to beware of false teachers of Defence, and howe they forsake theire owne naturall fights; with a breife commendation of the noble Sciennce or exercisinge of armes. By George Siluer, gentleman. Dedicated "To the right honnorable my verie good lord Robert, Earle of Essex and Ewe, Earl Marshall of England," &c., &c. Small 4°. 1599.

> [*MS.* 47 *pages.*
> With "*Epistle Dedecatorie (ff.* 4–6) *to Robert* [*Devereux,* 2nd] *Earl of Essex. Probably the actual presentation copy, having Essex's coat-of-arms at f.* 3 b, *and that of Knollys* (*Lettice, daughter of Sir Francis Knollys, was mother to Lord Essex*) *at f.* 7 b, *both in colours. There is also a pen-and-ink drawing of a fencer with sword and dagger at f.* 23. *Printed at London,* 1599 ; *the last part (ff.* 42–46 b) *entitled,* "*A breife note of three Italian teachers of offence.*" *Reprinted in the* "*Antiquarian Repertory,*" Vol. I. (1801), p. 165.]
> (*In the British Museum.* 34,192.—*Other works on Fencing by the same author are in Sloane MSS.* 376. *ff.* 1, 5 b, 32 b. *Paper ; ff.* 46. A.D. 1599.)

—— (—). — Brefe Instructions upon my Paradoxes of Defence for the true handlynge of all manner of weapons, together with the fower growndes and the fower governors, which governours are left out in my Paradoxes, without the knowledge of which no man can fight safe. Folio.

> [*MS.; 17th century.*]   (*In the British Museum. Fol. 5 b. Sl. 376.*)

SILUER (George) **[SILVER]**. — Rules of Defence to be Observed in Open Fight, &c.

> [*MS.; 17th century. Apparently by the same author. One chapter is entitled "Sundry Kinds of Play or Fight. Thornborow."*]
> (*In the British Museum. Fol. 32 b. Sl. 376.*)

SILVER (George). — Paradoxe of Defence, wherein is proved the true ground of fight to be in the short ancient weapons, and that the Short Sword hath the advantage of the long sword or long rapier, and the weaknesse and imperfection of the rapier fight displayed. Together with an admonition to the noble, ancient, victorious, valiant, and most brave nation of Englishmen, to beware of false teachers of defence, and how they forsake their own naturall fights; with a brief commendation of the noble science or exercising of arms. 8°. 1599. *London.*

> [*Woodcuts in the text. One chapter is entitled " Sundry Kinds of Play or Fight."*
> " *Saviolo seems to have remained unconquered. He was the hero of the silk button. The cutting of an adversary's doublet points on his body in un-ruffled sequence, preparatory to sending him to his account, was his speciality. Silver records the feat grudgingly, yet in detail, in his account of Saviolo's fight with another very tall man of his hands, Master Bartholo-mew Bramble, swordsman in Coventry, which encounter was the result of Bramble's hasty behaviour in emptying a blackjack full of October over the airified foreigner. The curious may find this account, which is very quaint but long-winded, in Silver's ' Paradoxe of Defence,' published as a counterblast to Saviolo's 'Practice, in two bookes, the first intreating of Rapier and Dagger, the second of Honour and Honourable Quarrels,' in the same year, namely, 1599."—Castle (E.), " The Story of Swordsman-ship." (" The National Review," May 1891.)*]

—— (—). — Brief Instructions upon my Paradoxes of Defence for the handling of all manner of weapons, together with the four grounds and the four governors, which governors are left out in my paradoxes, without the knowledge of which no man can fight safe ; together with admonitions to the gentlemen and brave gallants of Great Britain against quarrels and brawls.

> [*MS. In British Museum. Sloane 376. (Copy of same in Captain Hutton's Collection.)*]

—— (—). — *ANTIQUARIAN* Repertory.—1807.

SILVESTRE (DIEGO). — Carrera de la lanza. 4°. 1602. *Naples.*

SIMON (HENRI) et T * * *. — Le faux duel, ou le mariage par sensibilité. Comédie en un acte, mêlée de vaudevilles. 12°. 1816. *Paris :* J. N. Barba.

SIMS (GEORGE R.) [" Dagonet "]. — *REFEREE (The).*—1890.

SINCLAIR [Capt. of the 42nd Regt.]. — Cudgel-playing modernised and improved ; or the science of defence exemplified in a few short and easy lessons for the practice of the broadsword or single-stick on foot. 8°. [1800 ?] *London :* J. Bailey.

[Coloured frontispiece and folding plate.] (*In Captain Hutton's Collection.*)

SINGLE COMBATS. — *HARLEIAN* MSS.

SINGLE-STICK EXERCISE of the Aldershot Gymnasium. Fcap. 8°. [N.D.] *London :* W. H. Allen & Co.

(*In Mr. J. R. Garcia Donnell's Collection.*)

SKETCH (The). — (Periodical.) Folio. *London :* 198 Strand.

[1895. *October* 2. Page 548. *The Foil at the Adelphi : a Chat with a French Fencer.*
  ,, ,, ,, 549. *Scene from the "Swordsman's Daughter." at the Adelphi :—The Duel in the Wood— The Duel in the Court.*
1896. *January* 1. ,, 514. *The Duel in " The Prisoner of Zenda " (prologue). From a photograph by J. Byron, New York.*
  ,, *April* 29. ,, 93. *The Petticoat Duellists.*]

SLICER (H.). — Discourse on Duelling. 1838.

SLOANE MSS. — " A byll declarying how a Fellen may Wage hys Battell with the order thereof." 17th century (*temp.* Eliz.).

[MS. In the British Museum. 1710, pp. 162–163.]

—— —. — "The Waye of Duells before the Kinge," by Elias. 16th century paper.

[In the British Museum. Ashmolean MS. 3420, pp. 1–8.]

—— —. — A note of all maisters' prizes, provost prizes, scholars' prizes, and other necessary matters, with the rules of the society, 1568 to 1583 ; and an account of chalenges plaid before King Edward VI., Philip and Mary, and Queen Elizabeth.

[MS. In the British Museum. Sl. 2530.]

SLOANE MSS. — Dr. Adair.   Short Directions for Fencing.
[*MS. In the British Museum. Sl.* 1198. 2.]

—— —. — No. 1198, folio 40, 23 lines.   [Fencing.]
[*About the end of the 17th century. MS. In the British Museum.*]

SOCIÉTÉ FÉDÉRALE SUISSE DE GYMNASTIQUE. —
GYMNASTE (Le). — 1859.

SOLDIER'S COMPANION (The), containing instructions for the
drill, manual and platoon exercise, as commanded by His Majesty.
45th edition.   12°.   *London :* Lane & Newman.
[*Frontispiece : " Manual Exercise." Dedicated to H.R.H. the Duke of York.*]

SOLDIER'S (THE) FAITHFUL FRIEND, being monition to
officers and private men in the army and militia, by J. H., Esq.
8°.   2 vols.   1766.   *London.*
[Pages 51-58.   *Duelling.*]

SOLERA (DON PEDRO DE). — Titulo de maestro de la filosofia y
destreza de las armas.   Folio.   1710.   *Madrid.*

SOLIÉ (ÉM.). — Le mot de la fin sur le duel.   Les gens de plume
et les gens d'épée.   8°.   1867.   *Paris :* Ach. Faure.

SONTAG (R.). — Der studentische Zweikampf, das Schlägerduell
und dessen Bestrafung.   4°.   1881.   *Freiburg :* H. M. Poppen &
Sohn.
[*Rede bei der öffentlichen Feier der Uebergabe des Provectorats der Universität Freiburg in der Aula am 7. Mai 1881.*]

SOSSA (DON MANUEL). — Nueva ciencia de la destreza de las
armas.
[*" Así citada y también con el nombre de Losa por Muchos escritores, pero no
hay tal obra.   Este Manuel Sossa era el Asentista de S. M. que costeó la
edición de la Nueva Ciencia de Pacheco."*]

SOUTH (R.). — Case of Duelling considered with respect to
Challenger and Challenged.   12°.   1773.

SOUTHERN LITERARY MESSENGER.   *Richmond, U.S.A.*
[Vol. XXIX. p. 348.   *" The Duel : a Tale."*
„   XXXII. p. 226.   *" Duelling."*]

SOUTHEY (ROBERT). — Commonplace Book. 4 vols. 1849–51.
London : Longman.

[Vol.   I. p. 512.   *Law against Duelling in James I.'s Time.*
  „   I. p. 556.   *Barbarous Custom of Duelling.*
  „   II. p. 20.   *Curse of Duelling.*
  „   II. p. 306.   *A Word to Duellers.*
  „   III. p. 229.   *Trying Request at Duelling.*
  „   III. p. 332.   *Duelling forbidden by Baldwin the Good in Flanders.*
  „   III. pp. 511, 677.   *Johnson's Sophism on Duels.*
  „   IV. p. 492.   *Effectual Sermon against Duels.*]

SOUTHGATE (HENRY). — Many Thoughts of Many Minds. 2nd
series. 8°. 1871. *London :* Charles Griffin & Co.

[Page 137. *Duels.*
  3rd edition. 8°. 1862. London: *Griffin, Bohn, & Co.* (Pages 171–172.
  Duelling.)]

SPAINE (Concerning Duells in).

  [*Harleian MS.,* Vol. III. p. 122. cod. 4176. art. 5.]

SPANISH SWORD-CUTLERS (List of), with their Blade-marks.
18th century.

  [*Spanish MS. In British Museum.* No. 20,790. f. 397.]

SPECTATOR (The). — (Periodical.) Folio. *London.*

[1711. *June* 6. No. 84. *A Discourse against Duelling.*
  „   „ 21.   „ 97.   *Pharamond's Edict against Duels.*
  „   „ 23.   „ 99.   *Chief Point of Honour among Men and Women.*
                  (*Duelling.*)
  1830. pp. 33, 244. *Duelling.*
  „   p. 828. *Law of Duelling.*
  1832. p. 874. *Duelling.*
  1841. p. 325. *Some Thoughts about Duelling.*
  1843. p. 634. *A Deed without a Name.*
  „   p. 661. *Substitute for Pistols.*
  „   p. 683. *What a willing Government could do to abolish Duelling.*
  „   p. 709. *The Progress of Opinion.*
  „   p. 827. *The Duel and its Perplexities.*
  1844. p. 34. *The Duel and its Lesson.*
  „   p. 204. *A Law impossible to Obey.*
  „   p. 254. *Colonel Fawcett's Widow : a Word for Women.*
  1846. p. 253. *"Absurd" Verdicts : the Gosport Duel.*
  1862. p. 343. *The Duel of the Ironsides.*
  „   p. 349. *Duelling on its Last Legs.*
  1884. p. 1072. *Duelling in Italy.*
  1890. p. 371. *Duelling with Limited Liability.*
  1892. p. 708. *Duelling.*]

SPIELMANN (M. H.). — *FURNISS* (H.). — 1889.

SPINAZZI (PIETRO) [Capitano]. — Il bersagliere in campagna ed istruzione sulla scherma della baionetta, corredato di tavole dimostrative. 1851. *Genova:* tipografia del R. J. de' sordomuti.

SPITTLER (L. T.). — *GÖTTINGEN.* — 1791–94.

SPORT (Der) in Musterblättern für Kunst und Gewerbe. Mit beiträgen von Guido Hammer, Moritz Ledeli, Franz Patek, Professor Otto Seitz, Anton Weinberger, Th. Zasche, etc. Folio. 1880. *Wien:* Thiel und Schkerl.

[8 *Lieferungen, mit* 40 *Tafeln. Fechtkunst.*]

SPORT (LE) À PARIS. — *CHAPUS (E.).* — 1854.

SPORTO (LO) ILLUSTRATO. — (Periodical). Caccia, ippica, scherma, ecc. 1881. *Milano.*

SPORTO (LO) ITALICO. — Giornale settimanale di scherma, ecc. 1894.

SPORTS (A New Book of). — Reprinted from the "Saturday Review." 8°. 1885. *London:* R. Bentley & Son.

[*Backsword and Schläger,* page 147. *Rapier and Dagger,* page 146.]

SPORTSMAN (The). — (Periodical.) Folio. *London:* 139 Fleet Street.

[1892. *February* 23. "*Assault-at-Arms at the Oxford University Fencing Club.*"]

SPRING (S.). — Sermon on Duelling. 1804.

(*In New York State Library, U.S.A.*)

STADLER (D.). — Tractatus de duello. 4°. 1751. *Ingolstadt:* Krüll.

[*Engraved frontispiece.*]

STANDARD (The). — (Periodical.) Folio. *London.*

[1890.	*Mar.*	13.	*The Abolition of Duelling.*
,,	*Sept.*	15.	*A Boulangist Duel.*
,,	*Oct.*	22.	*Duels in Hungary.*
,,	*Nov.*	14.	*Duel between M. Déroulède and M. Laguerre.*
1891.	*Jan.*	2.	*Count Deym's Duel.*
,,	*Feb.*	7.	*Duelling in Hungary.*
,,	*April*	1.	*Duel between Prince Vadbolsky and M. Monossoff.*
,,	*May*	18.	*Duel in France between M. Bazire and M. Gungl.*
,,	,, ,,		*Duel in Rome between Signor Barzilai and Cáptain Bozzi.*
,,	,,	23.	*Duel in Tunis between M. Mussali and M. Carbonaro.*
,,	*June*	17.	*The O'Gorman Mahon* [vide *Mahon (O'G.)*].
,,	*July*	23.	*M. Ugron, Radical Deputy, Hungarian Chamber, challenged to fight a Duel by the Officers of the Austrian 79th Regiment of Infantry.*

STANDARD (The) (*continued*)—

1891.	*Aug.*	15.	Duelling in Hungary. (*A Duel between M. Rohonczy and M. Gajary, two Deputies of the Hungarian Parliament.*)
„	„	21.	Dr. Tanner, M.P., challenged to a Duel.
„	*Sept.*	14.	Duel at Pesth between the Editor of the "*Hirlap*" and a M. Sarkany.
„	„	19.	An Italian Duel (*with Sabres, between General Gandolfi and Deputy Franchetti*).
.	*Oct.*	1.	Duel between General Boulanger and M. Floquet.
„	„	17.	Review of Captain C. A. Thimm's "*Bibliography of Fencing and Duelling.*"
„	„	24.	A Duel with Pistols in Hungary between Count H—— and First-Lieutenant Von L——.
„	*Nov.*	6.	Professor Hartl's Corps of Viennese Fencing Ladies.
„	*Dec.*	21.	A Duel in Hungary. (*Baron Fejervary and Deputy Ugron.*)
1892.	*Jan.*	21.	A Duel between M. Delpech and M. Castelin, with Swords.
„	*Feb.*	20.	Englishmen and Duels. Question asked by Mr. Esslemont in the House of Commons.
„	*Mar.*	16.	A Duel with Swords between M. Isaac, formerly Sub-Prefect of Avesnes, and the Marquis de Morès.
„	*April*	30.	Another Duel at Ostende. (*Mr. Harry Vane Milbank and a Frenchman [Duc de Morny (?)].*)
„	*May*	9.	A Duel with Swords between Lieutenant Ovary and M. Horvath, a member of the Lower House of the Hungarian Diet.
„	„	13.	Fatal Duel in Germany between an Officer of the 106th Regiment and a Law Student named Netche.
„	„	19.	Extraordinary Series of Duels. (*MM. Roulez, member of the École d'Escrime Française, and Blondin, Dumoulin, Leclerc; the three latter were all wounded.*) [*See also "Pall Mall Gazette." May 20, 1892.*]
„	„	23.	The Reported Duelling. (*M. Roulez.*)
„	„	25.	Duelling in Hungary. (*Between Dr. Alexander Karsay and Baron Bela Aczel.*)
„	„	30.	Duelling in Paris. (*M. Burdeau and M. Couturier, fought with swords; the former was run through the wrist. Another duel was fought between a German officer, M. Oudet, and a French officer; the former shot through the stomach.*)
„	*June*	21.	Duelling in France. (*Captain Cremieux Foa and M. Drumont; four shots were exchanged without result.*)
„	„	24.	Fatal Duel in France. (*Marquis de Morès and Captain Meyer; the latter was run through the right lung, and was killed.*)
„	*July*	11.	Duelling in Greece. (*Between Alfred Bey, Secretary of the Turkish Legation, and a Greek cavalry officer; the latter was seriously wounded.*)
„	„	„	A Duel with Pistols between Mayor of Madrid and a Municipal Councillor. Two shots exchanged; neither combatant wounded.
„	„	14.	Duelling in Athens.
„	*Aug.*	20.	Duels in Germany.

STANDARD (The) (*continued*)—

1892. *Aug.* 30.   *The Morès-Meyer Duel.*
  „   „   31.   *Ditto.*
  „   *Sept.* 15.   *Continental Duelling.   (A duel on the Dunes near Was-senaar, between Baron Gärtner von Griebenow, Secretary of the German Legation, and Marquis d'Alcedo, Secretary of the Spanish Legation at The Hague, was fought with pistols; the latter wounded in the right hip.)   (A duel with pistols between M. Gerville Réache, Deputy for Guadaloupe, and M. Souques, a Conservative General Councillor for the same colony; the former wounded in right arm.)*
1893. *Dec.* 7.   *Leader on the subject of a new edition of Mr. Egerton Castle's "Schools and Masters of Fence."*
1894. *Oct.* 1.   *Duelling on the Continent.*]

STANTON (Samuel) [Lieutenant in the 97th Regiment]. — The Principles of Duelling.   8°.   1790.   *London.*

STANZAS ON DUELLING; inscribed to Wogden, the celebrated Pistol-maker.   4°.   1783.   *London:* Kerby.

STAR (The). — (Periodical.)   Folio.   *London.*

[1890. *Dec.* 30.   *Making Mystery of the Duel.*
1891. *Mar.* 24.   *One Editor kills Another, and a Third is wounded.*
1892. *June* 3.   *A Paris Duel with Bloodshed in it.*
1895. *Aug.* 13.   *Fencing at the Tivoli.*
1896. *Jan.* 7.   *A New Army Sword.*]

STATISTICA DELLE CAUSE delle Morti Avvenute in tutti i Comuni del Regno nell' anno 1887.   4°.   1890.   *Roma:* Tipografia Elzeviriana nel Ministero delle Finanze.

[*Statistica dei duelli durante il decennio dal giugno 1879 al luglio 1889.*]

STATUTI E REGOLAMENTI della società di ginnastica e scherma di Brescia approvati nelle adunanze generali dei soci del Aprile 1872 e del 10 Gennajo 1875.   8°.   1877.   *Brescia:* F. Apollonio.

(*In Mr. J. R. Garcia Donnell's Collection.*)

STATUTS ET RÈGLEMENS faits par les maistres en fait d'armes de la ville et Fauxbourgs de Paris.   Pour le maintient de leurs privilèges octroyez par les Roys.   Verifiez par Nosseigneurs du Conseil.   4°.   1645.   *Paris:* P. Moreau.

STATUTS ET RÈGLEMENS faits par les maîtres en fait d'armes de la ville et Fauxbourgs de Paris, 1644, publiés par Henry Daressy.   1867.   *Paris:* Vasseur.

STEELE (SIR JOHN). — The Court of Honour, or the Laws, Rules, and Ordinances established for the Suppression of Duels in France. Translated from the French, with Observations thereon. 1720.

STEIN (RICH.) [Lieut.]. — *AZÉMAR (Baron D').* — 1860.

STEINMETZ (ANDREW). — The Romance of Duelling, in all Times and all Countries. 2 vols. 8°. 1868. *London:* Chapman & Hall.

(*In the British Museum.* 2238. *bb.* 4.)

—— (—). — The Gaming Table: its Votaries and Victims in all Times and Countries, especially in England and France. 2 vols. 1870. 8°. *London:* Tinsley.

[*Bungay printed. Chapter on Duels.*]

STEPHAN (D. G.). — De duellis. 1781.

[*Mentioned in Max Perl's Catalogue.* Berlin. 1895.]

STEPHANI (RITTER HNR.). — Wie die Duelle, diese Schande unsers Zeitalters, auf unsern Universitäten so leicht wieder abgeschafft werden Können; nachwiesen. 8°. 1828. *Leipzig:* Brockhaus.

STEPHENS (THOMAS). — A New System of Broad and Small Sword Exercise, with Instructions in Horsemanship. 12°. 1843. *Philadelphia.*

—— (—). — A New System of Broad and Small Sword Exercise, comprising the Broad Sword Exercise for Cavalry and Artillery, and the Small Sword Cut and Thrust Practice for Infantry and Navy. 2nd edition. 8°. 1861. *Milwaukee:* Jermain & Brightman.

[62 *illustrations.*]

STIGLIANO (A. COLONNA DI). — Dialogismo sul duello. 8°. 1878. *Napoli.*

[55 *pages.*] (*In the British Museum.* 8425. *ff.* 23.)

STJERNSVARD (G. M.). — Handbok uti Gymnastik och Bajonett Fäktning. 24°. 1843. *Stockholm.*

[2 *plates.*]

STOCKEN [Hauptmann]. — Uebungs-Tabellen für den systematischen Betrieb der Gymnastik und des Bajonnetfechtens bei der Infanterie. 1te und 2te Auflage. 1862. *Berlin:* Schroeder.

STOCKEN [Hauptmann]. — Uebungs-Tabellen für den systematischen Betrieb der Gymnastik und des Bajonnetfechtens bei der Infanterie. 3te Auflage. 1864. *Berlin:* Schroeder.

———— . — Uebungs - Tabellen für den systematischen Betrieb der Gymnastik und des Bajonnetfechtens bei der Infanterie. Nebst einem kurzen Lectionsgange für den Unterricht im Stoss- und Hiebfechten. 4te Auflage. 8°. 1867. *Berlin:* Schroeder.

———— . — Lectionsgang für den Unterricht im Stoss- und Hiebfechten als Anhalt für den Lehrer. 8°. 1867. *Berlin:* Schroeder.

———— . — Uebungs-Tabellen für den systematischen Betrieb d. Milit. Gymnastik. 6te Auflage. 8°. 1869. *Berlin:* Schroeder.

STOCKHOLM. — Daggers in the Hammer Museum.
(*In the Art Library, South Kensington Museum. Portfolio* 499.)

"STONEHENGE" [**WALSH** (J. H.)] and **WOOD.** — Archery, Fencing, and Broadsword. 18°. 1863. *London:* Routledge.

STOTHARD (C. A.). — The Monumental Offices of Great Britain. Folio. 1817. *London:* Printed by J. M. M'Creery.
[*Monumental effigy in Malvern Abbey Church, Worcestershire, the round "buckler" is slung across the right shoulder by a guige. The weapon borne by the figure is probably that known in contemporary writings as the "bisacutum."*]

———— (—. —). — Ditto.   With Historical Descriptions and Notes by Alfred John Kempe, F.S.A.   A new edition, with large additions by John Hewitt, Esq.   4°.   1876.   *London:* Chatto & Windus.

STOWE MSS. — The Antiquitie, Vse & Ceremonies of Lawfull Combats in England.   Written by Sir Francis Tate, of the Middle Temple, London.   13° Feb. Aⁿᵒ 1600.
[*MS. In the British Museum. 568. f. 102.*]

———— —. — Of the Antiquitie, Use & Ceremony of Lawfull Combatts in England.   By ——— Davies.   1601.   Pr. ibid. p. 190.
[*MS. In the British Museum. 569. f. 35.*]

———— —. — Of the same.   By James Whitlocke.   1601.   Pr. ibid. p. 190.
[*MS. In the British Museum. 569. f. 35.*]

STOWE MSS. — [Of the Antiquity, Use & Ceremony of Lawfull Combats in England]. By Sir Robert Cotton. 1609. Pr. ibid. p. 172 ; the date, however, being given as 1601.

[*MS. In the British Museum. 569. f. 35.*]

——— . — Cases in which Duels are allowed by "la loy lombarde."

[*Fr. MS. In the British Museum. f. 74. b. (Stowe Cat. xvi.)*]

——— . — "Duello Foyl'd." By Edward Cook.

[*MS. In the British Museum. 569. f. 41. b.*]

——— . — "Modus faciendi duellum coram domino rege." *Temp.* Richard II. Begins, "Premierement les quereles et billes."

[*Fr. MS. In the British Museum. 140. ff. 136-141.*]

——— . — Concerning Duellos in Spaine. By Sir Henry Wotton.

[*MS. In the British Museum. 569. f. 70.*]

STRADA (ENRICO) [Generale di Cavalleria]. — Scherma e tiro. 1870. *Napoli :* tip. Strada.

STRANTZ (GUST.) [Prem. Lieut.]. — Leitfaden zum Stossfechten, Schlagen und Turnen für die königl. Militär-Reitschule zu Schwedt. Gr. 8°. 1861. *Berlin :* Springer.

STRECKER (E. W.). — Utrum duellum sit licitum. 1741. *Erfurt.*

[*Mentioned in Max Perl's Catalogue. Berlin. 1895.*]

STRICT (A) ENQUIRY into the Circumstances of a late Duel ; with some Account of the Persons concern'd on both Sides. To which is added the Substance of a Letter from General MacCartney to his Friend. 8°. 1713. *London.*

STRICTURES ON DUELLING selected from the most Authentic Authors ; with Additions by a Gentleman, late of the University of Oxford. 8°. 1792. *London :* Walter.

STRÖMBORG (N.). — Gymnastik-lära, efter P. H. Ling och G. Branting 1ª Häftet, Fäktlara. 8°. 1857. *Stockholm :* Ostlund & Berlingska.

STRUTT (JOSEPH). — Horda Angel Cynnan ; or a compleat view of the manners, customs, arms, habits, &c., of the inhabitants of

England. From the arrival of the Saxons till the reign of **Henry the Eighth.** 3 vols. 4°. 1775–76.

> [*Plate LIII. shows mode of fighting tournaments on horseback.*]

STRUTT (JOSEPH) [Engraver]. — Angleterre ancienne, ou tableau des moeurs, usages, armes, habillemens, etc., des anciens habitans de l'Angleterre. 2 vols. 4°. 1789. *Paris.*

> [*Ouvrage traduit de l'anglois par M. B. * * ** (i.e., *A. M. H. Boulard.*) *Avec beauc. de planches.*] (*In the British Museum.* 10,349. *h.* 9.)

—— (—). — Glig - Gamena Angel - Deod, or the Sports and Pastimes of the People of England, from the earliest period to the present time. Royal 4°. 1801. *London :* Printed by Bensley.

> [60 *coloured plates.*]

—— (—). — Sports and Pastimes of People of England. With a copious Index by Hone. New edition. 8°. 1850. *London :* Tegg.

SUISSE (Le Gymnaste). — *GYMNASTE (Le).* — 1859.

SULLY (MAXIMIL.). — Œconomies.

> [Vol. I. p. 301 ; Vol. III. p. 406 ; Vol. VI. p. 122 ; Vol. VIII. p. 406 ; Vol. IX. p. 408. "*Duelling.*"]

SUN (The). — (Periodical.) Folio. *London.*

> [1891. *June 2. An Unfortunate Duel.*
> 1894. *Oct. 3. Sarcey's Duel.*
> 1895. *Mar. 6. Harry Alis's Fatal Duel.*
>   „   *May 8. Missed!* ("*American Plan*" *of Duelling.*)
>   „   *June 4. Duelling Weapons.*]

SUN MAGAZINE (The). — (Monthly). 8°. *Paisley.*

> [1890. *September. Duelling in the Army.*]

SUNDAY SUN (The). — (Periodical). Folio. *London.*

> [1891. *May 24. Carolina Planters fight a Duel.* (*Between Mr. P. H. Cheatham and Mr. John Wately.*)
> 1891. *June 21. The Last of the Duellists.* (*The O'Gorman Mahon.*)
> 1892. *November 6. Russians Described by Themselves :* * *VIII. The Story of a Duel.*
> * "*The Queen of Spades, and Other Stories.*" *By Pushkin. Translated by Mrs. Sutherland Edwards. Chapman & Hall.*]

SUNDAY TIMES (The). — (Periodical). Folio. *London.*

> [1890. *September 21. Note on a French Duel in* "*Echoes of the Week,*" *by G. A. S*[*ala*].
> 1892. *June 26. Duelling.*]

SURDUN. — Notice biographique sur Jean-Louis et son École. 8°. 1866. *Montpellier :* Ricard.

> [*Avec portraits, dont un sur cuivre ajouté.*]

SUSIO (G.). — I tre libri della ingiustitia del duello, et di coloro, che lo permettono. 4°. 1555. *Vinegia:* Gab. Giolito.

[*Folding plate of Man and Woman Combat. Another edition appeared in 1558.*] (*In Captain Hutton's Collection.*)

SUTCLIFFE (MATHER). — Practice, Proceedings, and Lawes of Armes, described out of the doings of most valiant and expert captains, and confirmed by ancient and modern examinations. Sm. 4°. 1593.

[𝕭lack=letter.]

SUTOR (J.). — New künstliches Fechtbuch, das ist : Ausführliche Deschription der Freyen Adelichen und Ritterlichen Kunst dess Fechtens in den gebräuchlichsten Wehren, als Schwerdt, Dusacken, Rappier, Stangen vnd Helleparten, im Fechten mit sein gewissen zu vnd abtritten auss den Lagern, auch Geschwindigkeit, beneben kurzer Erklärung einer sehr nothwendigen Instruction, sampt viel schönen, gantz nützlichen vnd zierlichen Figuren eygentlich fürgestellet. Nun aber allen vnd jeden der löblichen Fechtkunst Liebhabern, zu sonderlichem gefallen in diese kleine Form gebracht vnd an tag gegeben, durch den Wohlerfahrnen vnd berühmten Freyfechtern Jacob Sutorium von Baden, etc. Gedruckt zu Frankfurt am Mayn durch Johann Bringern, in Verlegung Wilhelm Hoffmans, 1612. Neu herausgegeben, wort- und bildgetreu nach dem Original. 4°. 1849. *Stuttgart:* J. Scheible.

[89 *woodcuts.*] (*In Captain Hutton's and M. Vigeant's Collections.*)

SUTORIUS (JACOB) [Freyfechter von Baden]. — New Künstliches Fechtbuch, das ist aussführliche Deschription der Freyen Adelichen und Ritterlichen Kunst dess Fechtens in den gebreuchlichsten Wehren, als Schwerdt, Düsacken, Rappier, &c., &c. 4°. 1612. *Franckfurt:* Wilhelm Hoffmans.

[*Gedruckt zu Franckfurt am Mayn durch Johann Bringern. 94 woodcuts. "Although Jacob Sutor belonged to the flourishing epoch of Fabris, Giganti, and Capo Ferro's teaching, the rapier-play he describes shows even less perfection than that of Meyer."—Castle's "Schools and Masters of Fence."*]
(*In the British Museum. 7905. bbb. 3.*)

SWETNAM (JOSEPH). — The Schoole of the Noble and Worthy Science of Defence. Being the first of any Englishmans invention, which professed the sayd Science; So plainly described that any man may quickly come to the true knowledge of their weapons with small paines and little practise. Then reade it advisedly, and use the benefit there of when occasion shall serve, so shalt thou be a good Common-wealth man, live happy to thy selfe and comfortable to thy friend. Also many other good and profitable Precepts for the managing of Quarrels and ordering thy selfe in many other matters. 4°. 1617. *London:* Printed by Nicholas Okes.

[Dedicated to Charles, Prince of Wales. 7 woodcuts.]
(In the Bodleian Library.)

SWIFT (T.). — Answer (An). 1794.

SWORD AND BUCKLER.

[MSS. In the Royal Library, British Museum. No. 14, E. iii., 13th century, and No. 20, D. vi.]

SWORD-BLADES. — The Case of the Governor and Company for making Hollow Sword-blades in England. [N.D.]

(In the Guildhall Library of the City of London. Fo. sh.)

SWORD-DANCE.

[MS. In the Cotton Library. Cleopatra, C. iii., 9th century. Woodcuts.]

SWORD-EXERCISE for Cavalry. 8°. 1799. *London.*

[6 engravings.]

SWORD-EXERCISE of Cavalry. 8°. 1805.

[Plates.]

SWORD-EXERCISE, Cavalry. 1842. *Bangalore.*

SWORD-EXERCISE for Cavalry, Rules and Regulations by H.M.'s Company. 8°. *London.*

[**SWORDS.** — Anelace, or Short Sword. South Kensington Museum Catalogue of Loan Collection, 1862 (pp. 366–367). 8°. 1862. *London.*

——. — Arab Sword, Turin. Reale Armeria.

(In the Art Library, South Kensington Museum. Portfolio 377.)

——. — ARNETH (J. VON). — Die Cinque, Cento, Cameen und Arbeiten des Benvenuto Cellini. Folio. 1858. *Wien.*

[23 plates. Sword by Cellini, plate 21.]
(In the Art Library, South Kensington Museum.)

[**SWORDS**. — Barbaric Swords. Used by Dyaks of Borneo; also from Timor, Rotti, and neighbouring islands. British Museum Series.

(In the Art Library, South Kensington Museum. Portfolio 519.)

———. — BEAUMONT (É. DE). — Une épée du XIIIe siècle.

[*" Gazette des Beaux-Arts,"* Vol. III. 2nd Series, p. 288. 8º. 1870. Paris.]

———. — Cingalese. Royal Armoury, Windsor Castle.

(In the Art Library, South Kensington Museum. Portfolio 2.)

———. — Cingalese. South Kensington Museum.

(In the Art Library, South Kensington Museum. Portfolio 265.)

———. — Cingalese. With Hilt and Scabbard in carved Tortoise-shell. South Kensington Museum.

(In Art Library, South Kensington Museum. Portfolio 110.)

———. — DAVILLIER (C.). — Recherches sur l'orféverie en Espagne du Moyen Âge et à la Renaissance. 4º. 1879. *Paris.*

[Swords and Daggers.]

———. — Découverte d'éspées en bronze à Alies (Cantal).

[*" Revue Archéologique,"* Vol. XXIV. p. 337. 8º. 1872. Paris.]

———. — Hotspur's Sword. In possession of Lord Leconfield.

(In the Art Library, South Kensington Museum. Portfolio 178.)

———. — Italian Renaissance Swords and Daggers. Milan Industrial Museum of Art.

(In the Art Library, South Kensington Museum. Portfolio 559.)

———. — Japanese. Royal Armoury, Windsor Castle.

(In the Art Library, South Kensington Museum. Portfolio 2.)

———. — Leases from the Company for making Hollow Sword-blades.

[*MSS. In the British Museum.* 1704, 1709. *Add. ch.* 24,473, 24,474.]

———. — List of famous Spanish Sword-cutlers, with their Blade-marks.

[*MS.* 18th century. *Spanish. British Museum.* 20,790. f. 397.]

———. — Oriental Swords and Daggers belonging to the Marquis of Hertford. " L'art ancien."

(In the Art Library, South Kensington Museum. Portfolio 366.)

[**SWORDS**. — Pre-historic. Biel, Swabian Museum.

——. — Pre-historic. Hammer Museum, Stockholm.
(*In the Art Library, South Kensington Museum. Portfolios* 334, 499.)

——. — Project de classification des poignards et épées en bronze.
["*Revue Archéologique,*" Vol. XIII. p. 180. 8°. 1866. Paris.]

——. — Renaissance. Germanischen Museum.

——. — Renaissance. "L'art ancien." Vol. III.

——. — Renaissance. Berlin, Royal Arsenal. Exhibition 1872.
(*In the Art Library, South Kensington Museum. Portfolios* 250, 366, 574.)

——. — Roman. Épée Romaine, fouilles d'Alise-Sainte-Reine.
["*Revue Archéologique,*" Vol. IV. p. 141. 8°. 1861. Paris.]

——. — South Kensington Museum. Catalogue of Loan Exhibition, 1862. 8°. 1862. *London.*
[Pages 353–355, 359–363. *Swords and Daggers.*]

——. — Worn by the Popes, belonging to M. Labouchère.
(*In the Art Library, South Kensington Museum. Portfolio* 366.)]

[*It is not intended to give a complete list of books on Swords, but the above are all interesting to the fencer.*]

SYLVA (D. DIEGO REJON DE). — *SILVA* (*Don D. R. de*). — 1697.

T. (E.) [Commandant]. — *ESCRIME* de chambre.

T. C. (D. D.). — *DISCOURSE* of Duels, &c. — 1687.

TABOUROT (JEAN). — *ARBEAU* (*T.*). — 1596.

TAGLIABUE (C. ANTONIO). — Il duello. Considerazioni filosofiche e storiche sul modo di reprimerlo e sradicarlo dalla società. 16°. 1867. *Milano.*
[*Another edition.* 12°. 1868. Milano.]

TAIT'S EDINBURGH MAGAZINE. 8°. *Edinburgh.*
[Vol. III. p. 355. *The Duellist.*
New Series. Vol. VIII. p. 97. *Duelling. By T. De Quincey.*
,,   ,, XVIII. p. 151. *Duelling in France and the United States.*]

TALHOFFER (HANS). — Kampfbuch. 1443.

[*MS. Gotha Bibliothek. Chart. 558.*]

—— (—). — A copy of the same. (Ibid. pergam. 114.) 1497.

[*The oldest MSS. of Fence known. They deal with the methods of carrying out a wager of battle, and the tricks of fight recommendable therefor; and pretty gruesome they are, as a rule.*]

—— (—). — Fechtbuch gerichtliche und andere Zweikämpfe darstellend. 4°. 1467.

[*268 plates.*]

(*In München, Hof. Bibl.* [*Codex, Juno, 394–395.*]
 „ *Wien.* [*Ambras. Sammlung, 55.*]
 „ *Berlin.* [*Kupf. Cabin., H.S. 125.*]
 „ *Gotha Bibl.* [*Codex memb., fol. 114.*] [*This copy bears the date 1467.*])

—— (—). — Fechtbuch aus dem Jahre 1467. Gerichtliche und andere Zweikämpfe darstellend. Herausgegeben von G. Hergsell. 4°. 1887. *Prag:* Calve.

[*With 268 plates.*] (*In Captain Hutton's Collection.*)

—— (—). — Fechtbuch [Ambraser Codex] aus dem Jahre 1459, gerichtliche und andere Zweikämpfe darstellend. Mit hoher Bewillig. d. k. k. Oberstkämmerer-Amtes herausgegeben von Hauptmann d. n. a. Ldw. Landesfechtmeister Gust. Hergsell. Gr. 4°. 1889. *Prag:* Calve.

[*Mit 116 Tafeln in Lichtdruck.*
Kämpfe mit langem Schwert in voller Rüstung, Tafeln 1–4. Mit Spiess und Schwert, Tafeln 5–12. Junker Königsegg, Tafeln 13–42. Degen, Tafeln 43–63. Ringen, Tafeln 64–81. Spiess, Tafeln 82–90. Spiess gegen Reiter, Tafel 91. Zu Ross mit d. Spiess, Tafeln 92, 93, 100. Zu Ross mit Spiess und Schwert, Tafeln 94–99. Zu Ross mit Schwert, Tafeln 101–105. Ringkämpfe zu Ross, Tafeln 106–112. Szenen aus dem Reitunterricht, Tafeln 113–114.]

—— (—). — Fechtbuch [Gothaer Codex] aus dem Jahre 1443, gerichtliche und andere Zweikämpfe darstellend. Herausgegeben von Hauptmann d. n. a. Ldw. Landesfechtmeister Gust. Hergsell. Gr. 4°. 1889. *Prag:* Calve.

[*Mit 160 Tafeln in Lichtdruck.*
Fechten zu Ross mit Spiess und Schwert. Kampffechten zu Fuss. Meister Otts Ringkunst. Kampf mit dem langen Schwert und Szenen aus dem ritterlichen Leben, Tafeln 1–13. · Kampf mit dem Stechschilde, Tafeln 14–24. Kampf mit Stechschild und Kolben, Tafeln 25–34. Mit Schild und Kolben, Tafeln 35–47. In voller Rüstung mit d. langen Schwert, Tafeln 48–63. Mit Spiess, Schwert und Dolch, Tafeln 64–73. Mit den Hellebarten, Tafeln 74–81. Mit Degen, Tafeln 82–125. Ringen, Tafeln 126–160.]

—— (—). — *HERGSELL* (*G.*). — 1887.

TALHOFFER (Hans). — *SCHLICHTEGROLL (Dr. N.)*. —1817.

—— (—). — *THALHOFER (K.) und ISNARDI (M.)*.—1838.

TALLEMANT DES RÉAUX (Gédéon). — Les Historiettes.
[Vol. X. p. 13. *"Duelling."*] (*In Captain Hutton's Collection.*)

TAMBORNINI (Carlo). — Trattato di scherma alla sciabola.
1862. *Genova.*

TAPIA Y SALCEDO. — Exercicios de la gineta. 1614.

TARDE (Gabriel). — El duelo. 8°. [1893.] *Madrid:* Impr.
de la Compañía de Impresores y Libreros.
[*350 pages.*]

TASSO (Torquato). — *BIRAGO (F.)*. — 1686.

TATE (Francis). — *ASHMOLEAN* MS. 856. 154.

—— (—). — *CODICUM* MS.

TATLER (The). — (Periodical.) *London.*
[1709. *June* 7. No. 25. *Duelling and its Terms explained.*
,,   ,, 9. ,, 26. *Duellers—how treated after Death.*
,,   ,, 14. ,, 28. *Duelling.*
,,   ,, 16. ,, 29. *Duel — Inquiry into the Genealogy of that Monster.*
,,   ,, 18. ,, 30. *Duelling.*
,, *July* 9. ,, 39.   ,,
,, *Nov.* 12. ,, 93. *Fencing—how learned by Mr. Bickerstaff.*]

TAVERNIER (Adolphe). — L'Art du duel. Préface par Aurélien
Scholl. Gr. 8°. 1884. *Paris:* Marpon et Flammarion.
[*Tiré à 500 exemplaires numérotés.*
*Illustrations de Blanchon, Feyen-Perrin, Genilloud, Gœneutte, Juzet, Lerat,
A. De Neuville, H. Pille, Ruzé, Willette, Yundt.*]

—— (—). — [Another edition.] Nouvelle édition. 12°. Illustré. 1885. *Paris:* Marpon et Flammarion.
(*In Captain Hutton's Collection.*)

—— (—). — Amateurs et salles d'armes de Paris. 1886. 12°.
Paris: Marpon et Flammarion.
[*Illustrations et eau-forte de Genilloud.*]

—— (—). — L'Art du duel. Préface par A. Scholl. Nouvelle
édition. 12°. 1888. *Paris:* Marpon et Flammarion.

—— (—). — *PRÉVOST (C.)*. — 1886.

TAYLOR (John). — *ROWORTH (C.)*. — 1804.

TAYLOR (W.). — Sermon on Duelling. 1838.
(*In New York State Library, U.S.A.*)

TEDESCHI (LELIO DE). — Raccolta delle fedi d' alcuni prencipi, et SS^{ri} italiani, che hanno conosciuto, et provato il suo secreto del securo modo di levar nell' atto di ferire, ò del parare la spada di mano all' avversario.   4°.   1603.   *Bologna.*

TEISSIER (C.). — Du duel, au point de vue médico-légal.   4°. 1890.   *Lyon.*

[*58 pages.*]

TEMLICH. — Anfangsgründe der Fechtkunst.   8°.   1776. *Halle.*

TERRACUSA (NICOLA). — La vera scherma Napolitana Rinovata.   Nella 1. si dichiarava le lezioni di spada sola.   Nella 2. quella di spada e pugnale.   E nella 3. quella di spada e brocchiere, spada e rotella ; e spada e cappa.   1725.   *Roma :* Pietro Ferri.

TERWANGUE (ADOLPHE). — Réflexions techniques et historiques sur l'escrime, par un ancien amateur.   8°.   1874.   *Lille:* Meriaux.
[*Another edition.*   12°.   1891.   Lille.   (*39 pages.*)]

TEXEDO (DON PEDRO) [de Taruel, Sicilia]. — Escuela en la berdadera destreza de las armas.   (Dedicated to Don Fern. Joach. Faxardo de Requesens y Zuñiga.)   Small 4°.   1678 (?).   *Palermo* (?).
[*Portrait of the author, and figures.*]

THALHOFER (KARL) und **ISNARDI** (MICH.). — Theoret.-prakt. Anleitung zur Fechtkunst à la Contrepointe.   Nebst. e. Anleitung zur Vertheidigung mit d. Säbel oder Degen den Bajonnetisten von Tallhofer.   Mit 1 Heft figuren.   Gr. 8°.   1838.   *Wien:* Heubner.
[*59 lithographed plates.*]

THEATRE (The). — (Magazine.)   8°.   *London.*
[1891.   *March* 1. } *Duelling on the Stage and off.   By Walter Calvert.*
„   *April* 1. }   (*With 3 illustrations.*)
S. 3, Vol. II. No. 12, pp. 347–350.   *Fencing and Fencers.   By A. Escott.*]

THÉAULON, MÉLESVILLE et **CARMOUCHE.** — Cinq heures du soir, ou le duel manqué.   Comédie-vaudeville en un acte.   12°. 1827.   *Paris :* Quoy

THEOLOGY OF DUELLING.
[*"Saturday Review"* (*London*), Vol. LIX., No. 376.]

D.Bailly fecit 16..

GIRARD THIBAULT
d'Anvers

GIRARD THIBAULT, d'Anvers. 1628.

THEORIE der Fechtkunst, eine analytische Darstellung sämmt-licher Stellungen, Stösse Paraden, u. s. w.   Nach dem Traité d'escrime par Chatelain, nebst einer Anleitung über das Hieb-fechten.   4°.   1819.   *Leipzig.*

THÉORIE PRATIQUE SUR L'ART de la savate (appelée chausson ou adresse parisienne) et de la canne avec démonstration expliquée de la leçon . . . par un amateur, élève de Michel, dit Pisseux, pro-fesseur.   8°.   1851 (?).   *Paris.*

THIBAUD. — Ars digladiatoria.   Folio.   1650.   *Amsterdam.*

THIBAULT (Girard). — Académie de l'espée . . . à pied à cheval. 1626.   *Paris* (?).

—— (—) [d'Anvers]. — Académie de l'espée, où se demonstrent par reigles mathématiques, sur le fondement d'un cercle mystérieux, la théorie et pratique des vrais et iusqu'à present incognus secret du maniement des armes, à pied et à cheval.   Folio.   1628.   *Leyde.*

[*Frontispiece, portrait of Thibault, 9 plates containing the coats-of-arms of the nine kings and princes who subscribed to this work. 46 copperplates, folio size, drawn and engraved by Crispin de Pas, Gelle, Nicol Lastman, Andreas Stockins, Ad. Mœtham, T. Van Paenderen, Role Beaudouc, Isel-burg, Wilhelm Delff, P. Sherwontors, Bolsworth, Crispian Queborn, Salomon Saurius, Schelderie, Egbert a'Paondoron, Petrus de Todo, Jacobus a'Borch, Scheltus, W. Jacobi.*

Privileges of Louis XIII., dated 1620, and of the States-General of the Low Countries, dated 5th June 1627.

The name of the printers and the place of impression is only to be found in a few rare copies, bearing on the last page this notice announcing the death of the author :—

" *Un advertissement au lecteur.*

" *Le lecteur sera adverti que l'autheur, ayant eu le dessein de produire la science de l'escrime à cheval avec celle à pied, comme il eu est fait mention au frontispice de ce livre, la mort l'ayant prévenu, ne l'a pu mettre en effect; mêsme l'impression du present livre eu a esté retardé iusques à present.*

" *A Leyde, imprimé en la Typographie des Elzeviers, au mois d'Aoust l'an* CIƆIƆCXXX."

Brunet gives the place of publication as Anvers. The date in the colophon of the copy in the British Museum (64. i. 3.) is 1630. The part of the work relating to the exercise on horseback was not published.

" *Can be reckoned, without exception, the most elaborate treatise on swords-manship, and probably one of the most marvellous printed works extant, from a typographic and artistic point of view.*"—*Castle's* " *Schools and Masters of Fence.*"]

—— (—). — Académie de l'espée. . . . 2nd edition.   Folio.   1668. *Bruxelles.*

[" *Perhaps the most curious matter in connection with Spanish fence is that the fourth book published in the French language is purely Spanish in*

287

reality. But this book is indeed a monument, one of the biggest books ever printed, and beyond compare the biggest book of fence. It contains forty-six folio copperplates, engraved by the most famous engravers of the day, which absolutely exhaust the system of Spanish fight. It was issued in 1628 by the Leyden Elzeviers, and took fifteen years to complete. Nine reigning princes and an immense number of private gentlemen subscribed to meet its stupendous expenses. When it was at last completed, the author, Girard Thibault, of Antwerp, died. It may be wondered whether his sudden death was caused by his realising at last the phenomenal silliness of his work."— Castle (E.), " The Story of Swordsmanship." ("The National Review,' May 1891.)]

THIBAULT (GIRARD). — *HUTTON (A.).* — 1892.

THIERIET. — *SATURDAY* Review.

THIMM (CARL A.) [F.R.G.S., late Captain 2nd London Rifles]. —A Complete Bibliography of the Art of Fence, comprising that of the Sword and of the Bayonet, Duelling, &c., as practised by all European nations, from the earliest period to the present day. With a Classified Index. 12°. 1891. *London :* Franz Thimm & Co.
[*Dedicated by special permission to H.R.H. the Duke of Connaught, K.G.*]

—— (— —.). — Bibliographie complète de l'escrime ancienne et moderne. Comprenant la pointe, la contre-pointe, l'escrime à la baïonnette, le duel, etc., telle qu'elle a été exercée par toutes les nations de l'Europe depuis l'époque la plus reculée jusqu'à nos jours, suivi d'un index classifié. 12°. 1891. *Londres :* Franz Thimm & Co. *Paris :* Librairie Fischbacher.
[*With the exception of pages* i–xii, *this is a duplicate of the English edition.*]

—— (— —.). — Eine vollständige Bibliographie der alten und modernen Fechtkunst aller europäischen Nationen, das Duell, der Gebrauch des Säbels und des Bajonetts, etc., inbegriffen. Mit einem classificirten Inhaltsverzeichniss. 12°. 1891. *London :* Franz Thimm & Co. *Leipzig :* F. Volckmar.
[*With the exception of pages* i–xii, *this is a duplicate of the English edition.*]

—— (— —.).—A Descriptive Account of the 16th Century Sword-play, by members of the School of Arms, London Rifle Brigade, under the direction of Captain Alfred Hutton, F.S.A., member of the Sports Committee, and Ernest Stenson Cooke, Esq., London Rifle Brigade, in aid of the Funds of the Royal Cambridge Asylum for Soldiers' Widows, given in the Albany Club Grounds, Kingston-on-Thames, on Saturday, July 6, 1895. With Notes on " Ancient

Fence," by Captain A. Hutton, F.S.A., and on the "Bibliography of the Art of Fence," by Captain C. A. Thimm, F.R.G.S. 4°. 1895. *Kingston-on-Thames:* Drewett & Sons, Printers.

THIMM (CARL A.). — *COURT* Circular.

—— (— —). — *DAILY* News.

—— (— —). — *LIBRARY (The).*

—— (— —). — *LIFE.*

—— (— —). — *SATURDAY* Review.

THINNE (FRANCIS) [Lancaster]. — Matters concerning Heralds and the Triale of Armes, and of Court Military.
> [*MS. In the British Museum. Stowe,* 569.]

THIRD (THE) UNIVERSITY OF ENGLAND.
> [*A curious black-letter book describing the schools and colleges of London in 1615, and giving details of the institution of that 'Normal' School of Fence, and the ordeal that any would-be teacher had to undergo before being 'passed' and permitted to call himself a master.*]

THOMAS (BRANDON). — *MARY (Jules).*

THOMAS (COMTE DU VERGER DE SAINT-). — *SAINT-THOMAS.* —1879.

THOMAS (L'ABBÉ ALEXANDRE). — Le duel et l'Église catholique. 8°. 1869. *Versailles:* Beau.
> [*3e édition.* 12°. 1881. Paris: *Librairie de la Société Bibliographique.*]

—— (— —). — Le duel, l'Église catholique et l'armée. Deuxième édition. 8°. 1871. *Versailles:* Paul Oswald.

THOMASE (EUDALDO). — Tratado de esgrima á pié y á caballo, en que se enseña por principios el manejo del florete, ó el juego de la espada que se usa en el dia, adornado con diez y seis láminas grabadas en cobre. 4°. 1823. *Barcelona:* N. Dorca.
> [*16 plates.*]

THONNINA (F.). — Discorso in materia di duello. 8°. 1557. *Mantua.*
> (*In the Art Library, South Kensington Museum.*)

THORNBURY (W.). — *CASSELL'S* Old and New London.

THORPE (T. B.). — *HARPER'S* Magazine.

THOU (J. A. DE). — Histoire universelle de 1543–1607. 16 vols. 4°. 1734. *Londres* (*Paris*).
> [Vol. IX. pp. 592–593. Vol. XV. p. 57. "*Duelling*."]

THOUGHTS ON DUELLING. 8°. 1773. *Cambridge.*
> (*In the Library of the London Institution. Reed Tracts.* Vol. 49 (Vol. 442), Art. 8.)

THOUGHTS ON DUELLING and the Christian Character. 8°. 1839. *London :* Longman.

THOUGHTS ON DUELLING and its Abolition. 8°. 1844. *London.*

THÜMMEL (C.). — Der gerichtliche Zweikampf und das heutige Duell. 8°. 1887. *Hamburg :* J. F. Richter.
> [32 *pages. No.* 4. *Deutsche Zeit und Streit-Fragen. Flugschriften zur Kenntnisz der Gegenwart. In Verbindung mit Prof. Dr. Kluckholm, Red. A. Lammers, Proff. DD. J. B. Meyer und Paul Schmidt hrsg. von Frz. von Holtzondorff. Neue Folge.* 2. *Jahrg.* 4.–10. *Heft.*]

THUREAU (PAUL) et **DESJARDINS** (ALBERT). — Projet de loi sur le duel.
> [*Conférence Molé fondée le* 19 *mars* 1832. *Trente-et-unième année. Projets de Louis et Rapports,* 1862. 8°. 1862. Paris : *Imprimerie de Léautey.*]

THURMAN. — Duellica.
> [*Mentioned in Max Perl's Catalogue.* Berlin. 1895.]

TICKNOR (GEORGE). — History of Spanish Literature. 3 vols. 8°. 1888. *Boston :* Houghton, Mifflin & Co.
> [*Duelos de amor y lealtad of Calderon.* Vol. II. p. 399.
> *Duels.* Vol. II. pp. 403–404 *and note.*
>   ,,   (*Last*), *by authority, in Spain.* Vol. II. p. 401 *and note.*]

TIDSKRIFT I GYMNASTIK, af T. J. Hartelius (o. L. M. Thörngren). 8°. 1876–85. *Stockholm :* C. E. Fritze.

TIETZ (FR.). — Ein Duell unter Cardinal Richelieu. Schauspiel in 3 Aufzügen. Frei nach dem Französischen. 4°. *Berlin :* Hayn.
> [14 *pages.*
> *Bühnen—Repertoir des Auslandes. In Uebertragungen herausgegeben von W. Both (Ludw. Schneider).* XIX. Bd., No. 148.]

TIMBS (J.). — Romance of London. 3 vols. Post 8°. 1865. *London :* Bentley.
> [Vol. I. p. 200. *Duelling.*]

TIMES (The).—(Newspaper.) Folio. 1831–95. *London*: Printing House Square, E.C.

[1831.	*April* 11.		*Duel between Mr. Tennyson and Major Johnson at Islington.*
,,	*July* 9.	,,	,,	*Mr. Trant and Mr. O'Connell.*
,,	*Aug.* 8.	,,	,,	*John Benison and Thos. Berry in Leitrim.*
,,	,, 10.	,,	,,	*Hon. James Wayne and Dr. Daniel, with broadswords, in New York.*
,,	,, 15, 18, 27.		*Duel between Mr. Bond and Mr. Ease; fatal to the former.*
,,	,, 16.		*Duel between an Officer of the Garrison at Gibraltar and a Ship's Officer.*
,,	,, 24.	,,	,,	*the Minister of Foreign Affairs in France and General Lamarque.*
,,	*Oct.* 25.	,,	,,	*the Hon. F. Greville and Mr. Jones at Tavern Spite.*
,,	*Nov.* 24.	,,	,,	*Mr. Beattey and Mr. M'Donagh in Phœnix Park, Dublin.*
,,	*Dec.* 16.	,,	,,	*Captain Nolan and George Browne at Phippsborough.*
,,	,, 16.	,,	,,	*M. Manguin and M. Viennett.*
,,	,, 16.	,,	,,	*two gentlemen from Edinburgh, in Linlithgow.*
,,	,, 31.	,,	,,	*Lieutenant-Colonel Sir R. Gill and D. Finlaison at Wandsworth Common.*
1832.	*Jan.* 16.	,,	,,	*two gentlemen near Castleknock.*
,,	*Feb.* 15, 16, 17, 18, 20, 21, 22, 25. *March* 12. *Duel between General Moore and Mr. Stapylton on Wimbledon Common; latter wounded.*
,,	,, 25.		*Duel between M. Ferrier and M. Abret; former killed.*
,,	*Mar.* 1.		*Release of General Moore on bail.*
,,	*May* 11.		*Duel between Lord Elibank and Captain Ainslie at Wormwood Scrubbs.*
,,	*June* 1.	,,	,,	*Mr. Reynolds and Mr. O'Farrell at Phœnix Park, prevented by the police.*
,,	,, 5.⎫ 6.⎭	,,	,,	*Captain Markham and Colonel M'Donald in Dublin; fatal to Captain Markham.*
,,	*Aug.* 6.	,,	,,	*M. Caste and M. Benoit in Paris.*
,,	,, 14.	,,	,,	*M. Meiffred and M. Carbonnel at Aix.*
,,	*Sept.* 15.	,,	*at Liverpool, in Mount Vernon Road, Edgehill.*
,,	*Oct.* 2.	,,	*between Russell Bowlby and Mr. Braddyll at Offerton.*
,,	,, 2.	,,	,,	*two Officers in Regent's Park.*
,,	,, 2.	,,	,,	*Sir H. Williamson and Mr. Braddyll.*
,,	,, 10.	,,	,,	*Mr. Steavenson and Mr. Surtees at Newcastle.*
,,	,, 22.	,,	,,	*Mr. Wynne and Mr. Scott.*
,,	,, 22.	,,	,,	*,, ,, ,, Mr. John Martin.*
,,	,, 24.	,,	,,	*Mr. Caruthers, of Mile End, and Mr. Hammock, in the Hackney Fields. Denied.*
,,	*Nov.* 17.	,,	,,	*Mr. Maltby and Captain Jackson at Bromley.*
,,	*Dec.* 6.	,,	,,	*Maurice O'Connell and Mr. Blennerhasset.*
,,	,, 14.	,,	,,	*Lieutenant Wm. O'Connell and Mr. Cornly in Greenwich Park.*
,,	,, 15.	,,	,,	*Captain Arcus and Mr. M'Donald in the North Road.*

TIMES (The) *(continued)*—

1832.	*Dec.* 19.			Duel between Mr. Ralph Jameson and Mr. Rierdon.
1833.	*May* 7, 9, 11.			Duel between John Power White and Mr. Weldon; fatal to the former.
,,	,, 11.			Duel at Meadlands about a young lady.
,,	,, 14, 15, 21.			Duel between Dr. Hennis and Sir John Jeffcott near Exeter.
,,	,, 17.			Duel between G. F. Johnstone and Mr. Clark; fatal to the former.
,,	*June* 7.	,,	,,	two gentlemen at Bolton, without powder.
,,'	,, 18.	,,	,,	the Marquis of Dalmatia and Colonel de Bricqueville.
,,	*July* 15.	,,	,,	Mr. Gallagher and Mr. Irison near Halifax.
,,	*Sept.* 21.	,,	,,	Mr. Rodda and Mr. Blavier in France.
,,	*Oct.* 7.	,,	,,	Mr. Phillips and Mr. Hawkins at Singapore.
,,	,, 24.			Order issued by the King of Bavaria against Duelling.
,,	,, 31.			Duel between Captain Racken and Captain Lalande.
1834.	*Jan.* 2.	,,	,,	Baron Biel and Mr. von Wachanhausen in Hanover.
,,	*Feb.* 3.	,,	,,	General Bugland and M. Dulong; fatal to the latter.
,,	*Mar.* 29.	,,	,,	M. Billiard and M. Schlesinger.
,,	*July* 1.	,,	,,	Mr. Robertson and Mr. Glashin's Second.
,,	*Sept.* 9.	,,	,,	a Preacher and a Lawyer at Teignmouth.
,,	,, 13.	,,	,,	two Midshipmen on board the "Atlante."
,,	,, 15.	,,	,,	two persons at Paris; both killed.
,,	,, 18.	,,	,,	Captain Ashe and Sir Charles Hampton near Kingstown.
,,	,, 18.	,,	,,	Prince Puckler Muskau and a German gentleman.
,,	*Oct.* 9.	,,	without Witnesses: a romantic affair.
,,	,, 23.	,,	between Alexandre Dumas and M. Gaillardet.
,,	*Nov.* 1.	,,	,,	Cornet H. and Mr. H. at Curracloc.
,,	,, 6.	,,	,,	Mr. Blackney and Horace Rochefort; refused by Mr. Blackney.
,,·	,, 21.	,,	,,	two Officers, with sabres, at Frankfort, in which one lost part of his nose.
,,	,, 25.	,,	,,	M. Thiers and M. Paira; refused by the former.
,,	*Dec.* 8.	,,	,,	Captain Morrison and Mr. Boyce.
,,	,, 16.	,,	,,	Mr. Hamilton and Mr. Wallesley in Belgium; to be a mortal combat.
,,	,, 17.	,,	,,	a Judge and an Advocate at Metz.
,,	,, 17.	,,	,,	two young gentlemen at Boulogne-sur-Mer.
,,	,, 24.	,,	,,	Lieutenant Whitting and Mr. Scobell.
1835.	*Jan.* 12.	,,	,,	Major von Brandenstein and the Prince of Attingen-Wallenstein.
,,	,, 16.	,,	,,	Mr. Edward Ruthven and Mr. Perrin the Lord Mayor.
,,	,, 23.	,,	,,	Mr. G., of Wimbledon Common, and a Military Officer.
,,	*Feb.* 5.	,,	,,	two Officers at Libourne, near Bordeaux; one killed.

TIMES (The) (*continued*)—

1835.	Feb.	7.	Duel, Singular, to put the rival into a bag.
,,	,,	19.	,, between Count de Langle and the Duke de Rovigo, with swords, at Meudon.
,,	Mar.	3.	,, ,, a Son of Neptune and a Knight of the Lancet, near Stevenage.
,,	,,	26.	,, ,, Hon. Colonel O. and Prince de L.
,,	April	2.	,, ,, Captain Beauty and Lieutenant Dickson at Kurnaul ; former killed.
,,	,,	6.	,, ,, Mr. Maccabe and Mr. Pomroi at Dolly-mount.
,,	,,	8.	,, ,, Alfred, a coloured man, and another servant.
,,	,,	10.	,, ,, Captain Count de Langle and the Duke de Rovigo, with swords.
,,	,,	13.	,, ,, Captain A. and a Liverpool Merchant at Old Oak Common.
,,	May	6.	,, ,, Lord Alvanley and Mr. Morgan O'Connell.
,,	,,	7.	,, Note on.
,,	,,	15, 18.	Mr. St. John and Count Caraffiano ; latter killed.
,,	June	9.	Duel between Sir Colquhoun Grant and Lord Seymour.
,,	,,	29.	,, ,, Mr. Murphy and Mr. Haire at Dublin.
,,	July	6.	,, ,, a young man and the brother of his intended, and killed.
,,	,,	6.	Second duel with the other brother, who also was killed.
,,	,,	16.	Duel between M. Crepu and M. Cerferr, Editors of Newspapers.
,,	,,	27.	,, ,, the Mayor of Castillon and a Physician.
,,	Oct.	7.	,, ,, Dr. Downing and Captain Burslem near Mitchelstown.
,,	,,	9.	,, ,, Dr. Malcolmson and Captain Urquhart at Poonah.
,,	,,	23.	,, Indian's Reply to a Challenge.
,,	,,	28.	,, between two Officers at Blackrock.
,,	,,	29.	,, Extraordinary, in the United States. The Challenged shoots his four Opponents.
,,	Nov.	17.	,, between Mr. Dickenson and Mr. Symons at Boulogne.
,,	,,	18.	,, ,, Mr. Powell and Mr. Downes at Ludlow.
,,	,,	21.	,, ,, Mr. Black and Mr. Roeback at Christ Church.
,,	,,	24.	Note against the Practice of Duelling.
,,	Dec.	18.	,, ,, Mr. Montague and Mr. Rooke at Calais ; latter killed.
,,	,,	28.	,, ,, two Polish Refugees at Brussels.
1836.	Jan.	15.	,, ,, Captain Everett White and Colonel Bellamy ; fatal to both.
,,	April	4.	,, ,, Marshal Moncey and Marshal Maison ; arranged.
,,	,,	4.	,, ,, Ensign Davies and Lieutenant Joy at Bangalore.
,,	,,	18.	,, ,, Lord George Bentinck and Mr. Osbaldeston.
,,	,,	22.	,, ,, two Soldiers, with swords and pistols.
,,	May	7, 9, 10.	Duel between Colonel Kerby and Captain Dickson at Chalk Farm.

TIMES (The) (*continued*)—

1836.	*June*	6.	Duel between *Mr. Daintree and Mr. Lindsell.*
,,	,,	21.	,, ,, *two Civil Servants in Brussels ; one killed and the other injured.*
,,	,,	21.	,, ,, *two gentlemen, in Jamaica.*
,,	*July*	4.	*Law respecting Duelling.*
,,	,,	7.	*Duel between Count Alfred de Thevenot and Mr. Henry Tyrwhitt.*
,,	,,	22.	,, ,, *a Pole and an Editor.*
,,	,,	23.	,, ,, *Mr. Key and Mr. Shearman.*
,,	,,	25.	,, ,, *M. Armand Carrel and M. Emile de Girardin.*
,,	,,	27, 28.	*Death of Carrel.*
,,	*Aug.*	1.	*Duel between Captain Lockhart and Mr. Kenrick.*
,,	,,	17.	,, ,, *John Magee and Andrew Morrow.*
,,	*Sept.*	29.	,, ,, *Colonel Quvell and Mr. Cunningham.*
,,	*Oct.*	11.	,, *at Red Post, near Newton.*
,,	,,	17.	,, *at South Moulton—Ludicrous.*
,,	,,	17.	,, *between Alexander Orme and T. J. Slack—Application to Prevent.*
,,	,,	20.	,, ,, *Lieutenant Clay and Lieutenant Davies.*
,,	,,	21.	,, *at Quincompoix.*
,,	,,	22.	,, *between M. Robert Cœur-de-Vey and M. Brock.*
,,	,,	22.	,, ,, *M. Goux and M. de Rosamel.*
1837.	*Jan.*	19.	,, ,, *Mr. Costello and Mr. Baker at Holyhead.*
,,	,,	20.	,, ,, *Major Andrews and Lieutenant Barker.*
,,	,,	26.	,, ,, *Commandant Parquin and Colonel Talandies at Strasburg.*
,,	*Feb.*	7.	,, *with small swords, in Paris.*
,,	*Mar.*	27.	*Duel between Mr. Herbert and another gentleman.*
,,	*April*	8.	,, ,, *Mr. Raystock and Mr. Wood.*
,,	*May*	2.	,, ,, *Lieutenant Elmslie and Lieutenant Wright.*
,, .	,,	12, 13.	*Duel at Hampstead Heath.*
,,	,,	13, 15.	*Note on Duelling.*
,,	*July*	8.	*Duel between Wyatt and Jameson ; former wounded.*
,,	,,	27.	,, ,, *two coloured boys.*
,,	,,	29.	,, ,, *Mr. Chalmer and Captain Berkeley.*
,,	*Aug.*	2.	,, ,, *two women.*
,,	,,	28.	,, ,, *Griffith and Kelly.*
,,	*Oct.*	10.	,, ,, *two Poles at Rochelle.*
,,	,,	26.	,, ,, *James Bradford and John M'Dermott.*
1838.	*Jan.*	27.	,, ,, *Dillon Browne and James Arthur Browne.*
,,	*Mar.*	6.	,, ,, *Captain Keating and Captain Hughes ; latter killed.*
,,	,,	20.	,, ,, *Mr. de Salis and Captain Duvernet.*
,,	,,	27.	,, ,, *Mr. Cilley and Mr. Graves.*
,,	*May*	4.	,, ,, *Mr. Pigott and Mr. Carroll at Newtown Park.*
,,	,,	10.	,, ,, *Mr. Rushout and Mr. Borthwick on Wormwood Scrubbs.*
,,	,,	10.	*Cooler for Duelling. Sentence on Mr. Cooke.*
,,	,,	24.	*Duel between Mr. Cilley and Mr. Graves.*

TIMES (The) (*continued*)—

1838.	*June*	23.	*Duel between Major Warde and Mr. Sweeney at Montreal ; fatal to the former.*	
,,	*July*	7.	,, ,,	*J. Starke and Lieutenant Roberts.*
,,	,,	14.	., ,,	*Mr. Sweeny and Lieutenant-Colonel Warde ; latter killed.*
,,	,,	18.	,, ,,	*Count de Mulinen and Baron de Hugel.*
,,	,,	25.	,, ,,	*Lieutenant Tarpin and Lieutenant Bailey.*
,,	*Aug.*	24.	,, ,,	*C. K. Ponsonby and Sidney Hardinge.*
,,	,,	25, 27.	*Duel between Mr. Eliott and Mr. C. F. Mirfin ; latter killed.*	
,,	,,	27.	*Sept.* 1, 3, 4, 10, 13, 29. *Duel Notices.*	
,,	*Sept.*	12.	*Neapolitan Decree against Duelling.*	
,,	*Oct.*	9.	*Duel between the Marquis of Waterford and Lord George Loftus.*	
,,	,,	30.	,, *with swords, in Philadelphia.*	
1839.	*Mar.*	19.	,, *at Stafford ; prevented by arrest.*	
,,	*April*	2.	,, *between Colonel Galleis and R. D. Browne.*	
,,	,,	6.	,, ,,	*Richards and Mannicks.*
,,	,,	9.	,, ,,	*Jackson and O'Connell ; prevented.*
,,	,,	12.	,, ,,	*Colonel Prince and Mr. Baby ; latter killed.*
,,	*May*	22.	*Duelling. Archdn. and Clergy of Bath on.*	
,,	*June*	5.	*Duel between Jones and Wilson ; latter killed.*	
,,	,,	15.	,, ,,	*Lord Londonderry and Mr. Grattan.*
,,	*July*	13.	,, ,,	*Lieutenant Sullivan and Mr. Norman.*
.,	*Oct.*	21.	,, ,,	*a Seducer and the son of the Seduced, in which both are killed.*
,,	*Nov.*	8.	*Sword of Bruce.*	
,,	*Dec.*	11, 14.	*Duel between Lord Loftus and Lord Harley at Boulogne.*	
,,	,,	24.	*Duel between Lord William Paget and Thomas Fieke at Wimbledon.*	
,,	,,	25.	,, ,,	*Mr. Darlton and Captain Bargewell on Hampstead Heath.*
1840.	*Jan.*	20.	,, ,,	*Mr. Mayo and Mr. Wakey ; declined by latter.*
,,	*Feb.*	13.	,, *near the Racecourse at Cheltenham.*	
,,	,,	19.	,, *between Prince Lichnowski and the Count de Bros Waldeck.*	
,,	,,	20.	,, ,,	*two gentlemen in May's Ground, Belfast.*
,,	*Mar.*	6.	,, ,,	*Prince Louis Napoleon and Count Leon.*
,,	,,	11.	,, ,,	*Ditto. Account of the proceedings.*
,,	,,	13.	,, ,,	*Mr. Henry Williams and Captain Ashton ; prevented by the police.*
,,	,,	18.	,, ,,	*Lord William Paget and Mr. Bell.*
,,	,,	20.	,, *at Pyrmont ; a singular position of all parties, each in different countries.*	
,,	,,	22.	,, *between the Hon. Captain Pelham and Lieutenant-Colonel Browne at Gibraltar.*	
.,	*April*	4.	,, ,,	*two Magistrates at Cashel.*
,,	,,	8.	,, ,,	*Captain Fleetwood and Mr. Brocksopp at Wimbledon.*

TIMES (The) (*continued*)—

1840.	April	11.	Duel between M. Desrenaudes and M. Audrey in the Forest of Vezinet.
,,	,,	11.	,, ,, Marquis de Rovigo and Alderic de St. Pierre in the Forest of St. Germain.
,,	,,	22.	,, ,, Prince Wallenstein and Mr. D'Abel.
..	July	1.	,, ,, two Passengers in a Stage-coach near Pero; both killed.
.,	,,	7.	,, ,, Mr. Garbornia and Mr. Kechoff; fatal to the former.
,,	,,	14.	,, ,, two gentlemen of England in the Forest of Fontainebleau.
,,	Aug.	26.	,, ,, M. Throult and Paulin Prae in Louisiana.
,,	Sept.	16, 17, 22.	Duel between the Earl of Cardigan and Lieutenant Tuckett.
,,	Oct.	10.	Duel between Lieutenant Tuckett and Earl of Cardigan; recovery of the former.
,,	,,	15.	Trial of Captain Tuckett.
.,	,,	21.	Duel between Lieutenant Herbert and Mr. J. P. de St. Croix at Guernsey.
,,	Nov.	13.	,, ,, M. Alluaued and M. Gazard at Limoges.
,,	,,	28.	,, fought at Dublin.
,.	Dec.	5.	Duelling in America. Wigfall v. Bird; latter killed.
,,	,,	16.	Duel between Mr. Browne and Colonel Fitzgerald.
,,	,,	18.	,, ,, a Hanoverian and a Bavarian Officer.
.,	,,	28.	Duelling—Belgian Law of.
1841.	Jan.	19.	,, ,, Ensign Bruce and Mr. Boyd, jun.; stayed by the magistrate.
,,	,,	25.	,, ,, Mr. L. and Dr. H. at Penicuik.
,,	Feb.	20.	,, ,, Mark Marsden and Colonel Patterson in Regent's Park.
,,	,,	24.	Proposal to establish a Society to suppress Duelling.
,,	Mar.	15.	Duel between Captain Browning and Mr. Willis; prevented by the seconds.
,,	,,	24.	,, ,, Samuel Hutchins and Mr. John Lalor in Boulogne.
,,	,,	24.	,, at Chalk Farm between two Foreigners.
,,	,,	31.	,, between Macklin, son of the Actor, and an Officer; an odd one.
,,	,,	31.	Duels in Mexico—the survivor has to pay all the victim's debts.
,,	April	7.	Duel between Judge Smith and Mr. M'Clernand.
,,	,,	16.	,, ,, Ditto. A fiction.
,,	,,	20.	,, ,, two Officers of the Cossacks at Warsaw.
,,	May	11.	,, ,, M. de Romans and a Captain of Cavalry at Saumur; desperate.
,,	June	3, 8, 10.	Duel between M. Lynch and Kelly in Galway.
,,	,,	25.	Duel between Mr. Gilbert Ainslie Young and Mr. Parks.
.,	July	5.	,, ,, Mr. Disraeli and a Radical Barrister; prevented by the Mayor.
,,	,,	26.	,, ,, Captain Fitzgerald and Mr. M. Sweeney; prevented by the police.

TIMES (The) (*continued*)—

1841.	*Aug.*	7.	*Duel between Henry Launcelot and Captain Bellgrave at Wormwood Scrubbs.*
,,	,,	9.	,, ,,	*Malachi Kelly and Mr. Lynch in Galway.*
,,	*Sept.*	8.	,, ,,	*Captain FitzRoy and Mr. Sheppard—Correspondence about.*
,,	,,	13.	,, ,,	*Lord Sussex Lennox and Captain Narcote at Malta.*
,,	,,	16, 23.	*Duel between M. Plowden, the banker, and Dr. Crook (fatal), at Leghorn.*
,,	*Oct.*	6.	*Duel between a Doctor and a Rustic, with lancets, at Middleton, by Wirksworth.*
,,	,,	19.	,, ,,	*Margo, at Cairo, with a renegade Frenchman.*
,,	,,	30.	,, ,,	*Alderman Newfort and Mr. Jason Hansard at Waterford; prevented by both parties being bound over to keep the peace.*
,,	*Nov.*	24.	,, ,,	*General Bonnet and another Officer; the former killed.*
,,	*Dec.*	17.	*Affair of Honour at Lismore.*
,,	,,	17.	*Duel between two gentlemen of St. John's College, with wood and red ink.*
,,	,,	31.	,, ,,	*Judge Tenney and Mr. N. C. Rowley, to decide on the decision of the Judge on Sir Rowley's Case.*
1842.	*Jan.*	28.	,, ,,	*General Levasseur and Commandant Arrighi at Marseilles.*
,,	,,	29.	,, ,,	*Prince Lichnowsky and Count Montenegro at Vienna.*
,,	*Mar.*	1.	,, ,,	*Captain Levick and Lieutenant Adams at Malta; fatal to the latter.*
,,	,,	7.	,,	*Note on.*
,,	,,	21, 26.	*Duel between M. Lacrosse and M. Garnier de Cassagnac.*
,,	,,	22.	*Duel between two young men, with one pistol, for which they drew lots, in Paris.*
,,	,,	30.	,,	*Trial of the survivor.*
,,	*April*	4, 5.	,,	*between Captain Macleod and Mr. Bennett; prevented by the magistrates.*
,,	*May*	6, 26.	,, ,,	*Lieutenant Johnson and the Duc de Calabritti at Palermo; fatal.*
,,	,,	17.	,, ,,	*two Sunderland Magistrates—Mr. Spoor and Mr. Wright.*
,,	,,	30.	*Duellist.*	*A lady on the Duel between Captain Best and Lord Camelford.*
,,	*July*	4.	*Duel between Owen Lynch and Malachy Kelly.*
,,	,,	16.	,, ,,	*Hon. Craven Berkeley and Captain Boldero.*
,,	,,	16.	,, ,,	*Ditto. Correspondence about the cause.*
,,	,,	16, 23.	*Duel between Sir George Hill and Mr. Boyd; arranged amicably.*
,,	,,	21.	*Duel between two French Officers in the Bois de Boulogne; fatal.*

TIMES (The) (*continued*)—

TIMES (The) (*continued*)—

1843.	Aug.	15.	*Duel defeated at Montrouge.*
,,	,,	25.	*Duelling. New regulations in the Prussian Service.*
,,	Sept.	1.	,, *The survivor to support the family of his victim.*
,,	,,	8.	*Duel in France, with billiard balls.*
,,	,,	14.	,, *between Prince Napoleon Bonaparte and Count de Laroche-Pouchin in Germany.*
,,	,,	15.	,, *Regulations concerning, in Prussia.*
,,	,,	15.	,, *between Mr. Heaston and the Hon. Alcee Labrouche at New Orleans; former killed.*
,,	,,	18.	,, *at Brighton between two Assistants of a Draper's Shop.*
,,	Oct.	2.	,, *between Lord Nugent and Mr. Dayroll; message withdrawn.*
,,	Nov.	5, 10, 21. *Dec.* 16, 19, 20. *Duel. Decent measure and Colonel Faucate—Notices about.*	
,,	,,	13.	*Duel between two Tailors in Paris.*
,,	,,	22.	,, ,, *a Captain and a Civilian at Haverford-west.*
,,	Dec.	21, 22. *Duel between Von Hater and Von Sarachaga.*	
1844.	Jan.	6.	*Duel between Mr. D. and Mr. P.*
,,	Feb.	15.	,, *at Brecknock Arms. Trial of Lieutenant Grant.*
,,	Mar.	2.	,, *between General Debuys and Mr. Richardson at New Orleans.*
,,	,,	9, 23. *Duel—Notes on.*	
,,	,,	12.	*Duel. Lieutenant Munro's Defence.*
,,	,,	13.	*Duel of Colonel Fawcett and Lieutenant Munro—Note about.*
,,	,,	15, 21. *Duel in America, at Washington; Mr. Cochran shot.*	
,,	,,	18.	*Duel of M. Haber. Sentenced to six months in a fortress.*
,,	,,	18.	*Duels—Number and Results of over 200, from George III. to the Queen.*
,,	April	15.	*Duel between Lieutenant-Colonel Fawcett and Lieutenant Munro. Mrs. Fawcett's account of the meeting and challenge.*
,,	,,	17.	*Duelling in the Navy — Admiralty Instructions forbidding.*
,,	,,	22.	*Duel between Count Schœnborn Wiesenfeldt and Baron Arnstein at Presburg.*
,,	,,	25.	*Duelling in the Army—Amended Articles of War relating to.*
,,	June	10.	*Duels in America.*
,,	Sept.	10.	*Duel—Almost one, in New York.*
,,	Oct.	26.	,, *between M. Theilfelat and the Baron de Leithardt at Königsberg.*
,,	Nov.	4.	,, ,, *Count Batthyani and Count Zichy.*
,,	,,	7.	,, ,, *two Pupils of the Polytechnic School; one killed.*
1845.	Jan.	21.	,, ,, *M. Rupperberg and M. de Landette at Mentz; proving fatal to latter.*
,,	,,	22.	,, *Triangular, at Nice.*

TIMES (The) (*continued*)—

1845.	Jan.	31.	Duelling—The Etiquette of.
,,	Mar.	15, 18.	Duel between M. Dujarrier and M. Beauvallon.
,,	,,	24, 25.	,, ,, Lord Tullamore and Mr. Ball; prevented by the police.
,,	,,	31.	Duel between Major Partlow and Mr. Burton at Augusta.
,,	April	12.	,, ,, the Duke of Rovigo and M. Perregault, with swords.
,,	May	8, 22, 24, 26, 28, 31. June 2, 4, 10, 16, 21, 24. July 4. Duel between Mr. Seton and Lieutenant Hawkey at Gosport.	
,,	,,	13.	Duel between a Portuguese and an Attaché of the French Embassy at Munich.
.,	June	11.	,, in Galway; prevented by the arrest of the party demanding a duel.
,,	,,	17.	,, between M. Grivas and General Strato.
,,	,,	27, 28.	Duel between General Grivas and M. Callergi; prevented by former's terms.
,,	Aug.	26.	Duel between an Englishman and a Frenchman in a dark room.
,,	Sept.	24.	,, ,, Lieutenant Tulloch and Mr. Nilson at Fultah.
,,	Oct.	15.	,, at Wetzler; Lieutenant von Negri killed.
,,	,,	23.	,, of two gentlemen of Boston; strange race in accepting.
,,	Nov.	4.	Duels. The King of Prussia's Order on the Treatment of Principals and Seconds.
,,	.,	16, 18.	Duel at Elstree, near Edgware; and Colonel Metcalfe killed.
,,	,,	24.	Duel at Gray between two French Soldiers.
1846.	Feb.	28.	,, between Mr. Hawkey and Mr. Seton at Gosport.
,,	April	6.	,, in America.
,,	,,	25.	,, Fatal, at Gosport.
,,	July	9.	Duelling in Germany.
,,	,,	10.	Duel at Stokes Bay. Trial of Captain Hawkey for being the Principal.
,,	,,	15.	,, Fatal, between two Soldiers at Bayonne.
,,	,,	22.	,, at Palmyra; both parties killed.
,,	Sept.	9.	,, between Prince of Tour and Captain Schneat; the Prince killed.
,,	,,	9.	Duelling at Baden. Buying an Adversary's Shot.
1847.	May	7.	Duel between M. de Pommereux and the Duke of Vicenza.
,,	July	13.	Aug. 21. Duel at Brecknock Arms. Munro gives himself up as Principal.
,,	Aug.	19.	Ditto. Trial of Munro.
,,	,,	23.	Ditto—Note on.
,,	,,	24, 31.	Sept. 7, 21. Ditto. Situation of Lieutenant Munro.
,,	,,	31.	Sept. 18. Duel, Fatal, at Metz.
,,	Oct.	8.	Duel, Fatal, in Mexico, between Lieutenant Munford and Lieutenant Mahan.
1848.	Jan.	20.	,, between two boys at Cheltenham.
,.	Nov.	24.	,, ,, Colonel Rey and Edmond Adam.
,,	,,	24, 25.	Duel between General Baraguay d'Hilliers and M. Goodchaux.

TIMES (The) (*continued*)—

TIMES (The) (*continued*)—

1852. *June* 7. Duel between Mr. Stevenson and Mr. Carrick at George-
 town.
,, *Oct.* 21, 27, 29. Duel at Englefield Green between two Foreigners.
,, ,, 25. Duel. Funeral of the deceased M. Cournet in Egham
 Churchyard.
,, ,, 25, 27. Duel—Notes on.
,, *Nov.* 6. Duel—French Translation of the English Account of.
,, *Dec.* 15. ,, between M. Kalargi and Count Medem near Pisa;
 fatal.
1853. *Jan.* 13, 14. Duel between Count Niewerkerque and Colonel Edgar
 Ney.
,, ,, 25. *Feb.* 1. Duel between M. Ropolo, a Piedmontese Officer,
 and Captain Gueritz, an Austrian Officer.
,, *Mar.* 24. Duel at Egham.
,, *May* 3. ,, between the Marquis of Suero and M. Salamanca.
,, *Nov.* 29. ,, ,, two boys in Paris.
,, *Dec.* 24, 27. Duel between M. de Targit and Mr. Soule in Madrid.
,, ,, 26, 27. ,, ,, the Duke of Alba and Mr. Soule in
 Madrid.
,, ,, 31. The "Debats" on the Duel.
1854. *Jan.* 17. Duel between M. Mouginot and Marceau.
,, *April* 19, 26. Duel between Mr. Breckinridge and Mr. Cutting, two
 Members of the United States Congress.
,, *July* 4. Duel between General Saunders and Judge Evans near
 the Alabama State Line.
,, ,, 4. ,, ,, Mr. Schlessinger and Mr. Ladd at New
 Orleans.
,, ,, 20. ,, ,, Mr. C. Stewart and Mr. J. B. Coker.
,, ,, 25. ,, ,, two Chinamen in California.
,, *Aug.* 29. Duel. Sensible one in America, by squirts instead of
 pistols.
,, *Sept.* 12. Sword v. Sickle.
,, ,, 15. Duel. Relic of one between the Duke of Beaufort and De
 Nemours in 1652.
,, *Dec.* 27. Duel between Achilles Kewen and Colonel Woodlief in
 California.
1855. *June* 30. ,, in Nottingham Park.
,, *July* 31. ,, between Count L. and Lieutenant Bomberger.
,, *Sept.* 12. ,, Mock, of Canterbury Barracks—Note on.
,, *Oct.* 3. ,, between two Editors in Mississippi.
1856. *Jan.* 30. ,, on the Ile du Roi.
,, *Feb.* 5. ,, between Captain Vigavano and a nephew of Baron C.
,, *Mar.* 11, 13, 14, 15, 20, 22. Duel between the President of Police,
 Herr von Hinckelday, and Herr von Roch.
,, *June* 11, 12. Duel between the English Vice-Consul and an Officer
 of the Staff at Valencia.
,, ,, 25. Duel between two Editors at Bayou Sara; Robertson killed.
,, *Aug.* 22. ,, ,, ,, Editors at Washington.
,, *Oct.* 7. ,, ,, M. Meissl, an Austrian Officer, and a
 Prussian Officer.
,, ,, 14. ,, at Charleston; death of Mr. Taber, the Editor
 of the "Mercury."

TIMES (The) (*continued*)—

| 1856. | Oct. | 20. | *Duelling on a large scale—100 on each side—to settle the question of Slavery, in Kansas.* |

1856.   Oct.   20.   *Duelling on a large scale—100 on each side—to settle the question of Slavery, in Kansas.*

,,   Nov.   10.   *Duel, Singular, at Memphis; ladies present.*

,,   Dec.   19.   ,, *between Austrian Officers at Vienna.*

1857.   Feb.   27.   ,,   ,,   *Judge Elmore and Mr. Kagia at Tecumseh.*

,,   Mar.   14.   ,,   ,,   *M. Hazenbrick and M. Kimborough; the former killed.*

,,   ,,   17.   ,,   ,,   *Colonel Asstalos and a Wine Merchant at Bordeaux.*

,,   ,,   21.   ,,   *Extraordinary and Fatal, at Winston, North America, both parties being fastened to a 2-inch oak plank, and the fight being with bowie-knives.*

,,   April 23.   ,,   *between a Native and an Austrian Officer at Milan.*

,,   Aug.   10.   ,,   ,,   *J. T. Walker and W. W. King at Howth; prevented by the police arresting the principals and their seconds.*

,,   ,,   19.   ,,   *Fatal, of two Pupils of St. Cyr School.*

,,   ,,   19.   *Duelling in France among the Pupils of St. Cyr School; eighty since January.*

,,   Nov.   4.   *Duel between Mr. Blair and Colonel Casey in California.*

,,   Dec.   24.   *Duello in Spain.*

,,   ,,   28.   *Duel between Count Cattanee and Captain Froidefont at Vincennes.*

,,   ,,   30.   *Duelling in Alabama. Oath administered to Governor Moore on his accepting office.*

1858.   May   19, 21, 22, 24, 27.   *Duel between M. de Pene and one by one a whole posse of forty noble Officers.*

,,   ,,   22, 25, 28, 29, 31. June 17.   *Ditto. The Investigator's Report.*

,,   Aug.   13.   *Duelling. Another "Anticipation" from "Pickwick."*

,,   Oct.   1.   *Duel between Mr. Wise, Editor of the "Enquirer," and Mr. Clemmens, near Richmond, North America.*

,,   ,,   14.   ,,   ,,   *Mr. Johnston, Editor of the "National," and Senator Ferguson, in California, on Angel Island.*

,,   Dec.   2.   *Duelling in Paris.*

1859.   Jan.   1.   *Duel in Belgium between two Officers of the 1st Regiment of the Line; fatal to one.*

,,   ,,   4.   ,,   *at Nice between a Frenchman and a Count.*

,,   Feb.   9.   ,,   *between Negroes in Virginia.*

,,   July   28.   ,,   ,,   *Mr. Wise and Mr. Aylett in North Carolina.*

,,   Aug.   25.   ,,   *Exciting, in Arizona.*

,,   Oct.   20, 25, 27.   *Duel between Senator Broderick and Judge Ferry at San Francisco.*

,,   Dec.   24.   *Duel between the Marquis de Galiffet and Count de Lauriston at Paris.*

1860.   Jan.   26.   ,,   ,,   *M. About and M. Vaudin in Paris.*

,,   May   3.   ,,   ,,   *Baron Meyendorff and M. Demidoff in St. Petersburg.*

,,   June   28.   ,,   ,,   *Ditto—Note on.*

TIMES (The) (*continued*)—

1860.	*Oct.*	5.	*Duel between a gentleman and a lady near Prussia.*
1861.	*Feb.*	12.	„ „ *Dr. Jones and Lieutenant Wilson at Delaware.*
„	*June*	3.	„ „ *General Manteuffel and Mr. Tiverton at Potsdam.*
„	*Oct.*	12.	*Duelling in Prussia.*
„	*Nov.*	7.	*Duel between M. Lauxe and M. Chambers in Arkansas.*
„	„	27.	*Duelling, New Mode of killing one's self.*
„	*Dec.*	28.	*Duel between M. Stevens and M. Gerome.*
1862.	*Feb.*	28.	„ „ *Lieutenant Bonin and M. de Roulet; fatal.*
„	*April*	18.	„ „ *Hughes and Rochfort at Clontarf; stopped by the police.*
„	*Sept.*	12.	„ *near Paris.*
„	*Oct.*	14.	„ *between M. Bottero and M. Bensa.*
„	„	27, 28, 30.	*Nov.* 1, 21, 25, 26. *Duel between the Duke of Grammont and M. Dillon at St. Germain.*
„	*Nov.*	1.	*Duels, Three, in one day, at Hasenhaide, between Artillery Officers and Students.*
„	„	8.	*Duel between two Sub-Officers in Nimes.*
„	„	10.	„ „ *Colonel Calhoun and Major Rhett at Charleston.*
„	*Dec.*	12.	„ „ *Menotte Garibaldi and Colonel Pallavicino.*
1863.	*Mar.*	3, 9, 23.	*Duel between two Members of the Spanish and Dutch Embassies near Vienna; fatal.*
„	*April*	6.	*Duel between Albert Wolff and M. Febore in Paris.*
„	„	19.	„ „ *M. Malato and M. Nicolosi.*
„	„	22.	„ „ *M. Koning and M. Lafont at Auteuil, with swords.*
„	*June*	3.	„ „ *Counts Wiclopolski and Branicki.*
„	*Sept.*	12.	„ „ *two Officers at Blois.*
„	„	18.	„ „ *ladies in Baltimore.*
1864.	*Jan.*	19.	„ „ *Counts Sternbach and Hohnstein at Freising.*
„	*May*	2.	*Duelling at Wilmington; fatal.*
„	*June*	11.	*Duel at Heidelberg—Extraordinary.*
„	*July*	1.	„ *between Martha Howell and Miss Johnson.*
„	*Aug.*	1.	„ „ *two Miners, with pickaxes, at Washoe.*
„	*Sept.*	9.	„ „ „ *Officers of the Russian Guards at St. Petersburg.*
„	„	29.	„ *at Jaroslav, and the daughter of the killed seeking to fight her seducer.*
„	*Oct.*	28.	„ *between Count de Fuerstenberg and M. de Hochwachter near Vals.*
„	*Nov.*	26.	*Duelling in the Russian Army.*
1865.	*Jan.*	19.	*Duel between the Duc de Montmorency and M. de Larochefoucauld.*
„	„	21.	„ „ *two Cattle-drovers, with knives, near Holyhead.*
„	*April*	10, 11.	*Duel between Baron Chazel and M. Delaert.*
„	*Nov.*	3.	*Duel between M. de Cadoudal and M. de Fleurant.*
1866.	*Jan.*	6.	„ „ *two lads at school near Darmstadt.*

TIMES (The) (*continued*)—

1866.	Feb.	2.	*Duel between Signor Botta and Signor Bottero, two News-paper Editors, at Turin.*
,, ·	April	6.	,, *Savage, at Point Chicot, Mississippi River.*
,,	,,	27.	,, ,, *Captain Norton and S. C. Price; leave England for France.*
,,	June	4.	,, ,, *M. G. de Coetlogon and M. A. de Bors.*
,,	,,	23.	,, *Modern English, at Newcastle.*
,,	Aug.	8.	,, *between Mr. Henderson Taylor and Captain Greenland near Memphis.*
,,	Oct.	5.	,, ,, *M. Save and Clement Duvernois.*
,,	,,	30.	,, (*fatal to M. Seguin) in France.*
1867.	Feb.	21, 28.	*Duel between Prince Solms and Count Wedel at Vienna; fatal.*
,,	Mar.	2.	*Duel between M. Kargenbauer and M. Schotschik.*
,,	,,	12.	,, ,, *Paul de Cassagnac and Henri Rochefort—Trial of.*
,,	,,	30.	,, ,, *Senhor Jose Julio and Senhor Sa de Moguerna.*
,,	June	14.	,, ,. *Viscount Latouche and M. Floquet.*
,,	,,	14.	,, ,, *the Editors of the "Soleil" and the "Pays."*
1868.	Aug.	4.	,, ,, *M. Barot and M. Jecker near Waterloo.*
,,	Sept.	28.	,, ,, *M. Rochefort and M. Baroche.*
,,	Oct.	7.	,, *French, between a Student and an ex-Naval Officer in the Bois de Boulogne.*
,,	,,	14.	,, *at Baden; fatal.*
1869.	Mar.	2.	,, *of three brothers against three brothers in Florida.*
,,	,,	4.	,, *between two brothers at Bermondsey.*
,,	,,	23.	,, *between Count de Jara and Don Celestino Olozaga; fatal.*
,,	,,	26.	*Duelling in Italy.*
,,	June	5.	*Duel—An Indo-American; fatal.*
,,	July	30.	*Duel between Mr. Reginald Russell and M. de la Paeze at Chantilly.*
,,	Aug.	7.	,, ,, *Paul de Cassagnac and M. Gustave Flourens at Paris.*
,,	,,	10.	,, ,, *two Editors at Marseilles.*
,,	Oct.	4.	,, ,, *Viscount Hallez Claparede and Count de Beaumont.*
,,	,,	18, 19, 27.	*Duel between Prince Metternich and M. de Beaumont.*
,,	,,	26.	*Duelling in France : Count de Beaumont and his enemies.*
,,	Nov.	6.	*Duel between Count Fitzjames and M. de Beaumont.*
,,	,,	9, 11.	*Duel between The O'Donoghue and Mr. Moore.*
,,	Dec.	22, 28, 31.	*Duel between M. de Mauguy and M. de Beaumont.*
1870.	Jan.	18.	*Duel between Count Moritz Hohenthal and Count Uxskyll at Berlin.*
,,	Mar.	14, 15, 17, 21, 22, 26.	*Duel between the Duke of Montpensier and Don Enrique de Bourbon.*
,,	April	27.	*Duelling—Marshal Prim on.*
,,	May	18.	*Duel between M. Bande and M. Soutzo.*
,,	,,	30.	,, ,, *Parisian Journalists.*

TIMES (The) (*continued*)—

1870.	June	2.	Duel between a Dancer and a Soldier at Vienna.
,,	Sept.	19.	,, ,, Captain Aitken and Mr. Cohen at Savannah; fatal.
,,	Nov.	8.	Duellist, Disabilities of, in Virginia.
1871.	July	28.	Duel between M. Delpech and Mr. Middleton.
,,	Nov.	17.	,, ,, Rotours and St. Leger at Lille, with swords.
,,	,,	21, 24.	Duel between Clemenceau and Poussarque, with pistols.
,,	Dec.	4.	Duel between two Newspaper Writers at Marseilles.
1872.	Feb.	20.	,, ,, Colonel de Beauffremont and Captain Bibesco.
,,	Mar.	25.	,, ,, M. Rogat and M. Richardet.
,,	June	3.	,, ,, Paul de Cassagnac and M. E. Lockroy at Vincennes.
,,	,,	24.	,, ,, M. Ranc and Ivan Woestine, Editors of French Journals.
,,	,,	26.	,, ,, the ex-King of Araucania and the reigning King, by lassoes; to come off at Christmas.
,,	July	3.	,, ,, M. Ordinaire and M. Cavalier, with swords.
,,	,,	9.	,, ,, M. Tirard and M. Aubert.
,,	Aug.	15.	,, ,, Vermersch and Lissogaray, two Communist Refugees in London.
,,	Sept.	2.	,, A Writer in the "Figaro" and his Victim.
,,	,,	16, 26.	Sword of the Black Prince—Notes about.
,,	,,	25.	Duel, with dagger-knives, by two Germans at Finsbury Park.
,,	Oct.	1.	Swords of the Black Prince.
,,	,,	9, 20.	Duel between Alexandre Girardin and St. Albin.
1873.	Mar.	3.	Duel between two women in Paris.
,,	,,	19.	Swords, New, for the American Army.
,,	April	21.	Duel between M. de Borda and M. Delpit in Paris.
,,	July	3, 10.	,, ,, General Campos and Colonel Vega.
,,	,,	3, 4, 5, 7, 8, 9, 10.	Duel between M. Ranc and Paul de Cassagnac.
,,	,,	21.	Duel between ex-Judge Cooley and R. Barnwell Rhett in New Orleans.
,,	Aug.	7, 9.	,, ,, M. Herve and M. Edmond About.
,,	Sept.	24.	,, ,, M. Braime and M. Gery Legraud at Lille.
,,	Oct.	8.	Duels in Spain.
,,	,,	16.	Duel in Italy ; ferocious.
,,	Nov.	28, 29.	Duel between Prince Ghika and Prince Soutzo in France ; fatal.
,,	Dec.	2.	Duel between General von Goelben and Marshal Manteuffel.
,,	,,	6.	Ditto. A Hoax.
,,	,,	16.	Duel in Kentucky.
1874.	Jan.	10.	,, ,, New Orleans.
,,	,,	27.	,, between two Parisians on the Swiss frontier ; the Doctor wounded.
,,	Feb.	9.	,, ,, Prince Soutzo and Prince Ghika—sentence on the survivor.
,,	,,	11.	,, in Indiana.
,,	Mar.	13.	,, between Schoolboys at Lincoln.

TIMES (The) (*continued*)—

1874.	Mar. 13.	Duel in *California ; both combatants killed.*
,,	,, 26.	,, *between Negroes in Georgia.*
,,	May 5.	,, ,, *M. Lehembre and M. Fontaines—funeral of the former.*
,,	,, 23, 25.	Duel between *Prince Metternich and Count Montebello.*
,,	,, 25.	Duelling "*à la mode.*"
,,	June 23.	Duel, *Bloodless, at Dresden.*
,,	July 4.	,, *Fatal, in Belgium.*
,,	,, 23.	,, *between a man and a dog at Montargis.*
,,	Sept. 5.	,, *in Louisiana ; both killed.*
,,	,, 15.	,, *Political.*
,,	,, 15.	,, *Sir Robert Peel never actually a principal.*
,,	Oct. 16, 17.	Duel between *M. Perrin and M. Gregori.*
1875.	Jan. 14.	Duel between *Colonel Tardy and Dr. Lay.*
,,	,, 14.	,, ,, *M'Donald and Texas at Jefferson.*
,,	,, 21.	,, ,, *Lieutenant von Garnier and Sub-Lieutenant Rau von Holzhausen ; fatal.*
,,	April 15.	Fencing *in France.*
,,	,, 21.	Duel *between the Editors of the "Pays" and the "Union."*
,,	,, 27.	,, ,, *the Marquis de Caux and an Aide-de-camp at St. Petersburg.*
,,	June 22.	,, ,, *Captain Mancini and M. Benati de Baylon.*
,,	,, 23.	,, ,, *Dr. Curtis and M. Cortereal ; and suicide of the victor.*
,,	,, 24.	Duelling. *Anecdote of the way it was suppressed in a French Regiment.*
,,	,, 24.	,, *A common-sense way of practising.*
,,	Aug. 20.	Duel between *two Doctors in Texas.*
,,	Nov. 16.	,, ,, *M. Mallet and M. Moreau at Courtrai.*
,,	Dec. 29.	,, ,, *Mr. Lilburne and the Marquis de Solfaga ; fatal.*
1876.	Feb. 2.	Duelling—*New Cure for.*
,,	,, 7.	Duel, *Strange, of a French Officer.*
,,	Mar. 29.	,, *between M. Feuilrhade and M. Olliviar at Longwy ; fatal.*
,,	June 26.	,, ,, *two Drovers at Colorado.*
,,	Aug. 3, 4.	,, ,, *Ducland and Cunes.*
,,	Dec. 15.	,, *at Mons ; both combatants arrested.*
1877.	Jan. 10, 11, 22.	Duel between *Mr. Bennett, of the "New York Herald," and Mr. Fred. May.*
,,	,, 31.	Feb. 3. Duel between *M. de Soubeyran and M. Pereire ; threatened.*
,,	Feb. 22.	Duel between *Count Narraskin and the Circassian Commander Cooynimski.*
,,	Mar. 9, 30.	Duel between *Herr Meyer and the Marquis de Compiègne.*
,,	April 2.	Duel between *the Marquis de Compiègne and Mr. Meyer.*
,,	May 17.	,, ,, *M. Pierantoni and Signor Albanese.*

TIMES (The) (*continued*)—

1877. Nov. 3. Duel at Athens ; Captain Bourbaki killed.
,, ,, 17. ,, between M. Targe and M. Mitchell.
1878. Feb. 1. ,, ,, W. S. Harley and Robert Fishburne near Savannah.
,, Mar. 4. ,, ,, M. Thomson and Paul de Cassagnac near Versailles.
,, ,, 14. ,, ,, Paul de Cassagnac and M. Andrieux at Chatillon.
,, April 10. ,, at Berlin between two Officers.
,, ,, 12. ,, Inciting to fight.
,, May 4. ,, between M. de Maille and M. Loisant, French Deputies.
,, ,, 13. Duelling in Italy—Association formed to protest against.
,, June 11. Duel in Nuremberg. Curious trial and result.
,, Oct. 26. ,, between two Creole gentlemen near Orleans.
,, Nov. 22. ,, ,, M. Gambetta and M. de Fourten outside Paris.
,, ,, 28. ,, ,, M. Dreolle and Gilbert Martin near Paris.
,, ,, 30. ,, ,, two Captains at Cherbourg ; one killed.
,, Dec. 2. ,, ,, General Chanzy's Orderly and an Algerian Editor.
,, ,, 4, 7. Duelling in France—Notes on.
,, ,, 20. Duel in Algeria, with the sabre.
,, ,, 27. ,, between the Comte de Bouville and M. Maigne.
,, ,, 31. ,, ,, Rogniot and Count Pairnett, with swords.
1879. Jan. 17. ,, ,, S. Bonacci and S. Indelli at Rome.
,, July 23. ,, ,, two Journalists in Paris.
,, ,, 28. ,, ,, an Officer and a Student at Wurzburg.
,, Sept. 4, 13. Duel between Comte de Vaysy and Baron de Vanloo.
,, ,, 8. Duel between Marquis of Olivares and M. de Bouvie.
,, ,, 18. ,, ,, two Editors at Paris.
,, ,, 24. ,, ,, Jules Simon and a Bonapartist Editor.
,, Oct. 23. ,, ,, Lieutenant Faltres and Adjutant Levy at Algiers.
,, Dec. 30. ,, ,, M. Humbert and M. Mayer at Paris.
1880. Jan. 1. ,, ,, Mayer and Humbert, two Socialist Editors ; both wounded.
,, ,, 13, 17. Duel between an Editor and a Member of the National Club, at Pesth.
,, ,, 26. Duel between M. Waddington's son and another young man.
,, Mar. 29. ,, ,, M. Krieger and M. Leezmann ; latter killed.
,, April 11, 16. Duelling in Germany.
,, ,, 20. Duel between Lieutenant von Werder and Baron von Leydewitz.
,, June 3. ,, ,, M. Henri Rochefort and M. Koechlin in Switzerland.
,, ,, 4. ,, ,, Ditto. Rochefort wounded.
,, ,, 14. ,, ,, M. Lauanve and M. Simon.
,, July 6. ,, ,, M. Pelletan and M. Godblewski in Paris.
,, Oct. 27. ,, ,, M. Gassier and M. Kiramon.

TIMES (The) (*continued*)—

1880.	*Nov.* 22.	*Duel between M. Demarcay and M. Ordiani.*		
1881.	*Jan.* 13.	,,	,,	*two German Noblemen, near Frankfort, with pistols.*
,,	*April* 7.	,,	,,	*a Jew and a Jew Baiter.*
,,	*July* ¦ 16.	,,	*at Bonn.*	
,,	,, 25.	,,	*between Signor Mario and Signor Levi.*	
,,	*Nov.* 14.	,,	,,	*M. de Cassagnac and M. de Montebello.*
1882.	*Mar.* 31.	,,	,,	*two Legal Officials at Munster.*
,,	*Sept.* 4, 5, 27.	*Duel between M. Richard and M. de Massas in Paris, with swords; latter killed.*		
,,	*Nov.* 21.	*Duel between Captain Emmerich and a Student named Meyer, at Wurzburg; former killed.*		
1883.	*Mar.* 21.	,,	,,	*Count Biclozersky and Prince Dondoukoff-Korsakoff.*
,,	*May* 25, 28.	*Duel between Lieutenant Schlager and the Editor of a Military Journal in Vienna.*		
,,	,, 28.	*Duel between M. Albert Delpit and M. Daudet near Paris.*		
,,	*June* 4.	,,	,,	*M. de Cassagnac and an old Sergeant-Major of Chasseurs.*
,,	*Aug.* 8.	,,	,,	*M. Soutou and M. Mayer in Paris.*
,,	*Oct.* 23.	,,	,,	*Count Batthyany and Dr. Rosenberg at Temesvar.*
,,	*Nov.* 27.	,,	,,	*Counsel Heumann and Police Commissioner Vay.*
,,	*Dec.* 15.	,,	,,	*Herr Hoisty and Herr Almassy.*
,,	,, 26, 27.	*Duel between a Russian and a Frenchman; frustrated by their arrest at New Brighton.*		
1884.	*Jan.* 10.	*Duel between M. Scholl and M. Dion.*		
,,	,, 30.	,,	,,	*M. Viette and M. Gras.*
,,	*Feb.* 28.	,,	,,	*Marquis Antaldi and Deputy Belgioioso in Rome, with swords.*
,,	*Mar.* 10.	,,	,,	*General Davil and M. Williams.*
,,	*April* 21.	,,	,,	*Casey, the Fenian, and a Captain Scully, an Irish-American, in the Bois de Boulogne.*
,,	*June* 9.	,,	,,	*M. Arene and M. Judet in Paris.*
,,	,, 27, 28.	*Duel between M. Lalon and M. de Veilpicard.*		
,,	*Sept.* 25.	*Duel between French Journalists in Paris.*		
,,	*Nov.* 3.	,,	,,	*M. Secretan and M. Ruffy; prevented by the police.*
,,	,, 11.	,,	,,	*M. Rochefort and Captain Fournier in Paris.*
,,	,, 19.	,,	,,	*M. Lehey and M. Saissy in Paris, with swords.*
1885.	*Feb.* 14.	,,	,,	*two Officers at Cologne.*
,,	*Sept.* 19, 25.	*Duelling at German Universities.*		
,,	,, 24.	*Duelling—Note on.*		
,,	*Oct.* 6.	,,	,,	
,,	,, 7.	*Duel between two Officers at Madrid; fatal.*		
1886.	*Jan.* 17.	,,	,,	*Signor Luzzatto and Signor de Paz, with swords.*
,,	*Mar.* 17.	,,	,,	*Prince Amadée de Broglie and Vicomte de Tredern.*

TIMES (The) (*continued*)—

1886.	*April* 26.	Duel between French Journalists in Paris.		
,,	*May* 8.	,,	,,	M. Rochefort and M. Portalis.
,,	*July* 30.	,,	,,	a Lieutenant and an Army Surgeon near Liège.
,,	*Aug.* 16.	,,	Challenge to fight.	
,,	*Sept.* 24.	,,	between Baron Lajthenyi and a Landowner.	
,,	,, 30.	,,	,,	M. Gariel and Captain de Valicourt.
1887.	*Jan.* 27.	,,	,,	M. Pherekyde and M. Fleva.
,,	*April* 6.	,,	,,	M. de Douville-Maillefeu and M. Sans Leroy.
,,	*May* 18.	,,	,,	Dr. Pattai and an Officer named Wolf, at Vienna.
,,	*June* 13.	,,	,,	M. Clemenceau and M. Foucher in Paris.
,,	*July* 25.	,,	,,	two Waiters in Hungary; curious result.
,,	*Aug.* 8.	,,	,,	M. Magnier and M. Reinach in Paris.
,,	,, 12.	Duels in Spain.		
,,	,, 17.	Duel between two Frenchmen in New York.		
,,	,, 22.	,,	,,	St. de Melleville and M. de Labruyere in Paris.
,,	,, 30.	,,	,,	M. Tassin and M. Jullien in Paris.
,,	*Sept.* 21.	,,	,,	General Naranjo and General Pridilla in Mexico.
,,	,, 21, 22.	Duel between General Rocha and Senor Antonia Gayon in Mexico.		
,,	*Nov.* 18.	Duel between M. Rochefort and M. Marouck.		
,,	*Dec.* 12.	,,	,,	M. Literaty and his brother-in-law at Budapest.
,,	,, 14.	,,	,,	Ditto. Death of M. Literaty.
,,	,, 17.	,,	,,	Ditto. Attempted Suicide of Madame Literaty.
,,	,, 17.	,,	,,	M. Edwards and M. Mayer in Paris.
,,	,, 27.	Duels in Hungary during the last six years.		
,,	,, 30.	Duel between M. Meyer and M. Ivan Westyne in France.		
1888.	*Feb.* 2.	,,	,,	M. Vignon and M. Bauer in Paris.
,,	,, 20.	,,	,,	Dr. Johannes Meisner and Herr Fischauer.
,,	*April* 30.	*May* 1. June 27. Duel between M. Dupuis and M. Habert in the Bois de Boulogne; former shot dead.		
,,	*May* 2.	Duel between Duc de Gramont and M. Rambaud in Paris.		
,,	*June* 12.	,,	,,	M. Arene and M. Weiller.
,,	,, 14.	,,	,,	General Boulanger and M. Floquet.
,,	*Sept.* 6.	,,	,,	M. Thuillier and M. Lejeune in Belgium; former killed.
,,	*Nov.* 21.	,,	,,	M. Yves Guyot and M. Andrieux.
,,	*Dec.* 1.	,,	,,	M. Reinach and M. Deroulede in Paris.
,,	,, 15.	,,	,,	M. Clemenceau and M. Maurel in Paris.
1889.	*Jan.* 15.	,,	,,	M. Rochefort and M. Lissagaray.
,,	*Feb.* 4.	,,	,,	M. Layuerre and M. Sigismond.
,,	*Mar.* 11.	,,	,,	Prince de Ligne and the Baron de Jonghe —Sentence on, for.
,,	,, 28.	,,	,,	M. Foucher and M. Lissagaray near Paris.

TIMES (The) *(continued)*—

1889.	*May* 22.	*Duel between M. Lockroy and Deputy De La Berge in Paris.*	
,,	,, 31.	,, ,, *M. Edinger and M. Goussot in Paris.*	
,,	*July* 13.	,, ,, *M. Laur and M. Thomson in Paris.*	
,,	,, 15.	,, ,, *M. Pierotti and M. Belz at Marseilles; former killed.*	
,,	*Sept.* 16.	,, ,, *M. Lalon and M. Canivet in Paris.*	
,,	*Nov.* 27.	,, *in Germany; fatal.*	
,,	*Dec.* 10.	,, *between Count Ladislaus Karolyi and Count Eugen Lazar at Budapest.*	
1890.	*Jan.* 25.	,, ,, *M. Edouard de Rothschild and the Marquis de Gouy.*	
,,	*Feb.* 3.	,, ,, *Marquis de Mores and Deputy Dreyfus at Lille.*	
,,	*Mar.* 4.	,, ,, *M. Rousselle and M. Humbert in Paris.*	
,,	,, 15.	*Duelling in Japan.*	
,, ·	*April* 11.	*Duel between M. Borriglioni and M. Edwards.*	
,,	,, 14.	,, ,, ,, *M. Maro in Paris.*	
,,	*May* 22.	*Sword—A Faulty.*	
,,	*July* 1.	*Duel between M. Fouquier and M. Laurent in Paris.*	
,,	*Sept.* 6.	,, ,, *M. Rochefort and M. Thieband; prevented by the Dutch police.*	
,,	,, 8.	,, ,, *Ditto, fought at Clinge.*	
,,	,, 8, 9.	*Duel between M. Mermeix and M. Labruyere.*	
,,	,, 15.	*Duel between M. Mayer Levy and M. Arnould Galopin.*	
,.	,, 16.	,, ,, *Señor Gonzalo Estera and Señor Gutierrez Najera in Mexico.*	
,,	,, 16, 17.	*Duel between M. Mermeix and M. Dumouteil.*	
,,	,, 22.	*Duel between M. Gonnonithon and M. Chiche.*	
,,	,, 22.	,, ,, *M. Millevoye and M. Canivet.*	
,,	,, 25.	,, ,, *M. Mermeix and M. Millevoye.*	
,,	,, 26.	,, ,, *M. Lutand and M. Vilfen.*	
,,	,, 27.	*Duelling in Japan.*	
,,	,, 29.	*Duel between M. Catulle Mendes and M. Carle des Perrieres in Paris.*	
,,	*Oct.* 22.	,, ,, *M. Reinach and M. Deroulede.*	
,,	,, 29.	,, ,, *M. Allard and M. Franckel; death of former.*	
,,	*Nov.* 13, 14.	*Duel between M. Deroulede and M. Laguerre.*	
,,	,, 15, 17.	,, ,, *Ditto. Consigned to Charleroi Prison.*	
,,	,, 19.	*Duel between M. Ephrusst and M. Treille.*	
,,	,, 19.	,, ,, *M. Lesenne and M. Laguerre at St. Cloud.*	
,,	*Dec.* 19.	,, ,, *Deputies Sonnino and Indelli in Italy.*	
,,	,, 19.	,, ,, *F. Rillet and Ciceron, with rifles.*	
1891.	*Jan.* 5.	,. ,, *Count Deym and Count Francis Lutzow in Vienna.*	
,,	,, 7.	,, ,, *M. Leveille and M. Roux at Limoges.*	
,,	,, 8.	,, ,, *Señor Canalejas and Señor Martos Fies in Spain.*	
,,	*Feb.* 10.	,, ,, *M. Lordon and M. Larroumet in Paris.*	
,,	,, 26.	*Swordsmanship at the Lyceum Theatre (Mr. E. Castle's lecture).*	

TIMES (The) *(continued)*—

1891.	*Mar.* 25.	*Duel between M. Drumont and M. Vonoven in Paris.*
,,	*April* 11.	,,	,,	*M. Jules Lemaitre and M. Felicien Champsaur.*
,,	*May* 9.	,,	,,	*Colonel W. Johnson and Major A. Sizmore at Knoxville, Tennessee; former killed.*
,,	,, 18.	,,	,,	*M. Bazire and M. Gungl in Paris.*
,,	,, 20, 21, 22.	*Duels and the German Emperor.*
,,	,, 23.	*Duel between M. Mussali and M. Carbonaro in Tunis.*
,,	,, 26.	,,	,,	*Baron Rudolf Kalnoky and an unknown Southerner at Chicago.*
,,	*June* 8.	,,	,,	*M. Catulle Mendes and M. Rene d'Hubert in Paris.*
,,	*July* 25.	,,	,,	*M. Simon and M. Chironte at Dunkirk.*
,,	*Aug.* 17.	*Duels in Budapest.*
,,	*Sept.* 4.	*Duel between M. Chas. Laurent and M. Rene d'Hubert in Paris.*
,,	,, 19.	,,	,,	*Baron Franchetti and General Gandolfi in Italy.*
,,	,, 21.	,,	,,	*M. Catulle Mendes and M. Viele Griffin in France.*
,,	*Nov.* 7.	*Duel of Admiral Beranger with a Newspaper Editor.*
,,	,, 9.	,, *between M. Harencourt and M. Carre.*
,,	,, 16.	,,	,,	*two Mexican residents in Texas.*
,,	*Dec.* 16.	,,	,,	*M. Charles Seller and Colonel Rudruzzi.*
,,	,, 17.	,,	,,	*Weaver and Bassett, for cheating at cards.*
,,	,, 21, 22.	*Duel between Baron Fejervery and M. Regron.*
1892.	*Feb.* 17.	*Duel between M. Gajary and M. Csavolsky at Budapest.*
,,	,, 17.	,,	,,	*M. Aurel Muennich and Kornell Abranaji at Budapest, with swords.*
,,	,, 20.	,,	,,	*M. Drumont and M. Isaacs.*
,,	*April* 25, 30.	*Duel between M. Burrows and Edward Fox in Ostend (two Americans).*
,,	*May* 13.	*Duel between an Officer and a Law Student at Leipsic.*
,,	,, 19, 21.	*Duel between four, one after the other, of M. Roulez, in the Bois de Boulogne.*
,,	,, 23.	*Ditto. Reported to be a hoax.*
,,	*June* 24, 25, 27.	*Duel between Marquis de Mores and Captain Mayer; latter killed.*
,,	*Aug.* 15.	*Duel between Baron von Garteur-Grieknand and the Marquis de Valladares.*
,,	*Sept.* 15.	,,	,,	*Gerville Reache and M. Souques near Paris.*
,,	*Nov.* 16.	,,	,,	*a white man and a negro in Florida.*
,,	*Dec.* 23, 26.	*Duel between M. Deroulede and M. Clemenceau in Paris.*
1893.	*Jan.* 31.	*Duel between M. Pinchon and M. Deroulede.*
,,	*May* —.	,,	,,	*Marquis de Breteuil and M. Camille Dreyfus.*
,,	,, 11.	,,	,,	*Dr. Ward and M. Gaston Méry.*
,,	*Dec.* 2.	,,	,,	*M. Etienne and M. Millerand.*
1894.	*Feb.* 17.	*A French Duel.*
1895.	*Jan.* 4.	*Duel between M. Tofani and M. Vergori; latter killed.*
,,	,, 6.	,,	,,	*M. Percher and M. Chatelier; former killed.*

TIMES (The) (*continued*)—

1895.	*Mar.* 4, 6.	*Duel between ditto. Funeral of Percher.*
	Feb. 14.	„ „ *M. Canrobert and M. Hubbard; latter wounded.*
„	*April* 18.	„ „ *M. Jules Huret and M. Catulle Mendes.*
„	*July* 13.	„ „ *M. Basset and M. Archain; former wounded.*
„	„ 13.	„ „ *M. Gerault Richard and M. Denoix.*
„	*Aug.* 26.	*Duelling in Mexico.*
„	„ 29.	*Duel between M. Alessandri and M. Benedetti; former killed.*]

TIMLICH (K.). — Gründliche Abhandlung der Fechtkunst auf den Hieb zu Fuss und zu Pferde. 4°. 1796. *Wien.*

[*55 pages. Mit Kupfern.*] (*In the British Museum.* 7908. d. 21.)

—— (—.). — Abhandlung der Fechtkunst auf den Stoss. Mit conrographischen Kupfertabellen. 12°. 1807. *Wien:* Tendler.

(*In the British Museum.* 7908. a. 87.)

TINDALE (W.). — A Treatise on Military Equitation. 8°. 1797.
[*Folding plates of horse, sword, and man.*]

TINTI (A.). — Sinossi della scherma di sciabola. 16°. 1880. *Modena.*

TIPTOFT (Sir John) [Knt.]. — *COTTONIAN* MSS.
[*Tib. C. i. B.* 28. (229.)]

TIPTOFT (John) [Earl of Worcester]. — Regulations concerning Tournaments.

[*Harleian MSS.*	Vol.	I.	page 18	cod. 69	art. 17.
	„	„ II.	„ 12	„ 1354	., 11 *et seq.*
	„	„ II.	„ 226	„ 1776	„ 43.
	„	„ III.	„ 316	„ 6064	„ 80.]

TOBAR (Don Pedro Mexía de). — Engaño y desengaño de los herrores [*sic*] en la destreza de las armas. 4°. 1636. *Madrid.*

TOLEDO (Frederick de). — Account of Tournaments.
[*Harleian MS.* Vol. I. p. 18. cod. 69. art. 20.]

TOLLIN (F.) [Fechtmeister]. — Neue illustrirte Fechtschule. Nach der neuen und naturgemässen Methode des Prof. Heinr. Ling dargestellt und mit zahlreichen, nach der Natur gezeichneten Illustrationen (in Holzschn.) versehen. 8°. 1851. *Grimma:* Verlags-Comptoir.

TOMEONI. — *DUMANIANT.* — 1800.

3¹3

TORELLI. — Giuoco d'arme da Torelli. 1632. *Venetia.*

TORELLI (CARLO). — Lo splendore della nobiltà napoletana, giuoco d'arme esposto a somiglianza di quello intitolato : le chemin de l'honneur. 4°. 1678. *Napoli.*

TÖRNGREN (L. M.). — Reglemente i bajonett och sabelfäktning för kongl. flottan. Enligt nådigt uppdrag utarbetadt. 12°. 1882. *Stockholm :* Norstedt & Söner.

[21 plates.] (In Captain Hutton's Collection.)

—— (—. —.). — Tilläggsblad för reglemente i bajonett och sabel-fäktning. [Omslagstitel : Supplement för Atlas till gymnastik reglemente för kongl. flottan.] Folio. 1882. *Stockholm :* Norstedt & Söner.

[6 plates.]

—— (—. —.). — *GYMNASTIK*-reglemente för kongl. flottan. 12°. 1879. *Stockholm :* Norstedt & Söner.

—— (—. —.). — *TIDSKRIFT* i gymnastik. — 1876–85.

TORRE (PEDRO DE LA) [Petrus de Turri]. — [1474 ?].
[Mentioned by Narvaez, Pallavicini, and Marcelli, but without sufficient data, and which I have been unable to trace.]

TORRENTE Y CAVADA. Discursos sobre el duelo.

TOUCHE ([PHILBERT] DE LA) [Maistre en fait d'armes à Paris et des pages de la Reyne, et de ceux de la Chambre de son A. R. Monseigneur le Duc d'Orléans]. — Les vrays principes de l'espée seule, dediez au Roy. Oblong 4°. 1670. *Paris :* François Muguet.
[Portrait of La Touche. 35 copperplates, out of the text.
"La Touche is the first to describe that curious mode of holding the rapier with both hands, which seems to have been in favour in France throughout the second half of the seventeenth century."—Castle's "Schools and Masters of Fence."]

(In Captain Hutton's Collection.)

—— ([—] — —). — *HUTTON* (A.). — 1892.

TOURNEMINE (PRE.). — Un coup d'épée. Comédie-vaudeville en deux actes. 12°. 1837. *Paris :* E. Michaud.

TOURNOI INTERNATIONAL Annuel d'Escrime de France. Rapport présenté au nom de la organisation, par M. H. Hébrard de Villeneuve, Président de la Société d'Encouragement de l'Escrime. 8°. 1896. *Paris :* Imprimerie Chaix.
[Siège du Comité : Hôtel du Figaro, 26 Rue Drouot, Paris.]

PHIL[I]BERT DE LA TOUCHE. 1670.

Maistre en faits d'armes à Paris et des pages de la Reyne, et de ceux de la Chambre de son Altesse Royale, Monseigneur le Duc d'Orléans.

TOURNOIS. — Cérémonies anciennes observées aux gaiges de bataille, querelles, cartelz, duelz, satisfactions, preuves anciennes par le fer chaud et tournois. 1096–1636.

> [*MS. In the British Museum.* 30,542 (*ff.* 333).]

TOWNSEND (W. M.). — A Few Famous Duels.

> [*Article in "The Argosy" (Monthly Magazine) (London),* Vol. **XXVI.,** September 1878, pp. 188–193.]

TRACTADO DE ESGRIMATE. 8°. 1842.

> [*Aos R. P. de V. M.*]

TRACTATUS DE PROBITIONE DUELLI auctore luca Florono de Solarolo Juris cons. ac. S. Martini de Formellino Fauen. 4°. 1610. *Venetiis.*

TRACTATUS EX VARIS JURIS interpretibus collecti. Folio. 1549. *Lugduni.*

> [Vol. XII. pp. 212–213. ALCIATI (ANDREE). — *Consilium in materia duelli excerptum ex libro quinto responsorum.*
> „ pp. 204–212. —— (—). — *De duello.*
> „ pp. 197–204. CASTILLO (JACOBI). — *De duello.*
> „ pp. 193–196. LIGNANO (JOANNIS DE). — *De duello.*]
> (*In the British Museum.* 5305. *i.*)

TRAITÉ DES ARMES et de l'ordonnance de l'infanterie, relativement au génie de la nation françoise. 8°. 1776. *Amsterdam et Paris :* Jombert.

> [*5 planches se dépliant.*]

TRAITÉ DU DUEL JUDICIAIRE, relations de pas d'armes et tournois ; par Olivier de la Marche, Jean de Villiers, Seigneur de l'Isle-Adam, Hardouin de la Jaille, Antoine de Salle, &c. Publiés par Bernard Prost. 8°. 1872. *Paris :* L. Willem.

TRAITÉZ ET ADVIS de quelques gentils-hommes françois sur les duels et gages de bataille, assçavoir : de Ol. de la Marche, de J. de Villiers, de H. de la Jaille, et autres escrits sur le mesme suiet non encor' imprimez. 12°. 1586. *Paris :* Jean Richer.

> (*In Captain Hutton's Collection.*)

TRATADOS VARIOS. Folio.

> [*MSS. British Museum.* Eg. 2057. *A miscellaneous collection of historical tracts and papers (mostly copies) relating to the reigns of Philip III., Philip IV., and Charles II.* (1615–96).
> No. 20 (f. 237). "*Cirimonial* (sic) *de Principes compuesto por Mosen Diego de Valera.*"
> No. 21 (f. 243). "*Trattado de los Rieptos y desafios por el mismo.*"
> (*The above two tracts are copied from the printed editions.*)]

TRATADOS VARIOS. — Tumbo del monasterio de Santa Ana de Valladolid. Tomo II. Folio.

[*MSS. British Museum.* Eg. 358. *Second volume of a collection of miscellaneous historical tracts* (1503–1770).

No. 4 (f. 16). "*Desafío del capitan Francisco de Monsalve, Caballero de la Orden de Calatrava, maestre de Campo y gobernador de Turene* (sic), *con Diego de Mazariegos y Guadalaxara* (1531)."]

TREITEL (L.). — Zur Duell-Frage. Ein Wort an Eltern und Erzieher. Gr. 8°. 1890. *Karlsruhe :* Bielefeld.

[*Aus :* "*Israelit. Wochenschrift.*"]

TRELON (O. DE). — Advis sur la presentation de l'édit de sa Magesté contre la damnable coustume des duels ; prononcé ou Parlement de Thólose les Chambres assemblées. 12°. 1604. *Paris.*

TRIAL of Captain Edward Clark, Commander of H.M.S. *Canterbury,* for the Murder of Captain Thomas Innes, Commander of H.M.S. *Warwick,* in a Duel in Hyde Park, March 12, 1749, at the Old Bailey, April 1750. Small 4°. 1750. *London :* M. Cooper.

TRIAL of David Armstrong against Buchan Vair and Gideon Vair for sending a Challenge to fight a Duel. 8°. 1823. *Edinburgh.*

TRIAL of James Stuart, of Dunearn, for Murder by Duelling. 1822.

TRIAL of Major Campbell for the Murder of Capt. Boyd in a Duel. 8°. 1808.

TRIBOLATI (FELICE). — Lettera bibliografica sopra un trattato di scherma alla sciabola di G. B. Viti. 8°. 1872. *Pisa :* Tip. Citi.

TRICHTERN (VALENTINO) [Stallmeister der G. A. Universität Göttingen]. — Curiöses Reit-, Jagd-, Fecht, Tanz, oder Ritter-Exercitien-Lexikon. 8°. 1742. *Leipzig.*

(*In the British Museum.* 7906. ccc. 5.)

TRIEGLER (JOHANN GEORG). — Ein neues Künstliches Fechtbuch. 4°. 1664. *Leipzig.*

TROWBRIDGE (J. T.). — *ATLANTIC* Monthly (The).

TRUMAN (B. C.). — Field of Honour : History of Duelling in all Countries. 12°. 1884. *New York.*

[599 *pages.*]

TRUSLER (DR. JOHN). — System of Etiquette, Maxims of Prudence, and Observations on Duelling, &c. 12°. 1826. *Bath:* Souter.

TURNKALENDER (ILLUSTRIERTER DEUTSCHER). 4°. 1888. *Berlin:* H. Lenz.

[*Böttcher. Grundzuge d. deut. Stossfechtschule u. d. französ.-Schule.*]

TURN-ZEITUNG (DEUTSCHE). — (Periodical.) 4°. *Leipzig:* Strauch.

[1831. S. 363. *Auffchlüsse über Fechthandschriften und gedruckte Fechtbücher des 16 und 17 Jahrhunderts, von Dr. Karl Wassmannsdorff.*
1884. S. 353–356. *" Ueber die Marxbrüder und Federfechter und über das älteste—bisher noch unbekannte-gedruckte deutsche Fechtbüch," von Dr. Karl Wassmannsdorff.*]

TVANOWSKI (M.). — Nouveau système d'escrime de la cavalerie, fondé sur l'emploi d'un nouveau sabre. 8°. 1834. *Paris.*

TWO ANGRY WOMEN OF ABINGDON (The). A comedy. 1599.

[*The following pathetic complaint is therein made: "Sword and buckler fights begin to grow out of use. I am sorry for it: I shall never see good manhood again. If it be once gone, this poking fight of rapier and dagger will come up; then a tall man, and a good sword and buckler man, will be spitted like a cat or a rabbit."*]

UEBUNGS - TABELLE für das Turnen und Bajonettfechten der Infanterie zusammengestellt von W. H. 16°. 1890. *Cöln:* Warnitz & Co.

UFFENBACH. — Fechten in England. 1706. *Wien* (?) : Lenz.

[*Refers solely to English Fencing.*]

ULLOA (MARTIN DE). — Disertacion sobre el orígen de los duelos y desafíos y leyes de su observancia, con sus progresos hasta su total extincion. 1796.

[*Disertacion leida en la tercera junta pública anual que celebró la Real Academia de la Historia (Madrid), que se imprimió en los "Fastos," Tomo III., y se reimprimió luego en las " Memorias " de dicha Academia, Tomo I. pág. 35.*]

(*In the British Museum. T. C. 3. b. 6.*)

UNDERWOOD (JAMES) [of the Custom House, Dublin]. — The Art of Fencing, or the Use of the Small Sword. Corrected, revised, and enlarged. 8°. 1787. *Dublin:* Printed by T. Byrne.

[*Dedicated to His Grace, Charles, Duke of Rutland.*]

(*In Captain Hutton's Collection, and in the British Museum.* 7907. bbb. 18.)

UNGER (F. W.). — Der gerichtliche Zweikampf bei den germanischen Völkern. 8". 1847. *Göttingen.*

(In the British Museum. 8706. d. 23.)

UNITED SERVICE MAGAZINE (The). — (Periodical.) 8°.
London.

> [1882. Vol. II. p. 81. *Duelling Days in the Navy.*
> 1888.   „   I. p. 48. *Swords. By A. T. Sibbald.*
>   „   I. pp. 99–209 ; Vol. II. p. 45. "*Duelling Days in the Army.*"
> 1895. *August* 10, 17, 24. *Sword and Pistol.*
>   „   *October* 12. *Infantry Sword Exercise.*]

UNITED STATES ARMY. Ordnance Department. Ordnance
Memoranda, No. 15. Report on a Breech System for Muskets
and Carbines, with a Report on Trowel Bayonets. 8". 1873.
Washington.

UNTERRICHTS-PLAN für den Betrieb des gymnastischen Unterrichts auf den königlichen Kriegsschulen, unter zu Grundlegg.
der allerhöchst genehmigten Abändergn. und Zusätze zur Instruction für den Betrieb der Gymnastik und des Bajonettfechtens bei
der Infanterie vom 19. Octb. 1860. Gr. 8". 1865. *Berlin :* v.
Decker.

URREA (Jerónimo de). — Desafio del Emperador y Rey Francisco y Juicios dél segun el duela. 4°. *Venecia.*

[*Mentioned in Leguina's "La Espada."*]

UTTENHOVEN (G. von). — Erster Unterricht der Rekruten,
oder Vorübung zur leichten Erlernung des Exercirens, Bajonett-
fechtens, &c. 8°. 1846. *Rudolstadt :* Renovanz.

V. (H. A.). — *FENCING (Three Treatises on).* MSS.

VADEMECUM FÜR DEN DEUTSCHEN CORPSSTUDENTEN.
10. Auflage. Mit Nachträgen bis Pfingsten, 1886. 16°. 1886.
Jena. (Leipzig : Rossberg.)

[*Mit* 18 *color. Steintafeln.*]

VAÏSSE (Jean Louis). — Messie et journaliste, polémique philo-
sophico-politique. Étude philosophique et morale. Le duel. 8°.
1871. *Toulouse :* Gimet.

VALDIN. 1729.

VALDIN. — The Art of Fencing, as practised by Monsieur Valdin. 8°. 1729. *London :* Printed for J. Parker.

[45 *pages. Most humbly dedicated to His Grace the Duke of Montagu. Frontispiece portrait of Valdin by P. Fourdrinier. Preface by Solomon Negri.*
In this book the author announces his intention to bring out a very elaborate and comprehensive treatise "after the manner of Salvator Fabris." This great work, however, does not seem to have yet been discovered.]
(*In Captain Hutton's Collection, and in the British Museum* [7906. df. 6].)

V[ALENTIN]I. — Gespräche und Briefe über die Ehre und das Duell. 2. Auflage. 8°. 1829. *Leipzig.*

VALETTE (A.). — Rapport sur le duel. 8°. 1858. *Paris.*

—— (—.). — *MOLINIER* (*J. V.*). — 1861.

VALLE (Battista della). — Trattato dell' arte militare libri III. et nel quarto si tratta dell duello. 12°. 1535. *Vineggia.*
[[*Woodcuts.*]

VALLÉE (Henri). — Le duel—ses lois, ses règles, son histoire. 12°. 1877. *Paris :* Defodon.
[*Another edition.* 8°. 1888. Paris : *Decaux et M. Dreyfus.*]

VALLETA (Josef). — Discurso sobre el duelo.
[*MS. En la B. Nacional, Madrid.*]

VALLETTI (F.). — Manuale di ginnastica secondo i principii di R. Obermann. 6a ed. 16°. 1884. *Torino.*

—— (—.). — Manuale di ginnastica femminile. 1892. *Milano :* Hoepli.
[*Di pag.* iv—112.]

—— (—.). — Storia della ginnastica. 1893. *Milano :* Hoepli.
[*Di pag.* viii—84.]

VALLO. — *VALLE* (*Battista della*). — 1535.

VALMARANA (Conte di G. C.). — Modo del far pace in via cavaleresca e christiana per sodisfattion di parole, nelle ingiurie frà privati. 8°. 1648. *Padova.*

VALORY [*pseudonyme de* M. Mourier]. — Le coup d'épée. Pièce en un acte. 12°. 1830. *Paris :* P. J. Hardy.
[*Représentée pour la première fois, sur le théâtre du Cirque-Olympique, le lundi, 22 février* 1830.]

VALVILLE [Maître en fait d'armes]. — Traité sur la contre-pointe. Oblong 4°. 1817. *St. Pétersbourg :* Charles Kray.

[*24 copperplates. In French and in Russian.*]

VAN BREEN (A.). — *BREEN* (*A. van*). — 1618.

VANDERHAEGHEN (FERDINAND). — Chef - confrérie de Saint-Michel à Gand. Historique de la Société d'escrime royale et cheva-lière de Saint-Michel de Gand. 8°. 1873. *Gand :* Hebbelink.

[*Avec vignette représentant l'extérieur de l'antique salle d'armes de Gand.*]

VANDERLINDE (LE DOCTEUR A.). — Le duel. 8°. 1866. *Bruxelles :* Olivier.

VANDONI (MARCO MARCELLO). — Elementi della scherma. 8°. [1750 ?] *Milano.*

[*Plates. 40 pages.*] (*In the British Museum. 7913. df. 15.*)

VASALLO (DON PEDRO). — Satisfaccion sin altercados. 4°. 1812. *Palma.*

VAUX (LE BARON LUDOVIC DE). — Les hommes d'épée. Préface par A. Scholl. 8°. 1881. *Paris :* Rouveyre.

[*26 engravings and portraits.*]

—— (— — — —). — Les tireurs au pistolet. Préface par Guy de Maupassant et lettre du Prince Bibesco. 8°. 1882. *Paris :* Marpon et Flammarion.

[*Illustrations de Berne-Bellecour, Manet, G. Bellenger, Jeanniot, F. Régamey, Stéphen, Jacob, etc.*]

—— (— — — —). — Les duels célèbres. Préface par A. Scholl. Grand 8°. Illustré. 1884. *Paris :* Rouveyre.

[1 *frontispice,* 24 *portraits sur chine ; en têtes, lettres ornées, et culs-de-lampe composés par Mesplès.*]

—— (— — — —). — Les femmes de sport. Préface par Arsène Houssaye, et lettre de Catulle Mendès. 8°. 1884. *Paris :* Marpon et Flammarion.

[*Portraits et figures.*]

—— (— — — —). — Les hommes de sport. Préface par Alexandre Dumas. 8°. 1888. *Paris :* Marpon et Flammarion.

[*Illustrated.*]

VEERE (Sir Francis). — *COTTONIAN* MSS.
[*Tit. C. iv.* 10. (510.)]

VELA. — [*SALVO (J.)* y *VELA*]. — 1744.

VELASCO (Don Luis Daza de). — De la destreza de las armas.
MS.

VELLA (Giambattista) e **CORRADINO**. — Parere di scherma
palermitano sulle divergenze tra i Signori Nicolò Abbondati e Blasco
Florio. 8°. 1857. *Palermo:* G. Meli.

VENDRELL Y EDUART (Liborio). — Esgrima del sable á
caballo. 4°. 1879. *Vitoria:* E. Sarasgueta.

—— — — (—). — Arte de esgrimir el sable, arreglaas. 4°.
1879. *Vitoria.*
[*Plates.*]

—— — — (—). — Esgrima de carabina armada con caballeria,
combate individual. 4°. 1880. *Vitoria.*
[*Plates.*]

—— — — (—). — Arte de esgrimir el palo.

VENEZIA (La). — (Giornale.) Folio. *Venezia:* Calle Castorta,
N. 3565.
[1891. *Giugno* 3-4. *N.* 152. *Anno XVI.* "*La scherma e gli schermitori
italiani.*"]

VENTURINI (Jh. G. Jul.). — Die Fechtkunst auf Stoss und
Hieb, in systematischer Uebersicht für Offiziere und zum Gebrauch
in Kriegsschulen. 8°. 1802. *Braunschweig:* F. B. Eulemann.
[*Copperplates.*
2. *Auflage.* 8°. 1809. Hannover: *Hahn.*]
(*In Mr. J. R. Garcia Donnell's Collection.*)

VEREIN DEUTSCHER UNIVERSITÄTSFECHTMEISTER. —
DEUTSCHE Hiebfechtschule.

VERGAGNI (Paolo). — De l'enormité du duel. La traduction
par C. . . . 8°. 1783. *Paris:* Guillot.

VERGER DE SAINT-THOMAS (Comte Du). — *SAINT-
THOMAS.* — 1879.

**VERHANDELING OVER DE DUELLEN OF TWEEGE-
VECHTEN.** 1791. *S' Gravenhage.*

VÉRITABLE (LA) POLITIQUE DES PERSONNES DE QUALITÉ. 1711. *Paris.*

[*Duels.*]

VERMEIL (A.) [Pasteur de l'Église Réformée de Bordeaux]. — Le duel, discours. 8°. 1838. *Paris:* J. Risler.

VERMONA (PAUL). — Le maître d'armes. Comédie-vaudeville. 8°. 1850. *Paris.*

[*Représentée pour la première fois à Paris, sur le Théâtre des Variétés, le 6 décembre* 1850.]

VERNEY (LADY F. P.). — *CONTEMPORARY* Review (The). — 1880.

VEROLINI (THEODOR). — Der Künstliche Fechter, oder des berühmten Fechtmeisters Theodori Verolini klare Beschreibung der freyen, ritterlichen und adelichen Kunst des Fechtens im Rappier, Düsacken, und Schwerdt wie dann auch mit angehängter Ring-Kunst; wie sich bei vorfallenden Gelegenheiten in allerley gebräuchlichen Wehren die angenehme Schüler zur Behendigkeit künstlich mögen abgericht, etc. Folio. 1679. *Würzburg.*

[*In mehr als* 130 *abgebildeten Figuren vorgestellet und in* 4 *Theilen abgetheilet.*]

VESTER (E. F. W.). — Einleitung zur adelichen Fechtkunst. 8°. 1777. *Breslau:* Korn.

VEYSSIÈRE (FRANCOIS DE). — *GAUTHIER (Paul).* — 1888.

VEZZANI (ANTONIO). — L'Esercizio Accademico di Picca. 8°. 1628. *Parma.*

[*Portrait and copperplates.*] (*In Captain Hutton's Collection.*)

—— (—). — [Another edition.] Small oblong 4°. 1688. *Parma:* Nella Stamperia Ducale.

[*Avec frontispice d'après Ferd. Bibiena par Nic. Alù et* 47 *figures d'après Phil. Bernouil par Nic. Alù.*]

VICTORIA. — Illustrierte Zeitschrift für vaterländischen Sport und kriegsgemässes Radfahren. 4°. 1895. *Berlin:* Hacke & Grützmacher.

[*Heft* 1 *appeared on the* 1st *October* 1895.]

VIDAL DE SAINT-URBAIN. — Cour d'Appel de Dijon . . . Discours . . . Le duel sous l'ancien régime et de nos jours. 8°. 1892. *Dijon.*

[75 *pages.*]

VIEDMA (Luis Dias de). — Epitome de la enseñanza de la filosofia y destreza matematica de las armas. 8º. 1639. *Cadiz:* F. Rey.

—— (— — —). — Metodo de enseñanza de maestros en la ciencia filosofica de la verdadera destreza matematica de las armas. 4º. 1639. *Barcelona:* Sebastián y Jame Matevad.

VIENNA, AMBRASER COLLECTION (Swords in).
(*In the Art Library, South Kensington Museum. Portfolio 210.*)

VIETH (G. U. A.). — Versuch einer Encyklopädie der Leibes-übungen. 3 Theilen. 8º. 1794–1818. *Berlin.*
[*Der I*ᵉ *Theil erschien* 1794, *der II*ᵉ 1795, *der III*ᵉ, 1818.
A short article on Fencing in Vol. II. p. 496.]

VIGEANT (Arsène) [Maître d'armes à Paris, né à Metz en 1844].
—La bibliographie de l'escrime ancienne et moderne. 8º. 1882. *Paris:* Motteroz.
[*Vignettes de Cheragay et A. Deville. Gravures sur bois de Pannemaker.*]
(*In Captain Hutton's Collection.*)

—— (—). — Petit essai historique : Un maître d'armes sous la Restauration. 16º. 1883. *Paris.*
[*With etched frontispiece (portrait of Jean-Louis) and vignettes.*]

—— (—). — Duels de maîtres d'armes. 16º. 1884. *Paris:* Conquet.
[*With frontispiece (portrait of Bertrand) and a few vignettes.*]
(*In Captain Hutton's Collection.*)

—— (—). — L'almanach de l'escrime. Dessins de Fréd. Régamey. 8º. 1889. *Paris:* Quantin.
[*Numerous photogravures. Eaux-fortes de Courtry. Avec une gravure en couleur, portrait d'après Chartran, gravé par Baude, treize gravures sur cuivre hors texte et nombre de vignettes exécutées par la maison Goupil. MM. François Coppée, Ducreux, Claude La Marche, Albéric Magnard, ont collaboré à cet ouvrage.*]

—— (—). — Ma collection d'escrime. Préface d'Émile Gautier. Poésie de Louis Tiercelin. Dessins de Fréd. Régamey. 8º. *Paris:* Maison Quantin.
[*Manuscrits, albums, livres, tableaux, aquarelles, dessins, portraits, estampes, armes, bronzes, objects divers. Cet ouvrage a été tiré a deux cents exemplaires numérotés. viii. et 134 pages.*]

—— (—). — La grammaire de l'escrime, manuel théorique et pratique, avec planches, vignettes et portrait.
[*In the press.*]

VIGEANT (Arsène). — *EUDEL (P.)*. — 1885.

—— (—). — *SAINT-ALBIN (A. de)*. — 1887.

—— (—). — *SATURDAY* Review, Nov. 6, 1866.

VIGGIANI (Angelo) [Bolognese]. — Lo schermo. Nel quale, per via di dialogo si discorre intorno all eccelenza dell' armi et delle lettere, et intorno all' offesa et difesa. Et insegna uno schermo di spada sola sicuro e singolare con una tavola copiosissima. 4°. 1575. *Venetia:* Appresso Giorgio Angelieri.

> [*9 copperplates, in the text ; ff. 84.*
> *The author's name was spelt Vizani, in accordance with the soft pronuncia-*
> *tion of the Venetians, among whom he had so long taught fencing.*
> *Although the first edition bears the date of 1575, it is known that in deference*
> *to the author's wish his book appeared long after his death, and that it*
> *was finished in 1560. The book "is divided into three parts, the first of*
> *which treats of the inevitable comparison between literature and the science*
> *of arms ; the second of offence and defence. . . . The third part treats*
> *pretty exclusively of fencing, and therein is to be learned that Viggiani*
> *taught seven guards.''*]
> (*In the Bodleian Library ; South Kensington Museum ; British Museum*
> [07,905. g. 2.] ; *and Captain Hutton's Collection.*)

—— (—). — *VIZANI (A.)*.

VILLALOBOS (Don Jimon de). — Modo de pelear á la gineta. 8°. 1606. *Valladolid.*

VILLAMONT. — *CAVALCABO (H.)*. — 1609. 1611.

VILLANNEVA (Don Luis). — Memorias sobre los retos, duelos y desafios y sobre el suicido. 1844. *Madrid.*

VILLARDITA (Giuseppe). — La scherma Siciliana ridotta in compendio, communemente detto il Nicosioto. Oue si mostra, come con un sol moto retto di Corpo, ed una sola retta unea di spada debba il cavaliero principalmente schermire. 12°. 1670. *Palermo.*

> [*3 plates. 53 pages. Dedicata al Sig. D. Francesco Grugno.*]
> (*In Captain Hutton's Collection.*)

—— (—). — Trattato della scherma Siciliana, ove si mostra di seconda intentione, con una linea retta : difendersi di qualsivoglia operatione di resolutione, che operata per ferire à qualunque, ò di

punta, ò taglio, che accadesse in accidente di questionarsi.   Con
expressione di tutte le regole che nascono di seconda operatione.
12°.   1673.   *Palermo :* Carlo Adamo.
[16 *pages.*]   (*In Captain Hutton's Collection.*)

VILLENEUVE (H. Hébrard de). — *ROBERT* (*G.*). — 1887.

—— (— —). — *HÉBRARD* de Villeneuve (H.). — 1894.

—— (— —). — *TOURNOI* International.   1896.

VILLERS (Jehan de) [Seigneur de l'Isle Adam]. — *MARCHE*
(*O. Le*). — MS.

VILLIERS (Jean de). — *TRAITÉS* et advis. — 1586.

—— (— —). — *TRAITÉS* du duel judiciaire. — 1872.

VINDICATION of the Memory of Major Alex. Campbell, containing a full Account of the Circumstances attending his Unfortunate Duel with Capt. Boyd.   1810.

VINGTRINIER [Ainé]. — *CAVALCABO.* — 1889.

VINKEROY (E. van) [Capitaine au Régiment des Carabiniers].
— Catalogue des armes et armures.   Musée Royal d'Antiquités et
d'Armures, Bruxelles.   8°.   1885.   *Bruxelles :* Zech & fils.

VITI (Giovanni Battista) [Studente all' Università di Pisa]. —
Breve trattato di scherma alla sciabola.   8°.   1863.   *Pisa :* Tip.
Citi.

—— (— —) [Avvocato]. — [Another edition.]   1864.   *Genova :*
A. Ciminago.
[*Seconda edizione, corretta.   Osservazioni in materia di duelli, etc.*]
(*In the British Museum.*   7907. *g.* 24.)

—— (— —). — Codice del duello commentato ad uso dei duellanti,
padrini, legali e magistrati.   16°.   1884.   *Genova :* A. Ciminago.
[181 *pages.*]   (*In Mr. J. R. Garcia Donnell's Collection.*)

—— (— —). — Scherma : Parte generale.   1 vol.⎫
         „   Teoria e pratica della ⎬ In the Press.
                 scherma.   2 vols.⎪
         „   Arte schermistica supe-⎪
                 riore.   1 vol.⎭
         „   L'opera intiera.

VITI (Giovanni Battista). — *TRIBOLATI (J.).* — 1877.

VIZANI (Angelo) [Bologna]. — Trattato dello schermo, nel quale discorre intorno all' eccellenza dell' armi et delle lettere et intorno all' offesa et difesa. 2nd edition. All' illustrissimo signore, il sig. conte Pirro Malvezzi. 4°. 1588. *Bologna:* Gio. Rossi. (See *Viggiani,* 1575.)

> [*The text is slightly altered from the 1st edition, and a portrait of the author added to the plates, with a new title-page and dedication by Cavalcabo.*]
> (*In the British Museum* [7905. bbb. 36.]*, and Bodleian Library.*)

—— (—). — Tratto dello schermo, nel quale discorre intorno all' offesa et difesa. 4°. 1688. *Bologna.*

> [*9 copperplates.*]

VIZÉ (Donneau). — Les nouvelles galantes, comiques et tragiques. 3 vols. 12°. 1669.

> [*Le duel.*]

VIZETELLY (Ernest A.). — The True Story of the Chevalier D'Éon: Man, Woman, and Diplomatist. 8°. 1895. *London:* Tylston, Edwards & Marsden.

> [*With important illustrations after Cosway, Angelica Kauffmann, and others.*
> "We are not quite sure that the work was really worth the doing, but at any rate Mr. Vizetelly's interesting and painstaking volume has settled once and for ever the vexed question of the sex of the Chevalier D'Éon, one of the strangest episodes of the curious and crooked diplomacy of Louis XV. of France. After reading the volume carefully, one can only wonder that there should ever have been any uncertainty on the matter at all. Mr. Vizetelly has traced with exceeding care the whole course of the Chevalier's career, from his birth at Tonnerre, when he was christened as a boy, to his death, which took place after he had for some years masqueraded as a woman. The inquiry into D'Éon's experience and life in Russia has been very thoroughly carried out, and the portrait which is given of the Russian Court and its perpetual intrigues at that time almost possesses a historic value. The very curious and tortuous episode of Louis' projected invasion of England is of great importance to the study of the relations between France and England at that time, and the glimpses we get, not only of the diplomatic methods, but of society on both sides of the Channel, is extremely interesting, and sometimes diverting. All the same, it appears to be quite clear that D'Éon not only had considerable natural abilities, but also that he met with great success in his diplomatic functions, so that his altered behaviour at the turning-point of his fortunes, and before he assumed the female habit, is not so easy to pardon as it is to account for. As we have already remarked, the task is hardly worth the time and trouble devoted to it, but Mr. Vizetelly has certainly accomplished it with final completeness.*]

It only remains to add that the get-up of the book is equally satisfactory, paper and print are alike excellent ; while, owing to the kind assistance of Mr. Joseph Grego, the well-known authority on French and English engravings of that period, Mr. Vizetelly has been able to include several rare prints which are almost unique ; at the same time the reproductions are marked by admirable technical finish."—" The Christmas Bookseller," 1895.]

VOET (PAULUS). — De duellis licitis et illicitis liber singularis. 12º. 1646. *Ultrajecti.*

(*In the British Museum.* 882. a. 16. (1.))

—— (—). — De duellis, ex omni jure decisis casibus liber singularis. 12º. 1658. *Ultrajecti.*

[*Editione iterata, auctus et emendatus.*]
(*In the British Museum.* 500. a. 17.)

VOLPINI (C.) [Colonnello]. — Manuale de Cavallo del Ten.   8º. 1891. *Milano :* U. Hoepli.

[*Con illustrazioni e 8 tavole.*]

VOLTAIRE. — Le siècle de Louis XIV. Œuvres complètes. 1785. *Basle.*

[Tom. **XXI.** p. 205, chap. xxix., *refers to the introduction of the bayonet in the French army.*]

VOM FELS ZUM MEER (Periodical).   8º.   *Stuttgart.*
[1891.   Heft I.   *" On Duelling."   By E. Eckstein.*]

VON WEST NACH OST (Periodical).   *Tokio.*
[*Contains an article by Dr. Mori, a Japanese gentleman, on the forms of duelling in vogue in former times in Japan.   "The Times" (Periodical), London,* 1890 (*September* 27), *reviews this article, and gives extracts therefrom.*]

VORSCHRIFTEN ÜBER DEN BAJONET - FECHTUNTER-RICHT für den Grossh. Badenschen Truppen.   1841.   *Karlsruhe :* Gutsch u. Rupp.

[6 *folding plates.*]
(*In Captain Hutton's Collection.*)

VORSCHRIFTEN FÜR DEN UNTERRICHT IM BAYONNET-FECHTEN der königl. Bayerschen Infanterie.   32º.   1843. *Amberg.*

VORSCHRIFTEN FÜR DEN UNTERRICHT IM FECHTEN und Voltigiren der königl. Bayerschen Kavallerie. 16°. 1845. *Straubing :* Schorner.

VORSCHRIFTEN ZUM GEWEHRFECHTEN. 8°. 1854. *Schwerin.*

VORSCHRIFTEN ÜBER DAS BAJONETTFECHTEN der Infanterie. Gr. 8°. 1876. *Berlin :* Mittler u. Sohn.

[10 *figures, in text.*] (*In Captain Hutton's Collection.*)

VORSCHRIFTEN FÜR DAS BAJONETTFECHTEN der Infanterie. Gr. 8°. 1882. *Berlin :* Mittler u. Sohn.

VORSCHRIFTEN FÜR DAS HIEBFECHTEN. Gr. 8°. 1884. *Berlin :* Mittler u. Sohn.

[35 *pages.*]

VORSCHRIFTEN FÜR DAS STOSSFECHTEN. Gr. 8°. 1884. *Berlin :* Mittler u. Sohn.

[34 *pages.*]

VORSCHRIFTEN ÜBER DAS BAJONETTFECHTEN.

[Heft. V. 25 *pages.*
Reported in catalogue No. 130, 1888, issued by A. Bielefeld, Karlsruhe.]

VOS (W. DE) en **HEYLUS** (C. G.). — Over de tweegevechten. 1805. *Utrecht.*

VULSON DE LA COLOMBIÈRE.—COLOMBIÈRE.

WAITE (JOHN MUSGRAVE) [Professor of Fencing, late 2nd Life Guards]. — Lessons in Sabre, Singlestick, Sabre and Bayonet and Sword Feats; or, How to Use a Cut and Thrust Sword. 8°. 1880. *London :* Weldon & Co.

[*With 34 illustrations.*] (*In Captain Hutton's Collection.*]

—— (— —). — Sword and Bayonet Exercise. [N.D.]

WALDERSEE (OBERST GRAF VON). — *ERSTE* Anleitung. —1850.

WALFORD (E.). — *CASSELL'S* Old and New London.

WALKER (DONALD). — Defensive Exercises. 8°. 1840. *London :* Thomas Hurst.

[*Figures, in the text.*] (*In Captain Hutton's Collection.*)
[*New edition. Containing Fencing, the Broadsword, &c. The only work,*

apparently, in which the rules of this now obsolete single-stick play ("back-swording") are set forth systematically. With 100 woodcut illustrations. 12°. 1842. London : H. Bohn.]

WALKER (John). — *GENTLEMAN'S* Magazine.

WALLENSTEIN (J. de). —*NORTH AMERICAN* Review.

WALLER (Max). — *DESMEDT (E.)*. — 1888.

WALLHAUSEN (Jean Jacques de) [Johann Jacobi *of Wall-hausen*]. — L'Art militaire pour l'infanterie, auquel est monstré : Le maniement du mousquet et de la pique, un chascun en particulier. L'exercice d'une compagnie d'infanterie toute parfaite. Belles et nouvelles ordonnances de batailles d'une compagnie et d'un régimen tout entier d'infanterie. La discipline militaire de l'infanterie, selon la nature de la vraye science militaire. Le tout représenté par belles figures gravées en cuivre, pratique, et descrit en language allemand, par Jean Jacques de Wallhausen, et traduit nouvellement en françois. Folio. 1615. *Oppenheim.* (Imprimé a *Franckeu*, par Uldrick Balck.)

[*Avec 35 plaques.*
L'épitre dédicatoire à Mgr. Maurice de Nassau, est daté Oppenheim ce 30 d'Aoust 1615, et signé Jean-Théodore de Bry.]

WALLHAUSEN (J. J. von). — Künstliche Picquen Handlung Darinnen Schrifftlich und mit Figuren dieser adelichen Exercisiren angewiesen und gelernt wird. Folio. 1617. *Hanover.*
[*15 pages. Engraved title-page.*] (*In the British Museum.* 8824. h. 7.)

[**WALSH** (J. H.)]. — *"STONEHENGE."* — 1863.

WALTHER (F. A.). — Critic über den studentischen Zweikampf. 8°. 1885. *Berlin :* W. Stute.
[*7 pages.*]

WARD (Robert) [Gentleman and Commander]. — Animadversions of Warre, or a Militarie Magazine of the truest rules and ablest instructions for the managing of Warre. In two bookes. Folio. 1639. *London.*
[Chapter lxxvii. pp. 222–225. *Contains the Pike Drill as performed by "The Buffs" at the Military Tournament, Agricultural Hall, London,* 1895.] (*In the British Museum.* 718. i. 19.)

WARE (H.) [Junior]. — Sermon on Duelling.   1838.

(In the New York State Library, U.S.A.)

WARREN (S.). — *BLACKWOOD'S* Magazine.

WASSMANNSDORFF (DR. KARL) [Heidelberg]. — Anleitung zum Gewehrfechten.   Den deutschen Turnvereinen gewidmet.   8°. 1864.   *Leipzig : Keil.*

[*6 figures.*]

—— (—. —). — Sechs Fechtschulen (d. i. Schau- und Preis-fechten) der Marxbrüder* und Federfechter aus den Jahren 1573 bis 1614; Nürnberger Fechtschulreime v. J. 1579 und Rösener's Gedicht: Ehrentitel und Lobspruch der Fechtkunst v. J. 1589. Eine Vorarbeit zu einer Geschichte der Marxbrüder und Feder-fechter.   8°.   1870.   *Heidelberg : Karl Groos.*

[* *In Germany flourished from the fifteenth to the end of the sixteenth cen-turies a powerful and imperially favoured guild, the Marxbrüder, or Associates of St. Marcus of Löwenberg, with its headquarters at Frankfort, and influential branches in various German towns.*]

—— (—. —). — Die Leibesüngen in den Philanthropinen zu Dessau, Marschlins, Heidesheim und Schnepfenthal.   8°.   1870. *Heidelberg : K. Groos.*

[*Sonderabdruck aus der d. Turnzeitung.*]

—— (—. —). — Die Ringkunst des deutschen Mittelalters, mit 119 Ringerpaaren von Albrecht Dürer.   8°.   1870.   *Leipzig :* Priber.

—— (—. —). — Das um das Jahr 1500 gedruckte erste deutsche Turnbuch.   Mit Zusätzen aus deutschen Fechthandschriften und 17 Zeichnungen von Albrecht Dürer.   8°.   1871.   *Heidelberg :* Karl Groos.

(In Mr. J. R. Garcia Donnell's Collection.)

—— (—. —). — Aufschlüsse über Fechthandschriften und ged-ruckte Fechtbücher des 16. und 17. Jahrhunderts in einer Besprechung von G. Hergsell: "Talhoffers Fechtbuch aus dem Jahre 1467."   8°. 1887.   *Berlin : Gaertner.*

[*Reprinted from the " Berliner Monatsschrift für das Turnwesen."*]
(In Mr. J. R. Garcia Donnell's Collection.)

WASSMANNSDORFF (DR. KARL). — Turnen und Fechten in früheren Jahrhunderten. Aufsätze zur Geschichte der deutschen Leibesübungen aus der Festschrift f. das 7. deutsche Turnfest zu München, 1889. Gr. 8°. 1890. *Heidelberg :* K. Groos.

[*Mit 7 Abbildungen und 1 Tafeln.*]

—— (—. —). — *AUERSWALD (F. von).* — 1869.

—— (—. —). — *DURER (A.).* — [1500.]

—— (—. —). — *EISELEN (E. W. B.).* — 1882.

—— (—. —). — *MONATSSCHRIFT* für das Turnwesen. —1892.

—— (—. —). — *PETTER (N.).* —1887.

—— (—. —). — *TURN-ZEITUNG (Deut.).* — 1884.

WATTS (H. E.). — The Ingenious Gentleman Don Quixote of La Mancha. 4°. 1888.

[Vol. IV. p. 194. *"Espada del Perrillo."*]

WATTS (ISAAC) [D.D.]. — A Defence against the Temptation to Self-Murther. . . . Together with some Reflections on Excess in Strong Liquors, Duelling, and other practices akin to this heinous sin. 12°. 1726. *London.*

(*In the British Museum.* 4408. aaa. 20.)

WAYNE (HENRY E.) [Brevet-Major, U.S. Army]. — The Sword Exercise arranged for Military Instruction. Published by authority of the War Department. 8°. 1850. *Washington :* Printed by Gideon & Co.

[23 plates.
In two parts, with separate title-pages :—
1. *Fencing with the Small Sword, arranged for instruction in squads or classes.* 1849. Washington. 62 pages. 11 plates.
2. *Exercises for the Broadsword, Sabre, Cut and Thrust, and Stick.* 1849. Washington. 43 pages. 12 plates.]

WECK (C. R. A.). — Bajonett-Fechtinstruction für die Königlich Preussische Infanterie. 8°. 1836. *Mainz :* F. Kupferberg.

[5 plates, containing 46 figures.] (*In Captain Hutton's Collection.*)

WEEKS (S. B.). — *MAGAZINE* of American History.

WEEMS. — God's Revenge. 1818.

[*Duelling.*] (*In New York State Library,* U.S.A.)

[**WEICKARD** (W. A.)]. — Point d'Honneur und dergleichen vom Duell, eine Beilage zum philosophischen Arzt. 8°. 1787. *Frankfurt :* Fleischer.

WEILAND (B.). — Anleitung zum Betriebe d. Stoss- und Hiebfechtens. Für Militärschulen und Turnanstalten, wie auch zum Selbstunterricht für Liebhaber der Fechtkunst zusammengestellt und bearbeitet. 24°. 1879. *Wiesbaden :* Limbarth.

—— (—.). — Praktisches Handbuch der Fechtkunst für Truppenschulen, Militärbildungsanstalten, Turnschulen und Fechtvereine, sowie Freunde und Liebhaber der Fechtkunst. Gr. 8°. 1885. *Wiesbaden :* R. Bechtold & Comp.

[*211 pages.*]

WEINBERGER (Anton). — *SPORT* (*Der*). — 1880.

WEIS (Giuseppe). — Istruzione sulla scherma a cavallo. 1829. *Napoli.*

—— (—). — Scherma della baionetta. 4°. 1830. *Napoli.*

WEISCHNER (C. F.). — Exercices dans les salles d'armes. 4°. 1752. *Weimar.*

—— (—. —.). — Die Ritterliche Geschicklichkeit im Fechten durch ungezwungene Stellungen. 4°. 1765. *Weimar :* Hoffmann.

[*Mit Titelkupfer und 30 Kupfertafeln, G. C. Schmidt.*]
(*In Captain Hutton's Collection.*)

—— (—. —.). — *HUTTON* (*A.*). — 1892.

WEISCHNER (S.) [Hauptmann]. — Uebungen auf den fürstlichen Sächsischen Hof und Fechtboden zu Weimar. Verb. u. verm. Auflage. 8°. 1764. *Weimar :* Hoffmann.

[*2te Auflage, 1765.*]

WEISKE (Jul.). — Commentatio de L. II. ad. Leg. Jul. majestatis, qua nihil inter perduellionem et crimen majestatis interesse probatur. 8°. 1833. *Leipsiæ :* Serig.

WEOBLY (Charles). — *MEDLAND* (*W. M.*). — 1808.

WERNER (J. A. L.). — Versuch einer theoretischen Anweisung zur Fechtkunst im Hiebe. 4°. 1824. *Leipzig :* Lehnhold.

[*20 copperplates.*]

WERNER (J. A. L.). — Die ganze Gymnastik. Gr. 8°. 1833. *Meissen :* Goedsche.

> [Page 236. *Fechten auf Hieb.*
> „   257. *Fechten auf Stoss.*]

—— (—. —. —.). — Militär-Gymnastik. 8°. 1840. *Dresden :* Arnold'sche Buchhandlung.

—— (—. —. —.). — Militär-Gymnastik oder zweckmässige Leibeübungen, wie sie der Soldat jeder Truppengattung in seinem militärischen Berufsleben unbedingt nothwendig hat. 2te Auflage. 8°. 1844. *Dresden :* Arnold'sche B.

> [8 *copperplates and* 400 *figures in text.*]

—— (—. —. —.). — Militär-Gymnastik, &c. Gr. 8°. 1850. *Leipzig :* Arnold.

WEST (R.). — *ATLANTIC* Monthly (The).

WESTERN ANTIQUARY (The). — (Periodical.) *Plymouth.*

> [Vol. I. pp. 73, 188. *"Duel, West Country."*
> „   VI. p. 49. *"Duel at Plymouth,* 1665."]

WESTERN LAW JOURNAL (Periodical). *Cincinnati.*

> [Vol. IV. p. 433. *"How Duelling is regarded at Common Law. Extracts from tract of Granville Sharp."*]

WESTERN MONTHLY REVIEW (Periodical). *Cincinnati.*

> [Vol. I. p. 543. *"Duelling."*]

WESTMINSTER BUDGET (The). — (Periodical.) *London.*

> [1893. *November* 17. *" The Polite Art of Fence." Portrait of Monsieur Bertrand.*]

WESTMINSTER REVIEW (Periodical). 8°. *London.*

> [Vol. IV. p. 20. *"British Code of Duelling."*]

WHITE (Rev. Hugh). — Duelling. 8°. 1843. *Dublin.*

(*In the Royal United Service Institution Library, Whitehall, London.* 8°. Pamphlets, 2nd Series, Vol. XL.)

WHITELOCK (James). — *ASHMOLEAN* MSS.

> [856. 149.]

—— (—). — *CODICUM* MSS.

—— (—). — *COTTONIAN* MSS.

> [*Tib. C. i. B.* 27. (205.)]

WHITELOCK (James). — Of the Antiquity, Use, and Ceremony of Combats in England.

[*Harleian MSS.*, Vol. III. p. 122. cod. 4176. art. 2.]

WIDVILE (Antony) [Lord Scales]. — An Account of the Duel between Antoine, Bastard of Burgundy, and Anthony Widvile, Lord Scales, fought at Smithfield in 1467, in the presence of Henry IV.

[*MS. In the British Museum.* 30,542. *f.* 146.]

WIELAND (Jh.). — Anleitung zum Gebrauch des Bajonets oder kurzer Unterricht des Wesentlichsten dieser Fechtkunst. 8°. 1826. *Basel :* Schweighäuser.

[*This work was issued in French, same date, size, and publisher.*]

WIESINGER (Dr. Alb.). — Das Duell vor dem Richterstuhle der Religion, der Moral, des Rechtes und der Geschichte. Gr. 8°. 1884. *Graz, Styria.*

[xii *and* 184 *pages.*]

WIESINGER (J.). — " Herr, wärest Du dagewesen, unser Bruder wäre nich gestorben." Rede, bei der Beerdigung des im Zweikampfe gefallenen K. Hauptmann's und Compagniechefs Herrn Otto Emmerich, gehalten in Würzburg am 21. November 1882. 2te Auflage. 8°. 1882. *Würzburg :* Stuber.

WILBERFORCE (William) [the Philanthropist]. — A Practical View of the Prevailing Religious System of Professed Christians, &c. 8°. 1797. *London.*

[Chapter iv., Section 3. *Duelling.*] (*In the British Museum.* 13. *a.* 13.)

WILD-QUEISNER (Rob.). — Das Duell. Ein Wort zur Beleuchtung desselben nach Ursprung, Form, Zweck und Nothwendigkeit für den Civil- und Militairstand. Gr. 8°. 1887. *Berlin :* v. Decker.

[23 *pages.*]

WILKINSON (Henry) [M.R.A.S., Gunmaker]. — Observations on Swords, addressed to officers and civilians, but especially to those who prefer a good sword to a bad one. 3rd edition. 12°. 1846. *London :* [The Author.]

[8*th edition.* 12°. 1862. London. 24 *pages.*]

WILKINSON (HENRY). — Observations on Muskets, Rifles, and Projectiles. 12°. [N.D.] *London.*

WILLARDS (COMTE DE NORD). — Essai sur l'art des armes, opuscule dédié au Maréchal de Turenne. 8°. 1672. *Paris :* Seneuse.

WILLIAMS (J. M.) [Judge]. — Charge—Duelling. 1838.
(In New York State Library, U.S.A.)

WILLS (C. J.). — *PALL MALL* Magazine. — 1896. February.

WILL (G. A.). — Historisch-diplomatisches Magazin für das Vaterland. 8°. 1780. *Nuremberg.*
[Bd. II. p. 513. *"Fechtschulen zu Nürnberg."* — Also p. 264. *"Marxbrüder."*]

WINDSOR MAGAZINE (The). — (Monthly Periodical.) 8°. *London :* Ward, Lock & Bowden, Ltd.
[1895. *April. "Famous Swords of Modern Warriors." (Sketches and descriptions of the famous swords in the possession of the Duke of Cambridge, General Lord Roberts, Lord Methuen, Sir Archibald Alison, Sir Evelyn Wood, and others, by Ernest W. Low. By special permission of their owners.) Illustrated by Miss Ada Clegg, Miss Low, and from photographs.*
1896. *May. The Canterbury Riding Establishment. Illustrations — "Ready for the Bayonet," "Lance Exercise," "Sword Exercise."*]

WINN (A. R. G.). — *ALLANSON-WINN* (R. G.). — 1890.

WINTGENS (W.). — Het duel. Beschouwingen meêgedeeld naar aanleidung van de uitdaging van Mr. W. Wintgens door Mr. H. J. A. Raedt van Oldenbarnvelt. 8°. 1865. *Utrecht.*
(In the British Museum. 8425. b. 52. (8.))

WINTZLEBEN (JONAS THOMSEN VON) [Hans Kongl. Majits til Danmark og Norgen. bestallter Premier-Lieutenant og Guarnisons-Fegtmester].—Den Adelige Fegte-Kunst i et kort Begreb : Eller Underviüsning i Stød og Hug, züret med behørige Figurer. 12°. 1756. *Kiøbenhavn :* T. L. Borup.
[*Frontispiece and 23 plates, containing 45 figures, out of the text.*]
(In Captain Hutton's Collection.)

WITZLEBEN (A. VON). — Deutschlands Militär. - Literatur im letzten Jahrzehent. 8°. 1850. *Berlin :* Mittler.
[Pages 78-79. *"Fechtkunst."*]

WODESTOKE (Thomas of) [Conestable of England, and uncle to Kyng Richard (the Second)]. — *ASHMOLEAN* MSS.
> [856. 383.]

WOGDEN. — *STANZAS* on Duelling. — 1783.

WOLFF (F. A.). —Specimen philosophium de duello.   1786. *Halle.*

WOLLEB. — Duell. 4°. 1629. *Basel.*

WOLLEY (C. Phillips). — *ALLANSON-WINN* (R. G.). — 1890.

WORCESTER (Earl of). — *TIPTOFT* (*John*).

WORLD (Periodical). *London.*
> [1753. *Nov.* 22. No. 47. *A remarkable duel in Moorfields.*
> 1755. *Feb.* 27. No. 113. *Duel between a man and a dog.*]

WORMS (Emile). — Les attentats à l'honneur : diffamation, injures, outrages, adultère, duel, lois sur la presse, etc. 8°. 1890. *Paris :* Perrin et Cie.
> [332 *pages.*]

WRIGHT (Francis Vere). — The Broadsword as taught by the celebrated Italian Masters Masiello and Ciullini of Florence. 8°. 1889. *London :* W. H. Allen & Co.
> (*In Captain Hutton's Collection.*)

WRIGHT (T.) and **HALLIWELL** (J. O.). — Reliquiæ antiquæ. 8°. 1845. *London.*
> [Vol. I. p. 308, *contain, a poem* "On Fencing with Two-handed Sword," *from Harleian MS.* 3542, *of the fifteenth century, in the British Museum.*]

WYATT (Sir M. D.). — Metal Work and its Artistic Design. Folio. 1852. *London.*
> [50 *plates.* (*Italian Silver Dagger, cinque cento.*)]

WYLDE (Zachary). — The English Master of Defence, or the Gentleman's Al-a-Mode Accomplishment. Containing the True Art of Single-Rapier or Small-Sword, withal the curious Parres and many more than the vulgar Terms of Art plainly exprest; with the names of every particular Pass and the true performance thereof ; withal the exquisite Ways of Disarming and Enclosing, and all the Guards at Broad-Sword and Quarter-Staff, perfectly demonstrated ;

shewing how the Blows, Strokes, Chops, Thro's, Flirts, Slips, and Darts are perform'd; with the True Method of Travesing. 8°. 1711. *York:* Printed by John White, for the author.

> (*In the British Museum.* C. 45. b. 2. [*This copy has an autograph dedication by the author.*])

XIMENÈS (GÉRONIMO). — Dialogo de la verdadera honor.

YÑIGUEZ (EUSEBIO). — Ofensas y desafíos. Recopilación de las leyes que rigen en el duelo, y causas originales de este, etc. 8°. 1890. *Madrid.*

> [190 *pages.*]

YORK (RICHARD, DUKE OF). — Account of Tournament on Marriage of.

> [*Harleian MSS.*, Vol. I. p. 17. cod. 69. art. 1-3.]

YOUNG (A.). — *OVERLAND* Monthly.

YOUNG (THE) DUELLISTS; or, The Affair of Honour. 8°. 1837. *London.*

YOUNG (WILLIAM) [Maître d'armes]. — The Fencer's Manual, being a series of Introductory Lessons to the Art of Fence. 8°. 1840. *Chatham:* James Burrill.

> [*With lithographic plates illustrative of the principal parades.*]
> (*In Captain Hutton's Collection.*)

ZASCHE (TH.). — *SPORT* (*Der*). —1880.

ZEA (DON FAUSTINO). — Titulo de teniente de maestro mayor de la ciencia de destreza de las armas á favor del Serenisimo Señor Don Francisco de Paula Antonio de Borbon. MS. Folio. 1847. *Madrid.*

ZEA (F. GÁLVEZ DE). — *GÁLVEZ DE ZEA* (*F.*). — 1855.

ZEIT UND STREIT-FRAGEN (DEUTSCHE). — *THÜMMEL* (*C.*). — 1887.

ZERSTREUTE FECHTART (DIE) der K. K. Cavallerie. Dargestellt nach den allerhöchsten Bestimmungen von einem K. K. Officier. 16°. 1861. *Wien:* Pichler's Witwe und Sohn.

ZETER (JACQUES DE). — *GIGANTI* (*N.*). — 1619.

ZILETTUS. — Tractatus universi juris. Folio. 1584. *Venetiis.*

[Tomus XII. pp. 284–293.　CASTILLO (JACOBI DE) [*alias de Villa Sanctæ*].
　　　　　　　　　　　　　　— *De duello.*
　　„　　pp. 309–313.　FERRETTI (JVLII) [*Rauennatis*]. — *De duello.*
　　„　　pp. 281–284.　LIGNANO (JOANNIS). — *De duello.*
　　„　　pp. 313–321.　MASS.E (ANTONIO). — *Gallesii civis Romani
　　　　　　　　　　　　　contra vsum duelli.*]
　　　　(*In the British Museum.*　499. *g.* 6.)

ZWANZIGSTE (DAS) JAHRHUNDERT (Periodical).　*Berlin.*

[1891.　*December* 15.　"*The Duelling Question,*" by *O. Beta.*]

ZWEIKAMPF EICHLER - BLUM. — Stenographischer Bericht über die Verhandlungen des Schwurgerichts.　1. und 2. Auflage. 8°.　1889.　*Berlin:* Reinecke.

ZWEIKAMPF (GEDANKEN ÜBER DEN), von einem Offizier. 8°.　1787.

[A Marxbrüder instructing a Pupil.　(Meyer (J.).　1570.)]

(From the illustration used by Mr. Egerton Castle in "Schools and Masters of Fence.")

338

INDEX

[NOTE.—Authors' names, words, or letters printed in *ITALIC CAPITALS* refer to the name, word, or letter under which the full entry will be found in the Bibliography.]

ARMES et ARMURES. — Bruxelles Musée Catalogue. *VINKEROY* (E. van).
BACK-SWORD. — [ENGLISH]—
　　——　　　1714.　*HOPE* (W.).
　　——　　　1738.　*MILLER* (J.).
　　——　　　1747.　*GODFREY* (J.).
　　——　　　1884.　*SATURDAY* Review. January 19.
　　——　　　1885.　*SPORTS* (A New Book of).
　　——　　　1889.　*HUTTON* (A.). "Cold Steel."
　　——　　　　"　　*ALL* the Year Round, 2nd Series, Vol. **XXXVIII.** p. 298.
BACK-SWORDING. — *WALKER* (D.).　1840.
BASTÓN. — *See* SINGLE-STICK [SPANISH].
BASTONE. — *See* SINGLE-STICK [ITALIAN].
BAYONET FENCING and BAYONET EXERCISE.* — [ENGLISH]—
　　——　　　1711.　*GUN* and Bayonet Drill. MS.
　　——　　　1735.　*FEUQUIÈRE* (Marquis de).
　　——　　　1805.　*GORDON* (A.).
　　——　　　1829.　*ANGELO.*
　　——　　　1853.　*BURTON* (R. F.).
　　——　　　1861.　*KELTON* (Lieutenant).
　　——　　　　"　　*M'CLELLAN* (G. B.).
　　——　　1865–1880.　*NATION* (The).
　　——　　　1867.　*HUTTON* (A.).
　　——　　　1868.　*MACLAREN* (A.).
　　——　　　1880.　*INFANTRY* Sword.
　　——　　　1882.　*HUTTON* (A.).
　　——　　　1884.　*ELLIOTT* (W. J.).
　　——　　　1885.　*MANUAL* Exercises.
　　——　　　1889.　*FOX* (G. M.).

---

* The short dagger fixed at the end of firearms, said to have been invented at Bayonne, in France, about 1647, 1670, or 1690. It was used at Killiecrankie in 1689, and at Marsaglia by the French in 1693, "with great success against the enemy, unprepared for the encounter with so formidable a novelty." The ring-bayonet was adopted by the British, 24th September 1693.

INDEX

INDEX

341

---

* The broadsword was forbidden to be worn in Edinburgh in 1724.

---

* Dagger, a word of Keltic origin : *dag* or *dager*, a dagger.　The words *dag*, for dagger, and *daggen*, to stab, occur in old Dutch.

INDEX

INDEX

355

DUELLING.—[ENGLISH] *(continued)*—

—— between Chanzy's (General) Orderly and an Algerian Editor. *TIMES* (The). 1878.

—— —— Chalmer and Captain Berkeley. *TIMES* (The). 1837.

—— —— Chatelier (Captain le) and M. Percher, "Harry Alis." *SUN* (The). March 6, 1895.

—— —— Chauvigny (M. de) and Mr. Lameth, 1792. *HAYDN*. 1892.

—— —— Chazel (Baron) and M. Delaert. *TIMES* (The). 1865.

—— —— Cheatham (P. H.) and Mr. John Wately, prominent Carolina planters. *SUNDAY* Sun. May 24, 1891.

—— —— Christie and Scott. *CASSELL'S* London. 1875.

—— —— Ditto, 1821. *HAYDN*. 1892.

—— —— Cilley and Graves. *TIMES* (The). 1838. March 27. May 24.

—— —— Claparede (Viscount Hallez) and Count de Beaumont. *TIMES* (The). 1869.

—— —— Clark (Captain E.), R.N., and Captain T. Innes, R.N. *TRIAL* of. 1750.

—— —— Clarke (Mr.) and George Payne, 1810. *HAYDN*. 1892.

—— —— Clay (Lieutenant) and Lieutenant Davies. *TIMES* (The). 1836.

—— —— —— and Turner. *TIMES* (The). 1849.

—— —— Clemenceau and Poussargue. *TIMES* (The). 1871.

—— —— —— and Foucher. *TIMES* (The). 1887.

—— —— —— and Maurel. *TIMES* (The). 1888.

—— —— Coetlogon (M. G. de) and M. A. de Bors. *TIMES* (The). 1866.

—— —— Coislin (Marquis de) and M. Testelin. *TIMES* (The). 1850.

—— —— Colt (Sir H.) and Beau Fielding. *LARWOOD* (J.). 1871.

—— —— Compiègne (Marquis de) and Mr. Mayer. *TIMES* (The). 1877.

—— —— Conroy (Lieutenant) and Lieutenant Hindes, 1817. *HAYDN*. 1892.

—— —— Contarini (Signor) and Marquis Dosi. *PALL* Mall Gazette. November 11, 1891.

—— —— Cooley (ex-Judge) and R. Barnwell Rhett. *TIMES* (The). 1873.

—— —— Costello and Baker. *TIMES* (The). 1837.

—— —— Crepu and Cerferr. *TIMES* (The). 1835.

—— —— Curran (Mr.) and Major Hobart, 1790. *HAYDN*. 1892.

—— —— Curtis (Dr.) and M. Cortereal. *TIMES* (The). 1875.

—— —— Dacosta (Lieutenant) and Mr. Calder. *TIMES* (The). 1843.

—— —— Daintree and Lindsell. *TIMES* (The). 1836.

—— —— Dalmatia (The Marquis of) and Colonel de Bricqueville. *TIMES* (The). 1833.

—— —— Darlton (Mr.) and Captain Bargewell. *TIMES* (The). 1839.

—— —— Davies (Ensign) and Lieutenant Joy. *TIMES* (The). 1836.

—— —— Davil (General) and Williams. *TIMES* (The). 1884.

—— —— Debuys (General) and Mr. Richardson. *TIMES* (The). 1844.

INDEX

INDEX

INDEX

DUELLING.—[ENGLISH] (continued)—

—— —— between Lützow (Count Francis) and Count Deym, the Austro-Hungarian Ambassador in London. *PALL* Mall Gazette. 1891.

—— —— Ditto. *STANDARD* (The). 1891.

—— —— Luzzatto and De Paz. *TIMES* (The). 1885.

—— —— Lynch and Kelly. *TIMES* (The). 1841.

—— —— —— (Owen) and Kelly (Malachy). *TIMES* (The). 1842.

—— —— M'Donald and Texas. *TIMES* (The). 1875.

—— —— M'Keon (Mr.) and G. N. Reynolds, 1788. *HAYDN*. 1892.

—— —— M'Lacrosse and M. Garnier de Cassagnac. *TIMES* (The). 1842.

—— —— Macartney (Lord) and Major - General Stuart, 1786. *HAYDN*. 1892.

—— —— Maccabe and Pomroi. *TIMES* (The). 1835.

—— —— Macduff (Mr.) and Mr. Prince, 1790. *HAYDN*. 1892.

—— —— Macleod (Captain) and Mr. Bennett. *TIMES* (The). 1842.

—— —— Macnamara and Colonel Montgomery, 1803. *HAYDN*. 1892.

—— —— Macpherson and Major Brown. *LARWOOD* (J.). 1871.

—— —— Madoz and Mora. *TIMES* (The). 1851.

—— —— Magee (John) and Andrew Morrow. *TIMES* (The). 1836.

—— —— Maginn (Dr.) and Mr. Berkeley. *CASSELL'S* London. 1875.

—— —— Magnier and Reinach. *TIMES* (The). 1887.

—— —— Maguire (Mr. E.) and Lieutenant Blundell, 1813. *HAYDN*. 1892.

—— —— Maille (M. M. de) and Loisant. *TIMES* (The). 1878.

—— —— Malato and Nicolosi. *TIMES* (The). 1863.

—— —— Malcolmson (Dr.) and Captain Urquhart. *TIMES* (The). 1835.

—— —— Mallet and Moreau. *TIMES* (The). 1875.

—— —— Maltby and Captain Jackson. *TIMES* (The). 1832.

—— —— Mancini (Captain) and M. Benati. *TIMES* (The). 1875.

—— —— Manguin and Viennett. *TIMES* (The). 1831.

—— —— Manteuffel (General) and Mr. Tiverton. *TIMES* (The). 1861.

—— —— Manuel (M.) and Mr. Beaumont, 1821. *HAYDN*. 1892.

—— —— Margo and a renegade Frenchman. *TIMES* (The). 1841.

—— —— Mario and Levi. *TIMES* (The). 1881.

—— —— Markham (Captain) and Colonel M'Donald. *TIMES* (The). 1832.

—— —— Marsden (Mark) and Colonel Patterson. *TIMES* (The). 1841.

—— —— Marson and M'Carty. *HARPER'S* New Monthly Magazine. Vol. XVI. p. 473.

—— —— Martin (S.) and Mr. Wilkes, M.P., 1763. *HAYDN*. 1892.

—— —— Maugny (M. de) and M. de Beaumont. *TIMES* (The). 1869.

—— —— Maxwell (Mr.) and Colonel Gurwood. *TIMES* (The). 1843.

—— —— Mayer and Humbert. *TIMES* (The). 1880.

—— —— Mayo and Wakey. *TIMES* (The). 1840.

INDEX

DUELLING.—[ENGLISH] (*continued*)—
—— between Raystock and Wood. *TIMES* (The). 1837.
—— —— Reache (Gerville) and Souques. *TIMES* (The). 1892.
—— —— Reinach and Deroulede. *TIMES* (The). 1888. 1890.
—— —— Rey (Colonel) and Edmond Adam. *TIMES* (The). 1848.
—— —— Reynolds (Mr.) and Mr. O'Farrell. *TIMES* (The). 1832.
—— —— Richardel (M.) and M. de Laborde. *TIMES* (The). 1850.
—— —— Richards and Mannicks. *TIMES* (The). 1839.
—— —— R—d—n and Captain Steward. *LARWOOD* (J.). 1871.
—— —— Riehard and M. de Massas. *TIMES* (The). 1882.
—— —— Rillet (F.) and Ciceron. *TIMES* (The). 1890.
—— —— Robertson and Glashin. *TIMES* (The). 1834.
—— —— Rocha (General) and Antonia Gayon. *TIMES* (The). 1887.
—— —— Rochefort and Baroche. *TIMES* (The). 1868.
—— —— —— and Captain Fournier. *TIMES* (The). 1884.
—— —— —— (Henri) and Isaac. *PALL* Mall Gazette. 1891.
—— —— —— (—) and Koechlin. *TIMES* (The). 1880.
—— —— —— and Lissagaray. *TIMES* (The). 1889.
—— —— —— (Henri) and Marquis de Luçay. *PALL* Mall Gazette. 1891.
—— —— —— and Marouck. *TIMES* (The). 1887.
—— —— —— and Portalis. *TIMES* (The). 1886.
—— —— —— and Thiebaud. *TIMES* (The). 1890.
—— —— Rochefouchen (General Count de) and M. Delmas. *TIMES* (The). 1849.
—— —— Rochonczy and M. Gajary. *STANDARD* (The). August 15, 1891.
—— —— Rodda and Blavier. *TIMES* (The). 1833.
—— —— Roebuck, M.P., and Mr. Black, 1835. *HAYDN.* 1892.
—— —— Rogat and Richardet. *TIMES* (The). 1872.
—— —— Roigniot and Count Pairnett. *TIMES* (The). 1878.
—— —— Romans (M. de) and a Captain of Cavalry. *TIMES* (The). 1841.
—— —— Ropolo and Captain Gueritz. *TIMES* (The). 1853.
—— —— Rossi (Count) and Prince of Canino. *TIMES* (The). 1851.
—— —— Rothschild (E. de) and Marquis de Gouy. *TIMES* (The). 1890.
—— —— Rotours and St. Leger. *TIMES* (The). 1871.
—— —— Roulez and four, one after the other. *TIMES* (The). 1892.
—— —— Rousselle and Humbert. *TIMES* (The). 1890.
—— —— Rovigo (Marquis de) and Alderic de St. Pierre. *TIMES* (The). 1840.
—— —— —— (The Duke of) and M. Perregault. *TIMES* (The). 1845.
—— —— Rupperberg and M. de Lavelette. *TIMES* (The). 1845.
—— —— Rushout and Borthwick. *TIMES* (The). 1838.
—— —— Russell (Reginald) and M. de la Paeze. *TIMES* (The). 1869.
—— —— Ruthven (Edward) and Mr. Perrin. *TIMES* (The). 1835.
—— —— —— (Mr.) and Mr. Close, 1836. *HAYDN.* 1892.
—— —— —— (—.) and Mr. Scott, 1836. *HAYDN.* 1892.
—— —— Sackvill (Sir Edward) and Lord Bruce. *SACKVILL.* MS.

368

INDEX

DUELLING.—[ENGLISH] (*continued*)—

—— between Sagasto and Mantilla. *TIMES* (The). 1852.

—— —— St. John and Count Caraffiano. *TIMES* (The). 1835.

—— —— Salis (M. de) and Captain Duvernet. *TIMES* (The). 1838.

—— —— Sarkany (M.) and Editor of the *Hirlap. STANDARD* (The). September 14, 1891.

—— —— Saunders (General) and Judge Evans. *TIMES* (The). 1854.

—— —— Save and Clement Duvernois. *TIMES* (The). 1866.

—— —— Schlessinger and Ladd. *TIMES* (The). 1854.

—— —— Scholl and Dion. *TIMES* (The). 1884.

—— —— Secretan and Ruffy. *TIMES* (The). 1884.

—— —— Seller (Charles) and Colonel Rudruzzi. *TIMES* (The). 1891.

—— —— Seton (Mr.) and Lieutenant Hawkey. *TIMES* (The). 1845.

—— —— Shelburne (Earl) and Fullerton. *LARWOOD* (J.). 1871.

—— —— Sheridan and Mathews. *ALL* the Year Round. Series 2. Vol. XXXVIII. p. 546.

—— —— Ditto. *CASSELL'S* London. 1875.

—— —— Ditto. *LARWOOD* (J.). 1871.

—— —— Simon (Jules) and a Bonapartist Editor. *TIMES* (The). 1879.

—— —— —— (M. Charles) and M. Chironte. *PALL* Mall Gazette. July 24, 1891.

—— —— —— and Chironte. *TIMES* (The). 1891.

—— —— Simpson and Griffiths. *TIMES* (The). 1842.

—— —— Sligo (Marquis of) and Mr. Higgins. *TIMES* (The). 1850.

—— —— Smith (Captain) and Mr. O'Grady. 1830. *HAYDN.* 1892.

—— —— —— (Judge) and Mr. M'Clernand. *TIMES* (The). 1841.

—— —— Smythe (Hon. G.) and Colonel Romilly. *TIMES* (The). 1852.

—— —— *Soleil* (Editors of) and the *Pays. TIMES* (The). 1867.

—— —— Solms (Prince) and Count Wedel. *TIMES* (The). 1867.

—— —— Somers (Patrick) and Mr. Verdon. *TIMES* (The). 1850.

—— —— Sonnino and Indelli. *TIMES* (The). 1890.

—— —— Soubeyran (M. de) and M. Pereire. *TIMES* (The). 1877.

—— —— Soutza (Prince) and N. Ghika. 1873. *HAYDN.* 1892.

—— —— Soutzos (Prince) and Prince Ghika. *TIMES* (The). 1874.

—— —— Spoor and Wright. *TIMES* (The). 1842.

—— —— Stackpole (Captain) and Lieutenant Cecil. 1814. *HAYDN.* 1892.

—— —— Stanfield and Sir R. Cardington. *TIMES* (The). 1842.

—— —— Starke (J.) and Lieutenant Roberts. *TIMES* (The). 1838.

—— —— Steavenson and Surtees. *TIMES* (The). 1832.

—— —— Sternbach and Hohnstein. *TIMES* (The). 1864.

—— —— Stevens and Gerome. *TIMES* (The). 1861.

—— —— Stevenson and Carrick. *TIMES* (The). 1852.

—— —— Stewart (C.) and J. B. Coker. *TIMES* (The). 1854.

—— —— —— (Lieutenant) and Lieutenant Bagnal. 1812. *HAYDN.* 1892.

—— —— Storey (Mr.) and Mr. Matthias. 1833. *HAYDN.* 1892.

—— —— Stuart (Mr. J.) and Sir Alexander Boswell. 1822. *HAYDN.* 1892.

—— —— Suero (Marquis of) and M. Salamanca. *TIMES* (The). 1853.

INDEX

DUELLING. — [ENGLISH] (continued)—

—— Brighton, at. *TIMES* (The). 1843.
—— British code of. *CHAMBERS'S* Journal. Vol. XLIV. p. 305.
—— Ditto. *DENNIE'S* Portfolio. Vol. XXXIII. pp. 239, 431.
—— Ditto. *LITTELL'S* Museum. Vol. VII. p. 317.
—— Ditto. *LONDON* Magazine. Vol. XI. p. 198.
—— Ditto. *WESTMINSTER* Review. Vol. IV. p. 20.
—— Broadswords, with. *ALL* the Year Round. Series 2. Vol. XXXVIII. p. 298.
—— Budapest, at. *TIMES* (The). 1891.
—— California, in. *TIMES* (The). 1854. 1874.
—— *CAMELFORD* (Lord). 1804.
—— Canterbury barracks, in (Mock). *TIMES* (The). 1855.
—— Cardigan (Earl) and Captain Tuckett. *ALL* the Year Round. Series 3. Vol. II. p. 323.
—— Carolina (North), code in. *MAGAZINE* of American History. December 1891.
—— —— planters' duel. *SUNDAY* Times. May 24, 1891.
—— Cashel, between two magistrates at. *TIMES* (The). 1840.
—— Chalk Farm, at. *CASSELL'S* London. 1875.
—— Ditto. *TIMES* (The). 1841.
—— Challenge made by the Earl of Northumberland against Sir Francis Veare. *ASHMOLEAN* MSS. 1602.
—— Charleston, at. *TIMES* (The). 1856.
—— Cheltenham, at. *TIMES* (The). 1840. 1848.
—— Cherbourg, at. *TIMES* (The). 1878.
—— Chivalry, in times of. *DORAN* (J.). 1856.
—— Circus incident. *PALL* Mall Gazette. April 25, 1891.
—— Cobbett's way of fighting. *TIMES* (The). 1843.
—— Code in North Carolina. *MAGAZINE* of American History. December 1891.
—— —— of honour. *NOTES* and Queries. Series 3. Vol. VIII. p. 253.
—— Cologne, at. *TIMES* (The). 1885.
—— Colorado, at. *TIMES* (The). 1876.
—— Combat, Laws of single. *CODICUM* MSS.
—— —— Regulations for the trial of single. *CODICUM* MSS.
—— Combates, A discourse touching the unlawfulnesse of private. *ASHMOLEAN* MSS.
—— —— in England (Antiquity, use, and ceremony of lawfull). *ASHMOLEAN* MSS.
—— —— —— Discourse of lawfulness of. *CODICUM* MSS.
—— *COMBATS.* MSS. in the British Museum.
—— —— *COTTONIAN* MSS.
—— Comedy of the duel. *ALL* the Year Round. New Series. Vol. XXVII. pp. 8–12.
—— Ditto. *APPLETON'S* Journal. Vol. XXV. p. 521.
—— Continental duelling. *STANDARD* (The). September 15, 1892. October 1, 1894.
—— Corsica, A duel in. *PALL* Mall Gazette. September 26, 1891.
—— Cowboys' duel. *BRADFORD* Citizen. 1892.
—— Criminal trials. *MEDLAND* (W. M.) and *WEOBLY* (C.). 1808.
—— Cure, New, for. *TIMES* (The). 1876.
—— Curiosities of. *ALL* the Year Round. Vol. LXV. p. 376.

INDEX

INDEX

DUELLING. — [ENGLISH] (*continued*)—
—— Russian army, in the. *TIMES* (The). 1864.
—— San Francisco, after Mexican fashion in. *TIMES* (The). 1851.
—— Sarcey's duel. *SUN* (The). October 3, 1894.
—— Scandinavian nations, among. *EDINBURGH* Review. Vol. XXXIV. p. 196.
—— Schlägerei. *SATURDAY* Review. December 5, 1885.
—— Scotland, Last duel in. *PEN* and Pencil. February 5, 1887.
—— Sermon against. *CHISHULL* (E.). 1712.
—— Ditto. *HOLBROOK* (A.). 1727.
—— Sermon on. *JONES* (T.). 1792.
—— Sheridan and Mathews. *ALL* the Year Round. Series 2. Vol. XXXVIII. p. 546.
—— Shorncliffe Camp, at. *NOTES* and Queries. Series 7. Vol. XII. p. 299.
—— Single. *COMBAT.*
—— —— combat. *BURETTE* (P. J.). [1740?]
—— Sober advice to duellists. *HONOUR'S* Preservation. 1680.
—— Spain, Duello in. *TIMES* (The). 1857. 1874. 1887.
—— Spanish Bourbons. *ATLANTIC* Monthly. Vol. XXV. p. 626.
—— —— duel. *PALL* Mall Gazette. March 27, 1892.
—— Spring Gardens, in. *CASSELL'S* Old and New London. 1875.
—— St. Cyr School. *TIMES* (The). 1857.
—— St. Petersburg, at. *TIMES* (The). 1864.
—— Stage combats. *DAILY* Telegraph (The). April 4, 1891.
—— —— duel, A fatal. *ST. JAMES'S* Gazette. April 2, 1891.
—— —— duels. *SATURDAY* Review. May 16, 1891.
—— ——, on the, and off. *CALVERT* (W.). 1891.
—— Students' duels, The Emperor William on. *ST. JAMES'S* Gazette. May 9, 1891.
—— Submarine duel (A). *NOTES* and Queries. Series 2. Vols. I., VI. pp. 412, 501.
—— Suppress, Proposal to establish a society to. *TIMES* (The). 1841.
—— Suppression, Association for the. *TIMES* (The). 1843.
—— —— of. *SEGA* (J.). 1830.
—— —— —, in France. *LAWS* of Honour. 1685.
—— Swiss frontier, on the. *TIMES* (The). 1874.
—— Tanner, M.P. (Dr.), challenged to a duel. *STANDARD* (The). August 21, 1891.
—— Texas, in. *TIMES* (The). 1875. 1891.
—— Theology of. *SATURDAY* Review. March 21, 1885.
—— Thoughts arising from. *ACCOUNT.* 1712.
—— —— on. *DUELLING.* 1839.
—— Tothill Fields, in. *CASSELL'S* Old and New London. 1875.
—— Townshend (Lord) and Lord Bellamont. *ALL* the Year Round. Series 1. Vol. VII. p. 214.
—— Treatise on. *BOSQUETT* (A.). 1818.
—— Trial by combat. *SATURDAY* Review. March 8, 1890.
—— *TRIAL* of David Armstrong. 1823.
—— *TRIAL* of James Stuart. 1808.
—— *TRIAL* of Major Campbell. 1808.
—— Trial. The Queen *v.* Young. *MONTHLY* Law Magazine. Vol. III. p. 209.
—— —— 1830, before Mr. Justice Bayley. *LEGAL* Observer. Vol. XLIX. p. 498.

2 B

INDEX

INDEX

INDEX

---

* In 1859 there were eight teachers of fencing in London; in 1872, ten. Fencing-schools, having led to duelling in England, were prohibited in London by Statute 13 Edw. I. (1285).

INDEX

393

INDEX

399

INDEX

INDEX

INDEX

INDEX

403

INDEX

INDEX

INDEX

INDEX

INDEX

INDEX

INDEX

INDEX

416

INDEX

---

* The word *fleuret*, like the Italian *fiorete*, was applied to the buttoned foil, on account of its resemblance to a flower-bud.

* Foil, a rebated weapon, from the old French *fouler, refouler,* to turn back.

INDEX

INDEX

---

* "Although the rapier is associated with Italian, Spanish, and French sword-play more particularly, the word is German : the *Rapier*, or *Rappir*, is mentioned in the earliest sixteenth-century German fence-books. The name applied simply to the walking-sword, and belonged to special fencing jargon, very much as *Schläger* does in our days. The rapier was the "rapper," the "scratcher," from *raffen*, or *rappen*, "to tear." The word has no connection with Italian or Spanish. In France *rapière* soon became a more or less contemptuous term, applied to an outlandish-looking sword."—CASTLE (E.), *The Story of Swordsmanship.* (*The National Review*, May 1891.)

INDEX

---

* "The word single-stick bears the same relation to the staff or two-handed stick as the back-sword did to the long-sword or two-hander.

"The single-stick or cudgel was, and is, the foil of the back-sword, and the staff replaced the long-sword in fencing practice. The French use to this day a wooden sword for sabre practice, very similar to the foil of the sixteenth-century *Düsack.*"—CASTLE'S *Schools and Masters of Fence.*

INDEX

INDEX

INDEX

INDEX

INDEX

INDEX

INDEX

APPENDIX.

" A duellist, a duellist! a gentleman of the very first house, of the first and second cause."—SHAKESPEARE, *Romeo and Juliet*, Act ii. sc. 4.

NOTES ON FENCING & DUELLING.

[Duels both in Germany and France have of late been so frequent that the following descriptions of encounters, culled at random from the press during the past few years, may not be without interest.]

[Ganando los grados al perfil. (Adapted from Girard Thibault. 1628.)]

433

2 E

INDEX TO THE NOTES.

INDEX TO THE NOTES

INDEX TO THE NOTES

INDEX TO THE NOTES

NOTES ON

FENCING & DUELLING.

THE ORIGIN OF DUELLING.

We must consider the story of refined fence in connection with an institution which has, beyond doubt, been the primary cause of its sudden development in the sixteenth century—namely, the custom of private duelling.

In the first place, it is necessary to draw a very broad distinction between the *duel* proper, and the fight in hot blood as a last resort of argumentation, as a vent to fury or hatred. This sort of fighting appertains to all ages, and will no doubt endure until at least man has been civilised out of all manhood. The duel is a fight in cold blood, for the sake, chiefly, of public opinion ; fought with much ceremonial, before witnesses, in accordance not with the dictates of passion, but with that of an artificial code of honour. In the history of the duel proper we shall find the history of fencing proper (as distinguished from mere fighting), with all its systematic niceties.

The origin of the duel is found in the development of certain social prejudices, which at first belonged only to Gothic nations, but which rapidly spread over Europe during the Middle Ages. These prejudices, which have, and not so very long ago, been killed in England only by the most stringent legislation, still remain strong enough in countries where the law has not ruthlessly stepped in to prevent their practical application, to completely overshadow the dictates of common sense, not to speak of morals.

It is a matter of general knowledge that the private duel is a bastard descendant of the Gothic " Wager of Battle," or " Combat under the Judgment of God "—in fact, of the judicial duel. Now, the ethics of the judicial duel were, for days of universal mystic belief, tolerably sensible. They were twofold—human and religious : human in the warlike tenet that man without courage does not deserve to live ; religious in the confident belief that in a combat arranged as an appeal to Divine judgment the defender of the right would not be worsted. But nowadays, when there are other

439

manifestations of manly courage conceivable than a constant readiness to stake a possibly precious life in support of any position, wrongly or rightly assumed (for this has come to be the essence of the "point of honour"), when no one, least of all, we may surmise, the professional duellist, could desire providential interposition, the custom becomes as meaningless, as illogical, as it is illegal and immoral. And yet the point of honour as it is now understood—that precious point of honour which has given employment to so many thousands of masters of fence from the six-teenth century to our own days, which has filled so many hundreds of books with nice and discriminating lucubrations on the best methods of getting into honourable difficulties by word of mouth, and out of them by deed of point or edge—this point of honour is the direct outcome of the old Gothic legal procedure. Your mediæval litigant asserted one thing, his adverse party asserted that this thing was not; whereupon the former announced his readiness to maintain his say 'with his body.' * Appeal to Divine judgment was made ; they fought ; the vanquished was adjudged guilty. — CASTLE (E.), *The Story of Swordsmanship.* (*The National Review*, May 1891.)

THE SINGLE COMBATS (SHAKESPEARIAN).

[*Privately printed.*]

The fighting of the Shakespearian era is so peculiarly adapted to stage display that it seems strange that it should not have been more cultivated ; it may, perhaps, lack some of the refined elegance of the modern French school, but the loss is more than counterbalanced by the varied beauty of the weapons and the picturesque movements of the combatants. "Romeo and Juliet," with its five distinct duels, offers a fairly wide field to the student of old sword-play.

In the squabble, which opens the play, between certain retainers of the two rival houses, armed, after the manner of serving-men, with broad-sword and hand-buckler, a shield which, from its small size and its light-ness, lends itself greatly to lively play, the vivacity of which was further enhanced by the habit of the players of "calling" each other with two little bright raps given on the buckler with the back of the sword.

We come next to the encounter which is forced upon Benvolio by "the furious Tybalt ;" this is played with the "short syngle sword," and has

* It is curious to note that the German corps-student, who piques himself on preserving the best traditions of the "point of honour," almost invariably caps the "countercheck quarrelsome" with the simple and dignified words, "Wir sind fertig,"—"We" (the noble corps-men) "are ready," *i.e.* "to maintain our say with our body." This is supposed to settle any argument.

been carefully arranged from a manuscript book in the British Museum, by George Silver, a famous English swordsman of Elizabethan times. Benvolio awaits the fierce charges of Tybalt in "true gardant fyght" (a kind of "hanging guard" very accurately described by Silver), parries his attacks, and drives him back with the riposte, ending the combat by seizing Tybalt's sword-hand, forcing it downwards, and presenting the point at his throat. These seizures or "gryps" were much used in Silver's time, and he devotes considerable space to them.

The two most important combats in the play are, of course, those between Tybalt and Mercutio, and between Romeo and Tybalt; the latter armed himself with the "case of rapiers," the play of which Romeo, being young and inexperienced, would probably not understand. This "case of rapiers" consisted of a pair of swords which were kept side by side in one scabbard, and were used one in each hand; they were not worn in the belt, but were carried by an attendant. Tybalt, however, happens to come first into collision with Mercutio, who is similarly armed, and he kills him somewhat treacherously. He is subsequently slain by Romeo, who, armed with rapier and dagger, awaits his charge, and slipping back his left foot into the position of the "under stop-thrust" (a trick of considerable antiquity), receives him on the point of his sword.

The remaining fight, between Romeo and Paris in the tomb of the Capulets, is played with rapier and dagger, and consists of only one *reprise* before the final *corps-à-corps* struggle, in which Romeo drops his rapier purposely, in order to overpower his enemy's left hand, on which he kills him with his dagger.

It is worthy of note that at this period of the art of fence there was absolutely no "lunge;" it had yet to be invented. The movements of the feet were mainly "passes," or steps forwards or backwards, and "traverses," or lateral steps; they were effected with more or less swiftness as occasion required, and an impetuous man would often, like Tybalt, actually "charge" his opponent.—ALFRED HUTTON.

ARTICLES OF WAR, 1844.

Every officer who shall give or send a challenge, or who shall accept any challenge to fight a duel with another officer, or who, being privy to an intention to fight a duel, shall not take active measures to prevent such duel, or who shall upbraid another for refusing or for not giving a challenge, or who shall reject, or advise the rejection, of a reasonable proposition made for the honourable adjustment of a difference, shall be liable, if convicted before a general court-martial, to be cashiered, or suffer such other punishment as the court may award.

NOTES ON FENCING AND DUELLING

HIS IMPERIAL AND ROYAL MAJESTY THE GERMAN EMPEROR, KING OF PRUSSIA, ON FENCING AND DUELLING.

" Pall Mall Gazette," March 12, 1890.

You will have heard some months ago that the Emperor takes fencing lessons every day. I am now in a position to tell you why he does so. It is not for mere love of the sport, but for medical reasons. He suffers sometimes from difficult breathing—a difficulty which riding on horseback rather increases than diminishes. His medical advisers have therefore suggested daily exercise at fencing.

" Pall Mall Gazette," March 29, 1890.

The Emperor has instructed an officer of high rank to report to him personally in regard to the extent of duelling in the Prussian army, and the number of deaths which have ensued through these "combats of honour." There is no doubt that his Majesty means to take the most stern and energetic means to suppress duelling, not only in the army, but among the students.—*Dalziel.*

" The Daily Telegraph," April 8, 1890.

According to the *Germania*, Kaiser Wilhelm is about to introduce new and more stringent regulations with regard to the practice of duelling amongst officers in the German army. It is said that for the future no duel shall be permitted to take place unless sanctioned by a court of honour, which will be presided over by two regimental colonels, and that the grounds for such a duel shall only be : (1) If a blow shall have been inflicted by the offending party, for which he shall not have offered an ample verbal apology ; (2) If a lady, a relation or the *fiancée* of the offended party, being an officer, shall have been insulted. No duel shall be permitted in future to take place as the result of a quarrel in a club meeting, messroom, or café, or any similar place of resort ; or if the opponent shall have already fought in three duels ; or if one of the parties shall be married and the father of a family. These regulations are regarded as the commencement of a reform in the present mode of settling quarrels in this country, even amongst students at the universities.

442

NOTES ON FENCING AND DUELLING

" *St. James's Gazette,*" *May* 9, 1891.

THE EMPEROR WILLIAM ON STUDENTS' DUELS.

The Emperor William arrived at Carlsruhe yesterday from Bonn, and was welcomed by his uncle, the Grand Duke of Baden, and enthusiastically received by the inhabitants. On the evening before leaving Bonn the Emperor spent several hours at the beer *commers*, which was held to open the summer session of the Bonn University, such symposia being always attended by all the corps or fighting clubs. Of these the crack corps is that of the Borussia, of which the Emperor himself, when studying at Bonn, was a nominal member ; but at this general *commers* he acted as chairman of the revels. In reply to the health of the Emperor, which was effusively proposed and drunk in what is called "a thundering salamander," his Majesty rose and begged to subscribe to every word which had been spoken in praise of all the habits and customs of German student-life and their educational importance. He said :—

" It is my firm conviction that every youth who enters a corps or beer-drinking and duelling club will receive the true direction of his life from the spirit which prevails in them. It is the best education which a young man can get for his future life, and he who scoffs at the German students' corps does not penetrate their real meaning. I hope that as long as there are German corps-students the spirit which is fostered in their corps, and which is steeled by strength and courage, will be preserved, and that you will always take delight in handling the duelling-blade. There are many people who do not understand what our duels really mean, but that must not lead us astray. You and I, who have been corps-students, know better than that. As in the Middle Ages manly strength and courage were steeled by the practice of jousting or tournaments, so the spirit and habits which are acquired from membership of a corps furnish us with that degree of fortitude which is necessary to us when we go out into the world, and which will last as long as there are German universities. You have been good enough to refer to my son (the Crown Prince), and I give you my hearty thanks for doing so. I trust that the young man, when he is advanced enough, will matriculate here and join your clubs, and that he will then meet with the same kindly sentiments that were extended to me. And now a word to those young freshmen who are but beginning to lead a corps life. Train your courage, your discipline, and your obedience, without which we cannot as a state continue to live ; and I trust that many officials and officers will emerge from your midst."

NOTES ON FENCING AND DUELLING

This remarkable speech by the Emperor was (the *Times'* correspondent says) applauded to the echo by his youthful hearers, though it is certain to provoke a bitter enough controversy in other quarters. The Emperor remained among the beer-drinkers and song-singers till midnight, and then withdrew with his brother-in-law, Prince Adolph of Schaumburg-Lippe, amid a scene of great enthusiasm.

"Pall Mall Gazette," 17th October 1889.

FENCING FOR EVERYBODY.

A VISIT TO M. B. BERTRAND.

The duel in the "Dead Heart" between Mr. Irving as Landry and Mr. Bancroft as the Abbé Latour has been universally praised. It stands out vividly as one of the finest and most thrilling situations of the play, and is without doubt the best stage duel that English playgoers have witnessed in a quarter of a century. Neither critics nor audience were prepared for such an earnest and realistic set-to, and it was clear, from the moment that the clerical Macduff began to "lay on," that Mr. Irving would have to look to himself. The issue, of course, is prearranged, but up to that point it is a downright match between the combatants, and it may whet the interest of future spectators to be assured that the duel is a rather dangerous one both for Mr. Irving and for Mr. Bancroft. If Mr. Irving, from any cause, should fail in his guard at a critical moment, Mr. Bancroft could scarcely avoid rattling him over the sconce, with a result that might recall a famous situation in "Don Quixote." By its vigour, its grace, its freedom from convention, and its almost painful air of reality, the Lyceum duel will take its place among the artistic traditions of that theatre ; and every actor should see it, for it has rendered the duel of convention impossible in the future.

Lyceum successes have started fashions before now in matters not wholly theatrical. The duel in the new revival may make fencing one of the *modes* of the coming winter. It is a day of partial revivals in various departments of athletics. The boxer, despite the muffled reproaches of a moral press, is hitting out in all directions. Noble lords are coquetting with the tricycle. Now fencing, considered merely as a pastime, appeals with special and peculiar force and directness to Society with the capital S.

It is of all physical arts the most graceful and the most refined. Skill in fencing assuredly requires a quick eye and a strong and supple wrist ; but it is upon just positions and graceful movements of the frame that success in the art is chiefly dependent. Show me a first-rate swordsman, and I will

444

DUEL IN THE "DEAD HEART."

Lyceum Theatre, London. 1889.

show you a man who carries his head well, and in whose gait, attitude, and gestures there is never a *soupçon* of awkwardness. Is not the very mention of the art suggestive of the antique graces of the Courts and *salons* of pre-Revolutionary France? And if manners are in question, what is a better educator than the foil? Every well-ordered *salle d'armes* is a school of polite behaviour. To lose one's temper in fencing is, very literally, to give one's hand away to one's opponent; and the swordsman bent on winning his duel would no more dare to let his temper get the better of him (let him be worse pressed than Christian by Apollyon) than Blondin would dare to take in reality the false step that he sometimes pretends to take in walking the tight-rope.

"My dear M. Bertrand, is not all this perfectly true?"—"*Mon Dieu!*" responded the *maître d'armes*, with a gesture perfected by fifty years of foil practice, "it is beautiful. Write it in the *Pall Mall Gazette.*"

"*A la bonne heure.* But I want to know why so little interest is taken in this beautiful art of yours by the young bloods of the town, who can find guineas enough and to spare for the professional bruiser."

M. Bertrand, in his leathern doublet, sitting cross-legged with his back to the wall of the fencing-saloon, a row of foils above his head, pushed his peaked cap on one side, shrugged his shoulders, and plucked at his white "imperial."

"But," he hastened to say with fine magnanimity, "*la boxe* is good. I do not despise it. *Du tout!* And it is one of your national games. We teach boxing here, you know, a little, though I do not use the gloves myself. As for fencing—well, many of those 'young bloods' you speak of are among my pupils; and fencing is on the way to be revived in London."

This is a subject on which M. Bertrand ought to be as well informed as anybody. His splendid saloon in Warwick Street, Regent Street, is the centre of fencing in London, as he himself has been for years one of the foremost *maîtres d'armes* of Europe. There are three other well-known and admirable fencing-schools in London—Angelo's, the London Fencing Club, and the Inns of Court Club—but the Warwick Street establishment has a *cachet* all its own. Outside of Italy, it is upon the French system that fencing is taught and practised all the world over (is not the very language of the art French, or of French derivation?), and in Warwick Street the French tradition is maintained in its purity. Your true French professor of the ancient school is not a fencing-master, he is a *maître d'armes.* His profession is his passion. "*C'est un métier de sentiment,*" insists Bertrand, who remembers that, on the other side of the Channel, fencing "*a toujours été reconnu comme une des plus brillantes manifestations de l'art Française.*" It is not enough with him when he has shown a pupil how to stand on guard, how to parry, and to thrust. He seems to bring

445

the mind into play. In all fine fencing, audacity and reflection march side by side. It is an intellectual no less than a physical exercise; and morals and æsthetics have their part in it: fencing, as the great *maîtres d'armes* of old understood it, is linked with the idea and institution of chivalry.

"*N'est-ce pas*, M. Bertrand?"

"*Mais oui. C'est vrai.*"

For forty years M. Bertrand has been the leading and most intelligent exponent in London of this admirable art. This sketch was begun with a reference to the duel in the "Dead Heart;" and intentionally so, because the main inspiration of that duel was M. Bertrand's. For weeks before the production of the play Mr. Irving and Mr. Bancroft were diligently rehearsing the duel-scene in Warwick Street. Just eight-and-twenty years ago M. Fechter and Mr. Hermann Vezin were rehearsing, in the same place and under the same tuition, the duel in "Hamlet." Charles Dickens and the Rev. J. C. M. Bellew (whose genius as a reader equalled Dickens's as a writer) were occasional witnesses of the rehearsals. Their names remind me how many famous men have handled the foil, or watched its handling, in Warwick Street. Some of the best swordsmen in the army had their rudiments, or (to quote Mrs. Major O'Dowd) their "finishing," from M. Bertrand. In the days when Napoleon III. was pondering the vanity of things monarchical at Chislehurst, his brilliant, impetuous boy was fencing with all comers at Bertrand's. Napoleon himself looked in frequently when the room was quiet; and the master remembers vividly the brusque "*Bon jour, Bertrand!*" with which the beautiful Eugénie used occasionally to present herself in the doorway. The Napoleonic affections of M. Bertrand are inborn. The *salle d'armes*, in its pictures, its sculptures, and its trophies, is eloquent of the associations that have contributed to its fame, and a museum in little of all that appertains to *l'escrime* as an art. In the forty years that have whitened the aggressive moustache and "imperial" of M. Bertrand, he has taught fencing to three generations of the bluest blood of England, and he is teaching now the great-grandchildren of his earliest pupils. *Par parenthèse*, he can tire out, foil in hand, the most stalwart fencer in his school—which, I think, says something for the art as a preservative of health and vigour. I questioned him on this point. "Go to the doctors and ask their opinion," answered M. Bertrand. "I class my pupils in three divisions. First, there are those who want fencing as a pastime, an accomplishment. Then there are the actors and the operatic singers, in whose art—whether they agree with me or not—a knowledge of the foil is absolutely indispensable. Thirdly, there are the people who are sent to me by the doctors. Half my pupils are ordered here by their medical men—overworked students; barristers and literary men whose livers have got out of order, hypochondriacs and

B. BERTRAND. 1889.

Professeur d'Escrime, à Londres.

sentimentalists of all sorts. *Voyez vous*, there is not a nervous disease of the century which is not curable by the fencing-master. Of all the physical exercises, this is the most thorough and complete. It calls into play every muscle in the body. It acts and reacts on every organ. Fencing is harder work than boxing, and more wholesome (though far less severe) than riding. And it is so enticing. That is half the good of it. It allures so much more than any gymnastic exercise. Advance a little in fencing, and you cannot leave it off. The first steps over, the task becomes a delight; the teacher has no longer any need to gild the pill."

We passed on to talk of the ladies. M. Bertrand—as your readers, I think, have been informed already—is instructor in fencing and gymnastics to the daughters of the Prince and Princess of Wales; and he numbers many ladies amongst his pupils. He is enthusiastic in his advocacy of fencing for ladies. My own mental attitude on the subject is one of unmitigated surprise that every woman with a pretty figure does not use the foils. *Mesdames*, have you never thought of the ravishing costume? Have you never seen a well-graced Amazon attired for the combat? If not, then you have never seen the most adorable garb that the woman of perfect figure can assume. How well they understand this in Paris! There the lady of fashion who fences (and her name is legion) bestows as much consideration on her *costume de l'escrime* as she does on those for the ball, the opera, the racecourse, and the drive—and she generally shows to supremely greater advantage in the former than she does in any of the latter. You should bethink you, ladies, that there are not too many physical exercises in the performance of which you can be nicely and elegantly assisted by the milliner or the tailor. In riding—yes, assuredly. In archery—well, if you would only dress for the part, which you seldom do. In cricket, lawn-tennis, cycling—h'm! But in fencing—*Parbleu!* you *must* have the milliner or the tailor, or both of them there, and with the daintiest and most admirable result in the world. After this it seems trivial to bring forward the merits of the foil on any other grounds; but ladies may take it, on the infallible word of M. Bertrand, that it braces and beautifies the "figure" as no other exercise does or can do.

"You say so, M. Bertrand, do you not?"

"I have said it for forty years," replied the *maître d'armes*, passing his hand over the scar which recalls to him the day when the foil was sometimes exchanged for the small-sword, and the lookers-on included a surgeon.

But the veteran returned again to the mimic duel in the "Dead Heart." He was proud of it; he could not get it out of his mind. "*Ce n'est une pas convention—c'est une réalité!*" he repeated. "You have seen it—very well; but I don't believe you understand it properly. *Tiens!* I shall show it to you again. Félix!" and he summoned his handsome boy, who is his right hand in the *salle d'armes.* M. Bertrand took Mr. Irving's part, and Félix Mr. Bancroft's, and they went through the scene. I was like the late King of the Belgians, having a choice performance all to myself, with no common people to spoil my enjoyment by applauding in the wrong place.

"The Standard," March 13, 1890.

DUELLING.

The abolition of duelling, accomplished in England nearly half a century since, is still a matter of doubt and discussion in Continental countries, and especially in France. A learned writer, M. Emile Worms,* has just proposed the remedy of extending the jurisdiction of the regular courts of justice in some form which would make them competent in affairs of honour. This is by no means so absurd as it may look at first, for a French duel is already very far removed from a free fight. It has an almost legal solemnity ; it begins with ceremonial visits, and ends in a *procès-verbal.* Another very learned Frenchman, M. d'Arbois de Jubainville, has compared some curious provisions of early Irish law with a well-known anecdote of the great Scipio's Spanish campaign, and concludes that the settlement of disputes by an appointed single combat was probably a very ancient Celtic institution. The modern duel, however, cannot claim any direct relation to this. It is not more than three centuries old—a fact strangely forgotten by the modern Frenchmen and Italians who profess to wonder how any society of gentlemen can exist without it—and its immediate origin is to be found in the knightly combats which were waged under the direction of courts of chivalry from the fourteenth to the sixteenth century. These, again, were a fantastic variation of the Trial by Battle, or " Judgment of God," as it was commonly called, which is one of the most singular features of mediæval law, and which nominally survived in this country down to the present century. But the true judicial duel was almost extinct in practice when the chivalrous duel became fashionable. We have to thank a British writer for distinguishing the several kinds of Trial by Combat as known in these islands, and tracing the fortunes of duelling from its first definable appearance till its abolition. Mr. George Neilson,† of Glasgow, in his book published under this title, has conferred a great benefit on both legal and military antiquaries ; and his subject, though much learning is needed for its adequate treatment, is popular, in so far as anything with fighting in it appeals to the natural man in persons who are not antiquarian lawyers or even students of history. He may claim, indeed, to appeal to

* Vide WORMS (E.). 1890   † Vide NEILSON (G.). 1890.

all those who know and love the Waverley Novels, for he discusses the combat between the Clan Chattan and the Clan Kay, described in "The Fair Maid of Perth," and made familiar by the magic of Sir Walter Scott to thousands of readers who would otherwise never have heard of it. Mr. Neilson finds in this, not a barbarous Highland custom tolerated for reasons of policy, but a regular example, though on an unusual scale, of the chivalric fashion of the fourteenth century, then at its height, which Scotland had the more easily adopted because of the standing alliance with France. Deadly as the fight was (and Scott exaggerated nothing), it probably saved more lives than it lost, for the feud between the clans was settled, and the peace was honourably kept, which is more than can be said of the results of some modern wars that have been far more costly.

Generally, however, the set duel of chivalry was single; the bad custom of seconds joining in the fight appears to have grown up in France about the end of the sixteenth century, in the period illustrated by Alexandre Dumas, perhaps not less veraciously—certainly with more pleasure to the reader—than by most historians. Chivalrous duels, moreover, were by no means usually fatal. Often the duel never began at all, but went off on some technical preliminary, as, indeed, was apt to happen with the older legal Wager of Battle. The king or prince who presided would stop the fight, and settle the matter in difference by his own award. Sometimes, when the duel was fought in complete armour, the parties found it impossible to do one another much harm. This happened in 1380, in a duel at Westminster, upon a charge by a knight against his own squire for the treasonable surrender of a castle in France. Chivalry prevailed against legal objections, and the knight's challenge was allowed. The knight and the squire fought long, and were so exhausted, though unwounded, that when they closed and fell they had to be lifted; but the squire was really and truly dead beat, for he could neither walk nor stand, and died the next day, to "the delight of the people and the grief of traitors." Quite different weapons were used in the older judicial duel, introduced into England under William the Conqueror. The champions were bareheaded, clad in leather, and armed with oblong shields, and a short staff tipped with horn, set crosswise like a pickaxe head. Mr. Neilson thinks the horn may go back to days before the age of iron; and some very ancient superstition may have lurked in the custom of having the men's heads not only bare but shaven. A fight of this kind is shown in the margin of a thirteenth-century legal MS. preserved in the Record Office, of which a fac-simile may be seen in Professor F. W. Maitland's * "Select Pleas of the Crown," edited for the Selden Society. Selden's† own tract on the duello is, by the way, the first work of authority on the subject in our

* *Vide* MAITLAND (F. W.).
† *Vide* SELDEN (J.).—1610.

language. Both combatants are of most villainous appearance, and if they were in truth such ruffians as they look, one cannot much regret the fate of the beaten one, who is seen hanging in the background. Such was the penalty of his defeat, or rather of the felony which the defeat of the accused party was supposed to prove. When these combats were seriously fought out, they appear to have been quite as brutal as the most recent revivals of prize-fighting, though it must be said, in justice to our ancestors, that far more effectual measures were taken to ensure fair play. The "fancy" of an assize town (if we may be allowed a venial anachronism) must, in the twelfth and early thirteenth centuries, have had a satisfaction unknown to later days in witnessing a sporting event which might last until the stars appeared, and which might quite probably end in some one either being killed or being hanged. The proceedings were the same, with minute variations, whether the subject of the duel were a disputed right to land, or a charge of felony brought in the form of an "appeal."

In the course of the fifteenth century, while the chivalrous duel of armoured knights was already past the height of its fashion, the regular legal duel had become so uncommon that the forms proper to its two varieties were apt to be confused in practice in the scattered cases that occurred. Perhaps the oddest of the ceremonies was putting a silver penny in every finger of the gloves which were exchanged before the fight. Yet, in the latest case of an appeal of murder—the case of Abraham Thornton, in 1817, which led to the abrogation of the old law—the challenger threw down in Court a gauntlet, specially made for the occasion, which had no fingers at all. Pennies meant a good deal more in the Middle Ages than they do now ; but far larger sums changed hands when a case appointed for Trial by Battle was compromised in the field. The king or the lord having jurisdiction was enriched, and the judges consoled themselves and the spectators by causing the champions to play a few turns before them, the horn tips of the staves being first removed, so as to make them comparatively harmless. A strange pastime for the judges of the land ; but who knows that the men of the twenty-third or twenty-fifth century will not look with as astonished eyes on the favourite sports of the nineteenth as we do on a mediæval Trial by Battle ? Stranger than all the ceremonies and incidents of these combats is the reason given for establishing them. Legal trial by combat in Western Europe dates from the year 501. The earlier forms of the "Judgment of God" were ordeal and oath. Their prevalence illustrates what is now a commonplace of legal antiquities, the extraordinary antipathy of semi-civilised systems of law for forming an opinion upon disputed matters of fact, and the willingness of mankind, in certain states of society, to resort to the most grotesque expedients rather than attempt that intellectual feat. In 501 Gundobald of Burgundy, well perceiving that enormous perjuries were committed in the decision of causes by oath, " thought that his subjects might as well risk their bodies as their souls, and he introduced, or re-introduced, the judicial combat." His example was followed all over Western Christendom, sooner or later, and Trial by Battle became a part of the accepted mediæval theory of Divine and human justice. No less a man than Dante gravely maintained; that the wars of the conquering Romans manifested the "Judgment of God" in a series of judicial combats, waged in all due form, for the empire of the world. But the institution failed in its immediate object of abolishing perjury, for in the later settled forms of Trial by Battle both combatants had to swear terribly, so that at least one of them must have been perjured. The well-meant reform of Gundobald has had its day, and expired ; but it was a pretty long day—a matter of seven or eight centuries. It remains for posterity to see whether trial by jury, now about six centuries old, will have a longer life, on the whole, than trial by combat. Meanwhile, we have experimented with many judicial ways of arriving at the truth. We have, at different times and in different courts, forbidden the parties to bear witness, compelled them, and allowed them. And what remains, unfortunately, most certain is that, all law reformers from Gundobald to Jeremy Bentham notwithstanding, false swearing is not yet extinct.

" Pall Mall Gazette," August 2, 1890.

A DUEL WITH CAVALRY SABRES.

A duel with cavalry sabres took place on Thursday, in Denmark, between Lieutenant Castenschiold, of the Danish Royal Dragoons, and the Russian Baron von Rathen. The quarrel arose about an equestrian performer in the Circus Busch at Copenhagen. The Baron received a cut across the forehead, but is in no danger.

" Pall Mall Gazette," August 27, 1890.

A DUEL OF A ROUGH-AND-READY KIND.

A duel of a rough-and-ready kind has been fought at Rowland, in Kentucky. Ross Hamilton and Robert Ferguson, deadly enemies, met in the street and produced their revolvers. They fired to kill, and both men were instantly killed.

" The Globe," August 28, 1890.

DUELLING IN THE FRENCH ARMY.

M. Millot and M. Baruti, two lieutenants of a regiment quartered at Belfort, fought a duel with swords on Tuesday, in consequence of a silly dispute about regimental matters. The former received a slash on the arm, which severed all the large blood-vessels. It is said that the bleeding was stopped with the utmost difficulty, and two hours were spent in stitching up the arm. The wounded officer is in a serious condition, though it is pronounced an even chance that he will recover. It is to be hoped, says the Paris correspondent of the *Daily News*, this unfortunate affair will draw attention to the present duelling regulations in the French army. They are a relic of barbarism and a disgrace. Duelling, though forbidden by law, is by custom compulsory in the French army, among the private soldiers as well as with the officers. If a bully in the regiment chooses to pick a quarrel with a raw recruit and insults him, the latter is bound to challenge him under pain of imprisonment, and the colonel himself appoints an officer to be present at the encounter. He generally attempts to ward off ugly blows, and this much may be said, that such duels seldom end fatally. As every Frenchman is now bound, *nolens volens*, to go through the army, the cruelty of compulsory duelling is far greater than in the old times of purchasing substitutes. M. de Freycinet, the Minister of War, is opposed to duelling altogether, and by a decision of his, only a few days old, it is rendered optional. This decision, however, does not take effect immediately. M. Paul de Cassagnac, who is perhaps more celebrated for his duels than for anything else, wrote the other day a strong article against the barbarous practice. He showed how fallacious was the idea that to refuse a duel was derogatory to a soldier's manliness, by the example of England, whose officers and men in time of war were not behind those of any nation in the accomplishment of their duty.

" Pall Mall Gazette," August 30, 1890.

FATAL MILITARY DUEL IN GERMANY.

A fatal duel with pistols has been fought in the forest outside Perleberg. The principals were Lieutenant von Forstner and Lieutenant Frenk, and the duel was conducted with deadly determination, there being no limit to the number of shots. Frenk was mortally wounded, two bullets lodging in his breast. Von Forstner, who sustained no hurt, continues to perform his duties as adjutant of the 35th Regiment.—*Dalziel.*

" Pall Mall Gazette," September 3, 1890.

DUEL BETWEEN AN EDITOR AND AN OFFICER.

A Toulon telegram from Reuter's agent states that, as a result of the dispute between some naval officers there and M. David, editor of the Republican journal *Var*, who declared that an officer ill-treated a soldier who failed to salute him, a duel took place yesterday between M. David and a sub-lieutenant, in which the former received three wounds.

NOTES ON FENCING AND DUELLING

" *The Times*," *September* 8, 1890.

HENRI ROCHEFORT AND GEORGES THIÉBAUD (DUEL).

PARIS, *September* 7.—MM. Henri Rochefort and Georges Thiébaud at last fought their duel yesterday morning, at Clinge, on the Dutch frontier. It was M. Thiébaud who took offence at an article by M. Rochefort, and demanded satisfaction. The result is that M. Thiébaud, in addition to the injury done to him by the newspaper articles of which he complains, has to suffer from three slight wounds. Will these three wounds prove that M. Thiébaud has been calumniated, or that M. Rochefort spoke the truth? To solve that question recourse must be had to one of those privileged men who are appealed to as arbiters in cases in which reason, justice, and good sense are of no avail.

This encounter, however, has made a very ingenious innovation in duelling habits. Twenty-five years ago, for instance, the challenge was concealed, because the Courts prosecuted for the offence, and occasionally pronounced condemnations. Since the Republic came into existence, however, there has been progress made. The duel is announced before it takes place, and the details are afterwards published. There is no concealment from the authorities. The details are supplied by the seconds, or in the *procès-verbal* of the fight. The Rochefort-Thiébaud duel has given a new form to this "judgment of God," which might be described as a "close of the century" form. The combatants took with them not only the two necessary doctors and the indispensable seconds, but, in addition, a journalist, the London correspondent of the *Figaro*. "Our London correspondent," says this newspaper, "will accompany the combatants and will give the incidents." In fact, the correspondent did accompany the duellists, and described how the party were stopped by the Dutch police, what were the events of the journey, and how the struggle was fought when swords had been crossed. It is clear that the last stage of development has not yet been reached. I believe that if the correspondent of the *Figaro* had not been taken by surprise when the new functions were imposed upon him, he would have had with him an instantaneous photographic apparatus, which would have caught the combatants in their various postures, and supplied the public with the means of almost witnessing the fight. A special photographic apparatus will no doubt be added next to the special correspondent, and the newspaper press will have the means of criticising duels just as it criticises artistic, musical, or dramatic entertainments. The process is one that should be encouraged, for when duelling has in this way been made ridiculous it will be abandoned. At present the practice is only barbarous, a logical conclusion which does not suffice to extinguish it.

NOTES ON FENCING AND DUELLING

" *The Times,*" *September* 9, 1890.

DUEL FOUGHT BETWEEN M. MERMEIX AND
M. DE LABRUYÈRE.

The *procès-verbal* signed by the seconds before the duel fought yesterday afternoon between M. Mermeix and M. de Labruyère, of the *Gil Blas*, stated that the fight was not to cease until one of the combatants found himself in a state of inferiority verified by the doctors. The encounter took place in the garden in front of M. Laguerre's house in the Avenue de la Muette. It is stated that M. Laguerre has two drawing-rooms, in one of which he received M. Mermeix and his seconds, and in another M. de Labruyère and his friends. Taking the party outside his house, he said : " The garden is at your disposal, gentlemen : at yours, M. de Labruyère, my old comrade on the *Cri;* and at yours, M. Mermeix, my colleague on the *Presse.*"

The duel took place in front of the house. The *Matin*, one of the leader-writers of which was a second of M. de Labruyère, gives the following account of it :—

The lot having fallen on M. Dreyfus to direct the proceedings, he placed the two adversaries, and uttered the customary words, " Allez, Messieurs." Forthwith the champions began to cross their swords, but without, however, approaching so closely as to give ground to fear a course forbidden by the rules. It must be believed that M. Lévy, one of the seconds of M. Mermeix, was deceived by some optical illusion caused by his excitement, for in a few seconds he began to call out, " You are hit, M. de Labruyère." "Wounded ? Where, then ? " asked the latter, stopping and turning away his sword, while the director of the fight, who had the sole right to do so, called out a vigorous " Stop." In spite of the loudness with which the command was uttered, M. Mermeix, so far from stopping, took a step backwards, and making a thrust at his adversary, who was completely out of guard, gave him a deep wound on the hand. The general scare may be imagined. Finding he was wounded under circumstances so unusual, M. de Labruyère called out, " It is abominable ; " while M. Mermeix, in utter confusion, explained nervously that, not having in his excitement apprehended in time the command to stop, he had unconsciously, by a reflex movement, wounded his exposed adversary.

The first moment of confusion over, M. de Labruyère, furious, and justly so, energetically expressed a desire to continue the struggle with the left hand. A discussion followed between the seconds, in the course of which one of those of M. Mermeix called out, " It is impossible ; the use of the left hand is forbidden." No time was lost in explaining to him

that the use of the left hand is only forbidden and becomes unfair if a treacherous combatant, or one under the influence of nervousness, employs it to paralyse the sword of his adversary, and to strike him without danger with the right hand. Finally, the seconds, on the formal advice of the doctors, decided to stop the fight, and proceeded to draw up the *procès-verbal*. It was announced this morning that M. de Labruyère demanded a new encounter with M. Mermeix. The *Paris* sent to M. de Labruyère to ask if this was the case, and received from him the following reply :—
" M. Mermeix has been guilty of an act of felony towards me. I will not fight with him again."

The *Cocarde* of this evening publishes the following declaration by M. de Labruyère :—

" On my honour I affirm that M. Mermeix took advantage in order to hit me at a moment in which, the fight being suspended by M. Maxime Dreyfus, who directed it, I had fallen back and stuck my sword in the soil. On the ground itself, and in the presence of the witnesses, I openly reproached M. Mermeix with this act, which I described as one *de forfaiture et de félonie.*"

" Pall Mall Gazette," September 13, 1890.

SHOULD WOMEN FIGHT DUELS ?

Mdme. d'Estoc is (says the Paris correspondent of the *Telegraph*) a worthy imitator of Mdme. de Valsayrie, the lady fencer and duellist. At the last meeting of the League for the Emancipation of Women, Mdme. d'Estoc proposed a vote of censure on the lady called "Séverine," whose article lately caused M. Mermeix to fight M. Labruyère. Mdme. Séverine was condemned by the whole assembly of women waiting for emancipation, because she did not take up the challenge of the author of the revelations of Boulangism, and meet him on the field of honour herself, instead of allowing an obliging journalist to fight for her. The resolution proposed by Mdme. d'Estoc was that every woman who does not assume responsibility for her actions, and who allows a man to champion her cause, is guilty of a deed of " inferiority."

" Pall Mall Gazette," September 15, 1890.

DUEL IN MEXICO.

It is reported from Mexico that a duel has been fought between Señor Gonzalo Estera, editor of the journal *El Nacional*, and Señor Gutierrez Najera, a prominent journalist, both of whom are members of the House of Representatives. Señor Estera was slightly wounded.

NOTES ON FENCING AND DUELLING

" The Standard," September 16, 1890.

A BOULANGIST DUEL.

Paris, *September* 15.—A duel was fought this evening between M. Mermeix and M. Dumonteil, Deputy of the Aisne. M. Mermeix was seriously wounded in the right side.

" Pall Mall Gazette," September 16, 1890.

DUEL BETWEEN BOYS IN BERLIN.

A desperate duel with rapiers was fought on Sunday between two Berlin schoolboys, named Oscar Lesch, aged fourteen years, and Hans Donner, aged sixteen. They are members of a Latin high school in Muskauerstrasse, and the fight took place in the garret of the school building. Young Donner was wounded in the face, his nose and half of his left ear being cut off. After the duel Donner walked to the police station, where his wounds were dressed by a surgeon. The police captain sent for the fathers of the two boys, both of whom are well known in Berlin society ; but no attempt was made to arrest Lesch, but Herr Lesch was advised to give his son a thrashing. There were no witnesses to the duel. The cause turns out to have been the attempt of Donner to supplant young Lesch in the affections of his sweetheart, a young girl named Bertha Rath.

" The Standard," October 1, 1891.

DUEL BETWEEN GENERAL BOULANGER AND M. FLOQUET.

It is remarkable that, for a fighting soldier, General Boulanger was not skilled in the use of arms. His duel with M. Floquet would have killed any other man than the General with ridicule. M. Floquet was then over sixty, and the General was easily disposed of by this aged lawyer, who ran his sword into Boulanger's neck. His behaviour in the duel has been freely criticised, but the following anecdote may throw a more favourable light upon it. Before the meeting, the General, who had never fenced since his cadet days at St. Cyr, was persuaded to take a lesson from a famous swordsman. The moment he stood on guard his instructor saw that he knew nothing about fencing. "You don't know how to parry," he said to the General. "No," was the reply ; "I charge." "Then you will spit yourself." "*Tant pis.* I have never had time to learn the simplest parade, and it would be absurd for me to try to fence in the regulation manner. I shall charge as I did just now." He had previously run himself on to his opponent's sword exactly as, a few hours later, he fared with M. Floquet.

NOTES ON FENCING AND DUELLING

" Pall Mall Gazette," October 30, 1891.

DESPERATE DUEL WITH DAGGERS.

A remarkable duel took place yesterday in the forest of La Rocca. The combatants were Count Bertazzoli and Signor Calderoni. They are both in love with the same lady. They agreed to fight, without seconds, a duel to the death. The weapons chosen were daggers. They met in the wood without witnesses, and were fighting for three-quarters of an hour. Both were stabbed in many places, but neither could kill or disable the other. With blood flowing from many wounds, they continued to combat till neither was able to stand, and, when found by servants, both were lying helpless. They were hurried at once to the hospital and treated, but their condition is critical.

" The Standard," November 6, 1891.

PROFESSOR HARTL'S CORPS OF VIENNESE FENCING LADIES.

EMPIRE THEATRE OF VARIETIES.—A very decided attraction was introduced last night, when Professor Hartl's Corps of Viennese Fencing Ladies made their first appearance on the boards. The corps consists of six young ladies, gracefully attired, part in blue and part in red, and all with yellow and black sashes. They go through all the exercises of the *haute école*, both with the foils and with fencing swords, in a singularly graceful and masterly manner, and the sword and dagger duels were particularly spirited. The young ladies can come to no harm in their rapid exhibition of swordsmanship, inasmuch as they are well protected with padded cuirasses of leather, and, where there might be danger, with masks. It is altogether a very interesting display, and cannot fail to be popular.

" Pall Mall Gazette," November 23, 1891.

MUNICIPAL DUEL IN FRANCE.

A Mont de Marsan telegram says :—A duel was fought to-day between the Mayor of Dax and the sub-Prefect, in consequence of disputes between the latter and the municipality. The Mayor was wounded.

A BRITISH VICE-CONSUL AS DUELLIST'S SECOND.

Considerable surprise is expressed in the English colony in Paris (says the *Chronicle's* correspondent), in consequence of the fact that Mr. J. F.

NOTES ON FENCING AND DUELLING

D. Bowden, the British Vice-Consul in Paris, has acted as second in a duel between a Mr. Lucas and a Mr. Chandor. The latter was wounded by his adversary, but is happily doing well. It is felt that if British consuls abroad disobey the letter and spirit of the law of England by accepting the etiquette of the duello, they are putting their fellow-countrymen abroad in a false and humiliating position.

" Sunday Times," September 21, 1890.

AFTER A FRENCH DUEL.

BY G. A. S[ALA].

After a French duel, if "honour has been satisfied," and nobody has been assassinated, a grand breakfast usually takes place ; and the *déjeûner à la fourchette* given by M. Rochefort after his last "terrific combat of two," is said to have cost the pugnacious Marquis de Luçay something like a hundred pounds sterling. But did you ever hear of a duel that cost £17,000 ?

" The Times," September 27, 1890.

DUELLING IN JAPAN.

A German magazine, *Von West nach Ost*, published in Tokio, contains an article by Dr. Mori, a Japanese gentleman, on the forms of duelling in vogue in former times in Japan. It would be an error, he says, to think that the duel is an exclusively Western institution ; Japan also has had its duels in the best sense of the word. There was the same high regard for personal honour, and the same single combat for life and death before witnesses and with equal weapons ; there was, above all, the so-called *ikki-uchi*, a single combat, fought very much in the style of the Homeric heroes, in front of armies arrayed for battle. Distinguished from this public combat was the duel for private reasons, which was generally considered an act unworthy of praise. But an offence directed against one in his capacity of *samurai*, or soldier was unpardonable. A challenge was given instantly by word of mouth, or subsequently in writing ; the choice of weapons was a matter of course ; the opponent had to be a *samurai ;* seconds were not named, the supposition being that a knight could not possibly act contrary to honour and be guilty of treachery when engaging in such a contest, a supposition rarely found erroneous. A variety of the duel was the slaying of an enemy in revenge, which differed from the Corsican vendetta in the prohibition of treacherous assaults. This was directed against the slayer of one's parents or prince, according to the Confucian

458

precept, "not to live under the same sky with the murderer of one's parents or lord." The law silently approved such an act, and in one case the authorities actually released a girl from prison to give her and her husband an opportunity of avenging the death of her brother on his murderer. Another custom was the vengeance inflicted on the seducer of a married wife by her husband, prevalent at one time in the 16th century; but it was soon disapproved and abandoned, it being wrong, according to the Sinico-Japanese idea of the time, to risk for the sake of an adulteress a life that was absolutely devoted to the service of one's lord. Any violation of the laws of honour recognised in these matters was usually punished by dismissal from the service of the prince to whom the offender had been attached. Occasionally parties, and not individuals only, engaged in such acts of vengeance, as, for instance, when, a youth or girl called upon their relatives for aid in revenging the death of a parent, or when two men were declared to be entitled to challenge one and the same individual. In such cases the challenged or outnumbered party had a right to select a corresponding number of helpers. Quite harmless, and not devoid of a certain sense of humour, were the acts of vengeance perpetrated by deserted wives upon their successors in the hearts and homes of their former husbands. According to the consideration the respective parties enjoyed in society, three, five, or more women were hired for the contest in question, an equal number for each side, and the sides were headed by the aggrieved lady and her successful rival. No man could take part in the proceeding except the old servants of the two houses, who transmitted the challenge and its acceptance. The choice of weapons rested with the deserted wife, who chose either sticks or the bamboo swords used in fencing. This contest was as interesting and harmless as it was emphatic and noisy; it relieved the pent-up hatred on the one side, and gave, perhaps, the *coup de grâce* to the honeymoon on the other. After some time, the middlemen who had effected the former and recent marriage stepped forward, and a reconciliation scene was enacted over the broken bamboo swords of the battlefield. This custom, however, had but a short duration at the end of the sixteenth century.

"*Pall Mall Gazette*," *October* 6, 1890.

DUELLING STATISTICS.

Statistics have been published concerning the duels fought in Italy during the decade from 1879 to 1889. Of course the list is not complete, as many contests took place that were not duly reported. Nevertheless we have before us full details concerning 2759 duels which took place in Italy at the period mentioned. Of this number ninety-three per cent. were fought with swords or rapiers, six per cent. with pistols, and one only with revolvers. Strange to say, no less than 3901 wounds were inflicted, so that several combatants must have been wounded more than once, and occasionally both combatants were hurt. Of these wounds 1066 are estimated as serious, and fifty proved fatal. Thus less than two per cent. of the combatants were killed. The danger of death is therefore not very serious : one man in fifty or sixty may be killed. In analysing the causes of all these encounters, it was found that thirty per cent. arose from political divergences of opinion, and newspaper articles concerning the same ; eight per cent. only of the duels were fought in consequence of some serious insult ; but ten per cent. arose out of discussions on religious topics, and nineteen per cent. from quarrels over cards and other games. It is also a curious fact that the number of duels is five times greater in summer than in winter—a self-evident proof that heat affects the temper—while in the Lenten season there are hardly any duels at all, which is perhaps an argument in favour of fasting. Out of a hundred duellists, it was ascertained that thirty were military men, twenty-nine were journalists, twelve were barristers, four students, three professors, three engineers, and three members of parliament.

" The Standard," October 22, *1890.*

DUELS IN HUNGARY.

At Pesth a duel with sabres has just been fought between two officers of the Honved army, which has resulted in one of the combatants, Lieutenant Lazar, having his arm cut off. Another duel, fought with pistols, between two officers of the common army at Kronstadt, in Transylvania, has also had serious results. One of the officers, Count Marenzi, at the second shot received a wound which it is feared may prove fatal.

" St. James's Gazette," October 18, *1890.*

A FRENCH OFFICER'S STRANGE STORY—MYSTERIOUS DUELS.

A court-martial was held at Toulon yesterday to investigate a mysterious and extraordinary case. About four months ago M. Charles Wernert, a sub-lieutenant of marines, disappeared from his regiment, and no trace of him could be found. A day or two ago he gave himself up ; his reason for doing so was, he said, that he had seen in the newspapers that he was accused of being a spy, and he could not submit to allow his name to remain under such an imputation. The story he told to the court was a strange one. Between his relatives and another family at Lyons existed a deadly feud. A duel arose out of it, which took place in the garden of Wernert's house, in the presence of seconds and a doctor. Pistols were at first chosen, but subsequently discarded on account of the noise they would make, and the combat was fought with swords. In five minutes Wernert had run his opponent through the body. He was carried to Lyons, and soon died. One of the deceased man's seconds then challenged the sub-lieutenant. The second encounter also took place in Wernert's garden at night, by the light of lanterns, in presence of seconds and a doctor. The challenger was fatally wounded, although this time Wernert was himself slightly hurt. Fearing that he would be compelled to appear before the assizes to answer for the death of his adversaries, when the whole family drama which caused the combats would be discussed before the public, he determined to fly. Had it not been for the accusation that he was a spy, he would not have returned, in order that the family secret might be left undisturbed. He declined at whatever cost to disclose the secret or the names of his adversaries. The charge on which he appeared before the court-martial was "illegal absence from duty." He was acquitted. The result was received with general satisfaction by the public and by Lieutenant Wernert's fellow-officers, who shook hands with him, and congratulated him warmly.

"Pall Mall Gazette," January 1, 1891.

A DUEL IN THE CAVALRY BARRACKS AT VIENNA BETWEEN COUNTS DEYM AND FRANCIS LÜTZOW.

As was indicated in the *Pall Mall Gazette*, it has been an open secret in London society that unfortunate differences of a personal character had arisen between his Excellency the Austro-Hungarian Ambassador, Count Deym, and Count Francis Lützow, who for some time had been one of the secretaries of the Austrian Embassy here, and whose mother is a sister of the late General Sir Francis Seymour, her Majesty's Master of the Ceremonies. Count Francis Lützow, the Honorary Secretary to the Embassy, married Mademoiselle Bornemann. Count and Countess Deym, for reasons of their own, thought fit to refrain from inviting Countess Lützow to gatherings at the Embassy, and from calling upon her. Resenting this as a slight, Count Lützow called the Ambassador to account, and sent him a challenge. Count Deym went to Vienna expressly to consult Count Kalnoky as to the possibility of his duelling with his secretary. The affair terminated in a duel on the 28th ult., at the Joseph-Stadt Cavalry Barracks at Vienna. His Excellency's seconds were Count Hans Wilczek and Count Charles Kinsky, one of the secretaries to the London Embassy; whilst General von Kodolitsch and Rear-Admiral Count Cassini, formerly Naval Attaché to the Austrian Embassy in London, acted for Count Lützow. Swords were the weapons. Both Counts are excellent swordsmen, and the fight went on without either hurting the other till the number of passages at arms previously agreed upon between the seconds was reached, and "honour," as the farcical phrase goes, "was declared satisfied." The parties to this bloodless duel were then reconciled (says the *Daily News*), and Countess Deym will, it is understood, in future receive Countess Lützow.

"The Standard," January 2, 1891.

COUNT DEYM'S DUEL.

Confirming certain rumours which have been current here for the last day or two, the *Neue Freie Presse* states that a duel has taken place within the past week in the suburbs of Vienna between Count Franz Deym, the Austrian Ambassador at London, and Count Franz Lützow, formerly Honorary Secretary at the same Embassy. The weapons used were pistols. Neither of the combatants received any injury.

The ex-secretary sent a challenge to his former chief in London some time ago, on account of differences of a private nature. The meeting was deferred, partly because it was a question whether an ambassador was bound to accept a challenge from an official subordinate like his secretary. Count Deym, however, thought good to give Count Lützow the desired "satisfaction," and accordingly the two diplomatists travelled direct from London to Vienna for the special purpose of fighting out their quarrel.

The differences between the two Counts have for a long time past been a topic of conversation in London society. All that need be said as to the nature of the quarrel is that it arose rather out of differences on points of form and etiquette than on matters of a more serious character. Count Franz Lützow, who must not be confounded with his brother Count Henry, the present Secretary at the Austrian Legation, left the Embassy, I believe, as far back as November 1889, in consequence of what he took as an offence from the Ambassador.

Count Deym had a private audience of the Emperor to-day, in order to explain the matter, and immediately afterwards left for his Bohemian estate, whence he will shortly travel direct to London to resume his post.

"Pall Mall Gazette," March 3, 1891.

A DUEL BETWEEN FENCING-MASTERS.

The prospect of a duel between the two foremost *maîtres d'armes* has occasioned some excitement in the sporting world of Paris. The meeting is to take place on March 8. The principals (says *Dalziel*) are M. Mérignac, reputed to be the most skilful of French fencers, and M. Vigeant, whose reputation as a swordsman is scarcely less notable. The interest attaching to a hostile encounter between two celebrated professionals is increased by the circumstance that it will be the first that has taken place between French *maîtres d'armes* for the last forty years at least. The rivalry between the two distinguished principals is of old standing, dating, in fact, from a public fencing bout which was fought some ten years ago, and its latest indication arises out of a refusal on the part of M. Mérignac to accept M. Vigeant as a second in a friendly encounter in which he was going to engage. Time will be called at intervals of five minutes, and the combat will continue until one of the parties has been disabled.

It is reported that the seconds having declared that neither party had insulted the other, the quarrel has been patched up.

"St. James's Gazette," April 2, 1891.

A FATAL STAGE DUEL.

The Manchester coroner investigated a case yesterday which disclosed an extraordinary accident on a stage. During the performance of "Romeo and Juliet" by some amateurs in the Manchester Cathedral Schools, the scene in which Mercutio and Tybalt fight a duel with swords was reached, when Romeo, as usual, parted the combatants as Mercutio fell to the ground, saying, "I am hurt. A plague o' both your houses! I am sped; is he gone, and hath nothing?" Both words and action being in the play, no notice was taken of them until blood was seen to be flowing from Mercutio's nose and mouth. He was at once taken to the hospital, but he died before reaching that institution. A *post-mortem* examination showed that a sword had penetrated his chest to a depth of seven inches. It had passed through the lung, penetrated the pericardium, and had wounded the left pulmonary vein. The deceased was Thomas Wilson Whalley, and he was nineteen years of age.

Ernest Thompson, who played the part of Tybalt, said that the duel scene was carried on in the usual way, with the exception that Mr. Bagnall, who was playing Romeo, came right in between himself and the deceased, instead of simply knocking up the swords. The witness made another lunge at the deceased, having to thrust right round Mr. Bagnall's body, but did not feel any resistance to the point of his sword. When he saw the deceased fall, he thought he must have hurt him. No one else could possibly have caused the wound. After he saw the blood flowing from the deceased's mouth, he fainted, and remembered nothing more. He had

had no experience with swords of the kind used in the performance, but had frequently fenced with foils. He had not the slightest idea that he had used sufficient force to cause any wound. When he lunged behind Mr. Bagnall he did not put the weight of his body into the blow.

The coroner pointed out to the jury that with a stiff arm and a slight lunge forward they could send any of the swords used in the performance through a man's body or through a door without feeling any resistance.

Walter Bagnall said he played the part of Romeo. In the duel scene, before he interfered, no unfair thrusts had been given, and no wound, so far as he could see, had been caused. He could not say with certainty whether he himself caused the wound when he threw up the swords.

The coroner said he did not suppose it was anything but an accident ; but there had been some degree of negligence on the part of every one who took part in the performance.

The jury returned a verdict of "Death from loss of blood from a wound received while taking part in a dramatic performance."

"*The Daily Telegraph*," April 4, 1891.

COMBATS ON THE STAGE.

To the Editor of "The Daily Telegraph."—Sir,—The accident mentioned in your yesterday's issue, where a death occurred on the stage, reminds me of an occurrence when I was playing Romeo to the Juliet of the late Miss Neilson, in 1879. Being my first appearance in the part, I wished to make the best impression I could, and attended the dress rehearsal fully equipped with dagger and a Damascus blade sharp as a razor. I was about to commence the duel with Mercutio when Miss Neilson stopped the combat, and entreated me to proceed no further, save with a blunted weapon.

I followed her advice. But a few years later, forgetful of her counsel, I was wounded at the Lyceum, when playing the same part with Mary Anderson, in falling upon a dagger, which pierced my side.

The moral is that in stage combats no weapon should be used that is pointed or sharp enough to inflict injury.—I am, Sir, your obedient servant,   WILLIAM TERRISS.

Lyceum Theatre, April 3.

"*Pall Mall Gazette*," May 16, 1891.

THE GERMAN EMPEROR AND DUELLING.

The *National Zeitung* and the *Freisinnige Zeitung* report that great dissatisfaction exists among the professors and University authorities at

NOTES ON FENCING AND DUELLING

Bonn, owing to the way in which the speech lately delivered there by the Emperor has been interpreted by the corps-students; the latter having become more arrogant in their demeanour, while the number of duels has greatly increased.—*Reuter.*

"The Daily News," May 18, 1891.

FENCING AND DUELS.

Fencing has, for some time, regained a little of its popularity in England. We never practically need the art in private life, for we never were so much addicted to duelling with the sword as with the pistol, and now we never "go out," at least in England. But fencing is an exercise so graceful, so healthy, so good for legs, hand, wind, and even brain, that its new vogue is well merited. Stage duels are no longer what they were in the days of Mr. Vincent Crummles : Mr. Irving, Mr. Forbes Robertson, and others use the sword as it ought to be used. Paris and Romeo, or Tybalt and Mercutio, meet like swordsmen, giving their "one, two, and the third in your breast," even if their practice is not in the old Italian manner, after the school of Saviolo (1595). Meanwhile duelling flourishes mightily on the Continent, in spite of Emperors and Ministers who try, what has been tried a dozen times, to put it down. On all these matters of point and edge Mr. Carl Thimm has lately compiled a pleasant and handy book, "A Bibliography of Fencing" * (Thimm), with a few anecdotes of the modern *monomachia.* This is as useful to the student as to the collector, though a chapter on that little understood matter, the Code or Law of the Duel, would have been a desirable addition. Novelists are sadly to seek in this knowledge. Mr. Froude, in his romance, "The Two Chiefs of Dunboy," has a duel in which, according to our humble theory, almost all possible errors are committed. To be sure, the fight was in Ireland, where very odd and lawless things have occasionally been perpetrated. The novelists' common error is to give the challenged party the choice of weapons. Scythes were once chosen at Oxford—"sharp work." But on the Continent it is not the challenged who has the selection. This would give a bully his opportunity. The bully strikes a man, is certain to be the challenged, and proposes his favourite weapon, be it sword, sabre, or pistol. Abroad, as a rule, the provoked or insulted man has the choice. New times have new manners. Once the left arm, cloaked, gauntleted, or armed with a dagger, might be used in parrying. Now any guarding with the left hand is forbidden. A nervous action of the left hand is natural to beginners, and thus a tradesman killed an officer a few years ago, meaning no harm. In sabre duels it is desirable to settle beforehand whether the point may be used. A death caused by the point when point is "barred,"

Vide THIMM (C. A.).—1891.

leads to some unpleasantness. The Englishman who may find himself drawn into a duel abroad will do well to study the laws of the game. In Germany, where an Englishman, provoked by a student, chose pistols, his enemy never came on the ground at all. Villainous saltpetre is a great leveller, and many a noisy bravo of the blade greatly dislikes facing the barrel.

Mr. Thimm's book is full of curiosities. For example, he mentions an extremely rare and early work of Jayme Pons,* published at Perpigñan in 1474. More information is much needed on this head; the original title is not given, nor the size or *format* of the volume. Bibliography should be done far otherwise than thus. The old books of all are pedantically fond of the Antiquities of the Duel. How did Cain and Abel arrange their affair, Cain being a churl and Abel a gentleman? Was David's conduct in the duel with Goliath exactly correct? The Philistine was, we are now told, of Greek stock. He could not have expected the use of a missile. Even Paris, a bowman, did not shoot at Menelaus in their duel under Ilios. David's duel, with the two unfinished affairs in the "Iliad," is the oldest of which we have any knowledge. That of Aias and Hector was fought in a very courteous manner, and the seconds separated the heroes before anything deadly was done. Duelling was extremely distasteful to Greek manners. Even in Homer it is rare, and business is not meant. In civil life it was practically unknown, or Demosthenes would never have been off "the ground." Had Mark Antony been allowed to challenge Cicero, had Catiline been permitted to send a friend to the orator's house, we must have missed a great deal of eloquence. Even the gladiatorial shows did not introduce duelling into Rome. Murders and mobbings were more in the classical taste. It is to the Northern Holm-gang, followed by the feudal Judgment of God, that we owe the modern duel. The most entertaining historian of the duello in its wildest vagaries is Brantôme,† and single combat never flourished more merrily than under Henri III. The Renaissance produced a poet who denounced the duel, a rhymer named St. Polycarpe, whose book is "Sonnets contre les Escrimeurs et les Duellistes" (Paris, 1588). But neither sonnets nor edicts have ever been of any avail in France. Even the articles of M. Paul de Cassagnac ‡ against the art in which he excels are fruitless. In France a duel is an excellent advertisement. Particulars are published, as if the affair were a match of sporting interest. The adversaries as a rule keep at a very respectable distance, foining at the hand and wrist, which are partly guarded by the large bowl-hilts. "First blood" settles most strife, and a stand-up fight with fists is really a greater trial of courage than an ordinary duel of courtesy. But "steel draws the hand of the heroes;" the fighting fever may come on, and

* *Vide* PONS (de M.).—1474.
† *Vide* BRANTÔME (Mémoires de).—1722.
‡ *Vide* JACOB (Jules). 1887.

accidents will happen, especially among bad fencers. As to pistols, they are dangerous toys, even at a "nice gentlemanly distance."

Of a Scot abroad, in New Caledonia, it is told that he is ready to meet any Frenchman with either sword or pistol, and, as he means business, he is fighting his way into the general affection. In 1890, M. Mermeix fought M. de Labruyère—a desperate encounter. It was to go on "until one of the combatants found himself in a state of inferiority verified by the doctors." Unluckily the duel had been stopped for a moment by a second ; one of the antagonists did not hear, or did not heed, when the umpire cried "Over !" and there was a lamentable accident. It may be credited that no treachery was intended. Every bowler knows how hard it is to stop the delivery of the ball when the batsman holds up his hand to show that he is not ready to receive it. M. Mermeix, we may suppose, was in the position of the bowler. Romeo's perilous practice of striking up the swords yet exists when duels are fought in the French army ; and, when the second tries to prevent too shrewd a stroke, this may do much more harm than good. For ourselves, nothing but a complete overthrow of civilisation can bring the duel back into our manners. It died more of ridicule than of fear. We are not a people to put up with duels of courtesy ; we used the pistol, and the pistol could not be stopped by a second because it was too well aimed. Few could spare and slightly wound an opponent with the pistol, as may so easily be done with the small-sword. There is no use in regretting the duel, though it might sometimes be convenient. It gives the bully too good an opportunity, as in the detestable case of Fighting Fitzgerald. Its disuse has not brought in the informal "shooting at sight" of America—much the worst form of duelling. Moreover, with the duel, horsewhipping has gone out, for it is notoriously cowardly to strike a man and then refuse him satisfaction. Of the English moderns who have tried to appeal to the duel, it may be said that they are not chiefly famous for courage and chivalry. Duelling in England died when it became "ungentlemanly." Abroad the right to fight makes every man a gentleman. It is a bequest of the French Revolution, which gave all an equal right to appeal to the sword—once a knightly weapon, now accessible to all.

" The Times," May 21, 1891.

DUELLING IN GERMAN UNIVERSITIES.

To the Editor of "The Times."—Sir,—Whatever the German Emperor has lately said about duelling in German universities, he has not said what most Germans would say and think.

I well remember the rules at Göttingen concerning duels. They took place outside the town at a short distance away, and we used to go out in the early mornings to this place, where no police ever appeared. Duels were winked at by the officers of the law, and are part and parcel of German life. During the days of the American Civil War I associated with one of the corps, and saw a vast amount of beer imbibed and blood shed.

The son of Count Beust met with an accident through the breaking-off of a sword, the piece entering his skull, but I was not present when this accident happened. He lay in danger for a long time. But I knew of no other dangerous case.

One Scotch gentleman, a Mr. Clarke, was constantly involved in duels, he being a member of a corps; but, with that exception, no foreigner was ever involved in a duel while I was at Göttingen. I may mention that this Scotch gentleman held his own in all the duels in which he was involved, his antagonists getting the worst of the fray.

Duelling in the town of Göttingen was not allowed, but every soul there knew where the duels were fought out. They took place in a large restaurant building, having a pleasant garden attached.

Whatever may be said against duels, they decidedly have not lessened German courage, and I believe a man who has gone through the ordeal is none the worse, be it for civil employment, or for "food for cannon," as they call it there. I met a highly intelligent chemist at Schuls in the autumn—a Swiss—who told me that in all his holidays he returned to the University, and made a point and practice to have one, two, or three duels every holiday.

At his University the rules were to fight with iron spectacles over the eyes, and bare neck; or without spectacles, and with silk handkerchiefs wound round the neck. To be without the latter made a deadly wound possible. To be without the spectacles made loss of eyesight possible. He said to me: "Say what you like against the practice, but to feel one-self man to man, with cold steel in one's hand, does one good; and the custom makes people brave in my eyes, and it is or has *etwas schönes* in it." His idea of a holiday may be peculiar. As to the sentiments expressed by the Emperor, any one who has lived in Germany takes such sentiments for granted. There are worse customs and habits than the German *schläger* duel or sabre duel.—Yours obediently,

ARCHIBALD CAMPBELL.

Coombe Hill Farm,
Kingston-on-Thames, *May* 20.

"*Pall Mall Gazette*," *May* 25, 1891.

AN AUSTRIAN BARON'S DUEL IN CHICAGO—ONE OF THE COMBATANTS SERIOUSLY INJURED.

Baron Rudolf Kalnoky de Korös-Patak, nephew of Count Kalnoky, Prime Minister of Austria, fought a duel at daybreak yesterday, in Jackson Park at Chicago, with an unknown Southerner, who is believed to be the son of a prominent citizen of Atlanta, Georgia. The weapons used were rapiers.

Baron Kalnoky arrived at Chicago a month ago. The object of his visit was a mystery to all except to Mr. Carlson, the manager of the Richelieu Hotel, to whom he partly told his story. He said he was at one time a staunch defender and passionate admirer of Queen Natalie of Servia during his visits to the Austrian capital. He had also been the chosen companion of the gay young Prince Imperial of Austria; and on the suicide of the Prince he was driven into wilder dissipations, and finally sought change in America.

By accident he met with Miss Mattie Atherton, a member of the Duff Opera Company during their last Chicago engagement, and fell madly in love with her. She kept before him the fact that she could never become his wife, because her heart already belonged to another, for whom she would soon quit the stage. Baron Kalnoky followed her from Chicago to Louisville, where he met another candidate for her affections. The rivals returned to Chicago together on Friday night, and dined at the Richelieu Hotel. Kalnoky's companion drank too much wine, and a quarrel ensued, the Baron knocking down his rival for speaking disrespectfully of the woman he loved. An hour afterwards a friend of the Southerner appeared with a note demanding a meeting. Kalnoky at once accepted, and details were arranged on Saturday night. Kalnoky's second selected rapiers as the weapons to be used, the Baron being unfamiliar with the use of the pistol.

Before the duel the Austrian expressed a desire to Mr. Carlson to die in the duel. If he did, he said, it would obviate the necessity of his taking his own life. His wild life had been the occasion of his being disowned by his own family, and suicide was the only recourse left to one who was without a home and without love. He then settled his bill, and left word that if he did not survive the duel all his belongings should be sent to the woman for whose honour he fought. At four o'clock yesterday morning he went to the rendezvous, taking with him a prominent young physician who resides in Prairie Avenue, and whom he formerly knew when the latter was a student in Vienna.

At 6.10 the combatants were facing each other, stripped to their shirts. After some sharp fighting the Southerner succeeded in inflicting a slight wound in the Baron's right leg. Later, the Baron, by a clever lunge, pricked the skin of his antagonist's shoulder. Up to this time both men had fenced with care. Suddenly, however, to the horror of the seconds, Kalnoky appeared to slip, and literally fell upon his adversary's sword, which entered his neck. A stream of blood gushed from the wound. The seconds at once stopped the combat, and the Baron's wound was dressed by his friend the physician. The Southerner fled. All attempts to identify him have failed. It is known, however, that he boarded the train for Cincinnati two hours later. The Baron's whereabouts is a secret. His friends say that his life is not in immediate danger, but Mr. Carlson fears that the Baron will make an attempt on his own life.

" The Pelican," June 27, 1891.

JAMAICA—SANGUINARY ENCOUNTER.

The average modern duel is invariably a tame affair, especially if it takes place on the Continent. In the Wild West of America things are a little more lively, but it is to Jamaica one must go to witness a real downright sanguinary encounter. Not long since four Jamaica gentlemen quarrelled about a lady, and arming themselves with machetas, a species of sharp and heavy sickle, they met one fine evening and proceeded to settle their mutual difference by hacking one another to pieces. Needless to add, the result of the conflict was of a very conclusive nature, for such was the fury of the fight that all four men expired in a few moments. What became of the lady is not stated. Possibly she is now consoling herself with a fifth admirer.

" Pall Mall Gazette," July 2, 1891.

SIR WILFRID LAWSON.

Sir Wilfrid Lawson said rather a good thing yesterday in connection with the German Emperor's recent defence of duelling and beer-drinking: "If these institutions are to be the pillar of the German nation, the national flag might come to be known as the ' Scars and Swipes.' "

" The Daily Telegraph," July 3, 1891.

DO WOMEN FENCE?

" Do women fence?" is a query which would meet with a decided affirmative by a casual spectator who had happened to look into Mr. M'Pherson's pretty gymnasium in Sloane Street yesterday afternoon, when the stronger and fairer sex was in a decided majority to witness the excellent fencing bouts afforded by M. Lamarle of Epernay, M. C. Dessort of Rheims, M. Oudart and M. Menu of Lille, Professor Bourgeois, Mr. Crackenthorpe, M. Le Gaudaurville, M. de Goncer, Mr. F. G. M'Pherson, Captain Vaughan Williams, and M. M. Waddington, son of the French

NOTES ON FENCING AND DUELLING

Ambassador. Keen appreciation of thrust and parry, defence and attack, was given by the ladies present, who included Lady Brassey, the Hon. M. Brassey, the Hon. Mrs. Thomas Grosvenor, the Hon. Mrs. Norman Grosvenor, and the Hon. M. Capell. The foreign visitors were delighted with the kindly reception given to them, and were much interested in the other contests—the boxing between Messrs. Ramplin, Parker, and Suttle, the sword and bayonet exercise of Messrs. Maclaren and Dimmock, and the Indian club act of Professor Cousin. Such an interesting exhibition might well be repeated in perhaps less trying weather.

" The Standard, July 23, 1891.

AUSTRIAN 79TH REGIMENT OF INFANTRY.

The officers of the Austrian 79th Regiment of Infantry, consisting of Croatians, stationed at Fiume, being offended by a speech recently made in the Hungarian Chamber by the Radical Deputy Ugron, sent two captains to Pesth to challenge him to a duel. M. Ugron accordingly named his seconds; but the latter held that a Deputy cannot be held responsible for what he may say in Parliament, except by the President of the House. The question was submitted to a Committee of Honour, consisting of twenty Deputies, who have now unanimously declared that M. Ugron cannot accept the challenge.

"Evening News and Post" (London), August 11, 1891.

WHY NOT REVIVE DUELLING?

" It is probable," says *Vanity Fair,* "that the total abolition of duelling in England, and the disfavour into which it has fallen abroad, are one great cause of the display of selfishness and ill-breeding for which we now look, almost as a matter of course, among well-dressed people. Sixty years ago a young man who at a crowded semi-public concert lounged the whole evening in an arm-chair, regardless of the beseeching glances of delicate girls and ladies old enough to be his grandmother leaning wearily against the wall, and wondering what price would be too high to pay for ten minutes' rest—sixty years ago such a fellow would have had the impropriety of his conduct pointed out to him in a manner that would have prevented him feeling any desire to sit down for some time, however many might be the seats available. And if in those days a wandering politician, however notorious, had sent a message by a servant to a lady to move her chair because she interfered with the amusement of the distinguished traveller and his friends, he would assuredly have spent part of his morning on shore, a few—a very few—yards from the muzzle of a pistol. However much contempt he might feel for his fellow-passengers, he would think several times before expressing it if he reflected that, though he did not consider them good enough to dine at his table, they yet thought themselves—and each other—quite good enough to insist on an explanation of his words, and that the failure to explain them satisfactorily might be punished by a bullet in a soft part of his body. Why not revive duelling, then?"

"The Standard," August 21, 1891.

DR. TANNER CHALLENGED TO A DUEL.

The Local Committee of "L'Union des Femmes de France" (Ladies' Ambulance Society) gave its annual ball last night in the *salons* of the Casino in this town [Boulogne]. The attendance was very large, and the English visitors were numerous. As usual at these gatherings, a great many military officers attended, as on these occasions the officers of the Reserve are permitted to appear in uniform. The heat of the *salons* necessitated some ventilation, and a window was thrown open, around which some English ladies and gentlemen gathered. An officer who was on the committee ordered the window to be closed, which was objected to by the British subjects, among whom was Dr. Tanner, M.P. He remarked to his partner, who was complaining of the oppressive heat, " I suppose the only thing that would make them open the windows would be the Prussians."

M. Jacques Picart, chef de bataillon in the 7ème Territoriale, who was standing by, caught the last word, and followed Dr. Tanner, at the same time using most insulting and offensive language to the honourable member for Cork. The latter, not wishing to cause a disturbance, walked away and took no notice of the angry soldier. The Frenchman, not to be put off, demanded Dr. Tanner's card, which the latter refused to give ; but upon Captain Villiot, commandant of the garrison here, who acted as M. Picart's second, demanding it, Dr. Tanner referred him to a friend.

A meeting of the seconds took place this morning, when the unfortunate affair was discussed. It is more than probable, however, that it will be amicably arranged, and that firearms will not be brought into requisition.

Thursday Night.—The anticipated duel between Dr. Tanner and M. Picart will not take place. At a meeting this afternoon the former expressed regret at having used the word " Prussien," which he withdrew. M. Picart apologised for the insulting words he had used. A *procès-verbal* of the proceedings was drawn up and signed by the parties concerned. It will not be communicated to the press.

NOTES ON FENCING AND DUELLING

DUEL BETWEEN MR. JOHN SCOTT AND MR. CHRISTIE (NOTES ON).

"Pall Mall Gazette," September 9, 1891.

One can hardly believe that the author of "The Angel in the House" was ever second at a duel. But so it is said. The late Mr. Joseph Irving, whose death we announced yesterday, used to tell that Miss Mackay, whom Dr. John Brown, the author of "Rab and His Friends," took to wife, was a niece of Mr. Scott, of the *Champion* newspaper and *London Magazine*, and author of sundry interesting books of Continental travel, and that he was ultimately killed in a duel by a Mr. Christie. Mr. Coventry Patmore was (the *Glasgow Mail* states) Scott's second at the tragical meeting.

"Pall Mall Gazette," September 11, 1891.

Mr. Coventry Patmore was never second at a duel. "J. D. C." calls attention to the paragraph quoted from the *Glasgow Mail* in this column the other day, and says that the duel between Mr. John Scott and Mr. Christie was fought in February 1821, while Mr. Coventry Patmore was not born till July 23, 1823 !

"The Herald," September 13, 1891.

THE ITALIAN SWORD-CANE FENCING FAD.

The Italian sword-cane fencing fad is being introduced in London, although it is hard to see of what use it will be in a country where the possession of a sword-cane is a crime. The fencer uses the blade to attack, and the sheath to assist in defence. The sheath is held in the left hand, and the blade in the right. When standing on guard the sword arm is farthest from the enemy—an exact reversal of the rule in ordinary fencing.

"The Standard," September 19, 1891.

AN ITALIAN DUEL.

The appointment of General Gandolfi as Governor of Massowah having been confirmed, Deputy Franchetti, who had charge of the Colonisation Office, has published a letter tendering his resignation, on account of a misunderstanding with General Gandolfi. The result of this difference was that a duel with sabres took place to-day between the General and the Deputy, in which the latter received a wound on the head. General Gandolfi has also offered to resign.

NOTES ON FENCING AND DUELLING

" New York Herald " (*New York*), *June* 2, 1891.

EMPEROR WILLIAM IS CHALLENGED TO A DUEL.

Herr Richard Goerdeler, a well-known German, who has filled many positions, and who is at present a professor of music at the Pennington Seminary in New Jersey, has leaped into sudden notoriety. It is not unusual for one man to challenge another to a duel, but it is quite unusual —in fact, unprecedented—for a private person to challenge a monarch to single combat. He says he has sent a challenge to no less a personage than Emperor William II. of Germany.

The story of Goerdeler's life, as he gives it out, is quite a romance. If true, his troubles have unbalanced his mind.

In 1862 Herr Goerdeler was a lieutenant in the Prussian army, and was brought at times into contact with Bismarck. On one occasion, the story goes, he learned that the Chancellor had ordered a cargo of arms to be shipped to the Confederate soldiers in this country, and had expressed a wish that they might be satisfactorily used for the purpose of boring holes in the Federal soldiers. In some way or other Bismarck learned that the young lieutenant had discovered this secret, and from that moment began to compass his downfall.

The first step was to get Goerdeler removed from the army, and in this the Chancellor easily succeeded. The next step was to ruin him socially and financially, and in this, too, Prince Bismarck was successful. Goerdeler was engaged to a handsome young girl, and Bismarck trumped up a charge of forgery against her, and finally induced her to marry another. Goerdeler's mother interfered when his *fiancée* was about to be prosecuted, and then Bismarck conspired against her ; but in this case her family connections, and the fact that she was the wife of a Prussian judge, rendered even his efforts nugatory. Goerdeler had some property, and even out of this the unscrupulous Chancellor succeeded in wheedling him.

At last the young man, driven to bay, determined to hit back, and the result was that he wrote a letter to the Emperor, in which he told his story, and asked for the Chancellor's arrest and trial.

To this letter he got no answer, but Bismarck was soon afterwards deprived of the Chancellorship, and Herr Goerdeler is said to be convinced that his old enemy's fall from power was the direct result of his appeal to the Emperor.

Even this amount of revenge, however, did not satisfy the ex-lieutenant. Having been obliged to give up a lucrative position in Berlin—that of representative of the Northern Pacific Railroad—he came to this country, and soon obtaining employment in the Insurance Department at Albany, set his brain to work at planning further schemes for his old enemy's ruin. He brooded long over the matter, and finally, after he had left Albany and secured a position as professor of music at the Pennington Seminary, he came to the conclusion that Bismarck and he could no longer remain in the land of the living, and that one of them must surely die.

He sent a long and imperative letter to young Kaiser Wilhelm, calmly informing him that he must either hang Bismarck or fight a duel with the writer of the letter. Full details of the proposed duel were given in the letter, and the Kaiser was made plainly to understand that Bismarck must be dead by the hangman's rope before July 18, or on that day he (Emperor William) must face Herr Goerdeler's pistol in a pleasant grove near Hamm, Westphalia. The duel is to be fought with hair triggers at eighteen paces.

No reply has yet been received from the Kaiser, and the cable has not yet announced the hanging of Prince Bismarck.

I went to Pennington and interviewed Goerdeler. He told me the challenge reached the Emperor on April 27 last, when the latter was standing alongside the bier of Field-Marshal Von Moltke. He intends sailing for Germany on June 27.

I found him in his den, a small, dingy-looking room, about eight feet by four, facing the campus of the seminary. He hailed me from the entrance to the dining-hall, and by his salutation had evidently preconceived what I was after.

" Do I look like a crank ? " said he, as he ran his long, bony fingers through his thin growth of hair, and, without waiting for an answer, invited me inside to his studio, as the place is miscalled.

" Sit down and I will tell you all about it," he mildly commanded me, and, before I had a chance to take my hat off, the Professor began rattling off a series of grievances against the Emperor, Prince Bismarck, and the members of the two distinguished families.

" Don't put me down as a crank, because I am not one," said he again; " but listen to what I say, and take notes of my story carefully."

I could hardly get a word in edgeways, the Professor talked so rapidly; but at last I was permitted to ask him how long he had been in this country.

" I am a native of Germany," replied the fidgety, spare-boned man, " and have been twenty-six years in this country. I have been a citizen of the United States twenty years, having been naturalised at Danville, Boyle County, Ky. I have been only one year in this seminary."

" And your age—about sixty, I presume ? " I said to him, because he looks fully that old.

" Oh, only fifty-two," said the Professor smilingly. The Professor is an ascetic-looking person, and just nervous enough to kick up a row on slight provocation, and fight it out with pistols or sabres, perhaps, if need be.

"Have you fought duels before?"

"Oh yes, I have : several while I was a student in the German university and an officer in the German army."

"How many men have you killed in your day?"

"None at all; but I have been wounded myself in the head with sabres several times. See that?" said he, as he pointed to a slight scar above his forehead; "that came from a sabre cut."

"You are a good shot, then?"

"Oh yes; pretty good. The Emperor, however, is a poor shot; but that gives him the best chance, because he is likely to fire last, and the last shot generally brings down the adversary."

"Well, what is your grievance against the Emperor?"

The Professor rattled off a long story, the substance of which has been given above. He said he was forced to resign from the Insurance Department in Albany on October 17, 1889, on the charge of having prevented the Harper's Mutual Reserve Fund from getting a permit from Berlin to do business in Germany.

"Bismarck," he continued, "had this charge preferred against me. Subsequently, Emperor William received a letter from me with a forgery enclosed, by which two Prussian judges, friends of Bismarck's boys, wanted to get my signature, in order to swindle me out of my inheritance. I requested the Emperor not to hush up this forgery as he did the one sent the imperial prosecutor, June 28, 1889, and which had cheated my sister, who is an inmate of a lunatic asylum in Germany, out of her means of support. The Emperor sent for Bismarck at once, and inquired what forgery I referred to. Bismarck told the Emperor a lie, that the forgery was my mother's; and she was the widow of a judge of the Superior Court, therefore nothing could be done.

"For casting a suspicion on my mother, I called out the Emperor; and my friends, among them being Baron Trebord, of Halle, Germany, are looking after my interests. Bismarck knows I am an energetic, ambitious man, and not intended to end my life as a music teacher. Bismarck thought I would make a rush for the Emperor, proclaim a German Republic, and announce to the world that hereafter the German people would govern themselves, and become a great and free nation. I deem it most likely that Bismarck will be placed on public trial, and the world will be the better for it."

"Your grievances seem to be more against Bismarck than the Emperor," I said. "Then why have you not challenged the Prince instead of the Emperor?"

"My answer to that is," replied the Professor, "that I deem it best to go to the head of the heap to get satisfaction. The Emperor is the responsible party, and he must fight me."

He made other charges against the Prince, among them being the comical one that he generally ate fifty eggs for his breakfast, while he would not permit a poor family to have a mouthful of meat.

The Professor seemed to be willing to talk all night about his grievances. I intimated that I had enough already to fill an entire page of the *Herald*, and as I was about to leave him he said—

"If the Emperor kills me, I will die shouting 'The German Republic for ever ;' and if I die, my death will be the signal for an uprising of the German people in favour of free government such as the world has rarely witnessed. My proposition for conducting the duel is that we shall stand at a distance of nine paces ; when the word of command is given, each must advance three paces, take deliberate aim, and fire."

The Professor retired to his den in a seemingly happy frame of mind.

To make sure that the *Herald* got his side of the story, Professor Goerdeler telegraphed a long statement last night to this office.

" The Times " (Weekly Edition), November 20, 1891.

THE SWORD.

Sir F. Pollock's Lecture.

On Wednesday, Sir F. Pollock * gave a lecture in connection with the Inns of Court Rifle Volunteers, in the School of Arms, Lincoln's Inn, the subject of the lecture being entitled "The Sword." Pointing out that the small sword of modern days was a late product of swordsmanship, he traced the development of the weapon through ancient and mediæval times, illustrating the subject at every step by the aid of an interesting and complete collection of swords and daggers of European as well as of Eastern types. Both the straight and the curved types were extremely ancient, and it was impossible to say which was the older ; among European nations straight swords had been the most prevalent form, while the curved form generally indicated an Eastern origin, and indeed it was still preferred by Eastern nations. The original European sword was a straight one, and through the Middle Ages it was straight and double-edged ; and, showing the modifications it underwent and the art of fencing itself as time went on, he mentioned that it was impossible to understand the Elizabethan literature without some idea of the rapier play of the sixteenth century. Out of the rapier play grew the brighter and finer methods of modern fence, the first step in the evolution being the discarding of the dagger which was used in the left hand. In the seventeenth and the early

* *Vide* Pollock (F.).—1890.

477

part of the eighteenth century there were a series of transition types, and then came in the French three-edged sword, the type of the French duel sword. Dealing with the development of the cut and point play, he observed that a certain tradition of broadsword exercise in this country had always enabled us to keep up a fair standard of sabre play, although in this regard the French, and probably the Italians, too, were our masters. The old Scottish broadsword, which came through a Venetian pattern, had shown great persistence of form, the present Highland regulation sword being of exactly the same pattern as one he exhibited, which was 250 years old. Coming to the modern cavalry sword, he shortly described the processes of manufacture, and spoke in commendatory terms of the weapon in point of balance, strength, and quality. With regard to the British bayonet, he stated that, having seen the latest pattern a few days ago, he was able to say that there very soon would be in the hands of British troops 300,000 sword-bayonets made with exactly the same care and subjected to the same tests, only rather more severe, as the very best sword-blades.

"Pall Mall Gazette," December 8, 1891.

A NON-DUELLING OFFICER EXPELLED THE ARMY.

Once more the question of "duelling in the army" is being discussed actively in military circles. A few days ago (says the *Telegraph's* Paris correspondent) a captain in an infantry regiment stationed in a country town, having been insulted grossly by a brother-officer, sent him a challenge in the usual way, but having for some reason or another failed to obtain the "satisfaction" desired, he went up to him in the presence of several comrades and boxed his ears soundly. Even this heroic measure, however, was powerless to attain the wished-for result. There is no knowing what development this quarrel would not have assumed had not the colonel in command of the corps got wind of the affair. He promptly addressed an ultimatum to the assaulted officer, to the effect that within the next forty-eight hours he must either make up his mind to accept the challenge or send in his papers. The latter alternative was selected, and the officer in question is retiring from the army. Duels between officers have been by no means of common occurrence of late years. It is conjectured that the officer who declined to fight was animated either by some scruple as to the lawfulness of the "duel" from a religious or moral point of view, or by the feeling that his would-be adversary was not worthy to cross swords with him. But whatever the motive may have been, the attitude assumed by the colonel as a rule is commended warmly ; and this fact shows that on occasion the "duel" is still regarded as compulsory in military circles.

NOTES ON FENCING AND DUELLING

"*The Hawk*," *February* 2, 1892.

PUNCH'S CARTOON ON GERMAN STUDENTS' DUEL.

I have been sent the following :—

BIRKDALE PARK, SMEDLEY HYDROPATHIC
ESTABLISHMENT, SOUTHPORT,
January 28.

DEAR HAWKSHAW,—Linley Sambourne has made an extraordinary mistake in yesterday's *Punch.* He represents two German students fighting with the French duelling sword and using the point. Now German students always fight with the *schläger,* and never thrust.

The hand which holds the weapon is raised above the level, and well in front of the head, and the blade comes down somewhat diagonally in front of the body. The cuts are delivered with the wrist alone. Had Mr. Sambourne consulted any work on the subject, he would have found that the combatants are very differently attired to the pair he presents to us. On the head is a cap with a strong peak to protect the eye ; a thick stock is round the throat.

Leathern trousers are worn, and the right arm is swathed in bandages which are so cumbersome that between the rounds the arm has to be supported. Nor do the seconds sit idly by, as represented in Mr. Sambourne's picture. They are extremely active, and, sword in hand, are prepared at any moment to interfere and intercept any blow not in accordance with the laws of the game. At one university, and one alone, has the point been used in my time, and there, I believe, it is no longer employed. That university is Jena, and the reason why the use of the small sword was allowed is an odd one. Jena was the great resort of theological students, and a theological student with a sword-cut on his face was not admitted into the ministry. Permission was therefore given by the student code to Jenaites to settle their disputes by running one another through the body.—Yours, R. K. H.

"*The Standard*," *February* 20, 1892.

ENGLISHMEN AND DUELS.

QUESTIONS IN THE HOUSE OF COMMONS.

Mr. Esslemont asked the Under Secretary for Foreign Affairs whether the British Vice-Consul in Paris acted as second in a duel fought in or near Paris last November ; and if so, whether any notice had been taken, or was intended to be taken, in regard to the Vice-Consul's conduct.

NOTES ON FENCING AND DUELLING

Mr. J. W. Lowther said that no information on the subject had been received at the Foreign Office, nor had any intimation reached the Secretary of State that any charge of this character had been made against the gentleman referred to.

Mr. Esslemont asked if the Under Secretary would be good enough to inquire if such a charge had been made. He would be glad to put him in possession of any information he had.

Mr. Lowther.—I should like to point out to the hon. gentleman that at present there is no evidence that any offence, punishable either by the law of this country or by the law of France, has been committed.

Mr. Esslemont.—I desire to point out—

The Speaker.—Order, order.

Mr. Esslemont.—I desire to ask whether, without reference to an offence, it is the fact that the Vice-Consul did act as a second in a duel?

Mr. Lowther.—I have already told the hon. member that we have not a shadow of a shade of evidence of any such fact.

Mr. Esslemont.—If I put the Under Secretary in possession of the evidence, will he not make an inquiry?

Mr. Lowther.—If the hon. member will bring forward his evidence, the Secretary of State will no doubt consider it—(hear, hear).

" The Standard," March 16, 1892.

DUEL BETWEEN M. ISAAC AND MARQUIS DE MORÈS.

A duel with swords took place in the vicinity of Paris yesterday morning between M. Isaac, formerly sub-Prefect of Avesnes, and the Marquis de Morès. The former was slightly wounded in the chest.

" Pall Mall Gazette," March 29, 1892.

A SPANISH DUEL AMID PELTING RAIN.

Don Jose Maria Beranger has been reinstated as Minister of Marine in the Spanish Cabinet. This gallant vice-admiral resigned his post at the beginning of last November, in order to engage in an "affair of honour" with the editor of the *Resumen*, which, even in the land of Don Quixote, seemed very similar to a dramatic farce. On the morning of November 6, at 10.50 A.M., in a quiet suburb of Madrid, the duel was fought amid pelting rain. At the word of command one pistol discharged, that of the editor hanging fire. No harm was done. "I have not come here for nothing," cried the gallant admiral. Again they set to work. A bullet whizzed past the admiral's ear, and honour was satisfied.

NOTES ON FENCING AND DUELLING

" The Standard," May 19, 1892.

EXTRAORDINARY SERIES OF DUELS.

A series of encounters, which are probably unprecedented in the annals of duelling, took place at an early hour this morning in a secluded part of the Bois de Boulogne.

The affair arose out of a quarrel which originated at the Opera during the first representation of "Salammbo" on Monday evening. Among the audience was a gentleman named Roulez, who is a prominent member of the Ecole d'Escrime Française, and who, in the business world, is well known as an inventor of telephonic apparatus. An altercation occurred between this gentleman, who is over fifty years of age, and some younger men. It ended in the former sending a formal challenge to three of the latter, MM. Blondin, Dumoulin, and Leclerc.

M. Roulez was represented in the matter by two of his relatives, and it was arranged that he should fight his three adversaries, one after the other, in the Bois de Boulogne this morning. The meeting took place accordingly. M. Roulez, accompanied by his seconds and a doctor arrived at the appointed rendezvous punctually at nine o'clock. He found his three opponents, who are all young men between thirty and thirty-five years of age, already in attendance, each being accompanied by two seconds and a doctor.

The preliminaries had all been satisfactorily arranged, and the combat was at once begun. Duelling swords of the regulation description were the weapons chosen. The first adversary M. Roulez was called upon to confront was M. Blondin, and the fight lasted only a few moments. Rapidly disengaging, *tierce quarte,* M. Roulez passed his sword through the body of his opponent, severely wounding him, and, it is reported, piercing one of his lungs. The seconds and medical men immediately intervened and stopped the fight.

The wounded man having been carried off the ground, M. Dumoulin, attended by his seconds, next confronted the victor. The second contest was almost as brief as, and ended not less decisively than, the first. M. Dumoulin received a thrust so skilfully and vigorously directed that the sword passed right through his arm, and wounded him slightly in the side.

Having thus effectually disposed of his first two adversaries, M. Roulez, after a short breathing space, again took up his position, and faced M. Leclerc. The latter, perceiving that he had to do with a fencer of extraordinary skill and endurance, did not long stand his ground. He began to retreat, defending himself as best he could against the furious

481   2 H

onslaught of the veteran swordsman, who, however, throughout the third combat, showed no sign of fatigue, but, on the contrary, pressed M. Leclerc so hard, and with such consummate mastery of the art of fence, as to corner him by driving him against a tree after he had retreated a distance of nearly two hundred yards. On coming in contact with the tree, M. Leclerc was unable any longer to act upon the defensive, and, on attempting to advance, he was wounded in the face by the sword of M. Roulez. This put an end to the combat.

But M. Roulez had not yet finished his morning's work. One of the seconds on the other side lost all patience on seeing the third encounter terminate as unfortunately for his party as the first and second. He assailed M. Roulez in unmeasured terms, and threatened him with personal chastisement. M. Roulez replied that this fresh insult could only be wiped out in the same manner as those which had led to the previous challenges. Swords were chosen on the spot, and it was determined that a fourth encounter should be held forthwith.

It took place accordingly, and in a few moments the last of the four opponents whom M. Roulez had been called upon to face was rendered *hors de combat*, receiving, like each of his companions, a somewhat severe wound. The four consecutive duels were fought within an hour.

M. Roulez, whose conduct from first to last was marked by extraordinary coolness, returned to Paris, and spent the day attending to his business affairs, keeping all his appointments as if nothing unusual had occurred. His exploit is the general topic of conversation all over Paris this evening, and in sporting circles especially it is commented upon as one of the most remarkable performances of the kind on record.

"Pall Mall Gazette," May 19, 1892.

FOUR MIGHTY MEN OF FENCE.

There was an assault-at-arms last night at St. Martin's Vestry Hall, when three French fencing professors of eminence in London—M. Bourgeois, of the Langham Chambers School ; M. Vital Labailly, of the Portland Road School ; and M. Danguy, of the Sloane Street Gymnasium — opposed the Cavaliere Eugene Pini, the most accomplished of Italian fencers, who has recently beaten all the greatest masters in Paris. Fencing, now that duelling has gone out, has almost ceased to be a pastime in England, but it is still a serious business in France and Italy. There has always been a great rivalry between the French and Italian schools of fencing. Their methods are different, though they both aim at the same results. The French begin with the foil, the Italians with extraordinary gymnastic.

exercises. Twisting and twirling till he suggested the popular idea of a dancing dervish, the Cavaliere Pini mostly had his French antagonists at his mercy—and they are the most accomplished fencers in England—within a few seconds. He gyrated unexpectedly, and his opponents found him within their guard.—" London Correspondence," *Manchester Guardian.*

" *Pall Mall Gazette*," May 20, 1892.

THE QUADRUPLE DUEL.

Considerable difference of opinion exists in duelling circles in Paris (says the *Chronicle* correspondent) on the etiquette observed in the quadruple duel successfully fought yesterday by M. Roulez. It is not likely that the parties will be prosecuted ; but it is felt that if M. Roulez had been killed in the fourth encounter, instead of wounding his adversary, a terrible responsibility would have fallen on the seconds. M. Roulez, though short-sighted, is one of the best swordsmen in France. In 1871 he killed a Prussian officer in an encounter with sabres on the Belgian frontier.

" *The Standard*," May 21, 1892.

THE REPORTED DUELLING.

PARIS, *Sunday Night.*—The romantic story of M. Roulez and four duels turns out to have been a hoax. M. Roulez has confessed in writing that his object in concocting this story was to turn the laugh against interviewing journalists. The irate pressmen with whose credulity he thus trifled retaliate by insinuating that M. Roulez's vanity at his skill in fencing drove him mad, and that he laboured under an hallucination that he had really fought with four men. An interview with a representative of the *Gaulois* after his confession would tend to confirm this supposition, for he affirmed that he had confessed to a hoax simply to get out of the fuss that papers were making about the business. The perfectly matter-of-course way in which utter disregard of truth is confessed to by one of the parties, and received as something quite natural by the others, conveys a moral that does not adorn the tale.

PARIS, *May* 21.—Soon after the *Temps* appeared last evening, giving an account of an inquiry made by its reporters into all the circumstances of the affair, and suggesting that the circumstantial narrative of his encounters put forward by M. Roulez was merely an effort of the imagination, journalists without number went to the house of that gentleman for the purpose of cross-questioning him as to the authenticity of his story. M. Roulez was out at the time, and was greatly taken aback to find his *salon* crowded with strange gentlemen, who immediately beset him with eager questions about the famous duel. A copy of the *Temps* was shown to M. Roulez, who said he could not understand how that journal could make the statements it did.

Asked as to the steps he proposed to take in the matter, he said he should write a letter at once to the paper, giving a denial pure and simple to its allegations.

The reporters proceeded to ply M. Roulez with questions on the details of his story, and when he declined to answer, said that they should be obliged to regard his silence as an admission that his narrative of the quadruple encounter was an invention. The rejoinder of M. Roulez was that it was a matter of supreme indifference to him what inference his interrogators might be pleased to draw from his speech or silence. "I only ask of you one thing," he added, "and that is to leave me in peace." "But," urged the inquiring press, "in any case you knew your own seconds." "I knew no one concerned in the matter," responded M. Roulez. "When the affair occurred I simply did what I thought to be my duty. The opinion of the newspapers disturbs me but little." He was then pressed to mention the name of the *danseuse* at the Opera who was said to have been the cause of the quarrel which led to the duels. M. Roulez said that her name was Verdan, and not Vaughan, as had been erroneously stated. On all other points he maintained an impenetrable silence.

Subsequently Mdlle. Verdan was interviewed. Her ignorance on the subject of the quarrel was complete. In fact, on Monday last she was not at the Opera at all, and was fined for her absence.

Meanwhile, all endeavours to discover the principals and the seconds in the celebrated encounters have proved futile. There is a general consensus of opinion that M. Roulez is the victim of an hallucination of the brain. Indeed, some of his friends have come forward to state that during the past few days his behaviour has been in several respects very strange, and they believe he is suffering from delusions.

Evening.—This evening's papers are of opinion that M. Roulez's statements as to his having fought a quadruple duel are purely imaginary.

The *Paris* announces that M. Roulez this morning requested one of his friends to demand explanations from four journalists, including the editors of the *Temps* and the *Gaulois*. About noon he called upon the same friend, and, finding him out, left the following note for him : "I am being made a fool of by the editor of the *Gaulois*. When I see you I will explain everything." The journal expresses the belief that M. Roulez is suffering from an affection of the brain.

NOTES ON FENCING AND DUELLING

The *Liberté* states that M. Roulez, in an interview with one of its representatives, said :—

" All the information which I have given is false. Whether I fought
or not does not concern anybody. I have attained my object, that is all.
I shall pursue my libellers. I shall kill or wound the editors of certain
newspapers."

The impression made upon the mind of the *Liberté's* representative
appears to have been that M. Roulez's mind was deranged.

Finally, the *Temps* publishes without comment the following letter from
M. Roulez :—

" I have been amusing myself for the last forty-six hours at the expense
of the press. All the accounts of the famous duels are imaginary. The
joke is at an end. If the journalists desire it, I will be at their disposal
to prove to them that I am still vigorous. The laugh is on my side."

May 22.—The *Gil Blas* states that M. Ranc, director of the journal
Paris, has sent his seconds to M. Roulez, who communicated to the press
what is now believed to be an imaginary account of duels between himself
and four other persons.

" *The Standard*," May 25, 1892.

DUELLING IN HUNGARY.

VIENNA, *Tuesday Night.*—A duel has been fought at Pesth between Dr.
Alexander Karsay, twenty-three years of age, a lieutenant in the Reserve,
and Baron Bela Aczel, a member of the National Casino, or Magnates'
Club. The cause of the quarrel was an insult offered by the latter to Dr.
Karsay's father, who had, although a Jew, been formally invited by the
Obergespan, or Lieutenant-Governor of the County of Pesth, to join the
Banderium, or cavalcade of magnates, which is to escort the Emperor-
King on his Jubilee. The Obergespan, M. de.Benickzy, acted as second
to Dr. Karsay. Baron Aczel's shot entered his opponent's right breast,
pierced the lung, split the breast-bone, and finally lodged in the left
shoulder-blade. Seeing Dr. Karsay fall, the Baron rushed to his side and
begged his forgiveness. The young man is not expected to survive.

VIENNA, *May 24.*—The War Office authorities have reversed the judgment of the court-martial at Agram, which some time ago condemned a
cadet and two lieutenants of the 101st Infantry Regiment to eight months'
imprisonment and loss of rank. The cadet had challenged a captain of the
same regiment to a duel for insults offered, the lieutenants acting as
seconds. The Vienna authorities consider that a cadet equals an officer
in rank and honour, and have reduced the sentence to two months in the

case of the cadet and one of the lieutenants, one lieutenant being set free, and the captain being confined to barracks for fifteen days.

According to military regulations, the prisoners are permitted to petition the Emperor for restitution of rank. The colonel of the regiment has been forced to retire on pension.

"The Standard," *May* 30, 1892.

DUELLING IN FRANCE.

The heat of the weather seems to have developed duelling proclivities to even a greater extent than is usual. Two deputies, M. Burdeau, formerly reporter of the Budget, and M. Couturier, fought with swords yesterday afternoon, and M. Burdeau, who was the aggrieved party, was run through the wrist. Another duel was fought between a German officer, M. Oudet, and a French officer, whose name is withheld. M. Oudet was shot through the stomach, and had to be carried off the field. The attacks of M. Edouard Drumont on the Jews are likely to lead to a series of duels between officers of the Hebrew persuasion in the French army on the one hand, and M. Drumont, the Marquis de Morès, and others, who claim to be the champions of Christianity. Captain Crémieu-Foa, a captain of dragoons, having had his attention drawn to sundry articles in M. Drumont's paper, *La Libre Parole,* has sent him a letter in which he says :—

"I regard myself as personally offended by your insults against the three hundred officers of the French army who belong to the Jewish faith. I call upon you to put a stop to this odious campaign, and warn you that, if you do not attend to this letter, I shall demand of you reparation by arms."

M. Drumont returned the following reply, which is also signed by "the Marquis de Morès *et ses amis :*"—

"MONSIEUR,—In your letter, received this day, you describe yourself as offended by articles which have appeared in the *Libre Parole* concerning Jewish officers in the army ; and, although you have not been mentioned by name, you constitute yourself the champion of all the Jewish officers in the active army. To this I will reply—First, you are not qualified to act as champion for the Jewish officers, since you are not the senior, nor have you been delegated. The articles are all of them signed. Having said this much, I will add that if the Jewish officers feel insulted by our articles, let them draw by lot such number of delegates as they think fit ; an equal number of French swords will meet them. As far as you are concerned, if as a Jew you challenge me, I hold myself at your disposition."

NOTES ON FENCING AND DUELLING

" The Star," June 3, 1892.

A PARIS DUEL WITH BLOODSHED IN IT.

In the environs of Paris yesterday M. Reymond—the husband of the lady who killed his mistress, Madame Lassimonne—fought a duel with M. Carle des Perrières, who, in an article in *Gil Blas*, had discussed the drama in a manner which M. Reymond regarded as offensive. Swords were the arms employed. M. Carle des Perrières was wounded in the breast at the beginning of the encounter, but in spite of this the duel was continued, he finally receiving a lunge between the fifth and sixth ribs, which put an end to the combat.

A Reuter telegram from Paris this morning says M. Perrières's wounds are very severe. Shortly after the encounter, while the surgeon was dressing them, the injured man fainted from loss of blood, and in the evening, when he was conveyed to Paris, he was in a high fever. It is stated that, after the first wound was inflicted, the doctor who was in attendance declared that the duel ought not to proceed. M. Defly, Madame Reymond's father, was also referred to in the article, and he accordingly sent seconds to M. des Perrières. The latter replied that he would be at M. Defly's disposal as soon as he had recovered from his injuries.

" The Standard," June 24, 1892.

FATAL DUEL IN FRANCE.

PARIS, *Thursday Night.*—A duel was fought this afternoon between the Marquis de Morès and Captain Meyer, of the Engineers, who is one of the Instructors at the Polytechnic School. The *rencontre* arose out of an unpleasantness at the Cremieu-Foa duel with Count de Lamoze, at which Captain Meyer and the Marquis de Morès were seconds. Captain Meyer was run through the right lung.

Later.—The *Courrier du Soir* announces that Captain Meyer died this evening of the wound he received to-day during his duel with the Marquis de Morès.

"Pall Mall Gazette," June 25, 1892.

THE FATAL DUEL—ARREST OF THE MARQUIS DE MORÈS.

The Marquis de Morès, who killed Captain Meyer in a duel, was last night arrested by M. Gorou. He is detained in custody. In the course of a statement the duellist said :—

NOTES ON FENCING AND DUELLING

"I am deeply distressed at what has happened ; but on my conscience I have nothing to reproach myself with. The duel was perfectly fair, and I feel sure no one will question that. My adversary was young, taller than I am, and a very expert fencer. At the Polytechnic School his mastery with the foils was universally known, and I was quite able to make out the usual practice of M. Meyer, whose length of limb enabled him to make a formidable lunge. I saw in a moment that he intended to run me through the abdomen, and knew quite well he did not intend to spare me. When I felt my sword was penetrating I immediately stayed my hand. Had I struck home I should have run him clean through the body."

"The Sunday Times," June 26, 1892 (p. 5).

DUELLING.

The duello is again the talk of Paris, and this time the absurd practice has ended in the death of a brave and brilliant officer. M. Drumont sheds numerous tears over Captain Meyer's coffin, and the Marquis de Morès declares that the encounter was carried out with due regard to loyalty. But he adds that the war to the knife, which the Drumont clan have begun, will be carried on to the bitter end. In other words, the French army, which in the midst of political dissension has always been united for the service of the nation, is to be endangered by a wilful and criminal vendetta between Christian and Hebrew officers. Happily M. Drumont will fail. The bravery of Jewish officers is as undoubted as their ability, and, as in the case of his other rumours, the editor of *La Libre Parole* has spoken without the slightest foundation. The Marquis de Morès is to some extent actuated by personal feelings. But if he has been a victim of a handful of energetic financiers, there can be no reason for slaying his fellow-countrymen with the same light-heartedness that he displayed on his ranch in Montana when dealing with niggers. The anti-Jewish crusade will fall flat in France. It is anathematised by the Catholic party, and it is not in harmony with the democratic instincts of the French people. The Rothschilds spend countless sums in discreet charity, and they are even now preparing to give their garden in the Rue Lafayette to the city of Paris. The other great French Israelites are equally philanthropic, and their patriotism is far more thoughtful and enlightened than the wild clap-trap of the Déroulèdists. The statistics at the Ministry of War show that the Jewish officers are noted for their scientific achievements. Captain Meyer himself was one of the most distinguished professors of the École Polytechnique. He dies a martyr to the great cause of liberty of conscience, which M. Camille Dreyfus advocated to-day at the

Chamber of Deputies. It is to be hoped that his blood, so wantonly shed, will bear good fruit, and that even M. Drumont will see that there are plenty of evils to redress without recklessly promoting hatred and discord between Jew and Gentile.

"Pall Mall Gazette," June 30, 1892.

THE RECENT FATAL DUEL IN PARIS.

The recent fatal duel in Paris is not to be wholly without result. M. Maxime Lecomte, senator for the Nord, is about to introduce a bill providing a maximum penalty of a year's imprisonment and a fine of 2000 francs for engaging in a duel. If the duellist shall have killed his man, the maximum penalty will be three years' imprisonment and 10,000 francs fine. It is, of course, not the first time that the anti-duelling party has made an attempt to pass a bill of this kind. A Commission of the National Assembly considered the question in 1851, and proposed a measure which served as the foundation of a bill which M. Herold introduced into the Senate in 1877. Another Commission was then appointed to consider M. Herold's bill, and that also reported in favour of a special law. Nothing was done, however, and, considering French sentiment and the records of public men as duellists, it is thought an exceedingly delicate matter for any Administration to tackle.

"The Standard," July 11, 1892.

DUELLING IN GREECE.

The affair of the duels arranged between two secretaries of the Turkish Legation and two officers of the Greek army has produced much excitement in Athens.

The first duel has been fought between Alfred Bey and a Greek cavalry officer, with the result that the latter was seriously wounded. Influence is being brought to bear to prevent the second intended encounter.

A DUEL WITH PISTOLS IN MADRID.

A duel with pistols was fought in the outskirts of Madrid yesterday morning between the Mayor of Madrid and a municipal councillor. Two shots were exchanged, but neither combatant was wounded. The dispute was afterwards settled on the field.

NOTES ON FENCING AND DUELLING

"*Pall Mall Gazette,*" *July* 19, 1892.

FATAL ACCIDENT TO A FENCER.

As Mr. C. Terry, a prominent physician at Fall River, Massachusetts, was taking a fencing lesson from Professor Castaldi yesterday, he met with a tragic accident. The button of the foil used by the Professor became detached, and before the accident was discovered the weapon pierced the doctor's mask, and entering his right eye, penetrated to the brain. Mr. Terry died within three hours.—*Reuter.*

"*Modern Society,*" *August* 13, 1892.

A SANGUINARY DUEL BETWEEN TWO YOUNG LADIES.

A curious incident happened the other day at Dos Agnas, a town near Valenza. A sanguinary duel took place between two young ladies who were in love with the same gentleman, and, of course, were jealous of each other. The duel was with pistols at twenty paces for the first shot, fifteen for the second, and ten for the third. As may be seen, the two lady combatants took the matter very much *au sérieux*, and after the third shot one of the duellists was seriously wounded through a ball piercing the right lung, and it is feared that the unfortunate girl will not live. She is only eighteen years of age, and her adversary nineteen. A curious detail concerning the duel was, that of the four ladies who acted as seconds, one was the wife of the alcalde of the town, and another a cousin of the fortunate man for whose *beaux yeux* the duel took place.

"*New York Daily Tribune,*" *August* 14, 1892.

DUELLING IN THE UNITED STATES NAVY.

There have been several duels between officers since the navy was first established, but the Blue-jacket has not been an advocate of them for the last eighty years. "Jack" has many superstitions, and a duel is perhaps one of the strongest incentives for him to "jump the ship," or, as they say in the army, "run the guard." This dates back to the time of the duel in 1812 between Midshipmen Charles Morgan and Joseph Rogers. They were both on the old frigate *Constitution*, and when lying off Sandy Hook they quarrelled, a challenge passed, they went ashore and fought the duel without seconds, and, to carry out the agreement that the survivor should bury his antagonist, Morgan buried the body of Rogers in the sand. A funeral service was held on the following day, and while the boats were on their way to the shore a sailor fell from the masthead of the frigate and was killed; a few minutes later another sailor fell, and received injuries from which he died on the following day; and while lowering him into the cockpit another sailor fell and broke his leg. Two days afterwards a midshipman fell overboard and was drowned, and in attempting a rescue a boat capsized, throwing the crew into the water, and they were saved with difficulty.

Morgan, who later rose to the rank of commodore, was a personal appointee of President Jefferson. One day, in 1807, Mr. Jefferson was driving alone on a country road in Albemarle County, Va., when he asked young Morgan to share the buggy with him as far as he was going. Mr. Jefferson was so attracted with the boy's manner, intelligence, and frankness, that he offered him an appointment as midshipman in the navy, and as the boy got out of the buggy Mr. Jefferson remarked, "Tell your father you have been riding with Thomas Jefferson, the President of the United States."

The boy replied that he would not think of telling his father, and, when the President pressed for a reason, said, "If my father should learn that I had been riding with President Jefferson he would give me the worst whipping I ever had in my life, either at home or at school."

"Well, come to Washington, anyway, and I'll give you a midshipman warrant," said the President. And he kept his word.

Another more recent case of a challenge to a duel was that which resulted in the court-martial of Major D. M. Cohen and Captain William B. M'Kean, of the Marine corps, both of whom are yet in the service. It was in August 1863 that Captain Cohen challenged E. A. Selfridge, clerk to the commandant of the Mare Island Navy Yard, and the challenge was delivered by Lieutenant M'Kean. The charge under which they were tried by the court-martial was "scandalous conduct, tending to the destruction of good morals." The sentence of the court was that Captain Cohen be "reprimanded," and that Lieutenant M'Kean be "admonished;" but Secretary Welles was so disgusted with the action of the court that he would not confirm the sentences, and added to his decision the following :—

"The decision of the court appears to be directly in conflict with that provision of the 'Act for the Better Government of the Navy' which makes it a punishable offence to send or accept a challenge to fight a duel, or act as second in a duel. If there was any offence committed by the accused, it consisted in a violation, or at least in a manifest evasion, of the law referred to. But, in the opinion of the court, violation or evasion of a law intended for the suppression of a moral offence is not scandalous conduct, tending to the destruction of good morals. The department cannot sanction a decision which would seem to indicate a deficiency in the moral sense as well as in the reasoning powers of those who pronounced it, and the tendency of which would be to encourage a disregard of the law."

It is pretty evident from this, that if Secretary Welles had been the court, he would have declared that a challenge to fight a duel would have been regarded as "scandalous conduct" worthy of worse punishment than reprimand or admonition.

"Pall Mall Gazette," August 23, 1892.

REPORT OF A DUEL BETWEEN TWO LADIES.

No small sensation has been made by the report of a duel between two ladies of the high Austrian nobility. The Princess Pauline Metternich, the Honorary President of the Vienna Musical and Theatrical Exhibition, and the Countess Kilmannsegg, the wife of the Statthalter of Lower Austria, and President of the Ladies' Committee of the Exhibition, had a fearful quarrel over some arrangements at the Exhibition. The affair was regarded as so serious that it could only be settled by blood. The ladies travelled to Vaduz, the capital of the little principality of Lichtenstein, on the Swiss frontier, the town which Prince Alois of Lichtenstein some time ago offered to the Pope as a city of refuge in the event of his being obliged to leave the Vatican.

The duel was fought with rapiers. At the third round the Princess was slightly wounded on the nose, and the Countess on the arm. Thereupon the two seconds, Princess Schwarzenberg and Countess Kinsky, advised them to embrace, kiss, and make friends; which accordingly they did. Their wounds were attended to by Baroness Lubinska, a Polish lady who has studied medicine and obtained a doctor's degree, whom they had prudently sent for from Warsaw to attend the duel.

THE MORÈS-MEYER DUEL.

"The Daily Telegraph," August 27, 1892.

Your readers will not have forgotten the excitement created here some months ago by the sad result of a duel fought between the Marquis de Morès and Captain Meyer. The death of the gallant officer, who was very popular, produced a very painful impression. The Marquis de Morès was arrested, and, after spending some time in custody, was released, and was permitted to make a journey to Switzerland. On Monday he is to be brought to trial at the Seine Assizes with tho gentlemen who acted as seconds in this unfortunate affair; and in all probability the proceedings will last for about two days, as a fair number of witnesses will be examined. M. Delegorgue will be the presiding judge at the trial, Maître Demange acting on behalf of the Marquis de Morès; while the counsel for the four seconds—M. Guérin, M. de Lamase, Captain Pouiade, and Captain Delorme — will be Maître Houdaille, Maître Bourdon, Maître Hugon de Scœux, and Maître Benoît respectively. It is understood that the judicial authorities decided on the prosecution on the ground that the duel was not justified by anything that had taken place between the two adversaries; that the Marquis de Morès was re-cognised as the offending party, though nothing had occurred to prove this; that no attention was paid to the fact that Captain Meyer was placed at a disadvantage owing to the fatigue to which he had been sub-jected that morning at the École Polytechnique; and also that the swords used were too heavy. As a matter of fact, the whole affair was the result of a miserable misunderstanding. A duel had already been fought be-tween Captain Crémieu-Foa and M. de Lamase, in which Captain Meyer and M. de Morès acted as seconds on the opposite sides. It was agreed that the official report of the affair should not be communicated to the press, and on its publication the Marquis accused Captain Meyer of being responsible for this breach of the arrangement. The Captain made no attempt to exculpate himself, and so the encounter took place, with the disastrous result, which found an echo even in the Chamber of Deputies. Soon afterwards the brother of Captain Crémieu-Foa came forward volun-tarily and declared that it was he himself who had communicated the official report to the newspapers; but it was too late—the mischief was done, and soon the mortal remains of the gallant officer were followed in mournful procession to the grave by sorrowing relatives and friends, in-cluding a number of the students of the École Polytechnique, by whom he was much esteemed. There were other questions behind all this, and in the Chamber of Deputies M. de Freycinet, the Minister of War, stated, amid loud applause, that all the officers of the army were equally re-cognised as French soldiers, no prejudice existing on the score of faith or creed. It is quite possible that more may be heard of this matter at the trial which is about to open; but, as party passion seems to have subsided to a considerable extent, we may perhaps be spared a revival of the extremely bitter controversy to which the unfortunate event gave rise. One direct consequence of this affair is now at least distinctly visible: it has helped to bring the "duel" into disfavour, if not into actual dis-repute. Private members have laid on the tables of both Houses of Parliament bills aimed at the abolition of an institution which is at last regarded by many Frenchmen as obsolete and barbarous, if not as abso-lutely ridiculous. Evidently the "duel" has seen its best—or, to speak

NOTES ON FENCING AND DUELLING

more correctly, its worst—days. Some of our authorities still consider that, under very exceptional circumstances, a hostile encounter may be justifiable, if not necessary ; but how often is recourse had to sword or pistol under these very grave conditions ? In the vast majority of cases the "duel" simply supplies the belligerents with an opportunity of bringing their names before the public through the medium of a *procès-verbal*, a very slight wound in the arm, which placed one of the combatants at a disadvantage, being the only damage done. It has even been suggested that the suppression of the official report would of itself deal a death-blow at the duel—at any rate, the institution is now on its trial in more senses than one, and, although it may linger on for a time, its fate seems practically sealed.

" The Standard," August 30, 1892.

PARIS, *Tuesday Night.*—The Paris Assize Court was occupied to-day with the trial of the Marquis de Morès and the four seconds in the duel between that gentleman and Captain Meyer. The defendants—the Marquis de Morès and his two seconds, MM. de Lamase and Guérin, and the seconds of the late Captain Meyer, MM. Delorme and Poujade—though virtually charged with being concerned in homicide, appeared quite at their ease in the prisoners' dock. After the reading of the long indictment, in which particular stress was laid on the inequality of the duel, owing to the heaviness of the weapons, and the stiffness of the right arm from which Captain Meyer was suffering, the Judge commenced the examination of the Marquis.

The questions put to the prisoner in the first instance seemed to have very little to do with the duel. He was questioned about his life in the army, his marriage, and his voyage to America, from whence he returned to France after losing a very large sum of money. The presiding Judge then put questions to the Marquis which induced him to explain all his numerous colonial projects, none of which was he able to carry out. Later on the prisoner admitted that he had been condemned to a fine of one hundred francs for the unlawful possession of arms. It was from that moment that he occupied himself with politics.

Being reproached by the Judge with having incited the people to the hatred of the Israelites, the Marquis replied : " I never incited to hatred. I pointed out the Jewish monopolists to popular justice. My object was to show that credit should not be in the hands of a few, but in the hands of all." He then explained that this first anti-Semitic campaign led to a duel between himself and M. Dreyfus, the deputy, who was wounded in the right arm, and then went on by giving his version of the circumstances which led to his arrest and condemnation for provocation to insurrection and pillage. He took this opportunity of protesting energetically against the accusation of having employed Martinet, the anarchist, as his agent.

The Judge.—You at that time incited the populace to the spoliation of the Jews.

The Marquis.—Spoliation is not the word. I said that it was necessary to institute in France a court of justice for the revision of certain fortunes. That has been done a dozen times in the history of France. I consider it is the duty of the State to effect that revision.

The Judge.—On the occasion of the marriage of Mdlle. de Rothschild you published a pamphlet against the Jews, and you hired people to hawk it about the Rue de la Victoire and in the vicinity of the synagogue. That pamphlet was entitled, "Rothschild, Ravachol, et Cie." Moreover, you were in the Rue de la Victoire yourself.

The Marquis.—I did not send hawkers with my pamphlet into the street, and if I was there it was because I wished to see how the public traffic would be interrupted for the benefit of the Rothschild family.

The Judge.—You commenced writing in the *Libre Parole* immediately after its creation. Very shortly after, various articles, entitled "Les Juifs dans l'Armée," were published in it under the signature of M. de Lamase. You must admit these articles were most violent and injurious for those at whom they were aimed. There were, moreover, superior officers, not Jews, who were attacked in them.

The Marquis.—I do not share your opinion. As for the articles, they were the true expression of what really occurred.

On the demand of the Marquis de Morès, all these articles were read in Court, after which the Judge said it was impossible for the prisoner now to deny their unjustifiable violence, especially as in them such high military authorities as General Farre, General Saussier, and General de Galliffet, who are not Jews, were attacked. The Marquis de Morès would not admit it. He said: "No; these articles appear to me moderate. Only compare them with what M. Reinach wrote in the *Revue des Deux Mondes* concerning the manœuvres in the east of France."

It was after the publication of the third article that Captain Crémieu-Foa and M. Edouard Drumont fought a duel, in which they were both wounded. On the following day, 21st June, M. de Lamase, who had signed the articles, challenged M. Crémieu-Foa, saying he had insulted him by choosing M. Drumont as adversary. M. Crémieu-Foa, according to the Judge, accepted the challenge on condition that a jury of honour should be appointed to decide whether M. de Lamase had not been disqualified for that duel by allowing M. Drumont to fight in his stead. In reply, the Marquis de Morès affirmed that there had never been any question of forming a jury of honour. The preliminaries of the duel, he

495

said, were prolonged by M. Crémieu-Foa pretending to be at Daumartin, whereas he was constantly seen in the Bois de Boulogne.

Long and complicated explanations were then given as to the publication of what took place at the meeting of Captain Crémieu-Foa's and M. Drumont's seconds, which led up to the fatal duel with the Marquis de Morès and M. Meyer, in which the latter lost his life. After light had been thus thrown upon the subject, the Marquis de Morès said he believed Captain Meyer was not sorry to find an opportunity of fighting with him. The seconds in this duel, before the encounter, demanded of Captain Meyer whether he would consent to the publication of a note in the press stating that it was not he, but M. Ernest Crémieu-Foa, who had communicated to the journals an account of the affair. He would not consent to it, and the duel took place. A great deal was then said about the heaviness of the swords at the duel. After the fatal wound had been given, the Marquis approached Captain Meyer, who shook hands with him. The Captain was conveyed to the hospital on a mattress, and died the same evening.

In court to-day the Marquis protested against the account of the interview published in a Paris journal, and said he wished to prevent the Jews from making the army, what they had made banking, their fief. He desired to express his regret at what had happened. He had always in his duels acted with the greatest loyalty.

The further hearing of the case was adjourned till to-morrow.

" *The Standard,*" *August* 31, 1892.

The trial of the Marquis de Morès and the four seconds in the Morès-Meyer duel was resumed to-day at the Paris Assize Court by the examination of numerous witnesses. Count Esterhazy, major in the army, had served as second in the Crémieu-Foa and Drumont duel. When he heard of the projected duel between M. Crémieu-Foa and De Lamase he was thunderstruck. In court to-day the witness said, " My indignation and that of all my fellow-officers was extreme at the news that the author of the article in the *Libre Parole* was a French officer, who did not shrink from insulting his companions in arms and two of our respected generals." Count Esterhazy did not act as second in that duel. The seconds were Captain Meyer and Lieutenant Trochu. Before it took place Count Esterhazy, nevertheless, heard Captain Meyer say, " In an affair like that it is not as second I should prefer to figure." In response to these sentiments the Count urged Captain Meyer to do his utmost to learn the name of the officer who had written the article, adding, " I am anxious to get the man kicked out of the army. I will have the two soldiers told off to do the dirty work stripped, in order that they may not soil their uniforms."

The most important portion of Count Esterhazy's evidence was, however, that which related to the weight of the swords used at the duel between the Marquis de Morès and Captain Meyer. The average weight of duelling swords was, he said, from four hundred and eighty to five hundred and thirty grammes. Those with which the duel was fought weight two hundred grammes more, which was a very considerable difference. The witness, however, declared that the Marquis de Morès could not be blamed for the weight of the swords, since it was the duty of Captain Meyer's seconds to refuse them if they considered them too heavy. Questioned as to whether he would have done so had he been second on the occasion, he said he would have done so, or at least asked Captain Meyer whether he accepted them. In reply to this declaration, Captain Meyer's seconds again affirmed they did not consider the swords too heavy.

Dr. Février, surgeon at the École Polytechnique, then related that ten days before the duel Captain Meyer had complained to him of a pain in the right arm, but that on the eve of the duel it seemed to be quite cured. He added that if he and the chief surgeon of the Polytechnic School had considered that the condition of Captain Meyer's arm put him at a disadvantage in his duel with the Marquis, they would have prevented the encounter. He also testified to the perfect loyalty of the Marquis during the duel. As soon as the latter felt his weapon touch his adversary he drew back sharply.

Dr. Faure, who was also present at the duel, said he did not notice that the swords were too heavy. As for the contest itself, he did not pay minute attention to it, but he added, " I shall, however, remember all my life that, when the wound was inflicted, the sword and arm of the Marquis de Morès were in an absolutely horizontal position. Captain Meyer must therefore have lunged forward considerably." Being asked whether it required great strength to inflict such a wound, Dr. Faure declared it certainly did not, and this statement was corroborated by Dr. Paquelin, the third doctor.

There was considerable contradiction in the evidence then given by four fencing-masters. Three of them, MM. Texier, Rouleau, and Senille, considered the swords too heavy ; whereas the other, M. Ayat, declared they were not abnormally so. He said that last year the Comte de Dion fought with swords weighing nine hundred grammes, and that he (witness) had at his fencing establishment swords weighing eight hundred and fifty grammes.

As for calling any swords abnormally heavy, it was going too far, as there was no normal weight for a sword. The military fencing-masters had expressed a contrary opinion, because they constantly used foils. It was here again pointed out that Captain Meyer always practised with foils. M. Texier, being recalled, said he maintained the opinion he had given, which was that a person accustomed to fence with foils was necessarily placed at a disadvantage with an adversary accustomed to wield the sword.

Some sensation was then caused by the appearance of M. Léo Taxil in the witness-box. He affirmed the absolute correctness of what he wrote in the *France Chrétienne* on the morrow of the Drumont-Burdeau trial. He said : " I was in the public hall of the Palais de Justice when, in the midst of a group of very excited Anti-Semites, I heard M. Guérin (one of the Marquis's seconds) talking angrily, with set teeth. He said, ' We must make an end of the Jews ; the masses are with us ; they will act.' I interposed, ' Then what you seek is civil war ? ' ' Yes,' replied he, ' and I will undertake to strangle with my own hands the first I come across.' ' Rothschild ? ' said I. ' Oh, he will be hanged to the lamp-post in front of his mansion. If we only had a good Jewish corpse, it would stir up the whole of France. The nation would be grateful to us for having rid France of the Jews.' A lady who was standing by said, ' That gentleman is a good Frenchman. I should like to shake hands with him.' And she did so. His name was Guérin. A workman then exclaimed, ' Hulloa ! Ravachol has been let out of prison ! ' "

Asked by the Judge what he had to say to this, M. Guérin replied : " I have promised to be calm ; I will do my utmost to remain so. I repeat that I contradict flatly all that this man has just said. I consider that what he has come to do here is infamous. That man is a scoundrel." This epithet was greeted with such loud applause in court that the Public Advocate demanded that the court should be cleared. In the midst of the tumult, M. Léo Taxil shouted, " The infamy is in having killed a French officer with the object of increasing the circulation of a newspaper."

The Judge.—M. Guérin, you are insulting a witness. The Public Prosecutor would be justified in taking measures against you.

M. Guérin.—I am ready to assume the responsibility for what I have said.

The Judge.—Withdraw the word " scoundrel."

The Public Prosecutor.—If M. Guérin does not withdraw the expression I will demand the application of the law.

As M. Guérin remained silent, the sitting of the court was suspended. The greatest excitement prevailed, and, during the absence of the Bench, amidst the ever-growing tumult were heard the epithets of " Dirty dog ! " " Wretch ! " &c., addressed to M. Léo Taxil.

On the resumption of the proceedings, the Judge once more urged M. Guérin to withdraw the insulting expression, which he ultimately did out of respect for the court. M. Léo Taxil being recalled, M. Demange, counsel for M. Guérin, asked the witness whether he was not the author of the book entitled *Amours Secrètes de Pie IX*. M. Taxil replied, "It is a work which was published by the Anti-Clerical publishing house of Madame Léo Taxil. I had nothing to do with that work." M. Demange then examined M. Taxil with regard to some questionable writings which had been attributed to him, but the matter had no direct bearing on the case before the Court.

M. Laffon, the Public Advocate, then made a long speech, in which he declared the present duel was not an ordinary encounter, but was the outcome of a campaign undertaken by the Marquis de Morès. It should therefore be punished. Captain Meyer's seconds should have exerted themselves more than they did to prevent the duel. It would have been easy to find a formula which would have satisfied all susceptibilities. As for the Marquis de Morès' seconds, they were not sufficiently impartial to act as such.

M. Demange, for the defence, reproached the Public Advocate with pleading against the *Libre Parole* and Anti-Semitism, and not against the duel. He had described the Marquis de Morès as wishing to have the corpse of a Jew to act as a signal for civil war. But, asked M. Demange, what proof was there of any such intention? There was only one witness, Léo Taxil, who had written or sold immoral works, and who at the present moment was a writer on the *France Chretienne*. There was only one question at issue : Was the duel loyal and fair? The answer must be— Certainly, yes. In that case it was impossible to convict. Captain Meyer, in shaking hands with the Marquis de Morès after the duel, absolved him. The shade of the victim protected him.

After pleadings from the counsel of the other prisoners, a verdict of not guilty was agreed to by the jury. The Marquis de Morès and the other defendants were therefore all acquitted.

" Pall Mall Gazette," September 8, 1892.

THE CZAR AND DUELLING IN THE RUSSIAN ARMY.

General Vannovski, the Russian Minister of War, contemplates issuing an order prohibiting officers in the Russian army from fighting duels, either among themselves or with civilians, unless the motive for the encounter shall have been previously submitted to a tribunal of honour composed of officers, or to the colonel of the regiment, with whom it will remain to decide whether the duel shall take place or not. In the event of a combat being pronounced necessary, the Minister of War will in each case apply to the Emperor to sanction the release of the combatants from all the legal consequences attending their action.

NOTES ON FENCING AND DUELLING

" The Standard," September 15, 1892.

CONTINENTAL DUELLING.

THE HAGUE, *Wednesday Night.*—Last night a duel between diplomatists was fought on the Dunes, near Wassenaar. The antagonists were Baron Gärtner von Griebenow, Secretary of the German Legation, and Marquis d'Alcedo, Secretary of the Spanish Legation. The witnesses were members of the Austrian, German, Spanish, and French Legations.

Señor Alcedo fired in the air, and Gärtner aimed at the ground, but the bullet ricochetted and lodged in his opponent's right hip. The Marquis was conveyed to his hotel at the Hague, and to-day the bullet has been extracted. The cause of the duel was a dispute of a purely private character.

The police of Wassenaar, as soon as they heard of the affair, went to the duelling ground and took down the names of those present. A judicial inquiry has been ꝑopened, as duelling is prohibited in Holland. The condition of the wounded Marquis is satisfactory.

PARIS, *Wednesday Night.*—A duel with pistols was fought to-day between M. Gerville Réache, deputy for Guadaloupe, and M. Souques, a Conservative General Councillor for the same colony. Two shots were exchanged. By the second shot M. Réache was wounded in the right arm. The bullet penetrated fourteen centimetres up the fore-arm and lodged in the muscles. The cause of the duel was a discussion in the colonial press, during which M. Souques considered himself insulted.

" The Daily Telegraph," March 4, 1893.

" HARRY ALIS " DUEL.

The funeral of M. Hippolyte Percher, better known as " Harry Alis," is to take place on Tuesday. The remains will be borne from the house in the Rue Vauquelin to the Gare d'Orléans, where addresses will be delivered, and will then be conveyed to Etampes, for interment in the local cemetery. The family had wished that a religious service should be held in Paris, but the rector of the parish has refused, as the Roman Catholic Church has very strict rules on the subject of duelling. Now the hope is entertained that the Bishop of Versailles, who is being strongly urged to grant the requisite permission, will not set his face against a religious ceremony at Etampes. M. Le Chatelier and his seconds have been questioned at length by the *juge d'instruction,* to whom they have given a full account of the tragic affair. The seconds of the unfortunate journalist, M. Paul Bluysen and M. André Hallays, both of the *Débats,* are to be examined to-morrow. Oddly enough, about eight years ago M. Percher contributed to the *Débats* an article on duelling, in which he ridiculed the "scratches" generally received in hostile encounters arranged on the most futile pretexts. M. Jules Simon, by the way, has just denounced duelling as a barbarous custom, and has said that severe laws should be framed against it. But how could this be done, he added, as Parliament itself sets the example, and deputies have elevated duelling to a kind of national institution? The only thing that can be hoped for at present is that arbitration may be resorted to more frequently. The story that M. Percher and his adversary, after being warm friends, had become bitter enemies, owing to divergences of opinion and rivalry in connection with colonial matters, is corroborated, and this fact probably explains why the quarrel could not be patched up. At the same time, it is positively stated that all the arrangements for the duel were conducted in the most careful and precise manner, and that nothing was overlooked.

"The Idler," March 1894.

HENRI ROCHEFORT ON DUELLING.

There are two things to be said about duelling. Firstly, that it is a very stupid form of either amusement or *passe-temps*. I speak as one who knows, for I have been engaged in affairs of honour ever since I was quite a lad. You see, the combatants are always so ill-matched. There is nothing very glorious in fighting a man who has never held a sword in his hand, whilst you yourself have made a science of the art of fencing. No; in duels, as in everything else, I have always held that there should be a system of handicapping. What happens when a race is in question? A splendid horse who has already proved what he can do is given a heavier weight to carry than the novice. Well, affairs of honour should be arranged in the same fashion. "Ah! you have spent some hours each day since you were a schoolboy in *salles d'armes*. Very well; *you* shall be given a short sword to fight with; and your adversary, who has no idea how to use the foils, shall be given the sharpest and longest lance that can be procured!" But this is not the fashion in which the thing is conducted at the present moment. It is as reasonable to ask me to attempt making shoes with a skilled cobbler, as to set two men to fight one another of whom only one knows in the least how to thrust and parry.

But the second, and by far the most important thing about modern French duelling is that it has become a great source of self-advertisement. Some individual wishes to become known in art, in letters, or politics; he has but to say something insulting of a leading personality, and the trick is done. Firstly, there is a duel, and perhaps a wound, and then many little paragraphs in the newspapers. I assure you that those who are in any way well known have to be most careful lest they should unwittingly aid some good-for-nothing adventurer to make his mark. Again—and this is especially the case where the well-known duellist is a journalist—supposing a man is always being attacked in a newspaper, if he can only persuade the writer of the articles to fight him, he will never again be spoken ill of by his one-time adversary ; for it is with us a law of honour not to attack a man with whom we have fought.

" The Idler," March 1894.

BRONSON HOWARD ON THE AMERICAN DUEL.

Once in a long time some earnest and enterprising duellist makes an effort to introduce into Italy what is called the " American duel." The Italian firmly believes—which belief, by the way, he also shares with the Frenchman—that when two Americans wish to fight a duel, they load one pistol, draw lots for it, and the winner shoots himself. Why this should be supposed to be the American way of duelling I cannot imagine. If there is any such thing as an " American duel," it is what is familiarly known as " shooting on sight." The challenger sends word to his enemy that he will shoot him the next time he sees him, and thereupon the latter arms himself, and takes his walks abroad with much caution, until the two meet, when both begin a brisk fusillade with their revolvers, and one of them is usually killed, together with from four to six of the bystanders. This sort of duel would never do for a sparsely-populated country like Italy ; and as for the other and falsely called " American duel," it lacks everything that could recommend it to the lover of athletic sports.

" The Daily Chronicle," April 20, 1894.

DUELLING IN THE AUSTRIAN ARMY.

In the Lower House of the Austrian Reichsrath yesterday, Count Welsersheimb, Minister of National Defence, said that in the past year he had inquired into 278 cases of abuse of power by officers. In regard to the question of duelling, the Minister observed that if laws imposing the severest penalties had not been sufficient to stamp out the practice in the past, it was certain that mere Parliamentary resolutions could not do so in the present. The idea that duelling was favoured in the army was quite incorrect, and, as a matter of fact, duelling had much decreased among military men, more so, perhaps, than among other classes of society. In conclusion, Baron von Welsersheimb said that as soon as a man injured in his honour could rely upon obtaining full satisfaction from the laws and from society, he would no longer wish to call out his enemy, and he who did so would certainly be regarded and treated as a murderer; but until that time arrived, the taking of the law into a man's own hands was certainly to be as far as possible restricted, but not altogether prohibited. The Minister's remarks were greeted with loud cheers.

" The Sun," October 3, 1894.

SARCEY'S DUEL.

It was at a reception in Paris. On the entrance of the great dramatic critic he at once became the lion. Knowing he was among friends, he talked freely. He told us of his duel with Hector Pessard, the musical critic and comic opera composer, who is a very charming man, by the way. Sarcey, in 1865, wrote a scathing attack on Girardin's paper *La Liberté*. Emile de Girardin objected on principle to duels, so the editorial staff, considering their literary style insulted by Sarcey, drew lots as to who would call him out and kill him if possible. The lot fell on Pessard. Now, Pessard and Sarcey were great friends; but it was necessary to obey the call of honour, so Pessard sent the challenge, which Sarcey accepted with dignity. The adversaries took off their coats and vests and faced each other sword in hand, when, lo, the four seconds took to squabbling over some detail. The dispute was long and ferocious, and the two adversaries fell into conversation, sword in hand.

Quoth *Pessard*—I am frozen. Would you mind if I put on my coat?

Sarcey.—A good idea. We can kill each other later.

Pessard.—Let me tell you, my dear Sarcey, how greatly I admire your talent.

Sarcey.—I can say the same to you; but why are we going to kill each other?

Pessard.—I don't quite know. It seems you grossly insulted me, and if I do not succeed in killing you, that you must certainly slay me in expiation.

Sarcey (meditatively).—I do not remember having insulted you; but if you say so, I suppose it is true.

In the meantime the four seconds were quarrelling furiously. One gentleman was shaking his fist in his opponent's face, and another was brandishing his riding-whip, whereupon Sarcey suddenly burst out laughing, and said—

"Come, Pessard, let us separate our seconds, and then, instead of cutting each other's throats, we will go and have some breakfast."

Which was no sooner said than done, and the two duellists have been fast friends ever since.

NOTES ON FENCING AND DUELLING

" The Daily Telegraph," August 21, 1894.

DUELLING IN RUSSIA.

Our St. Petersburg correspondent writes :—" The new law promulgated lately by the Emperor of Russia himself, according to which duelling is obligatory upon officers of the army, not only whenever they themselves fancy they have been insulted, but likewise whenever anybody else thinks they have, is already bearing fruit. Detailed accounts reach St. Petersburg every other day of duels between young officers who are intimate friends, and never dreamt of offending each other, simply because, when joking among themselves, one of the party said or did something which in the opinion of somebody else ought to prove insulting. Thus, we read of one young man being shot by another, whose best friend he is, and with whom he had no quarrel of any kind, being compelled to call him out by the officers' 'Court of Honour,' which has been instituted in accordance with the recent imperial law ; and of another promising young fellow in the south, who is now disabled for the rest of his life because forced to fight with a comrade who never said a cross word to him. In all these cases the alternative is fight or leave the army, and no one dares to choose the latter. At least, no one had the courage necessary before last week, when a very interesting case unfolded itself in the city of Kertch. At a ball given by the local club there, the leader of the dancers was a young Lieutenant P., who took possession of two vacant chairs—one for himself and one for his partner—in the vicinity of the orchestra. He then left the room for a moment, and on his return found the chairs occupied by a young civilian and his partner. He requested the latter to vacate the chairs, and have others brought in their stead. But the civilian politely but firmly refused. 'I took possession of these chairs long ago,' he explained, 'before you came to them, and I cannot give them up. I am quite willing, however, to go and order a pair of chairs for you, which will be brought to you in half a minute.' Thereupon the officers, who constituted more than half of the guests, threatened to leave the club in a body unless the young civilian was expelled then and there. The club committee refused to expel him, having no ground for such an extreme measure, and the officers forthwith left the club-room and retired. Next day the commander of the regiment, informed of what had taken place, convened the Court of Honour and laid the matter before them. Among the witnesses were the young civilian and the lieutenant. Both deposed that no insulting or even impolite language had passed between them, and the former further declared that nothing was further from his intention than to wound the feelings or reflect upon the honour of the lieutenant. The Court of Honour, however, decided that Lieutenant P. must challenge the young civilian to a duel within five days or else leave the army. The young man, who was a favourite in the service, at once informed his superiors that he would send in his resignation, but would under no circumstances challenge a man who had done him no wrong. He had no abstract objection to duelling itself, which, since the new imperial ukase, has been taken under the wing of the Orthodox Church, but he has a decided objection to kill or maim in time of peace a man who has done him no ill whatever. The affair is causing a great sensation in military circles, where not one in a thousand would venture to imitate the example which most people admire as heroic."

" The Daily Telegraph," February 11, 1895.

DUEL BETWEEN M. CANROBERT AND DEPUTY HUBBARD.

General Billot has declined to arbitrate in the affair between M. Canrobert and Deputy Hubbard, as he himself took part in the debate at the Senate on the Marshal's funeral. It is, however, now settled that the duel is to come off. As M. Hubbard is at the present moment indisposed, the date of the encounter is to be fixed later on. The rapier is the weapon selected, and the fight will continue until one of the combatants is, in the opinion of the surgeons, placed in a position of inferiority.

As has been already stated, this quarrel has arisen out of the discussion in the Chamber. There has been another affair, owing to some comments made by Deputy Julien Dumas on the virulent speech against Canrobert delivered by M. Delpech in the Senate. M. Delpech sent a couple of friends with a demand for an explanation to M. Julien Dumas, who immediately selected his seconds. It has, however, been decided that there is no valid ground for a duel, so this incident at least has had a pacific termination.

February 14, 1895.—This morning a duel was fought between Lieutenant Canrobert, son of the late Marshal, and M. Hubbard, a member of Parliament. The affair arose out of some remarks made by the Deputy in the course of a speech during the debate about the funeral of Marshal Canrobert. M. Hubbard's observations on the career of the deceased veteran were considered offensive by M. Marcel Canrobert, who sent his seconds, M. Lefrançois and the Comte d'Apchier, to the Deputy. The duel was fought on the St. Ouen racecourse at eleven o'clock. Swords were used, and the principals attacked each other with impetuosity, the seconds having had to interfere. During the second engagement M. Hubbard received a deep puncture in the breast, and the duel was discontinued. The Deputy's wound was attended to on the spot, and he walked with considerable difficulty to his cab.

NOTES ON FENCING AND DUELLING

" The Daily Telegraph," March 2, 1895.

FATAL SWORD DUEL.

M. Hippolyte Percher, of the *Journal des Debats* and the *Journal Egyptien*, better known under his *nom de guerre* of "Harry Alis," was killed to-day in a duel at the Ile de la Grande Jatte, in the Seine, by M. le Chatelier, formerly a captain in a infantry regiment, and now director of the Société des Études of the French Congo. The quarrel had arisen out of a letter addressed by M. Percher to the Captain. The seconds who were appointed vainly endeavoured to patch up the affair, and a meeting was decided upon, Colonel Baudot and Commandant de Castelli acting for M. le Chatelier, and M. Paul Bluysen and M. André Hallays, both of the *Journal des Débats*, for M. Percher. The encounter took place at eleven o'clock this morning, swords being the weapons employed. M. Percher was almost immediately hit in the right arm-pit, his adversary's sword going clear through his body. Uttering the exclamation, "Je suis mort," the unfortunate man fell to the ground, and expired a moment afterwards. The sword had penetrated both lungs, and had pierced the left arm-pit as well. The duel had come off in the dancing-room of an establishment called the Moulin Rouge, on the Ile de la Grande Jatte. At the outset, M. Percher was placed with his back to the door, the choice of positions having been determined by tossing up a 5f. piece. He was at some disadvantage, as the floor slants, and is rather lower on that side. The proprietor of the establishment says that from the manner of the principals when they arrived he augured that the duel would not be an ordinary affair, as they seemed very resolute, and adds that he observed to his wife, "One of them will not leave the house alive." While awaiting the investigation by the Police Commissary, who had been hurriedly summoned, the corpse was laid on a mattress on the billiard-table. It had been arranged that the adversaries should remove their shirts, as M. le Chatelier was wearing a very thin and light one, and M. Percher one with a thick and stiff front, so the latter only had on a flannel waistcoat. One of M. Percher's seconds remained by the body, while those of M. le Chatelier went in search of the Police Commissary, their principal staying in the carriage which had brought him down. The Commissary questioned the seconds and seized the swords, and he was followed by a *juge d'instruction* and another official. Meanwhile friends had called to prepare the mother and widow of the dead man for the terrible news, saying that he had been wounded, and was being tended at the office of the *Journal des Débats*. M. Percher appeared to have had no presentiment of impending evil, as he simply said this morning that he was going out for a few hours. The affair, of course, has produced no little sensation. M. Percher, who was one of the founders of the French African Committee, was a hot opponent of the British occupation of Egypt. Both here and on the banks of the Nile he conducted a violent campaign against England. He had been connected at one time with Dalziel's Agency, and latterly was a leading member of the staff of the *Journal des Débats*. He was in his thirty-eighth year, and was a Knight of the Legion of Honour.

It was after an animated press controversy with Captain le Chatelier in regard to concessions in the French Congo territory that M. Percher had written the letter which caused so much offence. In it he had said to Captain le Chatelier, "I hope that if you will have the goodness to remember that you are an old officer, you will have recourse to more frank methods, and then you will see that you do not frighten me." The seconds were sent immediately on receipt of this defiance. The letter has been seized by the Police Commissary, who has also procured copies of the *Journal des Débats*, in which M. Percher's articles and the Captain's reply are to be found. M. le Chatelier, whose rapier was almost twisted by the force of the thrust, has assured the official that he had no intention of killing his adversary, but meant simply to wound him in the arm. Now it is rumoured that there had been for some time a feud between the two men. The combat was directed by M. Paul Bluysen, one of M. Percher's seconds, and it was but a moment after he had uttered the usual "Allez, messieurs," that his principal, who had opened the attack, received the fatal thrust. It was almost under identical conditions that Captain Meyer was killed by the Marquis de Morès in a duel that took place at the Casino de la Grande Jatte, situated only a few yards from the Moulin Rouge. The corpse was conveyed this evening to the house near the Panthéon where M. Percher lived, the sad news having previously been broken to the mother and widow.

"*The Daily Telegraph*," July 1, 1895.

DUEL BETWEEN A MINISTER AND A PRIVATE SOLDIER.

A duel between a Minister and a private soldier seems rather an incongruous proceeding, but the private soldier happens to be a Deputy, and it was not he, but the Minister, who sent the challenge. The affair arose out of an incident during the visit to Rheims of Senator Gadaud, Minister of Agriculture. M. Mirman, who represents Rheims in the Chamber, is now serving in a rifle battalion stationed at Vincennes, and, when M. Gadaud visited Rheims last Sunday, a Municipal Councillor protested against this, and asked him to draw the attention of the Minister of War to the fact that the town was unjustly deprived of his services

NOTES ON FENCING AND DUELLING

in Parliament. M. Gadaud answered that in former days Republicans deemed it an honour to enter the ranks of the army, and that he was sorry to see that now a Republican did not care to be a soldier. M. Mirman sent the Minister so strongly worded a letter on the subject that he lost no time in demanding satisfaction. There were some difficulties about the date, owing to M. Mirman's time being occupied by his military duties, and there was a talk of postponing the encounter till September, when he will leave the corps. Eventually, however, arrangements were made for the duel to come off last evening, and it took place on the Gravelle Plain, on a ground belonging to the Ministry of Agriculture. Senator Dusolier and Deputy De la Batat were M. Gadaud's seconds, while Deputies Millerand and Pierre Richard acted in a like capacity for their Socialist colleague. M. Mirman, who was in uniform, received almost at the outset a thrust in the right arm from his adversary's rapier, and, after the opinion of the doctors had been taken, the duel was brought to a close. It has been asserted that M. Gadaud resigned his portfolio in order that he might fight, but this was not the case. He informed his colleagues of the impending encounter at the Cabinet Council held yesterday, and some of them suggested that he should take this step, but he declined to do so. M. Floquet's duel with Boulanger in Comte Dillon's garden at Neuilly, when the then President of the Council wounded his adversary rather badly, will be remembered ; and on Christmas day last year M. Barthou, then in office, exchanged shots with M. Jaurès. Going further back, we have the De Fourtou-Gambetta affair in 1877 ; about ten years later the duel between Boulanger, while Minister of War, and Baron de Lareinty. M. Gadaud considered that there were sufficient precedents ; but, as M. Mirman is at the present moment above all things a private soldier, this is certainly a remarkable case, to which, by the way, M. Mirman might appeal if he took it into his head to send to his chief, the Minister of War, a challenge, with which General Zurlinden would certainly deal in a very different manner.

"*The Daily Telegraph,*" *March* 27, 1895.

DEATH OF M. PERCHER.

The tragic death of M. Percher at the Ile de la Grande Jatte a few weeks ago drew public attention to the melancholy consequences to which duelling may lead, and another dangerous affair has now occurred to support the outcry raised in certain quarters against a practice which is denounced by so many as barbarous and unworthy of an enlightened age. An encounter has just taken place at Constantine, in Algeria, between M. Souleyre, a Government engineer, and M. Masson, the manager of the

NOTES ON FENCING AND DUELLING

Silhouette, described as a satirical journal, who had written the article therein which had given offence. M. Souleyre is an able swordsman, but he was transfixed by his adversary's rapier a moment after the encounter had commenced. He fell down in a swoon, and was borne to his home in a dying state.

"The Daily Telegraph," April 15, 1895.

A DESPERATE DUEL.

BERLIN, *Sunday Night.*—At a retired spot on the borders of the sylvan environs of the German capital the Berliners' Easter festival was this year ushered in, early on Saturday morning, by one of those sanguinary encounters between two private individuals which, though prohibited by the strict letter of the law, are sanctioned by usage in this country, and winked at by the supreme authorities of the land. In the evening the sweet music of the Paschal peals of the municipal churches was harshly interrupted by the jarring cries of the newsboys proclaiming to the sauntering holiday crowds that "a desperate duel had taken place between Herr von Kotze, Master of Ceremonies to the Court, and another high Court functionary."

This second individual was, as the initiated knew, Baron von Reischach, one of the Kaiser's Chamberlains, and Court-Marshal to her Majesty the Empress Frederic. No extraordinary excitement was evoked in Berlin by the news that two personages of high rank had taken the law into their own hands to vindicate "their honour" by murderous methods, as such things are regarded in a different light over here—especially by those mainstays of the crown who are now clamouring, in the so-called interests of "order, religion, and morality," to have stricter powers put into the hands of the police, in order that liberty of speech and writing may be further restricted in Germany. After the holidays, when the newspapers reappear, publicists of Liberal, Radical, and Socialist tendencies will point out the mockery of this state of things ; but the incident itself will excite no general indignation, and will only form the topic of eager gossip in society and in the clubs. Meanwhile, a brief reference to the past history of this case is necessary.

This day ten months ago was handed to Kaiser Wilhelm, as he was on his way to lay the foundation of the new Protestant Cathedral in Berlin, a report, in which Herr von Kotze was accused of being the author of a series of missives of an exceptionally filthy kind received during many months past by some of the best-known ladies in Berlin society. His Majesty, placing credit in the evidence laid before him, gave instant orders that his servant should be divested of his honourable position and be transported to prison, adding that he should be treated like the vilest criminal, a sentence which he undoubtedly deserved if guilty. He was incarcerated for sixteen days, when it was discovered that the proofs preferred against him were not of so convincing a nature as the Kaiser had been led to suppose. The matter was then handed over to the slow and unbusiness-like examination of a military court, the accused holding the titular rank of an officer of the reserve ; and for ten weary months he and his wife have been banished from society with this fearful charge hanging unproved over their heads, all the members of his family meanwhile insisting as strongly as possible on his innocence.

During the trial it was said very openly that the actual culprits—for it was admitted that there were more than one of them—would never be publicly named, and the real truth is not likely to be known until the loathsome story has long been forgotten. It is fair to the accused and to his wife, both of whom have been subjected to so many months of torture, to say that they have not sought to inculpate anybody else, of whatever rank or station, amongst those whose names have been mentioned as the guilty parties.

After long and tedious deliberations and examinations, the military court last Tuesday pronounced the accused to be not guilty. The result was laid before the Kaiser, who, admitting thereby the injustice of the too impulsive words he used ten months ago, instantly indorsed the judgment, which was forthwith without delay communicated to Herr von Kotze. As soon as he was a free man, cleansed from the stain that had been inflicted upon him, he took the only course open to men of honour in this country. He sent to Baron von Reischach the first of a series of challenges to a duel, which, before his acquittal from the charges, nobody would have accepted.

The encounter took place, as above stated, on Saturday morning. The conditions were of an especially severe kind. The combatants were to fire at one another at a distance of fifteen paces with duelling pistols until one of the combatants should fall or be disabled. Herr von Kotze was severely but not dangerously wounded in the upper part of the leg at the eighth shot, his antagonist escaping unhurt. The wounded man was removed to the Royal Clinical Hospital, where he is likely to remain for six or eight weeks. He was in a satisfactory condition to-day, and his wound is said to be not dangerous.

The Kaiser, on hearing of the result of the duel, sent one of his aides-de-camp, Count von Moltke, to Herr von Kotze's house to inquire, and later in the evening caused a floral arrangement, in the form of an Easter egg, to be conveyed with his congratulations to the patient at the hospital, as a token of his rehabilitation to imperial favour, and as a sign of his, the Kaiser's, satisfaction that the duel had not ended fatally.

NOTES ON FENCING AND DUELLING

I happened to meet Frau von Kotze to-day, and am therefore able to vouch for the accuracy of the above details. By an incredible mistake, the Berlin papers state that it was Baron Reischach who was the challenger. It would be satisfactory to be able to think that, since Herr von Kotze has been declared not guilty by the court, and his sovereign has indorsed the verdict in a specially gracious manner, this unhappy affair might be terminated.

There is, however, unfortunately, every reason for supposing that other duels will follow in connection with it as soon as the patient shall have sufficiently recovered. It is no secret that the Duke of Ratibor, the contents of whose telegram on the subject ten months ago were especially offensive to the accused, will be challenged, and many others are also named. If nothing is done to put a stop to this wholesale, and, as matters now stand, obligatory butchery, it may very likely happen that the man who has been pronounced innocent will fall a victim to one or other of his opponents. The severe conditions observed on Saturday will certainly be demanded in the contemplated encounters. This would be a strange irony of justice; and, should nothing be done to avert it, there would be a danger at the present moment, when an effort is being made to repress a political party in the State, on the ground that it acts contrary to the interests of morality, order, and religion, that public indignation might be aroused. In general, there is absolutely no sympathy between the nobility and the people in Germany, and it would take a good deal to stir the latter to interest themselves in the repression of the vices of their haughty superiors in rank ; but a series of such flagrant evasions of the law as that now contemplated may perhaps make the powers that be in Prussia as alive to the folly of duelling as it is certain to make the masses clamour for an equality of justice.

" The Sun," May 8, 1895.

" MISSED ! "

Mr. James Payn tells this story of the "American plan" of duelling, wherein the two duellists, with one second, meet within doors, and draw lots for who shall shoot himself. On a recent occasion A. and B. having had a "difficulty," A. was the unlucky man, and retired for the purpose of self-destruction into the next apartment. B. and the second, both very much moved by the tragedy of the situation, remained in listening attitudes. At last the pistol-shot was heard ; they shuddered with emotion and remorse, when suddenly in rushed the supposed dead man, triumphantly exclaiming, "Missed !"

NOTES ON FENCING AND DUELLING

" The Sun," June 4, 1895.

DUELLING WEAPONS.

The weapons generally used at duels on the Continent are the sword and duelling-pistol. The sword has a triangular blade, thirty-two inches long from guard to point. For over a foot it is hollowed out like a bayonet. The point and edges are very sharp. Sometimes curious results follow wounds with the rapier. A New Orleans gentleman was run through the right lung in a duel, the steel coming out three inches under his shoulder-blade. At the time of the fight he was thought to be in the last stage of consumption. He not only got over the thrust, but the wound cured him of the dread consumption as well. The counter - irritation relieved the lung of its inflammation and effected a perfect cure.

The pistol used in the duel is not the military arm, nor the revolver, but a very carefully made and wonderfully accurate weapon known as the duelling-pistol. For many years the length of this arm was a matter of grave discussion at all the clubs in England and on the Continent. At first the duelling-pistol had a twelve-inch barrel, and carried twenty round bullets to the pound. But in 1810 the elder Devisure, with his confrère, Lepage, at Paris, and Manton and Egg, of London, the most eminent pistol - makers of their respective countries, fixed the actual length of the duelling pistol-barrel at nine inches, and there it has remained for eighty-five years. A case of the best pistols costs from twenty to thirty pounds.

" The Star," August 13, 1895.

FENCING AT THE TIVOLI.

Boxing and wrestling have both had a turn on the music-hall stage, the former, fortunately, having but a short life, while the latter caught on from the first, and has increased in popularity ever since. But good as the wrestling is, and popular as it has become, Mr. Dowsett has probably done wisely in looking for something else as a novelty to present to his audience, and he has found just the right kind of experiment in a display of graceful and skilful fencing between two young ladies and two male colleagues. One or two little matters require alteration, as was inevitable in an entirely new presentation, an important item being the provision of a darker background and floorcloth, against which the motion of the gleaming foils may be more clearly visible than they were last night. Then the display work, with its word of command, might well be omitted, and a couple more combats substituted, the latter having proved far more interesting and exciting than any other portion of the exhibition. The Indian club and bayonet exercises might be omitted altogether, as the former is not quite so complete as that with which Morris Cronin made us acquainted, and the latter is somewhat dull to those who can see a Guards regiment do the British bayonet exercise in whole companies, with all the dash and display for which they are famous. The remainder of Mr. Dowsett's programme is made up of favourites of the halls, most of whom have a new song or two.

" The Daily Telegraph," September 2, 1895.

"THE SWORDSMAN'S DAUGHTER" AT THE ROYAL ADELPHI THEATRE.

On Saturday evening the favourite "temple of melodrama" in the Strand was thronged from floor to ceiling by a sympathetic and demonstrative audience, gathered together in the depth of the dead season in order to greet with loud acclamations the latest dramatic combination of striking situations produced for public delectation by the enterprising management of the Adelphi Theatre. The new piece, translated from the French and adapted "to the usages" of the British stage by Messrs. Brandon Thomas and Clement Scott, was written three years ago, in collaboration, by MM. Jules Mary and Georges Grisier, and given for the first time on October 13, 1892, at the Théâtre de la Porte Saint Martin, in Paris, where it was favourably received, despite the audacious absurdity of its closing scene, and enjoyed a long and prosperous "run." *Le Maître d'Armes* — a title honourably associated with the patronymic of one of its authors — has been anglicised into "The Swordsman's Daughter;" but the original plot has not been meddled with by the adapters, who have confined their labours to abbreviating the piece judiciously, though as yet insufficiently, and to substituting vigorous and impressive lines for the often windy and wearisomely spun-out dialogue with which the first and third acts of the French play are disagreeably over-weighted. The story of *Le Maître d'Armes* is not a pretty nor a probable one. Its intrinsic offences, however, if not its most glaring improbabilities, are intelligently minimised in the English version. Briefly synthesised, it runs as follows :—

Vibrac, the most skilful and popular fencing-master of Paris, and the founder of a school of arms which has developed into a fashionable club, has an only daughter, to whom he is devotedly attached. During a professional tour in Russia of a twelvemonth's duration he intrusts his beloved child to the care of an amiable elderly lady, the mother of his favourite pupil, the Count de Rochefière, a fascinating but unprincipled yachtsman. Madame de Rochefière is so thoroughly subjugated by Madeleine Vibrac's beauty and charm of manner, that, falling dangerously ill, she urges her son to take the fencing-master's daughter to wife. As a matter of fact, Henri pledges himself solemnly to Madeleine in the presence of his dying parent, who joins their hands, blesses their prospective union, and then expires. On the strength of this pathetic troth-plighting he promptly seduces the defenceless girl, committed to the guardianship of his honour, and loses no time in abandoning her. The liaison is attended by the usual consequences of such lamentable indiscretions. A child is born—fortunately for Madeleine, before her father's return to France; and, with the aid and connivance of a good-natured doctor, also one of Vibrac's pupils, she contrives to conceal the birth. When the great swordsman comes back from St. Petersburg, in failing health, father and daughter emigrate, for change of air, to Dieppe, their native place, where they lodge in the house of one Olgan, a pilot of local renown, who had conceived an ardent passion for Madeleine Vibrac some years previously, when he and she were boy and girl. Olgan is loved by his foster-sister, an orphan named Thérèse, whom, however, he regards exclusively from a fraternal point of view. His heart is true to Madeleine, who in secret returns his affection, having never really cared for her betrayer, though she had yielded to his perfidious solicitations. She consents to stand godmother to Olgan's new pilot-boat, which is on the stocks ready for launching; but when he subsequently asks her to marry him, she refuses, for reasons that will be obvious to any scrupulously right-minded person. Meanwhile her child, which has been put out to nurse, is attacked by some infantile ailment, and the woman in charge of it, having heard that Mdlle. Vibrac and her father are staying at Olgan's cottage, hurries thither to apprise Madeleine that her little one's life is in danger. Just as the discovery of Madeleine's ruin appears inevitable, Thérèse interposes to save the object of Olgan's adoration from disgrace, claims the child as her own, and takes to herself the whole burden of Madeleine's shame. The truth, however, is accidentally disclosed a little later at the close of a superb assault-of-arms, given on the premises of the fencing-club, which owes its genesis to Vibrac's famous school. Vibrac, just after the terrible revelation has reached his ears, is on the point of playing a final bout "for the gallery" with his daughter's seducer, when he is stricken down by palsy.

Meanwhile De Rochefière has been overheard, while speaking in disparaging terms of Madeleine, by Leverdier, a naval lieutenant, whose life Olgan has saved prior to the action of the story, and who, cognisant of his friend's deep attachment to the swordsman's daughter, challenges the dissolute yachtsman to mortal combat. They meet, and at the close of a hard-fought duel—most realistically counterfeited on the Adelphi stage—De Rochefière inflicts a deadly wound upon his adversary, after having disarmed him. To this homicidal act, strictly prohibited by the code of duelling, formal exception is taken, with the result that De Rochefière, on the point of leaving France, is arrested, and ultimately arraigned at the Paris Court of Assize on a charge of murder. Vibrac, in the meantime, has partially recovered from his paralytic stroke, and, as soon as the faculty of speech has been in some measure restored to him, has compelled his daughter, on pain of incurring his curse, to disclose the name of her seducer. Having done this, she attempts to commit suicide, her effort in that direction being frustrated by Olgan, who persuades her to become his wife. In Vibrac, however, the resolve to be avenged upon De Rochefière has worked a complete cure of his malady. It has transpired that his testimony as an expert in swordsmanship may exonerate the slayer of Leverdier from the crime of which he is accused, and the president of the fencing-club, a grotesque but well-meaning personage, exhorts him to appear in court as a *témoin à décharge*, or witness on behalf of the prisoner, to declare that the fatal thrust had not violated any law of the *duello*. Seeing his way to achieve the vengeance upon which his soul is set, Vibrac consents to testify in that sense. He applies to be examined on the technical point in his capacity as *maître d'armes*, is duly summoned to the trial, and when in open court suggests to the jury that the contested pass should be illustrated in their presence by fencers of equal force—for instance, his "best pupil," De Rochefière, and himself! This amazing proposal finds favour with jury and judge alike, the latter—himself a member of the fencing-club—decreeing that the interesting experiment shall be tried with the very swords used in the real combat, which are among the *pièces de conviction* actually in court. At the instance of the presiding judge the prisoner then steps down from the dock, takes off his coat and necktie, turns up his shirt-sleeves, and engages in a desperate bout of "sharps" with his whilom instructor, who audibly warns him to defend himself, inasmuch as he—Vibrac—means to kill him. The mimic duel, of course, results in the death of De Rochefière, transfixed by the same disputable "stoccata" that had proved fatal to the intrepid but unskilful Leverdier. Vibrac is avenged, the court rises, and the curtain falls.

There are several good and sufficient reasons for the genuine success achieved by this astounding play on Saturday evening, and for the exceptional popularity which it is obviously destined to attain. In the first place, it offers the irresistible attraction of such a profuse display of fine fencing as has seldom, if ever, been presented on the boards of an English theatre. The assaults-of-arms that held the audience breathless in the second act were delivered by genuine French "masters" of the very first flight, and were fought out with a skill and vivacity beyond all praise. Both the mock duels, moreover, were admirably contested by the British actors who sustained the parts of Vibrac, De Rochefière, and Leverdier. There were two comic encounters, besides, between Mr. Harry Nicholls and Mr. Webb Darleigh in the corridor of the fencing-school, and between Mr. Fitzgerald and Mr. Porter in the *salle d'armes*, the fun of which was perfectly natural and unforced. It may be hoped that the magnificent foil and rapier play at the Adelphi will stimulate a healthy revival in this country of the most elegant, graceful, and fascinating of physical exercises, which of late years has somewhat fallen into desuetude among the gentlemen of England, whose forefathers at one time ranked among the most accomplished European swordsmen. Secondly, the new drama has been staged and mounted with excellent taste, and, as the familiar saying goes, "regardless of expense." The seaside "set," with its cosy tile-faced cottages, quaint old round signal-tower, and broad-beamed fishing-smacks, is a picture rife with charm and verisimilitude; and so is the tranquil woodland glade, scene of the desperate combat between Leverdier and De Rochefière in the third act. Thirdly, the cast is an efficient one, and all its members fill the rôles assigned to them with adequate intelligence and unflagging energy. As Vibrac, Mr. Terriss is no less dignified than passionate. Discreetly restrained during the first, second, and third acts, his fervid temperament has its own way with him and with the audience in the last scene but one, throughout his painful struggle to shake off the numbness with which paralysis has smitten his once lithe and supple limbs. To Mr. Harry Nicholls' genial and spontaneously humorous impersonation of an utterly impossible French baron are due the few flashes of mirth-moving gaiety that relieve the prevalent gloom of the piece. Miss Millward is a uniformly pathetic Madeleine; Mrs. Brooke a sufficiently brusque and bustling old housekeeper; Miss Featherstone an irreproachable, though blighted, orphan girl. Of the remaining characters, Jean Olgan is robustly represented by Mr. Charles Fulton, and Tommy Wilkins, an Anglo-French jack-tar, no less so by Mr. Julian Cross. Mr. Abingdon plays the "villain of the piece," Henri de Rochefière, with appropriate heartlessness and malignity, and the subordinate but highly useful parts of the kindly doctor and the chivalrous naval lieutenant are admirably sustained respectively by Messrs. Crauford and Sternroyd. "The Swordsman's Daughter" will not be the worse for the judicious but liberal excision to which its present superfluities will doubtless be subjected in the course of the present week. Even as it was produced, "with all its imperfections on its head," it was undeniably a strong, deeply emotional, and intensely interesting play, advancing many indisputable claims to a widespread and enduring popularity.

NOTES ON FENCING AND DUELLING

" The Sun," *September* 2, 1895.

PEOPLE OF TO-DAY.

Monday Morning.—Lord Chancellor Halsbury's hobby is sword exercise.

" The Daily Telegraph," *October* 8, 1895.

THE HISTORY OF THE SWORD.

A correspondent writes : "Sir Richard F. Burton tells us, in his entertaining 'History of the Sword,' that the history of that weapon is identical with the history of humanity itself. The sword is not only the oldest, the most universal, and the most varied of weapons, but it is the only one which has lived through all time. It was, adds Sir Richard, the favourite arm of the heathen gods, a gift sent down from heaven which made Mulciber divine. More than any other metallic implement now in existence it proclaims that man's civilisation began as soon as he learnt how to light fire and how to keep it alight. Before he could make weapons through the aid of fire, our primal ancestor lived the life of the lower animals. The first effort of human technology was, in short, to make weapons which taught man that he was lord of the universe. This long exordium in praise of the 'white arm,' as the French call it, will lend additional interest to the announcement that a new pattern sword with a steel hilt has been invented, or rather perfected, at the Royal Military Gymnasium, Aldershot, and is about to be served out to the officers of our infantry regiments, which now carry swords with brass hilts. The weapon is adapted for use in the new sword exercise, which requires greater dexterity and rapidity of hand than its predecessor, and necessitates a stronger and more effective protection in the hilt than the worn-out weapon used at Waterloo and in the Crimea afforded. Nothing is more discouraging to a soldier than to find, when he has dealt his adversary a mighty blow with the sword, that the blade twists or the hilt comes off in his hand. Who that has read Sir Walter Scott's novels can forget the tribute repeatedly paid by the 'Wizard of the North' to old Andrea Ferrara, the maker of those wondrous Spanish blades with which duels were fought when that old-fashioned system of settling quarrels between individuals was in universal use ? With the abolition of duelling, proficiency in wielding the sword has gone out of fashion among British officers, few of whom could emulate the skill shown by the late General M'Murdo when, as a young man, he accepted the challenge of a skilled Sikh warrior to fight him with the sword shortly before the battle of Meeanee, and killed his adversary in sight of the two armies. Let us hope that the adoption of a new sword exercise and a new hilt will stimulate officers to learn the deft use of the oldest weapon wielded in war."

" The Daily Telegraph," November 25, 1895.

DUEL BETWEEN M. ALBERT CARRÉ AND M. POSSIEN.

Duels have been rather frequent of late, the most important being that between M. Albert Carré, manager of the Vaudeville and Gymnase theatres, and M. Possien, a journalist. The encounter took place in the neighbourhood of Paris, swords being the weapons chosen. At the third pass M. Possien received a thrust in his right fore-arm, and, on the decision of the doctors present, the combat was stopped, the wounded man being declared incapable of continuing the fight.

" The Daily Telegraph," December 2, 1895.

DUEL BETWEEN BARON BOISSY D'ANGLAS AND VICOMTE DE VOGÜÉ.

Yesterday morning, at the back of the grand stand on the Longchamps racecourse, a duel was fought between the Baron Boissy d'Anglas, a well-known Radical Deputy, and the Vicomte de Vogüé, also a Deputy, and a member of the French Academy. The dispute arose out of a newspaper article in which the Vicomte deemed himself to have been slightingly referred to, and he accordingly sent his seconds to his brother member of Parliament. Swords were the weapons chosen, and at the second encounter the Radical Deputy pierced his opponent's lip. The duel was at once stopped, as the wounded man was declared incapable of continuing the combat with advantage.

" The Daily Telegraph," December 18, 1895.

ASSAULTS BETWEEN FRENCH AND ITALIAN SWORDSMEN.

The fencing world in Paris has for the last week been deeply interested in a series of assaults between four picked French and Italian swordsmen. Two of the agile fencers, an Italian and a Frenchman, had proved themselves such expert masters of the art, that their meeting, fixed to take place on the last evening, aroused even more than ordinary interest.

NOTES ON FENCING AND DUELLING

Unfortunately the assault did not take place, as the Italian master met with a nasty accident. He had paid a visit to a friend, who is by no means a proficient fencer, and the two had a bout. Suddenly the friend lunged hard and touched his opponent, who gave a cry and staggered back. On examining the foil, it was found that the button had come off, and the point had pierced the Italian's side, inflicting a painful but not a serious wound. The tournament in question was organised in order to decide whether the French is superior or not to the Italian school. Opinions are about equal as to their relative merits, with a slight leaning in favour of the Gallic methods.

" The Sun," December 19, 1895.

PRINCE BISMARCK'S DUELS.

Prince Bismarck has fought twenty duels and was wounded but once. That time he was slightly cut by the sword of his adversary, which flew from its socket and struck him in the face.

" The Daily Telegraph," December 21, 1895.

DUEL AT BUDA-PESTH.

Baron Josika, the Hungarian Court Minister, has left Buda-Pesth for Vienna, to make a report to the Emperor upon the scene which occurred in the Lower House of the Hungarian Diet on Friday, when M. Perczel, the Minister of the Interior, was reprimanded by the President for calling Baron Andreansky an insolent fellow on account of a remark made by the member implying that the Minister countenanced corrupt electoral practices. Many Deputies are of opinion that the President in calling the Minister to order acted somewhat hastily, considering that M. Perczel, by publicly apologising for the expression used by him, had given ample satisfaction to the House. As the result of the incident a duel was fought on Saturday at Buda-Pesth between Baron Andreansky and M. Perczel, swords being the weapons chosen. Baron Andreansky was severely wounded in the head.

" The Star," January 7, 1896.

A NEW ARMY SWORD.

A new pattern of sword has been approved for officers of infantry of the line, except rifle and Scottish regiments. It is described as having a steel half-basket hilt, pierced with scroll design and royal cipher, and crown chased ; the grip is to be of black fishskin, bound with three strands

519

of silver wire, back chequered to pommel, with flat part near guard for the thumb; straight blade, grooved, and spear-pointed. The blade is to be 32½ in. long, and 1 in. broad at the shoulder; the hilt 5¾ in. to 5⅞ in., and the grip 5 in., and the weight 1 lb. 11 oz. to 1 lb. 12 oz. without scabbard. Officers of rifle and Scottish regiments are to alter their swords to the new length of grip.

" The Daily Telegraph," January 14, 1896.

M. GEORGES DE LABRUYÈRE.

Next to the arrest of M. Jacques Saint Cère, *alias* Rosenthal, that of M. Georges de Labruyère, of which you were informed yesterday, has created the greatest excitement. This journalist is one of the best-known men in Paris, and was noted on the Boulevards and in the cafés for his cavalry-barrack manners. He formerly served in a hussar regiment, and has fought several duels since his entry into the ranks of the press. After having been a Boulevard reporter, he joined the staff of the *Cri du Peuple*, which was founded by the Communist Jules Vallès. That paper passed into the hands of Madame Séverine, the noted lady journalist, when her friend Vallès died, and M. de Labruyère became her right-hand man. Séverine wrote the leaders, and when her pen turned out gall and bitterness, the ex-cavalry corporal was ready with sword or rapier to defend the lady editor from hostile attacks. M. de Labruyère was also for a time in chief charge of that lively Boulangist sheet the *Cocarde*, which went down in the shipwreck of the party whose interests it upheld. In his journalistic capacity the ex-director of the *Cocarde* has had to fight about twenty duels. One of the most terrible of these encounters was in August 1887, when M. de Labruyère fought Lieutenant de Melleville of the First Dragoons. The lieutenant pierced his opponent's right lung during a sharp attack. Almost immediately the journalist put the point of his rapier through the officer's left lung. The two men were carried half dead off the field. The quarrel was of the most trumpery kind, the officer having been attacked in an article for an insult to a commercial traveller. Some years after, M. de Labruyère had a duel with M. Mermeix, who had been violently attacked by Madame Séverine for his revelations about Boulangism. Mermeix was victorious; but a second duel having been decided upon, he was seriously wounded. In December 1890, M. de Labruyère made a sensation by his description in a newspaper of the escape from Paris of the Pole Padelewski, who murdered the Russian General Seliverstoff in a Boulevard hotel. M. de Labruyère helped the Pole to escape into Italy, whence he went to Texas, where he committed suicide. On returning to Paris, M. de Labruyère was tried, and condemned to thirteen months' imprisonment, but he was acquitted on appeal. M. Henri Rochefort relates in his paper to-day that it was he who, when in London, furnished funds for the escape of the Pole, and he makes certain statements about M. de Labruyère's connection with the affair, which, to say the least, are startling. This, however, has nothing to do with the Lebaudy case, and it is yet difficult to see how any of the charges which have caused the arrest of the ex-director of the *Cocarde* can be brought home to him. It is true that his friend, Madame Sévérine, frequently denounced Max Lebaudy and others as squanderers of money; but she maintains that when M. de Labruyère was approached by a person who suggested that the millionaire should be called upon to square his opponents, he indignantly spurned the offers of the tempter. Madame Sévérine expresses confidence in the ability of her partner to clear himself from all the accusations, and says that she herself is perfectly calm in the midst of the storm.

" The Daily Telegraph," January 31, 1896.

THE DUEL À *L'AMÉRICAINE.*

Certain Anglo-American customs and expressions have within late years been introduced into this country, but the duel *à l'Américaine* is comparatively new here. Passers-by in the Square Monge were astonished last evening at a sudden outbreak of firing, and a commissioner of police narrowly escaped being shot, several balls passing in unpleasant proximity to his ears. He made chase after one of the disturbers of the peace, but failed to catch him. The other, however, was captured. He is a youth of eighteen, who goes by the appropriate name of " L'Indien." No information could be got from him ; but, despite his silence, the story has come out. Three young men had each fallen in love with the same damsel, who disdained their advances, and roused their jealousy by going off with a more agreeable swain. Afraid of the consequences, she persuaded an intimate friend to create a quarrel among the lovers, in the hopes that they would kill each other and leave her free. It was in the public square that the fight occurred—two of them emptying their revolvers at each other ; whilst the third, armed with a dagger and a six-shooter, kept watch, as he said, to stop any one interfering. The whole band, including the young lady and her friend, have been arrested, and are now awaiting further events at the depôt.

" Reynold's Newspaper," March 1, 1896.

A ROMANTIC DUEL IN REAL LIFE.

A duel with revolvers took place on Sunday between two young Paris workmen in the Belleville quarter, to decide which of them should marry a girl with whom they were in love. Four shots were exchanged, and as the last one was fired the police appeared on the scene. The spectators somewhat ignominiously took to flight, with the exception of one of the combatants, named Marchand, a young man twenty-five years of age, who was left lying on the ground severely wounded in the shoulder.

" The Daily Telegraph," March 23, 1896.

DUEL BETWEEN GENERAL MOCENNI AND SIGNOR BARZILAI.

ROME, *Saturday.*—Immediately after the reading of the minutes in the Chamber of Deputies to-day, a sharp altercation took place between General Mocenni, ex-Minister of War, and Signor Barzilai. General Mocenni denied a statement made by the latter to the effect that he (General Mocenni) had proposed the recall of General Baratieri after the defeat at Ambalagi, but that Signor Crispi and other politicians had opposed the suggestion in view of General Baratieri's influence as a Deputy. Signor Barzilai, on the other hand, adhered to his assertion. In the lobbies there is some talk of a duel between Signor Barzilai and the ex-Minister.

ROME, *Sunday.*—A duel was fought this morning between General Mocenni and Signor Barzilai, as a result of yesterday's altercation in the Chamber of Deputies. Signor Barzilai was wounded in the left cheek, while his opponent was unhurt.

" The Daily Telegraph," April 7, 1896.

DUELLING IN GERMANY.

Our Berlin correspondent writes :—On Easter Eve last year Herr von Kotze, formerly one of the Chamberlains of the Prussian Court, who had been boycotted by society for about nine months on suspicion of being guilty of a series of vile and obscene actions, but had just been acquitted, had a duel with another Court functionary, and was wounded in the thigh. As consolation, the Kaiser bestowed on him an Easter egg made up of flowers, and his Majesty's sister, the Hereditary Princess of Saxe-Meiningen, sent him her congratulations on his escape from his adversary's bullets. Society in general did not, however, think he was sufficiently acquitted of guilt, and an early opportunity for re-boycotting him was seized. One of his alleged calumniators was a Herr von Schrader, also a Court functionary, whom Herr von Kotze thought it

would be beneath his dignity to meet in a duel. He accordingly instituted legal proceedings against him. Both of them, however, wearing the
King's uniform, it was held, according to the custom of their country,
to be derogatory to submit a "case of honour" to the civil courts of
the land, as amongst men of this kind such matters can only be settled at
the point of the sword or at the mouth of a pistol. Herr von Kotze was
cut by his relatives and acquaintances, and condemned by the military
Court of Honour to be defrocked of his uniform—in other words, to be
declared an outcast. The Kaiser intervened, and so far quashed the
decision of the court—the chief members of which thereby considered
themselves mortally offended, and resigned their commissions—as to let
Kotze off with a warning. This meant that he was again reinstated to the
rank of a gentleman ; whereupon, as is commonly reported, he has challenged Herr von Schrader, his dire enemy, to fight a duel on "the severest
conditions," and the consequences can easily be conceived. Pending the
settlement of this "honourable" dispute, two other cases of duelling have
been reported in the public papers, both of which are specially character-
istic of the notions of the form of "honour" inculcated into the minds of
Teutons of the higher grades of society. A certain Captain von Hünerbein
challenged, and the other day fought, his father-in-law, the latter having
grievously insulted him in the presence of a number of other people.
Some details connected with the actors of this tragic domestic drama are
interesting. Herr von Hünerbein is a man enjoying the respect of his
friends, who are pretty numerous ; but his wife, as is recorded, failing to
appreciate his good qualities, and desirous of being divorced from him,
succeeded in having her spouse confined in a madhouse as a lunatic, and
deprived of all right to administer his own property. Her father, Herr
von Sprenger, is put down as one of the richest sugar-refiners and largest
landed proprietors in Silesia. The husband appears to have obtained his
release from confinement only to be wounded by his irascible father-in-law,
but not mortally. We now come to the most deplorable case of the three.
Some months ago a Dr. Zenker, a highly popular, amiable, and learned
lawyer, residing in Potsdam, discovered that his wife had been misconduct-
ing herself with a naval officer, holding the rank of lieutenant on board
the Imperial yacht *Hohenzollern*—a Herr von Ketelhodt by name—whose
acquaintance she had made at a watering-place. Dr. Zenker received
proofs of the guilt of his wife with the said officer, but the latter denied
the charge "on his word of honour." Proceedings for divorce were insti
tuted by the injured husband ; but the social customs of the country were
not satisfied with this. Any man of his social position in Germany would
be considered bound to challenge the seducer under such circumstances ;
but, as he happened to be a lieutenant in a regiment of the Landwehr, the
subject had to be laid before the district Court of Honour. That body

decided that Dr. Zenker—the lawyer—must challenge to a duel the seducer of his wife, Lieutenant von Ketelhodt. Had he not done so, he would have been simply cashiered as officer, and, according to the customs of the country, condemned to social ostracism. The duel took place, and Zenker was shot dead.

"The Daily Telegraph," April 11, 1896.

DUEL AT POTSDAM (BARON VON SCHRADER AND BARON VON KOTZE).

The long-expected duel between Herr von Kotze, formerly one of the Chamberlains to the German Imperial Court, and Herr von Schrader, one of his aforetime colleagues, took place to-day at a secluded spot near Potsdam. This time it was not the unhappy Herr von Kotze who was shot, but his antagonist, who some two years ago so brutally maligned him. Herr von Schrader received so severe a wound in the abdomen that he had to be taken to the hospital, where Professor von Bergmann, who was instantly summoned from Berlin, performed an operation, assisted by several other surgeons. The patient is said to be in a dangerous condition.

In order to explain the cause of this duel, I must remind you of the story told in your columns a year ago. Herr von Kotze had been accused nearly two years ago of being the actual writer, or an accomplice in the writing, of a series of loathsome and obscene letters sent to the highest ladies in the land frequenting the Berlin Court. The Kaiser, on hearing the charge, declared he should be punished like an ordinary criminal, and he was forthwith arrested as he was preparing to attend in his official capacity the ceremony of laying the foundation-stone of the Berlin Evangelische Cathedral. After being socially boycotted for nine months, and having during a part of that period suffered imprisonment, the official was acquitted by the military court, the inquiry having been held with closed doors.

On the morning of the publication of the acquittal, as he was socially bound to do according to the code of honour in Germany, he challenged his chief calumniator, Baron von Reischach, a member of the household of the Empress Frederick. The duel took place on Easter Eve, and Herr von Kotze was slightly wounded and taken to the hospital. The next morning he received the congratulations of the Kaiser and an Easter egg, composed of flowers, as a social whitewashing, together with the felicitations of the Hereditary Princess of Saxe-Meiningen, his Majesty's sister. The other nine duels which German honour required Herr von Kotze to fight were happily prohibited, so that his certain death was avoided.

Subsequently, however, he committed the offence, unpardonable for a

Prussian officer, of bringing an action at law before a civil court for calumny against Herr von Schrader, also a retired officer, and the military court appointed to consider this outrageous infringement of military etiquette decided, after lengthy proceedings, that he should have his uniform taken from him, and thus be *declassé*. The Kaiser, however, would not confirm the decision, and merely gave Kotze a "warning." The civil case never came off; but it has long been known that Herr von Kotze was consequently forced to challenge Schrader. The result of to-day's duel is as above stated.

The conditions under which the duel was fought were exceptionally severe—namely, ten paces' distance, both combatants to fire together at the word of command of the umpire, and the duel to continue until one of the combatants should be totally disabled. All efforts made to effect a reconciliation before the duel proved, of course, futile, as did an endeavour to moderate the conditions. The duel took place at 7.30 this morning. Only one shot was exchanged, and the wounded man was removed unconscious from the scene of action. Major-General von Bissing, the Commander of the 4th Cavalry Brigade, was Schrader's second.

As the result of the encounter, Herr von Kotze will, of course, have to go to prison again, this time in a fortress. People are curious already to know what steps the Kaiser will take, and what will be done with the seconds, who are usually consigned to fortress confinement also.

The *Vossische Zeitung*, reflecting the opinion of the right-minded minority of the Berlin upper classes, says to-night: "We regret that this bloody duel, of which influential circles undoubtedly knew, was not prevented. When will this unhappy Kotze affair be terminated? Are there to be any more victims? And what has been proved by the issue of this *rencontre?* That one of the two combatants was right and the other wrong? What a mockery there is in this example of law-breaking by officials of the Court when the people are called upon to join the struggle in defence of religion morality, and order! And yet people are surprised at the spread of social democracy!"

"The Daily Telegraph," April 13, 1896.

THE GERMAN COURT DUEL (DEATH OF BARON VON SCHRADER).

Baron von Schrader, the duellist wounded in Friday morning's encounter with Herr von Kotze, succumbed on Saturday evening, owing to the effects of his wound, having suffered, during his moments of consciousness, excruciating pain. Even the Conservative press is indignant that matters were allowed to drag on so long, and to terminate, for the present at least, so tragically. The majority, however, of the class of society in which the two combatants moved are still of opinion that a duel was the sole possible issue to the quarrel between them. Schrader undoubtedly acted, from his point of view, *bonâ fide* in making the accusation ; and he was so obstinately positive of the truth of the grave charge he made that nothing and nobody could induce him to admit, even to his best friends, that he had been deceived. Notwithstanding that he possessed no positive proof whatever against Kotze, he insisted that it was Kotze's place to prove his innocence—a strange frame of mind, especially when not one person who knew Kotze well believed for one moment that he was guilty. The military court, after hearing evidence, delayed their decision for nine months ; but they acquitted him last year at Easter, and there is not a shadow of doubt that he is innocent. But the gist of the whole thing lies in the fact that Kotze was imprudent, and had made a number of enemies ; hence, when suspicion was laid at his door, he had but few friends to plead his cause.

If the case had been brought before a civil court at the proper time, the guilty parties would probably have been easily discovered, and the innocent man would have been cleared. Everybody knows that there were reasons for not taking this course, and that the more cumbrous and less reliable procedure was adopted.

The offence Schrader committed in persisting in an unjust accusation was not, in the eyes of sensible men, one deserving the penalty of death, but it was one which, according to the code of honour accepted in this country, involved the necessity that he, the accuser, and the accused should risk their lives in a combat of chance. Despite popular indignation, which is at fever-heat just now, it is very doubtful whether any measures can be taken for the suppression of duelling in Germany.

A COMING DUEL (PRINCE DE SAGAN AND M. ABEL HERMANT).

Little else is talked of to-day save the dispute between the Prince de Sagan and M. Abel Hermant, author of the play, "La Meute," recently produced at the Renaissance. The Prince maintains that he and other members of his family, one of whom had dealings with the late Max Lebaudy, have been represented in the play under veiled names, and he has accordingly sent his seconds to the author. M. Hermant has already been in much hot water owing to his books. His novel dealing with army life, the "Cavalier Miserey," was burned on a dunghill, before a whole regiment, by its colonel, and the author was challenged by an officer. The two combatants were wounded in the encounter. Another novel dealing with university life was publicly burned in the grounds of the Normal School. M. Hermant is thirty-four years old, and before embarking in the particularly thorny branch of literature which he has chosen, that of the *roman à clef*, wrote verses which offended nobody. He is now in trouble with the leading sportsman of France, the accredited champion of the turf and arbiter of elegance, the glass of fashion and the mould of form. Charles Frédéric Boson, Prince de Sagan, is sixty-four years old, and is the son of the Duc de Talleyrand Périgord by his first marriage with the Duchesse de Montmorency. The Duc de Talleyrand is also Duc de Valençay, and Herzog von Sagan in Silesia. The Prince de Sagan, who married the daughter of Baron Seillière, has two sons, Elie and Baron de Talleyrand de Périgord. The Prince de Sagan sent his seconds, the Comte de Dion and General Count Friant, to M. Hermant yesterday, and the author at once referred them to his friends, M. Jules Ricard and M. Gustave Guiches. After a good deal of negotiation, it has been arranged that the duel will take place to-morrow morning at a certain spot in the outskirts of Paris, where the combatants will face each other with pistols.

" The Star," April 13, 1896.

DUEL BETWEEN BARON VON SCHRADER AND BARON VON KOTZE.

The death of Baron von Schrader, in consequence of a wound received in the recent duel with Baron von Kotze, has evoked a strong agitation in Germany against the practice of duelling, so common in that empire. The Baron leaves a widow with three children. The eldest son was begged by the father just before death to promise not to call out Von Kotze. During the evening a telegram was received from the Kaiser, inquiring after the welfare of the wounded man, and expressing his sympathy.

The *Chronicle*, however, declares that the duel must have received the express sanction and countenance of the Emperor, otherwise the combatants would never have enjoyed the services of two such distinguished seconds as they had—one of them a particular favourite of the Emperor. Besides this, the surgeon in attendance was the regimental doctor of the Hussars of the Guard, Dr. Timann—the regiment in which his Majesty himself rose from the rank of lieutenant to that of colonel, and of which he still by preference wears the scarlet uniform. Duelling is clearly forbidden by the laws of the land, but his Majesty has repeatedly pardoned noble duellists for pinking plebeian adversaries. One bellicose official was also promoted. On no one will the latest episode have produced such a revolting impression as on the Empress Frederick, seeing that the victim of Herr von Kotze's bullet was one of her own Court Chamberlains, and her especial favourite.

The *Volk*, in a trenchant article, says the nation especially is pained by the frequent extensions of the royal pardon to duellists—acts which are in sharpest contrast to the feelings of the people.

" The Star," April 13, 1896.

MAINLY ABOUT PEOPLE DUELLING.

The question of duelling has been raised again in Germany in an acute form by the death of Baron von Schrader at Berlin on Saturday evening.

Baron von Schrader met Herr von Kotze, his colleague in the office of Master of the Ceremonies in the Prussian Court, in a duel on Friday, and received his adversary's bullet in his abdomen. The surgeons who attended him had no hope of saving him from the first.

Continental duels—those in France especially—are usually more comic than tragic ; but duels in which serious injuries have been inflicted have of late been more unpleasantly common, and in one or two notorious instances death has resulted. Early in the present year a Hungarian land-owner had his jugular vein severed by a young lieutenant, and not very long before a French naval officer shot the Paris journalist M. Percher through the lung. There was an inquiry into the Percher affair, and a scapegoat was made of the keeper of the restaurant in which the shots were fired.

Occasionally France has the excitement of a lady duellist. Mdme. Astie de Valsayre, a skilled fencer, is one of them. She has two sons, and is called "a good fellow."

" The Daily Telegraph," April 14, 1896.

THE GERMAN DUEL (BARON VON SCHRADER AND BARON VON KOTZE).

An immense amount of sympathy is being shown in Berlin Court circles for the family of the deceased Baron von Schrader. It is said that the Empress Frederick repeatedly inquired about him as he lay in a dangerous condition after the duel, and sent a most touching telegram of condolence to his widow upon hearing of her loss. A number of the leaders of Court circles here have also expressed their sympathy. For the last few months Baron von Schrader had been in disgrace at Court, in consequence of the

518

part he had taken in regard to the baseless calumny against Herr von Kotze. He wrote a letter to the Kaiser just before he started for his duel, and this letter was, in accordance with the wish of the deceased, sent to his Majesty after his death. It is not supposed that its contents will be made known. Everything connected with this shameful scandal ought, in the opinion of all right-minded Germans in this capital, to have been repressed at once, so that the blood of innocent and misguided men need not have been shed, whilst persons whose names will not be mentioned are escaping unscathed.

Kotze is liable to three years' imprisonment in a fortress, but will, it is supposed, be pardoned.

A funeral service is to be held over the deceased's remains in the garrison church at Potsdam before their removal to the family country seat. It was at first intended that this function should take place in the royal parish church, the Church of Peace, where Kaiser Friedrich is buried, but the permission was subsequently cancelled.

"The Daily Telegraph," April 14, 1896.

DUEL BETWEEN THE PRINCE DE SAGAN AND
M. ABEL HERMANT.

Unusual interest was aroused in the duel between the Prince de Sagan and M. Abel Hermant, which came off this morning. Neither the descendant of the great Talleyrand, nor the dramatist who was accused of having drawn the portrait of the Prince in the play "La Meute," received a scratch, and a bloodless encounter was the meagre result of all the talk and excitement. In the early morning many curious persons assembled around the club-house, wherein the President of the Société d'Encouragement usually resides, in the hope of seeing him drive out to shoot and be shot at. The sportsman left the place about half-past seven o'clock for a "constitutional," in order to steady his nerves for the pistol-match to which he had challenged the dramatist. After his walk the Prince returned to the club, and having taken some light refreshment, he entered his carriage. Those who had the patience to wait outside 1 Rue Royale saw that the descendant of Talleyrand was carefully dressed, and wore a big black cravat, hiding his shirt-front, which was thus prevented from being a mark for his adversary. Outside 24 Boulevard des Capucines a hired vehicle awaited the novelist-dramatist. The two adversaries then drove in their separate carriages to where the seconds resided, and shortly after eleven o'clock the duel took place in the park of Saint-Ouen. Only a privileged few, like Prince Murat, the Duc de Montmorency, and the

Comte de Breteuil, were permitted to enter the grounds, a rigorous janitor sternly closing the gates in the face of those who were clamouring for admittance. Comte de Dion directed the arrangements, and made the combatants rehearse at twenty-five paces before firing ; that is to say, he repeated the words of command, and caused the principals to move in accordance with his instructions, as if they were being drilled. M. Hermant, like the Prince de Sagan, was arrayed in black, and the latter wore the round glasses called shooting spectacles. When the words "Are you ready" were uttered, it was noticed that M. Hermant replied "Yes" in a firm voice, while the Prince seemed to hesitate, and at last answered in a low tone. Four bullets, none of which took effect, were exchanged at the twenty-five paces, and then the principals separated without shaking hands. They thus neglected the custom among adversaries after a duel. It appears that the Prince de Sagan wanted eight bullets to be fired, but he was overruled by the seconds. The leading sportsman left the ground accompanied by his friends as soon as he had put on his overcoat ; but M. Hermant, before driving away, chatted for a few moments with those around him. Thus terminated an encounter which might have had tragic consequences, for pistol duels, although much ridiculed, have sometimes led to fatal results of late years.

"The Daily Telegraph," April 21, 1896.

DUELLING IN GERMANY.

The interpellation on the recent duel scandals was brought forward in the Reichstag to-day by Dr. Bachem (Centre), who, referring to the public indignation aroused by the duels, called upon the House to take action to prevent similar occurrences. He dwelt more particularly on the condemnatory attitude maintained in this matter by the Protestant clergy and the association of German nobles, who sought to improve upon the Courts of Honour, and stated that the practice of duelling was strongly condemned by almost the entire German press. "How is it," inquired the speaker, "that Herr von Kotze was allowed to depart? and was the duel directly attributable to the verdict delivered by the Court of Honour?" He maintained that duelling should be punished by imprisonment, and eventually by hard labour, and, pointing out how the late Prince Consort had combated the practice in England, he expressed the hope that the Emperor would also find means of removing the evil in Germany. (Loud cheers.) Dr. von Boetticher, Secretary of State, declared that the Imperial Chancellor, who was prevented by indisposition from attending the sitting, most sincerely regretted the late duels, but the authorities could not be blamed for having been unsuccessful in preventing them. (Murmurs on the Left.) People bent on fighting duels would always find means of carrying out their intention. The Imperial Chancellor, he continued, was earnestly considering what measures to adopt in order to ensure greater respect for the law among all classes, but he had as yet come to no final decision, and consequently he was not in a position to make any further communications on the subject to the House. The debate on the interpellation was then proceeded with.

Herr Rockert (Freisinnige) maintained that some improvement must be made in the military Courts of Honour. Herr Schall (Conservative) supported Dr. Bachem's contentions, and maintained that the power of the Courts of Honour should be increased. Herr Bebel remarked that the Social Democrats did not object to the so-called upper classes undertaking the task of mutual destruction. The middle classes, he maintained, aped the evil habits of the aristocracy. Duels were increasing in number because duellists were confident of being acquitted if brought up for trial.

The Reichstag at this stage adjourned until to-morrow, when the motion on duelling brought forward by the Freisinnige party will also be discussed.

" The Daily Telegraph," April 22, 1896.

DUELLING IN GERMANY.

The Reichstag to-day, on the proposal of Dr. von Bennigsen, decided to discuss the motion brought forward by the Freisinnige party in connection with the interpellation of the Centre on the recent duels. Count Bernstorff declared that his party had confidence in the intention of the Government to deal seriously with the question. Dr. von Bennigsen observed that he had hoped for a long time past that duelling would be abolished in Germany, as it had been in England, on political as well as on other grounds. The speaker denied that Herr Bebel had any right to express indignation at acts of violence, since it was he who in 1875 commended the Paris Commune to the Reichstag as an example. Dr. von Bennigsen concluded by declaring that the views at present held regarding the mode of satisfying injured honour must undergo a change, and that existing penalties for libel and insulting language were inadequate.

Herr Grober, of the Centre, condemned the students' sword duels, which, he said, were simply a preparatory training for serious duelling.

The House afterwards proceeded to discuss various substitute motions proposed by Herren Rickert, Lenzmann, Adt, Bachem, and Bernstorff. Herr von Bennigsen supported the motion of Herr Adt (National Liberal), that the Reichstag shall call upon the Federal Governments to energetically combat the illegal practice of duelling with all the means at their disposal. Herren Bachem, Rickert, and Bernstorff subsequently withdrew their motions in favour of that proposed by Herr Adt, which was eventually adopted unanimously amidst general applause.

" *Reynolds's Newspaper,*" *April* 26, 1896.

DETERMINED DUEL IN HUNGARY.

A determined duel was fought this morning between Baron De Fejérváry, Minister of National Defence, and M. Bernat, member of the Lower House of the Diet. Pistols were the weapons first chosen ; but as the shots exchanged were without effect, the duel, in accordance with the conditions previously arranged, was continued with swords until one of the combatants was disabled. M. Bernat received a severe cut across the right temple, and fell to the ground.

" *The Sketch,*" *April* 29, 1896.

THE PETTICOAT DUELLISTS.

If Mrs. Grundy knew history, which she does not, she would cease to attribute any new development of her sex to the flightiness of that much-abused quantity " the present generation." Once upon a time there was a certain Lady Almeria Braddock. She was visited, one afternoon in 1792, by a certain Mrs. Elphinstone. In the course of a *tête-à-tête*, which was not quite amiable, Mrs. Elphinstone declared to her ladyship, " You have been a very beautiful woman." The preterit petrified her ladyship. " You have a very good autumnal face even now," Mrs. Elphinstone went on, " but you must acknowledge that the lilies and roses are somewhat faded. Forty years ago, I am told, a young fellow could hardly gaze upon you with impunity." Whereat her ladyship declared she was not yet thirty. Mrs. Elphinstone at once cited Collins, the Burke of the day, who stated that her ladyship had been born in 1732, and was therefore sixty-one. That was the finishing touch, and the ladies adjourned to Hyde Park to have it out about Mr. Collins. They first set to with pistols at a range of ten yards, and Lady Almeria got a bullet whizzing through her hat, while her own shot was of no avail. The seconds then proposed a reconciliation ; but the Lady Almeria would have none of it, unless her opponent admitted that she had been to blame in questioning her veracity. Mrs. Elphinstone indignantly refused, and drew her sword, to her sorrow, for she was wounded slightly in the sword-arm. Lady Almeria was satisfied, and a concession having been drawn up in terms agreeable to both of them, the ladies curtsied to each other, and, in the words of the chronicler, " quitted the field with honour." Mr. Gilbert might have used the incident after this fashion in the metre of one of his jingles in "The Grand Duke ; or, the Statutory Duel : "—

About a century since,
    The code of the duello
Was full in force, and made a corse
    Of many a strapping fellow.
The man you made to wince
    Demanded satisfaction,
And would not wait to hear you state
    A nominal retraction.
The code of honour left no doubt
For him : but he must call you out—
    He scorned a libel action.

And now and then this law
    Was put in force by ladies.
Did one offend, her foe might send
    Her straightway down to Hades.
For, when the weary jaw
    Ran short of slanging fuel,
She did not tear the other's hair,
    But went and fought a duel.
This remedy conduced to sport,
And far excelled a legal court,
    Although it might be cruel.

When Mrs. Elphinstone
    Did chaff the fading Braddock
About her age, she had to wage
    A fight by Hyde Park paddock.
Since nothing would atone
    Short of a desperate battle,
The Lady B. made Mrs. E.
    Regret her tittle-tattle.
For slanders cease to be a joke
Whene'er you find the women-folk
    Such fiery kittle cattle.

The woman of our time
    May boat and fence and cycle ;
Once in a way (see Jones's play)
    An Angel ruins Michael.

NOTES ON FENCING AND DUELLING

> She's even known to mime,
> On various occasions,
> In mannish clo'es, and goodness knows
> How many more sensations.
> But women who are labelled New
> Have yet to learn a thing or two
> From bygone generations.

" The Star," April 30, 1896.

DUEL BETWEEN BARON FEJÉRVÁRY AND M. BOGDAN KORBULY.

In his latest duel with swords, the Hungarian Minister of National Defence, Baron Fejérváry, severely injured his adversary, M. Bogdan Korbuly, editor of the *Nemzet.*

" The Daily Telegraph," May 11, 1896.

THE COMBATS IN "ROMEO AND JULIET."

A few important alterations have been made in the cast of " Romeo and Juliet," to be produced next Friday afternoon at the Prince of Wales Theatre. The characters of Mercutio, the Friar, and the Nurse will be taken respectively by those excellent and experienced artists, W. H. Vernon, Arthur Stirling, and Mrs. E. H. Brookes. A remarkably clever young musician, William Wallace, whose symphonic poem, " The Passing of Beatrice," made a considerable stir at a recent Crystal Palace Concert, has specially composed a Pavane, which will be played on the stage in the ballroom scene after the manner of " house music."

But perhaps the most interesting feature of this revival to archæologists will be the combats in " Romeo and Juliet," which have been arranged by that learned authority, Captain Alfred Hutton, and will probably be given accurately for the first time in the history of the stage. Captain Hutton has issued a very valuable memorandum on the subject, from which I extract a few interesting notes. The chief combats are fought with "rapier and dagger." The "fiery Tybalt" arms himself with a "case of rapiers," which means a pair of swords kept side by side in one scabbard, and used one in each hand. They were not worn in the belt, but carried by an attendant. Tybalt kills Mercutio somewhat treacherously, but he gets his quietus from Romeo, who, "armed with a rapier and dagger, awaits Tybalt's charge, and slipping back his left foot into the position of 'under stop thrust,' a trick of considerable antiquity, receives his enemy on the point of the sword." Captain Hutton goes on to say :—

NOTES ON FENCING AND DUELLING

" The fighting of the Shakespearian era is so peculiarly adapted to stage display that it seems strange that it should not have been more cultivated ; it may, perhaps, lack some of the refined elegance of the modern French school, but the loss is more than counterbalanced by the varied beauty of the weapons, and the picturesque movements of the combatants. 'Romeo and Juliet,' with its five distinct duels, offers a fairly wide field to the student of old sword-play. In the squabble which opens the play, between certain retainers of the rival houses, they are armed, after the manner of serving-men, with broadsword and hand-buckler, a shield which, from its small size and its lightness, lends itself. greatly to lively play, the vivacity of which was further enhanced by the habit of the players of 'calling' each other with two little bright raps given on the buckler with the back of the sword.

" It is worthy of note that at this period of the art of fence there was absolutely no 'lunge ;' it had yet to be invented. The movements of the feet were mainly 'passes,' or steps forwards or backwards, and 'traverses,' or lateral steps. They were effected with more or less swiftness as occasion required, and an impetuous man would often, like Tybalt, actually 'charge' his opponent."

" The Star," June 3, 1896.

SWORD-FENCING MATCH (SIGNOR GRECO AND M. RUE).

PARIS, *June 2.*—At the International Fencing Tournament to-day chief interest centred in the evening display, in the course of which Signor Greco, the celebrated Italian fencing-master, was to measure swords with M. Rue, the champion of the French school. The hall was crowded with spectators, those present including Count Tornielli, the Italian Ambassador, who occupied a box with General Billot, the Minister of War. The appearance of Signor Greco and M. Rue in the arena was the signal for loud cheers. The bout was of a spirited character from the opening. Signor Greco never kept still, and vigorously attacked his opponent, who awaited his assaults calmly and parried well. The first point was in favour of Signor Greco, but as the Italian had hit below the line the point was marked as doubtful. M. Rue, who at the opening had remained on the defensive, changed his tactics, and attacking his opponent vigorously, forced him to break ground, and scored a point with one of the straight lunges for which he is famous. Signor Greco, on his part, also made some good hits, but at the end of the encounter M. Rue was declared the victor by eleven hits against six.—*Reuter.*

NOTES ON FENCING AND DUELLING

" The Star," June 5, 1896.

THE "FINEST SWORDSMAN IN THE ARMY" LOSES HIS RIGHT EYE.

A serious accident befell Sergeant B. Foerster, first-class instructor of gymnastics and fencing, at the Military Tournament yesterday morning. The sergeant, who is officially described as "the finest swordsman in the army," has become the victim, so to speak, of his own art. He was standing watching the sabre-play between two swordsmen, and had silently advanced to the close left rear of one of the combatants, when this combatant, in throwing back his blade over his left shoulder to take a cut at his antagonist, struck its point into Foerster's right eye, quite destroying it. It was really the sergeant-instructor's own blame, as he had given the swordsman at whose hands he suffered no sign of his presence on the fencing-ground. Foerster was at once removed to a hospital in a very collapsed state, and this morning the damaged orb is to be completely removed. Provided the other eye does not suffer from sympathy with its destroyed companion, it is probable that he will be preserved to the army, of which he is so distinguished an ornament; but, in any case, he will be well provided for, especially as he is a married man. Before joining the Army Gymnastic Staff, Foerster—a Baltic Province man by origin—had been in the Life Guards.

" Pall Mall Gazette," June 5, 1896.

THE FENCING TOURNAMENT IN PARIS.

PARIS, *Thursday Night.*—The decisive assaults between amateurs admitted to the competition after selection were begun this evening. In the contest between Mr. Wigram (England) [Captain H. H. Wigram, Scots Guards] and M. Herisson (France), the latter was successful, scoring six points to the Englishman's two. Another Englishman, Mr. Norbury, then entered the lists, his opponent being Lieutenant Senat, one of the best French amateurs. This bout proved one of the best of the evening, although Mr. Norbury only scored two points against nine placed to the credit of his opponent. Both combatants were warmly cheered. Among the other assaults worthy of mention were those between Mr. Clay (England) and M. Breitnayer (France), in which the latter scored fifteen points against the former's five; and between Signor Burba (Italy) and Captain Debase, in which each scored three hits. In the course of this contest Captain Debase, in delivering a somewhat violent thrust at the mask of Signor Burba, slightly grazed the latter's forehead. Signor Burba insisted, nevertheless, on continuing the bout, but it is generally admitted that he did not show his usual form. Lord Dufferin, who was among the spectators, took a lively interest in the contest.

"*The Daily Messenger*" (*Paris*), *June* 16, 1896.

DUEL BETWEEN M. DE SAINT-ALARY AND M. SAINT-VALÉRY.

M. de Saint-Alary fought a duel yesterday morning at ten o'clock with M. Saint-Valéry, on the subject of an article which the latter had written in *Paris Sport*. The duel, which was fought with rapiers, had a more serious termination than usual, for, in the first round, M. Saint-Valéry was badly wounded in his right side, and M. de Saint-Alary received a slight wound in his chest. The former was taken to his mother's house at Passy, where his friends explained to his mother that he had been the victim of a bicycling accident. The wound, say the doctors, is not in itself a very serious one, but it seems to have already produced complications. M. de Saint-Alary's wound was not sufficiently serious to prevent him from leaving for Ascot, where Omnium II., the cause of this quarrel, is running on Thursday in the Gold Cup.

"*The Daily Telegraph*," *June* 23, 1896.

DUEL BETWEEN LIEUTENANT BUCH AND LIEUTENANT LUEHRING.

A duel was fought yesterday upon the Kummersdorf shooting-ground near Berlin. Lieutenant Buch, of the 9th Regiment of Artillery, shot dead Lieutenant Luehring, of the 6th Regiment of the same branch of the service.

"*The Daily Courier*," *June* 25, 1896.

A HIT—A PALPABLE HIT!
An Automatic Electric Recorder.

On Tuesday night, at 10 Warwick Street, Regent Street, the *salle d'armes* of the veteran fencing-master M. Bertrand, an exhibition was given of an exceedingly clever invention. Every one who has watched a bout with the foils knows that the task of judging the hits is with a pair of amateurs difficult enough, and with a well-matched pair of *maîtres d'escrime* well-nigh impossible. To accomplish his responsible work satisfactorily, it is necessary for the judge to possess the eye of a hawk and the agility of a tiger in order to keep the lightning-like movements of both points well under observation. The invention is the work of Mr. Little, the well-known amateur swordsman, and is designed to do away with this uncertainty and useless expenditure of energy. It is hardly necessary to say that the inventor has called electricity to his aid. Briefly, the invention consists of an automatic electric recorder. The instrument is fastened to the wall and connected with the collar of the combatant, from whence the current is conveyed down the sleeve into the handle of the foil. The blade of the foil pressing into the handle completes the connection; the current is conveyed to a bell in the instrument, and thus each hit is recorded. At the exhibition the invention proved an unalloyed success, and ought to be a boon both to competitors and judges—to the former on account of its certainty, and to the latter because it not only lightens their labours, but also frees them from any suspicion of partiality.

"The Star," June 29, 1896.

TO PUT DOWN DUELLING.

BERLIN, *June* 29.—A memorial has been drawn up in the Ministry for War in favour of the extirpation of duelling in the army. It is intended to take action in affairs of honour on the lines customary in England.— *Central News.*

[Figura che ferisce di passata mentre che l'aversario cava per ferire.— ALFIERI (F. F.).—1640.]